P9-DXM-318

MVFOL

CHANGING LIVES

Women in European History
Since 1700

CHANGING LIVES

Women in European History
Since 1700

Bonnie G. Smith
University of Rochester

D. C. Heath and Company
Lexington, Massachusetts   Toronto

For Don

Cover: Sonia Terk Delaunay, "Study for Portugal," 1936–1937, Gouauche on
   paper, 14¼" × 37", The National Museum of Women in the Arts, Gift of
   Wallace and Wilhelmina Holladay. Detail

Copyright © 1989 by D. C. Heath and Company.

All rights reserved. No part of this publication may be reproduced or transmitted
in any form or by any means, electronic or mechanical, including photocopy,
recording, or any information storage or retrieval system, without permission in
writing from the publisher.

Published simultaneously in Canada.

Printed in the United States of America.

International Standard Book Number: 0-669-14561-0

Library of Congress Catalog Card Number: 88-82180

10 9 8

PREFACE

This book tells the story of women from the eighteenth century to the present. It introduces many famous women and describes the lives of the not-so-famous in the hope that some of those lives will strike the reader's imagination. Reading history is an imaginative undertaking by which we make contact with those who lived in the past. That contact should arouse our curiosity and even our passions so that we want to learn more. In the case of women, there is indeed much more to learn.

The reasons for studying the history of women—or of any group, for that matter—are legion. History provides us with rich pictures of the way people created cultures and societies. It allows us to recapture some of the ways they addressed the problems of life and the problems of living in groups. The critical memory that we call history shows us their aspirations and their art. We rely on historical memory the way we rely on our individual memories to give us pleasure but also to show us the dense nexus of culture and power in which we must forge our own lives.

Over the centuries the idea of "woman" has signified something immutable, ahistorical, and constant. This book, in contrast, portrays historical, changing lives, all the while it charts moments of stasis and sameness. Women's lives changed within networks of multiple relationships, and so this study deals with men, with children, with questions of nationality and class, and with issues of economics, politics, reproduction, and culture. Women's history is thus contextual and must be multifaceted in its approach to individual and collective life. We try to see from many points of view and to shift our analytical focus to capture both that fleeting thing we call "life" and that ever-changing construct we call "society." Women's history, then, builds on positive information or facts that are sometimes characterized and trivialized in the term "herstory." Such information, however, when posed against the facts we have had about men's lives, makes us see people whose history is "gendered." Male and female inhabit the same terrain, but always marking out and empowering a sense of "gender" or "difference." Yet even when we deploy that information about women alone, for itself, we act as if women had a narrative historical being. In this regard, writing about women's lives also means changing history.

In compiling this particular study I have had a good deal of help; first, from my students who have asked questions and aroused my curiosity with those questions. Cathy Mason has assisted in the questioning process and additionally has done research for this work. Jean De Groat prepared many versions of the manuscript in an expert and informed way. Nicole Tietjen and

Patience Smith did bibliographical work and provided moral support. I particularly thank Karen Potischman, James Miller, Susan Gleason, and Linda Halvorson for developing this book from its inception to its completion. Thanks also go to Mary Lang for researching the photographs and to Henry Rachlin for designing the book. Mary Jo Maynes provided excellent critiques of the entire manuscript (twice) and Karen Offen gave particularly good advice about the initial content and style of the second half. I am also grateful to those who reviewed the manuscript in its early stages: Myrna Chase, Baruch College; Deborah Hertz, SUNY Binghamton; Ann R. Higginbotham, Eastern Connecticut State University; Lynn Hunt, University of Pennsylvania; Catherine M. Prelinger, Yale University; Leila J. Rupp, Ohio State University; Londa Schiebinger, University of Georgia; and Jane Slaughter, University of New Mexico. Finally, Donald Kelley not only inspired this book on women (as he has every other one of mine), he also read and criticized it.

CONTENTS

CHANGING LIVES
Women in European History
Since 1700

PART

I

Life and Death in
the Eighteenth Century

To late twentieth-century people, the eighteenth century appears an unfamiliar world. It was an age in which most Europeans lived on the land with little margin in the struggle for survival. Ordinary folk knew only a perilous existence in which climate, war, disease, and even the monetary demands of landowners and kings could cut short their pathetically short life expectancy of only a few decades. Technology, transport, cities—none of these existed in their modern form. A few great cities—like London with one million inhabitants at the end of the century, and Paris or Naples with a half million—had teeming populations, but the vast majority of cities were very small by today's standards. Serving as administrative and market centers, they were nonetheless heavily dependent on the countryside. Cities offered possibilities for lively cultural exchange, but their economic life developed slowly. Government officials and guilds—that is, trade associations of master artisans—regulated and often hobbled manufacturing, commerce, and urban politics. Infectious disease was ever-present, childbirth dangerous, malnutrition commonplace, and famine a real possibility.

At the heart of this bare, survival economy lay a careful monitoring of women's and men's relationships. Work had its male and female spheres. Rituals, laws, and lore explaining such gender organization dominated daily life. Marriage, childbirth, and indeed all reproductive acts had to be strictly controlled because they largely determined whether a community would survive. This was equally true of the high-born royal family and of the humblest peasant household. Family rule and family landholding alike were signs of success in reproduction, and people often likened the hierarchical social order of the day to the male-dominated household.

Eighteenth-century society, however, was not static. New ideas about pol-

3

itics and competing ways of producing goods undermined this way of life. Expanding commerce, the spread of individualistic values, and pressure for a more representative form of government eventually helped ignite the American Revolution in 1776 and the French Revolution of 1789. During this revolutionary era, which stretched into the early nineteenth century, Europe's population exploded, city life flourished in new ways, and the old society of guilds, aristocrats, and kings trembled. Europeans began to escape from the treadmill of an agricultural and reproductive system geared to bare survival. As a new, more productive economic order took shape, some people called for change not only in the way nations should be governed but also in the way women and men should get along.

Time Line

- **1715** Death of Louis XIV of France
- **1718** Lady Mary Wortley Montagu introduces smallpox innoculation into England
- **1720** Russian decree ends requirement that wife follow husband into exile
- **c. 1738** Maria Agnesi begins *Istituzioni analitiche,* her study of integral and differential calculus
- **1740** Maria Theresa succeeds to Habsburg throne of the Austrian Empire
  War of the Austrian Succession
- **1756–1763** Seven Years' War
- **1760** Anna Morandi Mohzolini becomes Professor of Anatomy at the University of Bologna
- **1761** Jean-Jacques Rousseau publishes the *Nouvelle Héloise*
- **1762** Catherine II (the Great) of Russia overthrows her husband and takes the throne
  Jean-Jacques Rousseau publishes *Emile*
- **c. 1765** Spinning jenny invented in England
- **1769** James Watts perfects the steam engine
- **1776** American Revolution begins
- **1778** Fanny Burney publishes *Evelina*
- **1779** Manchester spinners violently protest the use of spinning jennies
- **1789** French Revolution begins
  Hannah More opens her first Sunday school
- **1791** Olympe de Gouges publishes the *Declaration of the Rights of Woman*
- **1792** Mary Wollstonecraft publishes *A Vindication of the Rights of Woman*
  Theodor von Hippel publishes *On the Improvement of Women*
  French reforms in marriage and divorce law
- **1793** Marie Antoinette, Olympe de Gouges, and Madame du Barry executed
  France outlaws women's clubs
- **1794** France bans women from public meetings and from assembling in groups of three or more
- **1797** Jane Austen completes *Pride and Prejudice* (published 1813)
- **1799** Napoleon Bonaparte comes to power in France (becomes Emperor Napoleon I in 1803)
- **1803–1804** Napoleonic Code promulgated in France; adopted in French-dominated countries
- **1807** Germaine de Staël publishes *Corinne*
- **1811** General Civil Code of the Habsburg Empire reasserts male authority over the household
- **1815** Napoleon defeated at Waterloo; end of the Napoleonic wars

I

Eighteenth-Century Worlds

An Early
Modern Marriage   Elizabeth and Johann Dietz continually caused an up-roar in the city of Halle. Johann thought his wife stayed out too late at night and once he beat her as she returned. Elizabeth thought her husband so miserly that she stored up money in secret. Her daughter by a first marriage also caused her concern, so Elizabeth helped her out financially, kept her company night and day, and thus further enraged Master Dietz. This brawling, screaming couple was often disciplined by town officials. After beating Elizabeth, Johann spent a humiliating time in the stocks, and somewhat later the city forced them to separate. Separation, however, hardly proved satisfactory, for Elizabeth "was unable to sleep of nights," while Johann found himself without a wife, with "much work on my hands, much cooking of food, and much anxiety." Finally and inevitably the pair reconciled, for one needed a spouse in the eighteenth century.

Johann Dietz, a master barber, had wisely married a barber's widow. As such, Elizabeth Dietz already knew how to care for the personnel of his shop, how to entertain officials of the barbers' guild, and how to spin and sew. "A clever and able woman and an excellent cook," Elizabeth was also capable of handling trusteeships and estate settlements and had a good eye for land deals. So important was a wife that Johann, though in his late sixties, remarried another craftsman's widow on Elizabeth's death and had four children. He and his new wife, he noted, had many a quarrel, which he attributed to her pregnancies and ill-temper.[1] According to court records and other sources, such stress and strain pervaded early modern marriage, with its divisions of tasks and fortunes.

In the eighteenth century, concern for social harmony made community leaders attentive to marriages and families as the key to the general well-being of individuals and society alike. Living in what was essentially an agrarian society, Europeans partook of a common struggle to get enough to eat and to replenish the population. The famines, plagues, and population decline of the seventeenth century lived in popular memory and still threatened every life.

Cities could thrive or perish, depending on the harvests, while political power derived from a steady population and from agriculture. The ruling aristocracies were those who controlled land and thus could lay claim to more of its harvest than anyone else. In Russia the wealth of sovereigns was based on land and serfs; in German states it depended on the ability to tax agricultural produce.

Even in the most rapidly urbanizing countries—England, France, and the Netherlands—more than 80 percent of the people still lived on the land and were therefore part of an agrarian routine, as well as an agrarian social, economic, and political structure. In general, the average woman had to both produce goods to sustain the family and reproduce children to repopulate it in order for society to survive. These activities, however, were hardly random. Like the Dietz couple, rural people participated in a gender system, a sexually determined arrangement of tasks and power that arose from the precarious conditions of both agrarian and urban life. Despite the tensions, men and women performed their distinct labors and ultimately relied on one another. They did so, again like Elizabeth and Johann Dietz, while being closely scrutinized and regulated by neighbors and kin with whom their lives intertwined. The centrality of household and community made urban and rural women's lives very similar.

Rural Women

Work and Days

In eighteenth-century villages the great majority of the people did the same thing—tilled the soil, tended animals, and performed all the other tasks of general farming. Villages did have some variety in the population—perhaps a shoemaker, some kind of store, and a blacksmith or other kind of artisan. They also had local aristocrats, nobility or gentry on whom all social prestige centered, while a handful of large farmers managed most of the land and hired large numbers of day workers and servants. Where rural people were still bound to the land by serfdom, for example, in Eastern Europe, conditions differed. Serf women owed the nobility several days of work each week in field and household service. Their lives could appear slavelike: "My little Pashinka is arriv'd this Eve," wrote an Irishwoman who made an unusual visit to Russia and received a serf girl as a gift, "she is now my *own property* for ever."[2] Little Pashinka owed her new mistress unceasing work and attendance.

The eighteenth-century woman was provincial, meaning that her frame of reference was centered on her house, her family, her land, and her village. Outside news arrived slowly and randomly, or often not at all. Daily activity took place in a well-prescribed area—the house, the courtyard, and sometimes at harvest season, the fields. Women were responsible for all activities within the house, such as the preparation of food and clothing. They and their young servants would spin yarn in the evenings and then get up early to tend the

These Irish women grinding wheat at home made an essential contribution to the family economy.

barnyard animals. The care of cows and chickens fell almost exclusively to women. They milked cows and performed the burdensome job of making cheese, often several times a week. They gathered eggs and also slaughtered, plucked, and prepared fowl. Although men usually slaughtered larger animals, such as pigs, women salted the meat or otherwise preserved it. In Southern Europe, where olives and grapes were major crops, women cared for young plants, tied mature ones, and helped with harvesting. During the day they took food to men in the fields, after having prepared it. In late summer the women joined men in reaping, stacking, and hauling the harvest. In addition, they gathered great amounts of grain by gleaning what remained after the harvest on large estates; this was their traditional right and duty. Harvest time, however, did not bring any reduction in the normal household tasks, such as baking bread and brewing, making soap and candles, collecting firewood, and tending fires. Household and barnyard activity made the household self-sufficient, a self-contained unit of production and consumption. Thus the entire rural population relied mostly on its own efforts for the necessities of life. A village might have a shoemaker and a weaver, but in almost every other way the family provided for its own needs. Each household produced raw materials and then processed them into a usable form.

Everyone's work in early modern times was tedious. Like men's, women's common tasks involved danger, repetition, skill, and physical strength. For example, cheese-making and butter-making in those households with cows entailed skilled and sustained milking because the greatest fat content was in the milk of a near-empty udder. Given the risk of souring or spoilage, dairying also demanded cleanliness of equipment—a cleanliness achieved only with a great deal of extra effort in those days of no running water or even wells. To make cheese, farmwomen needed first to induce fermentation and to separate curds from whey. The curds were then chopped and sometimes rechopped and placed in molds or dishes so that additional separation and the action of fungi could occur to drain off lactose. The aging process required long periods of time—sometimes two years—and great physical effort in turning the large wheels of cheese, scrubbing and treating the cheese with various solutions, scalding it, and putting weights on it. The process also might be in vain—the cheese was susceptible to invasion of bugs, worms, and insects.

Textile production, which, like dairying, occurred simultaneously with dozens of other daily tasks, took place year-round. Making linen, a common textile of the day, involved first planting flax and later harvesting it by pulling the plants out by the roots. Then women put the flax through a series of water treatments followed by a rolling process, in order to soften the fiber and then to separate it from the woody stalk. These two procedures took weeks or even months. In silk production, which thrived in Italy, women and children contributed all the labor for the process of raising silkworms. They harvested leaves from mulberry trees, nurtured the silkworms' eggs until they formed cocoons, and gathered up the raw silk. Once raw silk, flax, or wool fibers were obtained, spinning followed. The most primitive form of spinning involved holding a distaff containing the fibers under one arm and pulling, stretching, and agitating the fibers in order to wind them into an ever longer thread on the spindle. Once a fairly long thread was achieved, the spindle was suspended from the thread in order to twist the thread. The twisted, strengthened thread was then wound up. From the sixteenth century on, various advances occurred in this procedure. The spindle was attached to a frame. Then a treadle was added to allow the spinning to occur mechanically, which freed the hands to feed the fiber more efficiently and ultimately, with additional improvements, to feed two fibers at once.

One road led away from these routines and toward the outer world—selling farm products at the fairs and markets that occurred regularly in cities and towns. A middleman or broker might pass through and buy the produce of the farmwife and her servants on larger farms. Even the impoverished serfs in Eastern Europe would sell milk to milkmaids to be taken to nearby towns. And many a farmwoman or her helper packed a basket on market days and rode or walked to town. Eighteenth-century records tell of farmwomen bringing a variety of produce, such as eggs, chickens, and cheese, to market. A Mrs. Pike, of Berkshire, England, was known for her pineapple-shaped cheeses, and others made theirs to look like rabbits or flowers. Turkeys and geese always sold well to townfolk, as did gooseberries, raspberries, apples, or fruit of any

Spinning was so consistently women's occupation that they are even today called the "distaff side," in reference to the spinning tool (here, held in the left hand).

sort, over which women had control because they tended the orchards. The return on the produce sold usually provided enough income to pay the rent or taxes on the farm or to make the small number of purchases required for the family.

Women increasingly did spinning for pay in midcentury. They, their children, and servants obtained raw fiber, especially cotton, and washed, picked, and combed it. Then they passed evenings spinning. The finished products were sent to town for weaving into cloth for the growing urban population. Activity of this sort—both the market transactions and the spinning—produced vital cash for taxes and rent. In fact, few rural households could have survived without women's cash contributions.

More necessary than cash contributions, however, were the women's productive activities of gardening, cooking, preserving, candle- and soap-making, and brewing. The farm economy did not supply the means for buying basic commodities, but even if money had been available, goods were not marketed on a mass basis that would make them accessible to the general population. As for men, they worked the fields, tended draft animals, raised buildings, repaired and built fences, and crafted and maintained equipment. They had neither the time nor the skill to perform household tasks. In other words, the rural economy operated with labor divided between the sexes. Both parts of this labor were needed to fill all of the household's needs. In such an economic system, neither half could do without the other. For instance, hardy farm widows, competent in many areas but not acquainted with the market in grain or in large animals, might hire male servants and field workers, but no one could replace the responsible male farmer. Likewise, a rural widower needed to remarry rapidly and might even arrange the new union at his wife's wake. A farmer had difficulty surviving without the household production and the cash contributed by the farmwife. What characterized rural life most of all was this sexually based division of labor, in which the halves were joined in an interlocking way. Only the full activity of each part united with that of the other ensured the family's survival. Historians have come to refer to such a situation as the subsistence family, or the family subsistence economy.

Certain aspects of caring for the household required comparatively little effort. For one thing, most rural people's houses were simple. A cottage or hut usually had floors of beaten earth and little furniture, so polishing and scrubbing were not common. The death inventory of an Italian peasant, who lived in the late eighteenth century near the present-day border of Yugoslavia, listed his possessions as "a table and some chairs and stools, a tripod and chair for cooking over an open fire, pots, kettles, tableware, and two wash tubs." No record of bedroom furniture survived, for his family and his descendants, right into the twentieth century, "slept on corn-shuck mattresses laid over boards and saw horses."[3] A general lack of implements, ornaments, and things in general characterized rural interiors. Although the kind of care associated with modern homes simply did not exist, the tasks of obtaining the basic ingredients of housekeeping—fire and water—were hard and time-consuming. Hauling water and wood, keeping fires going, and cooking in fireplaces demanded a great deal of energy and fell to women's domain.

As far as clothing was concerned, the utmost simplicity prevailed. Peasant men wore a tunic with wrapped leggings or stockings, all of which were knit or sometimes woven at home, or they wore plain, loose trousers. Women generally opted for simple garments too, though some travelers' diaries tell a different story. Those passing from Northern Europe to Italy noted such adornments as bracelets, ribbons braided through the hair, straw hats, and lace collars. A military man in Austria in 1809 saw fairly elaborate garb on peasant and artisan women: "a brown apron, short, very pleated and bordered with two ribbons or braid. The vest is gray or blue, and decorated with four rows of silver buttons."[4] Generally women wore ankle-length garments, an apron, and a vest. Wooden shoes, or sabots—fashioned at home during the winter—protected the feet. Usually clothing did not require particular skill to make; in fact, sewing, except of aristocratic costumes, remained relatively rough well into the nineteenth century. Because people wore the same clothing day-in and day-out, laundry was minimal. When it was done, however, the procedure, like other household tasks, took time.

Cooking involved an intense and unceasing preparation just to have primary foodstuffs, such as cheese, butter, bread, and beer. Peasants in Lithuania were noted eating "black rye bread, sometimes white, eggs, salt-fish, bacon, mushrooms; their favorite dish is a kind of hodge-podge made of salt or fresh meat, groats, rye flour, highly seasoned with onions and garlick [sic]."[5] People consumed their food without ceremony, especially when they ate in the fields. The common custom of housewives' standing in attendance while husbands and farmhands ate may have been due to the dispatch with which people put away food and the rarity with which ceremony accompanied meals at the common table. Rural people placed little importance on intricate interiors, elaborate clothing, and a varied diet because their first imperative was survival. Spinning, not elaborate sewing; milking, not fancy cooking: women spent their time at a subsistence level of endeavor.

In the mid–eighteenth century people lived at a subsistence level because so much of their labor, their produce, and their cash income went to the lord or landlord, the church, and the government. Where serfdom or customary obligations remained—and this was true for a good deal of Eastern Europe—families gave up large portions of the harvest to the landholder. Olive oil, chickens, grain, any amount of game (where peasants could hunt and trap), wine, and similar items went to the landholder, and thus depleted the family's larder and deprived its members of nourishment. Rural people owed service to the lord in the form of daily labor; three days a week or even more during harvest season was customary. Not escaping this service, women left their own demanding sphere to work as domestics or field workers for the aristocratic family. Government also took its toll in the form of a range of taxes, from which the nobility was often exempt. For example, in France, salt, a necessity for preserving food, was heavily taxed; so was the use of roads. Finally, the church took its due in the form of tithes and fees. In sum, the common rural household of the eighteenth century struggled against nature and society simultaneously. The struggle left them poorly fed, housed, and clothed, with varying degrees according to local and natural conditions. Women's struggle had a double nature since they were expected to work and to reproduce the working population.

Reproduction

That women give birth to children is a biological fact. Yet reproduction itself has a history that is cultural and economic as well as natural. Pregnancies, though major biological events, had economic and political repercussions; thus reproduction stands as a major social concern throughout history. In the eighteenth century women's reproductive role was a coordinate of their productive life. By bearing children rural women provided the family with workers, who would grow increasingly more productive as the older generation weakened. In a subsistence economy every mouth and every pair of hands made an important difference. So rural families monitored fecundity and sterility alike as part of their effort to ensure familial and community survival. For this reason, customs and rituals developed around childbirth, as did myths, superstitions, and storytelling. In other words, although reproduction was personal and biological and although it had economic repercussions, it also formed a set of social practices, directed by community life and inherited wisdom. These practices worked on the individual mother to give the experience of childbirth in those days its unique historic shape.

The individual woman's body differed in some respects from that of the typical modern woman. As a result of poor nutrition and inequitable distribution of food, women of that time were even slighter in stature compared to men than are women of today. Many historians see this as a phenomenon occurring in early modern times, not throughout human history. That is, epidemics of disease and famines in the fifteenth through eighteenth centuries gave rise to a belief that women needed less food. The account book of a Norwegian minister of the eighteenth century shows that loaves of bread baked for his male workers weighed three pounds and those for women, two. Even as late as the turn of the twentieth century social investigators found that it was common for men to take half the food at table and leave the rest to be divided among women and children.

In addition, the reproductive years of women were shorter but more dangerous. Nutrition and general health affect age at menarche. From the sixteenth through the eighteenth century women began menstruating at age fourteen to sixteen, whereas thirteen to fourteen was common from Greek times right through the Middle Ages and then again in the late twentieth century. Early modern women also reached menopause earlier, somewhere in the early to mid-forties instead of the late forties to early fifties. Finally, women living in rural communities of Western Europe began experiencing sexual activity around the age of twenty-six. This factor, along with the low age of menopause and the higher age of menarche, obviously contributed to contracting the range of childbearing years. Poor nutrition made those years even more dangerous. As the standard of living in rural areas of Europe fell with changes in agriculture, problems with childbirth increased. Small bone structure automatically meant a more difficult birth. Deficiencies in nutrients not only made bones smaller but could deform them, again making pregnancy riskier.

Although childbirth at this time appears fairly crude by modern standards, it in fact occurred amidst elaborate rituals and was subject to intervention from the village midwife. While neighbors coached the woman in labor, the midwife provided the most authoritative guidance. Usually a woman beyond the childbearing years, the midwife possessed experience and a headful of lore, techniques, and recipes for easing birth and for remedying its attendant, minor problems. By encouraging the individual mother in her duty of replenishing the working population, she served an additional function as a representative of the wider community. Many of the midwife's practices were benign or helpful, while others were harmful or even lethal. Clearly the midwife lacked modern scientific knowledge, and certainly she intervened radically into the birth process by pushing, pulling, massaging, and reaching into the birth canal to grab the infant or afterbirth. Yet physicians, who were starting at this time to claim a greater role in obstetrical matters, did much the same. For every tale of a midwife pulling off a child's head or arms because of her enthusiasm for intervening, there is one of a doctor pulling out a woman's uterus. Midwives had the worse record, but that was because there were more of them and be-

A Doctor Criticizes Midwives

Male doctors heartily criticized women health practitioners in the eighteenth century both to advance science and to advance themselves. At the time English Jeanne Stephens had gained international prominence for her experiments in dissolving kidney stones, while Dorothy Erxleben received her doctorate in medicine in 1754 from the University of Halle after years of successful practice. Among midwives themselves, Madame Leboursier du Coudray of France worked many improvements in assisting at childbirth. Most notably, she designed a cloth mannequin with removable fetuses, reproductive and other organs which allowed her and other expert midwives to teach their skill. Yet the renowned Swiss physician Auguste Tissot (1728–1797) found the general run of midwives wanting and proposed his own substitute treatments.

> The need for enlightened midwives in most of the country and I dare say in all of Europe is a well-known misfortune, which has the most disastrous consequences and which demands the full attention of the government.
>
> The errors they commit during deliveries are infinite and too often irremedial. We need a book expressly to give precise directions to alert them and we need to educate midwives fit to understand them. I will mention only one of their practices which does the most harm: it is the use of warm remedies which they give when the delivery is particularly painful or slow—such things as castor oil, safran, sage, rue, oil of ambergris, wine, theriaque, wine prepared with aromatics, coffee, liqueur of anis, nuts, or fennel and all other liqueurs. All these things are true poisons, which, far from speeding up the delivery in fact make it more difficult by inflaming both the uterus, which can then no longer contract, and all the parts, which serve as a passage and which as a result swell and then make the way narrower. At other times these warm poisons produce hemorrhages which can kill the mother in a short time.
>
> One saves both mothers and infants by the opposite treatment. As soon as a healthy women finds herself in labor and if that labor appears excessively painful and difficult, far from encouraging premature efforts by the remedies I just mentioned, which will end everything, one should order the mother to be bled in the arm which will prevent inflammation, which will stop the pain, and which will relax the body and make it more favorably disposed. One should give no food during labor except a little bread soup every three hours

and water thickened with flour. Every four hours one should cleanse the passage with a mixture of mallow and oil. .. , rub it with a little butter and place compresses of hot water on the abdomen.

Source: Extracts from *Oeuvres choisies de Tissot,* ed. M. J. N. Halle, 11 vols. (Paris: Allut, 1810) 1:446–448.

cause they attended more births. Only in difficult or critical cases did doctors come into play.

In a situation where childbirth itself was precarious, rural women had to produce enough children to ensure family survival. This meant achieving just the right fertility level to compensate for high rates of infant mortality. Most demographers agree that under average conditions during this period, 50 percent of children did not survive to adulthood. Where new methods of farming increased agricultural produce, survival sometimes increased to 60 percent. In seventeen years of marriage, the Italian peasant mentioned earlier and his wife had eleven children, only three of whom reached adulthood. Of the eight who died, several died within a few months, others at one, two, and seven years. The mother herself died in her thirty-sixth year, at the birth of the eleventh child. Most of the children died from "weakness," typhoid, and other conditions associated with poor nutrition, lack of sanitation, and epidemics of disease. The mother died during a famine. Men, women, and children all lived close to the margin; death was a common denominator. The high death rate meant that a high rate of reproduction was necessary to ensure replacement of the current generation and a basic supply of labor. Thus infertile women in Catholic countries worshiped the belt that encircled the Virgin Mary's pregnant body, kissed church door locks that symbolized to them the opening and closing of birth passages, and made special devotions and pilgrimages in order to get pregnant.

By contrast, where prosperity from better farming techniques resulted in better health and lower infant mortality, families lowered the numbers of children desired. A high age at marriage constituted a major means of controlling fertility. The fact that the average age at marriage slowly increased in the early modern period to a high of twenty-six in the eighteenth century has been explained as the result of a general population increase that needed curbing. As the food supply improved for well-off peasants, so did fertility. So in certain areas or among certain families affected by this new prosperity, age at marriage increased to curb excessive population growth. Other historians suggest that the higher average age at marriage resulted from bad conditions and a declining standard of living. Because trends in population, prosperity, and mortality were localized in those days, adjacent villages could experience similar trends—such as a rising age at marriage—for opposite reasons. The following tables show how different demographic conditions could exist within a single region and how they varied by occupation and gender.

Economic and social demands shaped reproductive practices in other ways. In countries where serfdom existed, the landlord wanted new families and increased population because a greater number of workers provided him with greater services. That is, children meant more hands, more household servants, more obligatory labor. A new family or household also meant an additional couple to tax. So landlords in areas such as Russia and the Hapsburg Empire controlled the age of marriage and lowered it by a variety of means. They might, for instance, levy an extra tax on fathers who had unmarried children above the age of thirteen. Such practices formed a way of encouraging marriage beyond the effect of community norms. In such areas the age at marriage was much lower than that in Western Europe. The average

Comparative Demographic Profile, Eastern Norwegian Towns, Eighteenth Century

Median Age at Marriage. First Marriages. Both sexes.

Men		Farmers	Cottars*	Miners/Ironworkers
Ullensaker	1733–1789	29.1	28.6	—
Nesodden	information lacking			
Bø	1727–1815	26.3	27.6	26.5
Sandsvær	1750–1801	29.2	29.2	27.1
Rendalen	1733–1780	28.2	33.3	—
Women				
Ullensaker	1733–1789	26.0	28.6	—
Nesodden	1710–1800	25.4	31.0	—
Bø	1727–1815	22.8	26.9	24.8
Sandsvær	1750–1780	24.7	27.8	26.3
Rendalen	1733–1780	24.5	30.5	—

Remarriage for Social Groups. Percentage. Both Sexes.

	Men				Women			
	Ullensaker 1733– 1789	Bø 1727– 1815	Sandsvær 1750– 1801	Ullensaker 1790– 1839	Ullensaker 1733– 1789	Bø 1727– 1815	Sandsvær 1750– 1801	Ullensaker 1790– 1839
Farmers	54	69	48	44	37	45	39	33
Cottars	67	70	50	55	39	36	26	25
Miners	—	67	67	—	—	14	31	—
Total	59	69	54	49	38	39	33	30

*A cottar is a tenant renting land from a farmer or landlord.

Permanent Celibacy. Percentage of Age Groups 45–49, 50–54 Not Married. Both sexes.

	Ullensaker	Nesodden	Bø	Sandsvær	Rendalen
Men	5.7	11.4	4.5	6.6	18.5
Women	4.3	10.3	9.8	9.9	10.7

Percentage of Brides That Had First Birth Before or 0–7 Months After the Wedding.

		Farmers	Cottars	Miners/Ironworkers
Ullensaker	1733–1789	26	58	—
Nesodden	1710–1800	29	49	—
Bø	1727–1815	33	47	67
Sandsvær	1750–1801	33	60	53
Rendalen	1733–1780	45	61	—

Survivors per 1,000 Liveborn Babies at Different Age. Different Social Groups.

		1 Year	5 Years	10 Years	15 Years
Ullensaker	farmers	802	637	593	569
	cottars	724	565	511	470
Bø	farmers	811	704	676	652
	cottars	804	705	655	626
	ironworkers	800	700	663	625
Sandsvær	farmers	835	737	704	690
	cottars	833	755	722	710
	miners	737	600	570	558
Rendalen	farmers	879	811	755	730
	cottars	841	732	620	588

Expected Numbers of Years Still to Live at the Age of 0. Both Sexes.

		1727–49	1750–69	1770–89	1790–1815
Bø	Women	38.3	39.2	41.8	41.7
	Men	36.6	37.3	39.7	39.6

Average Number of Children per Family. Different Social Groups and Total.

	Farmers	Cottars	Miners	Total
Ullensaker	4.31	3.51	—	3.91
Nesodden	no information			
Bø	4.90	3.60	—	4.20
Sandsvær	4.44	3.10	3.95	3.86
Rendalen	5.02	2.78	—	3.85

Source: Sølvi Sogner, *Scandinavian Journal of History,* 9 (1984) 2: 121, 123, 125, 128, 130, 131.

Estonian woman, for example, married around the age of twenty and bore roughly 8.5 children (although approximately two-thirds of them died before the woman reached menopause).

Contraception provided yet another way of fine-tuning reproduction to fit social and economic needs. Powders, potions, and ablutions after intercourse formed one set of practices women employed. They also tried to block the cervix with mechanical devices or gumlike materials. The simplest means—that is, changes in the practice of sexual intercourse itself—were probably also used. By the eighteenth century, France and areas of England experienced a definite decline in fertility. Both the greater age at marriage and this decline in fertility indicated that the practice of birth control was common. Although wars probably separated couples and thereby impeded conception, a portion of the population must have practiced coitus interruptus, or withdrawal before ejaculation. This technique requires male cooperation, so some historians have ruled out its extensive use. These historians argue that men had little concern for the dangers to their wives of childbirth and none for the discomfort; thus, they had little reason to end intercourse prematurely. However, the consequences of fertility affected men as well as women in this subsistence economy, so it is likely that this method was used. A man's need for a live and healthy wife to run his household may have tempered his desire for momentary pleasure.

Finally, abstinence was the simplest of methods. Letters from concerned mothers to their married daughters urged them and their husbands to refrain from sexual relations because childbirth was so dangerous. Whenever possible women took trips to visit their families after childbirth; this, too, constituted a way of limiting family size. In addition women who breast-fed their children became pregnant less rapidly than those who did not. In some cases such infertility resulted from taboos against sexual intercourse with lactating women. Where custom prescribed a nursing time of two years or more, couples observing this taboo could space children effectively. Yet, balancing work life with reproductive demands could determine what form of contraception obtained. In some areas of Finland mothers were too busy to breast-feed and so had servants feed infants cow's milk from animal horns. Such a decision based on work needs then affected methods of population management. Whatever the method and whatever the needs of any particular locality or family, couples and communities in the eighteenth century spent a good deal of energy, if unconscious energy, manipulating population.

Because reproduction influenced family survival, women worried whenever their pregnancy threatened to upset the balance between resources and human claims on them. In this situation, they took stern measures to prevent unwanted pregnancies from reaching full term. Someone in every village knew about abortifacients—oils, herbs, vegetable substances, or even animal parts that were thought to induce abortions. Most commonly tried were ergot (a fungus that developed on diseased grains), the savin plant, the herb rue, and tealike infusions and oils derived from any number of other herbs. In fact, the herbs used had some effectiveness—most of them (or their chemical equivalents) have since proved to affect uterine conditions. By causing contractions of one kind or another at certain stages in pregnancy, they probably had the intended effect in a good number of cases. To induce miscarriage women also beat themselves, hurled themselves down stairs, jumped from high places, and vigorously rode animals. Massaging the uterus was thought by some to be effective, and tight binding of the abdomen was a widespread practice. Some historians believe that more intrusive, mechanical ways of ending pregnancy had no following; the risk to the mother was too great.

Poor couples and single mothers often gave newborns away. Europe teemed with foundling hospitals accepting unwanted infants. In the country-side especially, women left their newborns on doorsteps of the church, of vil-lage notables, or of parish overseers. In towns or villages servants could usually only keep their jobs if childless, and in the countryside the pauperization of many rural workers due to the ongoing streamlining of agriculture made aban-donment a necessity. Illegitimacy, on the rise in the eighteenth century, also contributed to the increasing popularity of the practice. On admission or open-ing day, crowds of women with their infants would press in around the gates of foundling institutions. One by one, the children passed through an admis-sions process, which sometimes required them to have identifying bracelets or lockets or body marks noted in case the parents should want to reclaim them—if, of course, the children survived that long. When hospitals became full and no more were taken in that day, women often despaired. One observer noted that "the expressions of grief of the women whose children could not be ad-mitted were scarcely more observable than those of some of the women who parted with their children."[6]

Rural Life: Patriarchy, the Family, and Social Order

The joint success of agricultural production and the reproduction of the pop-ulation ensured the survival of society. These two efforts were coordinated through the family. People worked as family units in so close a way as to make the survival of single people difficult. No more than 10 percent of the adult population was unmarried, and most single adults lived in some sort of familial or otherwise organized situation. Family decisions influenced reproductive al-liances and regulated social behavior in such matters as visiting, participation in ceremonies, and the like. There was also a wider reliance of family members on one another in political and social affairs. Families wielded local power or, when welded into a pressure group, influenced decision-making.

For all these reasons prudent marriage was a necessity. Because survival was so precarious, seeking proper alliances made as much sense among peas-ants as among princes. A marriage could unite adjacent fields, for example, or identical village interests. Common decisions about the timing of pasturing on commonly held fields or meadows or about harvesting were reached more eas-ily among allies and kin. Parents also looked for hard-working daughters-in-law or sons-in-law. Because households produced just enough to survive, they considered dowries in arranging marriages. Potential husbands might bring a field, money, livestock, or furniture. The most eligible wives were those who had accumulated savings from their years as servants and whose parents had other goods to offer, such as livestock or furniture. Through extra work over the years a young woman was expected to have laid by household linens and some clothing. Help in harvesting, common boundaries, and common kin were other factors that played their parts. In other words, the goal for an arranged marriage at the lower social levels was to set a couple along the road to productive and reproductive survival with the necessary tools. At the same time, those arranging the marriage looked to strengthen their own ties, as well as those of their children, by intensifying the support of a network of kin. To this end, women's gossip at fountains or evening work sessions provided information about such matters as property, the size of dowries, and character. Finally, marriage brokers, relatives connected with the church, or village notables also might negotiate the transaction to prevent sentiment from damaging family interest. Thus marriages were arranged with an eye to grim necessity.

A demanding economic situation led to a tightly structured family life and also nurtured the age-old institution of patriarchy, or the rule of fathers. European patriarchy rested on legal systems and principles developed in classical times and incorporated into law from then on. The Roman law of *patria potestas* or "paternal power" originally gave fathers the right of life or death over their children; a father could also sell his children into slavery. This paternal power extended to control over all members of the household, including wives and slaves, and over all family property. Similarly, the subsequent law of the Germanic tribes in early medieval times developed the concept of *mundium,* a form of guardianship, especially the authority of men over women and children. Finally, the sense of patriarchy was enhanced by the predominant system of primogeniture, which meant that the eldest son inherited the greatest share or even all of the family property.

By the sixteenth century, this severely patriarchal system had gradually weakened. Unmarried women or widows came to have some freedom from the control of men. They might have property in their own name or participate in councils or other kinds of civic meetings. Children also acquired some rights in relation to their fathers, first in the realm of their bodily safety and then in the realm of marriage. In the latter case the competing authority of the church led to ideas of consent and affection in the sacrament of marriage. The church fathers maintained that force should not be at the basis of this sacramental tie, but rather the free will of the individual. In some countries, however, the most extreme paternal authority was reaffirmed and deference characterized children's behavior. Polish boys and girls writing home closed their letters with "My lowest prostrations at your feet, honorable, omnipotent lord," or "Well-wishing son and footstool."[7] Women and children often did not sit in the presence of men, and in Eastern Europe children were not supposed to turn their backs to their fathers.

The perceived incapacity of the married woman also received legal sanction. In general, a married woman had few rights with respect to property, participation in judicial procedures, and so on. In certain areas special laws allowed them to own property, but sometimes their husbands controlled it. In any event, married women usually had no legal status. As the famous English jurist Blackstone put it, "By marriage the very being or legal existence of a woman is suspended, or at least it is incorporated or consolidated into that of the husband, under whose wing, protection and cover she performs everything, and she is therefore called in our law a *feme covert*."[8]

In the eighteenth century society on the Continent and in England became conscious of growing numbers of infractions against patriarchy. Clandestine and unsanctioned marriages particularly menaced the social order. For example, English couples eloped to Scotland or to areas of London such as Fleet Street that were historically exempt from normal requirements in marriage procedures. In other countries young people moved to cities and often took up residence with a partner, perhaps of a different social station, without parental permission. Like Samuel Johnson, many thought women in such cases should be severely punished "so as to deter others from the same perversion."[9] Families saw such infractions not only in personal terms but in terms of economic and political well-being. On another level, because people believed that the family was the center of all order, they reasoned that lack of respect for the father indicated lack of it for the lord, for the king, and for God. Disobeying one's father was therefore not merely a private act but heresy and treason. Thus, the monarchical state had good reason to enforce patriarchy in the household. In short, patriarchy worked on the personal level, on the familial level in terms of local power, on the state level in terms of social and political control, and at the spiritual level, because the church adhered to a male hierarchy and a masculine deity.

Some historians believe that the eighteenth century witnessed some tightening of older customs that gave women some official participation in power, for example, the severe curtailment of their prerogatives in making wills and in their legal standing when widowed or when their husbands were away or incapacitated. Other historians see a softening of patriarchy in Russia in the eighteenth century. Specifically, Westernization led to some control by wives of their property, to their exemption from an old rule about following their husbands into exile, and to freedom for some serf women who married free men. The Russian situation demonstrates the lack of uniformity in the details and evolution of patriarchy. It remained, however, the most common social and political form, one that made sexual difference the major controlling force in human society.

Within the family, patriarchy meant that the husband and father controlled decision-making and had ultimate authority. When areas of work required explicit coordinating, the male head of the family took charge. No country in Europe escaped from this arrangement of familial power. Indeed, patriarchy went back to the earliest societies and produced a whole range of proverbs and common wisdom, such as "A good horse and a bad horse need the spur; a good wife and a bad wife need the rod." Many of these proverbs spoke of women's inferiority in ways that announced her need for rule by men: "Where there's a woman, there's no silence."[10] But by the early modern period some advice urged moderation in patriarchy: "Just as a woman's body does not permit her to do the same physical labor as a man, neither does a woman have it in her heart to be as patient and long-suffering when adversity strikes. . . . Therefore, let the husband be the voice of reason and wisely spare his wife punishment, willingly bearing what fortune brings so that they may live together in peace."[11]

Sometimes the patriarch shared his power. For example, some cultures accorded both mother and father prerogatives over children and servants. "Father and mother are visible gods," one saying went. Another, from the sixteenth century, was

> A good child does always
> his mother and father obey.
> A bad one, even when beaten,
> rebels and goes astray.[12]

In the Eastern European and Mediterranean areas the extended family allowed for two lines of authority based on age and gender. Households usually combined several families, containing a father and mother plus all sons and their wives or a group of brothers and their spouses. Such combinations came into being to benefit the overlord's need for well-organized service and to protect any single family from failure due to these demands or to military conscription. Although a male commanded the total enterprise, a female line of control also existed. The father or oldest brother coordinated the work of sons, brothers, and any day laborers or servants; and the mother or oldest female spouse oversaw daughters-in-law, sisters-in-law, and any hired women. In directing some strangers, the mother-in-law organized a different kind of group from the collection of sons led by their father.

Daughters-in-law in the extended family—the *zadruga* it was called in the Balkans and in Hungary—had a particularly difficult time. First, unrelated to anyone, they entered a household of related men in a society where men ruled. They also entered as young women into a unit where age was of some importance. Thus, the daughter-in-law stood at the bottom of several hierarchies and bore a heavy charge to obey, to work, and to reproduce. Daughters-in-law also maintained connections with their former home, sometimes by tending part-time a plot of their mother's land and receiving the harvest. The daughter-in-law's relationship with men in the family was especially problematic. Fathers-in-law so regularly made sexual advances that this abuse often had a name of its own in local dialects. Husbands continued to beat their wives even when this long-established privilege was forbidden by law. In Hungary, failure to conceive was remedied by forcing the woman to have sexual relations with other men in the family. A widowed woman could expect her brothers-in-law to try to cheat her and her children of their inheritance and thus of the wherewithal to survive. Nor were mothers-in-law known for giving assistance. They might try to steal clothing, linens, or money from a dowry trunk. In some cultures, women worked to eliminate this abuse by placing clear markings on spoons, dishes, linens, chairs, and every other item a daughter-in-law legally had a right to. Even when a woman rose to the top of her ranks, she could lose her privileges when her husband died. From being the woman in charge of the women workers, she would become a subordinate sister-in-law if her husband's death put a younger brother-in-law in charge.

Rural Life: Community

Agricultural practices connected families to one another in a community. First, community members jointly controlled land on which animals were pastured or from whose woods people gathered fuel. Second, farming decisions about planting and harvesting were communal ones because animals had free run of all land between harvest and replanting. If nothing else bound people together, these two practices ensured that the community reached into family life to shape the behavior of individuals. This closeness reduced individual autonomy.

The community affected many young women's lives directly for the first time when they were sent out into other households to work as servants and began living according to the rhythms of other families. Another vigorous intrusion of the community into private life occurred in courting. Young people followed community patterns when they participated in Maypole dances, St. Valentine's Day observances, or other intersexual rituals. On St. Valentine's Day young men and women exchanged small gifts, messages, or favors—none of which indicated love or a definite move toward mating. Instead, such rituals of youth channeled sexual feelings, and young people's sexual feelings manifested themselves along the lines set out in these ritual practices. Such observances constituted the framework of young sexuality. Where marriage occurred late, young men and women formed themselves into groups, sharing friendships while monitoring and regulating premarital encounters. Some historians maintain that in Scandinavia and England, parents surrendered much of their involvement in matchmaking to the unmarried segment of the community, even to the point of allowing for individual choice as long as the rest of the youth approved.

What courting rituals did couples follow? How did they act toward one another in order to cement an alliance? Rural people gathered in the evening in barns, where the body heat of the animals warmed the company. Women—old and young—would do their spinning, sewing, and mending on such occasions. Young men and women would see each other and get acquainted. Often such *veillées* or *Spinstubbe* were segregated. While men played cards or games, women worked and circulated information about the habits, property, and so on, of eligible males. Dancing might occur, offering youth a chance to mingle, or young men would accompany young women home. In these ways, couples formed out of sex-segregated groups. Another courtship ritual was "bundling," or keeping company by sharing a bed that had a divider down the middle. Youth monitored these practices to ensure that they followed community norms and rituals. If couples transgressed against community opinion or that of their families, they would be loudly censured with a charivari, a noisy show of displeasure, or other public demonstration of disapproval. In Württemberg in 1759, a group of women beat a young man almost to death for his conduct at a *Spinstubbe*. The women claimed they "should have injured him even more,"[13] for the man had violently intruded on their activities in order to court an uninterested young woman. Disapproval might also be manifested, for example, if a very young man wooed an older woman or a widow. Misalliances invited not only family wrath but community censorship.

Premarital sex alone, however, usually aroused no such censure and was even customary. Premarital sex was only subject to community approval of the suitability of the partners in the union. In many parts of agrarian Europe premarital intercourse was supposed to result in pregnancy. This "testing" or "trying out" allowed the prospective husband and the community to gauge the woman's ability to reproduce. During this period 54 percent of all first children in one Danish county, for example, were baptized less than nine months after their parents' marriage. When pregnancy occurred before a couple had set up a household, the community as well as the family generally made sure that a marriage took place quickly. In this way new unions prevented a growth in the number of people unconnected to a predictable family structure—as illegitimate children or infertile women would be—from disrupting the smooth functioning of community life.

During the important events in women's lives—marriage and childbirth—they were enveloped by the attentions and rituals of the female community. Neighbors and female relatives surrounded the bride at her marriage, escorted her, prepared her clothing, prepared the nuptial bed, serenaded or charivariied her. During childbirth the already familiar midwife represented the community at its strongest. That is, she symbolized its accumulated knowledge, however primitive and incorrect, and its intervention at a crucial point—the birth of new souls, of new hands. Other women joined the midwife and together they took charge of the event. "I was banished before the bed was prepared," an early modern Nuremburg lawyer wrote; "Frau Margrethe Endres Tucherin, Ursula Fritz Tetzlin, the widow Magdalena Mugenhoferin and Anna the midwife assisted my wife."[14] Such women stoked fires, fetched water, and generally filled the room where the birth was taking place. They claimed the mother's body and the event by their presence. At this moment stories about other births were exchanged, and proverbs and lore were used to explain any unusual aspect of the birth and gauge its progress. The baby's appearance also involved a ritual. First, witnesses examined the baby's general demeanor, position at birth, the sounds he or she made, and explained these in light of past experiences and lore. The afterbirth was, in some cases, burned in a ritualized way, while the mother sweated under heavy coverings. In other words, reproduction occurred as a biological or physiological function that was wrapped in communal ritual. It took its coloration and meaning from these rituals. Never isolated, childbirth adhered to mechanisms of female sociability and control.

Villagers worked together, watched each other, and celebrated as a group. One communal activity was the annual hiring fair where young people—male and female—displayed themselves so that farmers would contract for their services for a year. Harvest time brought more community celebrations and so

Cross-dressing was part of public ritual in early modern society. In this picture the priest and the barber are dressing as characters from Don Quixote.

did Plough Day in the spring. Weddings took place according to agricultural time: for example, in the Riazan province of Russia in 1782, 57 percent of all marriages took place in the fall, at harvest time; virtually none occurred in the busy summer months. The religious calendar also influenced the timing of weddings: no one got married during Advent (December) or Lent (March). Human affairs moved to the beat of agricultural and religious rhythms.

The most important festivity in pre-industrial Europe was Carnival, the pre-Lenten period when people in towns, cities, and villages turned out for the wildest of festivals. The highlights of Carnival were pranks, masquerades, gluttony, and excesses of many kinds. In most cases these elements of Carnival signaled an inversion of normal life, as did celebrations and rituals in general. People lived for this respite from their daily hardships and toil; they lived, some historians have said, for celebration. Thus, Carnival and similar festivals brought a joy and excess not prevalent in daily life, and marked a departure from the normal by emphasizing the abnormal. Most prominent among these abnormalities were those related to the body, beginning with excessive eating and drinking and ending with bodily violence. In between were mock sexual inversions and exaggerations. In Valencia, Spain, each neighborhood sent a huge wooden or wax *falla* or phallus to the March festival, and in other celebrations enormous phallic symbols, pig bladders, horns, and huge sausages were paraded through the streets. Men dressed up as women, and women as men. In some areas, celebrations had moments when women ruled the festival or seemed to gain the upper hand. In Spain a regular feature of festivals saw women pouring buckets of water from balconies onto men in the streets below. Such manifestations of sexual role inversion allowed for organized release of sexual tension. Even the *Spinstubbe,* a time not quite like ordinary work time, could erupt occasionally into an outburst of cross-dressing.

The playing out of misrule and abnormal sexual roles shaped normal sexuality into the controlled patterns of a society that had to be highly organized for survival purposes. Carnivals, festivals, and other special occasions allowed sexual and bodily expressions momentarily to take hold of society, to have their moment of glory. The costumes that emphasized the sexual, the color and glitter, the aspect of orgy, and the filling of public spaces with uncontrolled bodies announced another way of life, another possibility for modes of living and being. Although the festivities of Carnival time and other occasions marked boundaries by transgressing them, they also resisted those boundaries and showed the possibility of redefining them. Therefore, even though the pre-Lenten Carnival declined as the most important celebration, the carnivalesque continued to play a role in other aspects of social life and in an ongoing array of popular holidays.

Aristocratic Women and the Political Elite

Noble families ruled over the village communities, over groups of villages, and sometimes over miles and miles of villages. Inheriting this right from preceding generations, the nobility adjudicated disputes, collected taxes and services, and took major parts of the agricultural yield as rent or as their customary share of the harvest. Even in areas where many of these powers had disappeared, the nobility constituted a social elite with political and economic power because they owned large stretches of land. At the apex of this inherited system of power stood the monarchy—an institution that had evolved from limited aristocratic landholding to dominion over entire kingdoms. Kings also inherited their right to rule, including their claims to dispense justice and to a wide range of offices, priveleges, and patronage.

Inherited rulership—whether local or national—symbolized the achievement of successful gender ordering that on the village level made for the stable replenishment of population. That is, aristocratic families survived or fell according to their reproductive stability. Passing through generations, kingly or aristocratic power incarnated the generalized maintenance of the species and thus of culture: a "power or principle . . . in the seed," as one seventeenth-century commentator put it.[15] At the same time the community owed these representatives of its reproductive success sustenance and thus its agricultural surplus as well as services. Often living in abundance and with excessive pleasures, the nobility and monarchs of Europe displayed all the goods that the community was capable of producing. In this way the body politic valued the monarchical and aristocratic forms of rulership as a synthesis of its productive and reproductive accomplishments. As the map on page 27 shows, countries like France, England, and Spain had consolidated monarchies, whereas the

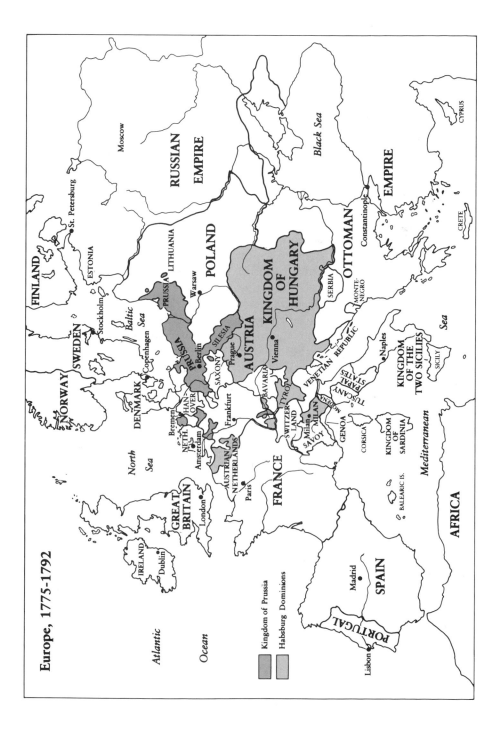

Europe, 1775–1792

German states were divided and the Habsburgs of Austria aimed at incorporating other kingdoms and principalities.

Birth-right or lineage—the political symbol of reproduction—determined where one belonged in the social order, whether one was common or noble. Although monarchs increasingly ennobled the very rich as a way of recognizing the achievement of great wealth, early modern social theory generally explained societies and civilizations as resting on a static kind of order with very little social mobility. In most countries these static social distinctions actually received legal classification in the concept of "estate" or "order." In Spain, for instance, there were four orders, while in France, three—the first estate or clergy, the second estate or nobility, and the third estate, which comprised the townspeople. While in England much of this precision was disappearing, in other places the nobility worked to fortify its legal position and prerogatives. Reinvigorating their claim to rule by finding a common ancestry, Polish nobles in the eighteenth century traced the origins of their estate to a single tribe, the Samartians. In addition, the nobility as a whole saw itself as possessing distinctive qualities such as virtue and courage. Nobility, according to one theorist, amounted to "a quality of superiority transmitted by blood."[16]

Given these beliefs, marriage constituted a major event in noble families. Family ties were at once political alliances, systems of clientage and patronage, and conduits of power. Extended kin groups at these upper reaches of society acted to exert or gain control of politics. Thus marriages served to maintain these alliances, to strengthen them, to enrich them, and even to extend them in new directions. To this end, family members kept track of their cousins and relatives to a degree that today seems quite remote. Family lore formed a kind of history that at least one or two members of the family had to specialize in. Indeed, official history for centuries amounted to narratives of marriages among noble and royal families. As people married, so power flowed. For this reason family councils, mediators, and royal ambassadors arranged marriages among the nobility according to strict principles and through careful negotiation. As a result personal interests of prospective couples carried little weight. Balking at a politically advantageous marriage, a young Polish noblewoman received this warning from her mother: "If you do not do my will you will not have God's blessing and I will wish all bad things on you, and even if you lie under a wall I will not know you; but if you do my bidding I will share my last crumb of bread with you."[17]

Marrying into an aristocratic family, a woman brought her monetary and landed fortune along with her family pedigree. As with peasant women, an economic contribution was essential, and never more so than in the eighteenth century. The rise of commerce made the noble way of life increasingly expensive. Writing in 1732, Lord Chesterfield described the importance of wealth in marriage: "If a marriage can be called 'good,' it's because of this, that there is something solid to it—money."[18] Moreover, the chase for heiresses formed a kind of melodrama the general public enjoyed. In England the *Gentleman's Magazine* ran a regular column giving dowry information and other juicy details of upcoming marriages among the elite. As for the family pedigree, it enhanced political power by intensifying the noble blood of the next generation.

Among the poorest aristocracy, wives performed the same kind of agricultural work that peasant women did. For the most part, however, the main responsibility of the noblewoman was breeding. Without the childbearing of a suitable aristocratic woman, the family line ended and with it generations of economic and political power. By contrast, a fertile woman of good pedigree ensured the maintenance of the blood line, of the "estate" or order, and of the principle of blood embodied in aristocratic succession. Rarely tending or educating children, they performed their job by breeding alone. The amount of reproduction involved varied in the eighteenth century. In England, for instance, the upper echelons of society produced somewhere between seven and eight children per family, while in France the number had dropped from more than six in the seventeenth century to two. Different authors have explained both trends as indications of greater parental affection; it is still undecided what such variations mean.

Bound up in the idea of noble blood, childbirth practices reflected the wide ranging power of the aristocracy. On the simplest level aristocratic women were better nourished and received better care. In addition, they benefited from gynecological improvements in medicine during the century. Reproducing the embodied power of an entire estate when they gave birth, aristocratic women found themselves performing a political act. A mid-century observer in the Kingdom of Naples noted the illumination of the castles on the birth of a royal child there. "Shouting, and candles, and torches, and coloured lamps . . . did their best to drive forward the general joy, and make known the birth of the royal baby for many miles round the capital; and there was a splendid opera the next night. . ." and after that a masquerade.[19] Royal childbirth called for official witnesses as well as the queen's ladies-in-waiting and midwives. Courtiers, senators, and the Chancellor, for instance, attended the delivery of Swedish Queen Sophia in 1778. Neither a personal act nor a simple summons to popular rejoicing, the lying-in of a queen or aristocrat called for male attendance precisely because of the political stakes involved.

Noble women and men cemented their difference from the lower classes with a distinctive way of life. In general, noblewomen hired wet-nurses for their infants. Breastfeeding would have made them too much like peasants. Moreover, taboos precluded sexual intercourse during the period of nursing and thus a woman was less sexually available for her husband. While the rest of society labored, the nobility followed the rituals of rulership and pursued all types of pleasure. Noblewomen in cities and those who took part in court life set cultural norms and fashions. Chateaus and palaces, whether urban or rural, constituted the center of social and political life. Attracting the ambitious and clever, courts fostered the arts, determined etiquette, fixed social standing, and radiated power through their ceremonies. Within the hierarchical ordering of status and place according to birth and familial power, aristocratic women took up the roles of ladies-in-waiting, readers to queens and princesses, keepers of the wardrobe, and other honorific but nonetheless im-

Artists and Pleasure in the Old Regime

Artists depended on aristocratic patronage in the eighteenth century. Among them Venetian Rosalba Carriera (1675–1757) made the pastel a popular medium for mythologies and portraiture, while Swiss artist Angelica Kauffmann (1741–1807) started work with her father in portraiture but then devoted a good deal of her time doing classical and historical scenes. Both travelled in the highest circles, but French artist Elisabeth Vigée-Lebrun (1755–1842) outdid them with her series of commissions from Queen Marie Antoinette and other important nobility across Europe. Vigée-Lebrun visually captured the pleasures of her time, but she also left written remembrances of how even a hard working artist, who from her teens had supported her family, enjoyed life.

Elisabeth Vigée-Lebrun, the great portrait painter, here portrayed by someone else.

The business of the day over, twelve or fifteen amiable people would gather to finish their evening in their hostess's home. The relaxed and easy gaiety that reigned over these light evening meals gave them a charm that formal dinners could never have. A sort of confidence and intimacy spread among the guests; and because well-bred people can always eliminate stiffness, it was in these suppers that Parisian high society showed itself superior to the rest of Europe.

At my house, for instance, we gathered about nine o'clock. We never talked of politics, but of literature or recounted the story of the day. Sometimes we amused ourselves with charades and sometimes [authors] read us a few of their verses. At ten we seated ourselves; my suppers were the simplest, composed always of a fowl, a fish, vegetables, and salad; but it mattered little, we were gay, amiable, hours passed as if they were minutes, and at about midnight, everyone departed.

One evening my brother was reading me the *Travels of Anacharis*. When he got to the place where a description of a Greek dinner appears, it explained how to make several sauces. I called my cook and we decided to have such and such a sauce for the fowl and another for the eels. As I was expecting very pretty women [for dinner], I decided to dress all of us in Greek fashions. My studio, full of everything necessary to drape my models, would furnish enough clothes, and the Count de Parois also had a superb collection of Etruscan vases. The charming Madame de Bonneuil arrived, then Madame Vigée, my sister-in-law, and soon both had been transformed into veritable Athenians. Lebrun-Pindar entered; we removed his hair powder, and I put a crown of laurel on his head. I also found costumes for Monsieur de Riviere, Guinguene, and Chaudet, the famous sculptor.

Besides the two dishes that I have already mentioned, we ate a cake of honey and raisins, and two plates of vegetables. We also drank a bottle of old wine from Cyprus that someone had given me as a guest. We spent a long time at dinner where Lebrun recited us several odes of Anacreon that he translated himself. I don't believe I ever had a more amusing evening.

Source: Adapted from Elisabeth Vigée-Lebrun, 2 vols. *Souvenirs* (Paris: Des Femmes, 1984) 1:85–88.

portant positions. Wealthy noblewomen danced attendance on monarchs, appeared at royal audiences, and generally participated in aristocratic display. Apparently useless, these displays were crucial as signals of the distance and difference in the aristocratic way of life. In demonstrating difference, courtlife thus manifested the order of a static society.

Constant pleasure shaped the wealthy aristocratic woman's daily life. Countess Stéphanie-Félicité de Genlis (1746–1830), for instance, spent her childhood taking minor roles in the plays her mother constantly put on at their chateau. Neighbors, servants, and guests all participated in this daily round of pleasure. Young Félicité loved fantasy and spent time every night "building castles in Spain."[20] Once married, she carried these habits into her new home. From morning to evening members of the household played tricks and pranks on each other, on itinerant craftsmen, or on passersby. In other palaces women sponsored days or even whole weekends devoted to blindman's bluff, pantomimes, acting out proverbs, or learning the latest dance. In addition, they smoked, drank, took snuff avidly, and amused themselves at gambling, cards, the hunt, and dancing. Princess Sapieha of Lithuania, for instance, was notorious for her gambling and was perpetually in debt because of it. In the parade of aristocratic frivolities, the noblewoman played her part. According to the Countess de Genlis, the aristocratic woman brought "gaiety, amusement, and joy" into upper-class life.[21] The aristocracy as a whole was highly made-up, with powdered hair and faces lavishly spread with paint and color, except where particularly strict Protestant standards, such as those of the Lutherans, had an effect. Noblewomen spent hours having their hair done into coiffures a foot or more high. Even among Lutherans, women decorated their faces with patches in the shape of stars, moons, or hearts, placed in rows leading out from the corners of eyes or mouth. The sexually enticing clothing of both men and women and the lavish adornment indicated a class of people made for pleasure and for domination, but not for work. Aristocratic women not only participated in those pleasures, they were responsible, as de Genlis noted, for inspiring and representing them.

Finally, the nobility—including its women—followed a different standard in its sexual practices. The quest for sexual pleasure could imbue aristocratic life, apart from its reproductive responsibility. Monarchs, for instance, had wives of the highest lineage for reproductive purposes and publicly acknowledged mistresses who took part in court ceremonies. Both the body's pleasures and the body's responsibilities received the highest form of recognition in this dual system. Yet the full exercise of pleasures only fell to the aristocracy. Commoners' deviations into adultery, for instance, brought community sanction and even legal prosecution. Aristocratic women, however, allowed themselves the noble privilege of sexual play, perhaps as much as noble men did. Adventures of the Duchess of Württemburg or of the Margravine of Bayreuth-Kulmbach, who sent seducers into her own daughter's bedroom, were common knowledge. The Countess de Genlis had a well-publicized affair with the Duke d'Orleans, while Catherine the Great openly kept a series of lovers. Later such behavior or the rumor of it would arouse people's political wrath and lead to revolutionary activism. For the moment, however, Countess Hopken at the

Swedish court happily and publicly posed nude for a statue named *Venus of the Beautiful Backside* and other women scurried into liaisons as their aristocratic due. The *cisisbo* in Italy and the *cortejo* in Spain were men who paid constant and public court to a favorite well-born woman while her husband went off with someone else. A range of such customs defined aristocratic sexuality and perpetuated a chivalric mode of sexual relationships.

Urban Women

After a hundred years of plagues, war, and famine, urban life prospered in the eighteenth century. Towns and cities grew in size, up to the limits of their walls or fortifications. For women, town life meant some release from the wearisome labors of agriculture. It offered certain conveniences, such as the ability to purchase food from markets, a greater variety of social events and entertainment, and the benefit of a dense network of neighbors. Because the townswoman usually worked with her husband in a craft or trade, her infants often were cared for by nurses. In addition, the urban woman could send her children to school for a few years until they could help in the family's business. Living in a town also meant access to news and information about political life. As a result, women as well as men were part of crowds and riots, which became frequent in some urban areas as the century wore on. Thus, the idea that urban life made one "free"—a notion born when serfs could gain their freedom by escaping to a town—had a wide meaning by this time. Towns offered the opportunity for those dissatisfied with the static aspects of agricultural life to expand their horizons and change their ways of thinking.

Urban women contributed to the family economy in a variety of ways. First, the dowry brought by the wife of an artisan often meant the difference between having a shop of his own or remaining a dependent laborer. Second, the work of wives and daughters allowed trades to flourish. These women packed, delivered, and sold goods; they cleaned the workshop and provisioned it with wood and water. In larger establishments the staff—journeymen, apprentices, and servants—required care in the form of feeding them, cleaning their clothes, and even caring for them when they were sick. Prosperous businesses, such as the barbershop of Johann and Elizabeth Dietz, meant more complicated households and more domestic work. In addition, women often entered into productive work in the craft. For weavers, they cleaned, carded, and spun raw materials; in metal trades, they did polishing and other finishing.

Some women pursued their own work, even when married to men in other trades. In textiles and clothing, they demonstrated the most independence. Seventeenth-century Florence saw women dominant in silk weaving, and in German cities they were most prominent in spinning. Women veil-makers, lacemakers, and glove-makers worked on their own. These particular crafts even gave rise to all-women workshops run by female masters, though only a few achieved any great success. A variety of other urban occupations, such as seamstressing, hat-making, and felt-making, attracted women, but in smaller numbers than did the production of cloth. In metal working only a few ran their

A Danish woman sells baskets. Market women and itinerant peddlers hawked every conceivable item.

own shops, mostly ones that made pins. They produced other small items such as candles and buttons. In the provisioning trades, women served as butchers, and many women hawked, peddled, or tended stalls in markets. They made and sold sausages, cleaned tripe, prepared springs for watches, stitched shoes, wound quills, told fortunes, and wove ribbons. Even in such unlikely occupations as masonry, women often performed unskilled, often heavy, work. Tax rolls show a few women represented in unusual occupations, such as barbering, hauling, and rag-picking. They and their daughters excelled at running tea-gardens, taverns, inns, and other institutions where people ate, drank, relaxed for a moment, or stayed the night. Women also might care for other's children—an estimated 5,000 wet-nurses out of a total population of 90,000 in Hamburg fed the children of busy urban craftswomen, as well as those of the nobility. In the urban environment, prostitution was another way of earning a living, but usually as a last resort. In all these cases, as in the rural one, women had the responsibility of supporting themselves and contributing to the family economy.

When widowed, a woman might carry on her husband's business. In trades ranging from clock-making to masonry, a woman might continue her husband's craft if she possessed either the necessary ability or the necessary personnel to help. The most abundant evidence of such efforts is found in the printing profession. Although generally they were not particularly well prepared for this work, since their literacy level was always less than men's, many printing widows seemed to flourish. Modifying their husbands' trademarks to indicate their new independence, they published books ranging from Greek-Latin dictionaries and theological treatises to popular works of entertainment and political propaganda.

For the most part, women in early modern Europe had a lower level of skill than men because they lacked training. They acquired what skills they had in a number of ways. Most often they learned to perform semiskilled tasks and those requiring little more than simple dexterity by working with their parents. If a woman married a man whose trade was different from her father's, she would undergo additional training so she could help out with her husband's particular business. In general, women trained by parents or husbands had lower levels of skills than those who had undertaken a formal apprenticeship. Although apprenticeships of three to five years or more were common for boys from artisans' families, apprenticeships for girls formed only a tiny percentage of the artisanal contracts. When a woman or girl became destitute, municipal authorities often came to the rescue by setting up and paying for an apprenticeship. Such arrangements were, however, somewhat chancy: a fifteen-year-old of good family officially complained that in her apprenticeship she "did nothing with fashion and hairdressing and instead acted as a servant."[22] More common than apprenticeship was the job of servant. Being in service might only mean domestic drudgery, errands, and provisioning the household, but could also mean learning certain aspects of household production. Religious institutions also provided training and even jobs.

Given the lower level of training for women, it is hardly surprising that they were less likely than men to have a craft or skill. When they did have a craft, working life coexisted with bearing and raising children and running a household. Missing out on an apprenticeship or trade meant missing out on an important form of organized group life—namely the journeyman's association or guild. Especially on the Continent, where guilds were the essence of community life, almost every male occupation had its guild, which shaped both work and professional identity. Women also had organizations based on their work. Feather workers, makers of artificial flowers, and women in various branches of textile and clothing production created associations of various kinds to give them an occupational identity and group strength. These groups, however, were not as numerous, as powerful, or as prominent as men's associations. Male guilds often barred women from their activities and especially inhibited single women by denying them connections with their corporations. Such connections usually were needed in order to obtain licenses and a range of other work permits. Thus, in 1738 Anne Calcott received a fine in Oxfordshire, England, for trying "Of her own proper Authority without any Lycence admission or allowance—to be a—Carryer Buyer and Seller of Butter Cheese Eggs Poultry and other dead Victualls."[23]

Male trade associations played a role in urban politics and also gave meaning to their members' lives; they shared a common patron or saint, marched together in civic festivals or religious processions, and followed a common set of rules, which even extended into the conduct of family life. In contrast, women's groups were usually less formal; for example, fishwives and market women banded together because of the proximity of their work and chose common saints or patronesses but did not receive the kind of external recognition awarded to guilds. Nor did they share in political power. Young male artisans of Europe made wandering tours of the country while they perfected their skills and made contacts. In the process they, like members of urban guilds, joined with other *compagnons* (the French word for these wandering artisans) in their work, relaxation, political and religious life, and even their sexual adventures and courtships. Women, however, never entered such a unified existence with other artisans; they returned to their families daily if they worked outside the home or never left it if they served as family helpers. As a result, they seldom exerted much economic or professional power.

The fact that women lacked clear occupational definition within towns worked to the benefit of the economic order. Whereas the guild structure's regulation of production, prices, wages, and entry to occupations created a rigid manufacturing situation, the unskilled nature of women's work allowed for flexibility. Women could fill a range of jobs and be sent out to work or be kept at home as circumstances required. Men had a clear sense of occupation and public status as artisans of such-and-such a guild. By contrast, women had a weaker public identity, and this gave the entire structure the flexibility to survive. When economic crisis or uncertainty arose, women often had their wages lowered by order of a guild or were even banned entirely from certain occupations. Records of German guilds, for example, show masters becoming less tolerant of widows maintaining their husband's craft. Leather workers protested against allowing women of an artisan's family to do unskilled work on belts because their cheap labor allowed the artisan to cut costs. From the fifteenth century on, women in the German cities of Leipzig and Göttingen were prohibited from weaving, and sixteenth-century regulations prohibited them from knitting hose on anything but needles. On the other hand, in Florence, for example, the number of women working in weaving had escalated by the eighteenth century as men abandoned it for more lucrative employment producing luxury items. The development of new commodities and new ways of producing them brought changing commercial patterns which unsettled Europe for both good and bad. This unstable situation prevailed right up until the Industrial Revolution. The result was a focus on women's work and an attempt to organize and contain it.

The gender-based division of occupations gradually became more pronounced as guilds sought to make work roles clearer in order to ensure their own well-being. By the eighteenth century widowhood spelled poverty in areas in which widows were restricted from continuing their husbands' trades. Municipal laws and trade regulations clearly shepherded women into lower paying positions and even less skilled ones. Although there were thousands of women weaving in Florence, they had virtually no representation in more prosperous crafts. In German cities, where they had once held various positions in the textile industries, women were mostly limited to spinning. These were the years when the word *spinster* started taking on less positive connotations, even though spinning was the source of women's livelihood and the repository of much of their talent. Spinning lost any economic importance it might have once had and became a kind of last resort. Thus, although town life offered women more variety than country life did, many observers sensed a decline in the position of women in the crafts. This sense of decline would have clear political import for the rise of protest and the beginnings of revolution.

Servants

On September 28, 1784, the Reverend James Woodforde noted in his diary that one of his maids had been unable to work for a week "owing to a bad thumb." A second maid, Molly Dade, was "very bad in a Cough. . . . She has increased it to day by easing the other maid in helping her and [the other maid] is so foolish as to tell Molly that she is in a Consumption—which makes the poor Girl very unhappy." For the next three weeks Woodforde noted the state of Molly Dade's health until finally, "though most willing to keep her," he sent her home to be with her parents; she did have tuberculosis. Molly's sister Betty replaced her, but the entries about Molly continued until her death a few months later. "As good a girl as ever lived. . . . I doubt not of her happiness in a future life."[24] Woodforde wrote copiously about his other servants, including details of their pregnancies, marriages, and love affairs. He commented on their personalities, noted the amounts of their wages and when he paid them, and delayed payment for sauciness but increased it if someone had shown particular kindness. Woodforde's diary exemplified master-servant relationships: they were personal and intense. The lives of servants and their masters intertwined in a complex way. In those days servants formed an official part of a household and the family. Servants belonged to a hierarchical ordering in the household in which they occupied the bottom rung. Similar to children and women, servants played a necessary role but an inferior one without full personal status. For all these reasons, the Reverend Woodforde had an intense interest in and felt a major responsibility for his servants. The intertwined relationships of masters and servants epitomized the "moral economy" of the eighteenth century. That is, work life bound people together along familial lines, on the basis of tasks well done, and according to principles of obedience, responsibility, and mutual obligation. Infused with personal and religious concern, the "moral economy" differed from the "cash" or "money economy" of the following centuries. These employers and employees had a relationship that was far removed from the relations of worker and industrialist that were looming on the horizon.

If not the most attractive job, being in service was a common one for both men and women. In European cities the servant class amounted at times to well over 10 percent of the population. Moreover, servants worked for a variety of masters. Rural households, like Woodforde's in England, and extended families in Eastern Europe kept servants to do farm work, dairying, and other commercial jobs such as spinning, as well as household chores. City dwellers used servants for artisanal manufacturing, for the ritual purposes of the nobility, and for the domestic chores of bourgeois and aristocratic households alike.

Men filled the highest ranks of service, which consisted of ceremonial positions serving the nobility. Wearing livery and acting as a kind of honor guard at entryways, on coaches, or on city streets, such men expanded the range of the symbolic power of the elite. In aristocratic households women held the lower end of service positions: cooks, scullery maids, and general household staff. Only a noblewoman's personal maid—one who dressed her, kept her company, and performed a range of intimate tasks—had a status approaching that of the male servants. The run-of-the-mill female servant performed a range of domestic work virtually without relief. Primitive equipment and conditions—cooking over fireplaces, few sanitary conveniences, and constant invasions of rodents and insects—existed in the nobleman's house as well as in the artisan's. Among servants performing household chores, only the cook had any degree of status. Her wages were highest, her authority greatest, and more of her needs were attended to. Most domestic servants received room and board but were paid only when they left a position or, where conditions were becoming modern, once a year. Servants who earned no wage at all sometimes received instead a sum of money when they married, for setting up a household of their own. Because of the variability of conditions, some urban servants constantly looked for better positions.

The purpose of entering service was to acquire, first, the means of survival, second, training in adult skills, and third, a dowry at the end of one's term. Urban servants had often left their homes because, for one reason or another, their families could not provide enough food for them. In rural areas young people training in other people's houses constituted a ritualistic labor exchange among farm families. For young women the skills learned and the dowry obtained in service increased the prospect of making a good marriage. The dowry accumulated over the years until one reached marriageable age and went to set up housekeeping; it was used to buy pots and pans, a straw mattress or bed, or some kind of household linen. Without this contribution from the female, a marriage could not take place. Sometimes women servants in better households earned enough to help an artisan establish himself. Studies show that women servants often married upward into the artisanal class, perhaps because they provided economic resources.

Service had certain perils. Although young women in their mid-teens usually found positions with farmers known to them or in houses recommended by family members, many were not that fortunate. Putting themselves up for hire at annual fairs, they might be hired by an unscrupulous master. Women walking to cities or villages in order to take positions as servants were the prey of robbers and seducers. Once in cities, seduction constituted a constant threat for the unprotected female servant, unless the family she lived with displayed particular diligence. The greatest danger came from male family members; the closeness of relationships in the eighteenth century made sex between masters and servants a regular occurrence and illegitimate children a problem—but only for the young women. The young female servant's twofold struggle to survive and at the same time accumulate a dowry was complicated by a host of other factors including sexuality, isolation from one's own family, and the intimacy of the household, which was supposed to serve as protection but, ironically, often did just the opposite.

Visions of Womanhood

Early modern attitudes toward women derived from many sources, but foremost among them was the Judeo-Christian heritage. Religious precepts explained everything: universe, politics, family, and everyday life. Moreover, the Bible said a great deal about women, beginning with the first woman—Eve. As the story went, she caused the fall of humanity when she tempted Adam with the apple. Thus, Eve became the archetypal woman, a corrupting temptress who dragged the human race into a state of sin and thus was someone against whom men should protect themselves. From Eve's act came the curse of labor: in the form of hard work for men and childbirth for women. The image of Eve dominated ideas about women despite the appearance of strong characters in the Old Testament, such as Ruth, Deborah, and Naomi. Moreover, other temptresses such as Delilah and Jezebel fleshed out this essentially negative image. The New Testament perpetuated a sense of women's unworthiness in relationship to the Christian church. This was especially the case with Paul, the early organizer of Christianity, in his pronouncements on church policy. In the first few centuries the church came to celebrate celibacy and to interpret fleshly contact as an evil that could be made right only by marriage. Celibacy and virginity remained the ideal. Paul's many letters to the first Christians also enshrined women's subordination: "Let your women keep silence in the churches: for it is not permitted unto them to speak," and "The head of the woman is the man. . . . The man was not created for the women; but the woman for the man." These and many other early Christian precepts shaped Western society; in particular, they were a basis of a powerful misogyny (hatred of women) at the heart of European culture.

Yet the church also claimed to have improved the lot of women. Jesus died for the redemption of all: "There is neither Jew nor Greek, there is neither bond nor free, there is neither male nor female: for ye are all one in Christ

Jesus." Not only did the soul, according to Christian doctrine, have no gender, but the particular attention Christ paid to women redeemed them and gave them stature. In addition, devotion to Mary, mother of Jesus, became an ever more important part of Catholicism. Conceived without sin and thus escaping Eve's legacy, Mary was venerated for her virginity, her maternity, and her status as queen of heaven and intercessor. Along with female saints and martyrs, but obviously surpassing them, Mary stood at the opposite pole from Eve and Biblical *femmes fatales*. Stories were passed down of famous medieval holy women, such as Hildegard of Bingen, Hroswitha of Gandersheim, Heloise, Radegond, and many others. Institutions such as convents and cloisters even allowed for the development of women's intellectual accomplishments and religious stature in the pre-industrial period. Thus, the church projected these two contradictory images of women, each equally powerful and simultaneously accepted in European culture.

Polarized images of womanhood in religious doctrine paralleled the two views of women in popular culture. On the one hand childbearing was officially hailed as an important function. On the other, all sorts of taboos grew up around women's bodily functions. After childbirth the female body was considered to be in an unclean state and in need of sanctification. Thus, women followed the ritual of "churching" after childbirth in order to regain purity. Folk customs reflected beliefs that menstrual blood and menstruating women posed dangers. Depending on the locality, various prohibitions developed around menstruating women: for example, in one place they could not take part in sowing; in another they could not take part in preserving—especially salting. Where metal-working was done, their presence reputedly generated rust or made a variety of tools so blunt that they would not work. More fundamentally, men believed that contact with a menstruating woman was somehow debilitating or even dangerous. Other kinds of sanctions and beliefs surrounded the lactating woman, whose breasts would be rubbed with her child's umbilical cord to transfer the life-giving power of the uterus that the cord symbolized. The breasts could be read for signs of problems, as could other parts of a woman's body. The virginal body of the young girl was somehow prized, but that of the sterile older woman was often frightening and seen as susceptible to corruption and even deviltry. The ultimate image of the polluting potential of women was the witch, who could infect, poison, and bedevil. The eighteenth century did mark a slow decline in the identification of old women and witchcraft—an identification which over the centuries had cost thousands of widows and older spinsters their lives. Despite the end in prosecutions for witchcraft, people maintained their beliefs in the unhealthy, dangerous, and even evil potential of women's bodies.

Official theories of reproduction and sexuality also conformed to hierarchical arrangements in productive life. Building on treatises as old as those of the ancient Greek physician Galen, many scientists still believed that reproductive organs were symmetrical in men and women. That is, any part of the male genitalia had its counterpart in the female. For example, ovaries and testes were the same, and the penis and vagina were convex and concave versions of one another. The clitoris was also equated with the penis because of its erotic sensitivity. By the eighteenth century, Galen's notions were more than 1500 years old, yet most medical people still adhered to them. Besides explaining physiology as an interlocking system of sexual difference, Galen's observations simultaneously conformed to the hierarchical nature of things: "The female is more imperfect than the male. The first reason is that she is colder. If, among animals, the warmer ones are more active, it follows that the colder ones must be more imperfect. . . . Just as man is the most perfect of all animals, so also, within the human species, man is more perfect than woman. The cause of this superiority is the superabundance of warmth, heat being the primary instrument of nature."[25] A woman's coldness was seen as underlying both her social and intellectual inferiority. It also explained why her reproductive organs were insulated within her body rather than being outside like the male's.

By the eighteenth century, scientists still asserted symmetry when they discussed reproductive processes. Instead of seeing an embryo as something transferred from the male to the uterus for gestation, the natural scientist and philosopher Gassendi maintained that male and female fluids both contributed to the creation of the fetus. An understanding that women in fact produced eggs led to further clarification of the process among the most advanced scientists. Conception, the great biologist Albrecht von Haller believed, resulted from orgasm within the male and female, a process that released both sperm and egg; release of the egg "is not performed without great pleasure to the mother, nor without an exquisite unrelatable sensation of the internal parts of the tube, threatening a swoon or fainting fit to the future mother."[26] In terms of women's sexuality this explanation allowed for and indeed demanded pleasure as a requirement for survival of the human race. At the same time, equality in this realm had little effect on general opinions about women. From woman's "weakness" due to childbearing came a pervasive inferiority. An influential writer alternately working in Sweden and France put it clearly: "As the female body is weak, so the intelligence is also."[27] According to these accounts women's inferiority was thus not first determined by law but by nature.

Popular Culture

The rituals, stories, and fairy tales that people invented and circulated reworked bits of everyday life into a rich culture. The hopes, fears, rules, and roles that oral culture expressed, in turn shaped life experience probably more than highly theoretical writings did. Concerns for pure and impure, for cleanliness and pollution were cultural matters, but they influenced popular behavior in powerful ways. Although the church had such ceremonies as confirmation, marriage, and churching, people set their own meaning to official rites. In Bulgaria the feast day of Saint Lazarus during the week before Palm Sunday afforded young women the opportunity to tour the village singing songs about

Dorothea Viehmann, the Fairytale-Wife, received a warm meal or other refreshment while she told her tales in the area around Cassel. One of her audience, Ludwig Grimm, also sketched this portrait.

love, marital happiness, and good health as a way of ensuring agricultural fertility.

> Blossom, lovely Basil tree!
> May your roots never wither!
> A lad will bring his true love
> To rest in your shade.[28]

Not only did folk rituals circulate ideas of community well-being and reinforce the taboos, but myths, stories, and tales made the popular culture richer. These myths and tales were portrayed in a number of ways, including street theater at festivals and wandering troupes in villages and cities. Wandering workers earned their bread not only by doing odd jobs at harvesting, but by story-telling. Dorothea Viehmann (1755–1815), a wandering German trader of dairy products, told fairy tales as well as sold produce to her customers. Another storyteller was blacksmith's daughter "old Marie" Müller (b. 1747) in the city of Cassel. The nights of communal work passed more quickly, more enjoyably, and more instructively when accompanied by the tales of village storytellers. This oral culture, along with the reading aloud of books in some places, disseminated the tales that shaped behavior and mentality while they also amused.

Popular plots have survived because of the work of folklorists who collected them in remote areas a century or more ago. The most popular characters were figures who are still well known today: Cinderella, Rapunzel, the victims of Bluebeard, and Sleeping Beauty. In the Cinderella tale the protagonist was victimized by a wicked stepmother—a stock character in those days of frequent and often quick remarriages. Cinderella was either overworked or undernourished, or both; this plight reflected common fears of women living on the edge of subsistence. In some versions Cinderella's first achievement was to acquire enough food; only later did she attract the prince. The rivalry between the purity of the heroine and the repulsiveness of an older woman provided the drama in most versions. Marriage was also a major concern in tales, and a rich one constituted the special dream of hard-working rural women. The prince could end the life of drudgery so graphically portrayed through the common motif of women spinning—spinning forced by evil dwarves, spinning as a sign of good character, and spinning in a desperate struggle to survive. Sexual fantasies and fears appeared in tales such as that of Bluebeard, who killed one wife after another until a wise one outwitted him. A story similar to that of Red Riding Hood revealed sexual fears of animality, passion, and violence, and of ruse in sexual matters. Finally, tales put actual situations into symbolic terms. The many wandering heroines and displaced brothers reflected a time when migration and precarious living conditions were common. In the close world of the villager or country worker, folk tales set out roles, laid out expectations, and also laid hopes to rest. Channeling emotions, stories added another dimension to the complex mental world of early modern people.

Upper-class women, such as Madame Le Prince de Beaumont in France and Frau Regierungspräsident Hassenpflug in Germany, for example, were some of the most important compilers of fairy tales in the mid–eighteenth century. In these days, the mental horizons of aristocrats often touched those of servants and tenants through shared stories and rituals. Yet the aristocratic woman also had extra layers of tradition in the form of chivalric rites and games, myth, and high culture. Despite the frank pursuit of sexual pleasure in aristocratic circles, a gloss of chivalric behavior remained. The fairy tales reveal an ongoing fascination with beautiful queens, fair maidens, and virginal princesses, who were often at the mercy of ogres, witches, or other demonic types. Release from a tormentor depended on the devoted attention of a hero. In contrast, a heroic male could be entrapped until a "lady" undid a magical spell through her love. Traditions of courtly love and chivalry revolved around unselfish and devoted attentions of a knight or nobleman to a highly placed woman. Such attentions were an indication of both the nobility of the man and the worthiness of the woman. Some noblewomen still wrote about this type of relationship in tales of courtiers secretly focusing all their best emotions on a princess, who was herself caught in the restriction that she only marry the most exalted of princes. Gallant acts and noble gestures traditionally infused male behavior toward women, whereas ideally, sacrifice and commitment were the motivations for these acts. In theory, then, the sensuality exhibited by the aristocracy was to some extent ennobled by a chivalric ideal, a belief system that remained powerful as an influence on gender relationships.

The culture of the marketplace, with its fairs and festivals, pervaded the world view of rich and poor alike, and provided additional social cohesion. Everyday versions of the carnival filled public spaces. Popular entertainers such as acrobats, wandering troupes of actors, singers and songsellers, marionettists, and magicians captured the culture's desires and fears. Observers applauded the freakish women, men, and children whose bodies displayed inverted sexual characteristics or were overfed or undernourished, gigantic or tiny. Farces and plays were filled with references to defecation or sexual behavior. In fact, the pervasive use of sexual references, double entendres, and sexual play appealed to both rich and poor, male and female. Through watching passion plays in the Easter season, watching buffoons assault one another, or applauding scatalogical dialogue, the public was reminded of the fundamental physicality of the human condition. For the well-born, public exhibitions and performances fueled their private theaters, which converted the same themes into lavish productions. For example, Alexander Pope's *Rape of the Lock* was a highly sophisticated version of popular skits featuring an assault on virginity. From the operas of Mozart to the comedies presented in the theaters of royal mistresses, which were farces about the body, sexual desire, and the entanglements of rich and poor—all these depended on and were nourished by the general culture of explicit physicality and publicity about the body. They highlighted and explained the common gender roles and sexual existence of both ordinary and well-born people.

Revolution in Agriculture

By the end of the eighteenth century, community ways of life and the interlocking nature of familial enterprise had already undergone several centuries of innovation in certain parts of Europe. Changes in agricultural methods eventually led to social changes as well. Interest in soil fertility and crop production developed in the seventeenth and eighteenth centuries and led to the introduction and acceptance of new crops and new ways of farming. Farmers began to grow turnips and certain kinds of grasses such as clover, both of which provided more abundant food for livestock. Clover also enriched the soil, ending the need to leave fields fallow in order to restore their stock of nutrients. These two new crops alone had notable consequences. First, since turnips grew well after harvest time, an innovative farmer would no longer allow other people's animals to run through his fields and eat up the profits of his enterprise. Moreover, not having to leave fields fallow meant that the community no longer had to make decisions about such matters. Farmers gradually became more individualistic and more production-oriented, working the land in new ways. Some innovations, such as drill-planting seeds instead of broadcast sowing them, did not have any immediate effect on the social structure.

But the increasing concern for productivity and the individualistic spirit of innovation caused a trend toward private, rather than communal, control of farming. The result was an enclosure movement, a tendency to fence in or enclose fields that over centuries brought about the conversion of some community land into private property. By fair means and foul, improving farmers dispossessed other less prosperous users of common land and made it their own. Once common land was no longer available to them, many of these users could not subsist. That is, when some farmers withdrew their land from common grazing or common agricultural cooperation, others were denied that bit of land use that made the difference between subsistence and failure. As a result of these agricultural changes, many self-sufficient farms failed, first in England and then later across the Continent. Although the small, independent family farm remains active right up to the present day, this way of life was diminished by the actions of more market-oriented landowners.

How did this affect women's lives? One effect was that their husbands often became day laborers, either part-time or full-time, for other farmers on a cash basis. Women and their daughters also were forced to take other jobs or to take in outside work. In particular, rural women and men turned to working for the growing number of textile manufacturers. Starting in the sixteenth century, merchants had developed another system for producing fabric. Instead of each family producing the fabrics it used, or artisans producing small quantities, textile manufacturers first bought up quantities of raw materials and then put them out in the countryside for home production. In the cities, guild regulations traditionally determined the size of woven material, the density of threads, price, and even the amount any artisan could produce in a single year. By moving their operations to the countryside, manufacturers escaped such regulations and could produce as much as they wanted of whatever they wanted. Once the raw material had been spun or the thread woven, the merchant or his agent reclaimed it for another process or for selling. This type of manufacture occurred across the continent, but especially in England. By the eighteenth century a whole range of out-work—lace-making, straw-plaiting, button-making, nail-making, pin-making, and many others—had become part of the household routine of women and children in rural families.

The interlocking nature of male and female production within the family remained. As day labor for large landowners replaced work on the family farm, families toiled together in agricultural gangs. A man's employment as a day laborer often depended on his ability to bring his family along to do the lighter or more tedious jobs such as weeding or spreading manure. Moreover, the amount of out-work that women took on in addition to household tasks could be varied, depending on how much their family's ability to generate income or produce had declined. Thus, these first slow steps in the modernization of rural life and its transformation into commercial farming did not end the tightly knit family economy. They did, however, introduce foreign elements into the rhythm of household production, such as the need to respond to the demands of employers—strangers whose interests and concerns were generally quite different from those of the family. Instead of achieving its own subsis-

A Women's Friendly Society

In the eighteenth century working people tried to protect themselves against the misfortunes of life by banding together in what were known as friendly societies. An offshoot of guilds, these societies collected regular sums from its members, but they also provided sociability. Some members of the upper class were interested in these societies because they could alleviate the problem of poverty in their localities. They also found the societies potentially dangerous because the social component might lead to political discussions. Here is one English observer's account of how a women's society operated late in the century.

Healthy women under 43 years of age are admitted, on paying 1s. 9d. entrance-money, 7d. box-money, and 1d. towards providing a doctor.* A member of 3 years standing is allowed, in case of sickness, 5s. a week for the first 10 weeks; and 3s. a week, afterwards; but no sickness, or lameness, in the time of pregnancy, entitles a member to relief from the Society; but if they are the consequence of pregnancy, such member is entitled to the allowance, to commence one month after her lying-in. £5. are allowed towards the funeral expences of a member, and £2. towards the funeral expences of a husband; but a member cannot receive the last allowance more than once in her life. Widows are allowed £2. on the death of a father, brother, etc. Members disclosing the secrets of the Society, upbraiding one another, refusing to be silent, after due notice, etc. are liable to a fine; the framers of these Rules, which are very minute, seem to have entertained strong ideas of the loquacity of the sex. The following Rule seems well calculated to punish dissoluteness of manners, among the female part of the labouring class. If any single or unmarried woman, having had a child, before she entered the Society, shall commit the same crime, when in the Society, she shall be excluded; or, if any married woman shall have a child in the absence of her husband, she also shall be excluded, provided she cannot satisfy the Society in six months. Members of 20 years standing are allowed 2s. a week for life, while the fund consists of £100. and upwards. For managing the concerns, and keeping the keys of the strong box of this Society, two stewardesses are taken by rotation, and continue six months in office; two collectors, who are chosen by the stewardesses, collect fines, etc: a beadle, and warden (both females,) are

---

*£ is the sign for British pound; s for shilling; and d for penny.

likewise taken by rotation; the former is the message bearer, and the latter inspects the public affairs of the Society, to see that the officers discharge their duty, and attends the door, on club nights. A committee, of six women, is taken by rotation from the roll, every six months, whose business is to determine all controversies, to accept members, with the concurrence of the stewardesses, and to give their assent to the lending or disposing of money, or other things, belonging to this Society. The club meets once a month at an ale-house in Wigton, the landlady of which is bond under penalty of 2s. 6d. to find them good ale.

Source: Frederic Morton Eden, *The State of the Poor: or, An History of the Labouring Classes in England,* 3 vols. (London: J. Davis, 1797) 2:59.

---

tence within the matrix of community life, the family became workers for wages. Independent to a large extent from neighbors but dependent on agricultural and manufacturing employers, families shaped their daily lives along external demands for their labor.

By the 1770s large segments of the population, especially in England and France, found themselves indigent. Two decades later Italian cities were overrun with beggars. Agricultural improvements had in fact boosted the population through better general nutrition. Although the new style of farming demanded many workers, it could not always absorb all of the population boom. Young women in particular started migrating toward towns and cities. As one Scandinavian minister noted, "farmers prefer male to female servants, so daughters have to seek employment elsewhere."[29] Where self-sufficiency declined, families had less need for the household services of daughters, unless there was work available in a cottage industry of some kind. Many men also took to the road for long periods of time as a way of finding work and reducing the number of mouths to feed at home. Officials increasingly noted in their records family breakups due to permanent male desertion. Migration, vagrancy, and begging became a way of life after mid-century, as more and more families slipped down into the ranks of the hopelessly poor. Estimates suggest that in areas undergoing modernization, as much as one-third of the population would have been so classified at one point or another in their lives. Where day labor became dominant, for example, in southern Spain, "wives and children are without work, and all, piled together in cities or large towns, live at the expense of charity. . . in terrible want out of keeping with the fertility of the soil."[30] Children became beggars, having received lessons from their mothers. Rural women knew the sources of charity around the countryside—the aristocratic homes, the servants, the landlords—and coached their children regularly in the ways of begging. Children, widows with children, and old women were dominant among the begging poor. In neither France nor England, where poverty was especially grave, did villages or towns or even cities have the funds to support the increasing numbers of poor.

An agrarian way of life was in the midst of a long-term transformation, leading to its slow demise as the predominant source of order in human affairs. The changes taking place throughout eighteenth-century Europe undermined the social structure on which aristocratic control of the land and politics had rested. Questions about a woman's role in the new social forms proved central. Agrarian society had demanded coordinated work from men and women, though within a patriarchal framework. Agricultural improvements affected women's work more dramatically. For example, wherever a single cash crop such as wheat became dominant, women lost their productive work in dairying. Wherever opportunities in cottage industry or service were also lacking, dire need set in. In one section of England women were especially destitute: "picking hops is women's only employment, except drinking tea and brandy very plentifully."[31] Thus, modern agriculture began blocking women from making their traditional contributions to survival.

At the same time urban women were enduring a stiff attack on their trades. From mantua-making to midwifery, their crafts were besieged by men, themselves hard-pressed in the fight for economic survival. The situation moved some women to comment on their losses, as did Mary Ann Radcliffe who wrote in the 1790s on "The Fatal Consequences of Men Traders Engrossing Women's Occupations." Commerce pressed its claims in opposition to a rural way of life. Communities and families had previously formed the context for a gender-based organization of work. Within this tight system, people enjoyed moments of release as well as certain frank expressions of sexual pleasure in carnivals or festivals. These outbursts had worked toward balancing society in what has been called a "moral economy." Feast and dearth, the privileged and the peasant, found equilibrium in the idea of reciprocity. Feudal obligations and social responsibilities, gender-based order and paternal power, reproduction of the population and production of its sustenance, interacted in special ways still associated with early modern life. Aristocrats at the end of the century would express their pity for those who had never tasted the sweetness of the old society. Rural people and artisans also fought to defend it. By this time, however, the ways of commerce had opened society to new influences and to a reevaluation of everything, from political rule to family structure. The rising population, as well as dislocation because of agricultural change, made people question the role of women and their relationship to childbirth and children.

NOTES

1. Bernard Miall, trans., *Master Johann Dietz* (London: Dulton, 1923), 249, 256, 275–76.
2. Martha Wilmot Bradford, ed., *The Russian Journals of Martha and Catherine Wilmot* (London: Macmillan, 1934), 131.

3. James Davis, *Rise from Want* (Philadelphia: University of Pennsylvania Press, 1986), 17.

4. Cadet de Gassicourt, *Voyage en Autriche, en Moravie, et en Bavière* (Paris: l'Huillier, 1818), 83.

5. William Coxe, *Travels into Poland, Russia, Sweden, and Denmark*, 3rd ed., 4 vols. (London: T. Cadell, 1787) 1:378.

6. Minutes of the Meeting of Incorporation of the Foundling Hospital, 25 March 1740, quoted in R. Paulson, *Hogarth: His Life, Art, and Times* (New Haven: Yale University Press, 1971), 2:39.

7. See Bogna Lorence-Kot, *Child-Rearing and Reform. A Study of the Nobility in Eighteenth-Century Poland* (Westport, Conn.: Greenwood, 1985), 34.

8. Quoted in Ray Strachey, *The Cause* (London: Virago, 1978), 15.

9. James Boswell, *Life of Johnson* (Oxford: Clarendon Press, 1934) 2:328–29.

10. Jean-Louis Flandrin, *Families in Former Times. Kinship, Household, and Sexuality* (Cambridge, England: Cambridge University Press, 1979), 122–23.

11. Steven Ozment, *When Fathers Ruled* (Cambridge, Mass: Harvard University Press, 1983), 57.

12. Quoted in Donald R. Kelley, *The Beginning of Ideology: Consciousness and Society in the French Reformation* (Cambridge, England: Cambridge University Press, 1981), 71.

13. *Amstprotokolle Laichingen*, vol. 1756–1968, November 29 and December 17, 1759, quoted in Hans Medick, "Village Spinning Bees in Early Modern Germany," Hans Medick and David Sabean, eds., *Interest and Emotion: Essays on the Study of Family and Kinship* (Cambridge, England: Cambridge University Press, 1984), 331.

14. Dr. Christoph Scheurl, *Schuld und Rechnungsbuch*, unpublished ms., Germanische Nationalmuseum, fol. 10, quoted by Merry E. Wiesner, "Early Modern Midwifery: A Case Study," in Barbara A. Hanawalt, ed., *Women and Work in Preindustrial Europe* (Bloomington: Indiana University Press, 1986), 104.

15. Gilles La Roque de la Lontière, *Traité de la noblesse* (Rouen: P. Le Boucher, 1734) preface.

16. Quoted in Ellery Schalk, *From Valor to Pedigree: Ideas of Nobility in France in the Sixteenth and Seventeenth Centuries* (Princeton: Princeton University Press, 1986) 144.

17. Przyjemski Collection, Pre-Modern Archives, Warsaw, quoted in Lorence-Kot, *Child-Rearing and Reform*, 53.

18. Letter of Lord Chesterfield to Baron Frederick William Torch, June 23, 1732, in Roger Coxon, *Chesterfield and His Critics* (London: George Routledge and Sons, 1925) 163.

19. Hester Piozzi, *Glimpses of Italian Society in the Eighteenth Century* (London: Seeley, 1892) 254–55.

20. Stéphanie-Félicité Genlis, *Mémoires*, 10 vols. (Brussels: P. J. de Mat, 1825), 1:28.

21. Ibid, 1:364.

22. Quoted in Arlette Farge, *La vie fragile: Violences, pouvoirs, et solidarités à Paris au XVIIIᵉ siècle* (Paris: Hachette, 1986), 130.

23. Quarter Session Bundles Epiphany–Easter 1738, Oxfordshire Record Office,

quoted in W. Twaites, "Women in the Marketplace: Oxfordshire c. 1690–1880," *Midland History* IX (1984):32.

24. James Woodforde, *A Country Parson: James Woodforde's Diary, 1759–1802* (New York: Oxford University Press, 1985), 91–94 *passim*.

25. Quoted in Julia O'Faolain and Lauro Martines, eds., *Not in God's Image: Women in History from the Greeks to the Victorians* (New York: Harper), 120.

26. Quoted by Thomas Laqueur, "Orgasm, Generation, and the Politics of Reproductive Biology," *Representations,* 14 (Spring, 1986):1–41.

27. Quoted in Paul Hoffmann, *La femme dans la pensée des lumières* (Paris: Ophrys, 1977), 34.

28. P. Dinekov, *Bulgarian Folklore* (1972), quoted in Nicholai Ivanov Kolev, "Festive Customs and Ritual Games on St. Lazarus' Day," *Journal of Popular Culture* 19, no. 1 (Summer, 1985)1:147.

29. Quoted in Bengt Ankarloo, "Agriculture and Women's Work: Directions of Change in the West, 1700–1900," *Journal of Family History* 4, no. 2 (Summer, 1979):115.

30. Olavide, intendant of Seville, quoted in Richard Herr, *The Eighteenth-Century Revolution in Spain* (Princeton, N. J.: Princeton University Press, 1958), 105.

31. Arthur Young, *The Farmer's Tour through the East of England (1771)* vol. 3, p. 48, quoted in Bridget Hill, *Eighteenth-Century Women: An Anthology* (London: George Allen and Unwin, 1984), 188.

SOURCES AND SUGGESTED READING

Ankarloo, Bengt. "Agriculture and Women's Work: Directions of Change in the West," *Journal of Family History* (1979).

Atkinson, Dorothy. "Society and the Sexes in the Russian Past," in Dorothy Atkinson et al., *Women in Russia* (1977).

Bottigheimer, Ruth. "Tale Spinners: Submerged Voices in Grimm's Fairy Tales," *New German Critique* (1982).

Burke, Peter. *Popular Culture in Early Modern Europe* (1978).

Czap, Peter. "The Perennial Multiple Family Household, Mishino, Russia 1782–1858, *Journal of Family History* (1982).

Fairchilds, Cissie. *Servants and Their Masters in Old Regime France* (1984). A thorough study of domestic relations in service.

Farnsworth, Beatrice. "The Litigious Daughter-in-Law: Family Relations in Rural Russia in the Second Half of the Nineteenth Century," *Slavic Review* (1986). Contains a survey of family relations in the pre-emancipation period.

Gavazzi, Milovan. "The Extended Family in Southeastern Europe," *Journal of Family History* (1982).

Gillis, John R. *For Better, for Worse: British Marriages, 1600 to the Present* (1985). Marital customs and relationships over four centuries.

Gullickson, Gay. *Spinners and Weavers of Auffay* (1986). An important interpretation of cottage industry.

Hanawalt, Barbara A., ed. *Women and Work in Pre-Industrial Europe* (1986). A major collection of essays on women's economic activities.

Hufton, Olwen. *The Poor of Eighteenth-Century France* (1974). Especially good on migration and begging.

Isherwood, Robert. *Farce and Fantasy: Popular Entertainment in Eighteenth-Century Paris* (1986). An engaging description of popular culture.

Kahk, Juhan, Heldur Palli, and Halliki Uibu. "Peasant Family and Household in Estonia in the Eighteenth and the First Half of the Nineteenth Centuries." *Journal of Family History* (1982).

Laget, Mireille. *Naissances. L'accouchement avant l'âge de la clinique* (1982). A survey of early modern childbirth practices, ritual, and lore.

Lorence-Kot, Bogna. *Child-Rearing and Reform: A Study of the Nobility in Eighteenth-Century Poland* (1985). An engaging analysis of child-parent relations and of women's lives.

Mitterauer, Richard, and Reinhard Sieder. *The European Family: Patriarchy to Partnership from the Middle Ages to the Present* (1977). A particularly good survey of changes in the modern family.

Plakans, Andrejs. "Seigneurial Authority and Peasant Family Life: The Baltic Area in the Eighteenth Century," *Journal of Interdisciplinary History* (1975).

Ransel, David L. *The Family in Imperial Russia* (1978).

Shorter, Edward. *A History of Women's Bodies* (1982). An important overview of medical theories and practices.

Stock, Phyllis. *Better than Rubies: A History of Women's Education* (1978).

Stone, Lawrence. *The Family, Sex and Marriage in England 1500–1800* (1974). A major interpretation of changes in family life.

Taylor, Peter, and Hermann Rebel. "Hessian Peasant Women, Their Families, and the Draft: A Social-Historical Interpretation of Four Tales from the Grimm Collection," *Journal of Family History* (1981).

Thestrup, Paul. "Methodological Problems of a Family Reconstitution Study in a Danish Rural Paris Before 1800," *Scandinavian Economic History Review* (1972).

Tilly, Louise, and Joan Scott. *Women, Work and Family* (1978). The classic study of the relationship between reproduction and production among French and English women.

Weisner, Merry E. *Working Women in Renaissance Germany* (1986). A rich description of working lives and changes in labor markets.

CHAPTER

2

Winds of Change

A Woman of New Interests Early in the eighteenth century Mary Pierrepont, a well-born young Englishwoman, wrote to Edward Wortley Montagu, her suitor: "I hate the man they propose for me. . . . I can think with pleasure of giving you with my first declaration of Love the sincerest proof of it. I read over some of your first Letters, and I formed romantic scenes to myself of Love and Solitude."[1] This secret correspondence led to the marriage of Mary and Edward after a great deal of parental haggling over settlements. This kind of marriage—to satisfy the couple's inclinations—formed part of a new pattern. In 1716 Lady Mary Wortley Montagu followed her husband to Istanbul, where they took up residence in the English embassy. She regaled London society with her letters about life in the harem, about the sultan and his ways, about the Turkish baths she frequented, and about the Turkish clothing she adopted, right down to the flowing trousers. On her return to England, Montagu introduced the practice of smallpox inoculation. This contribution and her general wit made her the center of court life. Known for her wide-ranging knowledge, Montagu was clearly a new kind of woman, one interested in science and different customs. Far from being provincial, she opened vistas for others of her society. Yet her wit and intelligence ultimately brought her one admirer who caused trouble. When she refused the advances of poet Alexander Pope, he began to attack her in verse, suggesting she was a lesbian—like the ancient Greek poet Sappho not only in mental gifts but in sexuality. Pushed to despair by the ongoing slander, Montagu abandoned England to live in Italy in the 1740s and 1750s, where she explored historic ruins, managed a farm renowned for its produce, and—some said—maintained her love life.

In her drive to see the world, to cultivate the land in new ways, and to pursue adventure, Mary Montagu embodied the changes that were sweeping through Europe. By the eighteenth century, the mental and physical horizons of the privileged classes were beginning to reach beyond the confines of village and manor: Montagu traveled with gusto and dressed in foreign costumes. People began showing great interest in the latest book and the latest invention: Montagu was among the first to spread news not only of goings-on at court or the newest novel or the latest verse, but of technology, science, and ways of living that offered to help people rise above the intimidating forces of the natural world. Witty and innovative, Montagu was a woman who was visible in the social structure by virtue of her achievements and her social leadership. Like her, other middle- and upper-class women began carving out a place for themselves in the intellectual world. Growing numbers of them wrote, performed, and painted. Perhaps as a result, the contradictory visions of womanhood* yield a particularly sharp debate over women's role. Pope's attack on Montagu formed part of this debate, even though it singled out a particular woman. Women's education, women's physiological and mental attributes, and the role of women in the family and in political life became part of a new intellectual agenda. Progress, science, wit, travel, writing, and new questions raised by new types of people marked this modern age. It was characterized not only by innovations in agriculture but by a series of other innovations, ranging from those in economics to those in politics and personal life.

Historians explain these changes as part of several movements. First, a commercial revolution had started two centuries earlier. The opening of the New World had increased foreign commerce and made available greater supplies of raw materials. Moreover, trade had picked up within Europe itself, especially in countries like England, where transportation had been made easier by improvements in harbors, canals, and new roads. Such efforts to stimulate commercial prosperity signaled a break with the old self-sufficient, static way of life. It indicated the presence of new types of men and women who took their cues not just from community and religious sources, but from market factors and the desire to make fortunes. Second, the steady rise of centralized government challenged the local authority of aristocrats and powerful church landlords. In place of these feudal or local prerogatives, theorists developed ideas of monarchical rule tempered by constitutions and codes of law. Universal citizenship for all men would replace privilege for certain groups. These changing ideas were conveyed by a European-wide movement known as the Enlightenment, which, throughout Europe, captured the imaginations of forward-looking aristocrats, social leaders, intellectuals, and members of the rising commercial classes. Influenced by the achievements of natural science in the past century, eighteenth-century thinkers began discussing the social and political order in ways that challenged the old order. Everything was open to discussion: industry and commerce, kingship and religion, the family and the place of women. Moreover, newspapers, salons, and novels brought the new ideas to a wide audience.

---

*See Chapter 1.

Commercial Revolution and the Rise of the Middle Class

Another eighteenth-century young woman, Christiana Spencer of Yorkshire, asked her father in London to send "salad oil, a Band of Sweet Soap, anchovies, capers, pickles, and tea and coffee."[2] Throughout Europe, but most conspicuously in England, people of means, like Christiana, were increasing their purchasing. They bought tobacco, chocolate, wallpaper, a variety of iron goods, and above all, muslins and calicos imported from the Orient. In fact, the most conspicuous consumption was of household items and materials for clothing, with the new, light cotton cloth a major item. Cotton clothing proved to be a vast improvement over the wool or linen garments that had been worn no matter what the season. The availability of cotton also started a trend of wearing underclothing that was changed more frequently than outer garments. A range of household linen developed, from table coverings to sheets, toweling, and pillows to window coverings. A wide variety of metal goods were available; for example, a firm in Birmingham, England, carried watchchains, buttons, snuff boxes, instrument cases, toothpick cases, cups, candlesticks, buckles, cufflinks, sugar jars, cruets, inkstands, and many other items made in a array of metals from silver to steel.

Eighteenth-century society saw a long-term increase in the quantity of goods consumed that were made outside the home—produced commercially and obtained with money. The growth of a cash economy had a host of consequences: a rising class of merchants and commercial people, urbanization based on commercial centers, new middle-class ideas and standards, and a change in the standard of living. Once commercially produced items became common in households, self-sufficiency started to decline and was replaced by a more widespread exchange economy and an interdependence of people, all of whom needed goods others could produce. Christiana Spencer's order to London, which she followed with others for cloth and clothing and chairs and bookcases, demonstrates that her household followed a way of life somewhat different from that of an older, self-sufficient home.

Like the agricultural revolution, the so-called commercial revolution had built up over several centuries, pushed along by merchant-manufacturers who are generally credited for developing it. Several aspects of the commercial revolution distinguish it from the trade that preceded it. These distinctions are important to understand because trade had existed almost since the beginning of history. Christiana Spencer's shopping list consisted of fairly ordinary goods, such as salad oil and soap. Many of the commodities made and sold in the eighteenth century were such staples of life as buttons, jars, and textiles. It is this ordinariness that distinguished such commerce from the older type of trade, which usually involved luxury goods such as silks and spices and affected only the highest levels of the nobility. The new kind of commerce touched not just the very rich and the town dwellers who had always depended on food markets; the commercial revolution reached into the countryside and

Chelsea-Ware, an eighteenth-century English china, was one of the products enticing well-to-do consumers of household commodities.

brought more levels of society—though obviously in differing degrees—into the market economy. When Christiana Spencer made out her shopping list, she demonstrated her dependence on the market for a number of goods. Less wealthy people had also become dependent, not for anchovies or silver snuff boxes, but for textiles or a pot. The agricultural revolution, as it took away access to common land and made people into day laborers, increasingly made the population dependent on the market, even for such necessities as food and clothing.

The commercial revolution established a prominent merchant class, interested in selling a wider range of goods on a grander scale. As a group, they fostered their interest in commerce in a variety of ways. In colonies in the New World, they laid claim to raw materials and made colonists a new market for their goods. From these interests developed the sale of textiles and iron goods to Africa, the selling of African slaves in the sugar islands or on the North American continent, and the exchange of goods and slaves for the many raw materials the Americans had to offer. The expansion of commerce occurred in the homeland as well and transformed—slowly to be sure—the face of Europe, beginning in the west with England, France, and the Low Countries and gradually spreading eastward. Although some areas remained virtually self-sufficient even into the twentieth century, commerce had made clear inroads into daily life by the eighteenth. Merchants profited from the agricultural revolution by utilizing the labor of surplus population and of those whose livelihood had been jeopardized by agricultural modernization. Since the beginning of changes in land use, merchants had been buying large supplies of raw materials for the production of textiles, putting them out to be spun or woven by women in the countryside, and then gathering up the yarn or cloth for sale or for further fashioning into a finished product. Some even started large textile workshops. The people who worked for the merchants received money for their work and thus were brought into the cash economy. Moreover, the time these people spent working for pay was time *not* spent in making something for themselves, either clothing or food. Rural people who participated in this kind of cottage industry, which is also called the putting-out system, had become part of the market and part of commercial expansion.

Both merchant-manufacturers and merchants involved in the colonial trade clearly had new values and aspirations. Unlike most of the nobility, their lives revolved around something other than pleasure, luxury, or prowess with a sword. Merchants valued hard work; they also valued the accumulation of money. Some aristocrats did, however, adopt this mentality; for example, Count Waldstein in Bohemia set up a huge workshop employing both his serfs and free artisans in producing woolen textiles, thus keeping "many from having to beg for their livelihood."[3] Moreover, although merchants generally participated in the religious life of their times, their aspirations were not limited to the goal of heavenly salvation. Success on earth strongly motivated them, and many sought to move higher up in the world by joining the aristocracy itself. In other words, the merchants, or the middle class, acquired a taste for upward mobility and believed in it more heartily than they believed in a static hierarchy and an unchanging social order. In addition, social position in the middle classes depended more on wealth and achievement than on breeding or bloodlines. However, these new middle class families still subscribed to the cultural values of the past to the extent of seeking ennoblement, often by marrying their children into the nobility. Thus, their view of the social hierarchy was complex—they could appreciate the value of social standing but could also visualize a social hierarchy based on different means, namely money rather than birth.

New values coincided with new ways of doing business. To accomplish their goals, the mercantile class challenged the restrictions established by the guild system. Merchants moved away from areas where guilds controlled manufacture and trade to towns with little regulation, or they sought to overturn guild privileges. Thus, merchants operated in new areas, employed new techniques, and bought, sold, and had manufactured as much as they could on whatever terms they could set. In other words, the values of openness to change, mobility, opportunity, and innovation operated for the merchant class in social and economic practices. These were the people who opened the way into the modern world.

The merchant-manufacturer's business employed all members of the family, even those outside the nuclear unit. In particular, the merchant relied on the work of his wife; in fact, a wife constituted such an essential part of any commercial undertaking that the relationship was symbiotic rather than a one-way reliance. In the home of François and Alexandrine Barrois in the textile city of Lille, France, for instance, a division of labor existed, but either member of the couple could take up certain of the other's tasks. For example, although François Barrois generally did the inspection of products, dyeing, and so on, his wife carried out many of these chores when he went off on sales trips. Selling was the major work of men, and such trips often took months at a time. While the men were away, their wives took care of the day-to-day aspects of running the business. Alexandrine Barrois always did the books, where she recorded the finished work, the price paid for it, and so on. Her general concern for finances often led her to propose financial speculations. For example, when her husband was off on one of his normal business circuits, she wrote to him about an opportunity to speculate in oil, and later about other commodities. Alexandrine Barrois did this kind of speculation as well as looking for new dyers, new finishers, and new methods of accomplishing tasks. She also raised three children during the course of these years and was able to do so because the merchant-manufacturer in those days ran business and home as one unit.

New norms attracted a variety of adherents, including aristocratic landowners. Many independent farmers, German aristocrats called Junkers, and the English nobility and gentry had moved toward modern agricultural practices that would net them more money. It was still uncommon for aristocrats to enter trade directly, however. Other values that became accepted by both upper and middle classes were new ideas about marriage and the family. The family order gradually acquired other than hierarchical attributes—though new and old ideas intermingled in the eighteenth century. The domestic couple was perceived as a "sweet community" in which a more than ordinary amount of agreement existed. Some could still see in this community a "commonwealth" with some degree of hierarchy by which servants and children were still bound to parents, and wives still subjected to husbands. Alexandrine Barrois called her husband "dear friend" and addressed him with affectionate words.[4] Their partnership in business life benefited from the closeness of their married relations. François Barrois had depended on his wife's dowry, but he also needed her skill, cooperation, and enterprise. Such reliance on qualities beyond dutiful toil gave marriage a different meaning. German Caroline Flachsland felt such closeness to her fiancé in all his endeavors that she always imagined his presence. After playing all his favorite songs, she could "see you sitting at the piano with me standing behind you full of feeling."[5] Among the aristocracy in England, parents gave children more choice in marriage; however, this did not mean the young people could marry anyone. They began looking among a fairly limited circle of appropriate partners, thinking about marriage as a future relationship with wider possibilities in it than the transmission of blood lines. A prospective partner's looks, accomplishments, and personality became important factors. In France a noblewoman showed that she looked on this new order of things with favor and disagreed with the old idea of extramarital pleasures: "The court is a dog of a place," the Marquise de Bombelles wrote to her husband, ". . . I feel certain that my lot should have been to be a good wife occupied solely with her husband, her children, and her household. For the pleasures of the court . . . have no attraction for me, and I have too bourgeois a way of thinking for that place."[6]

Development of the State and of Centralized Government

The rise of the middle class and the consolidation of government occured in tandem. For several centuries monarchs had been attempting to consolidate governmental power by creating bureaucracies under their control, developing devices of indirect and direct taxation, and gaining control of the administration of justice and of armies. In the late sixteenth century, Queen Elizabeth I prepared England for prosperity by keeping watch on the budget, by sponsoring trade and commerce, by managing and maneuvering around Parliament, and by squelching schemes that certain noblemen devised to limit her power. In general, controlling the nobility and curtailing its many prerogatives formed a central part of making coherent governmental structures. Standard and unified governmental policy, in contrast to the varied regulations imposed by the nobility, allowed trade to flourish. By supporting state power, merchants avoided local restrictions and tolls and eventually benefited from national transportation systems. Conversely, commerce generated revenues for nation-states. Thus, modern economic systems and modern political systems appeared together on the European horizon.

State formation came about in different ways and at different times. In seventeenth-century England groups of merchants and landlords restrained monarchical power with a constitution, which gave new rights to representatives of the political and economic elite. In other countries, however, such elements did not yet exercise authority on their own behalf. Instead, absolutism prospered. In some absolutist states, the rulers themselves tried to modernize the society and economy without losing power to the forces of constitutionalism. Such rulers were called enlightened despots, and among the most famous of them were two women, Catherine the Great of Russia (1729–1796) and Maria Theresa of Austria (1717-1780).

Born a German princess, Catherine the Great had no right to the Russian throne. In fact, she usurped it from her husband, Peter III, and most people believe she had him killed during her coup in 1762. At the time, however, Peter had also been trying to get rid of Catherine; in their struggle she clearly had the superior mental resources and determination. Like most royal marriages, theirs had been arranged—in this case by Peter's aunt, Elizabeth, Empress of Russia, who had used the occasion to foster goodwill with the German states. Married at fifteen to the intellectually limited but tyrannical Peter, Catherine spent a good deal of time reading political classics such as Machiavelli's *The*

Prince and works of political reformers such as Montesquieu and Cesare Beccaria. Catherine became one of the most cultured people of her day and corresponded with some of Europe's great thinkers, among them Diderot, Voltaire, and Friedrich Grimm. In her memos, treatises on government, and notes for future programs, she manifested a forward-looking spirit that showed the influence of the more progressive social and political thinking current in Europe at the time. Meanwhile she lived life to its fullest as Empress and constantly admitted to the imperial boudoir men who would become her most trusted advisers or allies. Catherine's greatest failure lay in her relationship with her son, who was raised by the former empress, Elizabeth, in the old ways of doing things. Despising his mother's programs and seeking to undermine her position for his own benefit, Paul constantly challenged Catherine's right to rule.

Catherine the Great was one of the most formidable rulers of the century. She tried to ameliorate the condition of the Russian serfs and to gain some control over the nobility. Influenced by Enlightenment literature on trade and national prosperity and by continuing evidence of the success of agricultural innovation elsewhere in Europe, she believed that more modern conditions of labor would bring about the kind of national wealth that existed in England and France. "Unfree hands do not work so well as free,"[7] she maintained. Moreover, she believed that removing the serfs' shackles to the land would improve city life as well and increase commerce. Yet although some serfs found their obligations lessened, for the most part Catherine dropped her plans whenever the nobility protested. Feeling that her grasp on power was looser than she wanted, Catherine heeded nobles' demands for continued control of agriculture and its laborers in return for their support of her military ventures. These included several wars against the Turks and the annexation of part of Poland. By these successes she substantially increased the Slavic population of Russia and its resources. Rationalization and standardization of provincial governance made the country more integrated, even with the new additions. Finally, Catherine continued Peter the Great's drive toward Westernization of Russia. Though she learned Russian well and adopted the Russian Orthodox religion, her goals proved more extensive than Peter's when it came to bringing in Western ideas.

Ruthless and reforming, Catherine ruled in an age of intellectual ferment. New thinkers and their ideas excited her. As a result she focused some of her prodigious energy on books, literacy, and education. A writer of satiric plays and an anonymous contributor to journals, she also spent thousands of rubles having leading books translated from Western languages and published. Catherine meant this effort to improve Russia generally, not to foster independent political thinking. The same was true with education, which Catherine also improved by promoting up-to-date methods, for example, in the teaching of reading. She set up the Smol'ny Institute for noble girls, where such subjects as languages became an accepted part of female education in a country hardly known for its enlightened ideas about women. None of Catherine's reforms ever reached full fruition, however, and her son and successor had little sympathy for most of them. Nonetheless, at Catherine's death Russia had definitely entered the ranks of the great European powers, and she herself had furthered the process of state formation.

In Austria, Maria Theresa proved to be a reforming ruler of a different style, though one just as committed to absolute power. Maria Theresa came to

---

Maria Theresa's Political Testament

Maria Theresa learned quickly about governing when Frederick the Great attacked her regime in 1740. In the War of the Austrian Succession that resulted, she faced shortages in her treasury, problems raising an army, and persistent resistance from the nobility. Some of her responses were dramatic: she pleaded for help from the Hungarian aristocracy by presenting her newborn son as a symbol of her fortitude but also of her royal maternity. In general, however, her actions on behalf of the Habsburg Empire were pragmatic. Her *Political Testament* of 1750–1751 analyzes the countervailing forces, such as the nobility, that stood in the way of centralized rule and the health of the empire as a whole.

> There are two real sources of abuses. The first, consisting in the innate selfishness and desire for dominion of various men by which the ministers of this land have made themselves wealthy and have consequently achieved superior sorts of exemptions and privileges, has redounded more to them and their families than to the commonwealth.
>
> The other source consists in that these ministers and leaders of the territories pursue their privileges and liberties so harmfully that preserving and defending the commonwealth is often impossible. To retrieve this prosperity from the possession of the Estates is our greatest need. Each nobleman should be forced to respect the ministry, its credit and absolute priority. The ministers themselves should accept the regime in order to preserve themselves and the state from ruin.
>
> The highly prized privileges of the nobility are founded on customs confirmed by our ancestors. In these various confirmations are written the words "well established custom." The continuation of these same privileges, however, can only be understood in terms of good laws and only in good, not evilly established customs.

Source: Adapted from "Politisches Testament von 1750–1751," in
Maria Theresia. Briefe und Aktenstücke in Auswahl, ed. Friedrich
Walter (Darmstadt: Wissenschaftliche Buchgesellschaft, 1968) 74–75.

the Habsburg throne in 1740 as the eldest daughter of an emperor who had no sons. This succession of a daughter was unusual but had been secured by the Pragmatic Sanction of 1713. The Sanction also declared that the collection of states held by the family were a single unit. Her accession was expected to provoke some kind of challenge to female rule and it was not long in coming. The attack on Maria Theresa's regime came from Frederick the Great of Prussia in the very year she took the throne. Other challenges followed, but the Austrians, led by this indomitable ruler, held out even though they lost the rich province of Silesia to Prussia. Maria Theresa became obsessed with the idea of regaining Silesia. Her alliances worked toward this end and resulted in what has been called the diplomatic revolution of the eighteenth century. Through her diplomatic maneuvering, Austria broke off connections with Great Britain and became allied with France, with one result being the marriage of Marie Antoinette, Maria Theresa's daughter, to Louis, the heir to the French throne. This alliance was one aspect of the rivalry between France and Britain for commercial and political predominance, which was to continue up through 1815. Fighting for control of central Europe, Austria struggled not to lose more to the Prussian army to the north. In the process, Maria Theresa rearranged the government, army, and judicial system and forged her country into a power to be reckoned with.

Maria Theresa inherited a realm in which the richest nobles controlled most of the land, kept private armies that constituted the military power, and paid no taxes. The War of the Austrian Succession taught her that this situation should change. Within a few years she had disbanded the private armies in favor of an imperial standing army and forced the nobility to pay for it. Although the nobility continued to wield a great deal of power, new sources of taxation and a standing army made the central government more effective. Above all, Maria Theresa sought to strengthen the state by strengthening the peasantry: "The sheep should be well-fed in order to make it yield more wool and more milk."[8]

A woman with complex programs, Maria Theresa tried to modernize her realm but at the same time maintained a strict adherence to Catholicism and a distaste for new intellectual ideas. Disdaining skepticism and free thought, she nonetheless believed that her subjects should be educated so that the country might prosper. By the end of her reign she had provided the Habsburg lands with the most extensive system of primary education in Europe and with other kinds of advanced schooling. She also encouraged trade, better use of land, and a score of improvements that might attract money from other countries into her own. For these and other reasons Vienna became a cultural center in the eighteenth century, especially for music and architecture. In fact, Maria Theresa had no true appreciation of art; rather, she was an upper-class patron who characteristically liked to receive pleasure.

While acting as a female monarch of unusual will and incredible self-discipline, she also guided her children's progress. Taking her son Joseph as coregent, she grew to fear his radical steps toward reform, which were to some

In 1741 Maria Theresa appealed to the Hungarian nobility for help. She dramatically emphasized the plight of her dynasty by displaying her infant son, the future Emperor Joseph II.

degree merely extensions of what she had started. She gave her daughter, Marie Antoinette, the most commonsensical advice about how to become pregnant. Their correspondence discusses menstruation, sexual behavior, and medical practices, all in the context of how to ensure breeding. Maria Theresa's sense of royal duty allowed her to increase the power of her line in terms of both aggrandizing the Habsburg throne and making the family reproductively successful throughout Europe.

All the while shaping these developments, the reigns of Catherine the Great and Maria Theresa in fact raised the question of future female rule. It hardly went unnoticed that they were women, and their ruthlessness or waywardness raised eyebrows. So too the influential royal mistresses in France came under question as somehow corrupting of government. While these debates were heating them up, people were revising their ideas about what society should be like. New ideas about strong, central governments that accompanied their growth for the most part proposed structures that in fact eliminated women's rule.

The creation of more organized and visible central governments altered the course of Western civilization. Not only did people look beyond their locality economically, they did so politically. Identification with a town or village gave way to some extent to identifying oneself as a French person or a Russian. These identifications were slow to develop. Even as late as the early twentieth century, governments were still trying to create a sense of national identity in some more remote populations, for example, in mountainous regions cut off from regular communication. The process began, however, in the eighteenth century and was important from then on. People started looking to the state not only for bread and relief in time of distress, but for more complex things such as rights, happiness, opportunity, representation, and equality. The rise of the nation-state also shaped women's political participation. Like the middle class in general, they would come to look toward the modernizing state as the agent of change. Women also began seeking a political identity. Before the century was over, they would engage the nation-state in a debate over citizenship, policies, and their rights.

The Enlightenment

The changes in commerce and government occured at the same time that new ideas were arising about the nature of the universe, of politics, of the family, and of gender. The development of Protestantism in the sixteenth century and the Scientific Revolution of the seventeenth transformed the way intellectuals viewed the natural world, the religious world, and human society. By the eighteenth century, the fascination with science and a growing belief in the powers of reason had produced a movement called the Enlightenment. Advanced by writers and thinkers known as *philosophes*, Enlightenment ideas applied reason and rational principles to discussions of religion or government. Like scientists they brought data to bear on analyses of society, commercial developments, and dealings in everyday life. These discussions amounted to programs for reform and even for revolutionary change. Reacting to social ills, the editors of the famous French *Encyclopedia*, published in mid-century, gave accounts of new discoveries and the latest philosophical opinion. Uncharacteristic of standard dictionaries or technical works, it also attacked as despotic and irrational a host of governmental practices and religious beliefs. Instead of touting the aristocratic way of life, it turned public attention to technology and commerce—once thought of as vulgar—and provided fine drawings of the latest machines and descriptions of the newest processes in manufacturing. The *Encyclopedia* was but one of many books, newspapers, and pamphlets that poured from the presses in the eighteenth century. That is, the Enlightenment aroused programs for change and new ways of thinking, but it was also a publicity campaign that welded provincial individuals into a farflung but united audience for political appeals. The boldness, wit, and sarcasm of *philosophes* and journalists made a host of new ideas irresistable.

Science

The Enlightenment depended on the Scientific Revolution of the previous century. Scientific discoveries such as the astronomical observations of Galileo and the formulation of physical laws by Isaac Newton constituted a revolution because they shifted the emphasis in scientific investigation away from religious explanations toward reliance on laws derived from observing the workings of nature. Newton's studies of motion, for example, demonstrated that principles such as gravity and inertia, rather than the spiritual qualities of objects, explained how these objects moved. Galileo used the telescope—initially believed by some to be a kind of diabolical instrument—to throw doubt on beliefs about the perfection of all heavenly bodies compared to the imperfections on Earth. Finding sunspots, craters, and all sorts of rough places on the moon, Galileo also discovered moons around Jupiter. All of these facts indicated both an unimagined, yet observable complexity in the heavens, which people had generally believed to be a mysterious and pure manifestation of the mysterious workings of God. In contrast, Galileo and Newton believed that the universe was knowable through the application of scientific methods and mathematics. Mathematics, observation, and regularity—these new precepts for studying the natural world challenged the authority of the church, of the universities, and even of governments, which often invoked irrational, arbitrary rules. Science made all traditional knowledge suspect and opened a way for new interpretations, including some about women.

By the eighteenth century science had become an engaging enterprise. Enlightened belief depended on a more widespread practice of and interest in science. In the case of women, many in the elite felt the lure of this new view of the natural world. Evidence comes from all quarters of such interest. For instance, a certain French noblewoman wanted neither jewels nor a lavish *objet d'art* for a wedding gift—instead she demanded a telescope. A Polish woman gathered minerals, skeletons and skulls, and experimental machinery to aid her in her scientific pursuits. As amateurs, women constituted an audience for science; they devoured such works as *Newtonianism for Woman*, published in Naples in 1737 and translated into English by the Bluestocking Elizabeth Carter. Other women also proved themselves by translating major scientific works; the most notable was Gabrielle-Emilie du Châtelet (1706–1749), who translated Newton's *Principia* into French. Others condensed difficult classics into works for the layperson. No one excelled in this type of enterprise more than Jane Marcet (1769–1858), who produced such best-sellers as *Conversations on Chemistry*. Finally, in the area of fostering scientific ideas, women such as Clelia Borromeo in Italy and Marie Lavoisier in France held scientific salons, where the newest inventions, discoveries, or theses were circulated and where scientific discourse was promoted.

Some celebrated women made their own discoveries and engaged in science at the highest levels. For instance, both du Châtelet and Lavoisier worked in physics and chemistry, respectively. In Italy, where the tradition of learned women remained powerful, Laura Bassi (1711–1778) held the chair in physics

The painting "Mademoiselle Ferrand Meditates on Newton" suggests how significant the new scientific spirit was in the lives of upper-class women.

at the University of Bologna. At the same institution, Maria Agnesi (1718–1799) succeeded to her father's chair in mathematics and natural philosophy. Agnesi received international attention for her work on conic sections and the versed sine curve, and her *Propositions* and *Analytical Institutions* (dedicated to the Empress of Austria) were hailed as the most complete of mathematical works. Unlike Bassi and Agnesi, German-born Caroline Herschel (1750–1848) was virtually uneducated, because her mother was adamantly opposed to education for women. Accompanying her brother William to England as his housekeeper, she soon became his assistant in astronomical studies. The couple built telescopes to make their own observations, which resulted in their discovering the planet Uranus. Night after night Caroline Herschel served as secretary, noting all her brother's findings and charting them. During lulls, she learned to sweep the sky with her own telescope. While her brother was on the Continent in 1786, Herschel made her first major discovery. Her report of the event reads as follows:

> Aug. 1 [1786]: I have calculated 100 nebulae to-day, and this evening I saw an object which I believe will prove to-morrow night to be a comet.
> Aug. 2: To-day I calculated 150 nebulae. I fear it will not be clear to-night, it has been raining throughout the whole day, but seems now to clear up a little.
> 1 o'clock; the object of last night *is a Comet*. [her emphasis][9]

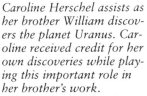
Caroline Herschel assists as her brother William discovers the planet Uranus. Caroline received credit for her own discoveries while playing this important role in her brother's work.

Although her discoveries were overshadowed by those of her brother, Caroline Herschel did receive some credit and celebrity. In 1828, she was given an award from the Royal Astronomical Society for her work on her brother's catalogue of star clusters and nebulae. In contrast, Sophie Duvaucel, stepdaughter of the famed paleontologist Georges Cuvier, was the major illustrator of his works but remained unrecognized. Women's enthusiasm for science often served the ambitions of the men in their lives. Yet it also opened avenues to enlightenment and the use of reason in a period when eager study and the pursuit of knowledge attracted men and women alike. This new field was yet ungendered.

Religion

The Catholic religion had played an important role in shaping beliefs about virtually everything. For example, it explained the social hierarchies on earth as part of a great chain of being, ordained by God's will and manifesting the hierarchical nature of creation. Kings and lower-level rulers received their responsibilities from God. The Protestant Reformation that began early in the sixteenth century challenged some of these social beliefs and raised issues that would last into the Enlightenment. Even where Protestantism did not take hold, it forced the Catholic church to rework many of its premises. First, Protestantism challenged the value of a celibate clergy. Martin Luther, a monk whose 95 Theses were posted on a German church door in 1517, ignited the fire of Protestantism. He announced that it was good to marry, and then he himself married a nun. As Protestants abandoned clerical celibacy, marriage gained a prestige denied by Catholic teachings. This prestige did not bring married women any explicit power, but it did enhance their role by enhancing the institution in which they performed it. Second, Protestantism emphasized the individual's direct relationship with God rather than one mediated by a clergyman. Although this stress on individualism in spiritual life opened the possibility of self-confidence to everyone, in theory it particularly liberated women as a group from male direction of their spiritual lives. Under Protestantism they could undertake crusades on their own.

Aware of these advantages, prominent women embraced the new religion from the beginning. In the sixteenth century Marguerite of Navarre (1492–1549), sister of the French king and queen of Navarre, sheltered persecuted Protestant leaders, while her daughter, Jeanne d'Albret (1528–1572) was a major force in the new faith. A century later Anne Hutchinson (1591–1643) and Margaret Fell (1614–1702) were among those women of the dissenting sects such as Quakerism to take leadership roles. Influenced by his wife Margaret, George Fell, founder of the Society of Friends or Quakers, explicitly encouraged female leadership. He explained that the coming of Christ had ended male supremacy over women: "There are Elder Women in the Truth, as well as Elder Men in the Truth; and these women are to be teachers of good things. . . . Deborah was a judge; Miriam and Huldah were prophetesses; old Anna was a Prophetess. . . . Mary Magdalene and the other Mary were the first preachers of Christ's Resurrection to the Disciples . . . they received the Command, and being sent, preached it; So is every Woman and Man to do."[10] Such ideas never became accepted social norms, but they created some ferment among women. At the instigation of Fell, Quaker women formed their own meetings, which lasted well into the eighteenth century both in England and in the North American colonies. Guided by the "inner light" and confident in their relationship with God, these women were effective as partners in commercial enterprises, as spiritual participants and even leaders, and as activists in political life. Moreover, the emphasis on preaching and on hearty individual faith demanded the education of women so that they could, for example, read scriptures.

By the eighteenth century these developments in religious thought and practice had aroused the interest of philosophers and had reshaped the thinking of ordinary people. For one thing, *philosophes* hotly debated religious issues while scorning superstitions, religious rituals, and practices such as torture for their irrational nature. The critic Voltaire wrote tracts against the Catholic church and what he saw as its backward, inhumane ways. In his satire *The Persian Letters,* the jurist Montesquieu ridiculed priests and popes alike as would-be magicians. For another, this open questioning accompanied a slippage in the usual acceptance of religious authority in everyday life. In France, the influence of Protestant ideas had infected faithful Catholics with an interest in popularizing religious knowledge and in intensifying the personal experience of faith. This version of Catholicism, known as Jansenism, produced violent demonstrations in Paris by male and female convulsionaries, who thereby testified to a faith that had become intense, demonstrative, and disorderly. More upper-class Jansenist women, finding the political order as distasteful as ordinary Catholicism, were emboldened by their religious fervor to criticize the government as well as ordinary Catholicism in the 1770s. Both the new rationalism in religion and the new fervor signaled that all was not well with the old way of doing things.

The Transformation of Political Thought

The winds of change brought with them a new political philosophy called liberalism. A replacement for theories of aristocratic or absolute monarchical power, classical liberal thought as it developed in the seventeenth and eighteenth centuries is not equivalent to current meanings of the word liberal. Instead liberal doctrine focused on ideas of rights, equality, and contractual government. Nothing affected women so powerfully as classical liberal thought, and nothing transformed ideas of government so much as the suggestion that it might be based on something other than arbitrary power. The greatest proponent of this new liberalism was the philosopher John Locke (1632–1704).

Reviewing the development of a prosperous, commercial society and the rise of middle-class activity, Locke—and an array of like-minded thinkers—posited that commerce as an activity would lessen the tendency of societies and their leaders to follow their passions when making public policy. He believed that commerce had a softening effect because it sprang from rational self-interest. By contrast, aristocrats and monarchs governed according to their will, their desires, and their interest in brutish military activity. Locke found the calculation involved in commerce a far healthier basis for government and for deciding on the fate of society. Giving credit to those new endeavors, he laid the groundwork for the theory of a new social order.

Like many revolutionary thinkers, Locke justified his theory by imagining what human life was like before society existed. That is, he constructed an imaginary "state of nature" in which, according to his theory, the primary human activity consisted of feeding and clothing the body. In other words, he saw the nature of life as it developed from this first necessity, as laboring, as economic, and as indisputably physical. The centerpiece of human endeavor was fostering one's existence through work, rather than nurturing one's immortal soul through prayer, contemplation, or any other spiritual activity. Locke and thinkers who followed him would emphasize the here and now, the activity of commerce and exchange, and the centrality and dignity of work in human life.

John Locke also brought up notions of equality, freedom, and property that in the eighteenth century formed the common coin of reform ideas. He saw human beings as born free and equal in so far as they had to nourish themselves, to mix their labor with the fruits of the earth, and thus to create property. Property, freedom, and equality therefore had an intimate connection in the philosophy of the up-and-coming commercial world. The idea of rationality—not necessarily connected to science—was also the basis of a different order of things. Locke posited that the human mind, blank at birth, slowly acquired sense impressions, which it continuously combined to form both moral and practical judgments. Human rationality had social purposes in that it freed people from control of their passions and led them to combine and form governments. Rationally recognizing the problem that some people might encroach on the rights of others, humans surrendered some of their freedom to a central institution of government, which would then regulate the system of property and exchange. This theory of contract, or compact, government grew in popularity among the educated elite during the course of the eighteenth century. In a contract system of government the political order was thought to rest on the participation of those with property, which might be goods or in the ability to sell one's labor. The new commercial society gained theoretical justification in these ideas of the propertied individual born free and equal in acquisitive rights, the rational nature of human life, and the contract theory of political rule. Adopting such ideas, Europeans (and colonists in the New World) moved toward a time when they would challenge aristocratic rule, monarchical theories of government, and values that gave emphasis to arbitrary will and the reign of passions.

The arbitrary rule of the sovereign or the noble was suspect in this new way of thinking, and so was the arbitrary power of the male in a household. Locke lashed out at the arbitrary power of the father as well as the arbitrary power of the king. He rejected the traditional theory in which "all power on earth is either derived from or usurped from the fatherly power."[11] Paternal or monarchical prerogatives implied that the earth had not been given to all people in common, that equality did not exist. Locke believed that human freedom predated human society and existed prior to human institutions, such as government or the family. For him both male and female possessed such equality and such freedom. The natural conditions, however, required modification by mind. Just as society could not exist with complete natural freedom and equality, so the family could not survive with *two* heads of household. Locke often posited an "ideal" world of equality, but he always came back to the real, "contingent" world. There, as far as the sexes were concerned, he found it "natural" that women should defer to male rule and men's greater physical strength, especially given female incapacity during childbirth. Locke's form of patriarchy was somewhat less arbitrary and more administrative; the father ruled in the name of family order. Thus, in the realm of gender relations, Locke began thinking about women in a practical, which is not necessarily to say a new, way. He arrived at some old conclusions but, also posited a world of rights, equality, freedom, commerce, and labor in which women had the same standing as men. Women would ultimately endeavor during the next centuries to give this theory practical reality.

Eighteenth-century thinkers partially built the Enlightenment by broadcasting liberal political theory. In particular they questioned the old order, including its static nature, its aristocratic privilege, and its general attitude that monarchs should rule by virtue of tradition and according to their whims. Instead of accepting government as God-given, the jurist Montesquieu considered all the systems of rule as fit topics for study and analysis. In his *Spirit of the Laws* (1748), he categorized and compared the features of monarchical, despotic, and republican forms in such a way as to call absolute monarchy into question. "Dare to know," wrote Immanuel Kant in German, meaning that people should think for themselves and use their reason to study social conditions.

Continuing the intellectual investigation of freedom, Catharine Macaulay (1731–1791) received great acclaim on the Continent and in the colonies for her English histories, in which she refuted the pessimistic and politically conservative work of philosopher David Hume. For Macaulay, history demonstrated the advance of reason and of liberty. Her interpretation coincided with the general denigration of despotism and popularity of liberal ideas while it made her one of the best-selling scholarly authors. These and many other writers slowly undermined centuries of monarchical rule and set the stage for further transformation of government.

Philosophical and Scientific Discussions of the Nature of Women

While rethinking the nature of society and government, philosophers explicitly addressed the question of women. As they developed new ideas of what it meant to be a human being, the gendered aspect of life was a crucial part of their speculations. In this rethinking process, however, they focused on women as the term in the gender equation through which all differences between the sexes could be explained. In this regard, Locke's thinking about the nature of rights in terms of male and female had been preceded in fact by the profound investigations of René Descartes (1596–1650), whose influence lasted well into the modern era.

A French philosopher and mathematician, Descartes posited thought as the major condition of existence. The spread of his formulation "I think, therefore I am" brought intellectuals to see the "rational" as being of primary concern and import. For Descartes, thought transcended gender and sexual difference. At the highest levels of being, male and female were equivalent because the most important, indeed the fundamental aspect of any human being was the aptitude for thought. Yet Descartes also believed that mind and body interacted and intersected in existence. Thus, in the case of women, their capacity to participate in thought depended on living according to the laws dominating the female body. Recognizing the real existence of the female body, Descartes conceded to it the power to disrupt the energy and functioning of thought. Nonetheless, as with men, the sexual aspect of women's bodies had no preeminence over thought.

Descartes's influence appeared to go in two different directions in subsequent philosophical and scientific writing. On the one hand, seventeenth century thinker François Poullain de la Barre saw only superstition and prejudice in ideas of women's inferiority. For him sexism was antiscientific. Another commentator, Marie Gournay, wrote in 1622 that the "human animal is neither male nor female."[12] On the other hand, medical men started emphasizing the bodily limitations on women in Descartes's formulation. By the eighteenth century their contribution to the debate over gender as interpreted through women's difference had become more influential than religious ideas of Eve's sinfulness or women's lust. Doctors discussing women found such theories antiscientific and invalid because they lacked clinical observation. With the prestige of science on the rise, medical men gradually replaced the clergy as interpreters of gender.

When doctors started postulating what women were, they looked to the most natural of manifestations—the body. Starting from this materialistic vantage point, they ended up with theories that emphasized difference rather than identity. For example, the great French scientist Georges Buffon placed women squarely in nature by emphasizing the role of their bodies. For Buffon, all human beings, as part of nature, were finite; their major activities were surrounded by the degeneration and regeneration of the species. This cycle of life and death made women's reproductivity central and obvious. Indeed, Buffon saw women as natural beings, defined by reproductivity and bathed in an attendant sexuality, instead of sharing mental capacity with men.

Sexuality itself, while superficially allowing of subjective feelings, merely served the end of reproducing the species. The Dutch scientist Hermann Boerhaave emphasized ways in which the bodily parts of women progressively adapted to this function. Moreover, anatomical depictions of skeletons exaggerated these newly important differences. For example, the drawings of a famous woman anatomist, Geneviève Thiroux d'Arconville, showed women as having a smaller head and a proportionately smaller rib cage than men, as well as a large pelvis to serve the reproductive function. Although by the 1790s a German anatomist had constructed a more accurate picture of the female skeleton, Thiroux d'Arconville's proportions remained the most influential. By the 1820s her viewpoint had been adopted in the anatomical work of John Barclay of Edinburgh, who added a child with skeletal proportions similar to those of the female. In this regard, science obviously reflected the commonly held attitudes about women. Demonstrating the pelvic capacity of women enhanced ideas of motherhood, and noting similar cranial proportions in women and children suggested similarities in intellectual ability. At the same time, the interest in gender differences and in actual physiology displaced the idea that woman was merely the derivative of man in an inferior form. Instead, woman's body became the site of newly valued qualities. The skin of women, physicians postulated, had more densely packed nerve endings, which made them more sensitive and more sentimental. In short, medical theory began attaching to the female body a host of important social attributes.

Nonetheless, medical men and other scientists faced the problem of wom-

Among Italian women university professors, Anna Morandi Mahzolini earned a reputation for innovative teaching of anatomy.

an's mind or soul. What was its relation to the bodily task of reproduction? Most agreed that in women the sexual aspect, or the "different", dominated over mind. Although virtually no one denied the presence of mind in woman, they argued about its capacity. For some physicians, woman's freedom was only negative. It existed in her mental capacity to deny her body's reproductivity and to attempt to live apart from its rules. Others saw the power of a woman's soul or mind as important in supplementing the work of the womb by exerting force on the fetus and on the developed child. The idea formed the basis of new constructions of motherhood. Other medical experts hedged, waiting for further scientific advances: "Perhaps one day anatomists will arrive at discovering the point where sex ends and at determining the point where woman ceases to be woman and begins to be man or human."[13] Still other physicians tried to distinguish between the reproductive condition of woman, which made her weak and physiologically inferior to man, and the social or moral condition of inferiority imposed by society. The widespread disagreement on this point indicated the instability of the definition of womanhood in the medical literature. Whereas reproductivity generally took on more significance, given the increasing power of doctors, the questions concerning woman's mind or soul remained unanswered and much debated. As a result, people could and did assert almost anything about women, even in the supposedly precise and scientific medical literature.

Although medical men set the agenda for less specialized Enlightenment thinkers, they put *philosophes* in a quandary. Believing in both science and reason, *philosophes* had a difficult time figuring women out. No one wanted to deny that women could reason, for this was the hallmark of the new age. Yet science had focused on the body and had stressed how reproduction reduced female capacity for thought. Consequently, philosophers such as Denis Diderot (1713–1784) saw women as imprisoned in their reproductivity even while advocating the development of their reason. Such views were pessimistic: aiming for reason, one should not have too high hopes for the outcome.

Other thinkers, such as Pierre-Antoine Choderlos de Laclos, took the insertion of women into nature to other extremes. Like Diderot, Laclos pointed to the sexual aspects of women's lives and the repressive nature of institutions arranged for organizing that sexuality, among them the middle-class household and convents. His famous novel, *Les liaisons dangereuses* (1782), showed how disastrous sexual encounters were in society as it was then constituted. For Laclos, the only answer for women lay in living the most natural and sexually unrestrained lives possible. A return to nature meant exercising to the fullest the sexuality that made up one's nature. Although Laclos was eccentric for his time, his theory as to women's best interests was reiterated as a minority position right up to the twentieth century, when it became dominant. In all events, in the eighteenth century, women's reason and women's reproductivity for the moment displaced all explicit concern about woman as Eve, about sexual temptation and irrepressible female sinfulness.

Social Structure

By the late eighteenth century, changes in the economy and politics stimulated rethinking the role of women in marriage and family life. In the seventeenth century, utilitarian explanations of marriage had described it as an institution that harmonized the sexes and that served the interest of each member of a couple. The family balanced personal interests just as commerce balanced those of property: both were part of classical liberal theory. This liberal view overshadowed the idea of marriage as a sacrament, but it was not unchallenged. A parallel "republican" theory specifically denied that marriage had to do with self-interest, agreement or contract, or harmony within the couple. In this theory marriage served a different end. By removing people from the sexual license and even brutality that existed in the natural state, marriage formed a society in which people were made moral, or virtuous. Moral sensibilities developed within the family and then radiated out into the public sphere. In fact, these affections and higher sentiments arising from the family constituted the only way of making the arena of commerce and worldly pursuits tolerable. Republicanism gave the roles played by women within the household a new cast by extending them beyond the realm of subsistence toward that of social benefit. Because women formed the characters of their children and shaped those of their male relatives for the public not just the individual good, their efforts served their "republic," that is, the good of the state. This republican cultural role meant additional responsibilities. Any activity injurious to matrimonial affections became a blow to public happiness as well, and the interests of the state came before all personal rights or claims. Adam Smith, the advocate of the free market in his *Wealth of Nations (1776), was a major proponent of the effects of private "virtue" on both private and public spheres. Women's adherence "to modesty, chastity, to economy" were not simply personal matters but reverberated widely.*[14]

The Rousseauean Doctrine

A little after mid-century, an egocentric and eccentric character named Jean-Jacques Rousseau (1712–1778) made some notable formulations about education, society, and the role of women. His ideas were bold, highly critical, and articulated in a way that caught the attention of intellectuals and would-be reformers. In his *Confessions* (1782), Rousseau expressed modern preoccupations with the self, inner feelings, and sentiments. Searching for authentic, natural relationships, he deplored overcivilized society that kept humans chained by unjust laws and customs. His *Social Contract* (1762) reiterated the notion of contractual government and also declared the existence, once the contract was made, of a "general will" embodying the collective desires and superior claims of the nation. Some of these ideas lay dormant until the French Revolution brought them to the fore.

Rousseau's *The New Heloise* (1761), however, immediately took Europe by storm and was followed by the popular *Emile* (1762). The impact of these books demonstrates what affected the European mind in those changing times and what subjects were preoccupying the reading public. Both posed questions concerning gender roles, marriage, and education. They began setting the agenda for change in manners and intellectual development, especially in children. *The New Heloise* repeated the medieval story of Abelard and Heloise, a tutor and his pupil who fell in love. In the original version, the tutor was castrated by his lover's kinfolk and the couple ended up in separate religious orders. Rousseau's story of the modern tutor St. Preux and his pupil Julie is about marriage and the family. Although Julie succumbs to her tutor's seduction, ultimately she is married off to a proper husband chosen for her by her father. While St. Preux is wandering through the world, Julie becomes an expert mother who breast-feeds her children and educates them. She is also an excellent wife and a doer of charitable works within her community. Nonetheless, Julie has to pay for initially breaking social and familial codes, and thus sometime after St. Preux returns to tutor her own children, she drowns. Rousseau's saga of love, motherhood, and death made tears flow, but it also aroused the admiration of women. Rousseau's Julie showed a woman in a powerful social role. As a mother, Julie was not the mere bearer of children, she also bore responsibility for each child's future development, for nurturing and education. This sustained connection, symbolized first in breast-feeding, put the acts of women into a new cultural context. Julie was clearly the party who enforced the social law and embodied virtue. In her later years she instilled in her children a sense of right and wrong. Not the law-giver, she served as the law-enforcer. Women recognized in all this an increment to whatever power they had before. This was true for both aristocratic women, for whom breeding had been a major function, and middle-class women, who had already begun to focus on family. Rousseau gave Julie her own sphere of influence, whereas St. Preux had the rest of the world.

Emile amounts to a protracted discussion of sex roles, in which men and women receive different educations to fit them for separate spheres. Before this, roles had centered on what appeared to be natural—breeding for the female and physical prowess for the larger, stronger male. As a boy, Emile goes away from civilization with a tutor to get his education. Rather than the old rote education with good measures of brutality thrown in, his innovative training for adulthood emphasizes development, self-control, and knowledge of practical matters. Through this formation Emile becomes a modern man, self-confident, self-governed, and walking with an assured—rather than an aristocratic—gait. But this "new" man needs a modern woman. Emile's future mate Sophie grows up in the countryside, not like a hothouse plant bred at court or chateau. Like Emile's, her ongoing education shapes her for the role she is to play in life, but her role is to be a domestic one. Women who read Rousseau's novel found the idea of women having a developmental capability a great advance. Many overlooked the limitations placed on Sophie's education; she received only as much as fitted her for obedient companionship. Moreover, they also overlooked the strict delineation in *Emile* of roles between man and woman.

Rousseau's novels offered explicit guidance to a society substituting middle-class values for aristocratic ones. Men and women throughout Europe took up what they conceived to be Rousseauean roles. Fashionable aristocrats advanced his themes; even Marie Antoinette, Queen of France, had a farm built for herself and her ladies-in-waiting so that they might retreat from the artificialities of court life. In so doing, they affirmed their connections with nature and with natural roles that had now been made cultural. Adherents to Rousseauean themes also joined him in distinguishing the public world from the private one or in institutionalizing the idea of "separate spheres" for women and men.

The Transformation of Culture

Rousseau's opinion that women should focus their attention on the private sphere served to develop republican sentiments about the home. It also addressed the powerful presence of well-to-do women in cultural life. Changing political and economic structures gave rise to new ways of disseminating ideas about these innovations. *Salons,* newspapers, learned academies, and intellectual clubs filled the need for sociability built around new ideas. Such instruments of cultural change generated excitement and passion. People coming together to hear letters read aloud, for instance, found new energy in free cul-

Salonières were at the center of Enlightenment political culture. Highly motivated to foster this new culture, they drew attacks nonetheless from Rousseau and later commentators for allegedly making philosophes *effeminate.*

tural exchange. While they did not dominate, women were prominent in almost all these ventures. Their prominence, while it made for social change, made some like Rousseau highly critical.

The Salon

The *salon*—a gathering of intellectuals, politicians, or cultural leaders to discuss current issues—wielded considerable power in the eighteenth century. In France the *salon* had developed an extensive influence over the past century. In the eary years *salons* helped rising men of wealth mingle with old members of the aristocracy; conversation, new ideas, and the refinement of manners held them together. The *salonière*, the woman who opened her home and often led the meetings, gained prestige not only for herself but for women in general. The *salon* formed part of several innovative trends, but primarily the rise of the middle class. By providing a place where the middle class could learn aristocratic ways and where aristocrats could be exposed to and involved with ideas, news, and technology, *salons* promoted social change. At the same time they intensified and even to some extent generated the debate over the role of women. *Salons* can be seen as a symbol of the gender changes that were also possible in this age of transformation.

Salons created a new place where cultural values were transformed. Ideas, insights, and discoveries received a hearing not at court, but in a wealthy woman's home. Proliferating across Europe, *salon* life came to flourish in Berlin, London, and Vienna as well as in Paris. People who came to a *salon* might play cards, but the central activity was conversation. This pursuit of intellectual stimulation in itself marked a slow transition away from aristocratic values, especially that of the primacy of sensual pleasure. Hostesses began arranging people into conversational groups by bringing in more furniture to place in clusters. The idea of intimate conversation even entered into home design, which began to mark out smaller public spaces in the homes of the great. In Mrs. Montagu's London home, guests sat in a semicircle facing the fire. She placed herself somewhere before the height of the curve. This asymmetry gave a new air, with the fire adding an informal touch. But the *salon* was not democratic; people were expressly invited, and invitations were prized. Those with wit, renown, or social standing could usually find a welcome. All, however, had to possess the ability to converse and contribute. An aristocratic background was not enough to ensure repeat invitations, nor could it make the *salonière* herself a success. She had to provide a fine gathering place, stimulating company, and some measure of personal accomplishment. Witty, ambitious, and engaging women became social leaders by means of their *salons*: first, Madame de Rambouillet; later, Madame de Tencin; and, in the *salon*'s mature, Enlightenment phase, Madame du Deffand, Julie de Lespinasse, and Madame Necker. Each of them differed somewhat in her background, approach, and reasons for forming such a circle. For example, Madame Necker, daughter of a Swiss parson, had almost no social standing, which was not generally true of *salonières*. But her husband was immensely wealthy, and she had intellectual accomplishments. The same could be said for the many Jewish women who ran *salons* in Berlin. Outcasts from a strict Prussian social order, they nonetheless constituted the major supporters of this institution in Germany because of their interest in learning.

Women who held *salons* rapidly became mediators, if not arbiters, of culture. In Weimar, Duchess Amelia helped make famous the poets Christoph Wieland (whom she chose as her son's tutor) and Johann von Goethe, the philosopher Johann Herder, and the novelist Jean Paul Richter. In Paris *salonières* determined the shape of the Enlightenment and gave publicity to its ideas. Madame de Tencin sponsored Montesquieu's *The Spirit of the Law*, and Madame de Pompadour, mistress of Louis XV, used her political influence to have his critics silenced. In *salons*, men of letters could test their ideas, meet influential people, and earn a reputation. Through the influence of French *salonières*, writers gained admission to the French Academy, the ultimate determinant of intellectual prestige. As one *salonière* put it, "It is through women that one obtains what one wishes from men."[15]

As Enlightenment ideas posed more and more of a challenge to the entrenched political order, *salons* and the *salonières* took on a more purposeful air. In Warsaw, Princess Sophia Czartoryska's circle spread learning and also constituted a faction for reform politics. Fanny von Arstein's Viennese *salon*, active from the late 1770s on, encouraged the Austrian Emperor to show greater tolerance of Jews. The *salons* of Berlin were subversive merely by providing an arena for intellectual talent in heavily censored Prussian society. The dominance of Jewish women there signaled a radical kind of openness. Serious books, news, and issues were talked about in *salons,* while pleasures of a trivial sort were virtually banished to the frivolous gatherings of the court aristocracy. Factions, philosophical forays, and literary adventures all developed with the *salon,* a domestic space in which women could play a public and political role. It promoted the new ideas and institutions that questioned political order throughout Europe; the *salonières,* especially those after mid-century, cleared the path along which the middle classes would triumphantly move toward revolution.

Bluestockings, Academies, and Freemasons

In 1768 Elizabeth Montagu, the famous hostess known as the "Queen of the Blues," described to her friend Mrs. Vesey the Christmas she had just spent "with the bluestocking philosophers. I had parties of them to dine with me continually, and ... I have got a new bluestocking with whom I am much pleased, a Mr. Percy who publish'd the Reliques of the ancient Poetry."[16] The Bluestockings in England formed a type of intellectual enclave similar to the *salon* but with a more self-consciously female orientation. Sometime after 1760 Elisabeth Vesey started gathering like-minded people in her "blue-room" or "green-room" or dressing room for conversation. Those invited included both men and women, but always a certain number of women formed the core. Mary Delaney (1700–1788), Elizabeth Carter (1717–1806), Elizabeth Montagu (1720–1800), Fanny Burney (1752–1840), and Hannah More (1745–1835) were an ill-assorted group if the criteria for judging were age, background, or interests, but they had one common bond—they rejected the older lifestyle of endless pleasure, primping, and uselessness. In its place they put study and the discussion of pertinent issues, and shaped their lives in some measure by these serious pursuits. Fanny Burney and Hannah More, the youngest of the Bluestockings, were famous for their writings. Elizabeth Carter first made a name for herself by translating Epictetus from the Greek and maintained her reputation with her fluency in many languages.

Such activity fed the debate over women, the limits of their ability, and what their horizons should be. The Bluestockings gave advice in these matters; for example, Hester Chapone's *Letters on the Improvement of the Mind Addressed to a Young Lady* (1773) made her famous as a well-spoken advocate of women's education. The Bluestockings participated actively in the intellectual society of the day by socializing and interacting with such luminaries as Samuel Johnson, Sir Joshua Reynolds, Horace Walpole, and others. Immortalized in Hannah More's poem *Bas Bleu,* the members of the group and all those who joined them for special conversations differed from the *salonières* on the Continent. That is, abhoring much about the condition of women, they especially disliked the fact that women were compelled to marry for money or social standing or to live useless lives. They made their own lives different by propagating ideas for change through their numerous writings and by being much talked-of examples. Yet, in spite of the Bluestockings' sense of humor, generosity, domestic skills, and genuine learning, the word *bluestocking* would be used in the next century to mean a pedantic, ugly, mannish, and overly educated woman. The original Bluestockings were none of these. Instead, like their counterparts running *salons* in the German states, France, and the Italian cities, they were a catalyst for the reassessment of traditional gender roles as well as social and political institutions.

Upper-class women, and even some of lower station, also became part of male-dominated intellectual circles. Scientific societies and learned academies developed throughout Europe to promote the dissemination of new findings and new trends in thought. Women attended these meetings and were sometimes elected members of such groups. One of the most respected of academicians was the relatively uneducated Corilla (Maria Maddalena Morelli, 1727–1800), crowned in 1776 by the Roman academy on the steps of the capitol for her powers of declamation and improvisation. Corilla served as the official poet of the Florentine court but also travelled to the major Italian cities to hold conversations with her admirers. Female Italian professors often entered academies, and one of them, Maria Agnesi (1718–1799), even sponsored Voltaire's membership. Membership in academies and the pursuit of knowledge were fraught with politics; for instance, in the career of Princess Ekaterina Dashkova (1743–1810), director of the St. Petersburg-based Academy of Arts and Sciences and first president of the Imperial Russian Academy. A learned woman, Dashkova had nonetheless participated in the coup that brought Catherine the Great to the throne. She and the monarch corresponded, sharing a common enthusiasm for knowledge. In her capacity as president of the Russian Academy, Dashkova played an important role in the production of the first Russian dictionary. None of this secured her position, however; she was exiled several times. What remained constant in her life was a commitment to learning, study, and innovation in the realm of ideas.

Princess Dashkova, the Russian Language, and the
Emergence of the State

Catherine the Great adopted the dissemination of knowledge as one way of bringing unity to her country and modernizing it. Sponsoring the translation of scientific works and philosophy, she also encouraged learned academies. She appointed Princess Ekaterina Dashkova to the presidency of the St. Petersburg Academy of Arts and Sciences in 1783 and then to the presidency of the Imperial Russian Academy. Dashkova saw the importance of both publishing and standardizing the Russian language to Catherine's state-building mission. Here is an excerpt from Dashkova's presidential speech at the opening of the Imperial Russian Academy.

GENTLEMEN,—A new instance of the solicitude of our august empress for the instruction of her subjects has this day assembled us together. That genius which has already diffused so many benefits over Russia has now given a proof of its protective energy in behalf of the Russian language, the parent and source of so many others. The riches and copiousness of our language to you are well known. They are such as will render justice to the varied treasures of antiquity. Our mother tongue unites not only these advantages, gentlemen, but even in all the subtleties of philosophy, in their affinities and oppositions, it furnishes appropriate expressions, and terms the most applicable and descriptive. But with such resources we have to lament the want of determinant rules—rules for the inflexions of words, as well as an authorized definition and limitation of their meaning. Hence have arisen those varieties of construction, those improprieties of imitation and foreign idiom, which have hitherto disfigured and depressed our language.

The object of the establishment of the Imperial Russian Academy is to render it perfect, to raise it to a standard of elevation suitable to the glorious age of Catherine II. This, gentlemen, must be the end and aim of the labours of a society founded and supported by her gracious protection. The different memorials of antiquity spread over the vast surface of the Russian empire, our numerous chronicles, those precious records of the great actions of our ancestors, of which few of the nations of Europe now existing can boast an equal number, present a vast field for our exertions, upon which we are led to advance under the guidance of the enlightened genius of our august protectress. The high deeds of our princes, the exploits of the past and the present ever-memorable age, present an almost boundless range of subjects worthy of our labour.

But, gentlemen, the first fruits of our endeavours, the first offering to be laid at the feet of our immortal sovereign, is a grammar of our language, exact and methodical, and a rich and copious dictionary.

Source: Memoirs of the Princess Daschkow. 2 vols. (London: Henry Colburn, 1840) 2:144–146.

The Freemasons, a secret society with esoteric codes and rituals, had begun in the early eighteenth century to promote ideals such as fraternity, progress, humanitarianism, and enlightenment in general. In some areas Freemasons (or

Masons) formed lodges that admitted both men and women. There women could participate not only in promoting enlightenment, but also in the power structure of the Enlightenment, because many of the most prominent reformers and thinkers belonged to the Masons. In France, some of these mixed-gender lodges spawned sisterhoods predominantly of women members. Within these sisterhoods there arose rituals that stressed the feminine, and even the feminist. One of the higher levels of female masonry took as its symbol Judith, the Old Testament heroine who assassinated an enemy leader and liberated her city. Another masonic level took the name "Order of the Amazons," in which senior members held military rank. At these higher levels of women's masonry, pro-female sentiments were felt and expressed. "Oh my sisters," announced a speaker in Dijon, "Let us rejoice in and honor masonic membership which avenges our sex for the multiple injuries which have been inflicted upon us for so long."[17] Governmental authorities generally disliked secret societies such as the Masons and perhaps would have preferred that women be barred from membership in academies; the reasons for this opposition lay in the academies' promotion of such concepts as liberty and equality.

The Quest for Education

Amelia, Duchess of the German principality of Weimar, and ruler there after her husband's early death, wrote:

> Never was education so little fitted as mine to form one destined to rule others. Those who directed it themselves needed direction; she to whose guidance I was entrusted was the sport of every passion, subject to innumerable wayward caprices, of which I became the unresisting victim. Unloved by my parents, ever kept in the background I was regarded as the outcast of the family.[18]

The duchess's complaints focused on her lack of good instruction for adulthood and her degradation as a girl in an aristocratic family. Forced by fate to rule, Duchess Amelia understood the magnitude of the problem of inadequate education. In the eighteenth century, people of all classes first learned in a domestic situation. Since the culture was, for the most part, oral, education took the form of learning while doing, in informal conversations or the storytelling of the *Spinstubbe* or in more formal settings such as the *salon*. Lower-class boys and girls trained as apprentices or learned household skills as servants. Only morality, deportment, catechism, and the like demanded special schooling or tutors. If people received any kind of institutional instruction, it was for these purposes. Although the wealthy might employ tutors or governesses for their children, many wealthy children spent time in convents or other boarding schools. Although literacy was increasing, the majority of women were illiterate in this century. Even the wealthiest and most prominent could not read or write well, the most notorious example being Marie Antoinette of France, who had fine powers of expression but made many errors in grammar and spelling.

This system produced a few women of exceptional learning. Apart from the Italian university women and practicing scientists, many others gained a reputation for both a breadth of knowledge and for specialized scholarship. The Empress Maria Theresa thought Luise Gottsched, renowned Austrian lexicographer, the most learned woman in the Germanies. Elizabeth Elstob's Anglo-Saxon grammar furthered language studies as did the work of increasing numbers of classicists. In France Madame Dacier, for instance, translated Homer. Others pursued a wide range of subjects in the Enlightenment fashion. The pleasure-loving Félicité de Genlis was an expert harpist, studied osteology, chemistry, and medicine, and wrote plays, histories, novels, and tracts on education. As for the classicist Elizabeth Carter, Samuel Johnson was amazed that she "could make a pudding as well as translate Epictetus and work a handkerchief as well as compose a poem."[19]

Despite such accomplishments, the level of women's knowledge remained low. In those circles influenced by the Enlightenment, the call for improved education was made forcefully. Some of the earliest educational reforms had aimed at curbing the pursuit of pleasure so dominant among the aristocracy and upper reaches of the bourgeoisie. At Saint-Cyr, a school for poor noble girls founded by Françoise de Maintenon, wife of Louis XIV, the curriculum emphasized household skills as well as obedience and a sense of woman's humble place in the world. Catherine the Great founded the Smol'ny Institute at mid-century. It stressed similar skills, but also offered a wider range of languages; in addition, the curriculum emphasized activity of a purposeful kind and the development of moral rectitude. In such schools, some aristocratic women prepared themselves for functioning in a world that was changing. Yet these innovations failed to address the quest for reason that so many felt necessary for all people in enlightened times.

Most of those raising the question of women's education did so with specific reference to Rousseau. Although approving of his general insistence on the developmental course of the human psyche and mind, some people, such as Catharine Macaulay in her *Letters on Education* (1787), disapproved of the scant attention he paid to the intellectual component in educating women. Moreover, Macaulay believed that women not trained to high standards of rationality, industry, and character would fail in all their responsibilities as adults. Macaulay and another advocate of women's education, the Marquis de Condorcet, proposed a system in which both sexes received the same education so that emphasis on sexual differences would give way to a common basis of reason.

A flood of tracts appeared during the latter part of the eighteenth century, and they proposed a number of educational systems. The most severe observations came from those who, like the Spanish writer Josefa Amar y Borbon, censured the self-interest of men in keeping women uneducated: "The men, not satisfied after having reserved for themselves positions, honors, compensations for their work, in other words everything that could excite the studiousness and dedication of women, have also deprived the members of our sex of the satisfaction of having an enlightened mind."[20] Amar y Borbon's *Dis-*

course in Defense of Women's Talent and Their Capacity for Government and Other Positions Held by Men (1786) and *Discourse on the Physical and Moral Education of Women* (1790) were the kinds of writings that aimed at gaining access for women to the rational aspects of the Enlightenment.

In some countries the importance of educating women so that they might better educate their children was recognized sooner than in others. Nowhere did this reform seem more urgent than in Poland from the 1770s on. After watching Prussia, Austria, and Russia divide up their homeland in a series of partitions, Polish reformers sought to rebuild their national strength. Improved education of the Polish citizenry, but especially of the aristocracy, was counted as a major step toward that goal. For example, Adam and Isabel Czartoryski not only educated their own children themselves; they took pupils from all classes into the school they founded on their estate. Early in the nineteenth century, Isabel Czartoryska (1746–1835) wrote the first book in Polish expressly for children. Particularly in Eastern Europe, nationalists focused on education, mothers' knowledge, and language in their drives for cohesion and political power.

Print Culture and the Rise of the Novel

As the print culture continued its dramatic rise, reading became a regular activity in more and more homes, with the novel growing in popularity. The result was a new, secular importance placed on reading as a skill necessary for personal enhancement and for social existence. Reading developed character, knowledge, and therefore inner confidence, and discussing the latest novel, newspaper story, or tract established new ties of sociability. Instead of relying on blood relationships as a common bond, the middle class took up reading and conversation as the basis of association. Reading together around the fire in the evenings bonded the family members in a sense of intimacy. Moreover, reading created, aroused, and fed sensibility—a trait appropriated by the middle class to distinguish themselves and increasingly used to mark out female from male. Women were known for being avid readers of certain types of books. As readers, they brought culture into the household.

At the same time, novelists, journalists, and writers of tracts and personal letters produced reams of words. Being published no longer depended exclusively on aristocratic patronage; those who could please a wide market could survive as writers. So talented women looking for work found it in this medium, which required no special equipment, workshop, or activity outside the home. Journalism in particular attracted women writers in good number. In England they wrote for *The Gentleman's Magazine, The World,* or *Fashionable Gazette,* and for a variety of papers intended only for women. Sarah Trimmer, a pioneer in the Sunday school movement, started *The Family Magazine* in 1788 to introduce more sober manners and new interests into the lives of the lower classes. This endeavor represented the spread of the print culture across class boundaries, for the purpose of forming bonds that would "better" the lower class. In The Hague, Madame du Noyer founded *The Quintessence*

A People's Poet

Anna Louisa Karsch (1722–1791) was the daughter of a Silesian tenant farmer. At sixteen she married a weaver, and later an alcoholic tailor. Both marriages were disasters, especially the second. During this time Karsch started writing poetry. Having discovered her talent, Berlin society hailed her as the "people's poet," a kind of rural innocent with words. This conception of Karsch's poetry fit in with the Enlightenment's interest in what "natural" people were like and how it felt to live close to nature. Karsch told them quite clearly in this poem.

> *To the Canon of Rochow, who said that love must*
> *have taught you to write such beautiful verse.*
>
> Weighted down with cares
> My youthful innocence sang its stammering song
> On many a summer's morn;
> Not for the rule of youth, No, but for the God who
> Looks down upon Humanity
> As on a hill of ants.
> Without feeling what I often describe,
> Without tenderness, I moved
> With the state of womanhood
> And motherhood
> Unloved, as in a savage war,
> A woman must kiss the
> Warrior who climbs the city walls,
> I sing songs for those who know love.
> Then I think of the dearest
> Of men, whom I always desire,
> Never find. No wife ever kissed so sadly
> Who kissed with Sappho's sacred fire.
> The lips I never felt.

Source: Anna Louisa Karsch, *Auserlesene Gedichte* (Berlin: G. L. Winters, 1764), 110–112.

of News, whereas German women contributed to a variety of journals, especially in the later part of the century, associated with the romantic movement.*

The women's magazines and papers that female journalists contributed to ranged from illustrated fashion magazines to those containing news and liter-

---

*See Chapter 3.

ature and raising an array of feminist issues. In England the most notorious of the explicitly feminist journalists was Eliza Haywood (1693–1756). A professional writer in many genres, Haywood tried launching two different periodicals for women, *The Female Spectator* (1744–1756) and *The Parrot* (1746). She forthrightly demanded an improvement in the condition of women and specifically queried the position of men: "Why then . . . do the Men, who are and will be the sole arbiters in this Case, refuse us all Opportunities of enlarging our Minds, and improving those Talents we have received from God and Nature."[21] Among the writings for women that appeared in Paris was the *Journal des Dames,* founded in 1759 as a "delicious nothing" for society women. The male publishers soon found the journal's character changed by a series of women editors who published writing about all the Enlightenment's projects and politics and who invited radical contributions. Soon the *Journal des Dames* had entered into such topics as woman's role, freemasonry, attacks on the government, and so on, although it often masked some of its most radical efforts with the usual society news and even praise for enemies.

All of the early female journalists were interesting personalities, leading irregular and often eccentric lives. Such eccentricity mirrored the position they were trying to create for themselves as women influential in a man's world. The medium they aspired to shape was a new and increasingly powerful one. In an age of reform when news was spread by print, their ambition—seen as an unfeminine trait—was more apparent than was that of women in other literary fields.

Letter writing constituted another literary genre, one the middle classes would tout as their own. Manuals for letter writing became almost indispensable for would-be intellectual women and men. Mary Montagu's letters from Turkey, for example, spread news and demonstrated an ability to grasp the world intellectually. Such news, as it passed through coffeehouse, club, and *salon,* sometimes pointed a finger at upper-class frivolity, at those who held onto privilege through tradition or force rather than knowledge or merit. It also bypassed literary censors. Letters also sprang from the interior space of an individual writer and gave news of families and home. A letter's sentimental and familial possibilities had first been apparent in the letters of Madame de Sevigné (1626–1696), that indefatigable purveyor of news from the court of Louis XIV to a daughter she desperately missed in the provinces. Later writers would discuss feelings and self-awareness—individualistic values that made up a new kind of consciousness. Generally, a letter signaled friendship and connectedness. Women were supposed to excel at making these sentimental and friendly connections because of a heightened sensibility their sex was supposed to possess. Intense concentration on the self, on the connections between people, and on society could lead to exalted thoughts. The letters of Berlin *salon* leader, Rahel Varnhagen Von Ense, reveal the kind of individualism sometimes articulated in letters: "I am as unique as the greatest phenomenon on earth. The greatest artist, philosopher, or poet is not above me. We are of the same cloth, in the same rank, and belong together . . . but life was assigned to me."[22] Letters connected women like the Bluestockings who were trying to form serious and substantial relationships by incessantly writing to one another. They alone among the century's great letter writers were ultimately seen as somehow unwomanly, caricatures, "Blues."

Women particularly stood out as early writers of fiction. Although the form had existed for centuries, in the eighteenth century it attained its ultimate triumph as the most popular form of reading material. The novel was a genre in tune with the new society—an inquisitive and more cosmopolitan one, fascinated by all sorts of human relationships among many types of people, not just the exploits of warrior-heroes. Neither limited in characters nor strict in form, novels could convey just about anything to their readers, including love stories, instruction in manners, new ideas, experiments in writing, and a range of feelings. Novels spread news and information and also evoked laughter, sorrow, delight, and desire. The increasing popularity of the novel was a small aspect of the new commerce that widened the range of available goods and opened towns and households to new experiences. With respect to novels, women were captivated readers, prolific writers, and fascinating subjects.

Being sentimental, mannerly, and expressive, most novels leaned toward a female sphere rather than the male one of history, politics, and war. Women shaped this development of the novel's focus on the private world. Madame de Lafayette's *The Princess of Cleves* (1678) provided a strong influence with its story of love among the supposedly unsentimental nobility. The eighteenth century brought more rollicking stories full of female adventure, wit, irony, mishaps, and always some kind of love, whether rational, passionate, unrequited, or misdirected. Isabel van Zuylen de Charrière, a Dutch woman who lived in Switzerland, wrote novels full of detailed accounts of everyday life. Two French best-sellers, Marie-Jeanne Riccoboni's *Letters of mistriss Fanni Butlerd* (1757) and Françoise Graffigny's *Letters of a Peruvian Woman* (1747), employed the popular epistolary form. The very exchange of something so intimate as a letter conjured up the private world these novels were evoking. Both novels use the theme of love, and the heroines of both refuse finally to enter unsuitable marriages. Some of the drama in the typical novel of the eighteenth century involves vicarious participation in the heroine's sorrows and reflections, and even sometimes in her ultimate resolve to remain celibate. The novel demonstrated that women had a private, inner world just as men did. Moreover, it reflected the dilemma inherent in the new marital customs, which allowed for affection and choice: the question was how to marry wisely, well, and with a partner one could love. Like Samuel Richardson's best-selling *Pamela* (1740) and *Clarissa* (1747), Fanny Burney's *Evelina* (1778) captured all these concerns. The heroine is harrassed by suitors, various acquaintances, and family members, while almost everyone misinforms and misleads her about the customs of marriage. The existence of several different ways of accomplishing a marriage made for mishaps and misfortunes in the story. Burney delighted audiences with the wit she brought to the general situation. Through all the twists and turns of the melodramatic plot, suitors and long-lost relatives provide immeasurable comedy and a good dose of eighteenth-century pleasure.

The typical novel also portrayed an array of forces working against the heroine. Human passions, male power, greed, and the new quest for money competed with a variety of community and parental interests in determining the heroine's ultimate end. Struggling through this matrix of adversity, the heroine usually developed a self, sometimes even a progressive and feminist self. In German author Sophie von La Roche's (1731–1807) *Story of Miss Von Sternheim* (1771), the heroine, Sophie, is the focal point of two intrigues: one, to make her a prince's mistress and the other, to dupe her into a false marriage. The latter plot succeeds, and Sophie spends the rest of the story escaping from its worst consequences, including imprisonment. Although she marries the friendly hero at the end, Sophie builds herself an admirable character along the way. She is not just virtuous, but intelligent and accomplished as well. In the midst of turmoil she calmly spends her time setting up schools, an effort that is in keeping with the new values of education and character development. Such activities sustain her, but what sustains her most is her own education and development of character: "Knowledge of the intellect, goodness of the heart—experience has proved to me even at the edge of my grave that you alone compose true earthly happiness!"[23] Throughout Sophie refers to the knowledge she has acquired as the center of her being. A new woman, she can triumph over the forces of male power and adverse conditions.

Other authors used the novel explicitly to decry male behavior in general. French novelist Riccoboni was very outspoken: "Look here you men! From what source do you derive the right to diminish where women are concerned the high regard you show one another? What law in nature, what legal conventions ever authorized this impudent distinction?"[24] Author after author similarly protested, complained, and demonstrated in their novels that women received shabby treatment in spite of their apparent merit.

The work of Jane Austen (1775–1817) displayed the whole range of dilemmas posed by living in a changing and tumultuous society. Daughter of an English clergyman, Austen wrote at the height of the revolutionary period,* but her novels posed the questions about marriage, money, and the situation of women that had been raised throughout the eighteenth century. Profoundly influenced by the work of Fanny Burney, Austen took the wit and comedy in Burney's novels and molded her own enduring masterpieces, such as *Pride and Prejudice, Emma,* and *Northanger Abbey.* Austen's heroines are unforgettable for their range of feelings, their humor and impertinence, and their naiveté amidst forces of greed and debauchery. Her heroines navigate the rough waters leading to matrimony; their course is especially rocky because they lack a prudent mother or even any mother at all. Regarding marriage as women's lot, although unmarried herself, Austen outlined the dangers clearly: passion, greed, and weakness of character. Foolish and uncontrollable people made disastrous unions. Austen never displayed sentimentality or undue sorrow over such cases but continued to concern herself with how a heroine might marry

---

*See Chapter 3.

German author Sophie von la Roche advocated the serious development of female character in her writing.

someone with the right amount of social status and a proper sensibility. Marrying correctly, Austen believed, ultimately produced happiness, even happiness of a romantic sort. Although she did consider feeling and personal regard as crucial to any union, she saw correct behavior and sexual restraint as essential to happiness. Placing priority on either passions or material interests would lead to the kind of chaos Europeans were experiencing at the time. Austen deplored excesses of all kinds, particularly because of the consequences to women, given their situation. Her novels were to have a lasting influence—pointing out women's dilemmas and urging self-control characterized women's novels thereafter.

Toward the Storm

The Enlightenment produced an atmosphere of criticism and cries for reform. It brought forth both programs advancing women's concerns and opposing arguments as to why those concerns had little legitimacy. A new science focused on reproduction, but some thinkers still criticized the social limitations placed on women and superstitions about gender. Novels, letters, *salons*, and scholarship drew attention to womanhood as a slighted, but worthy part of humanity. Writers from mid-century on took delight in pointing to great women of the past. Classical Greek writers such as Aspasia, Sappho, and Hypatia were celebrated anew; so were rulers such as Elizabeth I and Marie de Medici and pious and scholarly women such as Heloise. This writing made an image of woman that was a secular, heroic one, based on accomplishments in human society.

The intellectually ambitious woman, however, did not serve the needs of commercial society for the kind of harmony that people believed resulted from the exercise of maternal virtue. Economic change produced poverty, migration, and social disorder. Increased instances of illegitimacy and family breakup threatened the social fabric. In the midst of this upheaval, women sensed their declining position. Enlightened ones noted missing ingredients in their lives in comparison with what men would reap in the new age of reason. Complaints from all quarters filled the air. Many enlightened people believed society could be improved if problems were dealt with rationally. Some thought that freer economic growth and improved mothering would stop most social problems including poverty, infant mortality, and illegitimacy. These two solutions went hand in hand and became ever more popular. As one Hamburg official explained, mothers were the "incubators of population" and thus of prosperity.[25] Like Rousseau's Julie, mothers would instill a system of internal control, of dos and don'ts, of restraint and calculation. No longer directed by their kin, women must choose the prudent path and serve as guides for society as a whole. Should society go wrong—economically, politically, or in other ways— the guides would have failed. In these difficult times motherhood and commerce were seen as forces that would restore sweetness and harmony to a world irrationally run by a corrupt aristocracy.

NOTES

1. Quoted in Iris Barry, *Portrait of Lady Mary Montagu* (Indianapolis: Bobbs-Merrill, 1928), 107.
2. Quoted in G. E. and K. R. Fussell, *The English Country Woman* (London: Orbis, 1981), 133.
3. Quoted in Herman Freudenberger, *Noble Entrepreneurship in Eighteenth-Century Bohemia* (Boston: Harvard Graduate School of Business Administration, 1963), 7.
4. Henry-Louis Dubly, *Le caducée et le carquois* (Lille: Mercure de Flandre, 1926), *passim.*
5. Caroline Flachstand to Johann von Herder, letter of May 6, 1771, *Herders Briefwechsel mit Caroline Flachsland* (Weimar: Goethe-Gesellschaft, 1926), 1:195.
6. Letter of the Marquise de Bombelles to her husband, May 31, 1781, cited by Cissi Fairchilds, "Women and Family," in Samia I. Spencer, ed., *French Women and the Age of Enlightenment* (Bloomington: Indiana University Press, 1984), 98.
7. Quoted from Catherine II, in Isabel de Madariaga, *Russia in the Age of Catherine the Great* (New Haven: Yale University Press, 1981), 464.

8. Quote from Maria Theresa in Jerome Blum, *The End of the Old Order in Rural Europe* (Princeton, N. J.: Princeton University Press, 1978), 221.

9. Caroline A. Lubbock, *The Herschel Chronicle* (New York: Macmillan, 1933), 153.

10. Quoted in Julia O'Faolain and Laura Martines, *Not in God's Image* (New York: Harper and Row, 1973), 265–266.

11. John Locke, *Of Civil Government, Two Treatises* (London: Dent, 1943), 57, quoting Sir Robert Filmer.

12. Quoted in Marjorie H. Ilsley, *A Daughter of the Renaissance: Marie le Jars de Gournay* (The Hague: Mouton, 1963) 207.

13. Dr. Roussel, quoted in Hoffmann, *La femme dans la pensée des lumières*, 143.

14. Adam Smith, *The Wealth of Nations* (vol. II, 47) quoted in Jane Rendall, "Virtue and Commerce: Women in the Making of Adam Smith's Political Economy," in Ellen Kennedy and Susan Mendus, eds., *Women in Western Political Philosophy* (New York: St. Martin's, 1987), 69.

15. Quoted in Roseann Runte, "Woman as Muse," in Spencer, ed., *French Women and the Age of Enlightenment*, 143–54.

16. Elizabeth R. Montagu, *Her Letters and Friendships from 1762 to 1800*, 2 vols, Reginald Blunt, ed. (Boston: Houghton Mifflin, 1926) 2:5.

17. Quoted in Janet Burke, "Through Friendship to Feminism: The Growth in Self-Awareness among Eighteenth-Century Women Freemasons," unpublished paper, 1986, 21.

18. Anna-Amelia of Weimer, quoted in S. Baring-Gould, *Germany Present and Past*, 2 vols. (London: C. Kegan Paul, 1879) 1:194–195.

19. Samuel Johnson, *Johnsonian Miscellanies*, 2 vols., G. B. Hill, ed. (Oxford, Clarendon Press, 1897), 2:11.

20. Quoted in Eva M. Kahiluoto, "The View from Spain: Rococo Finesse and Esprit versus Plebian Manners," in Spencer, ed., *French Women and the Age of Enlightenment*, 402–403.

21. *The Female Spectator*, 1746, quoted in Mary R. Mohl and Helene Koon, eds., *The Female Spectator: English Women Writers Before 1800* (Bloomington: Indiana University Press, 1977), 230.

22. Rahel Varnhagen, *Rahel, Ein Buch des Andenkens für ihre Freunde*, Karl August Varnhagen von Ense, ed. (Bern, Switzerland: Herbert Lang, 1972), 1:266, quoted in Kay Goodman, "Poesis and Praxis in Rahel Varnhagen's Letters," *New German Critique* 27 (Fall, 1982), 131.

23. Quoted in Ruth-Ellen B. Joeres, "'That girl is an entirely different character!' 'Yes, But Is She a Feminist?'" Observations on Sophie von la Roche's *Geschichte des Fräuleins von Sternheim*" in Ruth-Ellen B. Joeres and Mary Jo Maynes, eds., *German Women in the Eighteenth and Nineteenth Centuries* (Bloomington: Indiana University Press, 1986), 147.

24. Joan Hinde Stewart, "The Novelists and Their Fictions," in Spencer, ed., *French Women and the Age of Enlightenment*, 197–211.

25. Cited by Mary Lindemann in "Maternal Politics: The Principles and Practice of Maternity Care in Eighteenth-Century Hamburg," *Journal of Family History*, vol. 9, no. 1 (Spring, 1984), 61.

SOURCES AND SUGGESTED READING

Alic, Margaret. *Hypatia's Heritage: A History of Women in Science from Antiquity through the Nineteenth Century* (1986).

Crankshaw, Edward. *Maria Theresa* (1969).

Gelbart, Nina Rattner. *Feminine and Opposition Journalism in Old Regime France* (1987). An exciting story of women journalists.

Hertz, Deborah. *Jewish High Society in Old Regime Berlin* (1988). A major study of the Jewish *salon*.

Hoffmann, Paul. *La femme dans la pensée des lumières* (1977). A survey of ideas developed by the major intellectuals during the seventeenth and eighteenth centuries.

Hunt, Margaret, Margaret Jacob, Phyllis Mack, and Ruth Perry. *Women and the Enlightenment* (1984). Interesting articles on England and the Netherlands.

Joeres, Ruth-Ellen B., and Mary Jo Maynes, eds. *German Women in the Eighteenth and Nineteenth Centuries* (1986). Important studies of women's writings and of women in daily life.

Laqueur, Thomas. "Orgasm, Generation, and the Politics of Reproductive Biology," *Representations* (1986).

Lindemann, Mary. "Maternal Politics: The Principles and Practice of Maternity Care in Eighteenth Century Hamburg," *Journal of Family History* (1984). On public policy and reproductive history in difficult times.

McKendrick, Neil, John Brewer, and J. H. Plumb. *The Birth of Consumer Society* (1985). A collection of articles on the desire for and production of goods in eighteenth-century England.

Madariaga, Isabel de. *Russia in the Age of Catherine the Great* (1981).

Mohl, Mary R., and Helene Koon, eds. *The Female Spectator: English Women Writers Before 1800* (1977). Excerpts from important writings.

Rendall, Jane. "Virtue and Commerce: Women in the Making of Adam Smith's Political Economy," in Ellen Kennedy and Susan Mendus, eds., *Women in Western Political Philosophy* (1987). A clear explanation of the difference between liberal and republican ideas of marriage and the family.

Rossiter, Margaret. "Women and the History of Scientific Communication," *Journal of Library History* (1986).

Schiebinger, Londa. "Skeletons in the Closet: The First Illustrations of the Female Skeleton in Eighteenth-Century Anatomy," *Representations* (1986). The story of the changing configuration of the skeleton as maternal ideology intensified.

Schwartz, Joel. *The Sexual Politics of Jean-Jacques Rousseau* (1984).

Sonnet, Martine. *L'éducation des filles au temps des lumières* (1987).

Spencer, Jane. *The Rise of the Woman Novelist from Aphra Behn to Jane Austen* (1986). An important overview of the period.

Spencer, Samia I. *French Women and the Age of Enlightenment* (1984). A major collection with information on a range of countries.

CHAPTER

3

The Age of Revolution

A New Role Emerges On October 16, 1793, thirty-eight-year-old Queen Marie Antoinette was guillotined before a cheering throng of Parisians. Dressed in white, her hair cut short by her own hand so that it would not get in the way of the executioner's blade, the queen was reportedly quite calm (although at the last minute she inadvertently stepped on the executioner's foot and asked his pardon). What calmed her was the thought that she would soon be with her loved ones in heaven, particularly her husband Louis XVI, who had met his death at the same spot some nine months earlier. Moreover, execution would blot out the indignities of her trial, at which she had been accused of numerous crimes, most notably of initiating her son into all sorts of sexual vices. The charges also included dealing with the enemy and influencing her husband to such an extent that in fact it was she herself who ruled. Scandal had dogged Marie Antoinette's frivolous youth and it was often scandal with a decidedly sexual ring, but it took four years of the Revolution to turn such scandal into crimes against the state. By this time people believed enough in a woman's duty toward her children and her subservience to her husband to sustain the conviction of Marie Antoinette. In December 1793, revolutionaries also convicted Madame Du Barry, mistress of Louis XVI's predecessor, ostensibly of spying for the British. The evidence and rhetoric, however, emphasized "the corruption of her life, the publicity and fame of her debauchery, her infamous prostitution."[1] Only a few years later, the English parliament made the first in a series of investigations into the sexual conduct of Queen Caroline (1768–1821). Expectations for noblewomen's behavior had clearly changed if they could be so easily brought down by charges focusing on sexual habits, familial hierarchies, and parental comportment.

The age of revolution—a period that began in 1776 in the English colonies and ended at the middle of the next century—rocked Western civilization. As monarchs were toppled and new men came to power, the revolutionary era ushered in novel forms of government, particularly republican and constitu-

On her way to execution in the
fall of 1793, Marie Antoinette
looked far different from the
glamorous queen of a few years
earlier. Her death symbolized the
end of noble women's
prerogatives and pleasures.

tional government. Although the centers of this drama were France and the
United States, the drastic changes there awakened debate in every country and
led to the further spread of revolutionary principles as French forces went to
war throughout Europe.

Drawing on Enlightenment philosophies and echoing the economic aspirations of the people, revolutionary movements encompassed all classes and
included both men and women. In France, women of the crowd and women
of the *salon* played their part in the Revolution by expressing political and
economic discontent in different ways. The age of revolution affected the political, economic, and social structure. It reached from the highest forms of
government and political thought to the family and transformed—if only temporarily—social roles. While politicians debated civil rights and constitutions,
people such as housewives, market women, and women writers were considering the inequities of women's lives. One result was that the role of the pleasure-loving aristocratic woman was swept away and replaced by that of the
virtuous and serious mother, who was to educate the modern citizen. By the
end of the revolutionary era, republican ideas on woman's role had not only

received an airing, they had become tenets of government and an important part of the new, nineteenth-century world view.

In the final analysis, the age of revolution struck blows at the old organization of agrarian society. The social and political order based on a subsistence economy was falling apart. Without a single political remedy, revolutionary leaders sometimes supported the monarchy and at other times did not. Most people agreed on the need for political and social change, but their disagreements about the exact nature of those changes made the French Revolution particularly bloody and protracted. They had various solutions for a new gender order to accompany changing productive circumstances and population growth. Only the dictator Napoleon at the turn of the century had enough force to set the French Revolution to rest and to establish a clear program. His celebrated code of laws substituted the rule of private property for feudalism. It formalized the republican idea of women's role instead of a liberal concept of women's rights.

Opening Shots

The rebellion of North American colonists against British rule involved, at first, a struggle for a degree of commercial autonomy. In fighting against a range of taxes and trade restrictions imposed after the French and Indian Wars (1754–1763),* colonists cast their protest in terms of natural rights to property and a political right to consensual government. Using liberal political language, they defined the reforms they hoped would end what they saw as the tyranny of British rule, especially personified by George III and his ministers. Finally, the conflict erupted into open warfare at the battles of Lexington and Concord in the spring of 1775. By the next year the colonists had declared their independence, and the British had invaded. In the midst of this full revolt, colonial leaders explained the principles on which they based their rebellion in a series of statements and documents such as the Declaration of Independence, their ideology taking on a clearer republican cast. In order to achieve independence, the new United States of America brought in monarchical France as its ally late in the 1770s, despite the fact that France's ruling principles were in direct opposition to those the new nation's leaders hoped to establish. By the 1780s the new principles, based on Enlightenment thinking and commercial values, were enshrined in a written constitution and later in the Bill of Rights.

Colonial women understood the new cause, and many of them supported it. Right from the start, for example, Mercy Otis Warren (1728–1814) in the colony of Massachusetts mocked the British king, his soldiers, and his appointed officials in anonymous pamphlets and plays. Former slave Phillis Wheatley (c. 1753–1784) wrote poetry whose themes were individual rights

---

*Known in Europe as the Seven Years' War (1756–1763).

and liberty, freedom and toleration. By the time the Revolution had begun, Abigail Adams had seen the relationship between the goals of men and the cause of women. When her husband John was away planning the new government, she wrote that he should "remember the ladies" in constructing the rights of citizens. She reminded him that, like George III, men would be "tyrants" over women. Maintaining a spirited correspondence with Mercy Otis Warren on these and other issues, Abigail Adams registered women's concerns during contested times.

Other women became activists in the colonial cause. For example, the domestic management of women was what made the boycott of tea and other goods possible. Household activity became politically oriented. Women also appeared in crowds protesting British rule. With their men away at war or government, women started taking charge of farms and businesses, often without having any prior experience. Their mental horizons expanded to encompass economic and political issues. Moreover, many were so dedicated to winning and concerned with making a contribution to victory that they formed local societies to raise money, collect supplies and bandages, and perform any number of small services. Women soldiers such as Molly Pitcher became legendary for their efforts, but their stepping beyond ordinary sex roles was merely a more extreme way of contributing. Most women during those revolutionary times experienced a new feeling of competence and developed a wider range of interests. Though they remained in the home, they began to look beyond its narrow realm to be interested in political events and participate in the life of the market with increasing vigor.

The French Scene

Giving support to the American Revolution wreaked havoc on the French treasury, and a series of bad harvests late in the 1780s caused widespread distress in French cities and countryside. Soaring bread prices not only made it difficult for people to buy food but stopped them from purchasing manufactured goods. Widespread underemployment in the cities thus followed. The powerful debated how to keep the government from going bankrupt and how to profit politically from the monarchy's distress. Both *philosophe* and bourgeois understood that outdated modes of taxation and finance caused problems in commerce and agriculture and undermined the general prosperity. When the bankers refused to grant more loans to the monarch until reforms occurred, Louis XVI called together the notables of France. Meeting in 1787, the great aristocrats of the realm refused to help in the belief that the power of the absolute monarchy should be weakened somewhat. Refusing to give up their privileged position of not paying taxes, they sought to enhance their own power. As a result, Louis desperately summoned the Estates-General to meet.*

---

*See Chapter 1 on the three estates that made up the Estates-General.

The Estates-General was a body representing the French people, and one the monarchy had prevented from meeting for a century and a half. In preparation, the people of France assembled in towns and cities to draw up their grievances and proposals. The *cahiers de doléance*, as these compilations are called, echoed Enlightenment philosophy but also put forth specific economic and political complaints. Women made contributions to the *cahiers de doléance* (though these were minimal) and sent petitions to the King. For example, the clothing, feather, and flower workers' guild asked for representation of their grievances because their guild paid taxes to the royal treasury. The flower sellers wanted their guild to be restored because competition had decreased their earnings. In general, women wanted protection both from the competition of other women and from the rising tide of men in what had been female preserves. By the time the Estates-General met in May of 1789, ordinary people had articulated the many issues that were on their minds. Like Enlightenment thinkers, they had brought personal issues onto the public stage. Most supported the monarchy, but they expected change.

Within a few weeks, the Estates-General moved toward revolution. The Third Estate and some reform-minded members of the other Estates of the clergy and aristocracy formed themselves into the National Assembly. The leading issue of this movement concerned the method of voting—whether it would be voting by Estate (which would have meant that the Third Estate and those interested in progress would always lose to the other two Estates) or voting by head (which would have allowed the Third Estate to win on issues because of the greater numbers of this Estate combined with the reform elements in the first two Estates). Rumors arose and persisted all summer that the king was massing troops to overturn the people's assembly and that in the countryside, the aristocracy was plotting against the peasantry. The result was a widespread uprising of farm people against the nobility, in which chateaus and land titles were burned. In mid-July Parisian men and women stormed and took over the Bastille prison—a symbol of despotism whose fall testified to the power and determination of the Third Estate. Frightened by these events, representatives of the aristocracy on the famous night of August 4 surrendered their privileges, many of which dated from medieval times. In the same month the National Assembly issued the famous Declaration of the Rights of Man and of the Citizen. This document announced the foundation of a government on new principles, including the sanctity of property, the notion of contractual government, and the doctrine that natural rights belong to all citizens. In these early days the revolution brought change on a variety of fronts. From the monarch to the Third Estate, no one was sure what would happen because so much spontaneous political activity was unprecedented.

Women were explicitly involved in this early ferment but in much smaller numbers than men. Supporting the citizens' army or National Guard, they took part in processions honoring the great events of August. In September one Madame Rigal urged her fellow artisans and silversmiths to contribute their money or their possessions such as jewelry to the monarchy as a way of restoring the nation's financial health. "Our sex is excluded from arduous la-

When market women marched to Versailles in October, 1789, they changed the character of the Revolution by bringing the King to Paris. In addition, they forcefully articulated ordinary people's needs for food and good wages.

bors, but it is allowed to engage in two very worthwhile occupations—the exercise of delicate virtues, and heroic sacrifices."[2] For Rigal, preserving the monarchy from bankruptcy meant preserving the revolutionary genius for resolving problems and righting wrongs. Just before the harvest, rioting broke out in Paris because the price of bread was rising sharply. Despite the ongoing progress of revolutionary debate and further revolutionary legislation, anger mounted and a crowd of market women and agitators gathered at the city hall on October 5 to demand help from the National Guard. From there they proceeded toward Versailles and gathered others en route until the marchers numbered between eight and ten thousand women. At their destination they presented their grievances concerning the scarcity of bread and its high price first to the National Assembly and then to the king himself. Not receiving any satisfaction, the crowd took charge of the royal family and forced them to move to Paris. In the process hesitant people were killed or wounded; the crowd was angered by those not wearing the revolutionary colors—red, white, and blue. In fact, their original wrath about bread had been fueled by rumors that soldiers in Versailles had desecrated the revolutionary colors. Thus, worried about the course of the revolution and the welfare of their families, the working women of Paris decided to bring the king and his family close to them, where he would be less subject to influence from aristocrats who, they thought, were probably hiding grain so as to starve the people back into submission.

The march to Versailles redirected the French Revolution. Bringing the king to Paris—and the National Assembly along with him—put events much more under the influence of the populace of Paris. From then on Parisians gathered to voice approval for or disapproval of proposals, projects, and legislation. The crowd displayed its muscle at crucial times not merely by gathering but by sacking monasteries and prisons and murdering or intimidating selected enemies. The march to Versailles also meant that women saw themselves and the issues that concerned them in terms of national politics. Their personal need for bread for their families no longer brought them simply to riot until the price fell or until they had confiscated enough to see their families through bad times. Instead they sought to influence policies permanently by bringing the king to where they might supervise his actions. He would especially receive protection from those of pernicious political intent, namely, the aristocrats. Recognizing their ability to influence the course of state affairs, indeed, seeing themselves as part of the state, women acted and thereby announced the arrival of a new order of things. The Enlightenment had brought about a cosmopolitan mindset while it challenged provincialism; working women in the march to Versailles and other actions in the revolution demonstrated that household issues were part of a bigger picture. They also manifested—as did all participants on the side of the Revolution—their belief in the rights of citizens, no longer mere subjects, to correct governmental policies and to exercise their strength in correcting it. In just a few months of revolution, the lives of "the people" had indeed been changed.

Middle-Class Demands and Liberal Voices

For more than a year after the March to Versailles, the working women of France were relatively quiescent, though never inattentive to what was happening. In the meantime, middle- and upper-class women had been focusing their attention on other mainstream revolutionary issues. The abolition of aristocratic privilege on the night of August 4 and the Declaration of the Rights of Man and of the Citizen opened new roads to the development of commercial and middle-class interests. Once the static nature of hierarchical, feudal society had been disrupted, reform after reform followed. The guilds were abolished, as was any kind of association for the restraint of trade (Le Chapelier Law, 1791); the clergy lost their privileged status and had to vow their allegiance to the nation (Civil Constitution of the Clergy, 1790). Women were delighted when the National Assembly compared the arbitrary privilege of the aristocrat with that of the father in the family. In the first year of the Revolution the National Assembly declared this kind of privilege over women and children at an end.

Middle-class women began connecting themselves with the revolutionary changes by asserting their right to property, to natural and political rights in general, to education, and to equality in both civil and marital realms. They took, in short, the Enlightenment ideas that applied to the political and social order as a whole and tried to make them policy in the sphere of gender as well. Some women saw these reforms as pertinent to their own interests. For example, a woman from the province of Normandy, petitioning early in the Revolution, saw the connection between the rule of property and the rights of women. Why, she wrote, shouldn't women with land or other goods, and particularly widows and unmarried women, have the right to vote? Keeping them without voice and without education only "destined them to provide the pleasures of the harem."[3] Some middle-class women who saw the revolution in Enlightenment terms maintained their *salons*. Marie Lavoisier, chemist, translator, and scientific illustrator, was one of these, as was Germaine de Staël, who aimed to propagate the reform ideas of her father, the king's former finance minister Jacques Necker.

To make their views known or to follow the course of events, women attended sessions of the National Assembly and also local meetings and political clubs. Clubs, such as the Jacobin, Cordelier, Girondin, and Monarchist, were schools of the Revolution in that proposals and new ideas were explained at meetings, which allowed for orderly groupings according to a commonality of ideas. Once the floodtide of change began, clubs gave direction to a society that had never before witnessed such innovation and movement. Women began forming women's clubs or converting older clubs to egalitarian meeting places for men and women alike. For example, the Fraternal Society of Patriots of Both Sexes contained some of the leading feminist revolutionaries. Later, the Society of Revolutionary Republican Women both organized women and made a series of demands that the Revolution broaden the scope of its benefits to include them.

Women also circulated petitions on a range of matters and took part in journalism. The most famous of these journalists was author and historian Louise Keralio-Robert (1758–1821), who before 1789 had anthologized the great women writers of previous centuries and who had advocated the primacy of reason over the passions and the necessity of education for women. The newspaper she launched in August 1789 at first described events particularly in anti-aristocratic terms. But soon Keralio-Robert became explicitly feminist, joining the Fraternal Society of Patriots of Both Sexes and proposing a number of reforms that would expand women's role in society. All these activities— writing, clubs, and *salons*—continued to promote change; give birth to new ideas, including some about a new role for women; and serve as springboards for politicians.

Although *salon* and club women debated issues generally without drawing specifically feminist lessons, beginning in 1791 some of them began making bolder statements. Etta Palm d'Aelders (1743–1830), a Dutch immigrant to France, spoke several times before the National Assembly proposing equal rights for women, especially in sexual matters. She condemned in particular a new adultery law under which only the accused woman would be prosecuted. Palm d'Aelders also suggested that women take official charge of public welfare in their districts by providing for relief, inspecting the wet-nursing system, and overseeing education. This suggestion carried overtones of the future— feminists of later generations would assert their competence in these areas and would support state action where public welfare was concerned. The sweeping proposals of Palm d'Aelders were echoed in those of Pauline Léon, who asked that women be armed and trained militarily so that their homes, not just the public places guarded by men, might receive protection from aristocrats and their troops. Other women would make similar requests throughout the Revolution.

Another bold statement came in the <u>Declaration of the Rights of Woman</u> <u>by Olympe de Gouges (1748–1793)</u>, in striking analogy to the Declaration of the Rights of Man. Daughter of a butcher and unhappily married, de Gouges came to Paris to seek her fortune by writing, notably for the theater, where she had some success. When the Revolution broke out, she supported it assiduously and founded the Club des Tricoteuses. Then, in 1791, she published the Declaration of the Rights of Woman, superficially a derivative document, but actually one that recast the terms of revolution so that gender became crucial. Containing a sample marriage contract based on egalitarian principles as well as an examination of liberty for slaves, the Declaration of the Rights of Woman became the prototype for feminist statements of principle. De Gouges maintained that the subjection of women marked the point where human beings deviated from nature. Animals, she noted, enforced no such subjugation. To follow nature, civil society should award women and men equal rights to property, participation in public administration, and just treatment; both sexes should be taxed equally, and the penal law should institute equal punishment as well. At the same time, however, de Gouges implied that men remained unfree unless women had freedom too: "Enslaved man has multiplied his strength and needs recourse to yours to break his chains. Having become free, he has become unjust to his companion."[4] She urged women to complete the achievement of freedom and justice by adhering to "the standards of philosophy" and by multiplying their efforts on its behalf. Another part of de Gouges's tract was an exhortation to Marie Antoinette to place herself as "mother and wife" at the head of the women's cause. Although this address to the queen resulted in de Gouges's being executed as a royalist a few years later, her reference to motherhood as that which made women the sex "superior in beauty as it is in courage" marked another example of arguments based on the combination of motherhood and equal rights. In the long run, Olympe de Gouges had pushed ideas of equal rights far beyond what the original proponents of rights had in mind.

Simultaneously, a somewhat incongruous voice was heard on the side of female emancipation. Marquis Donatien de Sade (1740–1814) had spent almost thirty years in the Bastille by orders of his parents and later of his wife's family. Married to enhance his father's fortune, de Sade had firsthand knowledge of patriarchal authority. While imprisoned for sexual offenses, he recognized the familial basis of tyranny. Like Buffon, de Sade accepted the natural entrapment of human beings within the cycle of life and death.* Artificial force, however, repelled him, including that imposed by the family and that inflicted on women. He used his prison years to write and, some said, to stir

---

*See Chapter 1.

up the mob below him on the streets around the Bastille. Among his prerevolutionary works was the pornographic novel *Justine,* the story of a girl's constant profession of virtue in the face of all sorts of outrages committed against
her. Her attitude, de Sade demonstrated, only led to victimization. During the
Revolution, de Sade changed his female characters and to some extent his
point of view. Eugénie de Mistival and Madame de Saint Ange of *Philosophy
in the Bedroom* (1795) and Juliette of *The Story of Juliette* find strength only
in their freedom from such concepts as virtue and familial obedience. Instead
they choose pleasure and power, which de Sade saw as the basic principles of
nature along with degeneration. In one work, de Sade explicitly demanded
freedom for women, citing principles announced in the Revolution: "It is
equally unjust exclusively to possess a woman as it is to own slaves; all men
are born free, all have equal rights . . . accordingly, no legitimate right can ever
be given to one sex, which would allow it to take possession of the other, and
never can one sex or one class arbitrarily possess the other."[5] The dark side of
his writings, however, portrayed women victimized at every turn by the superior physical force of men. In actuality, men orchestrated the Sadean world—
its liberty and its license. During the Revolution, de Sade gained his freedom
and even became a minor official, but he was reincarcerated in 1803 for his
eccentricities. His proposal of sexual pleasure as a liberating force in women's
lives reemerged only many decades later, still carrying the same disturbing implications.

Liberal Legislation

Revolutionary legislators attempted to restructure such institutions as marriage and the family in light of changing beliefs and liberal principles. The
goals of these legislators were to reduce the arbitrary power of the father and
to strengthen the ties of the individual to the state by weakening those relationships that competed with the social contract. In April of 1789 a group of
women had petitioned the Estates-General for marriage reform: "Marriage is
a union. People who intend to enter this state must be suited for each other
and not constrained by the will of their parents to marry someone they find
repugnant."[6] Convinced that individual liberty and marital love were desirable,
deputies enacted new laws on marriage and divorce in September of 1792. The
new law of marriage prescribed a civil service and civil registration of the act.
Although one motivation for this law was to reduce the Catholic Church's
power, the deputies also wanted to remove other mediating elements, such as
guilds and family, that stood between the state and the citizen. Civil marriage
allowed citizens to see how marital love was allied to love of the state. More
concretely, it allowed governmental supervision of individuals and their conjugal lives. The law also reduced the age of consent to twenty-one for women
and twenty-five for men, so that those in love would be able to escape parental
control earlier. This provision sprang from beliefs that the power of the father
must be reduced and that love should be allowed to flourish.

Divorce also became a viable option. Revolutionaries believed that what made marriage thrive was mutual attraction and sentiment. If those things disappeared, couples should separate and form new attachments. Divorce legislation provided for three scenarios: first, divorce by mutual consent; second, divorce when only one party wanted it; and third, divorce because of abandonment, emigration, imprisonment, and the like. Because legislators were also eager to reduce the power of the judiciary, arbitration in the first two types of action consisted mainly of extended family councils. Yet no matter what those councils ultimately decided, a couple received a divorce after some stipulated amount of time had passed.

Legislators also tried to eliminate inequalities in the family. One of the first acts in this area dismantled the system of the *lettres de cachet* by which a parent could have a child (of whatever age) imprisoned. Other laws were meant to reduce the distinctions between legitimate and illegitimate children. "The welfare of the state corresponds with the justice and humanity," announced revolutionary leader Maximilien Robespierre (1758–1794), "in giving illegitimate children the same help that the law gives others."[7] Between 1790 and 1793, a round of legislation attended to these concerns. It provided, first, for less legal distinction between the illegitimate and legitimate because these distinctions were "unnatural." As a result, illegitimate children could inherit from both parents. Moreover, these children and their mothers could press suit against the supposed father for damages and support. These laws pressed responsibility on men while reducing arbitrary authority. Next, legislators reduced testamentary authority by decreeing that all children should inherit equally. Parents could no longer favor one child over another; thus ended the dominance of the eldest son or the system of primogeniture. Moreover, legislators expressly stated that sisters and brothers should inherit equally. These provisions represented attempts to attain the revolutionary idea of a nation of citizens of similar wealth. Once the provisions were in force, women sued actively for equal inheritance. Because the laws were made to be retroactive, they could overturn previous agreements such as dowries and other settlements in which parents had made daughters surrender all rights to legacies. Of all the revolutionary legislation affecting women, this law was among the very few that survived. The course of events was moving in other directions even as liberalism was being carried to its logical conclusions in this family legislation. The quest for virtue, which became a symbol of the Revolution, ultimately curtailed freedom.

Republican Ideals and Revolutionary Symbols

The slogan of the French Revolution was "Liberty, Equality, Fraternity." None of these terms received so much discussion as the first—"Liberty." For aristocrats liberty meant a restoration of its old liberties, that is, the old privileges they had lost to the absolute monarchy. For many in the Third Estate liberty consisted of those liberal rights that each person received at birth from "nature" and that were enshrined in the Declaration of the Rights of Man. Still others saw liberty as the product of reason, which released people from ignorance and thus from the political or spiritual control of others. Finally, liberty could also develop when one lived in a republic and received rights as a condition of citizenship. As the revolution progressed these many complex meanings intersected, so that people could be celebrating many forms of liberty simultaneously.

Olympe de Gouges, who had invoked rights from nature, had also invoked those owed mothers because they gave birth to citizens. In this instance, she alluded to republican rights that sprang from contributing to the state. De Gouges was hardly the first to examine the republican content of liberty in terms of what it would mean for women. In the turmoil just before the meeting of the Estates-General, a group of women from Grenoble connected the political condition of France to maternity in a letter to the king: "We would not be able to resolve to give birth to children destined to live in a country compliant with despotism."[8] Breaking the power of patriarchal aristocrats and the king seemed to demand a counteremphasis on motherhood. In public ceremonies, mothers, pregnant women, and nursing women received a special place, special costume, and special recognition in the spoken program. Even Marie Antoinette knew the symbolic power of motherhood in the new regime. Pressed to appear on several occasions by menacing crowds, she usually came out displaying at least one of her children. Invocations of motherhood were made in the most trying times, when women were called to arms or at least to making a contribution to the continuation of the Revolution. Older women were idealized as mothers of the generation of heroic men fighting for the cause: "Mothers of one generation, you are even more so of the generations to come."[9] At a festival in 1793, water flowed from the breasts of an enormous maternal statue, while deputies from around France drank symbolically of it. Clearly, motherhood had made an imprint on the new regime, but its message had not yet worked itself out completely. Believing in a new female power based on reproduction, liberal women revolutionaries used motherhood as a claim to political influence. Their claims received some credence so long as the concept itself remained elastic. Motherhood did not yet mean the confinement of women to a rigidly separate sphere. At the beginning, it meant liberty.

Liberal ideas had carried the Enlightenment along, but republican ones stemming from interpretations of classical times became increasingly prominent in the Revolution. According to these, participation in civic or public life was what allowed individuals to become human in the most complete sense. Only then would the true moral and rational terms of existence be fulfilled. The full participation in a social role required the strenuous application of moral and rational faculties, and this was called virtue. Anyone who was unable or unwilling to perform this public function fully lacked virtue and complete liberty, for the autonomy of the individual derived from and at the same time was a condition of complete virtue and unhampered performance of pub-

Revolutionary artist Jean-Louis David portrayed an ideal republican mother in this painting of Madame Seinzat and her child (1795).

lic duty. The French revolutionaries promoted the display of virtue, both in public rituals and in daily personal interactions. For example, men and women alike greeted each other with the word "citizen"—*citoyen,* or *citoyenne* in the case of women. This announced their new status as participants in the public order and stamped private identity with the mark of the state.

The revolution came to imprint many personal goods with images of politics. Plates, plaques, buttons, and jewelry appeared in red, white, and blue—the revolutionary colors—or appeared emblazoned with flags, slogans, and politicians' pictures. Objects of everyday life testified to support for the new state's policy. Because marriage had been made a public act, it too received certification by the state. Festivals celebrated virtue and reason, once talked of as acts performed by individuals but now monitored by the government. Finally, images of women were used to symbolize the new government, reason, virtue, and liberty on a wide array of seals, in public ceremonies, and in statuary. In both Europe and the new United States, women's bodies stood as metaphors for republicanism.

In their private lives women adapted their clothing and manners to fit republican themes. Goddesses, maidens, and heroines represented the intangible aspects—reason and virtue, for example—of the Revolution's rule. Dressing in what was presumably the garb of the ancients or of goddesses, women

took white as their revolutionary color—symbolic of purity but also in imitation of classical statuary—and adorned it with red, blue, and white ribbons or
cockades. Allusions were made especially to Roman times. Not only did
women try to dress like Roman matrons, they arranged their hair in classical
styles and aimed to recapture a simplicity that was not only Roman but natural
in their entire appearance and habits. Madame Roland, for example, eliminated long-winded, mannered closings to her letters with this remark: "Simply,
adieu. The wife of Cato does not amuse herself by sending compliments to
Brutus."[10] In other words, she equated her husband and his fellow politicians
with Roman senators and intended to imitate their simplicity. Women often
referred to themselves as Portias or Cornelias, after devoted wives and mothers
of ancient times. The heroism of such women ensured rights for all; their public demonstrations of virtue served to guarantee liberty. Speaking about equality between men and women, Etta Palm d'Aelders said: "Will you make slaves
of those who have contributed with zeal to making you free? Will you stamp
a brand on the forehead of a Clelia, a Veturia, a Cornelia? No. No. Conjugal
authority should be only the consequence of the social pact."[11] Women, like
men, looked to ancient Rome for ideals for social and political life: purity,
simplicity, naturalness, law and law codes, citizenship, and virtue. These qualities marked the contrast between the new regime and the eighteenth-century
monarchy and aristocracy.

Thus, women such as Palm d'Aelders justified their public activities in
terms that were republican, Roman, and virtuous. They knew that unequal
laws about men and women prevented the equal display of virtue. A dependent—child or woman—could hardly be free or virtuous, or perform a social
role fully. So women marched to Versailles and demanded price controls as
part of their republican duty to break the reign of inequality in both the political realm and the marketplace. These republican ideals, however, soon came
to be used against women.

Finally, politicians in the new age used sexual imagery to stir up public
passions against the opposition. Women's sexuality, which had long aroused
fear, moved to the fore in political literature during the Revolution. Just as de
Sade spoke of sex using the language of liberty, so depictions of sex became
intertwined with issues of public policy. Those opposed to the revolutionaries
were often portrayed as sexually promiscuous or deviant. Most notably, Marie
Antoinette, although a fairly good mother and wife by aristocratic standards,
appeared as quite the opposite in revolutionary portrayals. In fact, in a famous
scandal during the 1780s, criminals had actually implicated the queen in the
theft of a diamond necklace. Although the queen had nothing to do with the
crime, the public came to associate her with the common prostitute who imitated her. From then on Marie Antoinette, mother of future kings, was known
as a "whore," and specifically as the "Austrian whore." Cartoonists and pam-
phleteers attributed a whole range of sexual aberrations to her—including having sexual relations with her brother-in-law and with her son. These depictions
worked to eliminate the sacred characteristics of monarchy. Other aristocratic
women were similarly depicted and caricatured as harpies, monsters, and sex-

ual deviants. The sexual pleasures once open to aristocratic women were shut down as their sexuality became criminalized in the process of being used as a symbol. The generalized sexual play so prominent in street theater changed as the sexual behavior of specific individuals now invited public scrutiny and public censure. Those so scrutinized were women with political influence, particularly the queen and prominent aristocrats.

The Terror and the Reign of Virtue

Republican symbolism, pageantry, and institutions really developed with the outbreak of war in 1792. By the spring of that year, Austria had come to the defense of the French monarchy, and France declared war on her. The demands of war brought tighter control of society and the economy, a search for internal enemies, and an ongoing discussion of how revolutionary and wartime policies could mix. Naturally the war brought hardships of many kinds, but the revolutionary government tried to convert privation into patriotism by declaring the war necessary to preserve the nation. When revolutionaries declared the monarchy at an end in the fall of 1792 and established a republic in its place, the republican concept of citizenship replaced the idea of being a king's subject and encouraged sacrifice. Citizens were part of the nation, and thus the fate of the nation was the fate of its citizens. Moreover, pride in their accomplishment made citizens not only anxious to preserve the new reign of justice but eager to spread revolution elsewhere. Sensing this revolutionary fervor, other European countries grew more fearful of France and joined forces with Austria. In defense, the French supported a stricter wartime government led first by the Girondist and then by the Jacobin party. Alongside this government arose the Committee of Public Safety, which ultimately pursued a policy dedicated to purging the enemies of Republican virtue and of victory in the war. This policy produced an increasing number of executions and was known as the Terror.

The Society of Revolutionary Republican Women took shape in the midst of this crisis. In particular, these women emphasized the promotion of virtue and thus took as their purpose: "to attend to public affairs, to succor suffering humanity, and . . . to banish all selfishness, rivalry and envy."[12] Believing in sacrifice for the nation, women's public role, and equitable sharing of both sacrifices and benefits for the good of the Revolution, this group helped propel radical men to leadership.

In 1793 the Revolutionary Republicans tried to convince the more egalitarian groups to oust the middle-class and mercantilist Girondins, who worried more about profits than about the hardships caused by high wartime prices. Along with many artisans and workers, the Revolutionary Republicans also fought for wage and price controls. But demanding more participation for the workers, the group soon challenged the growing power of the Jacobins and the rigid rule of the Committee of Public Safety. The Revolutionary Republicans pressed for more democracy and for visible demonstrations of revolutionary fervor. Those who failed to display the revolutionary symbols and colors were objects of their disapproval. Walking through markets, members of the

A Revolutionary Death

In the summer of 1793 the French government arrested Olympe de
Gouges, the fervent revolutionary. She believed herself imprisoned unjustly and had the following "Political Testament" tacked on walls
throughout Paris. In it she enumerated her contributions to the cause.
Not only had she given money, she had provided gaiety with her plays.
Justifying her conduct and condemning the Terror, de Gouges also
showed herself ready to die like a good republican for the cause of the
nation's well-being.

> My son, the wealth of the whole world, the universe in ser-
> vitude at my feet, the daggers of assassins raised at me, noth-
> ing can extinguish the love of country that burns in my soul;
> nothing could make me betray my conscience. Men deranged
> by passions, what have you done and what incalculable evils
> are you perpetrating on Paris and on the whole of France?
> You are risking everything; you flatter yourselves into think-
> ing that it is only a question of a great purge to save the pub-
> lic; let the departments, infused with terror, blindly adopt
> your horrible measures.
>
> If, by a last effort, I can save the public welfare, I want
> even my persecutors, as they destroy me by their furor, to be
> jealous of my kind of death. And if one day French women
> are pointed out to future generations perhaps my memory will
> equal that of the Romans. I have predicted it all; I know that
> my death is inevitable; but it is glorious for a well-intentioned
> soul, when an ignominious death threatens all good citizens,
> to die for a dying country!
>
> I will my heart to the nation, my integrity to men (they
> have need of it). To women, I will my soul; my creative spirit
> to dramatic artists; my disinterestedness to the ambitious; my
> philosophy to those who are persecuted; my intelligence to all
> fanatics; my religion to atheists; my gaiety to women on the
> decline; and all the poor remains of an honest fortune to my
> son, if he survives me.
>
> Frenchmen, those are my last words, listen to what I am
> saying and reach down into the bottom of your hearts: do
> you recognize the austere virtues and the unselfishness of a
> republican? Answer me: who has loved and served the nation
> more—you or I? People, your reign is over if you fail to stop
> yourselves at the edge of this abyss. You have never been
> grander or more sublime than in the majestic calm you have
> kept during this bloody storm. If you can preserve this calm

and this august kind of supervision, you will save Paris, the whole of France, and republican government.

Source: Adapted from Marie Olympe de Gouges, *Politische Schriften in Auswahl*, ed. Margarete Wolters and Clara Sutor (Hamburg: Helmut Buske Verlag, 1979) 202–206.

society checked that other women conspicuously displayed the revolutionary colors. In so doing, they often provoked fights, especially with commercially minded women who opposed price controls. Such disturbances caught the attention of the public and of officials, whose main goal for civilians during wartime was that they remain peaceful and productive. The Revolutionary Republican Women had different goals, the foremost of which was to move the Revolution constantly toward greater democracy.

Finally, in late 1793, the Society of Revolutionary Republican Women adopted as their symbol the red cap (commonly called the Phrygian cap) worn by male revolutionaries, and encouraged other women to do likewise. Because this cap originated in classical times, wearing it signaled one's adherence to ancient beliefs in a public role and citizenship. The Revolutionary Republicans grafted these classical beliefs onto an eighteenth-century situation and assumed that all of them could and must apply to women as well as to men. With this act of cross-dressing, that is, of adopting for women what was male, the Revolutionary Republican Women crossed the line of what was seen as acceptable behavior by their male peers. They had made a crucial mistake in assessing the nature of republican virtue. Misjudging its applicability to their own search for power in the public sphere, the Revolutionary Republicans sought gender equality and the fiscal well-being of all French people, which they saw as crucial to the general public welfare. The French Revolution, however, was not about these matters; instead its main goal was ending the "feudal system" and the rule of aristocratic privilege. Revolutionaries aimed for government based on a more widespread male consensus and for a gender organization of clearly defined, separate spheres that would exclude queens and aristocratic women from power. Therefore, politicians interpreted women's clubs, particularly this one, as disturbing to republican order and safety.

At the end of October of 1793, the National Assembly took up the question of women in politics. Adhering to republican ideas, its official spokesman announced that nature intended women "to begin the education of men, to prepare their children's minds and hearts for public virtues." Such a charge constituted the cornerstone of the republic, and any dereliction of this duty could even be interpreted as treasonous. In fact, this was in the case of Marie Antoinette, executed only two weeks earlier for corrupting her son. Women's fitness for their task, the government spokesman said, rested on morality: "Does the decency of a woman allow that she show herself in public or that she compete with men?"[13] Again, the crimes of the queen were illustrative—she had governed her husband and had played a public role instead of a private one, and therefore was immoral. For the French legislature, republicanism meant that women's contribution lay exclusively in nurturing children. Thus, the National Assembly outlawed women's clubs and specifically banned the Society of Republican Revolutionary Women. Because women should not be active citizens, no good purpose could result from their meetings. The male legislators believed that they disrupted the republican order, based on women's seclusion, their private virtue, and their personal morality. At first, women were merely banned from clubs. In the next year, the assembly banned them from attending any public meetings and from assembling in groups. Simultaneously, however, stricter control of prices by the radical wing of the Jacobin party, by then in charge of the government, attracted women's unofficial support and decreased their resistance to the other legislation. Thus, a combination of bloodshed and legislation helped to usher in domesticity.

Protest, Opposition, and Counterrevolution

During the revolutionary era, French women lived through a war against external enemies and a civil one among those for and against the Revolution. The entire situation was complicated by the unevenness of market conditions in pre-industrial society and by the disturbances to normal production and distribution caused by revolution itself. Unlike other eighteenth-century wars, which were limited in scope, the French Revolution gave birth to a modern kind of warfare in which the military and those on the home front interacted on a wider scale. The *levée en masse* summoned all citizens, male and female, young and old, civilian and soldier, to service for the nation. This meant directing one's productive energy toward winning the war; it meant doing without basic commodities so that the army might be provisioned; it meant giving up those possessions that might be made into cannons or shot or any of a number of other useful items. Even before war was actually declared, the working women of France had endured serious hardships. For one thing, the rather rapid decline of the aristocracy followed by the fall of the monarchy meant that people employed—as many women were—in the luxury trades such as silk production, dressmaking, millinery work, and so on, were at best only semi-employed if not altogether unemployed. Once war broke out, putting up with shortages served to test patriotism. For those not participating patriotically and in a public way, the guillotine could be waiting.

Opposition to the Revolution broke out almost immediately. Some of the counterrevolutionaries still had affection for the monarchy; some for the aristocrats who provided them with a living. Protests intensified after the Civil Constitution of the Clergy, which demanded that priests take an oath of allegiance to the new regime. Many women were angered by this disturbance of their religious life. The appearance of revolutionary officials in any town sometimes stirred up menacing crowds of inhabitants. In Sommières in the winter of 1791, townspeople stoned officials several times to keep their church from changing its ways. Women declared that they would defend their religion "with the last drop of my blood." One screamed, "Let them come, let them come those guys, we'll cut their throats. We won't lose our religion!"[14] For this particular incident, women's reasons for resistance differed from men's. The latter explained their actions in terms of showing who was boss; they had scores to settle with the newcomers to power. Whereas men chose their sides according to old patterns of political and economic allegiance, women constantly invoked religion and the obedience due first to the priests, then from the priests to the bishops, and so on.

Despite such gender-based differences, all counterrevolutionary townspeople came from the lowest segments of commerce and trade. Neither middle-class nor professional, they generally worked in crafts or in agriculture, or as proprietors of small shops. The women worked as spinners, domestics, or laundresses. Few were literate. In other words, defense of religion was really a defense of an older way of life, with its guilds, its predictability, its social allegiances and alliances. For these women, the church constituted an entire culture, a notably oral one that spoke to them not just about spiritual matters but about life in general. The Revolution's offering of bookish Enlightenment, free trade, and representative politics had little to attract their interest or adherence.

Resistance on a massive scale broke out in the west, in the south, and in other scattered areas until a majority of the provinces were in revolt against the revolutionary government. Historians have yet to find a definite role played by women in these uprisings. Peasants often fought close by their fields, then hid their weapons—which were almost anything. Some armies were formed, headed by aristocrats. In the Vendée uprisings in the west, whole families sometimes joined these armies. Once the revolutionary government had decreed a war to the death with counterrevolutionaries, it became imperative for whole villages of people to keep on the move. The republican armies pillaged entire towns and killed their inhabitants. Stories abound of heroines on both sides of these uprisings. Any such visible participation in this kind of disturbance fortified republican belief that reestablishing social order meant sending women to their proper sphere. The effects of the Vendée were serious because of the loss of human life and because of the excuse it gave for the Terror. The counterrevolution was feared by the revolutionaries because it might lead to their downfall. To galvanize the people's will against this antagonist, they urged more and more virtue and practiced more and more terror. Once counterrevolution and foreign invasion diminished as threats in 1794, the Terror ended. Who would rule in France remained a question for several more years.

The Spreading of Revolution

Events in France attracted worldwide attention right from the beginning. Not only did monarchs grow fearful, some common people did as well. Many others, however, embraced the ideas of liberty and equality that the Revolution seemed to embody; some even rushed to France to witness events firsthand. Among these was an Englishwoman, Helena Maria Williams (1762–1827), who sent back voluminous eyewitness reports. Like the French, Dutch women participated in political clubs and prorevolutionary demonstrations. When a revolution against Austrian rule erupted in Belgium in 1789, women played important roles. They identified with the state and made the cause of national independence their own. The Countess d'Yves provided important propaganda against "sovereigns who force their subjects to submit to the yoke of despotism."[15] Another Belgian, Jeanne de Bellem (1734–?), produced many prorevolutionary pamphlets. In addition, some women fought in the revolutionary army, and others attacked Austrian soldiers by hurling stones at them from windows.

As the French armies moved into the German and Italian states, they generated revolutionary fervor in these new locales. Overnight, whole territories opted for revolution, and all the visible manifestations of the new regime, such as liberty trees, Phrygian caps, and tricolored banners, appeared. In Germany, clubs sprang up immediately to debate revolutionary policies and to spread revolutionary principles. Among the members were many German women, who were called *Klubbisten*. In Italy, similar occurrences greeted the approach of the liberators from the north. Clubs, festivals, and other signs of civilian acceptance appeared. One of the most prominent female Italian revolutionaries was Eleanora Pimentel (1752–1799), a Neopolitan journalist whose newspaper, the *Monitore,* related news of republican triumphs. Pimentel supported democratic types of reform. She believed that public education was a necessary innovation if the revolution were to receive popular support. The situation in Italy was not favorable to revolution, she believed, because the illiterate and uninstructed populace knew little of print culture and of enlightened ideas. A freemason and club member, Pimentel hoped for a transformation of Italy evolving from her version of French ideas. This promise never materialized. Instead, the Italian monarchy reasserted itself temporarily in 1799 with a bloodbath that brought about the execution of Pimentel among many others.

Mary Wollstonecraft (1758–1797) is seen as the most important advocate of the French cause, being in favor of reforming society in general and then of reforming the situation of women. Wollstonecraft tried earning her way in the world as a teacher and then as a writer and journalist. She produced several important books on the much-debated topic of women's education. After the Revolution broke out, she defended the new freedom in *A Vindication of the Rights of Men.* In 1792 she published the enduring *A Vindication of the Rights of Woman,* which was a *tour de force.* Written hurriedly but with passionate feeling, it combines strong commitment and specific ideas for reform. Wollstonecraft challenged the minimal education Rousseau had envisioned for

---

Mary Wollstonecraft Opposes "Pretty Femininity"

The early accomplishments of the French Revolution made people optimistic that they could create a rational new world. Mary Wollstonecraft was one of those so inspired. She believed that the role of women could be converted from one of mere display and sexuality to a responsible and social vocation. This excerpt from her famous *A Vindication of the Rights of Woman* captures her intense feeling about the degradation that aristocratic values brought women.

My own sex, I hope, will excuse me, if I treat them like rational creatures, instead of flattering their *fascinating* graces, and viewing them as if they were in a state of perpetual childhood, unable to stand alone. I earnestly wish to point out in what true dignity and human happiness consists—I wish to persuade women to endeavour to acquire strength, both of mind and body, and to convince them that the soft phrases, susceptibility of heart, delicacy of sentiment, and refinement of taste, are almost synonymous with epithets of weakness, and that those beings who are only the objects of pity will soon become objects of contempt.

Dismissing those soft pretty feminine phrases, which the men condescendingly use to soften our slavish dependence, and despising that weak elegancy of mind, exquisite sensibility, and sweet docility of manners, supposed to be the sexual characteristics of the weaker vessel, I wish to shew that elegance is inferior to virtue, that the first object of laudable ambition is to obtain a character as a human being, regardless of the distinction of sex.

Youth is the season for love in both sexes; but in those days of thoughtless enjoyment provision should be made for the more important years of life, when reflection takes place of sensation. The woman who has only been taught to please will soon find that her charms are oblique sunbeams and that they cannot have much effect on her husband's heart when they are seen every day, when the summer is passed and gone. Will she then have sufficient native energy to look into herself for comfort, and cultivate her dormant faculties? or, is it not more rational to expect that she will try to please other men?

Why must the female mind be tainted by coquettish arts to gratify the sensualist and prevent love from subsiding into friendship, or compassionate tenderness, when there are not qualities on which friendship can be built? Let the honest heart shew itself, and *reason* teach passion to submit to necessity; or, let the dignified pursuit of virtue and knowledge raise the mind above those emotions.

Source: Extracted from Mary Wollstonecraft, *A Vindication of the Rights of Woman*, ed., Carol H. Poston (New York: W. W. Norton, 1975) 9–10, 27, 31.

women. Instead, even more emphatically than Rousseau, she underscored the interdependent importance of virtue, reason, and motherhood in the lives of women. Her concept of virtue obviously stemmed from republican notions about the strength of character necessary for performing social roles. The role Wollstonecraft envisioned for the majority of women included motherhood, but she also mentioned political participation and activity in the economic sphere. These were expressions of, and constant replenishers of, virtue. At the same time, Wollstonecraft advocated that women be educated for reason rather than trained to please men. Only through the development of intellectual skills and moral character would they be competent in their maternal and wifely roles. Such education not only better enabled a woman to educate her children, but also helped her to fulfill the role of companion in marriage. Instead of viewing marriage as just a sexual union, Wollstonecraft thought marriage had to have a basis in compatability and equal training of both partners to reason. Without equal training, men dominated because of their superior education. This led many women to try to rule through cunning and craft, traits Wollstonecraft saw as ignominious in the new, enlightened age. Even worse, cunning and crafty women hardly made suitable mothers, because their dependence on deception indicated a lack of virtue.

Wollstonecraft was a powerful advocate of women in the late eighteenth century. She pleaded for motherhood to be recognized as a public contribution and a social position that in turn had individual power. She thus set out some of the lines of argument of later feminists. Unlike Rousseau, Wollstonecraft started with women themselves and did not merely derive a "Sophie" from an "Emile." Likening women to the aristocracy, Wollstonecraft decried their similarly decorative dress as only emphasizing their decadence. She cast the old regime and monarchy as "womanly" in their theatrical, artificial ways. She also compared women to the military, dependent upon the government for place and service and thus unfit for virtue because of that dependence. Clearly, "femininity" grew from women's weakness and inferior status. Motherhood, on the other hand, far from being a source of inferiority, equaled virtue and led to clear claim by women to things public or to a powerful sphere of influence. In her *Historical and Moral View of the Origins and Progress of the French Revolution,* Wollstonecraft described civilization and patriotism as "but the expansion of domestic sympathy." In other words, civic virtue had a domestic, female source, not one that started in the public world. She described "liberty with maternal wing . . . soaring far above vulgar annoyance, promising to shelter all mankind."[16] Thus, Wollstonecraft displayed strong convictions that were based less in liberal principles than in classical republican ideals. In this respect, her ideas approximated those of Mercy Otis Warren, who castigated Americans in her *History of the Rise, Progress and Termination of the American Revolution* (1805) for turning toward commercial gain and away from republican concerns with virtue. Wollstonecraft, however, connected virtue squarely with the reform of women's situation.

While Wollstonecraft pursued virtue, she also fell prey to her sentiments

Intellectual Mary Wollstonecraft endeavored to turn women toward republican virtue and to make republicanism serve the interests of women. Attacking aristocratic values, her Vindication of the Rights of Woman *called for modernizing gender relations.*

and romantic feelings. First she had fallen in love with a married man. Hurrying to France to avoid temptation, she observed the Revolution up close. Then she fell in love again, this time with Gilbert Imlay, an American writer with whom she had a daughter, Fanny. Frequently abandoned by Imlay as he pursued other women and his business dealings, Wollstonecraft despaired: "I have looked at the sea, and at my child, hardly daring to own to myself the secret wish that it might become our tomb."[17] After returning to London and attempting suicide several times, she continued her association with English radicals such as Thomas Paine and William Godwin, who were spreading revolutionary ideas in Britain. Ultimately, Godwin and Wollstonecraft entered into a love affair and then married after she became pregnant in 1797. After giving birth to her second daughter (who would later write *Frankenstein*), Wollstonecraft contracted puerperal fever and died shortly thereafter. William Godwin felt compelled to publish his wife's posthumous works, including *Maria, or the Rights and Wrongs of Woman* (1798), in which Wollstonecraft

pleaded vigorously for sexual rights for women. The story of a woman de-
ceived by both her husband and a lover hired to seduce her, *Maria* exposed
women's vulnerability. The ideology of separate spheres defined men as chivalric protectors of those without political representation. Instead, men were
predators. Next, Godwin wrote his wife's biography. Full of admiration, he
told her life story in full, not omitting her love affairs and illegitimate child.
This biography stirred up public outrage against Wollstonecraft and her
works. From then on, she had a reputation less as an author than as a "fallen
woman" who dared to write.

Wollstonecraft's *Vindication of the Rights of Woman* evolved from the
excitement generated by the French Revolution with respect to women's role.
Others urged their full emancipation with equal vigor. In 1792 a German mag-
istrate, Theodor von Hippel (1741–1796), published his *On the Improvement
of Women*, a work that took less a republican position than a liberal one. For
von Hippel, labor was the basis of all fulfilling activity, and therefore work—
and not merely housework—should be part of women's lives. Von Hippel believed women should have roles in the public world, including administrative
positions. Referring specifically to France, where the revolutionary government had failed to accord them rights from the start, von Hippel chastised men
as tyrants. He also revealed the true nature of the much touted ideal of chivalric protection. He saw chivalry and the idea of guardianship as mere slogans
to justify the enslavement of women and the stunting of their lives. Von Hippel
demanded that women, like men, participate not in this kind of partial existence, but in "universals."

At virtually the same time, the German journalist Marianne Ehrmann
(1755–1795) adopted a more republican line, supporting women's education
as a benefit to society in many ways but especially as a means of improving
their performance in domestic roles. Ehrmann, like other women writers before and after her, felt it necessary to apologize for her "unwomanly" (that is,
atypical for a woman) life. She did emphasize, however, that an increase in
literacy might have a beneficial effect in several areas. Her compatriot, Emilie
Berlepsch (1757–1831), wrote direct attacks on society. Catching the revolutionary mood, she emphasized rights and individual self-sufficiency. And she
went further, to attack misogyny, which she called "the widely disseminated
poison of injustice toward us."[18] This was typical of the charges people began
to make against men in the few years when tyranny was on the defensive.

Thus, throughout Europe, writers, politicians, and ordinary people
equated the overthrow of kings with the demise of all sorts of inequity. As
revolution spread through countries, it also spread its influence to cover a host
of topics. Among these were the rights of women and opportunities for gender
equality. Revolution as rights and revolution as motherhood—the two interpretations coexisted in the discussion of women but with growing tension. Yet
the expansiveness of such fervor and the range of ideas were already narrowing
in France, at least as far as matters other than the overthrow of the aristocratic
regime were concerned. The focus of the Revolution determined the blueprints
for the arrangement of society and of gender relations in the future.

The Napoleonic Synthesis

By summer of 1794 French troops had been victorious enough over the would-be undoers of the Revolution that the Terror met its end. This victory did not mean that the French armies were decommissioned; they were sent to Egypt, Italy, and other places in need of new political ideas and specifically, places under Austrian or British control. The rule of virtue and the price controls and wartime stringencies diminished in France because neither the people nor the merchants would put up with constant regulation. During the next five years France had several governments—a Directorate, the Convention, and the Consulate. None of them ruled easily because social and political turmoil continued. High prices led to continued marketplace riots and confiscations of goods. City women demanded bread and other commodities for their families at a just price. In the countryside the so-called White Terror, directed against Jacobins, erupted to settle the score left by revolutionary executions and confiscation of property. Families sitting at dinner might be dragged out into the streets and killed if anyone associated them with revolutionary stridency. Former officials went into hiding. Asceticism in the name of the Revolution all but ended. In towns and cities, a new social fashion arose—men dressed in old regime splendor and spoke in affected, outmoded accents. Women of the middle and upper classes, particularly those of leisure, transformed the Roman-style garb they once wore to signal virtue. They began to wet their garments to make them cling to their bodies, or they exposed their bosoms or wore transparent clothing in a revival of sexually enticing aristocratic fashions. The political arena became populated by mistresses and adventurers, but none was successful in holding on to power. The uncertain climate invited a strong man, and Napoleon Bonaparte accepted the invitation.

A military hero, Bonaparte had taken Switzerland and Italy for France and tried to take Egypt. He also put down the worst riots against the post-Terror government by firing on the Parisian crowds. Yet Bonaparte was a committed revolutionary and wanted to see the Revolution not only work but spread. His military mindset was tinged with his commitment to new ideals. Far from being a member of the high aristocracy who would have a traditional right to military command, Bonaparte sprang from the impoverished nobility of Corsica, only recently made part of France. Working his way up to a generalship through talent, he clearly represented certain values of the new liberal world. For one thing, he was a self-made man and at the same time a military man, above parties and factions. His military prowess and revolutionary language appealed to those who feared a return of royalty.

A combination of old and new, of liberal and conservative, Bonaparte struck the right note. Aware, even if only intuitively, of the meaning of the Revolution, he appropriated its main goal: the overthrow of feudalism and the consolidation of private property. As a military man, however, he favored hierarchy and therefore allowed the aristocracy to return and even created new positions of honor for his own followers. Bonaparte also recognized the divi-

Civilians and the Revolutionary Wars (1792–1815)

The revolutionary wars continued the struggle between the French and British for control of commerce and for political domination. As armies traveled the Continent, civilians had to adjust to survive. Polish-born Johanna Schopenauer was in Weimar during the battle of Jena (1806) and described the entry of French troops into the town in a letter to her son. All members of the house had to have their wits about them, for pillage and death were ever-present dangers and, in the case of this household mostly of women, so was rape.

> The dreadful cry was heard in the streets, "the French are coming!" Hundreds of men rushed by to the market-place, which is not far from us. Now all hope was gone: we clasped each other's hands in silence. The cannons again roared, nearer and nearer, awfully near. The floor shook, and the windows rattled. How near death was to us! We no longer heard any single report, but the hissing and rattling of the balls and small-shot which flew over our house and onto the houses and the ground fifty paces from us, without our being hurt thereby: God's angel protected us. Peace and calm were suddenly restored to my heart, I drew my Adela to my bosom, and sat down with her on a sofa, hoping that a ball might kill us both,—at all events that neither might have to weep over the other. Never was the thought of death nearer to me, and never was it less formidable. Throughout the day, and even at that sad moment, Adela did not lose her self-composure. Not a tear did she shed, nor a cry did she utter: when her feelings became overpowering she drew herself nearer to me, kissed me, drew me close to her, and begged me not to distress myself. Even now she was quite still; but I felt her delicate limbs tremble with a feverish chill, and heard her teeth striking against each other. I kissed her and begged her to compose herself, for if we died we should die together; she ceased to tremble, and looked affectionately up in my face. It was nearly eight o'clock. I insisted on it that we should sit down properly to dinner; none of us had tasted anything all day but a few cups of broth and a glass or two of wine, and had endured this distracting anxiety besides. Just as we had seated ourselves at dinner, there was a cry of fire, and a column of flames, like Mont Blanc, burst forth. We saw plainly that it was not quite close to us, but there was a cry—"the castle's on fire!" and again, "the city is set fire to in four places!" There was no wind; we put our trust in God, and were more calm.

Soon after an attempt was made to force open the front door. Sophy and Conta ran down, and persuaded the ferocious men,—how, I cannot to tell,—to come under the window. They demanded bread and wine quickly; both were handed to them out of the window. They were merry; they sang, and drank Sophy's health; she was obliged to drink theirs in return, and then they went away. This was repeated several times. We had all crowded into a small back parlour not to let any light be seen: I had laid Adela on a bed; I sat down on it with a purse containing a few crowns in my hand. Now we heard their wild voices down-stairs:—"Du pain, du vin, vite, nous montons!" and Sophy and Conta bid them welcome in a most amiable manner. Sophy said,—she had been waiting for them a long while, and had cooked in readiness, so they had better be quiet. The table and all was ready, and thereupon she set out the bread and wine, and roast meat before them. Conta, who passed for her husband, did his part: the savages became tame; they ate, drank, and got quite tipsy. Just fancy their hideous faces, their bloody swords drawn, the white smocks they wore on such occasions, all sprinkled with blood, their savage merriment and conversation, and hands dyed red with blood. I had only a momentary glance from the stairs at them: they were ten or twelve in number. Sophy was joking, and laughing with them below. One grasped her round the waist. Then Sophy fetched Adela, who spoke to them very respectfully, and begged them to leave, because she was very sleepy; the wretches yielded to the child's request and went off.

Source: Excerpts from Johanna Schopenauer, *Youthful Life and Pictures of Travel*, 2 vols. (London: Longman, Brown, Green, and Longmans, 1847) 1:279–288.

sive nature of enforced secularism. To heal that breach, he allowed the Catholic Church to maintain its dominance over religious life, yet he himself controlled its appointments and other institutional regulations. A new court life came into being, bringing with it new allegiances as well as renewed business prosperity. By sponsoring industry and commerce, Bonaparte earned the homage of entrepreneurs and industrialists. He appealed to all types of people—from the modest farmer who could identify with his rise to fame, to the merchant who appreciated a good business head.

From 1799 Napoleon Bonaparte ruled as consul with two others; in 1804 he became emperor. From then on, he tried to forge an imperial domain, one that spread across Europe, with enlightened revolutionary rule for all. The

Roman motif he chose for himself echoed the symbols of the Revolution. He saw himself as a new Justinian, that is, a lawgiver who would consolidate the major ideals of the new regime into a code of rational laws echoing the Enlightenment desire for government intelligible to all citizens. In 1804 the final form of the Napoleonic Code appeared, which was analogous to the Roman formula. The bulk of this code concerned private property and all the methods for acquiring, increasing, mortgaging, and selling it. But the first two sections—those on citizenship and the family—were just as crucial to the Napoleonic scheme of things. Familial and civic discipline combined with a working plan for property summed up middle-class interests. Republicanism moved into the family, and liberalism remained the value system of those in the public and economic sphere. Virtue applied to women, whereas rights belonged to men.

Revolutionaries had not been unopposed when they began applying liberal principles to the family. The ideas of giving rights to women, maintaining equality between spouses, and recognizing the claims of illegitimate children were blamed as sources of revolutionary troubles and excesses. No one felt this more strongly than did the jurists who, along with Napoleon, sat for more than a year formulating the Code. Like the revolutionaries, their touchstone remained the Roman republic—and this, ironically, as Napoleon was making himself an emperor. For these men, the patriarchal family remained the basis of national health and social order. The republican patriarch, they pointed out, embodied the ideal citizen, having rights, capable of self-rule, and possessing a well-defined relationship to the state. When the Republic became the Roman Empire, the rise of prosperity robbed families of their stable center. Women came to possess excessive dowries and inheritances, with the result, the Napoleonic magistrates believed, that they controlled men and exercised their sexuality to no good end. License, not virtue, had come to govern the Roman Empire and created a situation of tyranny and excess. The codifiers sought to preempt such a result by creating a "proper" system of laws. They drew from the Roman example the lesson that the husband should be the administrator of the family and its goods. Thus, they formed the law of the family around the "marital power" of the husband, giving him administrative sway over his wife, his children, and all property. They believed that ensuring a consolidated family would ensure a gender-based social order similarly administered by men.

Specific provisions carried out this general vision. First, women acquired the nationality of their husbands upon marriage. This made a woman's relationship to the state an indirect one because it was dependent on her husband's. Second, a woman had to reside where her husband desired. Women could not participate in lawsuits or serve as witnesses in court or as witnesses to civil acts such as births, deaths, and marriages. Such a reduction in woman's civil status enhanced that of the individual male. Moreover, the code reduced, if not eliminated, male accountability for sexual acts and thrust it squarely on women. For example, men were no longer susceptible to paternity suits or legally responsible for the support of illegitimate children. Women were weakened economically if they bore illegitimate children, whereas men were not so affected if they fathered them. Finally, female adultery was punished by imprisonment and fines unless the husband relented and took his wife back. Men, however, suffered no such sanctions unless they brought their sexual partner into the home. The sexual behavior of women was open to scrutiny and prescribed by law, whereas that of men, almost without exception, had no criminal aspect attached to it. Thus male sexuality was accepted with few limitations, but women's was only acceptable if it remained within strict domestic boundaries. The Napoleonic Code institutionalized the republican responsibility of women to generate virtue—a term that began to acquire sexual overtones to its civic definition.

The Napoleonic Code also defined the space women would occupy in the new regime as marital, maternal, and domestic—all public matters would be determined by men. This circumscription was made more effective by the way the property law undercut the possibilities for women's economic independence and existence in a world beyond the home. In general, a woman had no control over property. Even if she was married under a contract that ensured a separate accounting of her dowry, her husband still had administrative control of funds. This administrative power of the husband and father replaced arbitrary patriarchal rule and was more in tune with modern ideas of government. Instead of serving the king's whim, governmental officials served the best interests of the nation just as the father increased the well-being of the family. This kind of economic control of women held in all classes. Women's wages went to their husbands, and market women and others engaged in business could not do so without permission from their husbands. Once a woman gained permission she did acquire some kind of legal status, in that a business woman could be sued. On the other hand, she had no control of her profits—these always passed to her husband, and court records demonstrate the continuing enforcement of this kind of control. Moreover, the husband's right to a businesswoman's property meant that the property passed to his descendants rather than hers. All of these provisions meant that, in the strictest sense, women could not act freely or independently.

The Napoleonic Code influenced many legal systems in Europe and the New World and set the terms for the treatment of women on a widespread basis. Establishing male power by transferring autonomy and economic goods from women to men, the Code organized gender roles for more than a century. "From the way the Code treats women, you can tell it was written by men," so older women reacted to the new decree.[19] Women's publications protested the sudden repression after a decade of more equitable laws. Even in the 1820s, books explaining the Code to women always recognized their anger. The justification for the Code's provisions involved reminders about men's chivalrous character and women's weakness. Arguments were based on nature both to invoke the equality of all men and to reinforce the consequences of women's supposed physical inferiority. Looking at nature, one writer saw in terms of gender man's "greater strength, his propensity to be active and assertive in comparison to woman's weakness, lack of vigor and natural modesty."[20] At the time the Code was written, the codifiers were looking at nature in two ways. In theorizing about men alone, nature was redolent of abstract rights. As far as women were concerned, however, nature became empirical in that women had less physical stature than men. Although short men were equal to tall men, women were simply smaller than men and thus were unequal.

According to jurists, therefore, women needed protection, and this protection was to be found within the domicile. The law, they maintained, still offered women protection from individual male brutality, in the rare cases when that might occur. Legislators thus used the law officially to carve out a private space for women in which they had no rights. At the same time, law codes were supposed to protect women from the abuses allowed in the first place. The small number of abuses that might result were not seen as significant drawbacks by the jurists. They saw the Code as "insuring the safety of patrimonies and restoring order in families."[21] It mattered little to them that the old regime carried over for women in the form of an "estate"—a term that indicated an unchangeable lifetime situation into which people were born and would always remain. Estates had been abolished for men in favor of mobility, but it continued for women.

By the time the Napoleonic Code went into effect, little remained of liberal revolutionary programs for women except the provision for equal inheritance by sisters and brothers. The Code cleared the way for the rule of property and for individual triumph. It ushered in an age of mobility, marked by the rise of the energetic and heroic. The Code gave women little room for that kind of acquisitiveness or for heroism. Instead, women's realm was to encompass virtue, reproduction, and family.

Romanticism

The Napoleonic Code seemed to enshrine reason and the principles of the Enlightenment, but other, conflicting tendencies took hold in certain avant-garde circles. Poetry celebrating nature was written by such poets as Samuel Coleridge, William Wordsworth, and William Blake. Not only nature but anti-intellectualism characterized their works, which demonstrated a distrust of books and teachers, of learned arguments and educational institutions. Love also edged reason out, for example, in Johann Wolfgang von Goethe's influential novel *The Sorrows of Youth Werther* (1774). This German master later produced *Hermann and Dorothea*, *Elective Affinities*, and *Wilhelm Meister*, all with themes involving love, nature and village life, and the plight of sensitive and sentimental people in the modern world. The triumph of Napoleon also consolidated the position of the romantic hero as the dominant figure in literature. Napoleon's rise ended the literary use of fantastic heroes, such as those in epics in which forces of good and evil or of religion were the motivating factors. Spiritually ordained heroes, whether princes or saints, had little place in the new literature; heroes in the revolutionary and Napoleonic periods were ordinary men who triumphed by their own efforts and led society through exalted times as well as terrifying ones. The stories that followed—such as those written by Stendhal—portrayed new kinds of men who were attempting to be heroes, sometimes succeeding, but also, like Napoleon, sometimes coming to a tragic end. The emphasis in Rousseau's *Confessions* on the misunderstood and sympathetic genius left a literary legacy of romance, tragedy, nature, heroes, and heroic misfits.

Anne-Louise-Germaine Necker de Staël (1766–1817) led the development of the Romantic movement in France during this era. The daughter of the famous banker and revolutionary minister Jacques Necker, de Staël was raised in an atmosphere full of ideas about politics, reform, and literature. Her mother ran a famous *salon*, where the foremost proponents of European liberalism congregated. After her marriage to a Swedish diplomat, Madame de Staël imitated her mother and became a *salonière* in her own right. During the early days of the Revolution, her *salon* was a political center for supporters of her father's ministry under Louis XVI. As the Revolution moved toward the Terror, de Staël returned to her estate in Switzerland (her father's birthplace), but remained a focus of intense intellectual activity. People flocked to her Swiss retreat then and in the various periods of exile that were to follow. When the Terror was suppressed, de Staël returned to Paris, only to leave when Napoleon refused her permission to live in his capital. From then on, de Staël became an opponent of the Emperor. As a romantic, she had once sought alliance with him, but Napoleon had little use for intellectual women like de Staël. He deliberately insulted her by staring at her bosom or by saying that he preferred women who had large families to learned ones. Until his downfall, de Staël had to travel constantly to escape harassment. Despite it all, she became a thorough romantic, writing about the imagination and heroes; however, her heroes were seldom French and were usually female. This birth of female heroes coincided with the publication of multivolumed biographical dictionaries of great women.

De Staël praised Rousseau, who, according to her, was a passionate man whose disturbed psyche found its relief in writing. More than once de Staël declared writing to be the solution to the heartbreak and troubles of her intense emotional experiences with many lovers. Although she elevated Rousseau, she simultaneously downplayed the great figures of the Enlightenment and their much vaunted reason. For her, their style betrayed a lack of freedom; she felt that irony and sarcasm had no place in the work of great writers but that authors such as Voltaire had to sully their talents with the use of such devices because of monarchical government and oppression. Light pieces, comedies, and plays had had to be written to please the frivolous people controlling eighteenth-century life—the so-called Age of Enlightenment. In fact, so disgusted did de Staël become with French arts and letters that she began turning toward Germany and Italy. Such a turn seemed heretical in this period. French thought and political theory had been triumphant, at least had captured worldwide attention. But de Staël visited German luminaries such as Goethe. She also praised Italian culture, including its music, poetry, and painting. This almost amounted to treason: had not the Germans contested the Revolution and Na-

Germaine de Staël posing as Corinne in a portrait by Elisabeth Vigée-Lebrun (1808). Although not beautiful, de Staël was spellbinding to many, as this depiction suggests.

poleon? had not the Italians had to be conquered to receive the benefits of freedom? Germaine de Staël brought these two cultures, so far removed from the dominant English and French ones, to the public eye in her two most influential books, *Corinne* (1807) and *De l'Allemagne* (1810). Both had a profound impact on culture in general, and both influenced women's writing for generations.

Corinne tells the story of an English-Italian genius, an orator celebrated throughout the Italian city-states, who falls in love with a visiting English lord. Corinne shows Lord Oswald ruins from the ancient and Renaissance cultures and in so doing arouses his esteem and love. The two go on a tour of Rome, Naples, and Venice, the description of which gave de Staël a chance to show Napoleon that his was not the first or the only triumphant civilization; before him had been the Romans, the Venetians, the Florentines—all of them freer than the French under imperial rule. After Lord Oswald returns to England, he jilts Corinne by marrying a far inferior woman as arranged by his father. The news makes Corinne mortally ill, but she lasts long enough to begin creating another female genius, Oswald's daughter. In the cult of heroism and genius developing at the time, *Corinne* held a high place. The novel was not only a popular success, it was enthusiastically received by intellectuals as well.

The values for which Corinne stood were those of the early revolution: freedom, reason, equality, and civility. To these, de Staël added passion, romance, and tragedy. The inspired, southern genius represented by Corinne received a battering from the cold Englishman, Oswald. Because Oswald married someone destined for him by his father, Corinne's plight could also be blamed on patriarchy and male betrayal. Thus de Staël successfully fused several situations: first, the threat to European cultural genius by the imposition of French law and customs; then, the destruction of intuitive genius by a mediocre and unfeeling northerner; and finally, the betrayal of a woman, and a woman of genius at that, by a man. Such a tale inspired writers such as Margaret Fuller in the United States, Anna Jameson in England, and dozens more across the Continent. *Corinne* provided inspiration not only for their writing but for living a passionate life.

In contrast to the public's reaction when *Corinne* appeared, Napoleon's was furious. The book's challenge was all too clear. And far more damaging was *De l'Allemagne*, which he banned from France. This work explains German culture to a European, in particular a French, audience and constitutes a kind of guided tour of the German states. Although to the French it seemed that all culture sprang from Paris, the heart of a bureaucratic and centralized state, de Staël showed them a more dispersed but no less admirable culture in Germany. Because the German states remained disunited, they produced, according to her, a more democratic and vital art. German art had its roots in the culture of the people and thus had an original rather than an imitative basis; no one merely imitated a work seen the night before at the theater. De Staël particularly praised those artists who could recapture the sentiments and feelings of a period in the past, those who could stimulate the imagination. Whereas many in the revolutionary period wanted to erase all previous history as a kind of nightmare of ignorance and superstition, romantics like de Staël felt its appeal. Not only did history provide lessons, but more importantly, it gave visions of other worlds. If one's political world was in shambles because of tyranny, if one could not embrace commercial or other materialistic values, one could turn, as de Staël did, to culture, especially to a foreign or exotic culture. Intellectuals unhappy with the modern world began retreating into the world of the imagination. Sentiment and feeling, aesthetic and cultural values could find expression there, unaffected by the philistines and tyrants of the new regime. De Staël was forced by Napoleon to retreat from politics, but her reaction shaped the modern artist's outlook on the world. Her message had a great effect on women as they became increasingly cut off from public influence. Thousands of women who took up their pens in the next centuries did so in imitation of the interior retreat celebrated so vividly by this female writer.

When de Staël looked to Germany for a different kind of inspiration, she chose well. Suffering repression alternatively at the hands of monarchs fearful of revolution and invading French armies, Germans had begun looking to the world of culture as the focus of intellectual activity when their own political discussion was out of the question. Moreover, cultural similarity became the ground on which Germans felt themselves united. Culture produced a new kind of individualism based not on rights but on feeling, sentiment, and the production of works of art. These ingredients had accompanied the rise of the novel. For the German romantics, however, sentiments and feelings had to reach new heights, so limited were the people from other realms of activity during this energetic age. Extraordinary and exalted feelings gave the individual a sense of worth surpassing even that achieved by fulfilling the role of citizen. Goethe's character Werther had felt similarly in the 1770s, but his feelings led to his suicide. By the Napoleonic period, the bliss aroused by art, nature, and life in general sustained the romantics instead of making them suicidal.

Fostering intellectual intercourse by taking up the role of *salonière* and willing hostess, German women continued to make *salon* life flourish in the beginning of the nineteenth century. But a transformation occurred in the *salon's* purpose. Instead of fixing on political reform, the German *salon* made ideas in and of themselves the principal topic. Unlike the most committed *salon* leaders of the mid–eighteenth century, these new *salonières* were not pursuing social reform as an outcome of conversation and intellectual exchange. Rather they sought to escape into ideas and find there not only rationality but emotional experience. Jewish women, especially in Berlin, dominated *salon* life perhaps because the *salon* offered such an escape from social reality. Women like Rahel Varnhagen, who had unrealistically fallen in love with officers and aristocrats considered inappropriate for Jewish women at the time, settled for creating unions of ideas.

Romanticism also promoted sexual passion and love. Friedrich Schlegel's *Lucinde* (1799) idealized his feelings for several women, and Goethe's *Elective Affinities* (1809) was built around a married man's passion for a young girl. Love became a feeling the heroine aroused in the hero; it had little to do with the fineness of sentiment of early novels. Women were portrayed as conduits of feeling and exaltation. For example, when Lucinde's "ample forms, her buxom charms aroused the fury of his love," she, as an object of passion, led the hero to experience feeling. The hero "enjoyed the sensation of the warm stream of delicate being," while his "gaze was ravished by the hues" of her skin.[22] Instead of being moderate and rational, love was an irresistible force unleashing itself in the male. Such arousal, the romantics made clear, was justified by the art that resulted from its excitement. Behind the artist was the inspiring woman, whose sexuality worked its way into art through him. Women were thus seen as being responsible for channeling passion into virtue and also into art.

Romanticism propagated relationships and marriages based on love rather than subsistence or dynastic goals. Caroline Michaelis Schelling (1763–1809) married three times, served as the major female symbol of the romantic movement, and was referred to simply as Caroline. Dorothea Mendelssohn (1763–1839) gained renown for falling in love with Friedrich Schlegel and for abandoning her husband, children, and religion for a free union with him. Despite the servitude that German wives appeared to endure, Germany seemed to be populated with this type of romantic heroine, whose ability to find and inspire

Caroline Michaelis Schelling, writer and romantic heroine, portrayed with loose garments and somewhat casual of demeanor.

many lovers and husbands was facilitated by easy divorce laws. States badly in need of soldiers, and therefore children, made divorce and remarriage relatively easy.

The romantic heroine could be many things in one, a model that was aspired to by Sophie Mereau (1773–1806), married twice and a poet of the Romantic movement, and the very fine poet Caroline Günderode (1780–1806), who stabbed herself because of unrequited love. In sum, romanticism appealed to women because it stressed *Bildung*, a central tenet of German cultural life that described an ongoing process of mental and spiritual evolution that they could experience. Although in fact quite male-oriented, romanticism nonetheless offered attractive possibilities to women.

Religious Solutions

While romanticism was developing gradually in reaction to the Enlightenment and to politics, an accompanying rise in religious fervor contributed to its vitality. Contemporaries attributed Goethe's romantic vision to the influence of his mother's intense and demonstrative piety. The new spiritual enthusiasm, like the romantic one, gave worth and stability to the individual in the face of political turmoil and pervasive economic dislocation. In England, the Methodist sect developed out of the preachings of John Wesley (1703–1791), and in Germany a revitalization of the existing Protestant sects occurred. In France, women prophets such as Catherine Emmerich (1774–1824) tried to oppose the progress of the Revolution with calls not to reform political life but to reawaken the soul. In the German states, Countess Julie von Reventlow and Princess Galitzine formed circles for common prayer and for learning how to probe the deepest recesses of the soul for signs of sin and spiritual feeling. Countess von Reventlow also took her prayerful mission into the countryside, to peasants and village artisans and especially to children. In fact, during the first waves of piety aristocrats and high members of the bourgeoisie were most often found doing the proselytizing. They favored a turning inward of men and women toward the family instead of rebellion, a scrutiny of one's inner life instead of criticizing the government, and enthusiasm drawn from spiritual fervor instead of from political activism. Thus, the religious reawakenings of the late eighteenth and early nineteenth centuries initially served the cause of conservatism and the goal of social peace. Restoring the faith that characterized the Middle Ages, when hierarchy prevailed, was a defense against revolutionary egalitarianism.

In the midst of growing commercial prosperity, rioting, and the threat of revolution, some in the English middle classes gained a sense of how religion could preserve social order. The case of Hannah More (1745–1833) demonstrates just how demanding the road to this kind of consciousness was. More and her four sisters ran a highly successful school for girls in Bristol. The sisters moved in good society, and were in great demand socially because of their acquaintance with celebrities and the high-born. Hannah More became the leader among the sisters by virtue of her literary ability as well as her engaging conversation. The great actor and playwright David Garrick befriended her; so did the Bluestockings and Samuel Johnson. For decades More lived a life of wit among writers and theater people, until she became caught up in the evangelical movement that flourished among the Anglicans like herself as well as among members of dissenting sects. More's acquisition of religious fervor transformed her life; "dear holy Hannah" she came to be called. More found the state of formal religion in England abysmal. Few practiced it, least of all the wealthy. Reaching her goal of establishing Sunday schools for the poor demanded relentless effort to overcome objections of the gentry, or, as she put it, "the petty tyrants, whose insolence I stroked and tamed, the ugly children I praised, the pointers and spaniels I caressed." Landowners saw her efforts both as wasteful of time that could best be spent working and as inspiring workers to want better things. More succeeded in opening her first school in 1789. [The first English Sunday school (1782) for the poor had been started by the highly religious Sarah Trimmer (1741–1810), who also wrote didactic children's books.] Scores more followed, started by More and others.

The Sunday school movement grew because, after their initial qualms, many of the wealthy saw these institutions as instruments of discipline. For their part, poor families were happy enough to have their children clothed by the Sunday schools, sometimes fed and even given cash incentives for good attendance. In addition, the children were taught to read, though only the best received instruction in writing. Annual festivals held by the schools often attracted more middle-class and well-to-do observers than children. Singing hymns and choruses of "God Save the King," the children constituted a living testimonial to the way a new society might look—sober, peaceful, and rejoicing in one's given social status.

As the call to revolution and radicalism rang ever more loudly, Hannah More intensified her missionary work. She read up on working-class struggles, on their family life, societies, and demonstrations. This intense scrutiny allowed her to write a series of tracts designed for the poor and discontented. Using colorful casts of working characters such as rat-catchers and fortune-tellers, More produced a stream of moral but interesting tales of working-class life and temptations, such as thieving and cheating. But the greatest temptations in More's eyes were discontent, unrest, and uprising. The good, like her character David Saunders the shepherd, raised children, despite having virtually no resources, and simultaneously maintained a God-fearing and politically respectful attitude. The worst, like character Tom Hod, a mason, wanted "liberty and equality and the rights of man." In More's works, the Tom Hods were ultimately proved wrong. She demonstrated that society could not exist without the gentry in the countryside who provided work or the rich folk in towns and cities who established hospitals and gave the poor charity. The message was that England had reached a state of social and political perfection: "We have a king, so loving that he would not hurt the people if he could; and so kept in that he could not hurt the people if he would. We have as much liberty as can make us happy, and more trade and riches than allows us to be good. We have the best laws in the world . . . and the best religion in the world."[23] Purchased in the tens of thousands to be distributed to the poor, More's tracts represent the antirevolutionary position held well into the nineteenth century: keep the infection from spreading by quieting political passions and channeling them into sociability. More laid out a road to religious and charitable deeds that was followed by many nineteenth-century women.

Revolutionary Results

The age of revolution and romanticism changed European society. It meant destruction of homes and lives; it generated an enthusiasm and exhilaration born of bringing down an old way of organizing society. Years of passion and struggle had destroyed, or at the least weakened, what remained of older patterns of controlling the land and politics. Thereafter, those who wanted aristocratic privilege and rule by the few would have to contain the forces of constitutionalism and republicanism. When the question of woman's rights and roles arose during those turbulent years, it was something to reckon with precisely because of the mood of change and the energy it brought with it. Throughout Europe, people commonly debated such topics as the education of women and their rights and duties. Instead of fulfilling a role in a tightly intertwined system of agricultural work, women became individuals with potential rights. Everyone saw possibilities for a new arrangement of the social order. Although many feared these new arrangements, some, including many activist women, pushed politicians to recognize the implications for women's freedom in the newly espoused creed of individual rights.

Such activism produced only a short-lived acquisition of political responsibility for women. From the women who marched to Versailles to those who asked for rights along with price controls, women made the French Revolution a democratic event; the definition of the "people," in whose name all action occurred, was thereby construed as meaning everyone instead of restricted to just men. Yet when those with interests in property triumphed, through terror at home and victory on the battlefield, it became clear that the issue of democracy was not the one being fought for. A return to normalcy meant reestablishing gender hierarchy as a sign that private property would be safe. The disorder that women in politics embodied had to be eradicated in favor of the order that their being at home seemed to ensure. It looked, indeed, as if nothing had changed, or even, given the Napoleonic Code, that things had changed for the worse.

The Revolution had given birth, or rather worldwide publicity, to liberal values in politics. It became clear what those values would signify for the relations between men and women and for the construction of gender identities in a modernized society. First more and more men would have their identities tied to political participation; such were the implications of republican values and contractual theories of government for them. At the same time, women's republicanism meant something different: "Women: Do you want to be republicans? Love, obey, and teach the laws that remind your husbands and children to exercise their rights."[24] This concept, subsequently called "republican motherhood," shaped women's lives in the nineteenth century. It enshrined Rousseau's ideas that motherhood had an explicitly cultural and political function. Women had a new relationship to the state and to social questions, and their new role demanded education. In the minds of many women, the concept of republican motherhood upgraded their position. Moreover, it seemed likely that, given the importance of women's work in the old regime, the acquisition of this kind of public recognition and public place would further empower them.

However, hopes for an increase in women's rights were shattered by the manner in which the new codes and the political aims of men restructured gender roles. The home developed as a politically and economically distinct area, separate from the ongoing activities of the market (that is, of property). Both the decrees of the National Assembly in the mid-1790s and the Napoleonic Code revealed, moreover, that this domestic arena had to be created through coercion. The Code determined the role of nineteenth-century women in two ways. First, it curtailed their property rights and thus forcibly removed them from the world of liberal values. Second, it restricted their sexuality and legislated obedience or self-regulation, in contrast to the old ways of the pleasure-seeking and overtly sexual aristocracy. The victims of all this were the aristocratic women—Marie Antoinette, Madame Du Barry, Princess Lamballe, and thousands of others. The great diplomat, Prince Talleyrand, understood this transformation when he said that the creation of the "proper lady" (*"la femme comme il faut"*) marked the end of the old regime.[25]

The romantic ideology with regard to gender roles complemented this curtailment of women's sexual and economic rights. For the romantics, women were the conduit to greatness; they aroused passion, mastery, and artistic genius. Men might control politics, economics, and the world of culture, but they could do so only if they could take inspiration from and have contact with this opposite kind of being. This interaction of opposites stood at the basis of nineteenth-century social constructs. Men carved out for themselves a universal culture, political world, and economic sphere in which they strove to excel. Women understood and even celebrated that universal world as republican mothers, but they participated in it on economically disadvantageous terms because of their being mothers, not workers. At the same time, women made this new confinement into something of their own—a world of domesticity. As the age of capitalism and industrialization progressed, men operated according to liberal tenets exclusively whereas women at various times would aim at both liberalism and virtue.

NOTES

1. Quoted in Olivier Bernier, *The Eighteenth-Century Woman* (New York: Doubleday, 1982), 93–94.

2. Quoted in Darline Gay Levy, Harriet B. Applewhite, and Mary D. Johnson, eds., *Women in Revolutionary Paris, 1789–1795* (Urbana: University of Illinois Press, 1979), 31–33.

3. Quoted in Paule-Marie Duhet, *Les femmes et la révolution 1789–1794* (Paris: Gallimard Julliard, 1971), 37–39.

4. Olympe de Gouges, "Declaration of the Rights of Women," in Levy, Applewhite, and Johnson, eds., *Women in Revolutionary Paris,* 92.

5. Donatien de Sade, *Three Complete Novels: Justine, Philosophy in the Bedroom, Eugénie de Franval,* Richard Seaver, tr. (New York: Grove, 1965), 318.

6. *Doléances des femmes de Franche-Comté* (Besançon, April 27, 1789), 25, quoted in James Traer, *Marriage and the Family in Eighteenth Century France* (Ithaca, N.Y.: Cornell University Press, 1980), 83.

7. Maximilien Robespierre, *Les droits de l'état des bâtards* (Arras: Académie des Sciences, Lettres et Arts, 1971), 74.

8. Quoted in Yvonne Knibiehler and Catherine Fouquet, *Histoire des mères* (Paris: Montalba, 1977), 156.

9. Knibiehler and Fouquet, *Histoire des mères,* 156.

10. Letter to Jean-Pierre Brissot de Warville, January 7, 1791, *Lettres de Madame Roland,* ed. Claude Perroud (Paris: Imprimerie nationale, 1902) 2:216.

11. Quoted in Levy, Applewhite, and Johnson, eds., *Women in Revolutionary Paris,* 76.

12. *Réglement de la Société Citoyennes Républicaines Révolutionnaires de Paris,* quoted in Levy, Applewhite, and Johnson, eds., *Women in Revolutionary Paris,* 161.

13. André Amar, quoted in *Moniteur,* XVIII, Séance du 9 brumaire, quoted in Duhet, *Les femmes et la révolution,* 156.

14. Timothy Tackett, "Women and Men in Counterrevolution: The Sommières Riot of 1791," *Journal of Modern History* (December, 1987), n. 30.

15. "Adresse à la Nation Belgique," quoted in Janet L. Polasky, "Women in Revolutionary Belgium: From Stone Throwers to Hearth Tenders," *History Workshop,* 21 (Spring, 1986): 90.

16. Mary Wollstonecraft, *An Historical and Moral View of the Origins and Progress of the French Revolution and the Effect It Has Produced* (London: J. Johnson, 1794), 19.

17. Mary Wollstonecraft to Gilbert Imlay, letter of June 12, 1795, in Ralph M. Wardle, *Collected Letters of Mary Wollstonecraft* (Ithaca, N. Y.: Cornell University Press, 1979), 291.

18. Quoted in Ruth Dawson, " 'And this shield is called self-reliance': Emerging Feminist Consciousness in the Late Eighteenth Century," in Ruth-Ellen B. Joeres and Mary Jo Maynes, eds., *German Women in the Eighteenth and Nineteenth Centuries* (Bloomington: Indiana University Press, 1986), 157–174.

19. Narcisse Carré, *Nouveau code des femmes* (Paris: Roret, 1828), 37.

20. F. A. Vazeille, *Traité du mariage, de la puissance maritale, et de la puissance paternelle* (Paris: l'auteur, 1825), 3.

21. Letter of J. E. M. Portalis, 6 February 1804, quoted in Lydie Schimséwitsch, *Portalis et son temps* (Paris: Presses modernes, 1936), 71.

22. *Lucinde,* quoted in Henri Brunschwig, *Enlightenment and Romanticism in Eighteenth-Century Prussia* (Chicago: University of Chicago Press, 1974), 237.

23. Cited in Mary Alden Hopkins, *Hannah More and Her Circle* (New York: Longmans, 1947), 206–208.

24. Quoted in Duhet, *Les femmes et la Révolution,* 206.

25. Cited in Anaïs Bassanville, *Les salons d'autrefois,* 4 vols. (Paris: Brunet, 1862), 1:1.

SOURCES AND SUGGESTED READING

Abray, Jane. "Feminism in the French Revolution," *American Historical Review* (1975).

Bianquis, Genevieve. *Amours en allemagne a l'époque romantique* (1961).

———. *La vie quotidienne en allemagne à l'époque romantique (1795–1830)* (1958).

Brinton, Crane. *French Revolutionary Legislation on Illegitimacy, 1789–1804* (1936).

Duhet, Paule-Marie. *Les femmes et la révolution 1789–1794* (1971).

Ferguson, Moira and Janet Todd. *Mary Wollstonecraft* (1984).

George, Margaret. "The 'World Historical Defeat' of the Républicaines-Révolutionnaires," *Science and Society* (1976–1977).

Gutwirth, Madeleine. *Madame de Staël* (1978). A literary study.

Hufton, Olwen, "Women in Revolution, 1789–1796," *Past and Present* (1971).

Kerber, Linda, *Women of the Republic: Intellect and Ideology in Revolutionary America* (1980). A sophisticated exploration of law and ideology in the revolutionary period.

Levy, Darline Gay, Harriet B. Applewhite, and Mary D. Johnson, eds. *Women in Revolutionary Paris, 1789–1795* (1979). A rich documentary source.

Norton, Mary Beth. *Liberty's Daughters. The Revolutionary Experience of American Women* (1980). An exciting portrayal of the ways in which women participated in revolutionary life.

Polasky, Janet. "Women in Revolutionary Belgium: From Stone Throwers to Hearth Tenders," *History Workshop* (1986). The movement of women into and away from revolutionary activity.

Rendall, Jane. *The Origins of Modern Feminism: Women in Britain, France and the United States* (1984). A major analytical and comparative study.

Tomalin, Claire. *The Life and Death of Mary Wollstonecraft* (1975).

Traer, James. *Marriage and the Family in Eighteenth-Century France* (1980). An important survey of revolutionary legislation and institutions.

PART

II

Work and Domesticity in Industrializing Europe 1815–1875

The nineteenth century has conventionally meant a world opened up to industrial change. Textile mills, railroads, and blast furnaces are some of its symbols, along with the drive to innovate and make money. Promoting ideas of individualism and progress, the age of revolution had paved the way for these stunning developments that make up the Industrial Revolution.

The Industrial Revolution, an ongoing process rather than an instant change, meant factory work and new patterns of labor for many men. Some women entered textile factories and those producing textilelike materials such as paper. Most, however, did not spend their work lives in factories. To the contrary, the Industrial Revolution promoted widespread home manufacturing and a continuation of labor segregation. The seamstress, the laundress, the porcelain painter, the straw plaiter—these were the common types of woman worker.

During the course of the century a great divide opened between those women who worked and those in the respectable middle class who did not. In place of the aristocratic woman and her pleasures, the middle-class woman developed the culture of domesticity resting on her household and family. The comforts of this way of life depended on servants and more abundant goods. But domesticity also involved an array of rituals such as charity work and upper-class etiquette that were closed off to working women. The high culture of the theater attracted the wealthy, whereas working-class women enjoyed a neighborhood culture of their own. Separated in new ways, both played their part in the intense urbanization then in progress, and both contributed to the lively life of the nineteenth-century city.

135

Industrialization and urbanization produced tensions, inequities, and anxiety, while also making for experimentation and adventure. Dislocated and impoverished, many urban newcomers lived in the utmost misery. Many kept alive the language and dreams of revolutionary Europe in an ongoing series of strikes, political movements, and new waves of revolution. Filled with ambition for liberty, working women started political groups of their own and engaged in political struggle. Simultaneously, middle-class women began organizing a mass feminist movement to obtain education, property and marital rights, and the vote. If the Industrial Revolution brought change to women's lives, we must look for that change less in the factory than in the home and the small shop. For political activity we look to street action and to the middle-class groups that first met in parlors before taking on Parliaments.

Time Line

- **1814** Eleanora d'Albedyhll publishes *Gefion*
- **1816** Sophie Germain wins Académie Française prize for her study of the mathematics of elastic surfaces
- **1818** Mary Shelley publishes *Frankenstein*
- **1819** Peterloo massacres in England
- **1830** French Revolution of 1830 and the founding of the July Monarchy
- **early 1830s** St. Simonian women active in Paris
- **1832** Amalie Sieveking founds the Female Association for the Care of the Poor and Sick in Hamburg

  George Sand publishes *Indiana*

  Great Reform Bill in England
- **late 1830s–1848** Chartist movement in Great Britain
- **1837** Queen Victoria assumes British throne
- **1839** Infant Custody Act in England
- **1842** Annette von Droste-Hulshoff publishes *Die Judenbuche*
- **1844** Vulcanization of rubber introduces possibility of more reliable contraception
- **1845** Božena Nemcová publishes *Granny*
- **1847** Emily Brontë publishes *Wuthering Heights;* Charlotte Brontë, *Jane Eyre*
- **1848** Revolutions erupt across the continent

  Queens College founded in England

  Newspaper *Voix des femmes* founded in Paris
- **1849** Louise Otto-Peters founds the *Frauenzeitung*
- **1854** Crimean War begins in which Florence Nightingale works toward modern nursing
- **1850s** Sewing machine becomes a consumer commodity
- **1857** Matrimonial Causes Act reforms divorce in England
- **1861** Alexander I frees the Russian serfs
- **1864** First Contagious Diseases Act passed in England, others in 1866 and 1869
- **1860s** Women begin attending medical schools in Switzerland and France
- **1865** All German Women's Union founded in Berlin
- **1866** Lette Society founded in Leipzig
- **1868** Alaide Gualberta Beccari founds *La Donna*
- **1869** John Stuart Mill publishes *On the Subjection of Women*

  Girton College founded
- **1870** Franco-Prussian War begins
- **1871** Women join in the formation of the Paris Commune
- **1871–1872** George Eliot publishes *Middlemarch*

The Rise of the Woman Worker:
The Early Years

The Working
Woman
Early in the nineteenth century, visitors to the Norwegian coast noticed an interesting phenomenon. In the countryside around port towns, men took care of the children and also tended barnyard animals. Decades later, German officials surveying work habits in the Oberlausitz region near the Polish border charted domestic chores that were performed routinely by men. What might be called a role reversal was not unusual in agricultural Europe at this time. While their husbands cooked, cleaned, and sometimes did the dairying, women were weaving, spinning, and sometimes trading in cloth. In the county of Hedemark in Norway, women produced 86 tons of linen cloth in 1804. In Sjudaradsbygden, Sweden, women had dropped linen production by mid-century for a brisk business in cotton, much of it going to local or regional markets. Four-fifths of the exporters of domestic textiles in the province of Turka in Finland were women from the lower classes, struggling against debt and the uncertainty of future orders to support their families. The increase in manufacturing and trade drew rural women to the production of textiles, sometimes to the exclusion of other endeavors. At the same time, more men competed for agricultural employment, and few found jobs readily in winter. Thus, a role reversal took place to some extent, and seemed unusual in a time when what was masculine and what was feminine was clearly defined.

"The woman worker, what a blasphemous word!"[1] So wrote French intellectual Jules Michelet, voicing the growing sentiment among the nineteenth century bourgeoisie that women ought not to be defiled by work. Women of the lower classes, however, needed to work to survive and did so in greater numbers than ever before. In fact, like the women in rural Norway, most did jobs for others and received pay instead of creating subsistence goods for their families. That is, they became more "workerly." Moreover, the range of women's work increased as factories dotted both urban and rural landscapes. Textile factories, factories for paper products, and later food-processing plants all attracted those in need of jobs. Cities also offered opportunities for employment, especially to those who found life on the farm too demanding or not reliable enough in providing regular work. Then there were women who combined a variety of tasks—countryside in the summer and factory in the winter.

The intense work life of women collided with attitudes such as those expressed by Michelet. The sense that working women were somehow unnatural, that they polluted society, and that they contributed to social disorder nonetheless gained ground. Republican ideas, enshrined by the French Revolution, affected the respectability of their productive activities. In this atmosphere of disapproval women tried to support themselves and their families.

Women's Work in the Nineteenth Century

The Changing Countryside

With the increased demand for commodities, jobs in rural manufacturing multiplied for farm people. Generally, women made textiles in their homes, either spinning or weaving for merchants as they had done a century earlier. Only the volume changed. From England to Russia women remained deeply absorbed in keeping their families alive, though now primarily through cottage industry. Local specialties existed, for example, women of the Hungarian *zadruga* often did straw-plaiting and embroidery. Around Moscow, many women made lace. According to 1861 figures, in Buckinghamshire, England, close to 3,000 women did straw-plaiting and more than 8,000 made lace. Embroidering, glove-making, needle-making, cigar-box-making, knitting, and a whole host of other crafts flourished in the countryside. Some women worked year round in these occupations, but others alternated such work with harvesting, domestic service in the household of a local landlord, and even work in factories. In many cases, a woman's chances for marriage depended on her having a marketable skill. In Denmark, where pot-making employed many women, people would say about a marriageable woman "she has no money, but she's good at clay."[2] Where once a rural woman might have had as a dowry a bit of land or a few animals, the reduction in common land and the consolidation of large commercial farms made this much less likely for the average woman. Instead, a reputation for hard work and dexterity replaced these tangible goods.

Rural enterprise changed the rhythm and scope of life. For example, this is a description of the routine of a Danish potter: "A pot-girl gets together with a man, with whom she makes an agreement that each gets half of what the pots are sold for, this is called 'sitting halves.' She makes the pots and fires them, but he provides the fuel for the kiln; he also provides her food, collects the clay out of the fields, and takes the pots to market. . . . A woman and a girl helping her could make about 12 or 14 wagonloads of pots in a summer."[3] Note that the Danish potter worked with someone outside her family; the girl who helped also might be a stranger. In addition, the potter calculated in terms of abundant production rather than in terms of enough for subsistence. Even

*In this early textile mill, the machines are arranged in regular order. The women op-
erators seem less orderly in their movements and spacing, especially in comparison to
later factory scenes.*

though these women lived in small villages, they had almost given up older
rural ways and were creating new ones. For example, constant activity at one
job narrowed the variety of skills rural women had, although it probably made
them far better at their specialties. The eighteenth-century rural woman mixed
farm, domestic, and manufacturing tasks, but a hundred years later rural people, like the Norwegian textile workers or the women weavers in the Oberlausitz, often did hardly anything but this kind of "outwork."

At the same time, farmers who had kept their lands and enlarged them
prospered from the rapid population increase and the growth of cities. More
people than ever needed to be fed, and many farmers thrived. In eastern Prussia, for example, the opportunity for commercial profit in farming led to the
reclamation of marginal lands. In France, where the Revolution had established peasant farmers' ownership of property, the mid–nineteenth century
constituted a successful time for those with sufficient amounts of land. Because
mechanization had not yet set in, intensive farming of marketable produce
demanded high levels of human labor and skill, particularly at harvest time.
Great teams of landless workers hired themselves out to harvest wheat. Paid
by piece rates, women could sometimes make as much as men, though usually
they worked as helpers to their husbands. Although women's gleaning rights
often disappeared in the wake of tough agricultural management, some women
did do field work for pay. In Sussex, England, the wife of a shepherd, Alice C.
Day, described her work as a harvester: "After an early breakfast, I used to

start with my children for one of the Hall fields, carrying our dinner with us. Even the toddlers could help by twisting the straw into bands and also by helping me tie up my sheaves. Many is the time that my husband came round to us when his own day's work was done, and we worked together setting up the shocks by moonlight."[4]

Because specialization increased profit, farms tended to concentrate in one crop, often to the detriment of women. Where new root crops such as the sugar beet and the potato became dominant, the onerous jobs of cultivation and weeding fell to women. Such work usually replaced barnyard responsibilities and dairying since many pasture lands had been converted to crop fields. Some kinds of specialization did enhance women's roles, however. In the 1830s and 1840s, Danish farmers had already turned their attention to commercial dairying. Until the development of factories for processing dairy products late in the century, dairymaids could earn more than the average farm worker. Teams of Polish and German migrant women workers were imported to do onerous field work in their stead. Some farm women became entrepreneurial themselves. Hanne Nielsen (1829–1903) traveled throughout Europe comparing cheeses to those produced on her farm. Unlettered, she gave as her formula for success "I see and I taste."[5] Her lasting contribution was Havarti cheese, named after the dairy she ran.

Where landed types such as Hanne Nielsen prospered, the old complementarity of the subsistence family flourished as well. This was not necessarily the case for the average rural woman, particularly in Eastern Europe. The increasing tendency of landlords to force their peasants to cultivate only a single market crop—sugar beets, for example—meant oppression for rural people who lacked even rudimentary civil rights. They also experienced both the continuing loss of common lands and forced labor for noble families, sometimes four days a week, and during harvest, for several solid weeks on end. Thus, they could not take advantage of opportunities town markets might have offered. Where most of the land was given over to the production of grain, the number of livestock that could be kept diminished, as did space available for household gardens. Itinerant food-sellers and village bakers provisioned families, and nutrition declined accordingly. Thus, in areas where job opportunities declined in the traditional areas and no new opportunities for work replaced them, women lost the wherewithal to sustain themselves and their families. Some did try to protect themselves: "My grandmother," one Rumanian recalled, "used to go to work for the noble family wearing huge leggings under her skirt, and while she worked she would stick grain into her leggings through a pocket, then three or four times a day she'd say she had to go home to feed her kids, and she'd empty those leggings so she could fill them up again."[6] Where such opportunity did not exist or where no outwork was available as an alternative to starvation, migration was the only answer. Migration to cities increased greatly in the nineteenth century, first in Western Europe where the rural population was legally free to move.

In contrast, serfdom persisted in most of Eastern Europe until mid-century: it ended in 1848 in the Austrian Empire and in Russia in 1861. Only with permission from the entire community could an individual leave. In extended families (the *zadruga*), migration to a city required the patriarch's consent. The first waves of migration after Russian serfdom ended predominantly involved men, who sent their wages back home. Left behind, women had to perform even more arduous labor than before because they replaced their husbands and brothers in the fields while continuing to carry out all the normal household chores. At the height of the harvest season, the strain of overwork often made women stop menstruating temporarily. This combination of absent, wage-earning men and women doing the farmwork did lead to some positive results, however. For one thing, the incidence of wife-beating greatly decreased. For another, women gained a measure of self-confidence from making independent contributions of a substantial nature to the family economy. Finally, observers noted that, in contrast to exclusively agricultural ones, households with such a mixed economy prospered: "Peasants no longer sleep on the stove or on planking between the stove and the ceiling . . . , but in separate beds with cotton curtains."[7]

In some areas, more intensive farming also encouraged a rising rate of illegitimacy. In the kingdom of Bavaria and the duchy of Styria, in Austria, for example, the number of illegitimate children soared from the beginning of the nineteenth century. Whereas the English rate of illegitimacy was 5 percent, Styria, where unused land was being newly farmed, had a ratio of 11.2 percent at the beginning of the nineteenth century and 27.8 percent in 1870. Rather than being simply a sign of the disintegration of village morals, rising illegitimacy was at least in part a response to the demands of agriculture. Certain areas faced the problem of labor shortages due to migration. Upper Styria, for example, was close to iron enterprises to which young men flocked for higher pay. Women with illegitimate children in such an area were sure of finding employment for themselves and their offspring because farmers were faced with an undersupply of workers. Villagers turned a deaf ear to rumors of illegitimacy that in other times might have spawned a charivari.

The rural scene in an age of industrialization was thus a mixture of new and arduous tasks, of poorer standards of living for many people, and of opportunities and ways of sexual behavior that differed from those of subsistence economies. The new ways did not completely supersede the old—traveling through Europe one might find both old ways of doing agricultural chores and new methods pushing out traditional ones. For many, however, the former complementarity of tasks had given way to a need for cooperation in generating income.

The Economy of Urban Life

Women and men crowded into cities throughout the nineteenth century, although not until the end of the century did a majority of Western Europe's population become more urban than rural. The great demographic spurt that had begun in the eighteenth century continued. In the German states as a whole, the population increased by more than 25 percent in the two decades before 1850. The population of England went from more than 8.5 million to over 13.25 million in the first three decades of the century. Such increases affected the cities more dramatically than the countryside. Large and small cities sometimes doubled or tripled in size. In the single decade of the 1830s, London added 130,000 to its population. Although many cities in Italy declined in population in the commercial age, the industrializing city of Turin grew from 86,000 in 1800 to 137,000 by 1850, and over 200,000 a decade later.

The nineteenth-century city pulsed with the same excitement as its eighteenth-century counterpart had. The growth of commerce and industry made cities magnets, particularly for single women and men. Once established, these new urban dwellers would send word back to cousins, siblings, and other relatives. Where agriculture was declining or tenuous, the pull of the city proved irresistible. Rag-pickers, fortunetellers, gypsies, street musicians, scissor grinders, actors, doctors, porters, thieves, and collectors of human excrement crowded in. "A wilderness of human beings" was how one young person remembered London in the 1820s.[8] Where industry dominated, migrants to the city could find work in mills. In new industrial towns, of every ten women working full time, as many as seven or eight were employed outside of factories. Those commercial and capital cities that had less to offer in the way of purely industrial work still had opportunities for employment in the crafts, in domestic service, and in a growing array of odd jobs such as laundering, cleaning, and selling.

Some aspects of the urban economy carried over from the eighteenth into the beginning of the nineteenth century. Market people remained a part of the population of towns and cities, as did such craftspeople as shoemakers, furniture-makers, goldsmiths, metal-workers, and tailors. The practice of a craft, however, had undergone a fundamental change, which affected women's role. The craftsworker's family still existed as a unit in which women might help in production. Craftsworkers as a group, however, were starting to lose control of their enterprises as the process of making any single item was divided into subprocesses.

During the century-long conflict culminating in the Napoleonic wars, governments needed cheap goods in quantity to supply their armies. One method they finally found was to subcontract the various operations that went into manufacturing a product. For example, shoemaking was broken down into cutting, sewing uppers to the sole, putting in eyelets, and so on. As guild structures disintegrated or were abolished, this type of system resulted in control of production being shifted to a middleman instead of a master craftsman. Ultimately known as a "sweater," this person gave the simpler tasks to the fairly unskilled and the more difficult aspects of making an item to the more skilled. Sweaters found in women the perfect employees for piecework. In the shoemaking process for example, women put in eyelets or did final polishing at home. In metal-working, furniture-making, and candlestick production, the last steps of applying finishes and polishing were often done by old people and women working in their homes. The same was true for tailoring, in which women did ordinary stitching, and the tailor then reclaimed the garments for the more intricate final steps.

Even though many production processes were divided, the men did not always do the most skilled work: in tailoring, men did the more complex work, but in furniture-making, women often did. Women also did porcelain painting at home and other kinds of design work on dishes, buttons, or pottery cast in the countryside.

The division of labor provided more job opportunities, even if poorer ones, for the unskilled. Newcomers, especially those from rural areas, could not fit easily into the established holistic practice of urban crafts. They arrived without specialized skills for manufacturing and without a trade. Moreover, in this age of migration, people hardly knew from one month to the next where they might be. Thus, piecework and jobs consisting of a single, easily learned process integrated the migrant more quickly into the urban workforce and allowed him or her to move from one job to another. The division of labor did mean that symbiosis in production had given way to a new relationship. A woman often practiced a type of craftwork entirely dissimilar from what her husband did. For example, someone in shoemaking might be married to someone in hatmaking. As the work of the artisan disappeared, men found other types of jobs, particularly in transporting goods, working on docks, or building the new buildings necessary to accommodate a booming population and a world of trade. Thus, men and women practiced the same trade less and less often, and their working lives meshed in fewer ways. It remained important nonetheless that each provide for his or her own sustenance and contribute to the family economy, which was becoming a wage or worker economy rather than a subsistence one.

The decline of artisanal families and the rural exodus made women a glut on the urban labor market. The cities abounded with women workers looking for subsistence. Lacking anything but domestic skills, these women drove down the price in the fields they entered. Nonetheless, it was still expected that women would continue to make their traditional contribution to the family economy even as the possibility for making such a contribution diminished. Many women had to struggle to find work lives that would allow them to make their necessary contribution. Occasionally a girl of twelve to fourteen would be given an apprenticeship by her parents. These young teenagers went into fancy dressmaking, millinery, or bookbinding—to name a few examples. Few parents, however, put money into such training for girls. Many women worked in sewing, both before and after marriage. Others further developed household activities into paying jobs. Sewing or garment-making and domestic service were the most common occupations, with cleaning and laundering close behind. All these occupations were flexible, but were devalued in terms of pay for that very reason.

Sewing

Sewing provided work for millions of women in the nineteenth century. Textiles came rolling off household looms and out of the new textile mills. The mechanization of production made possible more complicated household linens, more intricate and abundant clothing, and more quickly changing fashions. For example, as cotton became more common, its lightness made it appealing in the summer as a replacement for wool and linen. Also, people began wearing underwear as a result of cotton's cheapness, suitability, and ease of care. Moreover, some people stopped making all their clothing at home, preferring instead to purchase standard-sized, ready-made garments. As a result, the demand for needlewomen mushroomed.

The needle trades offered some variety in the level of skill required, the pay, and the conditions of work. At the top, a woman could, for instance, own an exclusive millinery or couturière establishment in a capital city. Patronized by the wealthy and powerful, an owner of such a shop might employ dozens of workers and apprentices. Such a position was rare, but proprietors, showroom people, and those in charge of the ordinary needlewomen in prominent dressmaking firms made a good living. Most women fell at the other extreme, sewing for a middleman at home or for an employer in a workshop. This kind of work meant the worst kind of exploitation. Although embroiderers and those who did very ornate or very complicated needlework fared better, the girls and women who made waistcoats, shirts, and other ordinary apparel barely earned enough to stay alive. Working at home, they spent much extra time fetching and delivering goods, cleaning and pressing, and buying thread, needles, and other equipment. Moreover, the piece rates they earned did not take into account their expenses for supplies or for light and heat used at home. Because married women needed the income from work so much yet needed to work at home so that they might care for their children at the same time, they were unable to secure better wages. Women working at home had the added disadvantage of being isolated from other workers with whom they might have gotten together to make demands more forcefully. Those in workshops, however, were treated no better by their employers, working long hours and even all night when necessary, but few or no hours if business was slow. Thus, besides making a third or less of what a typical male worker made, a seamstress also had to expect no work for five or so months a year. In the so-called dead periods, after seasonal clothing had been made and purchased, almost all needlewomen suffered unemployment. At these times, more than any other, women drove each other's wages down even further by competing for the small amount of remaining work.

In the 1850s, the American Singer sewing machine began appearing in European homes. Those who earned money by sewing at home realized they had to have new machines to meet competition from factories and workshops. Having a sewing machine at home seemed a sensible thing to do because it could be used for both paid and domestic work. Late in the century, a Transylvanian peasant woman bought a sewing machine using money she had accumulated to buy a bit of land. She figured the machine would be more profitable. Yet some historians maintain that the sewing machine meant further impoverishment of homeworkers. In Germany, for example, only 25 percent of the seamstresses with a machine earned more than 7 marks per week. The average cost of maintaining a single woman worker was 6.35 marks at the time, so most women would not be able to keep up a minimum standard of

Sweated Labor in London

Henry Mayhew was an English journalist determined to investigate the lives of the poor. From his first columns on working-class life in London he became known for the way he reported his subjects' verbatim accounts of their lives. This excerpt written in 1849 was part of a series describing "slopwork" or "sweated" labor. Getting their work from a "sweater," women could work at home and also keep track of their family's well-being. By the time Mayhew did his reporting, however, all informants noted that their pay was declining whereas "sweaters" themselves seemed to earn more and more.

I do the "looping." The looping consists in putting on the lace work down the front of the coats. I puts it on. That's my living; I wish it was not. I get 5d. for the looping of each coat; that's the regular price. It's three hours' work to do one coat, and work fast to do it as it's done now. I'm a particular quick hand. I have to find my own thread. It costs 1½d. for a reel of cotton; that will do five coats. If I sit down between eight and nine in the morning, and work till twelve at night—I never enters my bed afore—and then rise between eight and nine again (that's the time I sit down to work on account of doing my own affairs first), and then work on till eleven, I get my four coats done by that time, and some wouldn't get done till two. It's an hour's work going and coming, and waiting to be served at the piece-master's, so that at them long hours it takes me a day and a half hard work to get four coats looped. When I first touched this work I could do eight in the same time, and be paid better; I had 7d. then instead of 5d.; now the work in each is nearly double in quantity, that it is.

I've got two boys both at work, one about fifteen, earning 3s. per week, and I have got him to keep and clothe. The week before last I bought him a top coat—it cost me 6s.—for fear he should be laid up, for he's such bad health. The other boy is eighteen years, and earns 9s. a week. He's been in work about four months, and was out six weeks. At the same time I had no work. Oh, it was awful then! I have been paying 1s. 6d. a week off a debt for bread and things I was obliged to get on credit then.

My last boy is only nine years of age, and him I have entirely to keep. He goes to the charity school. It lets him have one coat and trousers and shoes and stockings every year. He wears a pinafore now to save his coat. My eldest boy is like a hearty man to every meal. If he hadn't got me to manage for him, may be he'd spend all his earnings in mere food. I get my

second bread, and I go as far as Nassau-street to save two or
three halfpence. Butter we *never* have. A roast of meat none
of us ever sees. A cup of tea, a piece of bread, and an onion,
is generally all I have for my dinner, and sometimes I haven't
even an onion.

Source: Adapted from Henry Mayhew, *The Morning Chronicle Survey of Labour and the Poor: The Metropolitan Districts* (Sussex: Caliban, 1980) I: 157–159.

living and pay the 1.50 marks weekly to buy a machine on time. At the same
time, piece rates declined precipitously with the introduction of the sewing
machine. Those not able to purchase a machine had to continue doing hand
sewing and therefore had an even harder time earning a living than the average
seamstress did.

For men, skill in operating new machines in factories led to increased
wages during the Industrial Revolution. For women, however, such skill usually meant little improvement, if any. Stuffed in inadequte flats, these workers
gained little benefit from technological change and probably saw their standard of living decline because of it. From being a respected male occupation
long before the Industrial Revolution, needlework had generally become a female occupation and had lost its capacity to sustain many of its workers—no
matter how hard they worked.

Cooking and Cleaning Commercialized

Domestic tasks made into commercial ones supported many wives and widows. Some women went out to do cleaning as many times a week as necessary
to get sufficient income. Others competed with delicatessens by cooking at
home and selling their food on the streets. Still others took in washing from
working couples or utilized their domestic skills in a variety of ways.

Laundering, an occupation that employed many women in the nineteenth
century, is a good example of the flexible kind of work that women with casually or seasonally employed partners needed. Women could work part-time
in laundries, as daily laundrywomen in the homes of their clients, or full-time
or part-time in their own homes. Laundering also followed seasonal patterns
and in some cases was migratory work. In England, some laundresses followed
their clients to vacation areas, moved to university towns during the academic
term, or went into the countryside to work for those doing fruit-picking, hop-
picking, or other kinds of harvesting. Doing other people's laundry in the home
often involved the entire family. Children gathered soiled articles from customers, and husbands sometimes helped by hauling water or wringing clothes.
Wet clothes filled all available space in small urban apartments, as did heat
and humidity from the process of hand laundering. In northern countries, laun-

dering could take several days because of dampness and cold. To get clothes clean in this unautomated process, the laundress had to soak and boil them. Washing clothes also involved many procedures such as blueing and starching that are hardly used today. Most of these steps amounted to unskilled but arduous work. After laundering came the more skilled task of ironing, which demanded attention in choosing the right type of iron and how hot it should be as it came from the fire. Fancy ironing even required a short apprenticeship, because mistakes ruined garments. Ironing clothing that had lace, fine fabric, ruffles, or pleats needed particular skill.

Among women who made a living from the commercialization of domestic skills, an occasional success story emerges. One example is that of Lucy Miller and her daughter, who started their laundering career in 1850 in Brighton. More than a hundred years later, their firm employed 200 people. Such triumphs, however, were scarce. Women's work seldom served to make them rich; it usually only prevented them from starving. The very need that drove women to work kept their wages low. Because the work they did served households and people rather than transport or industry, it was ill paid even though arduous.

Domestic Service

Young rural women or those moving from town to town would often put themselves into the service of the urban middle class, who increasingly wanted their needs taken care of by others. To members of the wandering female population, the middle-class home seemed a repository of both virtue and stability. As service was in the process of being transformed into a less masculine occupation, the bourgeois home offered fewer ceremonial positions. By the nineteenth century employers clearly associated domestic service with work. In the 1860s one-third of all young women aged fifteen to twenty-four in London were servants and in mid-century Paris there were 111,000 domestics. Yet only miniscule numbers of those serving as domestics in large cities had been born there. Clearly, migrants to urban areas looked to service as a means of support. With rhythms resembling those of the rural life they had left, the middle-class household seemed more familiar and more welcoming to many young women than a workshop or factory.

The average servant worked from twelve to eighteen hours a day, with one day off a month—if the family adhered to that particular custom. Because most households that employed servants only had one or two, each servant performed a wide variety of chores. Usually rising about five, she prepared fires, polished shoes, cleaned stoops and steps, and then awakened and helped her employers. From then on, her chores involved shopping, cooking, cleaning, and possibly child care. The middle-class home had access to few ready-made goods, except men's clothing, so servants preserved fruit, made liquors, and killed and plucked animals. They also blackened stoves, cleaned grates, and trapped mice, rats, and other pests. Their work had virtually no limit because there were no regular hours. Clearly defined as being apart from the family, servants slept in attics or cellars, and in the former case sometimes had little more than a ladder to reach their beds. Before the rebuilding of cities and the expansion into suburbs, the urban middle-class family was hard-pressed for space and paid dearly for what it had. The servant's standard of living was the first to be affected by this scarcity. Although members of the middle class may have talked about morality, their treatment of servants was not affected: they crowded servants, forced them to share beds, and provided them with little in the way of heat, light, or human sociability.

In spite of the hardships, people remained domestics because the standard of living they obtained in service was higher than that for most other occupations. Servants earned a meager wage, which was often saved up for them until their departure, but they also received room and board. The quality of what was provided varied, but it could be quite good and, in many cases, was at least better than what the struggling rural family, the seamstress, or the casually employed had. Servants also were clothed, sometimes cared for if sick, and received other fringe benefits. In addition, as in the previous century, service was a clear road to upward mobility. In the mid–nineteenth century, servants married later than the average working woman. They thus limited their fertility and accumulated a dowry—both factors that allowed them to improve their social position. Living with the middle class, servants were in general more literate than the working population and often acquired other skills that permitted them to get better jobs. Finally, a high percentage of servants married above their social origins into the lower-middle, or shopkeeping, class. In short, a servant who succeeded in her job was likely to move up a bit in the world because of it.

Service in many ways carried forward the old moral economy into a world of new values. Not bound to the clock or the machine as in a factory, servants worked in the household space doing tasks that people had been doing for centuries. Their work hours, like those in an older way of life, lasted as long as the work did. No factory whistle or bell regulated the end of their day. Nor was their remuneration fixed by the hour. Even though the monthly or yearly salary might be rather small, it was supplemented by gifts, tips, worn clothing, and various payments for any number of reasons, such as the expenses for the burial of a parent. A servant also had a degree of social life not allowed to factory workers. She could talk to people while shopping, gossip with servants in adjacent buildings, and socialize with delivery people. Her everyday life thus had a measure of diversity. Although servants had to face whimsical or cruel employers sometimes, their work had little to do with making profit. The servant continued to produce only use value for the household, nothing for exchange. Like servants of old, the nineteenth-century servant also provided status for the family that engaged her. Because the upper-middle-class woman led an increasingly leisurely life, the servant furnished a reverse image, emphasizing her employer's removal from productive activity, her separation from the economic sphere, and her sole function of bearing children. Like servants of

earlier centuries, whose numbers and liveries added to the powerful appearance of their aristocratic employers, the nineteenth-century female servant still
created an aura for the middle-class woman.

Prostitution

Prostitution offered women yet another way of making a living. Observers in
the nineteenth century counted prostitutes in major European cities in the tens
of thousands and declared the number continually on the rise. Prostitution
supplied the money needed by many migrants to the city. Working at jobs
paying less than a subsistence wage, some women made prostitution an occasional occupation in those times when their wages failed to feed them or when
unemployed. Many seamstresses, for example, resorted to prostitution in the
slow season. Migrant women were particularly likely to support themselves by
prostitution. Far away from familial or community control or help, they took
up the occupation or were lured into it. Servants seduced by masters or women
impregnated and then abandoned by their lovers found their only recourse in
prostitution. Indeed the majority of prostitutes fit the profile of a single young
woman from the outlying areas of a city, whereas others were the daughters of
urban artisans in declining trades. Far from having an irregular background,
prostitutes were rarely illegitimate or from the very poorest families.

Desperation was hardly the only motive for becoming a prostitute. Some
women found that prostitution paid relatively well and was thus a way to
achieve an acceptable standard of living. Able to make in a single night the
normal wages of a week, these women exchanged sex for small improvements,
tiny pleasures, and at least temporary ease. A traveler in Sweden noted that
prostitutes there "preserved some decency" because they also worked "as
seamstresses, or servants, or shopwomen."[9] Not only in Sweden but everywhere, some city women exchanged sexual favors for meals, nights out, or
gifts. Wives who were unable to make a sufficient contribution to the family
economy in other ways sometimes tried prostitution. Just as the lack of property and job opportunities drove middle-class women to marriage, so low
wages drove working-class women to selling sex as the only way of improving
their situation. Once in prostitution, they sometimes found it a tolerable "life"
and one with an interesting culture of its own.

Women who dealt in commercial sex did so to different extents, beginning

---

Regulating Prostitution in Vienna

The modernizing state focused on prostitution in the nineteenth century. Defining, regulating, treating, and punishing prostitutes employed lawmakers, lawyers, police, doctors, and many other lower

public officials. The process of regulating prostitution also affected prostitutes and in less obvious ways many other members of society. Prostitution, as defined in regulations like those that follow, set behavioral boundaries and also marked off who would have the right to judicial processes. As this excerpt shows, the police, not the judiciary, dealt with prostitutes and worked with sets of procedures and guidelines to determine their fate.

Instructions for Police Treatment of Prostitutes, 1852

1. Under the designation prostitute is understood to be every woman who seeks business by exposing her body for sale in lewdness.
2. Under what circumstances the prostitute is officially conducted to the criminal court and what penalties in all other cases remain under police jurisdiction is determined by penal law.
3. The prostitute falls into the realm of police correction when she:
    a. walks the streets, that is, she walks in such a way as to enlist business from men;
    b. loiters for the same end on doorsteps in allies or in open spaces;
    c. has her residence in a house or part of the city in which are gathered such women of a conduct similar to those of a bordello or in a region known for its lewd manners;
    d. lures people in a shameless way from a window or from an openair part of the house, or otherwise offends public decency, and not only in a criminal way.
4. Every one who is defined under these as a streetwalker and who is held in detention is subject to the following proceedings:
    a. a medical examination;
    b. an inquiry into her present situation, and
    c. her past, in order to
    d. conduct an investigation into her methods of earning a living and her personal relationships.
5. Should such a female qualify as a prostitute and be found ill, she must first of all go to the hospital or according to the circumstances to an investigatory hospital and after a successful cure further investigation will be undertaken.

Source: Excerpted from Josef Schrank, *Die Prostitution in Wien* (Wien: Genossenschafts-Buchdruckerei, 1886), 316.

with the woman who merely exchanged sex for treats or gifts. Other working women took up prostitution casually, as the need for extra income arose. Full-time prostitutes ranged from those working independently as streetwalkers to those in teams operating in boarding houses or hotels. The most organized worked in brothels, or bordellos, where they often received clothing, wages, meals, and medical care. At the top of the scale, some women were mistresses, sometimes in long-term relationships, of wealthy, prominent, or powerful men. An experienced and talented woman could also own and manage her own house of prostitution. In brothels, prostitutes developed a way of life that included special nicknames, networks for assistance, rituals for meals and recreation, and a good deal of eating and drinking. Many had someone to care for them, whether in or out of a brothel; streetwalkers came to rely on men for protection and sometimes for permanent companionship. In 1830 "pimps, some twenty in number, lying in wait" at a Parisian cafe, proceeded to attack two guards taking one of their women to the police.[10] Where prostitution was not regulated and scrutinized by medical officials working for the state, police often extorted protection money from streetwalkers and madams. In parts of Italy before government regulation, the police or their wives actually ran the houses of prostitution.

Although many prostitutes moved into more socially acceptable occupations by their late twenties, their working lives before that had elements of risk, crime, and contact with the police. Full-time prostitutes reinforced the popular association of their way of life with criminality by engaging in a variety of antisocial behaviors. They harangued passersby with vulgarities and engaged in theft, pickpocketing, and street fighting. The prostitute always appeared well represented among those arrested for small crimes and disorderly conduct. Instead of regarding prostitutes in strictly moral terms, middle-class society increasingly viewed them in terms of deviancy and criminality, and thus within the purview of the police and health officials. Although prostitutes created their own culture, their "deviant" way of life served several purposes. It marked the boundary beyond which women could not stray in their sexual lives while also absorbing the supposedly excess sexuality of "respectable" males. Thus prostitution functioned to remake definitions of male and female from the French Revolution onward.

With the urban environment changing so rapidly, the middle class suspected and feared the poor. Fear colored their view of new inhabitants and day laborers, whom they connected with all the dangers that city life seemed to hold: if disease and crime stalked the urban scene, then it was the poor who spread all these. The popular novels of the day, such as Charles Dickens's *Oliver Twist* (1837–1839) and Victor Hugo's *Les Misérables* (1862) equated working-class life with a subterranean world, particularly that of the sewers, and with the criminal element. The prostitute stood out as a symbol of danger. Recalling the old Eve myths, the middle-class believed the prostitute led men to forget themselves and submit to irrational passions, when they should be led by the rationality so honored in the industrial age. The prostitute, in their view, spread disease and threatened the lives of families, and her very existence as a single woman living beyond the confines of the home was a sign of disorder. The ultimate outcast, she served to warn other women of what unlimited sexuality meant in postrevolutionary society.

An attempt to bring order to disorderly, hypersexual women led to an array of regulations in almost every country by the 1860s. This regulation took its broad outlines from Napoleonic legislation that required prostitutes to register with the police and submit to medical inspection for sexually transmitted disease. In 1802 Napoleon had instituted a dispensary for prostitutes in order to give his soldiers maximum protection from syphilis and thus help to ensure that they would stay well enough to fulfill their duties. The system spread to other countries. In the 1850s Camillo di Cavour, premier of the Kingdom of Sardinia, also wanted to get his troops in shape before trying to unify Italy. He thus announced a stringent program, first in Sardinia and then as the law of the land when Italy unified in 1860. Cavour's program surpassed the usual inspections by regulating clothing, pay, and living conditions for prostitutes. German cities and states modeled their program after the French one, and in 1864, 1866, and 1869, the British Parliament passed the Contagious Diseases Acts. By this time roundups, registration, examination, incarceration, and treatment of prostitutes, and sometimes even any women on the streets, were regular occurrences in many cities. Most regulatory systems ignored the clients of the prostitutes, although some armies regularly inspected soldiers for disease. Instead, attention was focused on the prostitute as the source of disease and the cause of social disorder.

The regulatory system worked to reorder sexual life in tandem with the reordering of productive life. When it came to prostitution, public health officials and police inspectors were utopians aiming at achieving a perfect sexual economy by means of the regulated bordello and hygienic treatment centers, often called lock-hospitals. Their vision of prostitution as a "necessary evil" combined a moral attitude with a disciplinarian one. They believed that sexual release was necessary for men and so was a rational program to accommodate it. Reformers saw the brothel as a place to order sex, comparable to the well-planned prison, hospital, or factory. Brothel design flourished in the nineteenth century, and by 1880 almost two-thirds of Italian prostitutes worked from "closed," or officially regulated, ones. The bordello would both control its inmates' behavior through its rational design and shield the rest of society through its frosted glass windows and relegation to certain parts of cities. Regular inspection would remove disease, a frightening nightmare to those who focused not on the body as a source of pleasure as had aristocrats, but on the harmonious, fit, and disease-free middle-class body. The regulation of prostitution was in fact typical of this age. Well-planned intercourse with the body of a healthy prostitute restabilized men by releasing their excess passions. Accomplishing this also meant gaining symbolic control over the working-class woman's behavior by clearly marking out the prostitute. The worst problem, said one small town doctor, was that "her childhood friends don't fear talking to her."[11] Regulating and criminalizing prostitution ordered social life into a system of fears and pleasures.

Industrial Work

From its beginning in eighteenth-century England, the Industrial Revolution transformed the way goods were produced, where and how many were produced, and the speed with which they reached the marketplace. The first steps toward industry involved the transformation of agriculture, allowing enough food to be produced to feed an industrial workforce. By destroying the household's self-sufficiency, however, the revolution in agriculture created consumers in the countryside as well as in cities. In addition the commercial revolution had for centuries been laying the groundwork by opening up markets, establishing trade networks, and ultimately developing consumer interest on a wider scale than had ever existed before. The success of commerce in turn generated capital and an interest in profit that led to industrial ventures. Opening factories, although not so costly at first as it would become in later years, took capital that would have been lacking in a society in which sufficiency had primacy. Having amassed capital, entrepreneurs were able to provide the financial ingredients needed for the daring enterprise of opening the first factories. Such an undertaking must have seemed foolhardy to many of their peers well into the nineteenth century. The same boldness that had conquered the New World produced the factory system. Finally, once these preconditions had created the climate in which industry could make its tentative beginnings, technology came into play.

Technological innovations took hold first in the area of textile production, a realm that had traditionally belonged to women. Innovations such as the flying shuttle, the spinning jenny, the mule jenny, and steam engine revolutionized the way goods were produced. The flying shuttle, invented in the 1730s, increased the speed at which woven cloth could be produced and multiplied the demand for spun thread. Women in the countryside, in need of income for their families, responded to that demand by taking up spinning. When the spinning jenny, a machine that was capable of spinning multiple bobbins of thread, appeared in the 1760s, it signaled the start of women's relationship with an ever more sophisticated technology. Soon two more machines, the water frame and mule jenny, appeared. Run by water or steam power, these machines allowed production to move into factories. Because the spinning jenny used human power rather than a large, centralized power source, it allowed spinning to remain a domestic activity. The use of a centralized power source, however, transformed production into a socialized undertaking performed by workers concentrated in a single location. By the beginning of the nineteenth century, the textile factory had become a feature of life in some areas of Europe. Continuing their association with textiles, women began working in factories and so did men. Many families could no longer survive on farm work combined with cottage industry.

The invention and spread of machines meant that industrial production could also be immensely speeded up through a division of labor, each machine operator performing a separate, specialized task. The nature of machines, however, offered the possibility of ending the sexual division of labor. Because these machines generated more energy than any single human being's muscle power, both men and women could tend them. In fact, in the 1820s and 1830s in England, women worked at spinning and at weaving, although men tended the largest of the mule spinners because of the strength it took. Women also preserved some of their prerogatives in the weaving industry in Lancashire throughout the century and were fairly well remunerated—an elite of women industrial workers. Yet in most instances work in textiles was segregated by sex, although the segregation varied by area. In some cities, women were segregated in spinning; in others, women performed certain aspects of weaving. The sexual division of labor did vary by locality or even by factory, but almost everywhere it did exist. In almost all cases, women did the poorest paying, and often the least skilled, work, such as the preliminary tasks of cleaning raw materials, or in weaving, tenting and batting.

Division of labor based on gender made the allocation of work processes seem arbitrary. In Troyes, France, for example, the hosiery manufacturers followed guild rules that had been set when hosiery was knit on small machines at home. These rules dictated that women should not tend the machines, though obviously they had tended them when men were out doing seasonal work in the countryside. When the craft became industrialized at mid-century, women were banned by the rules from machine work of this type. They could do the preliminary task of winding spun thread on bobbins—the lowest paid and most demeaning work in the factory. At the other extreme, they also did the highly skilled reworking of dropped stitches in the finished hose. Although this task received better pay, the wages hardly reached a level commensurate with the skill demanded of the workers doing it. Some accounts show that the average female industrial worker earned about two-fifths of a man's wages. Sexual segregation of jobs allowed this sort of financial discrimination, not based on skill level but simply on gender.

Women began working in factories early in life, and many continued to do so even after marriage. In France, the 1866 census revealed that women made up 45 percent of all workers in textiles, 41 percent of all workers in rubber and paper, and 20 percent of all those in fine metalworking. The majority of women workers were young and unmarried. The Lancashire mills had girls who began working at an early age—say ten—to help their families and often to work with them. Even after the domesticity of women became a goal throughout Europe, in this area of England, between 33 and 40 percent of married women worked in the mills. Women might stop working in the mill in their late thirties or forties, when their children became old enough to contribute to the family economy. From then on, a mother's job involved keeping the rest of the family fit for work by doing washing, cooking, and generally making their work life possible. In short, because working women had familial commitments, which detracted from their definition as workers, their work life was subject to reproductive patterns. This affected the general advancement of women in industry, the skill level they might attain, and their power to negotiate conditions of work and remuneration.

Industrialists worried endlessly about making production profitable. To

Working women in Manchester had a lively street life as shown in this depiction of a second-hand clothing market.

succeed, they believed it necessary to enforce strict discipline and to work people to their utmost. Entrepreneurs had to transform rural people into industrial ones. Accustomed to performing a variety of tasks, new factory workers struggled to learn to do one repetitive task, to work by the clock and by the rhythm of the machine. The work day in factories began in the small hours of the morning, and industrialists imposed strict fines on anyone who was a minute or so late, as well as on those who talked or committed any other kind of act that seemed to detract from production. Missing a few minutes' work could mean losing a day's or even a week's wage. Such fines and restrictions served to break workers' connection with rural time, where holidays, weather, or some community event meant time off. Signs of intoxication also produced fines. The rural habit of observing "Saint Monday," when people recovered from the weekend binges, lingered on. Many in the working class used alcohol, which was often the centerpiece of sociability.

Although a gender-based division of labor had existed in agricultural work, men and women had harvested together and done other types of work in common. Factory owners attempted to channel the abundant sexual energies of young men and women into work. They did so by segregating the sexes

Coal haulers needed strength and endurance. Such women disturbed new gender ideals, while they served the rise of industry.

in as many ways as possible. In Catholic areas industrialists often engaged nuns to impose industrial discipline and to preserve sexual decorum. In textile factories and in foundries, women and men both worked wearing as little clothing as possible because the heat of the machines and the humidity necessary for manufacturing cloth was so great. Any relaxation of discipline would lead to catastrophe, so industrialists believed. In all, the discipline of the clock and the machine, the system of minimal wages and maximum fines, the rule of sexual repression, and sobriety constituted a system of forced production. Industrial workers, insofar as they acquiesced to this regime, were a new breed.

Work in foundries, in tanning, and in coal mines was dirtier and more apparently masculine than work in factories. Yet women were found at the anvil or in the pit. An estimated 6,000 women worked in English mines in the 1840s, and in Upper Silesia (now part of Poland) women constituted more than 7 percent of mineworkers. Like textile work, mining had a familial dimension. For instance, miners needed someone to haul coal, so they hired young members of their own families, more often than not girls and young women, to carry, haul, or push baskets of coal from the site to the top of the pit. With straps or chains around their bodies, they walked bent over to get as quickly as possible through the narrow, steep passages. Other young women bailed water from the pit—a task not unlike that of moving coal but less remunerative. Although girls seemed to dominate in this activity, some women moved coal when their children were still too young to work and so did coal miners' widows, suddenly left without a source of support. Because of the intense heat in the mines and the strenuous work, women wore trousers and little else. Some faced harassment because of their dress, but many received protection from family members and others fended for themselves. They worked a twelve-hour day, and often well into the night, to meet quotas for their team. Rarely earning enough to maintain themselves on their own, coal-mining women generally operated within a family economy. To outsiders, they seemed filthy and oddly dressed, denizens of a subterranean world. They attracted the attention of travelers, reformers, and moralists for looking so unlike other women. An American described Lancashire women as "plunging here and there as if engaged in some bedlamish saturnalis" (sic). Their activity had "the element of wild and awful grandeur in it."[12] An outcast from the world of virtue, the pit woman served as yet another antithesis to the proper lady. Her means of livelihood soon attracted governmental investigation.

The Structures of Everyday Urban Life

Work lives, whether in handicraft or industry, proceeded in the midst of ongoing change in the way people lived. The old community cooperation and regulation diminished, and thus, so did old ways of regulating marriage and fertility. The age of invention meant changes in the home, but also new problems and pollution in living areas. These changes, along with changing work patterns, restructured the rhythms of life. The culture growing from urban change served as a thick envelope for experience. Working women lived with their songs, sayings, and attitudes toward their complex world of work. But they also felt the heavy hand of official culture, which viewed the woman worker suspiciously and sought to remake her life.

Fertility, the Household, Health, and Poverty

As urbanization transformed Europe, so it transformed the way individuals lived. This transformation encompassed household technology, health, and poor relief, but it began with changes in marital practices and fertility. In England, the pioneer in industry, the age of marriage for women dropped from 26.2 years at the beginning of the eighteenth century to 24.9 years at the end. In the first half of the nineteenth century it plunged still further, to 23.4 years. The age for men fell accordingly. No longer relying on property to sustain them, landless urban laborers married earlier, apparently with more concern for personal feelings and attraction. Some of the urban poor lived in free unions, avoiding the legal or religious formalities of family life. To some extent religious fees and legal restrictions hampered marriage. Before 1850 in the north German city of Bremen, for example, a couple only qualified for a church wedding if they had a net worth of approximately three times the annual wage of a domestic servant. In some cases free unions appealed more to casual laborers than to industrial workers. Better paid and working in familial units, the factory family remained an interlocking productive institution for a good part of the century.

Free unions helped produce a soaring illegitimacy rate. In France it doubled in the last half of the eighteenth century. By 1816, illegitimate births in Paris were almost 40 percent of total births though they dropped to 32 percent by the mid-1850s. In Vienna there were more illegitimate than legitimate births in some years during this period. Along with free unions, economic vulnerability under the new productive system increased the risk of sexual abandonment. Whereas once communities and families had enforced the rule of marriage and fidelity, now such enforcement began to lapse. Single women congregated in cities, outside traditional community boundaries, where a different kind of sexual ethos prevailed. As noted earlier, even in rural areas the rationale for legitimacy sometimes lost its force.

Household life, whether the result of free union or of marriage, took on a distinctive form in cities. The spread of transportation systems—first canals, then railroads—and the invention of new products combined to bring innovations to daily life. Towns now enjoyed easier connections with other towns and cities, from which inhabitants received new products. A major change involved the substitution of coal for wood, twigs, dung, and other primitive heating materials. Wherever coal was introduced, the household economy changed, for heat became a purchased commodity rather than something procured directly by household labor. By the mid–nineteenth century, Europeans used more efficient stoves, sometimes freestanding and sometimes in the form of inserts in their fireplaces. The stove eliminated the cauldron and made baking at home easier. Reducing some of the hazards of open-fire cooking, the stove raised the standards for everyday cooking as well as increasing the efficiency of heating. With this improvement in cooking methods, however, came a need for more complicated cleaning procedures, including scraping out the flues, degreasing the surfaces, and blackening. All these procedures constituted a daily ritual in nineteenth-century households with stoves. Procedures for other household tasks changed as well. By mid-century, well-to-do city dwellers were starting to get piped water in their residences, while the poor had readier access to public water supplies. Although an increase in commodities meant more things to clean, cleaning supplies improved through new methods of obtaining washing soda and new soapmaking techniques. Dozens of types of irons and innovations in washing procedures allowed nineteenth-century people to attain new levels of personal cleanliness. At the same time, the Industrial Revolution created more dirt in both mining towns and industrial cities, where soot and other kinds of pollutants blackened windows, household linen, and clothing.

Such innovations made household work less dangerous and each procedure less onerous, but they also made for more work in general. The sewing machine is a good example. A standard fixture in many homes, even in those that could ill afford it, the sewing machine represented extra income to the lower-middle classes and convenience to the bourgeois household. It increased the amount of sewing done for a normal family, however. The housewife who possessed such a machine increased her labor and upgraded her standards of comfort and hygiene. Women's willingness to change household procedures for providing nourishment, clothing, shelter, and health care allowed the start of a gradual spread of the consumer side of manufacturing. This flexibility moved the Industrial Revolution along through the purchase—no matter how small— of new commodities.

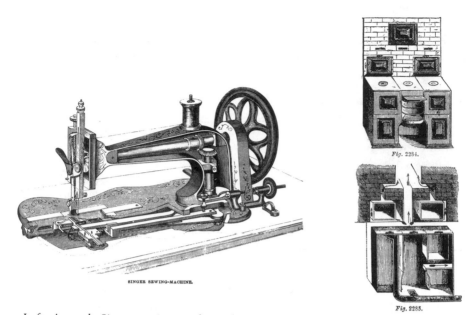

Fig. 2284.

Fig. 2285.

Left: An early Singer sewing machine, decorative and even dainty in design to fit the image of the home—not the image of work. Right: The stove was a major improvement in household technology. In particular, it lessened the possibility of dangerous accidents and made food preparation far less burdensome than it was with a fireplace.

By the 1850s working class health conditions had deteriorated markedly. The rapid influx of rural people to the cities had by this time become an avalanche that taxed urban resources. Slums proliferated, and overcrowding was a way of life. Not until later in the century did building at all catch up with population growth. Many towns and cities still retained their medieval walls, which hindered the movement of air. Nor had sanitation facilities greatly improved: human and animal excrement and waste of all kinds lay around in open depositories or just anywhere. As a result, cholera and typhoid were rampant from the 1830s until the 1880s. For women, urban filth increased the risks of childbirth, and bad nutrition lowered resistance to post-partum infections.

The Industrial Revolution impaired the working-class diet. Urban workers, especially those squeezed by the new methods of production, suffered substantial dietary deterioration. Malnutrition produced rickets as a general problem among the working population. Resulting from a lack of vitamin D, rickets posed specific problems for women's health. It caused deformed pelvises, which meant difficult pregnancies at best and fatal ones at worst. Those affected by rickets also might have small or deformed chest cavities, which in turn increased the risk of tuberculosis and other chest ailments. In the nineteenth century, tuberculosis was a common cause of death, and the consumptive seamstress or flower vendor remains one of the poignant images of the time.

Working conditions caused other health problems. Textile production required a warm, damp atmosphere. Women generally stripped down to work in factories or workshops and often stood half-clothed in pools of warm water. Leaving work during the winter months, they went out into the cold still insufficiently clad. These women's resistance to diseases was low, and they were exposed to bacteria constantly: drinking water contaminated by leakage from piles of rotting refuse and eating food contaminated by insects. Machinery also proved dangerous. At the beginning of the mechanical age, few factory owners concerned themselves with industrial safety. Workers of both sexes were victims of frequent industrial accidents affecting limbs or fingers. As for women, their breasts or long hair could easily get caught in machinery; if hair was caught, the scalp might be ripped off. Spending long hours tending machines or sewing caused skeletal deformations and thus difficult pregnancies. Dust from textile production, especially prevalent in silk and cotton manufacturing, caused damage to the skin and internal organs. Seamstresses working by dim light to save money could eventually go blind, and laundresses suffered from ulcerated skin and varicose veins. In short, nearly every occupation was detrimental to health. Productivity was the only priority, however, and only later did the workers' well-being get any attention. For a time, the crowds of wandering poor and the vast migration into the city provided industrialists with an unlimited supply of labor.

Poverty continued to increase. In the early nineteenth century, city officials estimated the number of poor in Florence to be somewhere around a third of the population, whereas charitable religious groups declared that some 55,000 of the city's 75,000 inhabitants needed some kind of relief, most often food. An older form of relief that continued was charity in kind, that is, donations of furniture, food, household linens, and so on, instead of money. Some religious institutions offered young women work or trained them in a craft. Young women might also acquire a small dowry by applying to a municipal fund or religious foundation established for that purpose. Other religious groups took in homeless women and gave them work to do. This activity by nunneries often provoked complaints, however, because the goods produced in their workshops competed with those of the already hard-pressed poor, especially when they sold goods below the going price. Instead of relieving poverty, nuns' charity may in this instance have contributed to it. Other sources of help included municipally controlled pawn shops, which women learned to use on a regular basis. The small amount families could get for basic household items often allowed them to survive a day or two. Old women generally constituted the largest sector of the poor. In Florence, widows headed one-third of the needy households. Their pitiful state classified them as among "worthy" or "deserving" poor—the only category the dominant institutions would aid. Officials of most charitable funds still subscribed to the morality of the pre-industrial world and applied its requirements to recipients of charity.

Some, however, were changing their attitudes toward the poor to fit the new ethos of money and work. The new attitudes appeared clearly in Britain.

For centuries, the British had provided relief using money collected from local taxpayers. In 1834, when the increasing numbers of poor threatened to overwhelm this system of relief, Parliament passed a New Poor Law amidst expressions of hostility toward the indigent. No longer the worthy objects of charity, the poor were shiftless, bad characters. Accordingly, parliamentarians granted relief to poor people only if they were incarcerated in workhouses. The mid-century workhouse arose out of the same sentiments as the brothel and other institutions of incarceration and control. In the workhouse, reformers hoped, the indigent would learn about work, diligence, prudence, and conformity. Local officials in England made a certain Mrs. Cooper "wear a Parish dress" even before she went to the poorhouse as a way of curbing her individuality.[13] To ease the organizational process, inmates entering as families were separated from each other. Men, women, and children had separate sections of the workhouse. In the case of unmarried or widowed mothers, who formed a good number of those forced to enter because of their circumstances, their separation from infants still occurred. Thus, the workhouse was supposed to eliminate the imperfections of human associations in favor of work and regular habits. In addition, it took the poor away from temptations of the world, such as "green tea, gin, and snuff,"[14] as one observer described the vices of a local laundress. Such vices did not exist in the workhouse; the people there knew only incessant labor and austere living. After this kind of regime, the poor were supposedly ready to live better lives in the outside world.

Viewing the Woman Worker

Middle- and upper-class Europeans were appalled at the social consequences of industrialization. Appraisal of the women worker came from almost every quarter of society. Early works with such a theme in England were Hannah More's *Lancashire Collier Girl* (1795) and Maria Edgeworth's *Castle Rackrent* (1800), which has a female servant as the protagonist. Elizabeth Gaskell's *Ruth* (1853) and Charlotte Tonna's *Helen Fleetwood* (1840–1842) had plots involving seduction, exploitation, and betrayal. Karl Gutzkow's *Knights of the Spirit* (1850–1852) described in detail the life of a working woman in Berlin and had many other characters from the lower classes. Fanny Lewald wrote essays about German working women from the 1840s on, and in the 1830s Luis Mülbach drew vivid literary portraits of servants' crushing lives. In his *Comédie Humaine* (1827–1847), Honoré de Balzac portrayed a wide range of women from aristocrats to servants and prostitutes, and Gustave Flaubert immortalized an unwed working mother, the humble Félicité in "Un Coeur Simple" (1877). In most of these works, the working woman was portrayed as a victim; her image was fixed as someone to be pitied because she had to work. While expressing sympathy, some people found demeaning consequences in women's work. First, they believed women workers often became immoral and transmitted this immorality to the next generation. Although prostitutes in fact generally came from respectable though poor families, these observers saw them as the result of generations of illegitimacy or deviancy on the mother's side. In this view, working mothers kept their children unclean and illiterate and pushed them, unintentionally, toward lives of crime. Moreover, the argument went, husbands whose wives worked often became alcoholics because no wife was at home all day exerting a controlling influence. For many, the women's work was a question of morality. The working classes in the nineteenth century seemed dangerous to those in power, and the working woman figured simultaneously as the symbol and cause of that danger. Outside the home she evoked memories of the stereotypically violent market women of the French Revolutionary mob,* diminished her maternal virtue, and thus aggravated the problem of morality.

The negative view of working women and their exploitation led to social investigation, which in turn supported charges of immorality. Louis René Villermé in France and later Henry Mayhew in England were the best known investigators of working conditions. In 1844, the Romantic intellectual Bettina von Arnim started her *Book of the Poor,* a sympathetic record of the way ordinary people lived in Berlin. After mid-century, the less sympathetic Frédéric Le Play and Wilhelm Heinrich Riehl influenced the rise of sociology directed toward research into familial forms and their deviation from imagined norms. They posited a golden age when wise patriarchs would rule over extensive families. Free unions, working women, and other symptoms of moral decay, they hoped, would disappear when the results of their sociological studies had been applied. At this time, the general study of population was developing. Researchers in Italy provided statistics about work, family, reproduction, and finances in various urban areas. Statisticians everywhere used their new skills to fulfill an interest in how the lower classes lived. Simultaneously, they produced special information about women and in particular about women as workers. The most famous of the studies done in the early industrial era was that based on hearings of the British Parliament in the 1840s. Parliament organized a commission to take testimony from working women and their children, as well as from their employers. These hearings arose from concern about the terrible conditions in which the working classes seemed to live and work. Getting people to talk about themselves and to reveal the details of their lives, researchers, parliamentary officials, and governmental agents drew a sordid picture of the working woman.

After targeting working women for study, governments felt compelled to produce legislation concerning them. Instead of improving working conditions generally, Parliament restricted women's work day to ten hours and banned them from work in the pits in the 1840s. Because their towns offered little beside mining work, the latter restriction was particularly disastrous. Thousands of women thus became unemployed. Women who had testified about conditions in the mines felt particularly betrayed; instead of gaining improvements in their working conditions, they lost their jobs. Such legislation became common across Europe. For instance, in 1868, legislation in Upper Silesia

---

*See Chapter 3.

banned women from pitwork. State and local governments were replicating the kind of restrictions guilds had formerly put on women's work. Although limitations on their roles had existed in the old regime of craft production, the new restrictions represented the authority of large sovereign states and thus had greater force. Moreover, the state purported to represent its citizens' opinions, from those of intellectual leaders such as Riehl to men of the working class. Women, announced the *Journal of Italian Workers Associations* in 1864, were not made for work: "An angel of peace, woman's heritage is love." Working men everywhere, particularly certain articulate leaders of those in the declining crafts, felt threatened by women workers, to whose low income level they might fall. Instead, according to Italian politician Carlo Cattaneo (1801–1869), their job consisted of making the home "a school of virtue, of gentleness, and of love."[15]

Republican ideology and republican-inspired laws applied more readily to middle-class women than to poor or working-class ones. The latter's motherhood involved not just caring for their children but earning money to support them. At their jobs, however, working women seemed unmotherly. The first labor legislation addressed the ideological aspect of the exploitation of women workers and in so doing impinged on the women's own idea of what motherhood involved—providing for their families. Making *working* women into an anomaly, legislators allowed them to receive lower wages and to be treated worse than before. Thus, legislation covering the woman worker, and the theory behind it, defined her as woman rather than worker and emphasized male-female differences rather than common working-class interests. Such early regulatory activity shaped everyday life and sowed the seeds of the welfare state.

Popular Culture and Women's Identity

Working women in the nineteenth century had a complex view of themselves and of their activities. "She's a good worker and occupies herself with her household and her son,"[16] so one Parisian defended her friend who had been arrested in 1834. Such a litany of virtues expressed a solidarity that came from shared activities of many kinds. Women who had work and motherhood in common formed neighborly groups united by their shared experiences. They enjoyed songs, poems, and stories that either celebrated life's texture or lamented its tribulations. One of the great London favorites was Thomas Hood's "Song of the Shirt,"[17] which movingly described the life of a seamstress:

> With fingers weary and worn,
> With eyelids heavy and red
> A Woman sat, in unwomanly rags,
> Plying her needle and thread—
> Stitch! stitch! stitch!
> In poverty, hunger, and dirt,
> And still with a voice of dolorous pitch
> She sang the "Song of the Shirt!"

Songs describing the working life of women were sold in single printed sheets and later entered into the oral culture of urban folk. Many French songs had themes related to festivals and household rituals, such as one about the coffee-pot and its centrality to daily life and sociability: "When something arises to bring us to grief, When sorrow deals us a blow, It's coffee that brings us re-lief."[18] In addition to being sung, lyrics appeared on textiles, plates, plaques, and other household objects. Popular songs were played and sung in cafés, music halls, dance halls, and clubs. Wandering minstrels, beggerwomen, and people out for a good time sang individually, in pairs, and in groups. Music was an important part of working-class life in the nineteenth-century city.

Socializing occurred in public places rather than in the small urban apart-ments. Spilling out into the streets, working people pursued what pleasures they had time for outdoors or in such spaces as dance halls. From Vienna to Paris, the urban dweller frequented a variety of establishments for dancing. The most modest was a single room in an apartment house fitted out with some benches and with a violinist. Families passed their evenings there, or often their Sunday afternoons. Other dance halls were more elaborate and had dance masters leading crowds of couples in a regular schedule of formal dances. Although men might pay a modest entry fee, owners regularly gave free admission to neighborhood women. Parks were another place in which to relax and seek amusement and became a major force in urban sociability. Parks such as the Prater in Vienna, the gardens of the Tuileries in Paris, and a variety of amusement "gardens" in London attracted working-class families and cou-ples, as well as prostitutes. Women and men found relief from toil in sampling the goods offered by vendors and watching the spectacles staged by entertain-ers. Joanna Stuwer was one of the earliest and most legendary of the enter-tainers in the Prater. A fireworks expert, her shows dazzled the public so effectively that "Bravo Stuwer" still describes something expertly done. Court-ship also took place in the natural surroundings of parks, in a place as far away from work as most people could ever get. Yet courtship songs often relied on work vocabularies, such as this one heard in parks in English industrial cities:[19]

> As I walked between Bolton and Bury, 'twas a moonshiny night,
> I met with a buxom young weaver whose company gave me delight.
> She says: Young fellow come tell me if your lever and rule are in tune,
> Come, give me an answer correct, can you get up and square my loom.
> I said: My dear Lassie, believe me, I am a good joiner by trade,
> And many a good loom and shuttle before me in my time I have made.

The natural setting, the group sociability, and the courtship in crowds repre-sented an urban transmutation of agricultural community.

Working women also had more and more contact with print culture. Those in cities had access to serialized books and periodicals. Many novels were first printed either in newspapers or in sections sold individually for a small sum. Although individual readers might buy these, more often cafés got them for the use of their clients. Servants read books belonging to their em-

Laundresses in Vienna at their "Sunday dance" show how work and sociability were intimately connected.

ployers, and workers in all occupations regularly kept books in their work-places. Every city had its popular magazine for working women, in which they could find not only the well-liked romantic stories but a variety of practical patterns for embroidery and other needlework. Working-class readers particularly liked romances and heroic stories: Anna Maria Jones's *The Gipsy Mother* and *The Ruined Cottage* were English favorites; and Sir Walter Scott's historic novels were extremely popular throughout Europe in the first half of the nineteenth century. Political belief sometimes developed from reading. For example, German socialist Ottilie Baader formed her political creed while listening to her father read political classics to her as she sewed to support the family. In previous centuries most had gained their political sensibility from oral culture, but workers in the nineteenth century turned to the print culture in great numbers. As schools promoted literacy for the masses, books and newspapers competed with the organized church, the *veillès,** and the marketplace as sources of information and beliefs.

The Industrial Revolution broke down the old power structures, including

---

*See Chapter 1.

the traditional churches. Scrambling to earn a livelihood, working people started reshaping social institutions into a culture more pertinent to their lives. In particular, they turned religion to their own uses. A popular form of religion developed as the most satisfying of all social practices because it combined song, oral culture, reading, and sociability. In England, the development of popular religion accompanied economic change, and this form of religion aroused the interest of both women and men. Unlike the mainstream religious awakening discussed in Chapter 3, which was engaged in by upper-class women such as the Countess von Reventlow and Hannah More, the new revivalism sprang from the rural homes of farmers and craftspeople. It attracted some industrial workers as well. Famous and influential preachers such as Elizabeth Gorse Gaunt (b. 1777); Hannah Woolley (b. 1770); Ann Cutler (b. 1759), also known as "Praying Nanny"; Mary Barritt Taft (b. 1772); and Elizabeth Tomlinson comprised the first generation of ministers inspired by revivalism. These preachers spoke directly to the plight of men and women in a time of social transformation and widespread poverty. They specifically addressed the conditions of women's lives, and sometimes served as midwives as well as spiritual guides: "We were with them in weariness and in painfulness, in watchings often, in fastings too."[20] Ordinary working women, whether farmers, craftswomen, or sweated workers, did not hesitate to speak out. At prayer meetings held in kitchens, barns, or meeting halls, they offered psalms, scripture readings, sermons, and prayers. For preachers and congregations, the Bible offered a message about a simple and certain existence that they saw as being undermined by new values. The female revivalist ministers preached family solidarity and cited the Old Testament's endorsement of women's preaching as justification for their leadership. It was precisely this leadership that alarmed local authorities—both religious and secular. Female preachers in primitive Methodism or other popular sects were upsetting for two reasons: they defied the gender order, and they awakened feelings of solidarity in the working class.

All evidence suggests that popular expressions of religious fervor converted official church doctrine into a people's culture. One example among Catholics was the annual pilgrimage from Vienna to the shrine of the Virgin at Mariazell. The pilgrims were mostly women, barefoot, dressed in austere pilgrim's clothing, and carrying shepherd's crooks with bouquets. One writer described their journey along a steep path and with miles of marching: "the pilgrims always ascend . . . chanting hymns; the young women allow their hair to hang down loose over their shoulders . . . and the more laboriously pious add to the sum of their good works by dragging after them a cumbersome cross."[21] Yet alongside these conventional manifestations of extreme piety by thousands of marchers, fights broke out. Competition for position and place, singing of secular songs, heavy drinking, and long evenings of merry carousing occurred, much to the amazement of the upper-class witnesses for whom piety had no such joyous accompaniment. For these few days, the dreary aspects of the urban worker's life were supplanted by joyful expressions of popular religious community.

Struggling to Change Their Destiny

People vigorously engaged in their work lives and gained a sense of self from what they did. The major components of most women's lives in those days—work and motherhood—constituted sources of identity. So, in the face of hardship, women fought for their livelihood and for a fair chance to raise their children and support themselves. They engaged in protests, political movements, and strikes. Some, however, had dreams and plans for radical change not only in their work lives, but in their personal ones. These plans led to experiments in living and working that horrified the respectable middle classes.

Work Actions and Popular Protest

The rebellious crowds of the eighteenth century continued to gather in the nineteenth. Food remained a scarce commodity for many people because of the still inadequate nature of transport and the uneven development of the market. Moreover, throughout the century the spread of industrialization affected regions in different ways. Although some were thriving, others were starving. Food riots continued to erupt, for example, in German states from 1830 to 1833, across Europe from Ireland to Silesia in 1846–1847, and in Italy in the 1850s. Conditions on the land still determined the well-being of those who farmed, and the great potato famine of the 1840s decimated populations.

New forms of action developed to protest the introduction of machinery and the rest of the industrial way of life that challenged their own. As early as the late eighteenth century, protesters in England—called Luddites—had broken machines. In 1779 thousands of spinners in the Manchester area rampaged through towns smashing all kinds of machinery except the smaller jennies. Their motives were clear: "being no longer able to endure the remediless cries of our husbands, wives, and children, and not having it in our power to put food in the mouths of those to whom, under God, we gave existence; in an unhappy hour of depression, prompted by want and poverty, we pulled down and demolished several of these Machines, the causes of our calamitous situation."[22] Weavers in Saxony in the 1830s and 1840s did the same. Such destruction erupted when workers found industrialization detrimental to their interests. Home workers and sometimes even factory workers would wreck machines to prevent them from destroying their livelihood. Such acts failed to halt the progress of industry. Instead, like the barn burners of the English agricultural disturbances in the 1830s, called "Swing Riots," the machine wreckers were imprisoned, deported, or hanged. Nonetheless, Luddism continued as a form of labor protest till late in the century.

Working people also set up new structures to shape their protest. Guilds had organized working life in earlier times. As productive conditions changed, workers tried to recapture the guild spirit and structure. With worker groups outlawed, in France by the Revolution and in other countries by governments fearful of revolutionary uprisings, workers often met in secret. Some set up mutual aid or "friendly" societies. Such groups provided the sociability and protection that had been benefits of the old guild system. Each worker contributed a pittance each month or week, and the common fund was used for specific needs or emergencies such as sickness, retirement, or incapacitation. In women's mutual aid societies, such money served similar ends or was given to aid those recovering from childbirth. Such women's organizations, however, were few and far between, existing only in cities such as Birmingham and Lyons and generally not for long. The short life of mutual aid societies and the small number of them reveal how difficult it was for women to contribute even a penny to a nonessential use, such as a fund not at their immediate disposal. As the guilds had, these societies sometimes took up a patron saint or perhaps had church sponsorship, further evidence of the close connection of religion, sociability, and work life. As an early manifestation of the commonality of workers, the mutual aid societies were an important intermediate step toward unionization. The societies relied on their own incredibly meager funds for relief, however. When unions developed, they marked a new era in worker organization, for they placed demands on employers and their profits rather than on workers and their limited means.

Some urban working women struck directly at unfair conditions. Their protests centered on technological innovations and on working conditions and hours. These workers also worried that machines would destroy job opportunities for their daughters. Parisian shawl-cutters and felt workers, for example, went on strike when their employers introduced cutting machines into workshops. In 1828, laundresses at the Salpêtrière Hospital in Paris went on strike over wages. Other workers struck, but generally in wildcat actions. Instead of forming long-term organizations directed toward obtaining better working conditions and pay, most women acted on the spur of the moment after they had reached the limit of their endurance. Craft workers were most likely to organize, duplicating the guild structure in an effort to counteract the negative effects of the piecework system. A few early workers' organizations formed in England, where the Owenite movement (see page 171) encouraged groups to improve their working conditions. The resulting "lodges" were as short-lived as the mutual aid societies. Industrialization was not far enough advanced to spawn powerful organizations. In fact, for the moment factory workers of both sexes were better paid than most other workers.

By the 1860s, however, women's efforts toward better working conditions and pay began to result in an organized status. An example from France is a strike late in the 1860s of silk-winders in Lyons that eventually mobilized some 8,000 women workers. Angry, the strikers harrassed those who continued to work. They attacked steam engines, but not the machines on which they worked. From workshop to workshop the strikers went, gathering support from people on the street and those in cafés. In some ways the event was like a festival. Banded together, the workers created an out-of-control atmosphere like that at Carnival. They laughed, made noise, and wildly called their bosses filthy names. Their menacing air was reinforcement for the view held by polite society that they were truly dangerous because they were working women. Their activities made the middle-class citizenry sit up and take notice: "Democracy is worming its way into the minds of the silk-winders," one commission feared. Others found the carnivalesque atmosphere "frightening in its implications for morality and public safety."[23] The women's actions also attracted the attention of male workers. In general, the working man was slowly adopting the attitude of his bourgeois counterpart—that women should remain virtuously at home and not compete for men's jobs. When a man returned home from work in need of sustenance, attention, and relaxation, the woman should be there waiting to provide them. Other men who observed the silk-winders' protest, however, saw the possibility of making allies of the strikers. They offered help from the strike fund of the new International Alliance of Workers, and the women became not just participants in a spur-of-the-moment strike but members of an international union. Many of the silk-winders received the 2 franc wage and time reduction of 2 hours that they had demanded, but such an outcome was an extraordinary event. In these early days of attempted organization, strikes usually failed and unions lasted but a short time. A feeling of solidarity among the workers remained nonetheless.

New Visions of Work

Although working women horrified some, they inspired others. For one thing, women themselves developed identities and goals different from those set out in republican ideology. As industrialists agitated for new rights for themselves, women also joined in their own political struggle. In addition, industry inspired visionaries who thought in terms of making society as efficient and organized as the modern factory seemed. For them, improvement in the condition of women was essential to any modernization of the social fabric. Loathing the effect machines were having on the general life style, Romantic writers and artists gave a new prominence to women and to love as the opposite of the mechanical. They focused on the female body, on things maternal and sensual as an antidote to the machine age. This transforming imagery served as a resource for women in thinking about themselves in new ways. Finally, as middle-class men accumulated money and effectively changed the material conditions of production, reformers demanded more and more power for themselves and for the bourgeoisie in general. The way in which they made these demands and their apparent, though gradual, success provided a model for action and a pattern for discourse that many working women found stimulating. In almost every sector of industrial society, currents of change were set off that eventually stirred working women's imaginations and benefited their collective interests. The thinking of reform socialists and utopians affected the ideas and concerns of working women.

Utopian socialists saw the gender question as central to social reorganization. In this depiction of Robert Owen's "ideal woman," note both the depravity she has escaped and the reformed dress, including trousers, she adopts (1846).

The Owenites

Most of the new visions resulted from people wondering what postrevolutionary and industrial society would be like. Some of these people envisioned a world of communal harmony and cooperation. Robert Owen (1771–1858), an industrialist who had made his fortune in the cotton industry, built utopian industrial communities in which production was made more rational, community life more intense, and education a universal benefit. Beginning with better housing, programs and clubs, and systems of benefits for workers, Owen's changes extended into sexual relations and the family. For Owen, as for many of his radical peers, the problems of married life mirrored those in all segments of society. Discontent in the family stemmed from human greed, or ultimately from liberal beliefs that the nature of humans was to be acquisitive. As a sort of republican, Owen preferred to think that the possesion of equal amounts of property would in turn create a more egalitarian kind of relationship between men and women. At the same time, Owen was an advocate of sexual freedom, who demanded an end to such social barriers as marriage, the elimination of the family unit because it blocked freedom, and the encouragement of sociability or sexuality to flow freely throughout society. For Owen, as for so many others, improvement in the situation of women would result from these general reforms. He did not see male domination as the basis of injustice. Rather, he thought pervasive liberal values were harmful to everyone. A turn away from individualism and toward a more community-minded ideal would bring liberation to all.

Owen attracted some adherents who were women. Anna Wheeler (1785–1848) came from an upper-class family but soon became an Owenite. With William Thompson, she co-authored a tract entitled "Appeal of One-Half of the Human Race, Women, Against the Pretensions of the Other Half, Men, to Retain Them in Political and Thence in Civil and Domestic Slavery." The tract espoused radical ideas of British writers who had been influenced by the French Revolution. It proposed that women be lifted from their traditional status as *femmes-covert* to a place where they would have an individual identity. In her writing and preaching, Wheeler took a slightly different tack from that of Owen. Seeing inequality in the family, she attributed it not to liberal values in general but to the inequality in the economic system that gave some groups of people power over others. For Wheeler, economic domination found a parallel and coordinate in gender domination. Wheeler and Thompson substituted the harmonizing and equalizing ingredient of love for this power and inequality. Like Owen, they believed in perfection and the kind of eighteenth-century happiness that logically resulted from egalitarianism, rights, and the application of science.

Frances Wright (1795–1852), another wealthy woman adopted the Owenite creed, including its disdain for legalized sexual relations. She set out to bring this utopian gospel to the New World and went so far as to purchase slaves to populate a model community at Nashoba, Tennessee. Wright did not believe in middle-class respectability and encouraged unconventional relationships in her community. Although Nashoba ultimately failed, Wright herself remained involved in struggles for women's rights and abolition but paradoxically married so that her child would not be illegitimate. Wearing trousers and living according to Owenite precepts, Wright combined radical behavior in everyday life with an ongoing activism against racial and sexual oppression.

Working-class pioneers also followed Owen's example, setting up all sorts of associations. Hat-makers, glove-makers, weavers, silk-workers, and a host of others were among those who organized into unions and cooperative workshops under the inspiration of Owenism. Several working-class papers were started, including the *Pioneer*. It carried articles in favor of women's rights, many of them written by Frances Morrison, a committed Owenite whose husband edited the journal. Even though Owen and his early followers advocated the rights of women, many craftsmen resisted putting these theories into daily practice. In the 1830s, male Owenites attempted to argue that women's working undercut men's earning power and thus their ability to support a family. But Owenite women used the popular media to respond that women not working and not unionized were "utterly scattered, each subject to her own husband."[24] The Owenite women also pointed to the many strikes they had participated in and supported as wives of northern textile workers and as workers themselves. They charged that men in the cooperatives made sure that women received lower remuneration for their work. An 1834 strike of tailors demanding an end to the piece-work done by women in their homes put solidarity and equality to the test. Splitting the Owenites and their "Consolidated Union" along gender lines, the tailors and their supporters ultimately destroyed the actively utopian aspect of the movement. What remained were ideals of solidarity and internationalism that would resurface as the background for a different kind of socialist theory.

Utopian Socialists in France

In Paris, new political theories of the mid–nineteenth century involved women, as they had during the Enlightenment. The restrictions of the Napoleonic Code were seen as unwelcome by many thinkers. Yet some also saw the Code as a model in that it was an example of the way in which society could be formulated on paper and changed. Several unusual thinkers undertook similarly to redraw society in the new regime. First, the Comte de Saint-Simon, then Charles Fourier, and finally Auguste Comte wrote what have become known as "utopian socialist" blueprints. They called themselves or were called socialists, just like many other writers on all sides of political questions, because they sketched out what society should be or what the social sphere would look like. They were utopian by virtue of their planned project for the perfect future.

Saint-Simon called for an inversion of the usual state of affairs in European society by emphasizing industrialists and technicians as the most important leaders of the next stage of progress. He saw that first theologians, then philosophers, and finally engineers and businessmen of all varieties had charted how society functioned in different historical periods. In his scheme, work had become the foremost value, and industrialists must replace other outmoded social leaders. In his later years, Saint-Simon believed that a spiritualizing force—poets, artists, and women—would have to be present alongside the progressive element in order that society could gain transcendent values. In the 1820s, his secretary, Auguste Comte, independently proceeded to expand on this vision. In particular, Comte saw the possibility of formulating precise social laws, or "positive" laws, through study. Social managers could then proceed to construct harmonious societies. Furthermore, Comte postulated that this harmony would be the result of balance in the social-sexual order, as woman's abundant love would be released to influence the world toward greater morality and virtue.

Charles Fourier, seemingly the most eccentric of these three, followed the same line of thought about social planning. However, Fourier's determining principle for social organization was the passionate, or what is now called the sensual. For him, the diversity of the human population was due to the existence of a number of emotional or personality types. A finite number of traits manifested themselves in predictable combinations. By identifying and manipulating these emotive types, the social engineer could construct a harmonious social order in which these types were matched and regulated. For Fourier, social problems arose precisely from mismatching personalities and occupations. His best-known match gave little boys, who loved dirt and muck, the job of performing the garbage-collecting functions of the utopian community.

All of these doctrines attracted women, particularly Saint-Simon's, which turned into a movement after his death in 1825. Young men of status, artists,

A Belgian Woman Attacks Poverty

Utopian socialism attracted many women adherents because it ad-dressed issues that were pertinent to their lives. Belgian activist Zoé Gatti de Gamond believed that only a reorganization of society would change things in women's favor. Attracted in particular by Fourier's program for social planning, she collaborated in founding a phalan-stery of her own. In an excerpt from one of her several books on how and why to start such new communities, Gatti de Gamond explains that women's poverty—that creation of the new regime—is at the heart of social problems.

> The most direct cause of women's misfortune is poverty; de-manding their freedom means above all demanding reform in the economy of society which will eradicate poverty and give everyone education, a minimum standard of living, and the right to work. It is not only that class called "women of the people" for whom the major source of all their misfortunes is poverty, but rather women of all classes.
>
> From that comes the subjection of women, their narrow dependence on men, and their reduction to a negative influ-ence. Men have thus materialized love, perverted the angelic nature of women, and created a being who submits to their caprices, their desires—a domesticated animal shaped to their pleasures and to their needs. Using their powers, they have split women into the appearance of two classes: for the priv-ileged group, marriage, the care of the household, and mater-nal love; for the other, the sad role of seduced woman and of the misfortunate one reduced to the last degree of misery and degradation. Everywhere oppression and nowhere liberty.
>
> The question is not to decide whether it is fitting to give women political rights or to put them on an equal footing with men when it comes to admission to employment. Rather the question exists above all in the question of poverty; and to make women ready to fill political roles, it is poverty above all that must be effaced. Nor can the independence of women be reconciled with the isolation of households, which prevents even the working woman from being independent.
>
> The system of Fourier, imperceptibly and smoothly intro-ducing associations within society, resolves all the difficulties in the position of women; without changing legislation or proclaiming new rights, it will regenerate them, silence the sources of corruption and reform with one blow education and morals with the single fact that results naturally from the associational principles of his system: a common education

and the independence of women assured by the right to work; independence rendered possible by the association of households, attractive and harmonious work, and the multiplication of wealth.

Source: Adapted from Zoé Gatti de Gamond, *Fourier et son système* (Paris: Capelle, 1841–1842) 247–266.

and intellectuals organized a community in Paris and proceeded to establish a system of cooperative farming and production. Moreover, they set out to reform sexual relations. Working-class women supported both aspects of this venture because they saw a possibility for improving working conditions and gaining a better personal life. In addition, female Saint-Simonians appreciated the principal of community leadership by both a Father (*Père*) and a Mother (*Mère*), though the male leadership professed not yet to have found a suitable female leader. For several months in the early 1830s, they enjoyed working, establishing relationships based on affection, and pushing their thinking about women even beyond that of the founders. Soon, however, French authorities grew anxious about this transgression of gender order. When the Saint-Simonians were prosecuted for loose morals, the men retreated by themselves in an act of purification that was to be followed by an exodus to the East to find the Mother.

Excluded from this demonstration of sanctity, working women such as Suzanne Voilquin, Claire Démar, and Reine Guindorf came into their own. First, they organized a women's newspaper that discussed associational principles for women. It articulated a program for group life by which women would explicitly unite because of their gender—not just in imitation of male political, military, and social institutions. The working-class Saint-Simonian women saw in their own sexual nature and reproductive lives a power, a commonality, and a *raison d'être* for unity. They also debated sexual practice: did the new restraints on sexuality since the Revolution make for women's oppression or for her protection? With respect to their quest for a new ideal woman, Claire Démar predicted that she would be "supremely shocking" because she was representative of "every nature, of every wish."[25] That is, finding the "Mother" and recognizing female power explicitly was something society was not prepared for. Démar also recognized a basic problem in what they were trying to do: "You call our program in your masterful tongue *our feminine shriekings*."[26] She realized that some men would question the legitimacy of women's even speaking about social issues.

Working for a living and constantly striving to support children, lovers, husbands, and relatives, Saint-Simonian women managed also to develop themselves as social activists and as autonomous individuals. For a while they accomplished their ends, including producing a newspaper and keeping a women's movement alive. But the objective circumstances in France in the

1830s were too much against them. Several, including Démar, committed suicide. Others, including Suzanne Voilquin, joined the crusade to the East in search of the Mother, or female leader. Arriving in the midst of a plague, the Saint-Simonians were decimated by the disease, along with Egyptian supporters of their industrial projects. Voilquin was more fortunate than many. Not only did she survive the plague, she learned medical skills, including midwifery. Virtually ignored, she carried what she called her "apostolate" or crusade on behalf of women to Russia. When she died in relative obscurity in Paris, it was after a lifetime of enthusiastic participation in the development of the women's movement.

The Saint-Simonian women's movement was the most sophisticated intellectually and doctrinally in its day. Unlike other women's activities, it addressed the total situation of women rather than focusing on working-class rights, abolition, health reform, or philanthropy. Moreover, it unified the economic, emotional, domestic, and political issues in women's lives. Saint-Simonian women tried to live by their principles and took risks—such as migration and economic self-sufficiency—that later feminists would merely discuss. Theoretically rich and wide-ranging, their movement also encompassed everyday practices. The aspects of communal living, emotional and economic liberation, and an appreciation of reproduction spread with utopian socialism to other countries and decisively influenced women's politics.

Flora Tristan

The most celebrated woman activist of the mid–nineteenth century was Flora Tristan (1801–1844). After attending Fourierist meetings in Paris, she later struck out on her own, touring the country with coherent programs for workers' liberation. Tristan saw the emancipation of women as a key to unlock a better future for the working class. She identified the economic competition of men with women as the foundation of all bad conditions for workers. Employers, Tristan reasoned, replaced men with women because they could pay them less and thus cut costs. Similarly children could ultimately replace both men and women. Tristan saw women's other role at the center of domestic life, as the foundation of a humane society. Because women were degraded in both endeavors, they eroded working-class strength. When ill-educated, legally inferior, and emotionally oppressed, women became shrews and damaged their families' humanity. Unequally paid, women pulled the entire working class down with them. Tristan did not conclude from this—as was common among later workers—that women should leave the workforce and make the home a shrine. Rather, she summoned the working class to unite (*L'Union ouvrière*) in the cause of women, which would in the long run be the cause of all.

Tristan's analysis was in many ways derivative, but her style was not. Physically beautiful and an inspiring speaker, she stumped the country and captivated one hostile audience after another. Her inspiration was seemingly fueled by the hardships in her life. Born wealthy, Tristan grew up as an illegitimate child because her parents' church marriage in Spain was not recognized by French law. On her Peruvian father's death, the French government confiscated his fortune. Tristan took up the kinds of jobs open to women of her background; she hand-colored lithographic plates and much later became a lady's companion. While a colorist, she married her employer. When they separated, French law decreed that she must surrender custody of her children, but she regained it when her ex-husband sexually abused his own daughter. To restore her fortune and to earn her living, Tristan traveled to Peru, London, and elsewhere and recorded her impressions in diaries and letters. Although her experience as a woman facing the legal and economic disadvantages of the time was not unique, Tristan worked the totality of her life into a powerful and unforgettable message. After her premature death from typhus, the workers of Bordeaux built a monument to commemorate her life. In so doing, they gave collective force to what had been an individual's crusade.

The Woman Worker and the Rise of Industry

Working women in the nineteenth century had a complex vision of their identity—one that included many roles: worker, sexual partner, mother, and neighbor. Claiming rights to work, justice, and equitable treatment, they formed groups, protested, and struck. Working women complained about their wages and opposed the conditions under which they labored. Their preaching, writing, protesting, and working, however, was seen as a threat to the social order. For one thing, their appearing in public contradicted the relegation of women to the private sphere and the new republican credo that women were essentially mothers. For another, the very visible poverty of working women made the official position of respect for the home seem ungenuine. Moreover, if enough people were to accept the working woman's reality, society would have had to treat her complaints as legitimate, and industrial profit and capitalist flexibility would have suffered. Not just gender order, but industrial "progress" rested on a general acceptance of woman's identity as a mother. Parliamentary commissions, protective legislation, incessant writing and sermonizing—all worked to define woman convincingly as mother, while ensuring somehow that she continued to work.

From their position as the most talked about and least prosperous segment of society, working women began to enter national politics, revolutionary movements, and feminist organizations. They challenged the new middle-class ideology that defined woman's role as that of the mother, in the home raising citizens and workers. According to that ideology, women's role as workers was "blasphemous." But, at the same time as working women were being deplored by the middle-class, the industrialists were using them to break down the crafts and keep down wages. Defined as mothers and not workers, women could legitimately be paid less because they were just amateurs or interlopers in a world not rightfully theirs. Though most women had to continue providing their traditional contribution to the family economy by working for pay, they had to do so in ways different from men and under adverse conditions. The variety of their work—in workshops, homes (theirs and others), factories, farms, or some combination of these—gave industry the flexibility to expand in good times by hiring women and to contract in bad times by firing them or reducing pay. Given proportionately lower wages, because industrialists believed mothers did not need to earn the wages of male breadwinners, women ensured the success of manufacturing and industry. Thus, the ideology of virtue sealed working women's poverty and allowed the Industrial Revolution to succeed.

NOTES

1. Jules Michelet, *La femme* (Paris: Hachette, 1860), 3.
2. Quoted in Joan Rockwell, "The Danish Peasant Village," *Journal of Peasant Studies*, vol. 1, no. 4 (July, 1974) 430.
3. Quoted in Rockwell, "The Danish Peasant Village," 430–431.
4. Quoted in David Hoseason Morgan, *Harvesters and Harvesting, 1840–1900. A Study of the Rural Proletariat* (London: Croom and Helm, 1982), 26.
5. Bodil K. Hansen, "Rural Women in Late Nineteenth-Century Denmark," *Journal of Peasant Studies*, vol. 9, no. 4 (January 1982) 231.
6. Quoted in Katherine Verdery, *Transylvanian Villagers* (Berkeley: University of California Press, 1983), 263.
7. Dr. D. N. Zhbankov, quoted in Barbara Engel, "The Women's Side: Male Out-Migration and the Family Economy in Komstroma Province," *Slavic Review*, vol. 45, no. 2 (Summer, 1986) 266.
8. James Burn, *Autobiography of a Beggar Boy* (London: Tweedie, 1855), 95.
9. Charles Loring Brace, *The Norse-Folk: or A Visit to See the Homes of Norway and Sweden* (New York, 1857), 260–261, quoted in Donald Meyer, *Sex and Power. The Rise of Women in America, Russia, Sweden and Italy* (Middletown, Conn.: Wesleyan University Press, 1987), 173.
10. Quoted in Jill Harsin, *Policing Prostitution in Nineteenth-Century France* (Princeton: Princeton University Press, 1985), 187.
11. Dr. Hippolyte Homo, *Etude sur la prostitution dans la ville de Château-Gontier* (Paris, 1872), 65, quoted in Alain Corbin, *Les filles de noce* (Paris: Aubier, 1978), 44.
12. Quoted in Angela John, *By the Sweat of Their Brow: Women Workers at Victorian Coal Mines* (London: Routledge and Kegan Paul, 1980), 27.
13. Quoted in Roger A. E. Wells, "Social Conflict and Protest in the English Countryside in the Early Nineteenth-Century: A Rejoinder," *Journal of Peasant Studies*, vol 8, no. 4 (July, 1981), 519.
14. Nancy Russell Mitford, *Our Village* (Oxford, England: Oxford University Press, 1982 [1832]), 19.
15. Quoted in Franca Pieroni Bortolotti, *Alle origini del movimento femminile in Italia, 1848–1892* (Turin: Einaudi, 1975 [1963]), 27.

16. Ordonnance de non-lieu (April, 1834). Archives nationales de France. Série CC602, n. 114. The author thanks Judith De Groat for this citation.

17. John Clubbe, ed., *Selected Poems of Thomas Hood* (Cambridge, Mass.: Harvard University Press, 1970), 305.

18. Quoted in Pierre Pierrard, *La vie ouvrière à Lille sous le Second Empire* (Paris: Bloudet Gay, 1965), 206.

19. Quoted in Martha Vicinus, "The Bury New Loom," *The Industrial Muse* (New York: Harper and Row, 1974), 40.

20. Deborah Valenze, *Prophetic Sons and Daughters: Female Preaching and Popular Religion in Industrial Religion* (Princeton, N. J.: Princeton University Press, 1985), 72.

21. W. Blumenbach, *Austria and the Austrians,* 2 vols. (London: Colburn, 1837), 2:199.

22. Ivy Pinchbeck, *Women Workers and the Industrial Revolution, 1750–1850* (London: Virago, 1969 [1930]), 151.

23. Claire Anzias and Annik Mouel, *La grève des ovalistes* (Paris: Payot, 1982), 95, 191.

24. Quoted in Barbara Taylor, *Eve and the New Jerusalem. Socialism and Feminism in the Nineteenth Century* (New York: Pantheon, 1983), 100.

25. Claire Démar, "Ma loi de l'avenir," in *Textes sur l'affranchisement des femmes (1832–1833),* Valentin Pelosse, ed. (Paris: Payot, 1976), 67.

26. Démar, "Appel d'une femme," in *Textes sur l'affranchisement,* 15.

SOURCES AND SUGGESTED READING

Bythell, Duncan. *The Sweated Trades. Outwork in Nineteenth-Century Britain* (1978).

Clark, Anna. *Women's Silence, Men's Violence: Sexual Assault in England, 1770–1845* (1987).

Dupâquier, J., et al., eds. *Marriage and Remarriage in Populations of the Past* (1981). Important data on Eastern Europe and Scandinavia.

Engel, Barbara. "The Women's Side: Male Out-Migration and the Family Economy in Komstroma Province," *Slavic Review* (1986).

Frader, Laura. "Women in the Industrial Capitalist Economy," in Renate Bridenthal, Claudia Koonz and Susan Stuard, eds., *Becoming Visible: Women in European History* (1987).

Gibson, Mary. *Prostitution and the State in Italy, 1860–1915* (1986). An important study of both prostitutes and those who sought to end the regulatory system.

Harsin, Jill. *Policing Prostitution in Nineteenth-Century Paris* (1985). The public behavior of prostitutes and their relationship to the police system.

Hausen, Karin. "Technical Progress and Women's Labour in the Nineteenth Century. The Social History of the Sewing Machine," in George Iggers, ed., *The Social History of Politics* (1985).

Hellerstein, Erna O., Leslie P. Hume, and Karen Offen, eds. *Victorian Women: A Documentary Account of Women's Lives in Nineteenth-Century England, France, and the United States* (1981). A pathbreaking collection, including many testimonies from working women.

John, Angela V. *By the Sweat of Their Brow. Women Workers at Victorian Coal Mines* (1984).

———. *Unequal Opportunities: Women's Employment in England 1800–1918* (1986).

Lee, W. R. "The Impact of Agrarian Change on Women's Work and Child Care in Early Nineteenth-Century Prussia," in John Fout, ed., *German Women in the Nineteenth Century: A Social History* (1984).

McBride, Theresa. *The Domestic Revolution* (1977). A statistical treatment of servants and their mobility.

Malcolmson, Patricia. *English Laundresses. A Social History, 1850–1930* (1986).

Mitterauer, Michael, and Reinhard Sieder. *The European Family* (1982). Particularly good data on Eastern Europe.

Moses, Claire G. "Saint Simonian Men/Saint-Simonian Women: The Transformation of Feminist Thought in 1830s France," *Journal of Modern History* (1982).

Phayer, Michael. *Sexual Liberation and Religion in Nineteenth-Century Europe* (1977).

Pinchbeck, Ivy. *Women Workers and the Industrial Revolution, 1750-1850* (1930). A richly detailed work.

Polasky, Janet. "Utopia and Domesticity: Zoé Gatti de Gamond," *Western Society for French Historical Studies Proceedings* (1985).

Quataert, Jean. "The Shaping of Women's Work in Manufacturing Guilds, Households and the State in Central Europe 1648–1870" in *The American Historical Review* (1985).

Segalen, Martine. *Love and Power in the Peasant Family: Rural France in the Nineteenth Century* (1983).

Sewell, William. *Structure and Mobility: The Men and Women of Marseille, 1820–1870* (1985). Particularly informative statistical data on migration and work.

Taylor, Barbara. *Eve and the New Jerusalem. Socialism and Feminism in the Nineteenth Century* (1983). A detailed study of British working women and their political aspirations.

Valenze, Deborah. *Prophetic Sons and Daughters: Female Preaching and Popular Religion in the Industrial Revolution* (1985).

Walkowitz, Judith. *Prostitution and Victorian Society. Women, Class and the State* (1985). A major revision of historical understanding of the modern state and prostitutes' lives.

CHAPTER
5

The Domestic Sphere in the Victorian Age

The Victorian Woman The nineteenth century opened with public and private enthusiasm for domestic life and particularly for motherhood. New law codes and revolutionary ideology had enshrined motherhood, and middle- and upper-class women rose to the challenge of meeting these ideals. "How I feel when I hold my little daughter in my lap, or lay her to my breast, you will not expect me to describe—how could I?" wrote Prussian-born Henriette von Willich in 1805. She was one of those making motherhood and domestic life into what she called a "sweet vocation."[1] Half a century later such sentiments were a staple of middle-class women's lives. By that time most of them did no productive work such as managing a husband's shop or assisting in his craft. These women devoted themselves instead to their families and homes, with varying degrees of intensity. Many of them filled their lives with rituals, symbolism, and meaning. For example, one German woman, Frau Kurz of Tübingen, found serving her husband's lunch so meaningful that it moved her to poetry. At the heart of this domestic world was the duty to bear and raise children, which women had so recently acquired as the activities most suited to them. Instead, however, of regarding reproduction as merely a natural function, they cast it as a complex cultural activity. The domestic world by the middle of the nineteenth century had become a system replete with rules and consequences.

In the English-speaking world, the age took its name from Queen Victoria (1819–1901), who ushered in a period of stability in English politics. Victoria's coronation marked the end of decades of royal misconduct. Adulterous kings and queens, none of whom showed any inclination toward public virtue, had preceded her. Illegitimate offspring and royal mistresses presiding over public functions had put the monarchy's future in doubt. When Victoria came to the throne, all that changed. Marrying soon after her accession to the throne, she and the Prince Consort, Albert, were models of marital stability and prudent rule. They obviously loved and trusted one another in domestic as well as political life. Although she bore a large brood of children, Queen Victoria took

Before her widowhood in 1861, Queen Victoria (with a portrait of Prince Albert on her arm) symbolized the power of virtue in service to the nation.

little delight in the process. She advised her daughter on her marriage to the Crown Prince of Prussia to postpone having children: "What made me so miserable was—to have the first two years of my married life utterly spoilt by this occupation! I could enjoy nothing—not travel about or go about with dear Papa [Prince Albert] and if I had waited a year, as I hope you will, it would have been very different."[2] In fact, she disliked infants; they reminded her of frogs, constantly flapping their arms and legs. In public, however, she gave the impression of maternal devotion by always bringing one or two of her children to carefully planned ceremonial functions. Victoria deliberately set an example of virtue and good behavior for her subjects. Thus, she installed a variation of the republican motif in a country devoted to pursuing wealth and plunder. In her lavish clothing, she symbolized the decorative aspects of womanhood. She also represented propriety, prosperity, and family. In this capacity, she became a symbol of the age, along with the machine.

The eighteenth century had created an ideal of modern motherhood, and the revolutionary period eliminated the aristocratic woman as an alternative model. During the Victorian period women and men inhabited separate spheres: women practiced virtue at home in their domestic, reproductive, and maternal activities; men worked in public, in the marketplace, and took part in representative politics. Coexisting with this ideology of separate spheres was one concerning women's unsuitability for work. Any production transferred from the home to the factory increased the difficulties urban women had in making their contributions to the family economy. This ideology first made working-class women into a disadvantaged group in the workforce. As the ideology gained expression in medical, poetic, and philosophical terms, it also encompassed the middle-class woman, who was seen as even more unsuited for work than her lower-class counterpart. "The family is the kingdom of women—her life," wrote one Russian author in 1850.[3] The middle-class woman who aspired to work at something other than child-rearing or who was totally untalented in domestic skills was seen as abnormal and inferior. Thus arose the first tensions concerning separate spheres for men and women. With provincialism and localism on the wane, some women wanted to inhabit and work in the public world. In addition, virtue was a serious matter, but ostensibly frivolous aspects of domestic life such as fashion and lavish interior decorating undermined the claims of the domestic sphere to virtue. From the domestic ideology also sprang the idea of charity, or helping one's neighbor, which led women out into the world. Domestic life thus gave rise to activities that conflicted with the very idea of "women's sphere."

Domesticity

The home, nineteenth-century people said, formed a haven for family members. It constituted an area of privacy and tranquility. After the tumultuous revolutionary period and in the midst of rapid industrial growth, the home sheltered the family from the worst disturbances that politics and economics might bring. As the century opened, the German author C. F. Pockels expressed this idea of a haven clearly: "When it storms in the world outside . . . when war threatens and all hope of a better world disappears, when one despairs of strength and courage, what more remains to the best of men than confident association with his household happiness, intimate contact with his noble wife, with her kindness and quiet goodness."[4] Pockels's sense of the home as a refuge was actualized in an Austrian style called *Biedermeier*. The designation *Biedermeier* applied to cozy domestic interiors of the period from the Restoration until the Revolutions of 1848.* Couples and their children passed their evenings and holidays together pursuing common activities. Gently curved furniture, simple but elegant plasterwork on ceilings, and austere fabric patterns signified the peacefulness of the household in the *Biedermeier* period. This tranquility and restfulness was expressed in the idea of "home sweet home" in England and in the revered status of the *foyer* or hearth in France.

---

*See Chapter 3.

The notion of the home as a haven was part of a middle-class perspective. Domesticity as an ideal was first pursued in the homes of prosperous farmers whose wives' productive functions were no longer necessary or in those of businessmen and professionals whose wives likewise did not work for pay or profit. One consequence of this perspective on the home was that it became an official view. Census-takers registered women who had no profession outside the home as being "without work" or "housewives," and sometimes they did not even bother to fill in the column about occupation. The outside world was concerned with economic activities; the home was concerned with moral undertakings—no matter how much actual work occurred there. The domestic world nourished the best in human feelings and concerned itself with human life. Women within it were expected to have little interest in anything else but this particular moral undertaking; nor were they to gain an aptitude for other things.

Regional variations existed in the practice of separate spheres. In Catholic Italy, for example, young women were sent to convents, supposedly for an education, though they learned little. Once married, they often shut themselves in, isolated in illiteracy and religious fervor. Hardly any opportunity existed for male and female worlds to mix. In contrast, the home could serve the political purpose of highlighting aristocratic wantonness. Sexually faithful and morally upright, the inhabitants of the middle-class home laid their claims to social leadership. The Evangelical movement in England that so energized Hannah More played a formative role in the development of a new moral code based in the home.* Emphasizing inner purity, upper-class evangelicals stressed the home as the place for cultivation of rectitude, a revived religious faith, and discipline. Moreover, the home ideally replaced the foppish, dainty ways of the aristocracy and instilled a kind of manners more in keeping with middle-class needs and with those of industry. A forthright concern for others and correct behavior guided familial society, where intimacy fostered the kind of behavior demanded in the outside world. The home thus served as a training ground for middle-class life.

These views expressed a sense of the home seen from the outside, sometimes by those who spent little time there. Another sort of domestic life was actually led by middle-class women. Their vision of the home was much more complex. For them, the home hardly constituted a refuge or a realm in which to prepare for a hard day in the outside world. For women, the home shaped their entire existence. In the daytime, the home was the scene of tumult and busyness, as the women prepared for the moment when the rest of the family members would return. A servant scurried about and toiled; the laundry woman came and turned the place inside out. Babies howled, and children carried on their disputes or frolicking. For certain periods, the household had as intense activity as anything the market place might produce. All this activity

---

*See Chapter 3.

Family life in the Danish upper classes, as elsewhere, involved a sentimentalization of children, particularly the youngest. Note the absence of grown men in the domestic scene, except in the portrait.

constituted an ongoing display of vitality—not of repose or relaxation. Women were also expected to prepare children morally to face adult life, educating, inculcating values, and showing a new generation what their duties were. Charged with the care of people and other responsibilities, women led a life at home far different from the common depictions of tranquility. Yet women's sense of duty arose from within domestic life and deviated from the rules of the marketplace: the home, wrote one advice-book author, "is not a place for laissez-faire."[5] The marketplace, however, was precisely that.

All domestic activity served a dual purpose. On the one hand, it reproduced the human population and made it ready for work by feeding, clothing, and sheltering. On the other hand, it had a symbolic side, indicating the presence of woman, reflecting her character, and converting her functions into cultural life. Both sewing and cooking are cultural manipulations of things nature provides. Cooking transforms raw foodstuffs into something dramatic, dainty, or mouth-watering. Cleaning and polishing also functioned to transform natural space into cultural space, which was controlled by women and indicated

their presence. Even changing the drapes—from summer whites to winter brocades—signified the changes in nature, fertility, and the freshness of the housewife. All of these drew attention to the woman of the house.

Converting the role of women from one aimed at subsistence and production to one having more abstract cultural and psychological components took
a good deal of effort. Growing in popularity from the 1740s on, so-called
advice books offered programs for organizing the home. These books either
addressed a limited topic such as cooking or etiquette or were encyclopedic.
For example, Hannah Wisnes, the wife of a Norwegian minister, published the
popular *Manual of Household Arts* (1848), which described the care of linens,
preparation of food for the holidays, and domestic utensils. The original edition also discussed brewing, slaughtering, and other tasks no longer performed
by many middle-class households, but was soon revised into a best-selling version intended for the less complex modern household. Isabella Beeton's classic
Book of Household Management (1861) ranged from cooking, which took up
thirty-seven of the forty-six chapters, to health and legal matters. Mrs. Beeton's
work gave a preliminary list of a housewife's virtues, which stressed early rising, frugality, limited acquaintances, an avoidance of "love of company for its
own sake," care in clothing, and "restraint in conversation."[6] This book's detailed explanations of the vices to be avoided were so full of supposed real-life
examples as to make a modern reader think her advice must have been sorely
needed. Beeton herself was obviously a hard worker, someone who didn't need
to be told how to make the household more accountable and more pleasant.
Born in 1836, she married in 1856 and died of puerperal fever after the birth
of her fourth child in 1865. By then she had put out two other books and had
published many articles in the magazines her husband owned. In her writing
she stressed the utilitarian side of housekeeping, which meant the strict supervision of servants, scrupulous keeping of household accounts, and performance of social and familial duties. Yet she also understood the cultural importance of knowing the "natural history" of vegetables and animals used in
cookery. In addition, she compared social customs: English women, for example, should only dip the tips of their fingers in finger bowls and not follow
the French custom of "gargling in the mouth" with the water at the end of
meals. Yet it was cooking that she emphasized in recognition that men now
had other places where they might get a tasty meal. She saw clubs, taverns,
and restaurants as "competition" that kept men away from home and their
families. By being made decorative and enticing, the domestic sphere could
offer men an attractive alternative to the outside world of industry and commerce.

Beeton and others outlined the sobering responsibilities of marriage and
household activity. Among the more specialized manuals, some stressed supervision of servants, whereas others focused on housekeeping routines and
chores including cleaning. Still others dealt with the handling of financial matters and recommended accurate recording of all domestic expenditures, right
down to the last penny. Beeton proposed that household accounts be balanced
at the very least once a month but optimally once a week. Other authors rec-

ommended noting all expenditures and keeping any receipts. These should be put in envelopes designated for specific categories, say, charity, household, food, and so on. In France, Madame St. Leger scrupulously kept such accounts in mid-century, including the preceding categories as well as ones for herself, her husband, and her son. Madame St. Leger kept track of even miniscule amounts such as a penny or two for someone who came to the door for charity. She noted everything spent on the maid's clothing, her aprons, bedding, a trip to visit her sick mother, and so on. She recorded amounts paid for baths, for special wine when someone was ill, and for rides in rented conveyances around town. At the same time that she kept detailed accounts of small expenses, she spent thousands on jewelry, hats, and lace. The purpose of account keeping—to keep track of and limit expenditures—conflicted with desires to decorate the body. This conflict reveals how different the household was from the world of industry and commerce; for household accounts, showing a profit was not a goal; nor for that matter was saving among wealthy women like Madame St. Leger. The ritual of showing accounts to one's husband on a regular basis perhaps had some importance: women reportedly grew anxious on the eve of such encounters. In the final analysis the account book, like many other domestic features, worked toward such serious ends as charting familial property and calculating the costs of raising a family, but also toward decorating the body and household space.

Managing the activities of servants was another domestic responsibility, though in Germany observers noticed husbands doing the hiring and sometimes even the managing. Most middle-class families employed only one woman, who did a range of work. Where there was more than one servant, households usually had a cook in addition to the general maid. In the wealthiest homes, teams of servants headed by a housekeeper performed all household work. Housewives were supposed to supervise certain activities closely. They counted sheets, silverware, and checked larders for supplies; most of these items were kept locked up. Preserving and making liquors were also tasks demanding strict attention to make sure servants performed the processes correctly. The function of servants in middle-class households was not decorative or symbolic but utilitarian. Servant's work, however, did have the symbolic purpose of making the housewife look like a person of leisure. That is, any work that the woman did was camouflaged by the presence of servants. Officially centered on nurturing and reproduction, "true" women did not work. The servant's importance as a symbol was also revealed by the one household activity that was forbidden to her—reproduction. The servant who became pregnant made a blot on the family and was usually forced to leave. Middle-class laws of the household made the worst offense of intimate relations between servant and master. The law of the master, however, and the law of the household expressly differed: masters seduced servants with impunity. Serving as the functional converse of the housewife, the servant emphasized her mistress's symbolic role by her own lack of reproductive effort and her attention to productive labors. Some books of advice to housewives published at the time emphasized the need for strict attention to servants' morality. Along with frantic letters written to relatives in the countryside asking them to find a girl who was reliable and obedient, such advice is indicative of the new high purpose of the home and of the housewife.

The Reconstruction of Childhood

For the concept of republican motherhood to be realized, there had to be children with special needs to which mothers would attend. Prior to this time, accounts of children had depicted them less as psychologically different beings than as ones whose attainment of adulthood depended only on growth in size and attention to duty. Many parents had put their children out with nurses so that both father and mother could proceed to do productive work in a craft or trade without interruption. Children went from a wet nurse's care into other people's shops, businesses, or farms to learn skills from adults outside their immediate families. Prior to the nineteenth century parental duty in terms of supervising emotional development had scarcely been conceived of, nor did people believe that children had special needs—other than learning a craft—that parents alone should care for. Republican motherhood changed these attitudes.

Rousseau had focused attention on education and child care and thus helped begin reconstructing the idea of childhood. The Swiss educator Johann Pestalozzi (1746–1827) stimulated the interest Rousseau had stirred up with his *How Gertrude Teaches Her Children* (1801). Pestalozzi particularly advocated carefully guided activity for children. Women following his precepts

---

A Russian Family

Sonya Kovalevsky, the great Russian mathematician, adored her beautiful and talented mother, but the latter showed a preference for her son and older daughter. In contrast, Sonya feared her father, whom she seldom saw in any case. Like many European fathers, General Krukovsky was a distant figure, but even in his absence he represented familial law and order. The relationship grew from nineteenth-century gender roles and family life. The following is Sonya's account of that relationship, as demonstrated by an incident when she was caught reading too much.

> In such cases, the governess had recourse to the most extreme measures: she sent me to my father with orders to relate my guilt to him myself. I feared this more than all other punishments.
>
> In reality father was not at all severe with us; but I saw

him rarely—only at dinner. He never permitted himself the slightest familiarity with us except when one of the children was ill. Then he was completely changed. We simply adored him at such times, and retained the memory of them for a long while. But on ordinary occasions, when all were well, he stuck to the rule that "a man must be severe," and therefore was very sparing of his caresses.

Hence, when the governess used to say, "Go to your father; make your boast to him of how you have been behaving," I felt genuine despair. I cried and resisted, but the governess was implacable, and taking me by the hand, she led me, or, to speak more correctly, she dragged me through the long suite of rooms to the door of the study, left me to my fate, and went away.

I knock, but very softly. Several moments, which seem to me interminable, elapse.

There is nothing to be done; I knock again.

"Who's there? Come in," calls father's voice at last from the study.

I enter, but halt in the semi-darkness on the threshold. Father sits at his writing-table with his back to the door, and does not see me.

"Who's there? What's wanted?" he cries impatiently.

"It is I, papa. Margarita Frantzovna has sent me," I gulp out in reply.

Then for the first time father divines what is the matter.

"Ah, ah! you have been naughty again, of course," he says, trying to communicate to his voice as stern an intonation as possible. "Come, tell your story. What have you been doing?"

After I told it, he responded, "What a horrid, naughty little girl you are. I am very much displeased with you," he says, and pauses because he does not know what else to say. "Go, stand in the corner," he pronounces judgment at last, because, out of all his pedagogic wisdom, his memory has retained nothing beyond the fact that naughty children are made to stand in the corner.

And so you may picture to yourself how I, a big girl of twelve—I, who a few minutes previously had been going through the most complicated dramas with the heroine of a romance perused on the sly,—I am obliged to go and stand in the corner like a foolish little child.

Source: Adapted from Sonya Kovalevsky, *Her Recollections of Childhood,* Isabel Hapgood, trans. (New York: Century, 1895), 46–49.

devoted more time to keeping their own children active and supervising them more closely. Pestalozzi's ideas also encouraged the formation of schools that taught industrial skills and crafts to the young. Charitable women started schools to teach knitting and other potentially commercial skills to poor children. Though these were seen as little more than workshops, some educational benefits did result. Moreover, the women teachers saw their connection with their small charges as an important social undertaking. Friedrich Wilhelm Froebel (1782–1852), a pupil of Pestalozzi, made that undertaking seem even more important. At his schools in various villages in the central German region of Thuringia, Froebel stressed the need for teachers to develop the inborn ability of each child. In his kindergartens, Froebel emphasized the nurturing aspects of child care. Rather than drumming in rote knowledge, adults should strive to know each child and how to motivate him or her. Like plants, children needed close attention at the various stages of their development. Each stage had its own inner logic, and only successful passage through each stage ensured a smooth path to adulthood. Of these stages, the most important was the first, those few early years when mothers and children should be as one. These ideas of Froebel ascribed a new importance to the connection between mother and child. Children needed to be studied so that their development and inner mental life could be understood. Only a watchful parent would have the requisite knowledge of such development, and mothers alone could undertake the earliest investigations and nurturing. Insufficient maternal attention prevented a child from reaching adulthood properly. Although Pestalozzi had stressed the importance of childhood education within the family as a whole, Froebel made it compelling that mothers attend to their children.

Extending the idea that education of children was best done by mothers, Froebel announced a need for maternal training and championed women as educators of children outside the home. He believed that women should undertake serious programs of study to prepare them for their role in childhood education. Then they would be eminently qualified to teach numbers of young children. He saw his task "to rescue the female sex from its hitherto passive and instinctive situation and, through its nurturing mission, to raise it to the same level as the male sex." Froebel's plan to train women to be professional teachers drew immense support from women and, in fact, started a movement in favor of women's careers. Teaching presented an alternative for females who admired domestic goals but hated familial confinement. Henriette Breymann, for one, saw "an entirely new age dawning for women."[7] Other commentators envisioned progress for Germany as liberal values developed because of this emphasis on childhood activity. Along with male members of the avant garde, some women lobbied hard for the spread of the kindergarten system. The foremost among these, Berthe Marenholtz-Bulow wrote and proselytized with an energy that seemed excessive to many in her aristocratic set. Some people, however, saw kindergartens as too radical, as a sign of revolutionary goals penetrating German life. They felt that women would become unsexed, that is, unfeminine, if they pursued work outside the home.

For the leaders of the kindergarten movement, the virtues of having

A German kindergarten filled with women and children and dominated at the center by a depiction of Friedrich Froebel offering direction.

women teach lay precisely in the fact that they would not only maintain but enhance the maternal role and spread feminine virtues. Far from unsexing women, the training for kindergarten work would consolidate their woman-hood and allow it expression. Teaching would be an extension of motherly activity into an acceptable realm. The middle class eagerly hired women who had received such training as governesses to give their children private instruc-tion. Middle-class women instituted a final step in the evolution of the kinder-garten by viewing the institution as a way of reaching the lower classes and of buttressing the familial role of women there. Although the kindergarten move-ment had started as a training of the inward, middle-class self, the implications and opportunities of the cause ultimately led those who took it up into wider realms. Like other aspects of domestic life, educating children could become the source of threatening changes.

As a result of these theories and also because of the lack of opportunity for productive activity, women of the middle and upper classes could turn to their children for an occupation. Although they often had help with the phys-ical aspects of child care, it was the developmental growth of children that concerned them. An upper-class French woman at mid-century saw herself as allied with her children's guardian angel. In this capacity, she scrutinized their characters, faults, and achievements. Even after her children went to nursery school and grade school, her motherly supervision continued. She listened to their lessons in the evening after letting them have a short period of amuse-ment. She also taught them to have a "profound affection for their brothers and sisters."[8] To remind herself of her resolve in these matters, this mother wrote down the plan she followed. Evidently, the educational mission of motherhood did not yet come naturally. Instead, a mother must plan her behavior, list precepts, and outline her goals with respect to her children.

Despite this new interest in motherhood, some middle-class and upper-class children still went to boarding schools at an early age—six or seven, for example. They also had nurses, governesses, and tutors as well as other part-time instructors. Middle-class children received this kind of intense general education, whereas formerly they might have served apprenticeships. But the important changes lay in the emotional concern that mothers started offering and the identification of women's role with this kind of attention. Once the "developmental" nature of childhood had been accepted, mothers could adopt and perfect a nurturing role.

Marriage, Fertility, and Sexuality

In 1851, Russian novelist Evgeniia Tur portrayed an upper-class woman's views about marriage as follows: "It had nothing to do with love . . . if she wanted to be free, it was necessary to have her own home and to marry."[9] In some social circles, like this Russian one, people associated marriage with freedom from parental control. Although marriage was increasingly a matter of the heart among the ruling classes, parents nonetheless played an important role in determining partners. Some chose mates for their offspring with virtually no consultation of the parties involved. Others trusted the social environment to protect their families from unsuitable matches. They believed that if young women were well chaperoned and only introduced to acceptable young men, they would marry properly. As long as these ground rules were followed, "love" and "sentiment" were allowed to flower.

Marriage, however, meant more than having one's "own home," as the Russian heroine dreamed of. It meant engaging in sexual relations and reproduction, and in the nineteenth century the setting for these functions differed from the agrarian one that dominated a century earlier. Changes in the productive system even influenced the number of children people had. Across Europe, couples had begun limiting the size of their families as early as the eighteenth century. For the most part this early limitation occurred in noble families. Although in some countries, notably Great Britain, the peerage did not start limiting family size until the mid–nineteenth century; in other places noble families felt the need to concentrate their wealth on fewer children. In Austria and its dependencies such as Hungary, in France, and in countries such as the Italian states affected by the Napoleonic Code and by other legal reforms, the upper classes were constrained to make all their children beneficiaries instead of just the oldest son. The end of primogeniture would have splintered familial wealth out of existence had the nobility not practiced birth control. Moreover, noble wealth not directed into new channels such as business and industry was already in danger of evaporating. The trend toward smaller families in the nobility is exemplified in a family of the old Venetian nobility, the Donà. This family had regularly produced eleven to twelve children per couple prior to the eighteenth century. Over the next two centuries, the average number of children dropped to eight, still a substantial family size but also a 33 percent reduction. By the twentieth century, the average number of children per couple in all branches of the family was two. Despite all evidence that in many areas the wealthy and upwardly mobile practiced birth control, the Victorian family still seems huge compared to today's typical family. Family portraits display numerous children, and prominent women often appeared surrounded by them. Both Queen Victoria (1819–1901) and Catherine Gladstone (1812–1900), philanthropist and wife of Prime Minister William Gladstone, had nine children, for example.

A similar reduction in family size occurred in the middle classes, also at least partly for economic reasons. Middle-class parents had adopted a manner of training that differed from the commercial and craft training of a century earlier. Instead of putting children into service or an apprenticeship, the middle class began to educate its young people until a fairly advanced age. Children became burdens on, rather than contributors to, the family economy. Because they were dependent for a longer time, they put a greater strain on the family budget. Simultaneously, the middle-class woman was making smaller contributions to the income of the family and using more of it to maintain her way of life as a reproducer and nurturer and perhaps as a symbol of financial security. Finally, the middle class had assumed a new social and political position, which meant money had to be spent on decorating, entertaining, and the like. Family economics made birth control a necessity. Reinforcing the economic motivation was the idea of the child as a special part of the social order, as a being in need of constant attention; the more children a woman had, the less individual attention each one could receive.

Family size did not decrease everywhere; some areas experienced rising fertility rates. In northern France, where families still controlled businesses long after stock companies became common, the number of children per family rose. There women in the generation born between 1780 and 1798 averaged 4.7 births; these women were often active in managing family-owned textile firms. After middle-class women in this area began leading exclusively domestic lives, the fertility rate rose to 6.3 births per woman for those born between 1849 and 1858 and to 7.3 births for those born between 1869 and 1878. Women in professional families averaged a smaller number of births, whereas those producing children to go into business were above average in their fertility. This French data clearly deviates from the norm. In England, although large families did continue to be prevalent among the wealthy, they were primarily the result of declining child mortality. In other words, women may have had the same number or even fewer offspring than earlier generations, but fewer of the children died. Once this demographic trend began adversely affecting family well-being, the English also limited their family size.

Birth control must have contributed to the reduction in family size because the age at marriage for women was gradually declining at this time in some areas and thus increased the number of childbearing years. Bourgeois women in Genoa, for example, typically got married at the age of 26.3 years between 1700 and 1749, at 22.7 years between 1800 and 1849, and at 24.7 years between 1850 and 1899. On the other hand, among upper classes in other parts of Europe, the age of marriage for women rose slightly during the nineteenth century and this served to limit these women's fertility. In other words, the ways of practicing birth control and whether it was practical at all depended on local customs and local wealth.

In the eighteenth century, reproduction was regarded as a pleasurable act that would have the instrumental end of replenishing the population. This view gave way to new values that stressed the long-term duties and responsibilities of reproduction, rather than its sexual pleasures. Clearly not all marital life was devoid of such pleasure: at the beginning of this period, German housewife Bettina von Arnim reported a rhapsodic relationship with her husband. Other women left records that attest to their passion and pleasure. But, at the other extreme, many women expressed their loathing of sex. Queen Victoria supposedly gave her daughter premarital advice about getting through sexual intercourse by "thinking of Britain." "Thinking of Britain" connected marital relations with civic responsibility and maternity; in no way did it acknowledge female sensuality. In Catholic countries mothers told their daughters to think of Jesus Christ or the Virgin Mary while "enduring" sexual intercourse. Women in the public sphere, such as actresses, dancers, and obviously prostitutes, sought out pleasure and were therefore outcasts from respectable, domestic society.

Liberal ideology posited a balance of self-interest and difference within the heterosexual economy. That is, men's excessive pleasure-seeking balanced women's anesthesia to pleasure in sexual relations. Young men "sowed their wild oats," whereas girls maintained their ignorance or innocence in sexual matters. Common wisdom suggested that women were more interested in the ultimate goal of intercourse: reproduction, not sexual pleasure, was what gave value to marital relations. Moreover, women's sexual pleasure was always alloyed by thoughts of the consequences of intercourse—pregnancy or disease were possible and either would be painful if not deadly. Queen Victoria complained about the fatigues and miseries of her first two years of marriage, all due to pregnancy. At that time, the only way to eliminate such consequences was to avoid sexual intercourse. For this reason, marriage was often problematic for women. Unlike the upper-class Russian who envisioned marriage as the beginning of freedom, many women saw it as a burden, especially in countries where the ideal of romantic love had not developed. In Catholic Italy or among middle-class French or Germans, marriage meant responsibility, childbirth, and physical suffering.

The sexual reserve on women's part did not mean that the Victorian age had no awareness of sexuality. In fact, it had a great deal. From the beginning of the century, statisticians collected data on marital status, fertility, and conditions of cohabitation, among other things. Catholic confessors' manuals from this time show an intense interest in the sexual sins—as opposed to other kinds—committed by parishioners. However, sexuality was relegated to a hidden and disguised status. Although people talked about their sexual lives in the confessional, to the census taker or recorder of vital statistics, or in medical manuals not for ordinary consumption, in general this topic was taboo. The male figure, despite ideology concerning its abundant sexuality, was hidden in somber, dark clothing that reflected his sober pursuits in the public world. At the same time, the reputedly asexual female body was displayed in plunging necklines, with bits of lace covering pushed-up breasts, and varieties of padding to emphasize the body's shape. Many in the middle classes strived to maintain a facade of uninvolvement with sexuality. For example, observers in Germany remarked on the single beds and separate rooms of married couples, which seemed to indicate a limited sexual life. There were, of course, national variations. In all countries, however, this appearance of sexual restraint coexisted alongside women's sexually enticing clothing and flirtatious behavior and a growing array of institutions such as census bureaus designed to chart the sexual pulse of populations. The culture of sexuality expressed a variety of paradoxes and contradictions.

Clothing, Sewing, and Gender Difference

In the course of modernizing production, men underwent a transformation in physical appearance. Early in the nineteenth century, men's clothing was still colorful, and the male body an object of display. Fashion illustrations from that time often pictured male and female figures on the same page, an indication of how accepted the peacock-like aristocratic male was. Prominent men wore fancy uniforms, corsets to improve their figures, and hose to display the shape of the legs. The nobleman appeared in public adorned and decorated— a sensual image. Except for military men in dress parades and court officials, these aspects of male dress had all but disappeared by mid-century. By the early twentieth century, even most kings and emperors wore full-length trousers and less form-fitting and elaborate uniforms. The multiple waistcoats, fancy buttons, flowing cravats, and equally flowing hair of middle-class men also disappeared during the nineteenth century. Business and professional men adopted the black suit, loosely fitted and without any decoration of metal, silk, lace, or other accoutrements of old regime garb. The male exchanged a made-to-order, form-fitting costume for ready-made wear. This standardization of dress accompanied the suppression of sexual display on the part of men. An occasional fancy button on a waistcoat, a small tie ornament, or cuff links were all that remained of sartorial ornamentation that drew attention to the male body. Overtly, it had become a productive rather than a sexual body, one intended for money making rather than for pleasure seeking.

In an era that stressed gender difference, women conformed to an opposite strategy in dress. As men's clothing became less sexual, women's became more so. Fashionable women's clothing in the first two decades of the century had lines that simply followed bodily contours, but from the 1820s on, skirts grew

The Countess of Castiglione, an intimate of French Emperior Napoleon III, displays the fashion of the 1850s. It included the constricted waistline, massive skirt, and voluminous sleeves—all of which shaped the body into a frail but imposing artifact.

fuller as bulky crinolines swelled the lower portion of the female silhouette. By the 1850s, hoopskirts constituted the standard underpinning of women's dresses. The hoopskirt caused a revolution in underwear by serving as a substitute for the weighty layers of petticoats and crinolines that had been worn. The desired effect of the bulkiness was the illusion of fullness in the hips—an effect also achieved by padding. When the hoopskirt went out, the artificial fullness was transferred to the bust and to the back of dresses in the form of bustles that made the buttocks into a prominent protrusion covered with swirls of fabric. In other words, clothing constantly reshaped women's bodies. It particularly drew attention to the sexual and reproductive parts, that is, to the breasts and the hips. The corset also aided in reshaping the figure. A garment made with whalebone or steel reinforcements, the corset laced below the breasts and around the waist with the help of metal eyelets that allowed the laces to be drawn tightly without tearing the fabric. Inserts were added to push up the breasts, and pads were attached at the hip area. These devices made the female body a kind of artifact that could be remade and redefined. In her dress, woman displayed her reproductive nature, in marked contrast to man. Thus, clothing expressed the gender order. Even among working-class people, fashion situated women in this order: observers noted, for example, Italian peasant women in the fields wearing crinolines.

Patterns of sewing clothing also followed gender differentiation. The construction of most men's clothing took place in the outside world, whereas women's was generally made at home. Men's and boy's socks were often knitted at home, but tailors did fine fitting of suits for middle-class men, and seamstresses made men's shirts, waistcoats, underclothing, and nightwear. On the other hand, women's clothing, except for especially fancy dresses made by couturières, was constructed at home. Seamstresses were hired to work in a household by the day. Housewives, however, usually participated in clothing construction, and many habitually carried a bag containing mending. In addition to doing regular maintenance, repairing tears, or sewing on buttons, women put a lot of effort and attention to keeping in style by giving new turns to flounces, new collars to dresses, new shapes to sleeves. A shift in fashion might require adding an overskirt of lace or different cuffs, buttons, or belt. Such newness testified to youth, freshness, and fertility. Change in dress took precedence in household activity. The reproductive body was so central to cultural ideology that women emphasized it by constant manipulations of its shape.

The Disruptive Consequences of Gender Difference

The Victorian middle-class home had many contradictory aspects and so did the lives of the women who inhabited it. Although primness, efficiency, and moral virtue formed one side of their lives and caring for children took up a great deal of some women's time, a more apparently frivolous side of domestic life existed with those aspects. The middle-class home grew more and more ornate as the century progressed. Lampshades were fringed; sofas were done up in brocade, braid, and ornate moldings; rugs were woven in floral patterns or made of animal skins; and wooden furniture was inlaid, heavily carved, or intricately adorned. Table settings called for silverware for each part of a meal or for different dishes, including salad forks, jelly spoons, fish knives, cream soup spoons, butter knives, mayonnaise spoons, berry spoons, and so on. Moreover, in order to sell more silverware, manufacturers increasingly differentiated between patterns for luncheon and dinner. New forms of dishes were invented to serve specific courses or to hold a particular kind of food. Household furnishings also became more varied in purpose and style, from tables for every kind of function—library, serving, hall, sideboard—to a range of cupboards, including armoires, what-nots, and china cabinets. This increasing complexity and cost of household decor as well as the lavishness of women's clothing went against the grain of society's emphasis on efficiency and cost-accounting. Women who noted every penny spent might also spend whimsically and even extravagantly on merely decorative fabrics and objects.

Household time, with its domestic celebrations, also stood in marked contrast to industrial time, with its undifferentiated days and seasons. Celebrations centered on births and marriages, that is, on events having to do with reproduction and sexuality. Moreover, families celebrated holidays by themselves, not in the community celebrations that accompanied such events in the past. Holidays such as Christmas were increasingly run by women and domesticated. Absorbed in her gift-making and decoration, Fanny Mendelssohn apologized to a friend late in 1828 for not writing: "In the last few weeks before Christmas women do really, like children, feel under a charm, and acknowledge no other interests and purposes than those of the needle."[10] The household's extravagance in comparison to the austerity of the factory or the bank had a celebratory air about it. "Never have I seen," wrote one woman of her house at party time "a similar state of inside-out."[11] In other words, women turned the world upside down at regular intervals. The lavishness, celebrations, and focus on reproduction and sexuality that characterized the middle-class home also suggest the world of the carnival. Only a permissiveness associated with carnival explains the existence of such household frivolities in direct opposition to the general severity of middle-class principles. The women whose sexual characteristics received undue emphasis from their clothing and the overburdened dinner tables throughout middle-class Europe revived the world of carnival at a time when industrialists wanted to eliminate such festivals from their employees' lives in the name of profit. As manifested in some households, the serious activities of republican motherhood coexisted with disruptive aspects of domesticity.

The Victorian household was ideally a nonproductive center; therefore, the perfect woman should adopt an image of repose and idleness to emphasize the complementarity of the home and the world outside. Florence Nightingale's mother and sister, for example, reportedly cautioned each other about overexertion when one of them left the sofa to arrange flowers. Delicacy was first a character trait but came to affect behavior. Such "delicacy" aroused concern for some whenever physical activity was suggested. The mother of Swedish author Fredrika Bremer (1801–1865) firmly opposed women's moving about any more than necessary. When Fredrika wanted to walk outside and exercise, her mother suggested that she move a bit behind her chair. Nervousness and fainting were other commonly accepted manifestations of women's weakness, in contrast to men's strength. Bad or even disagreeable news, shocking sights, or poor manners could cause fainting. Many middle-class women experienced recurring headaches. Jane Carlyle (1801–1866), married to a tyrannical genius, suffered from them; so did Sophie Vrau-Aubineau after being forced into retiring from her position as head of a textile firm in Lille in 1861. Some physical infirmities such as tearing in childbirth or a prolapsed uterus resulted from poor gynecological and obstetrical treatment. Standards of modesty and fashion also contributed to women's physical debilitation. Heavy underclothing suspended from the waist impeded easy movement and was something of a drag on energy; corsets adversely affected inner organs, respiration, and circulation. In short, a range of factors—physical, social, and ideological—went toward creating the languishing woman as both an ideal and a reality. Many of the problems women had with their bodies led them to seek a variety of cures, even within quasi-religious movements. Health cures, resorts, and sanitoriums flourished to treat the nervousness and debility of the middle class, especially its women. Pills, salves, and gynecological devices also catered to those who believed they led to better health. Some women, such as the poet Elizabeth Barrett Browning, moved from one part of Europe to another in search of a climate that might be beneficial to their health. Later, health reform and feminist ideology would tackle the complex dimensions of what had become a way of life. In the meantime, delicacy and sickness served to focus attention away from male concerns toward the female. Even so powerful a woman as Queen Victoria had "sick headaches," temper tantrums, and fits of weakness in order to get her way. Mary Wollstonecraft's observation that women used crafty behavior to overcome their powerlessness in relation to men remained pertinent long after her death.

Rules and institutions developed to structure the contact between men and women in order to minimize the possibility for conflict and overt sexual activity. Men had their clubs, taverns, cafés, and other private institutions, as Isabella Beeton so clearly reminded her readers. Women visited members of their own social class and sometimes formed intense friendships. Both men and women of the middle and upper classes participated in mixed social events, such as dinner parties, balls, and weekend visits in the country. All these occasions took place according to strict rules. For example, when paying a formal call, women followed standards governing how long to stay, whether to accept a cup of tea, at what moment to leave a calling card, and how long after an event such as childbirth, marriage, death, or betrothal one should pay a visit. Similarly, mealtime called for careful behavior, especially when non–family members were present, or the meal marked a special occasion. Around the natural process of eating, rules were imposed about such things as when to begin, when and how to use silverware, and where to seat people around the table based on gender, family relationships, and rank. Like clothing and home decoration, etiquette singled out the woman of the house as the central character in the event. The hostess maintained control over the natural process of eating through rules of etiquette that all accepted as the proper way to behave.

High-society functions were subject to the highest degree of detailed preparation in matters of clothing, etiquette, decor, and food. The guest list reflected social class and one's rank within it: a hostess invited politicians, professional men, and perhaps some intellectuals or artists. An English woman described women's place on the guest list: "Besides these eminent people there was usually a sprinkling of women famous for their beauty, wit, or both, who either gave the conversation a sparkling turn, or were wise enough not to interrupt good talk, and who accordingly sat looking statuesque or flowerlike."[12] Many attractive women assumed a statuesque or flowerlike demeanor in order not to appear to be trying to attract men sexually. When the waltz became popular after mid-century, some middle- and upper-class women protested that it would incite sexual behavior, which they believed had no place in public. For this type of middle-class woman, the physical contact between man and woman that waltzing involved was threatening; it was a reminder of the disturbing natural world of sexuality and reproduction—a world her cultural activities tried to control, while at the same time she allowed it to flourish.

Troublesome Women

Not all middle-class women followed the prescribed societal norms scrupulously. Many who made names for themselves did so partly because they broke the social codes governing women's conduct. German revolutionary and author Louise Aston (1814–1871) smoked cigars, wore men's trousers, and denounced religion. In France, novelist George Sand (Amandine-Aurore Dupin, 1804–1876) dressed as a man in order to get better theater seats at cheaper prices; she also wore men's clothing when in the country, as her grandmother had, for riding and hiking.* Sand, too, smoked cigars. Mathilde Anneke (1817–1884) also wore men's clothing when riding during the revolutions of 1848, and Italian secret society member Bianca Milesi cut her hair off so as to travel more freely. Both smoking and cross-dressing were fairly common among women who had practical or ideological reasons for breaking conventions about what women should do. More consequential transgressions were those of women who became part of illicit relationships or gave birth to children out of wedlock. Though not married to George Lewes, English author George Eliot (Marian Evans, 1819–1880) insisted on the legitimacy of their partnership.* George Sand's daughter Aurore was certainly the product of an adulterous relationship, and so was the daughter of Italian journalist and political leader Christina Belgiojoso (1808–1871). Author Daniel Stern (Marie d'Agoult, 1805–1876) had several illegitimate children fathered by the composer Franz Liszt. Prominent Italian feminist Anna Mozzoni (1837–1920) had an illegitimate daughter, and French author and feminist Hortense Allart (1801-1879) had two illegitimate sons. Some of these women were consciously applying the liberating ideas of the Romantic Movement concerning sexual love and passion. In all cases, however, they were assuming a male role. Often adopting a male pseudonym to hide their female identity, they also adopted the stance of men who parented illegitimate children without qualms. So many prominent women of this time pursued some kind of sexual adventure that the breaking of norms in one's personal life seems almost a prerequisite of achievement in the public sphere.

Even conventional unmarried women defied the Victorian social order. Although it was acceptable for unmarried men to roam the world, engage in business, and lead a celibate life, middle-class women attempting to do any of these were seen as odd or defective, even though unmarried women constituted

---

*See Chapter 6 for general discussion of their writing.

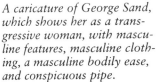

A caricature of George Sand, which shows her as a transgressive woman, with masculine features, masculine clothing, a masculine bodily ease, and conspicuous pipe.

a potential financial and social burden to their families. The existence of large numbers of unmarried women was perceived as threatening, particularly in Germany and England. In these places, observers gave dire estimations of the effect of the excess of unmarried women. Recent studies show that the excess was due to the higher age of marriage in these areas: in both countries, more than 70 percent of women were still unmarried at age twenty-five, whereas a lower age at marriage prevailed elsewhere. Studies show that higher rates of celibacy existed among the middle rather than working classes. Among workers, marriage and cohabitation were necessary to produce the income to survive. The expense of setting up a household that met middle-class standards cost more than many middle-class couples could afford, given that the man had to generate all the income. So the middle-class spinster plagued the European scene, though more prevalently in some areas than in others.

The main problem concerning middle-class spinsters was what they might do in a world so fixated on the necessity of heterosexual and nuclear households. The middle-class spinster could not generate income, either for herself or for the household she inhabited. She could and often did become a kind of beast of burden in a parent's or sibling's home by performing all the tasks of a high-level servant. She could keep busy doing the endless round of supervising servants, care of children, and many other activities. Spinsters also fulfilled other needs of various family members, for example, by serving as a kind of secretary to a father or brother or lavishing extra love and attention on chil-

A Swedish Woman Decides to Remain Single

Most people married in the nineteenth century, though an important minority did not. Sometimes families kept at least one daughter single to care for aging parents. The middle class increasingly could not provide dowries for all its children. Other women chose celibacy, like Swedish author Fredrika Bremer (1801–1865) who even before writing the great novel *Hertha* refused one marriage offer after another. The following letter to her married sister Charlotte in 1829 also shows how important a role parents played in arranging marriages, while it demonstrates also Bremer's resolve not to marry.

I then asked [Father] if he wished me to read the newspapers to him. He answered with a gentle "No," but said that he had something for *me* to read, and went into the next room and returned with a letter, which he gave me; the handwriting was unknown to me. I went into the drawing-room and read, to my astonishment a very well-written offer of marriage. . . . The letter is otherwise very good, and I was really sorry for the man, that he should have addressed the wrong person. Having read the letter, I returned it to my father, who asked me what he was to answer. Without the slightest hesitation, as you may well imagine, I begged of him to say, "No, I thank you most humbly!" This morning my father sent for me, read me his answer, and asked me whether it was according to my wish. It contained many good things, but others which might have been left out. But it would never have done for me to make any remark. Afterwards I agreed with my mother and sisters, that, in order to enjoy life's mediocre happiness . . . one would do wiser to take [a man like the one who had proposed], than many another one with greater external gifts and large estates,—provided *nota bene*, one intends to enter into the holy state of matrimony, which I pray, together with all the tortures mentioned in the Litany, to be spared from.

Source: Life, Letters, and Posthumous Works of Fredrika Bremer, Charlotte Bremer, ed., Fredrik Milow and Emily Nonnen, trans. (New York: Hurd and Houghton, 1868), 140–141.

dren in the family. Successful men of Victorian times often had a spinster relative working behind the scenes. On the other hand, the spinster could interfere with the functioning of nuclear families. Her own emotional needs could disrupt the life of a couple, and her very presence was detrimental to the ideal of intimacy and privacy. Even a well-liked sister of a wife or husband broke into the heterosexual dyad the century demanded.

The spinster without means had little opportunity for extricating herself from her penurious situation. The only plausible option was serving as a governess or lady's companion. In England in any given year there were more than 25,000 governesses, and lesser numbers could be found across the Continent. French and English governesses were more and more in demand as the middle class developed in other countries, such as Russia, because Western European women had superior educations early in the century. Women whose families could not support them or those suddenly on their own turned toward the position of governess, but always with great reluctance. One man described the predicament of his six unmarried sisters in the 1860s:[13]

> My father, who was certainly quite advanced in his ideas, never for a moment contemplated that any of his daughters should learn professional work with a view to earning their living. . . . After a restless night of anxiety over some failure among his investments, and dread lest he should not be able at his death to leave the girls a competent income, he would come down to breakfast looking the picture of misery. . . . There was only one conclusion—"the girls would have to go out as governesses." Then silence and gloom would descend on the household. . . . To be a governess—that was to become a pariah.

The governess in the nineteenth century personified a life of intense misery. She was also that most unfortunate individual: the single, middle-class woman who had to earn her own living. Although being a governess might be a degradation, employing one was a sign of culture and means. With skills in such areas as languages, music, art, geography, and history, the governess could teach these things to children of the middle class. The creation of the developmental child helped to define the Victorian mother, but other aspects of Victorian ideology allowed for surrogates in the job of fostering children's development.

The psychological situation of the governess made her position unenviable. Her presence created practical difficulties within the Victorian home because she was neither a servant nor a member of the family. She was from the social level of the family, but the fact that she was paid a salary put her at the economic level of the servants. Stories abound of bad treatment from both sides of the household: ostracism by servants and exploitation by mistresses or seduction by masters. Some governesses were treated as part of the family circle, whereas others only inhabited it when summoned like the other domestics. The typical governess also had financial worries—how could she provide for any period of unemployment, for sickness, and for her old age? Many governesses had to send much of their pay to support widowed mothers and siblings still at home. The governess's situation aroused sympathy in certain middle-class women, who saw it as a fate they had fortunately avoided. While novels publicized the governess's plight, philanthropists aimed at practical remedies. In England, a Governesses Benevolent Association arose along with the establishment of Queen's College in 1848. The college offered courses to upgrade women's skills so that they might be more competitive in the job market and be able to demand better treatment and wages. This was the start of a drive to improve job opportunities for those middle-class women who did not live within a nuclear family.

Victorian Constructions of Womanhood

In the eighteenth century, myths, religious doctrine, and folklore defined cultural notions of womanhood. Avant-garde writers and women novelists writing at the end of that century had challenged some of these ideas; they had even posed alternative interpretations. New views were added in the nineteenth century and formed the climate of opinion within which women constructed their lives. For one thing, the "evil woman" became a common figure in literary works, the visual arts, and in that important art form, the opera; a series of bewitching, castrating Carmens, Delilahs, and Salomes had popular representations. Two of the century's most prominent poets wrote of women whose wily ways would bewitch men to death. German Heinrich Heine immortalized the "Lorelei," a legendary woman whose sirenlike song lured a boatsman and his passengers to their deaths. John Keats, who wrote romantic poems about Grecian urns and lovely women, sounded a cautionary note in his verse about a knight at repose in the arms of his beloved. When his dreams came, they were nightmares:

> I saw pale kings, and princes too,
> Pale warriors, death pale were they all;
> They cried—"La belle dame sans merci
> Hath thee in thrall."[14]

Such was the fate awaiting the trusting lover who put himself in the hands of innocent-looking women. In this world of domestic tranquility and reason, men feared the thralldom represented by irrational passion for a woman, who might not be trusted. At the same time, poets and artists found the irrational element in love and women an irresistible subject. Shakespeare had immense popularity across the Continent during the first half of the nineteenth century. His heroine Ophelia particularly attracted those who looked for the mad and irrational in women. An artistic heightening of the powers and perils of hysterical, erotic, or crazy women delineated the separate spheres of normality more clearly. Some poets thus refurbished the image of Eve as dangerous to man, whereas the German Romantics continued to celebrate the good woman's inspiring and normative love.

Nineteenth-century medical practitioners, newly influential arbiters of women's personality and place, investigated female physiology and sexuality. The leading discovery concerned the true nature of the human ovum. The work of Dr. Karl von Baer in the 1820s and subsequent studies produced a theory of spontaneous formation and release of eggs. Earlier theory had described ovulation and conception as caused by sexual orgasm, but now some German physicians, foremost among them Theodor Bischoff, found that that was not the case. Experimenting with female dogs, Bischoff discovered that the female body regularly produced and expelled eggs from the ovaries. Such a finding theoretically separated reproduction from pleasure and also gave a certain bodily autonomy to the generative powers of women.

A second focus of attention was on menstruation. To the end of the nineteenth century, physicians could not decide whether menstruation revitalized the uterus to receive the fertilized egg or represented the destruction of an unused uterine lining. Perhaps because of the lack of any resolution, the debate attracted more and more interest. Most scientists saw the human female's periodic cycle as totally different from that of animals. Ovulation, they thought, did not occur during women's menses, nor in animals was there the kind of menstrual flow. Moreover, during menstruation women did not experience the "heat" that female animals did. Thus, the differentiation of woman from animality was clear. Amidst these debates and studies, menstruation came to categorize and determine femininity in new ways. Medical literature began describing women's physical and mental health as a product of their menstrual cycles; so did educators and a host of other commentators. Woman's incapacity and irrationality were conjured up as by-products of an inescapable physical process.

Ideas of male reproductive and sexual attributes developed in coordination with ones about the female. First, the theory of the spontaneously released ovum served to disconnect sexual pleasure from the process of reproduction, with the result that the reproductive aspects of sexuality gained centrality. As motherhood gradually reached a major position in cultural ideology, so did the importance of male potency, as demonstrated by the fathering of children, grow. The definition of potency began to be associated with the male's ability to effect pregnancy, to engender life, rather than with sexual prowess that had marked out the aristocratic male of the eighteenth century. Particularly in medical and prescriptive literature, all sorts of transformative attributes were ascribed to semen. It could, first of all, impregnate, but in so doing it worked other effects on a woman. Some thought the female personality was revitalized by contact with semen, even if pregnancy did not result. Second, semen appeared to control a man's physical well-being. Excessive loss was thought to weaken him, whereas conservation and moderation would preserve vitality and youth. Likewise, impotence, the inability to muster semen and to create a new life, was seen as a dangerous condition. The impotent, semenless male would slowly degenerate into a being without desire, without power, without honor—in short, a female. Some doctors even stated that the impotent male would take on the sexual characteristics of a woman, including a shrinking of the genitalia and such secondary qualities as a high voice and general fleshiness. Assigning such vital qualities to sperm led to the view that masturbation was dangerous. Masturbation was considered the deadly enemy of potency and was thus the subject of much anxiety in the construction of male sexuality. All sorts of contraptions, such as belts to confine the penis and urethral rings with spikes in them, were devised to inhibit or prevent male masturbation. Those engaged in the attack on masturbation warned of madness, sickness, sterility, and impotence. Doctors likewise warned that female masturbation, provoking pleasure alone, had similarly pernicious effects. The Victorian obsession about this one sexual practice was the negative counterpart of the high value placed on potency and semen. Defining respectable women as those who could be impregnated without experiencing pleasure, middle-class men feared a pleasure that could come from their own bodies when no reproductive act was involved.

New medical theories invigorated popular literature in the nineteenth century. The scientific study of ovulation meant that it was no longer necessary to see such events as menstruation and pregnancy in mystical and superstitious terms. Because scientists had established that menstrual blood did not represent a purging of women's noxious humours, people could have concluded that it had no power to spoil preserved foods and the like. The set of breakthroughs in the 1820s through the 1840s that explained bodily functions held the potential for removing pregnancy from the realm of mysterious empowerment. For the most part, no such demystification occurred. Instead writers converted scientific theories into a new form of rhapsody.

Foremost among these popular writers was Frenchman Jules Michelet (1798–1874), who took all his cues on women from the medical literature. He saw the complex functioning of the ovaries and especially the ripening of the eggs as a sign of woman's total involvement in love. This reproductive apparatus, according to him, had a determining influence on woman's being because it imposed a permanent wound that resulted in regular illness and a monthly flight into another world. Pouring forth, menstrual blood revealed an all-encompassing infirmity and was an indication of women's true nature. Michelet was unique in that he boldly expressed concern for women's sexual pleasure. Yet his foremost theme was woman's body as a reproductive tool for building the French population. Michelet's influential writings coincided with others that focused on the physical differences between the sexes and on women's reproductive mission.

John Ruskin (1819–1900), the prominent English art critic, also described women's nature. In his popular lecture series, Ruskin developed a major Victorian theme: reading and books as a means of communicating with kings and other great historic figures. His talks were also about gender, for education or knowledge had, as always, a close connection with sexual issues. Ruskin concluded that in literature, as in life, woman played a redemptive role or, as he put it, a queenly one. Woman was "incomparably just and pure," meant not for worldly place but for the chivalric role as the "lady" to whom the knight willingly subjected himself. This relationship, for Ruskin, involved an "eternal truth." He also rhapsodized about the home—an entity present wherever woman was and infused with her "majestic peace." Anything that marred that peace destroyed the nature of womanhood, and vice versa, for the two in fact constituted one entity. Thus, Ruskin, like Michelet and many others, spoke of women in metaphorical terms and equated them with blood, home, peace, angels, and myriad other entities.

Whereas medical men saw women in terms of their physiological functioning, literary intellectuals turned that functioning into symbol and metaphor. Once enshrined in this metaphorical world, real women had difficulty in demanding rights, opportunities, property that would give them subsistence, and so on. Such demands, as Ruskin and others maintained, were destructive of the recreative powers of women, of their tending of the gardens—the only shelter in a world "torn up by the agony of men, and beat level by the drift of their life-blood."[15] The reproductive trials of women, the real pain and danger of childbirth, were put by these male writers into a world beyond science, reason, and liberal ideals. Such were the poetic renderings of domesticity that originated outside the confines of the home. They express the excessive terms in which intellectuals constructed women's nurturing role in the industrial age.

Women and Print Culture in the Victorian Age

Nineteenth-century middle-class women became increasingly avid consumers as well as producers of the print culture, as did working women. In Western Europe, they became more literate along with society in general. English teenager Kate Stanley, for example, reported on her reading in her letters to family members. Eighteen in 1860, she had read Jane Austen, John Stuart Mill's *On Liberty*, *The Life of Mary Anne Schimmelpennick*, Horace Walpole's *The Castle of Otranto*, Thomas Macaulay's speeches, Harriet Grote's *Life of Ary Scheffer*, George Eliot's *The Mill on the Floss*, Sydney Smith's *Memoirs*, and other historical, fictional, and biographical works. However, her parents censored her reading. For example, in the biography of Schimmelpennick, a Quaker woman, some chapters were prohibited as being religiously suspect. More strictly raised young women, such as the writer Ida Hahn-Hahn (1805–1880) in Germany, found their reading restricted to works like the encyclopedia. On the other hand, another German, Louise Otto-Peters (1819–1895), had a different experience. Novelist, newspaper editor, and feminist leader, Otto-Peters described a household in which reading aloud occurred all the time: "When vegetables were being cleaned or fruit being prepared for bottling, there was always a recitation from English as well as German novelists, whether they liked it or not: Walter Scott, Cooper and Bulwer, Wilhelm Hauff, Ernst Wagner, Henriette Hanke, Caroline Pichler, Rellstab, Sealsfield, and others lost none of their dignity in the process."[16] Although opinion varied on the acceptability of novels, reading was an important ingredient in the middle-class family's cultural life. Sitting around a table in the evening, the family read together. As domestic missionaries for culture, women read in order to lead the family and to cement it together. In addition, private reading formed an important link in the chain of virtue.

The ideal of domesticity was promoted in growing numbers of magazines, from which many women received ideological visions. From its eighteenth-century beginnings, journalism had grown and now aimed at a mass audience. Magazines appeared as regular monthly, quarterly, or annual issues. At the beginning of the century, *The Book of Beauty* presented poems and illustrations to English women, and other annuals included empty pages for personal entries. These lavish volumes served multiple purposes, including that of being decorative since they were bound in leather, silk, or other luxurious fabrics. Display, introspection and self-expression, sentiment, and instruction—the annual filled all these functions for middle-class women. Monthly magazines such as the *Journal des dames et des demoiselles* (*The Magazine for Ladies and Young Women*) or *Lady's Magazine* included a great variety of material. Such journals presented verse, short stories, and even serialized novels, as well as advice, news from capital cities, recipes, housekeeping hints, fashion news and illustrations, and society gossip. Some magazines focused on either the serious or the frivolous side of domesticity. For example, certain ones were devoted mostly to fashion, whereas others, such as religious journals for mothers and families, emphasized the religious education of children, spiritual life, and familial duties. These might contain inspirational fiction. The fashion journals, meanwhile, documented the rhythm of change that characterized domesticity. Domestic journalism wove the strands of women's individual lives into a pattern that showed a complete picture of the inherent contradictions of middle-class home life. Beginning in 1853, *Die Gartenlaube* (*The Arbor*), for example, brought the colorful and cultural aspects of life into the fairly strict and serious German household. Along with the novel, the magazine tuned its female readers into a national or even international print culture. The private world—the separate sphere—had its own public representation in domestic journalism.

The domestic novel was a genre read by great numbers of women. Much like the detective novel, which began its climb to popularity at about mid-century, the domestic novel was set in a world of order—a woman's or familial world, that is. In these stories, a young girl, woman, or matron starts out on the road of life, love, or marriage. Fairly soon, however, the heroine's universe falls into chaos, and friends, family, or husband betray her. The question arises whether the heroine will survive, especially since among those plotting against her are often women themselves, but her opposites. In a typical story, a contrast is set up from the start with two little girls—one blonde and the other brunette, for instance—representing good and evil. The blonde girl is weakened by being an orphan, living with stepparents or in a boarding school or some similarly hostile environment, an environment that is not familial. By the end of the novel, the good young woman has triumphed by becoming a bride or head of her family. Things fall into place, and the characters in the story recognize the heroine's goodness, morality, strength, and centrality to all their lives. In fact, the heroine conquers all, especially evil women and men of almost any character. This conquest establishes her heroic stature, the heroism of a woman in the private sphere who has struggled and been born anew. The domestic novel portrayed an important myth that explained the rise of domestic culture in the triumph of the good woman.

Authors were of every nationality. Some immersed themselves in charity and religion; others lived a normal middle-class life except that they needed to earn money for their families. If the latter was the case—the situation of many writers—their offerings varied from novels to popular histories and biographies. Sometimes they included advice, cooking, and etiquette books in their repertoires. Thousands of women in these conditions tried their hand at authorship, always with either a desire to write or to earn money. Among the most famous and successful were German authors Marie Ebner-Eschenbach (1830–1916), Fanny Lewald (1811–1889), and E. Marlitt (Eugénie John, 1825–1887); French writers Mathilde Bourdon (1817–1888) and Josephine de Gaulle (1806–1886); and such English writers as Charlotte Yonge (1823–1901). Although not always following the pattern of the domestic novel, most of them held up the domestic sphere as an ideal for women. In the process, many also criticized the marketplace and men.

Some women writers condemned the new age of aggressive invention that inflated people's belief in what the individual was capable of doing. Mary Shelley (1797–1851) did so in her novel *Frankenstein* (1818). The daughter of Mary Wollstonecraft and William Godwin, she had run off at age sixteen with Percy Bysshe Shelley, who was already married. Encouraged by him to write, she produced a series of novels; the first was *Frankenstein*, which became a classic. Dr. Frankenstein exemplified the egotist of the new age, who separated himself from the world of virtue and of family. His boundless self wanted to reach beyond nature and humanity. His success in this pursuit led to the creation of a dreadful monster. Because his birth circumvented the natural role of woman, the monster performed all sorts of horrid deeds, including the murder of all those Frankenstein loved. Despite the horrific nature of his creation, Frankenstein continued in his ambitious but destructive course, and the monster lived on as the creature of someone else's will. He performed his murders while thinking of the love denied him in his monstrous state: looking at a sleeping woman, he contemplated her capacity for love. Because his creator would not provide him with a loving companion, the monster's revenge follows: "if I cannot inspire love, I will cause fear."[17] Both Frankenstein and the monster were beings without families, most notably without mothers, as were many other characters in the book. Mary Shelley thus depicted the horrifying aspect of a world without women—a world that was increasingly male-centered would become one of murderous violence. In writing this ghastly tale, she continued her mother's criticism of male-dominated society and reiterated her idea that females were isolated and even alienated from everything that stood for accomplishment and creativity in industrial society. But Mary Shelley also saw the maternal love as the keystone to order and well-being.

In this age of print culture, journalism had an impact and allowed women to comment directly on public life. The cheap daily paper entered circulation as printing costs became lower and lower, beginning in the 1830s. The appeal to the masses through print echoed the rise of the citizen's role in public life as the century progressed. An informed citizenry could and did have an effect on public events. The influential nature of journalism attracted all sorts of writers, including many women. Some made their reputations through newspaper writing, and others merely enhanced theirs. George Sand, Daniel Stern, Louise Otto-Peters, Mathilde Anneke, and Christina Belgiojoso, for example, published mostly political commentary, although some also excelled in fiction. Writing under pseudonyms, women could express their political opinions and chronicle political movements even though they supposedly had no public existence. Working-class women such as Pauline Roland supported themselves by writing, sometimes supplementing this enterprise with sewing or other kinds of craft work. Mary Russell Mitford wrote vignettes about her village so as to earn money to support her parents. Other women wrote book reviews, translations, commentaries, and other small pieces as a way to earn a living but also as a road to public impact. The revolutions of 1848, the unification of Italy, the modernization of the German states, and finally the women's movement itself (see Chapter 6) came into being on this wave of journalistic writing.

Religion

Religious fervor played a powerful part in Victorian women's lives, but among the middle class it tended to divide men from women and to reinforce their separate spheres. Enlightened rationalism and secularism influenced men who were attuned to making money, fostering commerce, and innovating in industry. These men believed in liberal principles as the foundation of their efforts and their successes. However, there was a religious revival in the late eighteenth and early nineteenth century, with the result that a Christian emphasis infused many lives. Protestant men were still able to see their constant business activity and drive to earn money as an expression of the will of God. Religious introspection led many to great deeds and earnest writing. Prime ministers prayed for guidance, and so did members of working-class congregations. But damage due to the Enlightenment and Industrial Revolution took a heavy toll and prevented religion from returning to its prerevolutionary status. Religion slowly changed, declined, and continued to be challenged.

Although some men turned from religion toward secularism, few women did. Instead religious observance among middle-class women increased in the modern world: their fervor resulted in prayer societies, charitable work, missionary activity, and intense personal devotion. To some extent, this religious observance marked women off from men: the churches became women's space. Whereas fewer men performed even the minimal religious duties, most women did and with obvious vigor. The message of the church—whether Protestant or Catholic—came to them in welcome terms. For one thing, the message coordinated well with separate spheres and the domestic ideology by stressing virtues and introspection. For another, religion had allusions to home and family. Since the marketplace tore men away from these structures, it is hardly surprising that other theories and philosophies attracted them. For women, however, religion remained vital.

For middle-class women, Christian virtues mirrored domestic ones: resignation, morality, inwardness, forgiveness, patience, poverty, and charity. At the same time, the vices denounced by religion, such as greed, fornication, falsehood, blasphemy, and impiety, characterized the world outside the home. Moreover, the biblical cast of characters included fathers, sons, and mothers along with a host of down-to-earth acquaintances such as craftsmen, neighborhood women, and local notables, which seemed similar to life in the home. Thus, expressions of belief in a power beyond, not in, the social and political order continued to be valid for women, whereas many men in the middle class had switched to a belief in their own powers on this earth. Raising children involved initiating them into this order by hearing their catechism studies, teaching them to read the Bible, praying with them, or taking them to church. Performing these duties reinforced the virtue women were supposed to have, and thus manifested heavenly and earthly virtue at the same time.

The church also absorbed women's physical and intellectual energy in a way no other institution did. The Catholic Church housed hundreds of thousands of women in its convents. In Italy, many entered as young girls, sent by their parents to avoid the cost of a dowry, whereas in France such a custom had to some extent died out. A life dedicated to the church offered an alternative—sometimes the only acceptable one—to marriage. Also, the church encouraged activity and even leadership in hospitals, schools, religious devotion, and a whole range of public missions. Even though Catherine the Great had disbanded religious orders, Russian Orthodox women organized vast agricultural communes that not only maintained the physical well-being of the sisters but also supported an array of devotions and charitable acts. For those women who had only lay status, the church, no matter what denomination, welcomed their inspirational thoughts, those that roamed beyond the confines of the daily world, their flights of feeling, and their serious commitment to an enterprise. For example, in Protestant countries women wrote popular hymns and religious poetry expressing their sorrows and tribulations, as well as the forgiveness, succor, and grace received from their religious experiences. The most popular of these writers was Felicia Hemans (1794–1835), who captured an array of feeling directed toward heaven but springing from women's concerns with life-giving, nursing, and death:

> Tremblers beside the grave
> We call on thee to save,
> Father divine!
> Hear, hear our suppliant breath!
> Keep us, in life and death,
> Thine, only thine![18]

Religion could also at times disturb the public peace and challenge the clear demarcation of separate spheres. By the mid–nineteenth century, certain branches of both Protestant and Catholic churches had taken up a social mission with the idea of bringing people to God and correcting the earthly order of things. The evangelical work of Hannah More and Sarah Trimmer, for instance, was an attempt to stop democratization and restore hierarchy. Organized religious practice accorded well with the new idea of citizen as encompassing those who believed in the same principles and submitted to a "general will." Also, Protestantism gave people a sense of an individual relationship with God, which fostered a certain amount of self-confidence when facing the outer world. People could prosper and acquire wealth with the belief that their prosperity was a sign of God's approval. Similarly, one could attack social problems with confidence that the social order could be remade according to godlier precepts. These beliefs affected both Catholics and Protestants. In Germany, for example, the German-Catholic movement began challenging the authoritarian government and the social structure. German-Catholic churches broke off from state support, began missions to help the poor, and even introduced the idea of female equality—not just in the spiritual world but in daily life. Some of these churches allowed women full voting rights in congregational meetings and accepted them on church-governing councils in the 1840s. The driving force of this movement was a desire to connect inner spiritual life with social practice; purging the individual of evil entailed purging the social order. By this movement, complicated theology diminished in importance, but the outward manifestation of religious energy gained. Catholic officials recognized that women's religion was intense, but they feared its uninstructed nature. A German-Catholic minister said of Emilie Wustenfeld, an influential layworker in the 1840s, that she had renounced the "images of divinity," while maintaining "her belief in the purpose and power of the godly in the world. . . . Devotion ceased but there remained the pious spirit . . . committed to the cult of human love."[19] Many women then, started converting their religious fervor to public deeds—some of which were disruptive and divisive. As in the case of Wustenfeld, they enthusiastically did good works in the name of religion while abandoning strict religious doctrine and study.

Annette von Droste-Hülshoff (1797–1848), considered the greatest female German writer of the nineteenth century, concentrated on religious and ethical themes. A spinster who lived with her family in Westphalia, she sometimes wrote about local customs and lore, like some of the Romantics. Yet Droste-Hülshoff departed from both the sentimental emphasis Romantics and religious writers often adopted and any commitment to public mission. Instead, her religious poetry and fiction emphasized evil and guilt. Humans in nature unleashed their awful powers in destructive ways. Her famous novella *Die Judenbuche* (*The Jewish Beechtree*) (1842) described the life of a man after he had murdered a Jew. Droste-Hülshoff focused on the protagonist's mental state during his adventures up until the moment he hangs himself at the location of the murder decades later. To her mind, human destructiveness in the face of

God gave rise to an overpowering guilt. Such guilt and the evil from which it sprang shaped existence to such an extent that the writer needed to portray it exactly to convey the sense of life. Although she tried to find in art a place free from the burden of sin, a refuge from human destiny, Droste-Hülshoff depicted the alienation and the absurdity of being that so many twentieth-century writers would dwell on. At the same time, her religious insight led her to understand how poor the condition of women was in her society. Speaking of the possibility of marriage, she recognized how it "crippled in intellect" those women who entered it; she believed if she married she would become "half-mad, truly dumb."[20] Integrity or wholeness of the spirit had to be grounded in integrity of the person—a quality married women could not achieve because their existence was given over to a husband and children. In the case of Droste-Hülshoff, religious feeling did not coalesce with conventional views.

Extrareligious movements such as mesmerism, spiritualism, and theosophy became the rage in industrializing society. In the 1840s, the Fox sisters drew crowds of admirers and believers in upper New York state because of the rappings and knockings they received from another world. In the same decade, writer Harriet Martineau (1802–1876) was cured of an acute illness by a mesmerist, who apparently removed her illness by passing his hands through the air around her body. Even though such activity seemed like quackery, Martineau believed mesmerism worked because its unknown processes were more advanced than scientific knowledge. Who knew, she wrote, "but that some new insight must be obtained by its means, into the powers of our mysterious frame."[21] Spiritualism, the belief in the ability to contact beings who were dead, and theosophy, a kind of spiritualism deriving from Hinduism, also gained many adherents among nineteenth-century women, especially those with feminist leanings. English women's rights pioneer Barbara Bodichon (1827–1891) tried rapping sessions and poet Elizabeth Barrett Browning firmly believed in the kinds of spiritualist manifestations that occurred during the séances she attended. Other women initiated movements on their own. Russian Helena Blavatsky (1831–1891) helped to found the Theosophical Society in the early 1870s, and she had among her admirers such activists as English social reformer Annie Besant (1847–1933). In many cases theosophy and women's causes developed an identical membership. French writer Julia Bécour, a convinced spiritualist, emphasized that spiritualism sought contact with the world beyond death "which is the leveller of being, the constant purification of the earth." She thought that spiritualism took people beyond secular concerns for wealth and power to a purer world where equality existed between the sexes. On earth, man is prideful, she wrote, and "thinks himself someone special, but in reality he is poor in the world of the spirits; he knows nothing beyond himself." Spiritualists stressed a world beyond the body: "Passions ruin the body and spoil the spirit."[22] Such a doctrine proved to be an encouraging pattern for living and one that women could and did preach to those around them. Like other forms of religious faith, spiritualism had its fervent supporters, who in many cases became activists and found themselves at odds with liberal values.

Charity and Reform

In the 1840s, English historian Lucy Aikin commented that what marked mid-century women from previous generations was their abundant charitable work. By the 1860s, there were thousands of societies designed to help the poor and working members of society. Middle- and upper-class women in-spected prisons, asylums, and workhouses; they ran, supervised, or financed primary schools; and most of all they visited the poor in their homes. Famous philanthropist Angela Burdett-Coutts (1814–1906), motivated by a deep evan-gelical faith, gave away more than three million pounds for schools, housing, and refuges for the poor. Even though men initiated or administered many charitable organizations, almost all of them admitted that women did most of the work, had most of the ideas, and were, in short, the prime movers behind charity. Their effort was such a commonly accepted part of life that printed guidebooks existed to tell how to make contacts with the poor—people from whom the middle classes had become almost completely estranged. It was this estrangement that had given rise to the new effort in the first place. Industrial-ization and urban growth had brought plenty to a few but misery to many. By mid-century, well-off people had begun separating themselves from poorer classes, both by an exodus to middle-class neighborhoods and by an emotional and psychological distancing. Once the separation was accomplished, many women wanted to build bridges back; indeed, the domestic and religious ide-ology demanded those bridges between classes. Charity provided the answer, especially to women who saw it as "the flow of maternal love."[23]

Activists in charity in the nineteenth century took their inspiration from a maternal, religious world view. Their interpretation contrasted with industrial values, liberal creeds, and analyses based on political economy. For religious people, God had created the universe, including human life, because of love. Christian love also served as the social glue that bound neighbor to neighbor, class to class. In industrial society, where classes lived separately, charitable acts—acts of *caritas*—were more necessary than ever to rebind one class to the other. For women, only personal contact manifested *caritas*; the bureaucratic relief administered by men was nothing without caring. In fact, wherever gov-ernments had organized such entities as workhouses or asylums, which oper-ated with paid personnel, women volunteers moved in with their own brand of help—personal charity. Sometimes at odds with men of their own class on this issue, these women nonetheless had their way because they were willing

---

A Guide for Charity Workers

Concepción Arenal (1820–1893), like thousands of European women, practiced charity and searched for ways to alleviate the misery of the poor. A Spanish reformer, Arenal also worked on upgrading prisons.

Her writing on social problems earned her many awards and an international reputation as an expert in the area of law, reform, and charity. Early in her career, Arenal produced a guide for visitors to the poor, which was reissued into the mid–twentieth century. *The Visitor of the Poor* (1860) tried to create in its readers a religious attitude toward those in need. She differed from later advocates of bureaucratic welfare who believed that poverty should and could be eradicated.

> It will be very difficult in visiting the poor to alleviate their sorrow and console their spiritual and bodily misery if first we do not form an exact idea of our respective positions, if we do not show humility and tolerance of feeling and thought; if we can answer exactly these three questions: what is sorrow? what is a poor person? what are we? If we give a true answer to each of these questions, if we think about and identify with them, if we visit the poor in such a spiritual condition, then we can do the most good possible.
>
> Sorrow is not a passing result of special circumstances or deplorable errors or a transitory state either for society or individuals. It is a necessity of our nature, an indispensable element of our moral perfection. Therefore we should not regard it as our enemy but as a sad friend who accompanies us on the road of life. Let us imagine, if we can, a society without sorrow. Expecting to see a house of delights, we will find a city of repugnant monsters. One who receives only pleasing sensations in life is hopelessly degraded physically and morally. Without struggle, without contradictions, without self-denial, without—finally—sorrow, neither morality nor virtue is possible.
>
> All the circumstances which appear to raise us above the poor are purely accidental. Our good fortune alone gives us any merit and only occasionally can we claim any worth beyond the use we make of our gifts. Before the throne of the divine judge we will have to defend ourselves far more than "those people" who are the objects of our charity. In order to enter the homes of the poor with humility of heart and of mind, we must decide whether in their place we would conduct ourselves better. In viewing their faults, vices, and crimes, we must ask ourselves this question: would the poor be what they are, if we were what we ought to be?

Source: Adapted from Concepción Arenal, *Obras completas. El visitador del pobre* (Madrid: Victoriano Suarez, 1934), 7–17.

to do the actual work. For administrators working under pre–welfare state policies, women's legwork and fund-raising helped compensate for the funds they could not get from government. Charitable efforts thus dominated women's engagement in social issues. Until personal charity was challenged by the welfare state, it remained religiously inspired and, in fact, mushroomed during religious revivals.

In Hamburg, Amalie Sieveking (1794–1859) began the Female Association for the Care of the Poor and the Sick in 1832. Moved by a conversion to religious fervor, Sieveking took it upon herself to supplement the inadequate relief provided by the city. She and her middle-class associates began to visit the sick and impoverished regularly and to provide them with both spiritual and material assistance. The Female Association distributed prayerbooks, but also found jobs, housing, and health care and in the process created the interclass ties of *caritas*. Overcoming opposition and resisting attempts to absorb it, Sieveking's society had more than eighty branches across the Continent by the time of her death. Similarly successful, Ellen Ranyard's (1814–1879) Bible and Domestic Female Mission hired working-class "Bible women" to sell Bibles and religious literature in London homes. Proceeds from these sales were combined with donations and went to provisioning the needy. Mrs. Ranyard's agents were trained in religion and domestic matters to prepare them for whatever situations they encountered. As the network grew, middle-class women joined its ranks as co-visitors and trainers and supervisors of the canvassers. Eventually, the Bible and Domestic Female Mission organized large numbers of women around religion, relief, and the management of substantial sums of money. Somewhat different because of their focus, the maternal societies in France organized women to provide assistance upon childbirth. Founded late in the eighteenth century on a somewhat tentative basis, the societies flourished after 1850, when the Empress Eugénie (consort of Napoleon III) became an active patron. Each group set its own bylaws, which generally included stipulations about personal visits, the amount of monetary assistance to each mother, and the items in each newborn's layette. These societies also had requirements concerning the character of the mother, the baptism of the child, and, where poverty was especially pronounced, the minimum number of confinements necessary before a woman could receive aid. At mid-century, Italian Laura Mantegazza set up day care centers, where working mothers could breastfeed their children during the workday and thereby embody the new brand of motherhood. Later she organized and taught in schools for the illiterate, where working women could improve their skills. In all this, Mantegazza practiced a personal charity by raising money herself and caring for her infant charges and pupils.

Charity led to reform, which became another watchword of the century. Whereas charity alleviated misery caused by social inequities, reform sought to change society. The changes might be minimal things, such as improvement in behavior, or they could be much greater. Among the many towering reform figures was Florence Nightingale (1820–1910). Her background would not lead one to expect the obsession of her adult years except that so many upper-

To the British, Florence Nightingale was the merci-ful "lady with the lamp." In reality, she was a tough-minded reformer. On her return from the Crimea she took to her bed with the claim to serious illness. Thus released from house-hold rituals, she wrote book after book on reform and lived to be 90.

and middle-class women took up the cause of improving society. Born to wealth, Nightingale led an intense social life with her mother and studied clas-sical subjects just as intensely with her father. While still a teenager, she heard a call from God and spent the next decade struggling between the demands of upper-class domesticity and her driving ambition to escape them. Many as-pects of household life infuriated her, including long meals, meaningless socia-bility, and insistence on attention to any number of rituals. She proposed var-ious projects to her parents, in particular that she train with a religious order for hospital service. They greeted this with rage and hysteria, for nurses came from the lowest classes, did menial chores only, and charged patrons for special services, including sexual ones. Nightingale's request to work in a hospital was tantamount to asking to enter a brothel, so similar were prostitutes and nurses to the middle-class mind. After various small stints at nursing—each the cause of a family uproar—her great opportunity arose with the Crimean War (1854–1856).

Great Britain claimed to be the most civilized country in the world, but its soldiers fighting in the Crimea were dying from lack of medical care, disease, and undernourishment. Using her political connections, Nightingale obtained a commission to raise a team of nurses, equip it, and lead it to Turkey. She also took with her a small fortune in funds. Nightingale's aims were threefold. First, she wanted to save soldiers' lives and improve their immediate lot. In this effort, although constantly thwarted by incompetence and corruption, she succeeded well enough to make her a national heroine. Second, Nightingale wanted to change the status of nursing. To accomplish this, she molded an untested collection of women into a squad disciplined to take doctors' orders and trained, if only by this experience, in health-care procedures. The upgrading of nursing that followed the Crimean experience resulted from the publicity generated by Nightingale as well as her subsequent role in establishing schools of nursing and nursing corps. Moreover, her best-selling *Notes on Nursing* (1859) caused changes in the kind of care sick people received. Challenging old superstitions, Nightingale advocated fresh air and sunshine, substantial nourishment, and friendly visitors to aid recuperation. When the Crimean War ended, England greeted her as a new Joan of Arc. Exploiting her considerable prestige, Nightingale spent the rest of her life on a final goal: modernizing the English army so that it was efficient, sanitary, and honest. This became an obsession, so hideous and brutal were the conditions under which the common soldier lived. In fostering the causes of sanitation and nursing, Nightingale was the first of many women whose initial moral commitment led them to science and knowledge.

Toward Political Activism

Florence Nightingale's life demonstrates how far charity and reform could take women from their starting point in the household. In their performance of charity, middle-class women entered the public space and places society deemed unfit for their angelic natures. Household values also led to public criticism of the industrial order and sometimes even led women to challenge what their husbands were doing. Moreover, charity work ultimately led some women to make speeches, organize working girls and women, and even run newspapers. Many published books about their ventures, which opened new vistas to other women. Books on such subjects as woman's mission, temperance, child poverty and neglect, and the general lack of sanitation in cities suggested that the analyses found in competing books on political economy were wrong. In this way, then, charity and reform work led to opposing positions on how society should be run even within the middle class. Though men and women shared many charitable beliefs, charity also created divisions between them when it came to such questions as how powerful women's influence should be and what values should govern society. Such controversy sprang from the notion of gender differences as demonstrated in the doctrine of separate spheres.

The home also contained its own contradictions in terms of virtue. The rituals involved in elaborate meals, for example, enraged Florence Nightingale, who was motivated by a sense of mission and an ideal of the purposeful aspects of women's nature. In many cases, a powerful sense of virtue actually moved women to leave the comforts of home behind. In a sense, Nightingale escaped from one domestic sphere to promote ideals of domestic life in the real world. So did thousands of other women who became activists, particularly feminist activists, from mid-century on. They took up the cause of unmasking domesticity's true nature, of revealing that the material abundance and rituals of the middle-class home were just camouflage for its deficiencies and for the impotence of the women who were bound there, especially middle-class ones. They also aimed at showing that it was the lack of influence and productive activity that generated women's discontent. Precepts of motherhood, moral superiority, religion, and virtue empowered women in unpredictable ways. Disruption sprang both from domesticity and from work outside the home. Often believing in liberal rights as well as virtue, women headed toward revolution, feminism, and an ever increasing public role.

NOTES

1. Letter of Henriette von Willich to Friedrich Ernst Schleiermacher, October, 1805, quoted in Gwendolyn E. Jensen, "Henriette Schleiermacher. A Woman in a Traditional Role," in John C. Fout, ed., *German Women in the Nineteenth Century* (London: Holmes and Meier, 1984), 89.

2. Quoted in Cecil Woodham-Smith, *Queen Victoria. From Her Birth to the Death of the Prince Consort* (New York: Knopf, 1972), 402.

3. V. Shul'gin quoted in Dorothy Atkinson, "Society and the Sexes in the Russian Past," in Dorothy Atkinson, Alexander Dallin, and Gail Lapidus, eds., *Women in Russia* (Stanford, Calif.: Stanford University Press, 1977), 34.

4. C. F. Pockels, *Versuch einer Characteristik des Weiblichen Geschlechts: Ein Sittengemälde* 5 vols. (Hanover: 1802), 2:232.

5. Mathilde Bourdon, *Politesse et savoir-vivre* (Paris: Lethielleux, 1864), 8, 122–123.

6. Isabella Beeton, *Mrs. Beeton's Book of Household Management* (London, 1880), i, 13.

7. Ann Taylor Allen, "Spiritual Motherhood: German Feminists and the Kindergarten Movement, 1848–1911," *History of Education Quarterly*, vol. 22, no. 3 (Fall, 1982):322.

8. "Plan d'education d'une mère chrétienne," in Anatole de Ségur, *Vie d l'abbé Bernard* (Paris: Bray et Retaux, 1883), 426–430.

9. Evgeniia Tur, *Plemiannitsa* (Moscow, 1851) 4:168, quoted in Jessica Tovrov, "Mother-Child Relationships among the Russian Nobility," in David Ransel, ed., *The Family in Imperial Russia* (Urbana: University of Illinois Press, 1976), 40.

10. Fanny Mendelssohn to Klingemann, letter of December 27, 1828, in Sebastian Hensel, ed., *The Mendelssohn Family, 1729–1847, From Letters and Journals*, 2 vols. (New York: Harper, 1881), 1:163.

11. *Le journal intime de Caroline B.* (Paris: Montalba, 1985), 50–51.

12. Lady Tweedsmuir, quoted in Leonora Davidoff, *The Best Circles. Society, Etiquette, and the Season* (London: Croom Helm, 1973), 26.

13. Edward Carpenter, *My Dreams and Days* (London: George Allen, 1916), 31.

14. John Keats, *Complete Poems and Selected Letters,* Clarence D. Thorpe, ed. (New York: Odyssey, 1935), 341.

15. John Ruskin, *Sesame and Lilies* (London: J. M. Dent, 1907 [1865]), 1–79 *passim.*

16. Louise Otto, *Frauenleben im Deutschen Reich. Erinnerungen aus der Vergangenheit* (Leipzig, 1876), 7–8, quoted in Renate Mohrmann, "The Reading Habits of Women in the Vormärz," in Fout, ed., *German Women,* 111.

17. Mary Shelley, *Frankenstein, or the Modern Prometheus* (London: Oxford University Press, 1969 [1818]), 145.

18. Quoted in Margaret Maison, " 'Thine, Only Thine!' Women Hymn Writers in Britain, 1769–1835," in Gail Malmgreen, ed., *Religion in the Lives of English Women, 1760–1930* (Bloomington: Indiana University Press, 1986), 36.

19. Quoted in Catherine M. Prelinger, *Charity, Challenge, and Change. Religious Dimensions of the Mid–Nineteenth-Century Women's Movement in Germany* (Westport, Conn.: Greenwood, 1987), 63.

20. Eda Sagarra, *Tradition and Revolution. German Literature and Society 1830–1890* (London: Weidenfield and Nicolson, 1971); and Annette von Droste-Hülshoff, *Sämtliche Werke* (München: Hanser, 1963), 877, quoted in Elke Frederiksen, "German Women Writers in the Nineteenth Century: Where Are They?" in Kay Goodman and Susan Cocalis, eds., *Beyond the Eternal Feminine: Critical Essays on Women and German Literature* (Stuttgart: Akademischer Verlag Hans-Dieter Heinz, 1982), 189.

21. Harriet Martineau, *Life in the Sick-Room,* quoted in Valerie Pichanick, *Harriet Martineau, the Woman and Her Work* (Ann Arbor: University of Michigan Press, 1980), 131.

22. Julia Bécour, *Les voix lointaines. Le stage. Paroles de là-bas* (Paris: Librairies des Sciences Psychiques, 1905), *passim.*

23. Quoted in F. K. Prochaska, *Women and Philanthropy in Nineteenth-Century England* (Oxford, England: Clarendon, 1980), 7.

SOURCES AND SUGGESTED READING

Adburgham, Alison. *Women in Print: Writing Women and Women's Magazines from the Restoration to the Accession of Victoria* (1972).

Allen, Ann Taylor. "Spiritual Motherhood: German Feminists and the Kindergarten Movement, 1848–1911," *History of Education Quarterly* (1982). On the government's view of kindergartens as subversive.

Banks, J. A., and Olive Banks. *Feminism and Family Planning* (1964). A classic study of the middle class in Britain and the financial impetus for birth control.

Davidoff, Leonore. *The Best Circles. Society, Etiquette, and the Season* (1973).

Davidoff, Leonore, and Catherine Hall. *Family Fortunes. Men and Women of the English Middle Class 1780–1850* (1987). A major interpretation of family structure and the control of public power.

Davis, James C. *A Venetian Family and Its Fortune 1500–1900: The Donà and the Conservation of their Wealth* (1975).

Foucault, Michel. *History of Sexuality* (1978). A reevaluation of Victorian sexual practice and of general theories of sexual liberation.

Ginzburg, Natalia. *The Manzoni Family* (1987). Fascinating letters of a very special Italian family.

Hartman, Mary S. *Victorian Murderesses* (1978). An interpretation of what murder meant to women in the nineteenth century.

Henry, Louis. *Anciennes familles genevoises, etude demographique xvi–xx siecle* (1956).

Jensen, Gwendolyn E. "Henriette Schleiermacher. A Woman in a Traditional Role," in John C. Fout, ed., *German Women in the Nineteenth Century* (1984).

Laqueur, Thomas. "Orgasm, Generation, and the Politics of Reproductive Biology," *Representations* (1986).

McLaren, Angus. *Birth Control in Nineteenth Century England* (1978).

Malmgreen, Gail, ed. *Religion in the Lives of English Women, 1760–1930* (1986).

Nye, Robert. "Honor, Impotence, and Male Sexuality in Nineteenth-Century French Medicine," *French Historical Studies* (1989). A major step in studying the construction of masculinity.

Pichanick, Valerie. *Harriet Martineau, the Woman and Her Work* (1980).

Poovey, Mary. *The Proper Lady and the Woman Writer* (1984). An important study of English novelists.

Prelinger, Catherine M. *Charity, Challenge, and Change. Religious Dimensions of the Mid–Nineteenth-Century Women's Movement in Germany* (1987). The political implications of charity.

Prochaska, F. K. *Women and Philanthropy in Nineteenth-Century England* (1980). An important survey.

Smith, Bonnie G. *Ladies of the Leisure Class: The Bourgeoises of Northern France in the Nineteenth Century* (1981).

Tovrov, Jessica. "Mother-Child Relationships among the Russian Nobility," in David Ransel, ed., *The Family in Imperial Russia* (1976).

Vicinus, Martha, ed. *Suffer and Be Still: Women in the Victorian Age* (1973). An important collection of essays on English women.

Woodham-Smith, Cecil. *Florence Nightingale* (1951). A detailed and engaging revision of the Nightingale myth.

6

Culture and Politics in the Nation-State

A Growing Activism   The French Revolution ushered in an age in which politics touched broad segments of the general public. The cause of justice and nationhood interested people in numbers unheard of in the days of monarchical or aristocratic absolutism. Now not only charity, but politics attracted women's activity. "My heart bleeds to see prolonged indefinitely this state of degradation among a people capable of heroic virtues and noble faculties,"[1] wrote Italian aristocrat Cristina Belgiojoso (1808–1871) as she reflected on the uprisings of 1848. From her twenties on, Belgiojoso participated in movements to bring about the unification and modernization of Italy. Pursued by the Austrian secret police under whose jurisdiction her native city of Milan fell, she lived in various countries from the 1830s on. Because the Austrian government confiscated her money until 1861, when the unification finally took place, Belgiojoso had to earn her living by writing or by farming, and sometimes she received contributions from her family. In any case, she always continued to work for her cause. In the 1840s in Paris, she started the newspaper *Gazetta Italiana* and by 1848 was editing three others published in various Italian cities. She produced histories of Lombardy and the House of Savoy, commentaries on Italian politics, and studies of the Middle East. Belgiojoso was seen as a romantic heroine by prominent artists of her time. Married to a syphilitic womanizer, she lived a mostly celibate life devoted to politics. Her headiest moments came during the revolutions of 1848, when she helped organize troops and hospitals in Naples, Milan, and Rome. Exiled once more after the uprisings were suppressed, she continued to write and agitate. Once Italy was unified, Belgiojoso added a final commentary to her arsenal of written works—a long tract on the condition of women. She particularly advocated education and fair treatment. The barbarity of women's status was a remnant of the backwardness she had worked to eliminate throughout Italy. Belgiojoso was elite by virtue of her birth and activist role, but she nonetheless manifested a political sensibility that became more and

Cristina Belgiojoso took up the cause of Italian unification but also made herself into a romantic heroine. She alternately adopted the pose of activist, invalid, and impoverished stoic.

more common among women. Attuned to national conditions and struggles, more women started to get involved in partisan politics, the causes of economic reform, and a variety of revolutionary movements. Women's political consciousness awakened and, as in the case of Belgiojoso, it often led from national politics to activism on behalf of women.

The rise of domesticity occurred at the same time as a struggle for liberalization of institutions and a further expansion of the state as an entity more profoundly affecting people's lives. The 1815 settlement at Vienna to end the Napoleonic wars had favored conservatism rather than progressive values. For one thing, it restored Louis XVI's brother to the French throne. Central Europe lived under the Habsburg police state, controlled by the arch-reactionary Austrian chancellor Clemens von Metternich. Italians hoping to move their society in revolutionary directions met in secret or lived in exile. Conditions in England were fairly liberal, but those in France were unsettled, with the potential for another revolution ever present. Throughout Europe, political movements and revolutions on behalf of a variety of causes kept erupting. Men and women chafed under restrictions and censorship, whereas workers felt the hardships of ongoing industrialization. A German woman, fighting in 1848 beside her husband against kingship and aristocratic control, expressed a common sentiment: "You know it was not war that called me but love; yet I must confess—hate, too, a burning hate generated in the struggle against tyrants and oppressors of sacred human rights."[2] This kind of liberalism was manifested in the revolutions of 1830, 1848, in the English Chartist movement, and in the French Commune of 1870. Nationalism also inspired activists who were struggling to unite the Italian and German states into nations that could take their place among the European powers. Many women favored the cause of nationalism. Identifying with the state and seeing themselves as having contributions to make, they supported this modern form. Particularism—that is, small states such as existed in the Germanies—seemed outmoded, and people associated it with backward, oppressive ways of doing things. Because aristocratic societies in the German and Italian states had paid no attention to principles such as rights and equal opportunity, they held little appeal for those who placed their hopes in constitutionalism and liberal government. Italian and German unification, occurring in 1861 and 1870, respectively, drew women's attention and effort and continued the process of politicizing them.

Revolutions and nationalist movements were tinged with feminism. Although the domestic sphere seemed to be women's destiny after the French Revolution and invoking the family seemed to some to be the only way of restoring order, resistance to the more oppressive aspects of domesticity soon developed. In England, where liberal legislation unfolded gradually, women demanded political rights as more and more men gained them. Across the Continent improved education for men prompted calls for similar opportunities for women, for schooling from the lowest levels to the highest. In addition, it became clear that the new economic opportunities were leaving women behind. In industrial society, millions of spinsters found themselves virtually penniless and unable to fend for themselves. This too became a cause. In all these movements, men joined with women. By mid-century, many felt that the underpinnings of gender order were slipping. Women were found in high places; it was the age of Queen Victoria, Empress Eugénie of France (1826–1920), and the beautiful, though eccentric, Empress Elizabeth of Austria (1837–1898). However, each of these women symbolized separate spheres and all the accoutrements of domesticity. Victorian society seemed a formidable fortress, but feminism began to meet it head on. In the revolutions of 1848 and 1870, women made economic and political claims. There was a woman's side to revolution and state formation. In addition, the march of everyday politics also involved women, pressing for education; for reform in marriage, divorce, and property laws; for better jobs; and for liberalized sexual mores. Feminism took on the nation-state and liberal society; it also challenged the economic order through political action. The Victorian Age has been called the age of equipoise, or equilibrium. Such a characterization hardly does justice to the activity that constituted the first major steps in the women's movement.

Print and Politics

Language and Nationhood

"Love for poetry in general, and patriotism in particular, has induced me to write,"[3] said Eleanora d'Albedyhll (1770–1835) about her powerful epic *Gefion* (1814), which recreated the world of the Norse gods. Her vision was pan-Scandinavian. That is, *Gefion* showed Sweden, Norway, and Denmark as countries with a common destiny by the beauty of their geography and by their culture. In a world dominated intellectually by the French, d'Albedyhll took as her theme the celebration of things Scandinavian. Polish author Klementyna Tanska Hoffmanowa (1798–1845) wrote, "In my youth I saw the harm done to our sense of nationality by our infatuation with everything French. So . . . I have directed all my efforts to provide as many books as I can, in Polish, for Polish children."[4] Both of these authors were pioneers in reawakening nationalism after decades of fascination with the French. They were joined by other women and men who saw history, custom and myth, and language itself as the foundations of nationhood.

The nineteenth century was an age of nationalism. Countries composed of weak and disunited peoples aspired to national unity and power. In the Habsburg Empire, Czechs, Poles, Hungarians, and many other ethnic groups longed for a glorious national existence such as the French had had. They chafed

---

Granny

First published in 1855, *Granny* inspired and delighted generations of Czech nationalists. Božena Němcová's classic is the story of an aged woman who is full of wisdom about people, customs and folklore, and the ways of nature. A friend of both ordinary folk and nobility, Granny lives a forthright, purposeful life in the midst of her children and grandchildren. Only one cloud darkens her old age: the fate of the Czechs. At home, her son-in-law speaks German, and her own daughter prefers modern ways of doing things to traditional ones. In her grandchildren, Granny sees a source of hope, and she instills in them national pride. The following scene takes place out-of-doors as Granny and her grandchildren look at the hilltops and woods around them. Pondering the spectacle of nature, one granddaughter, Babbie, recounts for the other children the story of the Sibyl—a female prophet or fortune teller.

"The Sibyl foretold that great misery would come on the Czech lands, that there would be wars and famine and plague. But the worst of all would be when father wouldn't understand son, or son father, or brother brother, and when neither word nor bond would be worth anything. That would be the worst of all, she said, and then the Czech earth would be scattered under the hooves of horses."

"You remembered it well. But God forbid it should ever come true," said Granny with a sigh.

"Oh, Granny, sometimes I'm so afraid I can't tell you! You wouldn't like the Czech earth to be scattered under the hooves of horses, either, would you?"

"Silly girl, of course I wouldn't! Don't we pray every day for the well-being of the Czech earth? Isn't this land our mother? Well, then, if I should see my mother falling into distress, do you think I could be indifferent? What would you do, if somebody was trying to kill your mother?"

"We should scream and cry," said the boys and Adelka.

"Ah, you're children," said Granny with a smile.

"We should have to go to her help, shouldn't we, Granny?" said Babbie, and her eyes were burning.

"That's it, child, that's it, that's the right of it! Screaming and crying don't help," said the old woman, and laid her hand upon her granddaughter's head.

"But, Granny, we're only little, how could we help?" asked John, who was annoyed that he should be dismissed as a mere child.

"Don't you remember what I told you about little David, who killed great Goliath? You see, even a little person can do much, if he has faith in God, you remember that. When you grow up and go out into the world you'll get to know evil and good, you'll be led astray and brought into temptation. Then remember your Granny, and the things she told you when she was out walking with you. You know that I left the good living the Prussian king offered me, and chose to work till I dropped rather than let my children be turned into foreigners and estranged from me. You must love your country like a mother, too, love her above all things, and work for her like good sons and daughters, and then the prophecy that frightens you will never be fulfilled. I shan't see you grow to be men, but I hope you'll remember your Granny's words," she concluded in a trembling voice.

"I'll never, never forget them," whispered Babbie, hiding her face in the old woman's lap.

Source: Excerpted from Božena Němcová, *Granny. Scenes from Country Life*, Edith Pargeter, trans. (Westport, Conn.: Greenwood, 1976), 195–196.

under repressive conditions, among them the imposition of German as the official language, ordered by the imperial government in Vienna. Thus Hoffmanowa decried not only an "infatuation with everything French," but the attempt by empires to eradicate aspiring nationality groups by eradicating their languages. In opposition to this attempt, a powerful literature developed in Czech, Slavic, Hungarian, and many other languages. Probably the best known of the nationalist writers was Božena Němcová (1820–1862), whose *Granny* (1855) became the most enduring piece of nineteenth-century Czech literature. Němcová focused on the unborn nation and on the women—patriotic grandmothers and mothers—who would forge a new state based on old traditions. The grandmother in the tale kept alive the Czech language, spun and sewed for her family, and maintained the vigor of her Catholic faith. When writing this chronicle of folkways, Němcová had traveled the Czech countryside, where she was regarded at first as an eccentric interloper. But ultimately she succeeded in making what Franz Kafka called the "only music of language, that of Božena Němcová."[5]

The Novel and Women's Sphere

The eighteenth-century novel had brought women's interests to the public eye, and nineteenth-century fiction continued to do so. Great women novelists in England and France filled the bookstores with their works. Although female novelists were commonplace, women's writing of a more serious sort sometimes was not accepted for publication or was not regarded as fitting. Whereas women's artistic activity in the eighteenth century had a dash and flair to it matching the adventurous and fluid temper of the times, those who wrote in the nineteenth century had clearly stepped out of the domestic sphere, and this made them bold and brazen. The high seriousness with which male writers were regarded contrasted sharply with the characterization of women novelists as "scribblers" and authors of "silly" works.

As if in acknowledgment of their misfit status, many women writers, including the best, took men's names as their pseudonyms: George Eliot, Currer Bell (Charlotte Brontë), Ellis Bell (Emily Brontë), Acton Bell (Anne Brontë), Daniel Stern, George Sand, Otto Stern (Louise Otto-Peters), and Paul Grendel (Julia Bécour). They adopted men's names because maleness gave legitimacy to their writing, especially if they were writing on serious subjects such as politics. Elizabeth Barrett Browning wrote a poem about the ambiguities in the life of French writer George Sand (1804–1876). Barrett Browning was fascinated by Sand and described her as "True genius, but true woman." The genius wandered back and forth between identities:

> Thy woman's hair, my sister, all unshorn,
> Floats back dishevelled strength in agony,
> Disproving thy man's name.

Browning sensed that genius that lived in memory after death was "unsexed."[6] Yet whether a man or a woman was the author of a work became and remained an important issue to nineteenth-century readers and critics. Charles Dickens, for example, suspected that George Eliot's *Adam Bede* was in fact the work of a woman, and Harriet Martineau maintained that Currer Bell's *Jane Eyre* was. The suspicion that a male name was being used by a woman author aroused commentary. Even though writing occurred in private, its publication meant entry into the outside world, and thus it was seen as more properly part of the male sphere.

Women writers were clearly in an ambivalent position. As women, they often admired many traditional values ascribed to womanhood, but by having a profession, they stepped beyond these values and moved into the world of men. Many women writers fulfilled the ideal of motherhood. As mothers or stepmothers, they received testimonials to their womanly goodness. This one, for example, is from George Eliot's stepson, Charles Lewes: "George Eliot found a ruined life and she made it into a beautiful life. She found us poor motherless boys, and what she did for us no one on earth will ever know."[7] Some authors, such as Elizabeth Gaskell (1810–1855), filled their letters with stories of their bouncing, blissful children. Other women writers were concerned about moving out of their sphere; for example, Charlotte Brontë worried about having written something "unfitting." The woman writer understood woman's world yet was separated from it by her writing, which gave her a man's perspective. Although active in the world of men, women writers still were able to see its problems, particularly its immorality and lust for gold. For example, Elizabeth Gaskell recognized the effects of the great divide between the sexes: "I would not trust a mouse to a woman if a man's judgment was to be had. Women have no judgment. They've tact and sensitiveness, genius and hundreds of loving qualities, but are at best angelic geese."[8] Gaskell wrote about daily life in an intimate, delightful way, yet she pointed out the problems of male-dominated society. *Cranford* (1853) portrayed a small village whose inhabitants had routines built around tea and card-playing and where a running thread of intrigue and foibles held the plot together. *Ruth* (1853), *North and South* (1855), and *Mary Barton* (1848) chronicled industrial and social problems of which she was acutely aware, given her vantage point in Manchester. In *Ruth* she shocked polite society by taking up the cause of the abandoned, unwed mother.

The name of George Sand (1804–1876) reverberated throughout the century as that of a problematic figure. A writer who led a notoriously unconventional life, she stood for both women's genius and women's dangerous side. Sand came from a distinguished lineage. One ancestor was the King of Poland, who fathered hundreds of illegitimate children, and another was famous eighteenth-century military hero, the Maréchal de Saxe. Sand's paternal grandmother had been a glittering figure of the old regime and her father had served Napoleon, but her mother was a working woman, low-born and poorly educated. This combination of backgrounds produced a writer and a rebel. The beginning of Sand's rebelliousness occurred when she left a tyrannical and brutish husband to live an independent life in Paris. From then on, she conducted various love affairs and became a leader of intellectual society and a talked-about figure. Whether seductively dressed as a woman or practically dressed as a man, Sand traveled, lived life to the fullest, and—most of all—wrote. In 1832, her first novel, *Indiana,* captured the imagination of the reading public. The story of a woman married to a boorish husband, *Indiana* dealt with the new ideal of romantic love and with passion. For those of revolutionary spirit, for those who waited for the day of liberation, this heroine's life demonstrated the possibilities that a woman could have a self based on intense feeling, could rebel, and could achieve happiness. The heroine's sense of self grew out of emotions rather than accomplishments; she then remained faithful to her strong feelings through actions. Sand created a series of such striving heroines, who sought love, who found or missed out on love, who asserted rights to sexual happiness, and who failed to find it with men. After this series of novels, Sand turned to a theme of the common people in novels about artisans and country types. In all of them, she stressed the strength of women. *La Petite Fadette* (1848) is the tale of an awkward, slovenly, and even witchlike girl who develops into a powerful, beautiful, and maternal woman. *François the Waif* (1847) describes the life of a poor rural teenager who raises an abandoned child and eventually marries him. Sand's stories were never ordinary—they contained muted incest and seductions of young people, and always promoted the cause of women. Her stories were important and gripping, and her life was too. The center of feminist attentions and allegiance, she often preferred the company of men and fought their political battles more often than she did those of women. Sand's life represented the dichotomy that characterized the lives of many women writers of the time.

The Brontë sisters—Charlotte (1816–1855), Emily (1818–1848), and Anne (1820–1849)—adopted male pseudonyms and often enfolded their identities as writers into male narrators. The sisters spent their childhood years in Haworth parsonage in Yorkshire, where they developed their writing skills by producing their own magazines and a series of fantasies about the kingdoms of Angria and Gondal. The Haworth parsonage was severe in its interior decoration—their father feared fires and therefore never allowed curtains. Outside was a stern landscape of moors and tumultuous, stormy weather. In this setting, the lives of the sisters evolved amidst eccentricities and tragedies. Their father shot off his pistol every morning to unload the bullets he kept on hand in case of local disturbance. He doted on his only son, Branwell (1817–1848), who also participated in the childhood writing but later became addicted to opium and alcohol. Having lost their mother, four of the five girls were sent off to school where conditions were so harsh that the two eldest died in 1825. Returning home, the survivors developed their writing, although occasionally one or another left to serve as a governess. In the mid-1840s, Charlotte undertook to publish some of their poetry as well as the novels she, Anne, and Emily had written. Her efforts led to the publication of *Agnes Grey* by Anne and the masterpiece *Wuthering Heights* by Emily in 1847, followed later that same year by Charlotte's *Jane Eyre. Jane Eyre* became a success overnight, very likely because it dealt with the plight of governesses, whereas *Wuthering Heights* took more time to achieve recognition. In the midst of these triumphs, Branwell died, followed quickly by Emily, and then, a year after the appearance of her *The Tenant of Wildfell Hall* (1848), Anne died of tuberculosis. Left alone, Charlotte continued to produce fine novels: *Shirley* (1849) concerned social questions, and *Villette* (1853) was about a young woman in love. Charlotte married her father's curate Arthur Bell Nichols in 1854; she died the next year of tuberculosis, near the end of a much desired pregnancy.

Wuthering Heights described the mystical and tempestuous love of the orphan Heathcliff for Catherine Earnshaw. Emily Brontë's poetry had already revealed that she thought in terms of the cosmic nature of human existence. Isolated from any society beyond her family, she was led by the intensity of her small world to connect its inhabitants, and everyone for that matter, to the most powerful forces of the universe. The passion between Catherine and Heathcliff was therefore pictured as immense and cosmic. Yet readers most appreciated the atmosphere of the Yorkshire moors, with its winds and apparent forlornness. They loved the homespun characters such as Nelly Dean, who told Heathcliff's and Cathy's story to the male narrator. The combination of the local and the ghastly made Emily fit into one branch of the Romantic school of novelists. The story, however, told much more than did those of most Romantics, for it relates the life of a young woman before her entry into marriage and patriarchal society. Growing up with and helping to acculturate the orphan Heathcliff, she is in a kind of natural state with him. However, the pair visits the home of the Lintons where, bitten by a dog, Catherine must stay to recuperate. Cosseted and pampered, she enters a more formal society, and eventually marries young Edgar Linton, the patriarch. Catherine falls ill in this setting, becomes pregnant, and dies after a stormy scene in which she and Heathcliff recognize themselves as each other's self. Inconsolable, Heathcliff sets out to ruin all who remain, including Linton's sister Isabella, whom he has married; their son; and Catherine's baby daughter, whom he blames for Catherine's death. Ultimately the cosmic vision of Catherine that so haunts his life also redeems it. Among the best English novels, this story of Catherine Earnshaw's power even after death dealt with issues of women, religion, and the ongoing struggles that made up human life. Brontë twisted all these themes into a story that confronted propriety by calling up individual and universal passions let loose on society. In the end what survived was a woman-created myth—that of successive generations of Catherines.

Jane Eyre told a less morbid, though only slightly less bizarre, story. The heroine experienced a miserable childhood like that of the Brontës and suffers as a governess, especially when the master of the house, Rochester, tries to marry her while keeping his legitimate but insane wife locked away in another part of the house. Charlotte's tale, like Emily's, had Romantic themes, such as conflagration, madness, darkly handsome heroes, storms, and human excess. Yet *Jane Eyre* also told the moralistic story of a woman who refuses to become a mistress, and later even refuses to become the wife of a respectable minister who only wants her services in his religious work. Intuitively demanding equality in her relationships, the heroine discovers her mature self and having achieved it, marries Rochester—now blind and crippled because he tried to save his wife from a fire in his home. The egalitarian theme of *Jane Eyre* reappeared in the social novel *Shirley,* in which a combination of powerless, but wealthy women and angry, starving working-class people provided a critique of the economic and gender order. Charlotte's Brontë's final novel, *Villette,* is her ultimate story of women's poor status in society. The heroine of the novel, Lucy Snowe lacks positive qualities such as money, good looks, family, or even an engaging personality. How does such a woman survive and especially how does she fare in the human quest for love? While Lucy Snowe sought emotional satisfaction, she also observed others involved in that quest. The book is full of couplings, potential marriages, and emotional wanderings, as well as various forms of human treachery. All of these serve as lessons helping Lucy to develop her self-control, which from time to time is undermined by the appearance of people she cares for or by nature: "I had feelings: passive as I lived, little as I spoke, cold as I looked . . . I *could* feel."[9] Rather than submerge her heroine in a Romantic vision, Brontë showed a woman trying to bring balance into her life. In this struggle, Lucy must avoid the excess feelings romance would bring, though she yearns to experience love. At the same time, she must confront the inequality of women's position in the social world. All these factors she recognizes as she narrates her own story. Narration, for Charlotte Brontë and for Lucy Snowe, allowed for a resolution of women's position. The literary progression from *Jane Eyre* to *Villette* mirrored Brontë's own progression from governess to woman writer.

Marian Evans (1819–1880), who took the pen name George Eliot, began her literary career with scholarly work—first a translation of David Strauss's *Life of Jesus* (1846), a study that denied Christ's divine aspects while stressing the ethical and human ones. She contributed to the *Westminster Review* in the early 1850s, became an assistant editor, and fell in love with its editor John Chapman. Later she also fell in love with the sociologist Herbert Spencer. Neither of these men appreciated her strong feelings. In 1854, she began living with George Henry Lewes, a renowned critic whose wife had left him for someone else. Divorce required an act of Parliament and cost a great deal of money; therefore, the two could not marry. They were shunned by many in polite society and even by family members. Eliot was a very moral person, who considered herself Lewes's true wife and conscientiously served as a loving stepmother to his deserted children and grandmother to their children. Lewes directed her to fiction after reading her prose, and once started, she produced a steady stream of excellent novels. In her novels Eliot portrayed the sad aspects of ordinary life, the fateful grinding down of one hope or ambition after another. This hardly fit the pattern of her own success in love and work. Even in her sixties, after Lewes's death, Eliot married another man, twenty years her junior. Her enormous success as a popular writer and her satisfaction in love made her life quite different from that of the heroines she created.

George Eliot aimed at a kind of clinical examination of ordinary people: parsons, country girls, and undistinguished aristocrats and scholars. This

George Eliot, whose Middlemarch *is judged by some to be the greatest novel of the nineteenth century, lived an unconventional life while endorsing conventions. The power of her novels redeemed her in the eyes of many contemporaries.*

theme was echoed even in her books' titles right from the first, *Scenes of Clerical Life* (1857). Though she employed down-to-earth characters, Eliot explored the great and dramatic questions of love and death, especially in relation to her female protagonists. *Adam Bede* (1859) recounts the story of unwed mother Hetty Sorel, who killed her illegitimate child and was then condemned to die. The classic *The Mill on the Floss* (1860) describes the spirited Maggie Tulliver, whose youth, much like Eliot's, involved an intense closeness to her brother. In these stories and in those to follow, Eliot examined the relationship of women to men and implicitly described the moral universe she felt had to be perpetuated. Many of her young women characters aspired to learning or some other kind of higher experience. Dinah Morris in *Adam Bede* is a woman preacher, modeled after Eliot's aunt. Both Celia and Dorothea Brooke in *Middlemarch* (1871–1872) strive for intellectual knowledge: Celia reads a lot and speaks of her attachment to *Corinne*—Madame de Staël's powerful portrayal of a woman genius. Nonetheless, most of Eliot's heroines end up renouncing this kind of achievement in favor of morality, sacrifice, and other manifestations of devotion to men and the social order. In *Middlemarch*, which many believe to be Eliot's masterpiece and perhaps the greatest novel of the nineteenth century, such a conversion takes place for Dorothea Brooke, who tries to get involved in scholarship by marrying the dried-up old scholar Casaubon and ends up a better human being. Eliot was critical of women's aspirations to be like men in their quest for place and money. Such ambition characterized Gwendolyn Harleth, the heroine of *Daniel Deronda* (1876), also a story about heroism among the outcasts of Victorian society—the Jews. Eliot's view was that acting on civilized values that included toleration and integrity was the destiny and duty of women in a world where men were ambitious. At the same time, Eliot undermined the idea of separate spheres by intermeshing men's and women's spheres of action in her novels and by making it difficult to tell which was one and which the other. Nonetheless, she described realistically a world in which men had most of the control and women had to help the system's victims and each other.

Thus, from the nationalistic novels of Eastern Europe to the Victorian classics of the West, women's voluminous writing delved into both the personal world and the political one. It critiqued the nature of society and human relationships, while portraying models—such as Granny—of what lives should be like. Ambitious and hard-working, women undertook aesthetically to instruct, engage, and entertain vast numbers through print.

Reform in England

The home of industrialization, England was the scene of political action and intellectual debate that centered on the effects of industrialization on the lives of women and men. The novelists Gaskell and Eliot were among those who described this phenomenon. Liberals, political economists, and philosophers of the time tried to explain the rules and norms for a new society in a way that would make for greater acceptance of them. They advocated a free market and free trade, and some, particularly Thomas Malthus and his followers, made dire predictions. Malthus noted the population explosion and predicted that working people would produce more and more children if their standard of living improved. He believed that ultimately this would lead to famine and disaster. To alleviate the problem, Malthus proposed programs of population limitation, especially for the poor. His theory became known as Malthusianism. From the early nineteenth century on, the population question took many forms. The ongoing interest and often heated debate about population grew from concerns about what reproductive organization should be like now that society could replace its members in abundance.

Harriet Martineau (1802–1876), who believed in an active type of religion, also participated in the discussion of social and economic laws. Martineau's desire to reach a large public coincided with her need to support herself from an early age. From 1832 until the late 1840s, she published a series of popular essays on economics, legal reform, and social change. Her message was a modern one that had originated with Locke and Adam Smith: the market economy with its balance of interests benefited most of society, unlike aristocratic negligence of commerce and protection of special interests. Martineau explained the utilitarian theory that governments should create social policy that benefited the majority. She consistently expressed a desire to help the "mass" of people. Selling tens of thousands of copies, her lessons on political economy in story form envisioned a society in which all classes could see that their best interests were attached to working for industrial development and an integrated market economy. At the same time she feared the consequences of rising population and advocated such remedies as emigration and higher ages at marriage. In her later years, Martineau expressed liberal feminist sentiments; before then she advanced the cause of liberal reform in general.

Whereas the elite discussed industrial society and its effects, the common people addressed the issues more actively. Influenced by the democratic aspects of the French Revolution, English working people, especially in the industrializing north, agitated for reform. Agreeing with the middle classes, they wanted an end to aristocratic domination in economics and politics. For example, just after the end of the Napoleonic Wars (1815) the government had passed a corn law, which kept the price of grain artificially high by imposing tariffs on imported grain. Such a tariff reflected the interests of large landowners and acted to the detriment of working people. So did the very limited right to vote and the lack of Parliamentary representation for newly enlarged cities. Many felt that universal male suffrage and free trade would change the situation and more adequately reflect the concerns of the British population. These beliefs constituted a political program known as radicalism. A number of radical organizations arose including dozens of "female reform societies," which were formed for the most part around 1819 by working-class women. The goals of these organizations generally entailed universal male suffrage, and their political pronouncements often contained statements about the soothing and consoling role of women. Not demanding anything for themselves, members of the female reform societies saw themselves as auxiliaries to their men. "Sharing and sympathizing in the pure patriotic feelings of . . . father, brother, or husband," members of the Blackburn Female Reform Society called the venture for universal male suffrage a "hallowed cause."[10] The radical movement made officials nervous, especially when it resulted in huge rallies. With the potential for revolution so much on the minds of those in power, an incident was bound to happen, and it did in Manchester in 1819. Troops fired on and wounded hundreds of people at a mass meeting, among them 113 women. After that, repressive laws attempted to control popular meetings and to censor the writing of agitators and to punish them.

The ongoing movement for political liberalism led to the Great Reform Bill of 1832, giving the franchise to middle-class men and proportional representation to newly populous industrial cities. The bill changed the political balance by taking away from landholders their traditional control of parliamentary seats. Just two years later, the middle class drove the New Poor Law through Parliament. This bill reduced the poor rates that the wealthy paid and forced indigent people to enter workhouses. It also brought about an uprising involving both men and women because the workhouse loomed large as a place where they or their kin might be incarcerated in hard times. For practically the rest of the decade, working women attacked the Poor Law as a political instrument that would destroy the family. In 1838, for example, they led several physical assaults on poorhouse officials and generally did everything in their power to prevent poor houses from functioning. Then women took an important political step when they moved from spontaneous action to political organization. In the mid-1830s, many anti–Poor Law societies were formed. They especially promoted the cause of mothers who would be separated from their children. Republican ideology influenced this struggle to maintain familial roles.

All these organizations, though unsuccessful in ending the workhouse system, became part of a strong working-class movement called Chartism in the late 1830s. Inspired by the electoral reform of 1832, by radical ideals, and economic distress, Chartists aimed to gain universal suffrage, to end property requirements for sitting in Parliament, and to accomplish other democratic political reforms. Women helped the cause by a range of auxiliary efforts— raising money, passing petitions for signatures, holding teas and other events to recruit new adherents. These women also demanded that the so-called "Charter" giving all men the vote include provisions for female suffrage. The initial demand grew out of the intense political activity of working women in the early decades of the century. Although men often urged an exclusively domestic life for women along with their removal from the workforce, they coupled that preference with an acceptance of suffrage. Women kept the Chartist movement going, and their efforts frightened the authorities. The *London Times* called Chartist women "hen radicals," and other papers demanded their removal from politics:[11]

> Women may influence great possess
> But on certain conditions
> And one of them is—they must ne'er
> Set up for politicians.

Chartism raised the specter of revolution. Although there were few women who spoke at rallies, those who did were said to resemble the "harpies" of the French Revolution. Chartist women also reintroduced certain disturbing ideas, particularly those of Mary Wollstonecraft, outcast earlier for her "whorish" ways. But the movement's impetus died down for several reasons. By the mid-1840s the very difficult economic conditions of five years earlier had improved. Moreover, the rhetoric of the movement in favor of domesticity seemed to influence the rank and file members to return to separate spheres. Nonetheless, the Chartist movement demonstrated women's profound interest in national issues and a new concern with the contours of state power. The politicization of working-class women was the lasting legacy of the movement, one that would affect middle-class women as well.

The Revolutions of 1848

While reform proceeded in England, revolution erupted elsewhere in Europe. Beginning in the Kingdom of Naples in January of 1848, it spread across the Continent. The causes were the restoration of monarchic governments that replaced the Napoleonic system and a desire for national unification. Also, workers everywhere had endured several years of miserable times, and agriculture had failed widely as well. Though run by conservative princes, countries and cities were bursting with new ideas, often as a result of economic development. The ruling elite tried to turn back the clock but failed miserably. They seemed only to antagonize the population while they remained in power. In France, a clique of powerful businessmen around King Louis Philippe had placed a stranglehold on growth and opportunity for people other than themselves. In the German states, the people wanted liberalism, national unity, and constitutional government, although many wanted protection for their threatened crafts. In Italy, issues similar to those in Germany came to the fore: nationalism, an end to Austrian control of the northern part of the peninsula, and social progress. Meanwhile, the Habsburg empire faced peasant, ethnic, and urban uprisings; it also faced the demands of Hungarian nobles who wanted a greater share of power. In early 1848 popular discontent grew and spread so rapidly that kings were either toppled from their thrones or they granted constitutions almost immediately. By spring, ministers such as Austria's reactionary Clemens von Metternich and France's François Guizot were forced out of power. Suddenly open to reform, most countries experienced a move toward more representative government based on constitutional guarantees of rights and regular procedures. This reforming period brought all kinds of demands, including those from women, who saw this time of flexibility as an opportunity to express their desperate needs.

Italy

The French occupation of Italy during the Napoleonic Wars had lifted many Italians out of their relatively backward state. The influence of such retrogressive institutions as the aristocracy and the Catholic Church had been drastically reduced. Then, in 1815 the defeat of the French at Waterloo restored all these reactionary forces. Chafing under them, some Italians formed secret societies to work for political change. Women had one of their own called the *giardinière* (the gardeners). In Rome, Napoleon's stepdaughter and sister-in-law, Hortense de Beauharnais, formerly Queen of Holland, held a *salon* that served the secret cause. So did other *salons* across Europe. However, police repression caused the fragmentation of the reformers into factions with differing plans for the creation of a new nation. Though committed to unifying Italy, activists were divided on who would head the new Italian state—the pope, the King of Sardinia, or representatives of the people? They differed on what kind of government would follow unification—constitutional monarchy or republic? Such divisions halted the revolution of 1848 before any of the goals had reached fruition. The revolutionary King of Sardinia surrendered to the Austrians; the pope refused to head any kind of Italian government; and the French entered Italy in order to put down the republic that had been established in Rome. There were also some positive results from the uprisings, however. The forces of the renegade military leader and patriot Giuseppe Garibaldi had excited the people, and the pope's renunciation of civil leadership had clarified his inability to champion the national cause. In supporting revolution, the people had demonstrated their belief in a unified Italy. Although the urban uprisings failed, the idea of national unity was stronger than ever.

The factors leading to revolution had to do with poverty and the hunger due to bad crop yields in 1846 and 1847. As in the French Revolution, economic hard times provided the impulse, and those most adversely affected acted first. In the fall of 1847, 200 women in Messina, Sicily, attacked the palace, tearing off the guards' royal insignia and roughing them up. When the revolution finally broke out in January, women filled the streets, carrying or wearing the Italian tricolor and chasing royal officials from their palaces. Besides these early manifestations in city after city, observers noted the participation of women by the thousands in pitched battles with the armed forces. For example, a woman of the common people named Rosa Donato was known throughout Sicily because she and two men had wheeled artillery around a city to hold off the royal forces. In greater numbers than women of any other country, Italian women entered the volunteer civilian guards and revolutionary armies. They helped to barricade cities and formed part of practically every armed force fighting to drive foreign soldiers from Italian soil.

The idea of creating a nation was inspiring. Household skills were turned into military services as women made bandages, knit stockings, and sent packages of food to soldiers. In addition, women collected money, mended and made uniforms, and volunteered to care for wounded soldiers. Hospitals in cities found scores of women from all classes ready to assist in nursing duties and to supply provisions. Wealthy women adopted soldiers' families and cared for their needs while the men were at the front. Thus, as in the French and American revolutions, women's daily work was put to use serving the state. Their political consciousness developed along with an allegiance to the nation. Denied ostensible rights, they still thought of themselves in terms of citizenship because their domestic work acquired political significance. Like others before them, Italian women became patriotic mothers.

Many women saw a connection between the work they did and the political quest for nationhood because of Giuseppe Mazzini, long the leading ideologue of a more spiritual form of Italian nationalism. Among the creators of competing programs for unifying and liberating Italy, Mazzini was the most charismatic. Mazzini had belonged to secret societies and moved into exile in London. From there he preached nationalism and republicanism, a combination whose radicalism disturbed liberals. A true republican, Mazzini had a special program for women, but it did not differ much from earlier republican ideology. His tracts and pamphlets called woman an "angel," an educator, and a necessary part of the cause of national unity and the development of self-government. Religious rhetoric and a sense of the historical grandeur of the Roman past infused all his pronouncements on unification. When speaking of women, he invoked the Virgin Mary and attributed divine purpose to the differences between men and women. At the same time, in a good republican manner, he gave the home an overwhelming importance. Because it was the birthplace of citizenship, his followers were "to sanctify the family, and to link it ever more closely with country."[12] The attraction of his program for women stemmed from the same interests that had led to the establishment of republican motherhood following the French and American revolutions. Maternity gained national and cultural purpose. In addition, his criticism of excessive individualism and materialism had an appeal similar to that of the theories of utopian socialists. Therefore, Mazzini's thought shaped Italian feminism from the 1840s on. After the revolution was put down in 1849 by various forces, including those of France and Austria, women continued referring to themselves as "citizen-mothers." They continued to struggle for nationhood, which was accomplished in 1861 with the formation of the kingdom of Italy.

France

The French monarchy fell in late February 1848. Eager for more liberty, a revolution in 1830 had established a constitutional monarchy called the July Monarchy. But democrats and businessmen remained discontented with its restrictions on progress. Rioting in cities and countryside over high prices and scarcity of goods also led to this new upheaval. Once in control, a provisional government declared universal male suffrage, and the working-classes demanded attention to unemployment. Believing in the primacy of work, workers petitioned the government to establish national workshops, where the unemployed could find work and where work could be better organized. Club life flourished again, and so did newspapers. Both spread revolutionary ideas as they had in 1789. Women were again part of the action. They too launched newspapers—the *Voix des Femmes* (*Women's Voice*) came into being in March—and formed clubs, such as the Club for the Emancipation of Women, the Committee for the Rights of Women, the Fraternal Association of Democrats of Both Sexes, and the working-class Vesuvians. Participating in street action, they all tried to reform their daily lives and those of their families. When national workshops for men came into existence, working-class women demanded ones for unemployed women as well. However, the workshops that were established mostly provided work sewing luxury garments. Running these workshops also became an issue. The leaders of the provisional government wanted them directed by middle-class women. Working women, however, demanded that they be directed by their own kind, who would know how such an enterprise ran, what its needs were, and what sort of discipline should be used. Why pay money to women who did not need it, when there were plenty of talented working-class women who could do the job as well

A woman of the people, "Mariane" represented the cause of French liberty in this painting by Eugène Delacroix. Such a depiction raises many questions about representation, the nation-state, and gender.

and needed the money to support their families? Such demands made working-class women seem uppity and disruptive to those higher up in the social hierarchy in place at the time.

French women also strived to obtain voting rights—truly universal suffrage. Women from the Committee for the Rights of Women petitioned the provisional government for the franchise. Then in an April issue of the *Voix des Femmes*, Eugenie Niboyet, a former Saint-Simonian, endorsed George Sand as a candidate for the new assembly, which would be the first elected under universal male suffrage. The endorsement of Sand by the women of the *Voix des Femmes* carried a strong emotional message based on the Saint-Simonian credo. For Niboyet, Sand was the perfect human entity: "The representative who united our sympathies, is by type masculine and feminine, male by virtue of virility, female by divine intuition, poetry: we have nominated Sand."[13] Sand embodied qualities admired by the Saint-Simonian women—she represented the Mother, who through childbirth and then nurture brought special qualities to the social order. Sand's writing they saw as expressing the poetry of that mission. Sand, however, scornfully refused the nomination by

Workers Petition the Government in Times of Distress

In 1848 Parisians joined to overthrow the monarchy of Louis Philippe. The times were troubled, people were out of work—a situation which in the past had led people to petition the monarch as one would petition a father. Now they brought their grievances to the new revolutionary government. In mid-March a group of rabbit fur cutters in the hat industry wrote this letter explaining their predicament. Their letter gives a picture not only of their distress, but it reveals the familial orientation of their goals and an old regime conception of craft as estate or *état*. Unfortunately, they addressed a government less paternalistic and far more business-oriented than the old one.

> Sirs,
>
> The women workers exercising the trade (*état*) of rabbit fur cutters for the hat industry, two or three thousand in number, all diligent and mothers of families, have the honor of showing that this trade (*état*), which is only practiced by women, gives them the wherewithal to live, to feed their children, and to give a trade (*état*) to their daughters, enabling them according to their ability to earn 10 or 12 francs per week, although now they are reduced to earning 50 or 75 centimes a day, which makes it impossible for them to earn their livelihood or that of their families. This state of things, Sirs, arises from machines which have been adopted by the richest owners . . . and which cause us the greatest injury, . . . aggravate our already sad position, and snatch bread from our mouths. In addition, for fifteen years, ten thousand foreign workers have arrived to bring misery to a trade (*état*), which once flourished but which now is almost extinct.
>
> For these reasons, the petitioners . . . beg the provisional government, from which all justice arises, to look with compassion on their unfortunate fate and to restore their livelihood by stopping these machines. . . . It is their most ardent wish and they have complete confidence that your humanity and your justice will not fail them and will protect them against the egotism of the wealthy cutters.

Source: Archives nationales de France, F/12 4898 Lettre des coupeuses de poil de lapin à Messieurs les Membres du Gouvernement Provisoire. Paris, le 13 mars 1848. Judith De Groat generously provided this document.

denying any acquaintance with these "ladies." At the time Sand's social circle included members of the provisional government, and her journalistic accounts of the revolution were appearing in several different newspapers. Because she was much sought after, Sand's scornful rejection was especially hurtful. Sand's rejection rested on certain liberal principles that she put ahead of the republican ideals of the *Voix des Femmes*. Not motherhood but civil rights interested Sand at this time. She objected to sitting in the assembly among men who had rights when women did not; she said a woman being there would constitute "the claim to represent something when you are not even the representation of yourselves."[14] In this regard a liberal, though she generally scorned the middle classes, Sand felt no solidarity with women who thought in terms of the unifying force of motherhood. In this clash, two branches of feminist thought showed a tension. This tension would plague later feminists throughout Europe.

The elections did not turn out as revolutionary women wanted. Small landowners from the country, those supportive of the monarchy, and business interests of all sorts voted in a mostly conservative assembly. From then on workers in Paris were at odds with the rest of the populace. Their proposals for reform had only their own support; their middle-class allies who had helped bring down the monarchy deserted them once the republic was ensured. Things went badly for women right from the start, for in the spring the assembly defeated a bill for women's suffrage by a vote of 899 to 1. Still women kept making demands. Seamstress Desirée Gay proposed a multitude of services for working-class women from her position on the national workshop council. More radical women led by Jeanne Deroin, also a former seamstress, started their own paper, the *Politique des Femmes* (*Women's Politics*). Before these efforts could be consolidated into a movement, the conservative government closed down the national workshops. This act represented the end of the alliance between workers and middle-class reformers. In protest, the workers took to the streets in June. There, in several days of fighting, volunteers from all over France who sought to restore economic order put down the workers' uprising. Part of that restoration involved a virtual reenactment of the gender aspects of the revolution of 1789. That is, at the end of June a new French government decreed an end to women's membership in political clubs and began harassing women's newspapers as well as political activists. Women playing a public role symbolized the disorderliness of a revolution that the men now in power wanted to put behind them.

The repressive mood seemed not to dampen some workers' activism. Jeanne Deroin (c. 1810–1894) announced her candidacy for the next assembly election in the spring of 1849. Her platform was a liberal one based on ideas of freedom and equality: both workers and women needed representation, and the interests of either group could only be represented by someone from the group. Her campaign was fruitless, but her activism continued. Deroin participated in the movement for establishing cooperative associations among workers. She was joined in this effort by Pauline Roland (1805–1852), another Saint-Simonian who had been living in such a community outside of Paris. Roland spoke to meetings of craft organizations and urged them to move beyond simple association toward organization of consumption. Roland also advocated "perfect equality" of the sexes in society and in marriage, "moral reform" of gender life, and the coeducation of children. Once cooperation had achieved the end of abolishing "industrial feudalism," as she called the nineteenth-century society in which she lived, then other remnants of injustice and feudal decadence would go as well.[15] Roland's ideas on gender shocked authorities and so did the organization she finally set up, the Union of Workers Associations. This organization of all the cooperatives planned a new society in which workers rearranged production and the moral aspects of their lives. In 1850, Deroin and Roland were both arrested for conducting political meetings and sentenced to six-month prison terms. The course of their trial indicated what worried the authorities. Roland spoke of her socialist interests, whereas the judge and prosecution also focused on her personal life and her interest in changing gender relations. Activist women seemed to pose a threat to society, especially to a government that was trying to stabilize itself.

In the late fall of 1851, Louis Napoleon, nephew of the emperor, staged a coup d'état while serving a term as president of the French republic. The next year he proclaimed himself Emperor Napoleon III. In the process of taking power, Napoleon III had the police round up people he perceived as dangerous; among them was Pauline Roland. Sent to a penal colony in Algeria, Roland died on her return from this second imprisonment. Deroin more prudently exiled herself from a country where ideas about gender equality were so threatening.

The German States

Revolution erupted in the German states for a variety of reasons. The desire for national unity and liberal measures intersected with the need for economic security. Reforms that had been instituted in the Napoleonic years withered away after 1815 and were replaced by political repression and censorship and by poverty for those crushed by the process of industrialization. The period between 1815 and 1848 abounded in criticism of the status quo and calls for action. In her notebooks on the poor, Bettina von Arnim (1785–1859) kept scrupulous accounts of the conditions among workers in Berlin. As journalists, other women protested being forced to write in "half words." "I believe," wrote one, "that where the censor generally has sway, the life and activity of peaceful citizens must be protected from the intrusions of unrestrained, insolent caprice."[16] Gatherings intended to build support for reform called on women to join in protesting the retrograde conditions in Germany. Working for education and enlightenment, women contributed to the birth of a new spirit of protest. Schooling, writings, and other activities manifested the liberal views that infected other European circles. Women translated foreign works with political messages, especially those exalting liberty. Kathinka Zitz-Halein, for example, translated Victor Hugo's plays, notably those criticizing absolute power. Constantly alert, women participated in circulating petitions and in protesting when economic conditions deteriorated or when those few liberties that did exist were threatened. They were active in building the energetic spirit of the *Vormärz*—which literally means the period "before March" 1848.

The *Vormärz* was characterized by middle-class reform; it also celebrated youth. The movement called Young Germany exalted the romantic spirit and the potential for creating a different society, including a new attitude toward women. The intellectuals, artists, and students who founded Young Germany borrowed heavily from the Saint-Simonians. Two novels written by Young Germans, Karl Gutzkow's *Madonna* and Theodor Mundt's *Wally, the Skeptic*, appeared in 1835 and portrayed a new kind of woman, who was both sensual and intelligent. Instead of the sober and phlegmatic persona of the typical German housewife, these heroines showed a deeper sensibility, which in turn liberated them from the tightness of domestic norms. Such novels appeared corrupt to officials but reflected the changes the Young Germans proposed. Dedicating her book *Correspondence of Goethe with a Child* (1834) to the movement, Bettina von Arnim became an important figure to the Young Germans precisely because she was a woman. Von Arnim displayed the middle-class conscience of the day and in this particular work captured the uniqueness

Women and men rioted together in the German town of Stetlin in 1847. Their object was to obtain bread from the bakery at affordable prices for working-class people.

the Young Germans attributed to their ideas. Granddaughter of novelist Sophie von La Roche, von Arnim interwove parts of letters Goethe had written her with fictions of her own. She presented a picture of Goethe as a stern figure obedient to the monarchy, whereas she, representative of the new generation, came across quite differently. Recapturing and to some extent inventing her childhood, she displayed childish innocence and truth in her letters. The book drew a stark contrast between two generations—in the context of the time, two political generations. Buying von Arnim's interpretation of Goethe, which critics said did not capture the complexity of his artistic and literary positions, the Young Germans made her *Correspondence* into a kind of testimony of youthful faith. In 1840, publication of von Arnim's *Correspondence with Günderode,* dedicated to university students, was marked by a torchlight parade. In this work, she used her friendship with the Romantic poet Caroline Günderode to voice liberated political ideas. Von Arnim maintained that in the best of worlds, the political person's inspiration came from religion and the universal truths of nature. Lifting resistance out of the dirty world of everyday political life, von Arnim instead placed it in a spiritual realm, the same exalted terrain on which the Young Germans focused their dreams.

The revolution that broke out in March of 1848 in cities throughout Germany was due more to bad economic conditions than to Romanticism. Disastrous harvests starved urban workers, and spreading industrialization put them out of work. During these disastrous times, the young Germans Karl Marx (1818–1883) and Friedrich Engels (1820–1895) began formulating their own variety of socialist analysis. In the mid-forties Silesian weavers revolted as mechanization drove down their income. In the spring of 1847, bread riots erupted as the price of grain and flour skyrocketed. In Stuttgart, women without bread to feed their families screamed at grain merchants in public and charivaried them. In other cities, women and men obtained flour through violence and then cooperatively divided it up to take to their families. As news of the workers' revolts in Paris and Sicily reached the German states, working-class political activity erupted: domestic servants formed unions and announced their demands; craftspeople demanded an end to mechanization; and mothers continued to ask for bread. In every city women were among those arrested for participation in crowds, strikes, and political protests. In Berlin, women were among those who died in the first attacks on demonstrators by soldiers. "For the first time," wrote Malwida von Meysenbug of her coming to revolutionary consciousness, "I thought seriously of the necessity for a woman to win economic independence through her own force."[17] Thinking in new ways and acting forcefully on behalf of their families' well-being, women were literally turning the world upside down.

Even before the uprisings of working-class women seeking food and employment, middle-class women recognized the importance of workers' lives to their own cause. Political poet Louise Aston wrote her "Song of a Silesian Woman Weaver," and Louise Otto had written about spinners. The revolution brought these and other middle-class women to the fore as journalists reporting on outbursts of violence and political events, such as the proceedings of the Frankfurt Parliament, which began meeting in 1848 to bring about the unification of Germany. In Frankfurt and other capital cities, women reporters wrote for a variety of papers, from the most conservative to the most radical. Claire von Glümer, journalist for the *Magdeburger Zeitung* (*Magdeburg Times*), was among the journalists who played a wider role. Glümer went to prison for her revolutionary activities; she also helped in her brother's escape from jail. Even prior to 1848, Louise Aston had been questioned by the police for her radicalism, including her advanced views on religion and women. For participating in the Berlin uprising, she was banished. Even though the number of banished women grew, other women progressed with the course of liberal revolution. In 1848, Mathilde Anneke published the first women's newspaper, but it produced only one issue. The next paper, Louise Otto-Peters's (1819– 1895) *Frauenzeitung* (*Women's Times*), lasted from the spring of 1849 until 1852, when it was banned. Otto-Peters's motto was that she would "enlist women for the kingdom of freedom." To do so she spread news of the international women's movement, ran book reviews, and provided information about the condition of women. A bourgeois in many ways, she nonetheless stressed a role for women that extended beyond the home. She had little use for "emancipated" women, those who rejected too much, transgressed gender lines, and were not religious. Supporting the working woman, Otto-Peters scorned the idle woman who dissipated her own energies. She stressed the social role of women—to deal with the problems of modern society, especially housing, women's poverty, and the generally deplorable plight of workers.

The revolutionary impulse was felt within households, from which public affairs were supposed to be banished. Those not on the barricades or running newspapers played other roles and built a revolutionary consciousness. The Humania Association for Patriotic Interests, founded in the spring of 1849, was an example of the clubs and organizations started by women to aid the revolutionary cause. Its leader, Kathinka Zitz-Halein (b. 1801), had joined the opposition in the *Vormärz* period. With the problem of refugees and impoverished revolutionaries looming large, she organized more than 1600 women of all classes into a group to make contributions and to distribute assistance. Comparing her co-workers' actions to those of women in the French Revolution, Zitz-Halein made women's charitable work into a political mission. Yet she too disliked the "emancipated" women made prominent by the revolution, and she had great distaste for those who took to the battlefields. She thought the type of effort she and her association engaged in was womanly and feminine in the best sense of the word. This position allowed the Humania Association to survive when other women's organizations were suppressed after the revolution and even after Zitz-Halein had resigned. The Humania Association, made up of many working-class women, continued its work until 1851, despite mounting problems. Its internal arguments over who would get aid and the localism manifested in its restriction on where aid would go have been seen by some historians as being indicative of the problems of the German revolutions in general. Members of the Humania Association, like the German population as a whole, had problems banding together for a common cause.

The German revolutions—and there were many because there were many German states—raised issues concerning work and wages, rights and liberty, and national unity. None of these struggles reached any satisfying resolution. Delegates from the various states who met at Frankfurt to discuss the question of unity ended up offering the crown of a united Germany to the king of Prussia, but he refused it. He saw the constitutional monarchy offered up by the nationalists as degrading—"a crown from the gutter" he called it. Moreover, as the Frankfurt representatives deliberated, they themselves used troops to put down workers' demonstrations. Finally, headed by the Prussian king, various armies dispersed the would-be unifiers of Germany, suppressed any lingering spirit of revolt, and generally used armed force to put things back the way they had been. Ringleaders were tried and executed; many men and women went into exile. The governments of individual states suppressed such signs of liberal activity as the Froebel kindergartens and training schools. The failure to achieve liberal goals and the suppression of the revolutions by the military affected the course of both German history and women's history. First, the military renewed its position of power, and industrialists proceeded with the process of modernization without democratization. The country continued to be governed by the Junker, or landed aristocracy, and the military. Consequently, the women's movement in Germany would have a somewhat different shape from those in more politically liberal countries.

The Birth of Modern Feminism

The modern feminist movement—a movement on behalf of women's interests—began in the nineteenth century. In earlier centuries, debates over women's role had occurred, and such debates continued. But in the nineteenth century, a critical development occurred. Organizations—some tentative, others failures, and still others successes—were founded to work for an array of causes related to women's condition and rights: the right to own property, marriage and divorce reform, an end to the double standard in sexual behavior, job opportunities, and health and dress reform. Such issues had been publicly raised by Saint-Simonianism, the Chartist movement, and the revolutions of 1848, and privately raised by thousands of incidents in domestic life. Now the issues seemed to coalesce, arousing women and men to commitment and activity in what was called at the time the "Woman Movement." The name captured the diversity in organizations, opinions, and styles. It also captured the sense of crusade that many women felt. For example, the Saint-Simonian Suzanne Voilquin, when she realized the situation of women, felt as if God had spoken to her. For Voilquin, as for hundreds of thousands who joined the "Woman Movement," feminism constituted a revelation. Moments of revelation sparked the energies of women throughout the course of the stormy years of the nineteenth century. As industrialization proceeded and the modern, republican family and the domestic sphere took shape, feminist organization was occurring along with these many other events. Taking women as its primary field of interest was what distinguished the movement as something revolutionary.

England

Feminists in England worked for numerous reforms, beginning with women's health and rights concerning their children and marriage, and then moving on to rights of property, work, and the vote. The kinds of reforms they undertook demonstrate how multifaceted the movement was. Improvements in sanitation and dress reform constituted a beginning point for a movement to make women healthier physically. The training of more women doctors was also seen by many as a step that would improve women's health. The reforms that focused on strengthening the body were followed by analysis of marriage, whose success, feminists maintained, depended on the woman's having an education equal to that of her husband. Equality in the family, in education, and in property rights would bring symmetry to the imbalance in marriage. Finally, English feminists pushed for jobs and suffrage, that is, for public activity balancing that of men. While acting on a variety of fronts for reform, English women were also developing several theoretical lines. The maternal aspect of womanhood appealed to many feminists as a special source of power for women: Barbara Smith Bodichon (1827–1891) and others talked about the humanizing qualities of women. Other feminists, such as Harriet Taylor Mill (1807–1858), promoted a pure liberalism based on equal rights and individualism. She branded republican ideas that women constituted a "sentimental priesthood" wrongheaded.[18] She rejected ideas of predetermined spheres or gender complementary because she saw them as ideological paths to unfreedom.

Early feminist actions aimed at gaining power for motherhood. In England, as in most countries, the law specified that men got custody of the children in the event of separation or divorce. Such legislation went against the formation of the mother-child dyad deemed so essential. A celebrated divorce case in the 1830s publicized this inherent contradiction. Caroline Norton (1808 1877), the brilliant and beautiful granddaughter of playwright Richard Sheridan, had unwisely married the poor and rather stupid George Norton, who had lied about his income. Earning her own living by writing, Caroline Norton attracted the attention of some powerful people, notably Prime Minister Lord Melbourne for whom she held political gatherings. George Norton saw an opportunity to turn a profit from the situation and instituted a lawsuit against Melbourne for alienation of affection. Though he failed in this legal action and in a subsequent divorce suit against his wife, George got custody of their three children and laid claim to her earnings. Caroline did not let her situation go unheard. In the late 1830s she wrote *Natural Rights of a Mother,* which brought about the Infant Custody Act of 1839, giving women custody of children under seven. After that age they might pass to their fathers. Like Olympe de Gouges, Caroline Norton extended liberal rights to maternity. In so doing, she converted motherhood, usually invoked both to prevent women from having rights and to maintain separate spheres, into a cornerstone of women's legal claims. Norton's efforts also helped move divorce proceedings into the courts. Up until 1857, when the Matrimonial Causes Act went into effect, divorce could only be obtained through a special and costly act of Parliament.

In the mid-1850s, a group of women organized to lobby for changes in the property laws. The Langham Place Group, so-called because it met at the home of Barbara Bodichon in Langham Place, attacked the propertyless situation of women, especially married women. The common law placed control of a wife's property in the hands of her husband. There was a procedure available in the equity courts by which a wife could keep her own property after marriage, but the process was costly and thus only the wealthy could take advantage of it. Reformers recognized that property—whether the ability to sell one's labor for a wage or the actual ownership of money or goods—was the foundation of modern society. Thus, those prohibited from possessing it were outside of the political order. Women's propertylessness meant impotence in the political realm. Following the method of the Chartists, women around the country circulated petitions, on which appeared the names of such luminaries as Elizabeth Barrett Browning, Elizabeth Gaskell, Jane Carlyle, and actress Charlotte Cushman, all impressive to the public. However, society's fears surfaced in the form of objections to this first major skirmish of organized feminism. Politicians announced that the family would come crashing down once women had property of their own. Once women were propertied, the family would work in a liberal way around each person's interest in property. With women committed to property instead of virtue, the family would lose its republican cast.

Why did organization for women's rights begin when it did in England and sustain itself in the quiet 1850s rather than in earlier, more tumultuous decades marked by reform societies, Chartism, and economic protest? One reason was that in the mid-1850s Florence Nightingale became the heroine of the Crimean War, and the recognition she won gave women's abilities new luster. In addition, the plight of working women had clearly surfaced. The lack of resources of surplus—that is, the tens of thousands of unmarried—women also made people feel something was wrong, and the Norton case and others aroused the sympathies of the public. At the same time, a committed individual, Barbara Smith Bodichon, came to the fore to lead in the development of English feminism. One of five illegitimate children of Richard Smith, a member of Parliament, she was a well-educated but highly unorthodox woman, with whom high society types often refused to associate despite her wealth and learning. Barbara Smith and her friend Bessie Rayner Parkes (1829–1925) did shocking things such as traveling through Europe together, refusing to wear corsets, and letting their hair fall naturally, held only by a ribbon. Drawn to the spiritualist belief in a better world, Smith started her activism working for reforms in education and property law; she then moved on to lobby for job reforms and took up the suffrage campaign. Finally, she helped in the founding of Girton College, one of the first all-women colleges in England. After a disastrous, adulterous love affair with the editor of the *Westminster Review,* she met an eccentric doctor, Eugene Bodichon, and married him. An accomplished artist, Bodichon said that she wished to have three lives, one to spend with Eugene, the other two for art and social action. Living an unusually independent life, Bodichon used her wealth and energy to work for a variety of women's rights, but she usually surrounded herself with many respectable collaborators to hide her involvement.

Knowing the influence of print, Bessie Rayner Parkes and Bodichon launched the *English Women's Journal*, which merged in the 1860s with the *Englishwoman's Review*. The *Journal* gave birth to a kind of employment agency, so numerous were the inquiries from desperate women looking for a variety of jobs. In every quarter of England people had been talking about better employment of women; now a middle-class group took up the cause. Training schools for legal work and the development of clerical and sales skills, a press, and other projects were instigated by the Society for Promoting the Employment of Women, headed by Jessie Boucherett (1825–1905). Boucherett reportedly came to feminism after reading about surplus women in Harriet Martineau's works and being overwhelmed on her first, accidental reading of the *English Women's Journal*. From then on Boucherett, like Bodichon, undertook to work for a host of reforms.

In the mid-1860s, a new round of reform, including the reform of suffrage, occurred. In a gradual, though not necessarily tranquil, process of democratization, the government allowed more men to vote and moved toward other social changes. Inspired by the extension of male suffrage, two groups, the Kensington Society in London and another group in Manchester, began campaigning for women's suffrage. After a good deal of discussion, they adopted the strategy of asking that the word "male" be changed to "person" in any suffrage bill. Although many women would still be excluded from voting because of income restrictions, it would give women the same voting eligibility based on property ownership as was afforded men. Instead of demanding suffrage for everyone, including all women, the suffrage societies adopted this more conservative strategy because they thought it had a better chance of succeeding.

The suffrage societies enlisted John Stuart Mill (1806–1873) in their cause. A member of Parliament, Mill stood out as the century's great philosopher of liberal values, expressed in such works as "On Liberty" (1859) and *Principles of Political Economy* (1848). Mill's father had been one of the developers of the utilitarian creed, which emphasized the state's role in formulating policies to ensure the greatest possible happiness in the social order. Jeremy Bentham, the main proponent of the utilitarian philosophy, had proposed the necessity of society's commitment to women's happiness since they constituted half of humankind. If women's needs received insufficient attention, then the sum of happiness in society would be decreased. Favoring education of the people at large to prepare them for political participation, Mill supported women's rights. His thinking on this issue first developed from utilitarian principles, but as he matured the energy he committed to the cause sprang from his relationship with Harriet Taylor. Mill and Taylor met when she was still married and maintained an intense friendship for almost twenty years while her husband was alive. Two years after he died, they married. Mill attributed the best of his work on a range of matters to Taylor, but he always kept some of the sentimental views on women that she so deplored. Even though he referred to women as the "softer sex" and approved the division of labor by which men worked and women tended the home, Mill believed in equal rights and took up the cause of suffrage in Parliament. Despite petitions with thousands of signatures in 1867, the female suffrage amendment was voted down in a 73 to 196 vote, whereas male suffrage was extended. Subsequently, the suffrage movement split over whether men should participate on its committees.

Property reform was brought up again, promoted by a large committee based at Manchester and headed by Lydia Becker (1827–1890), along with educational reformer Elizabeth Wolstenholme-Elmy (1834–1913). Mill also supported this reform in debates in Parliament until he was not reelected in 1869. The battle reached a preliminary resolution with passage of the Married Women's Property Act of 1870. Though insufficient, the act did allow women to keep the wages they earned after marriage. A woman's savings and other property still went to her husband upon marriage, though property inherited after marriage was the wife's. Clearly, neither the property battle nor the suf-

A cartoon of John Stuart Mill and the English suffragists. Mill himself is shown somewhat at a loss about the situation, which confounds normal usage and habits.

frage campaign had been resolved. After he left Parliament, Mill continued to work for the feminist cause, notably by publishing his famous essay *On the Subjection of Women* (1869). His points in the essay were those he had expressed in Parliament. First, the social order's imperfections resulted from the unequal situation of women. Domestic happiness and social good would increase when men and women were equal instead of one being a tyrant, the other a slave. As for the argument that male supremacy was natural, Mill asked: "Was there ever any domination which did not appear natural to those who possessed it?"[19] *On the Subjection of Women*, like Mary Wollstonecraft's *A Vindication of the Rights of Women*, became a classic in feminist theory.

During these struggles feminists also pursued an ongoing commitment to upgrade women's education, notably at higher levels. A radical idea, this educational reform drew dire warnings from physicians and clergymen about the consequences of developing women's minds. Later in the century, men in English universities were so opposed to the idea of women's education that they rioted against their admission. At stake was whether women might enter the world of high culture and compete for leadership. As society increasingly depended on technological, scientific, linguistic, philosophic, and other skills, women without education remained distinctly at a disadvantage. Lack of Latin and Greek alone, for example, could keep women from qualifying for higher professional training or careers. Thus, women were effectively barred from many careers and jobs by being excluded from educational centers such as universities. Recognizing this, feminists established institutions of higher education for women. The founding of Queen's College in 1848 was followed soon after by that of Bedford College to teach women general subjects, not just to prepare them to be governesses. Essentially these were secondary schools, but they offered training for women that was virtually nonexistent elsewhere. Soon after, Frances Buss (1827–1894) opened the renowned North London Collegiate School for Ladies. Along with Dorothy Beale (1831–1906), principal of Cheltenham Ladies' College, Buss spent her life fighting to upgrade such private schools and the status of women teachers and to open established universities to women. The achievements of Buss and Beale were so extraordinary and their energy so single-mindedly devoted to an educational mission that this verse about them was published:

> Miss Buss and Miss Beale
> Cupid's darts do not feel
> How unlike us
> Miss Beale and Miss Buss.[20]

Simultaneously, others aimed at opening up universities to women. For example, Elizabeth Blackwell (1821–1910) had been determined to become a physician in the belief that women doctors would improve women's health, and her education was financed largely by Barbara Bodichon's father. Elizabeth Garrett Anderson (1836–1917) and Sophia Jex-Blake (1840–1912) also pursued a single-minded quest to obtain a medical education in England and then to help others do so.

The campaign to penetrate those age-old and virtually sacrosanct institutions, Cambridge and Oxford, raised major questions about education in general. Allowing women access to universities constituted part of a broad national mission to modernize education as society was modernizing. In the nineteenth century these universities employed hundreds of professors who had little intellectual qualification. Moreover, the curricula stressed Greek and Latin rather than more practical subjects such as science, mathematics, languages, and the like. For women, universities did not serve as places to pass time or sow wild oats. The interest of women lay in upgrading their education, so high standards and top performance on examinations were stressed for all women entering university programs. Higher education drew only women of serious purpose and high intelligence. Sarah Emily Davies (1830–1921), while working to reform the university examination system, opened an annex for women in 1869 near Cambridge. Ultimately this annex, supported by a whole host of women, became Girton College. At Cambridge, Henry Sidgwick, professor of moral philosophy, aimed at upgrading the education of women as part of upgrading the university curriculum in general. In 1871 he opened a women's college—Newnham College—which offered a serious course of study in modern subjects. In no instance did women's academic work lead to a university degree. Yet even without degrees the women's colleges became more and more popular because they opened the world of education and professional opportunity to women.

To society, the most disturbing aspect of the movement to reform the gender order was the crusade against the Contagious Diseases Acts, which provided for the inspection of prostitutes for venereal diseases.* Reformers, sometimes intuitively, centered their attention on prostitutes' situation as indicative of a more general problem facing women. Although the crusade was the effort of many men and women, it became associated with the leadership of Josephine Butler (1828–1906). The lively daughter of forward-thinking and religious parents, Butler married a clergyman who supported her activities. For a time president of the North of England Council for the Higher Education of Women, Butler had made prostitution and the repeal of the Contagious Diseases Acts her main cause by the late 1860s. Religion fortified her mission. She wrote: "You remember how sweet and lovely Jesus always was to *women*, and how He helped their *woman* diseases, and how respectful He was to them, and loved them and forgave the sins of the most sinful! And He was born of a woman—a woman *only*. No man had any hand in *that*! It was such an honour to women."[21] Although Butler sounded conventionally religious, her crusade proved iconoclastic. It brought the issue of sexual behavior out in the open and attacked the double standard in sexual and economic matters and civil rights. The campaign gained support from such celebrities as Elizabeth Blackwell, Florence Nightingale, and Harriet Martineau. Nonetheless it outraged Victorian society and even disturbed many feminists, who felt that broaching

---

*See Chapter 4.

such an "unladylike" topic was inimicable to their cause. Talking explicitly, Butler attacked the easy sexual access to women's bodies and asked for self-control on the part of men. Her promotion of self-restraint instead of state intervention in sexual matters put her in the vanguard of sex reformers who sought internalization of sexual norms and who talked more openly about sex. Called a "shrieking sister" for her denunciation of the Contagious Diseases Acts, Butler advocated a self-policing population. At the same time, the publicity she gave sexual matters made their regulation more accessible to policy makers, social reformers, and theorists.

The German States

Conditions were detrimental to the birth of a feminist movement in the German states, which seemed committed to eighteenth-century forms of provincial autonomy and aristocratic rule. Nonetheless, after much repression of women's activities in the 1850s, an organized movement emerged a decade later. In 1865, at least three discrete efforts to improve the status of women began. A former Austrian army officer, P. A. Korn, who had adopted many ideas concerning women's emancipation while in America, started the first of these and the one about which the least is known. He and his wife returned to Berlin,

In the German states a woman also symbolized the nation. Holding sword, book, and shield in this depiction from the 1840s, she is surrounded by male artifacts as signs of power.

where they founded a newspaper, the *Allgemeine Frauenzeitung* (*General Women's Times*), which lasted almost ten years. Meanwhile, in Leipzig, a women's educational union, sponsoring an array of programs to train, house, and find jobs for women, issued a call for a general meeting of German women. This lead to the formation in 1865 of the All German Women's Union (Allgemeiner Deutscher Frauenverein), headed by Louise Otto-Peters, who started another newspaper called *Neue Bahnen* (*New Roads*). This paper, like the Leipzig group and the national organization, stressed education, or *Bildung*. This goal held great importance in German intellectual life, for *Bildung* signified an overall spiritual shaping of character as well as intellectual growth. Thus, reform in education could emphasize breaking down institutional doors and building curricula, or it could refer to the particularly German emphasis on a rather isolated undertaking with little actual social consequence except as regarded the individual's spiritual life. The co-editor of *Neue Bahnen*, Jenny Heynrichs, wrote in a similarly bifurcated way about work, for example: "Work, liberating and liberated work is the slogan of our association." She advocated work especially for single women so that they might feel themselves "a link in a chain that holds society together," but also develop an inner self that was "content, fit, strong."[22] Members of the union thus moved in two different directions as the movement came to be the largest women's movement in the German states. Rejecting male membership, the All German Women's Union spurned P. A. Korn's offers to merge. Another organization was founded in Berlin in 1866 by Dr. Adolf Lette. Led by several men, the Lette Society aimed at improving the economic status of women particularly by finding "suitable" jobs for those "redundant" spinsters in the middle class. The society started schools to teach commercial skills, art, domestic technology, making of artificial flowers, and printing. For those needing suitable housing it provided a boarding house, restaurant, and cooperative store. The Lette Society differed from the All German Women's Union in both its admission of men to high office and its explicitly practical bias.

Early German feminists did not confront their government with demands for suffrage, property rights, or admission to universities. Indeed, until the unification of Germany in 1870 (see map on page 255), there was no single government to petition. Even after 1870, the German empire created under the leadership of Prussia was not a government based on individual rights. The result of Prussia's victory over France in the Franco-Prussian War, united Germany was built on military power. Patriotic and cautious, German feminists were self-aware: "The conservative character of the German reformers has been criticized. They have been found too timid, too considerate of old prejudices, too slow, too circumspect. The stricture arises mainly, however, from an imperfect understanding of the situation in this country."[22] The German situation, as they called it, resembled the women's movement in other countries in one respect: the national political context influenced the tactics leaders took and the goals they set for themselves. Moreover, even though the organizations made no daring forays into political reform as the English feminists were doing, Louise Otto-Peters noted that the mere existence of the organizations

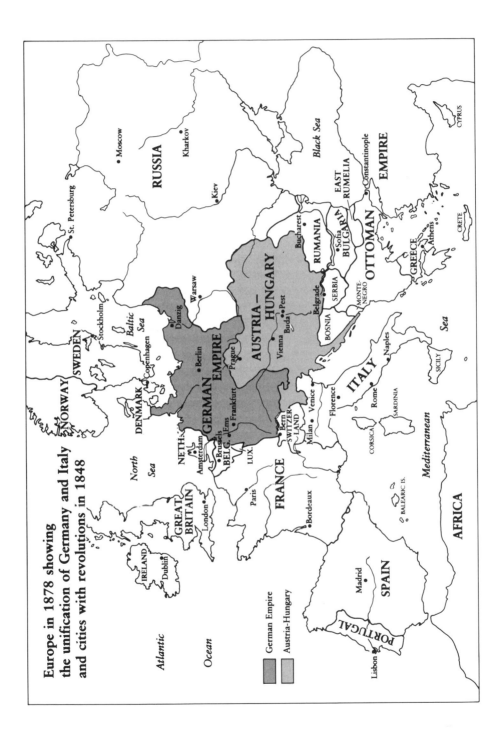

Europe in 1878 showing the unification of Germany and Italy and cities with revolutions in 1848

meant something: "The union (*Vereinigung*) is an end in itself and not just a means."[23] Since censorship and police interference in meetings could still occur in Germany, women's recognizing common interests and joining together was an important first step.

Italy

The revolution of 1848 had aroused Italian women to fight in the name of patriotism and unification. They continued to do so in a new round of warfare that drove the Austrians out of all of northern Italy except Venice. The Kingdom of Italy came into being in 1861 (see map on p. 255) under the leadership of liberal forces in Sardinia, and the unification proceedings drew activists from around the world. Englishwoman Jessie White Mario (1832–1906) and the American feminist Margaret Fuller (1810–1850) were among those who came to participate. Like Fuller and White Mario, women journalists spread information about this event, the culmination of a cause that was dear to liberal hearts. Meanwhile, Italian women fought in large numbers in the army of Garibaldi as it invaded the south. Others formed the Feminine Committee of the Italian National Society, which was larger and more active than the main organization. After the wars of liberation were over in 1861, they continued to raise money for families of soldiers and other victims of the conflict. Mazzini's idea of the citizen-mother inspired even those who did not subscribe to his spiritual brand of nationalism.

Involved in these political struggles, women expected a good deal from the new nation. Rhetoric such as that of Mazzini aroused expectations that the nation would reward women with civil rights. The new constitution, proposed in the early 1860s, however, proved once again that gender difference underlay formation of the modern nation. Under Austrian law, women who owned property had had certain rights to local political participation. In some Italian states, women had controlled their own dowries and property. The new constitution changed all that by imitating the provisions of the Napoleonic Code. "Once more I reflect with bitterness," wrote one woman on hearing about the new Italian code, "on the inequality in the roles of men and women." She wondered when Italy would ever "educate a new generation to new ideals."[24] The fact that the new code called for regulation of prostitution made others eager to fight rather than support a united state. Only one ray of hope glimmered as the parliamentarians organized the new state: Deputy Salvatore Morelli vocally took up the feminist cause. In 1861, Morelli published *Woman and Science Considered as the Only Means for Resolving the Problems of the Future*, which said that continuing social disharmony would result from the inequalities in women's condition. During his four terms in the conservative Parliament, Morelli pushed for women's suffrage, women's access to careers, divorce reform, and the deregulation of prostitution.

Although there was no national women's organization in Italy until the 1870s, activity on behalf of women's rights accelerated in the years prior to them. First, a series of local papers developed to discuss the woman question.

Feminism in the New Italian Nation

Anna Mozzoni was the most famous name in nineteenth century Italian feminism. She connected the rights of women with the right of Italy to exist as a nation. While speaking of rights, she also spoke of certain qualities women possessed that would enhance national life and ensure national survival. This excerpt from her first published writing about women, *Woman and Her Social Relations* (1864) explores the inequities in society's apportionment of rights and duties.

The revision of the Civil Code by the Italian Parliament has placed in my mind the following argument: woman, excluded by worn out customs from the councils of state, has always submitted to the law without participating in the making of it, has always contributed her resources and work to the public good and always without any reward.

For her, taxes but not an education; for her, sacrifices but not employment; for her, strict virtue but not honor; for her, the struggle to maintain the family but not even control of her own person; for her, the capacity to be punished but not the right to be independent; strong enough to be laden with an array of painful duties, but sufficiently weak not to be allowed to govern herself.

I begin with the principles that all rights and all duties have as their foundation and rationale to serve as the force which gives the conscience its ostensible legitimacy. This principle holds for each human being of whatever sex and I do not see for what reason this faculty should be in one case exercised freely and sometimes with force and in the other case buried and entirely suffocated. This occurs so much that in the miserable conditions in which society has cast her, woman, deprived of half her wealth, weakened because of the degrading work actually given her, finds herself dragged down to the fatal necessity to destroy herself through trade in her unhappy body.

Humanity and the nation, civilization and morality, need women on their side.

Source: Adapted from Anna Mozzoni, *La liberazione della donna,* Franca Pieroni Bartolotti, ed. (Milan: G. Mazzotta, 1975), 34, 57–58.

Of these, *La Donna* (*Woman*), founded in 1868 by the eighteen-year-old republican Alaide Gaulberta Beccari, became the most influential. A Venetian whose family fortune was lost in the war with Austria, Beccari maintained that

she had been a feminist since childhood when she started working as her father's secretary. Not just woman's role, but the social situation in general upset
her: "Above all I felt myself stirred to rebellion when I learned of some brutal
husband who had beaten his wife."[25] *La Donna* published the writings of feminist journalists and literary people from all over Italy, but its primary message
remained clearly that of the Mazzinian citizen-mother. Ermina Fua-Fusinato
directed her efforts toward primary education, which she saw as a key to improving the position of women. Minimalist in her feminism, Fua-Fusinato disliked, as did many activists, the idea of the emancipated woman who would
neutralize gender. Sarah Nathan, mother of twelve and an ardent follower of
Mazzini, aimed at spreading the Mazzinian ideology in working-class sections
of Rome. She did so believing it furthered women's role as "initiators of the
future."[26] She also favored education for all women because it would make
them thoroughly alert, knowledgeable, and active as republican mothers. In
this regard, Nathan, like so many other leading Italian women, rejected the
Catholic idea that women's education should involve only lessons in religion
and in obedience, which the new government seemed to have adopted. Finally,
Anna Mozzoni (1837–1920) attacked the Catholic Church, the new code, and
the new constitutional monarchy as responsible for the repression of women.
Mozzoni also translated John Stuart Mill's *On the Subjection of Women*.
Among the many Italian activists, Mozzoni came closest in these early decades
to organizing women into a movement.

Russia

Alexander II freed the serfs in 1861 and in so doing released a current of reform
energy. Russian difficulties in the Crimean War made it apparent how much
the country needed to catch up with developments in the West. For one thing,
this meant improving the labor supply—a goal Catherine had set a century
earlier. Liberation of the serfs encouraged modernization in various other
areas. Liberal and scientific ideas began to permeate Russian middle-class circles, though this class remained small. At the same time, emancipation of the
serfs burdened some noble families financially and made it necessary for their
daughters to consider working. Even women who remained domestic were
receptive both to ideas about early childhood development and their role in it
and to the more radical ideas of John Stuart Mill concerning women's suffrage.
The czar himself initiated secondary school courses for women, and university-
level education for women started in special lecture series, the Bestuzhev and
Alarchin courses. Many Russian women went to universities outside their own
country. Zurich particularly attracted them because of its medical programs
and also for the advanced political life that developed there.

One of the most famous of the foreign-educated women was Sofia Kovalevskaya (1850–1890), who ultimately produced theorems in partial differential equations. Winning the first doctorate in mathematics awarded to a
woman in modern times and holding a professorship in Stockholm, she reflected the new state of affairs. To pursue her mathematical degree, Kovalev-

Russian mathematician Sofia Kofalevskaya broke with her family to pursue an intellectual career. Her doctoral thesis earned her a degree summa cum laude *and placed her at the forefront of European science.*

skaya had married in order to escape her traditional family. Her marriage was a phony one, that is, a marriage to a politically liberal young man. Acting on the principle that it was necessary to break authoritarian institutions, he married her but made no sexual demands so that she might escape patriarchal control. Although Russian women could own property, in all other matters they lived under strict control of their fathers and within a circumscribed vision of what women should do. Women were often beaten or confined to the home. Kovalevskaya's sister, Anna Korvin-Krukovskaya, had infuriated her parents with her constant reading: "She never keeps anyone company, never does needlework, never takes walks."[27] Repression often led to rebellion. When higher education was periodically refused them—for example, the Medical Surgical Academy in St. Petersburg admitted women in 1861, but stopped in 1864—women fled to Western Europe. When parents forbade study or membership in intellectual or political circles, young women left home, most often by entering into a phony marriage. The idea for this widespread practice came from Mikhail Mikhailov's writings against the family and the repressive situation faced by women and especially from Nikolai Chernyshevskii's *What Is to Be Done* (1863). This novel, inspired by George Sand, focused on the aspirations of a young heroine, her escape into a phony marriage, her constant search for a useful life, and her eventual discovery of love.

After going through with a phony marriage, young Russian women often lived in communes—many of them male-dominated—and adopted an entirely new way of dressing to indicate their liberation. These women changed their clothing to simple dark dress upon leaving their families; they cut their hair short and wore blue glasses—the sure sign of an emancipated woman. Those driven to support liberal principles in an autocratic political setting gained the name nihilists. They rejected old forms of authority—from the father in the family to the Czar or "Little Father" of the empire, as he was called. Thus, young Russian women took the most extreme form of escape from the severe repression of the home—assuming virtually new identities and turning the custom of marriage upside down. Such women set a trend; by breaking with the family they opened the door to a complete break with society. These early generations of Russian women who acquired political and classical educations matured in two directions. Some developed into terrorists and revolutionaries. The average young woman persisted longer in Russia's radical movements than the average man because her education entailed a more radical rebellion. Others of the early generations became professionals, particularly teachers and doctors, and many of these led the Russian women's movement in the 1890s. Thus, the early days of women's activism in Russia saw them struggling to become educated, but also to transform radically the structures of everyday life. Unorganized at first, Russian feminists would take different roads toward social change.

France During the Second Empire and the Commune

Once in power, Napoleon III tried to erase memories of 1848 by supporting industrial development and the institution of free trade policies. He also forestalled any future revolutions by rebuilding Paris with straight streets that were too wide for barricades and that made the city accessible to coordinated troop movements. This rebuilding provided jobs, which increased his popularity. Like other leaders, Napoleon III set France on the course to modernization by instigating up-to-date water supplies, sanitation, and the like. However, he also reestablished a clear gender order, notably in his marriage to the elegant and beautiful Eugénie (1826–1920). The empress came to represent the height of womanhood at mid-century. Dressed in hoops, crinolines, and silks, Eugénie set fashion around the world and simultaneously helped the French silk industry. She also served as a symbol of motherhood in her apparent constant attention to their only child. A new-style empress, Eugénie constantly had her son at her side in portraits, and the whole family sometimes posed together. The empress was pious and charitable, visiting orphanages and sponsoring hundreds of philanthropic societies around the country. Believing in the importance of improved education for women, Empress Eugénie even sponsored advanced courses taught by university professors and sent her nieces to attend them. Devoted to the Catholic faith, she was a contrast to her husband, the womanizing emperor. Eugénie attracted admiration internationally and was respected by many feminists for her motherly behavior and fortitude in the face of her husband's philandering.

Unlike England, France was not a good setting for the development of feminism in the 1850s; there was particular hostility to women's rights because they were regarded as a sign of turmoil in general. In caustic attacks, the working-class leader and anarchist Pierre-Joseph Proudhon (1809–1865) showed a profound disdain of women. Unlike Jules Michelet, who built an appealing ideology of womanhood, Proudhon wrote explicit attacks on their aspirations to equality. His argument, simply put, asserted women's moral, physical, and intellectual inferiority. No metaphors made it more palatable: women belonged in the home breeding; only men had the ability to run the world. Proudhon's blatant misogyny, influential because of his ties to working men and intellectuals, rekindled women's activism in the unpropitious atmosphere of post-1848 France. Juliette Lamber (b. 1836) and Jenny d'Héricourt both affirmed women's capacity and deplored the lack of opportunity for that capacity to manifest itself. At the same time novelist André Leo (pseudonym of Léodile Bara de Champceix, 1832–1900) produced several works advocating such reforms as divorce. Those with working-class interests, such as the former Saint-Simonian Elisa Lemonnier (1805–1865), set up industrial schools for girls.

Late in the 1860s, Napoleon III relaxed some of his political restrictions. In this more favorable atmosphere, Maria Deraismes (1828–1894) became involved in the fledgling women's movement. Wealthy and well-educated, she was an author and lecturer on a variety of subjects. Once censorship relaxed, she began talking about the condition of women. The Society to Claim the Rights of Women had been founded sometime in the mid-1860s, and Desraimes supported it. She saw women's rights, however, as a buttress to the family's importance and the role of women in it. Like Julie Daubié, who in 1866 wrote about the inescapable net of women's poverty that limited their pleasures and possibilities, Deraismes continued the focus on poverty of Fourierists and Saint-Simonians. For all its limitations, this newest round of French feminism relied on the earlier tradition.

In 1870, the Franco-Prussian War brought down the Second Empire. By September, the French had declared a republic; the siege of Paris followed. Fearful of losing yet another republic and its benefits and not willing to go back to the old way of doing things, the people of Paris rose again and in March 1871, formed the "Commune," as this revolutionary government was called. Communard Louise Michel wrote: "On . . . the eighteenth of March, the people wakened. If they had not, it would have been the triumph of some king; instead it was a triumph of the people."[28] Pleas went out asking the provinces to join the new society and to help protect Paris from the wartime government at Versailles, which had replaced the captured emperor. From then on, the Versailles government, headed by Adolphe Thiers, attempted to put the Commune down by force. In the development and maintenance of the communal spirit, the women of Paris, particularly seamstresses, laundresses, and other working-class women, played such an important role that they entered French political mythology, even though at the time they were vilified by many as bloodthirsty whores. These women recognized that this loosening of the political fabric might make a place for women. At first, women's role in the Commune's struggles was a traditional one. They served as nurses and provisioners of the troops that now made up a working-class national guard. They then took on less traditional roles—women lugged ammunition, cared for weapons as well as for the ill, served as scouts, and placed themselves in the way en masse of enemy troops to keep them from firing. The strategy of placing women's and children's bodies in the way of oncoming troops only worked in the first days of the Commune. After that women were fair game to the opposing troops since their leaders recognized that Commune women were as committed and active as the men.

The establishment of the Commune had come about after the first elections under the Thiers government had produced a radical city council in Paris. Most middle-class people had evacuated the city before the siege, so the city fell under the control of the workers, who had their own priorities. Among male workers, women's economic condition was of little interest. Women, however, saw a chance to remake their lives in tandem with communal attempts to change the face of society. Several groups organized themselves into workshops in which they could work on sewing for the Commune. The goal of these shops was not just to provide work but also to get a wage better than the starvation one that middlemen had formerly paid. Issues concerning women's dual responsibility for work and family life also came to the fore. In response, the Commune provided some piecework to be done in homes at a more equitable rate. Getting such concessions and raising such issues in the midst of a civil war amounted to a great achievement. Usually, under wartime conditions, concern with the mundane issues of daily life and work was put aside. In this situation, however, improvements occurred because women played a visibly important role in the war effort itself while they kept civilian life going. Moreover, with battles occurring in Paris and the surrounding countryside, this particular war did not separate the genders or emphasize separate spheres. Rather the Commune amounted to a joint effort in which working men and women shouldered subsistence and military efforts together.

In these struggles many women came to the fore. The illustrious figure of Louise Michel (1830–1905) towered above all others as a leader and a fighter. A schoolteacher who had come to Paris during the Second Empire, she had increasingly involved herself with political causes that would lead to social reform. Believing in popular activism, she became a leader in the Commune because of her constant participation and enthusiasm. Michel, it was said, appeared everywhere, especially wherever the cause faced difficulties. Another leader, André Leo, novelist and journalist, stressed the importance of women's issues in planning reforms. Moreover, she saw, as did many others, that women were essential to the cause: other revolutions had failed because most women found them irrelevant to their concerns. Elizabeth Dmitrieff believed in people liberating themselves and so founded the Union of Women for the Defense of Paris and the Care of the Wounded. Exhibiting a participatory style, the Union consisted of committees in each section of Paris, which met each day to chart arrangements for maintaining "the cause of the people, the Revolution, and the Commune."[29] Although a few of the leaders were middle class, the Commune thus had thousands of working-class women supporting it in clubs, workshops, and rescue work.

At the end of May, the Versailles government finally put down the Commune and established the Third Republic. A great deal of blood was shed, tens of thousands of communards were slaughtered, and many were arrested. The women of the Commune acquired the name *petroleuses,* or incendiaries, for in those last days, the city of Paris burned. Many of the fires were started by the government troops to burn out the revolutionaries. Other fires were started by the communards to keep the troops from using buildings to shoot from. In any event, the name *petroleuses* lived on as an appellation of working-class women. Many of the female communards were summarily executed; others, such as Louise Michel, received sentences to life at hard labor in penal colonies in Guiana and New Caledonia. The sentences were harsh and completed the defeat of French working women.

Although the French gloried in their revolutionary tradition, certain aspects of that tradition bothered them. Liberalism, legal reform, and progress gave the French pride, but the attendant disorder and violence sullied their history. Thus, the aftermath of revolution again heard paens raised to the family as the source of tranquility, order, and stability. In contrast, working women were seen as rowdy and upsetting of the social order. Those who played a role in public—like Louise Michel, Olympe de Gouges, and George Sand—brought violence, whereas women serving the republic within the family meant social peace. This political reasoning, which characterized every administration since the Napoleonic one, made it impossible for there to be any French political heroines. Having been labeled as harpies, women fighting for liberal rights became anathema to good citizens. Indeed, all the works of George Sand except *François the Waif* were banished from public libraries and schools. Instead, standard reading for women consisted of classical stories of female virtue and duty. Even as France became more secular, women were supposed to model themselves after saints, pious queens, and other appropriately devout women. Many female leaders, especially the working-class incendiaries who had fought for freedom and economic well-being, were eradicated as positive historical figures. If women were not completely decorous and ladylike, their personal lives counted against them to discredit their political acts. This fate arose from the fundamental construction of modern society. That society now clearly depended on men pursuing self-interest in the economic world and on women rejecting self-interest in the name of the family that was the heart of the republic. The reestablishment of that separation after war or revolution meant the reestablishment of the ordered polity.

The Drive for Equality and Citizenship

State power had grown enormously by the last quarter of the century, and women's interest in politics had increased commensurately. Like men, they were patriotic, involved, and active. Women writers reached large public audiences, and they chose to discuss important issues. Yet published writing and public activism by women were still regarded as irregular by most people, even by some women writers and activists. Discussions of the woman worker and of the middle-class "angel in the house" marked out women as something apart from the male norm. Events through the whole course of the nineteenth century, even the growth of feminism itself, pointed to the difference of women. Asserting women's distinctness was the foundation of male citizenship in the new nation. Women's special political impotence, ritually reasserted in such acts as closing Froebel schools or defeating proposals for suffrage, visibly bound men together as equal participants in the modern state. Separate spheres indicated women's difference, as did their lack of rights. Lower wages for women also marked a divide, and the republican ideology of sacrifice to a common good pertained to women, but to men only in wartime.

Because women were designated as different, they engaged in concerted campaigns during this period to show their equality, their sameness, and their coordinate status as citizens. Many others so marked out—the Irish, for instance—engaged in the same kind of struggle to have the state acknowledge their equality and treat them accordingly. When revolution erupted, it summoned women to assert their interests as mothers and workers. In the aftermath of revolution, however, they saw their quest for fair wages to support their families smashed. Yet middle-class women, especially those interested in rights and identity as citizens of the nation-state, still had some hopes left. Many moved into politics through the Woman Movement. Once started, this campaign gathered momentum. Right from the start, the women's rights movement had a broad platform and attracted a variety of adherents. Dominated by the urban middle class, it appealed nonetheless to many others, including some men and larger numbers of working women later in the century. At the same time, new organizations and new enthusiasms besides feminism vied for their allegiance.

NOTES

1. Beth Archer Brombert, *Cristina: Portraits of a Princess* (Chicago: University of Chicago Press, 1983), 192.

2. Lisa Secci, "German Women Writers and the Revolution of 1848," in John C. Fout, ed., *German Women in the Nineteenth Century* (London: Holmes and Meier, 1984), 157.

3. Quoted in Adolph Burnett Benson, *The Old Norse Element in Swedish Romanticism* (New York: Columbia University Press, 1914), 87.

4. Quoted in Bogna Lorence-Kot, "Klementyna Tanska Hoffmanowa, Cultural Nationalism and Womanhood," *History of European Ideas*, vol. 8, no. 4/5 (1987):445.

5. Franz Kafka, *Letters to Milena*, quoted in Milada Souckova, *The Czech Romantics* ('S-Gravenhage: Mouton, 1958), 163.

6. Elizabeth Barrett Browning, *Complete Poetical Works* (Boston: Houghton Mifflin, 1900), 103.

7. Quoted in Edward Wagenknecht, *Cavalcade of the English Novel from Elizabeth to George VI* (New York: Henry Holt, 1943), 321.

8. Quoted in Elizabeth S. Haldane, *Mrs. Gaskell and Her Friends* (New York: Appleton, 1931), 285.

9. Charlotte Brontë, *Villette* (Boston: Houghton Mifflin, 1971 [1853]), 93.

10. Quoted in Malcolm I. Thomis and Jennifer Grimmett, *Women in Protest 1800–1850* (London: Croom Helm, 1982), 99.

11. Quoted in Dorothy Thompson, *The Chartists. Popular Politics in the Industrial Revolution* (New York: Pantheon, 1984), 147.

12. Giuseppe Mazzini, *An Essay on the Duties of Man Addressed to Workingmen*, quoted in Susan G. Bell and Karen M. Offen, eds., *Women, the Family and Freedom: The Debate in Documents*, 2 vols. (Stanford, Calif.: Stanford University Press, 1983), 1:386.

13. *Voix des Femmes*, April 6, 1848, quoted in Claire Goldberg Moses, *French Feminism in the Nineteenth Century* (Albany: State University of New York Press, 1984), 140–141.

14. Quoted in Curtis Cate, *George Sand* (New York: Avon, 1975), 592.

15. Edith Thomas, *Pauline Roland. Socialisme et Feminisme au XIXe siècle* (Paris: Marcel Rivière, 1956), 116–148.

16. Quoted in Stanley Zucker, "Female Political Opposition in Pre-1848 Germany," in Fout, ed., *German Women*, 139.

17. Quoted in Franca Pieroni Bortolotti, *Alle origini del movimento femminile in Italia 1848–1892* (Turin, Italy: Einaudi, 1963), 29.

18. Harriet Taylor Mill, "The Enfranchisement of Women," quoted in Jane Rendall, *The Origins of Modern Feminism* (London: Macmillan, 1985), 311.

19. John Stuart Mill, *On the Subjection of Women* (Arlington Heights: Crofts, 1980), 11.

20. Quoted in *The Europa Biographical Dictionary of British Women* (London: Europa, 1983), 35.

21. Quoted in Elizabeth Longford, *Eminent Victorian Women* (New York: Knopf, 1981), 115.

22. Jenny Heynrichs, "Was ist Arbeit?" *Neue Bahnen* (1866), quoted in Eleanor Riemer and John Fout, eds., *European Women. A Documentary History* (New York: Schocken, 1980), 53.

23. Anna Schepeler-Lette and Jenny Hirsch, "Germany: A General Review of the Women's Movement," in Theodore Stanton, ed., *The Woman Question in Europe* (New York: G. P. Putnam's Sons, 1884), 145.

24. Quoted in Ruth-Ellen Boetcher Joeres, "Louise Otto and Her Journals: A Chapter in Nineteenth-Century German Feminism," *Internationales Archiv für Sozialgeschichte der deutschen Literatur* 4 (1979):122.

25. Grazia Pieratoni Mancini, *Impressioni e ricordi 1856–1864* (Milan, Italy: Cogliati, 1908), 329, quoted in Bortolotti, *Alle origini*, 41.

26. Quoted in Judith Jeffrey Howard, "Patriot Mothers in the Post-Risorgimento," in Carol R. Berkin and Clara M. Lovett, eds., *Women, War, and Revolution* (New York: Holmes & Meier, 1980), 248.

27. Quoted in Barbara Engel, *Mothers and Daughters: Women of the Intelligentsia in Nineteenth-Century Russia* (Cambridge: Cambridge University Press, 1983), 66.

28. Bullitt Lowry and Elizabeth Ellington Gunter, eds. and trans., *The Red Virgin: Memoirs of Louise Michel* (Mobile: University of Alabama Press, 1981), 64.

29. Quoted in Edith Thomas, *The Women Incendiaries*, James and Starr Atkinson, trans. (New York: George Braziller, 1966), 75.

SOURCES AND SUGGESTED READING

Adler, Hans. "On a Feminist Controvery: Louise Otto vs. Louise Aston," in Ruth-Ellen B. Joeres and Mary Jo Maynes, eds., *German Women in the Eighteenth and Nineteenth Centuries* (1986).

Banks, Olive. *The Faces of Feminism: A Study of Feminism as a Social Movement* (1981). Explores three streams of feminist impulse in Britain.

Boralevi, Lea Campos. "Utilitarianism and Feminism," in Ellen Kennedy and Susan Mendus. *Women in Western Political Philosophy* (1987).

Bortolotti, Franca Pieroni. *Alle origini del movimento femminile in Italia 1848–1892* (1963). The classic study of Italian feminism.

Burstyn, Joan. *Victorian Education and the Ideal of Womanhood* (1984).

Calapso, Jole. *Donne ribelli. Un secolo di lotte femminili* (1980). Activism, protest, and feminism in Sicily.

Drewitz, Ingeborg. *Bettina von Arnim* (1969). A biography of the romantic heroine and writer.

Engel, Barbara. *Mothers and Daughters: Women of the Intelligentsia in Nineteenth-Century Russia* (1983). A major investigation of the homelife of rebellious Russian women.

Gilbert, Sandra, and Susan Gubar. *The Madwoman in the Attic* (1979). An encyclopedic study of British writers.

Gorham, Deborah. *The Victorian Girl and the Feminine Ideal* (1982). Particularly interesting testimonies of childhood.

Hayek, F. A. *John Stuart Mill and Harriet Taylor: Their Friendship and Subsequent Marriage* (1951). Important letters and joint writing, particularly on marriage and divorce.

Herstein, Sheila. *A Mid-Victorian Feminist, Barbara Leigh Smith Bodichon* (1985).

Holcombe, Lee. *Wives and Property: Reform of the Married Women's Property Law in Nineteenth-Century England* (1983). A detailed political study.

Homans, Margaret. *Bearing the Word: Language and Female Experience in Nineteenth-Century Women's Writing* (1986).

Howard, Judith Jeffrey. "Patriot Mothers in the Post-Risorgimento: Women after the Italian Revolution," in Carol Berkin and Clara Lovett, eds., *Women, War, and Revolution* (1980).

Joeres, Ruth-Ellen Boetcher. "Louise Otto and Her Journals: A Chapter in Nineteenth Century German Feminism," *Internationales Archiv für Sozialgeschichte der deutschen Literatur* (1980).

Lipp, Carola, ed. *Schimpfende Weiber und patriotische Jungfrauen: Frauen im Vormärz und in der Revolution 1848–49* (1986). A collection of exciting articles on the political and cultural role of women in the Vormärz and during the Revolution of 1848 in the German states.

Lorence-Kot, Bogna. "Klementyna Tanska Hoffmanowa, cultural nationalism and a new formula for Polish womanhood," *History of European Ideas* (1987).

Moses, Claire Goldberg. *French Feminism in the Nineteenth Century* (1984). An important survey.

Rendall, Jane. *The Origins of Modern Feminism: Women in Britain, France, and the United States, 1780–1860* (1985).

Stites, Richard. *The Women's Liberation Movement in Russia. Feminism, Nihilism, and Bolshevism, 1860–1930* (1978). A classic study.

Thomas, Edith. *The Women Incendiaries* (1966). The ordeal and excitement of the Paris Commune.

Thomis, Malcolm I., and Jennifer Grimmett. *Women in Protest 1800–1850* (1982). Varieties of English working-class activism.

Vicinus, Martha, ed. *A Widening Sphere: Changing Roles of Victorian Women* (1980). An important collection of articles on English women.

Zucker, Stanley. "German Women and the Revolution of 1848: Kathinka Zitz Halein and the Humania Association," *Central European History* (1980).

PART

III

A World Torn Asunder
1875–1925

People called the time before World War I (1914-1918) the *belle époque,* or the good old days. Artists portray the end of the nineteenth century as one of color and gaiety. Working-class couples danced in outdoor beer-gardens or sat laughing in cafes. The upper classes serenely strolled the parks or rode in carriages.

For all the beauty of this artistic vision, the turn of the century in fact hummed with such new inventions as the telephone and the automobile. An age of iron and steel, it ushered in blast furnaces, denser railroad networks, and chemical industries. Governments also embarked on campaigns to subject the peoples of Asia, Africa, and Latin America to their political and economic control—a campaign called imperialism.

Along with all of this came a burgeoning urban working class, subject to the insecurities of industrial advance and innovation. Driving industry to success, workers felt a rising discontent that generated strikes, hard negotiating for better working conditions, and a taste for new kinds of socialist politics.

Women faced the problem of raising children and of supporting themselves in this rapidly changing world. In an age of modern inventions, they continued to perform a range of tasks at home and also worked—some say more than ever before—in sweated jobs. Demands on their time increased, for the state needed healthier citizens in this competitive age. If governments sought to bring foreign people under their control, they also aimed at educating and shaping the working mother to take better care of the workforce. The welfare state took shape from this need to organize reproductive tasks.

Many women also became "modern"—as modern in appearance and world view as industrial society itself was becoming. A few took off their corsets, wore loose clothing, and refused to marry. They entered new professions such as nursing, office work, and teaching. Breaking with patriarchal customs, they used birth control devices, talked openly of sexual options, and spread feminist organization until, by 1914, millions of women belonged to activist groups, including socialist ones.

Beneath the tranquil surface of the *belle époque* lay a host of disturbing factors. Socialism, feminism, and imperialism called the liberal order into question and provoked tensions. Poverty made workers discontent, while "new" or modern women threatened beliefs about gender. In the summer of 1914, after the assassination of the heir to the Habsburg monarchy seemed to upset international order as well, the nations of Europe declared war on one another. Much of the citizenry gladly embraced this chance to set things aright.

Yet the industrial revolution had also made the forces of destruction as powerful as the forces of production. The war soon became a mass slaughter, which provoked even more suffering. In Eastern Europe, this suffering turned into the Russian Revolution. By 1920, after just a few short years of war and revolution, people could rightly look back on the years before the war and call them "the good old days." European society—its sensibilities, its politics, its gender balance—had changed for good.

Time Line

- **1872** Infant Life Protection Act in Britain
- **1873** European depression begins
- **1874** English Factory and Workshop Acts "protect" women's work
  J. J. Lawson patents the chain driven bicycle
  E. Remington and Sons markets its first typewriter
- **1877** Annie Besant and Charles Bradlaugh tried in London for distributing birth control
  literature
  Vera Zasulich assassinates governor-general of St. Petersburg
- **1878** German government passes insurance legislation for workers
- **1879** Henrik Ibsen publishes *A Doll's House*
- **1881** Sophia Perovskaya executed for assassinating Tsar Alexander II of Russia
- **1882** Aletta Jacobs founds first birth control clinic
- **1884** Reform of divorce law in France
  Friedrich Engels publishes *Origin of the Family, Private Property and the State*
  Sonya Kovalevskaya appointed to Chair of Mathematics in Stockholm
- **1886** Final repeal of the Contagious Diseases Acts in England
  Emilia Pardo Bazan publishes *The Manor of Ulloa*
- **1891** German protective legislation limiting women's work and mandating maternity leave
- **1894** Havelock Ellis publishes *Sexual Inversion*
- **1895** Mutual Philanthropic Society founded in Russia
- **1900** Sweden mandates maternity leaves without compensation
- **1903** Marie Curie shares Nobel Prize in Physics with her husband, Pierre Curie
  Women's Social and Political Union founded
  Aimee Duc publishes *Sind es Frauen*
- **1904** First International Women's Suffrage Alliance meets in Berlin
- **1905** Bertha von Suttner wins Nobel Peace Prize
- **1906** Women in Finland obtain the suffrage
  Sibella Aleramo publishes *Una Donna*
- **1909** Selma Lagerlöf wins the Nobel Prize in Literature
  French Union for Women's Suffrage established
- **1911** Marie Curie wins Nobel Prize in Chemistry
- **1912** Reform of Russian inheritance laws favoring women
- **1913** Women in Norway obtain the suffrage
- **1914** Irish women found Cumann na mBan
  World War I begins
- **1915** Women pacifists meet in the Hague
  Women in Denmark and Iceland receive the suffrage
- **1916** Easter Uprising in Dublin
- **1917** Russian Revolution begins
  Women in the Netherlands receive the suffrage
- **1918** World War I ends
  Women in England receive limited suffrage
- **1919** Rosa Luxemburg and William Liebknecht murdered
  Women in Germany receive the suffrage
- **1920** Russian law legalizes abortion
  Women in Austria receive the suffrage
  French law makes distribution of birth control information a crime and abortion a
  capital crime

Working-Class Life in the *Belle Époque*

A Question of Overwork In 1905, Emma Ihrer (1857–1911), founding editor of *The Woman Worker* and head of the Berlin Women Workers, summoned the German working class to liberate itself from overwork. Focusing particularly on women's problems, she saw the solution as choosing "one occupation, according to . . . ability and inclination—whether it be a profession *or* raising children *or* dealing with the house. . . . It's in this three-fold workload that the difficulty lies."[1] Ihrer was one of many working women who became political activists in the age of rapid and ubiquitous industrialization. By the end of the nineteenth century, mining, metallurgy, and chemicals dominated heavy industry. Railroads and railway travel were commonplace, and automobiles and electricity were making their debut. Buildings made with steel dotted the urban landscape, and chemical technology brought advances to many enterprises, ranging from commercial farming to weaponry. As industry flourished, finance and banking did also; stock markets and complex accounting procedures took control of business life and gave birth to the bureaucratic management of business. Few enterprises were run by a single owner; such owners were supported or even supplanted by managers and staffs of office workers. In the midst of the rapid transformation of society, the triply burdened lives of working women as outlined by Ihrer seemed little affected by modernizing trends.

By the start of the twentieth century, the number of women workers had grown, along with the dramatic increase in the European population. In 1910 in the Habsburg empire, around 900,000 women worked in factories, and in the French urban center of Lillé-Roubaix-Tourcoing, about 70,000 women worked in textiles alone. At the turn of the century, Scandinavia, northern Italy, Russia, and especially Germany were rapidly developing their industrial capacity. Women continued to dominate both in domestic service and in textiles. In Italy in the last quarter of the nineteenth century, the percentage of workers in the silk industry who were women increased from 60 to 70 percent; in cotton it went from 50 to 61 percent, and in wool from 31 to 45 percent.

Cotton mill in Lancashire, England in 1902. By this time, machines are more densely placed and dominate factory space and their tenders. Still, workers are moving about more than they would in the future.

In England, they were 49 percent of the textile-producing workforce in 1851; they constituted 57 percent in 1911. In the Moscow area in the 1880s, consumer demand created employment for about 35,000 women who made gloves and beads, wove rope sandals and fishnets, knitted an array of products, and treated cotton thread—all at home. In places such as the Czech areas of the Habsburg Empire, women could even be found working in heavy industry: there they constituted 30 percent of foundry workers. In Eastern Europe, most women remained on the land, but industrialization and urbanization still touched their lives. Mechanization changed many longstanding roles in agrarian life.

The problem of overwork pointed out by Ihrer was hardly diminished because of industrial modernization or the increase in consumer goods. Household chores and child care remained onerous. Though in some areas working wives and husbands shared chores—as had the Norwegian cottagers described earlier and the Oberlausitz weavers—in general responsibility for the domestic sphere fell to women. In addition to housework and child care, many women worked outside the home or took in piecework to earn money. In 1899, 37 percent of jute spinners in Bremen and of textile workers in Roubaix in northern France were married. Of all early twentieth-century Russian factory women, half were married. Even as more women were entering the workplace, governments began to demand improved standards of care in the domestic sphere. Because high child mortality rates threatened economic development by depleting the potential workforce, politicians resolved that working-class mothers should solve the problem by paying more attention to conditions in the home. Thus, as working life drew in more women, domestic life became more demanding. Working women sought solutions to their dilemma in politics and trade unions; many found the new socialist ideology attractive. But for most of them, neighbors and family, networks, gossip, domestic rituals, and public celebrations were their sources of sustenance and the culture that made a life of toil worth living.

The Conditions of Working Life

Urban Work

In urban areas, women's work at the turn of the century was diverse, but still defined by traditional gender-based notions of roles. A microcosmic view of the workforce in the highly industrialized German city of Düsseldorf in 1905, the year of Ihrer's summons, shows roughly 9,000 female domestic servants. Another 3,000 women worked in laundry and clothing work, 3,000 were employed in commerce, 1,200 served as chambermaids and waitresses, 1,500 were in factory textile work and food processing, 267 worked in the dominant metallurgy industry, and 71 in the wood industry.[2] Industrial cities with textile, carpet, or food-processing plants had a high number, sometimes even a majority of women workers in their factories. In general, women filled completely different productive roles than did men. Though machines offered the opportunity to neutralize gender in the workplace, custom shaped the most rational and modern of spheres—the industrial one. As in Düsseldorf, domestic work, clothing, textiles, food, and laundry were women's province in the world of advancing industrialization, as they had been centuries earlier.

Because of the gender division of labor, for women industrialization did not necessarily mean work with heavy machinery in factories. Continued mechanization reduced the need for human muscle power and made most factory work less labor-intensive. Much of women's work, however, remained unmechanized and therefore continued to be labor-intensive. In the early eighteenth century, the first improvements in weaving processes spurred domestic spinning. The subsequent mechanization of spinning led to a proliferation of handloom weavers. Similarly, the wave of industrialization in the late nineteenth century left in its wake pockets where labor-intensive processes predominated. Women in Normandy, for example, made boxes for cheese at home, and their involvement in this work increased along with the processing of food products in factories. Throughout Europe, women were employed making cartons and boxes by hand, knotting fishnets, seaming stockings, making buttonholes, making cutlery, rolling cigars, and painting on china. In general, later phases of industrialization are characterized by intensive capitalization; that is, large amounts of capital are needed to purchase machinery. But women's work often did not reflect this trend either, although it has been interpreted as the dominant one of the time.

Berlin homeworkers decorating chocolate. Notice the complex interior with many accoutrements of domesticity.

Most women who worked for pay did not do so in factories. For example, fewer than 20 percent of German women workers accomplished their productive activity in factories, and most of those worked in textile factories. Instead, employers gave women work to take home, labor-intensive work that did not require the powered machinery of the factories. Many manufacturers split their workforce into home workers and factory workers. The garment industry offers a perfect example of this phenomenon. Some workers were employed at sewing machines in workshops, and other workers did sewing at home where they performed either unmechanized processes such as buttonhole making or processes similar to those done in the factory itself. One consequence of these work patterns was that women's working life was less socialized; work was less often done in large groups and more often performed in relative isolation. Another result was that they could not develop a knowledge of machinery and technology. Except for those who had sewing machines, many never learned the skills of industrial production. Thus, for a high proportion of the population, working life had a different coloration than has usually been suggested. Isolated, seldom working with machinery, performing most tasks with their own physical dexterity or skill, such women maintained older work patterns. The piecework that women did in the home—making buttonholes, for exam-

Active Female Population in Certain Industries in Spain, 1900–1930

Industries	1900		1910		1920		1930	
	Total female workers	% active women in industry	Total female workers	% active women in industry	Total female workers	% active women in industry	Total female workers	% active women in industry
Pottery and ceramics	751	0.41	647	0.33	831	0.29	516	0.15
Food	20,240	11.05	15,470	7.9	8,574	3.03	13,068	3.7
Leather, fur, etc.	291	0.16	182	0.09	2,375	0.84	8,427	2.38
Electric					643	0.22	735	0.21
Iron and other metals					6,394	2.25	4,918	1.39
Books	592	0.32	1,675	0.86	1,789	0.63	666	0.19
Wood	1,178	0.64	1,834	0.94	649	0.23	5,948	1.68
Metallurgy	586	0.32	347	0.18	533	0.19	128	0.04
Furniture	739	0.40	1,302	0.66	1,315	0.46		
Paper					6,341	2.24	4,045	1.14
Chemicals					4,085	1.44	3,481	0.98
Tobacco*	2,502	1.37	2,164	1.1	11,960	4.22	12,570	3.56
Textiles	51,519	28.14	50,290	25.7	123,680	43.7	115,361	32.66
Clothing and hair	92,974	50.79	99,245	50.72	86,013	30.39	90,415	25.6

*For 1900 and 1910, chemicals were included in tobacco without indications of number of workers.

Source: Rosa Capel Martinez, *El trabajo y la educcación de la mujer en España* (Madrid: Ministerio de Cultura, 1982), 118–119.

ple—was just as monotonous and just as fragmented as factory work and per-haps more physically wearing since factories incorporated advances in produc-tive mechanisms. To some extent, one might conclude that, working in a home or craft environment, women substituted for machines.

Whether women did piecework at home or worked in textile or food-processing plants they earned one-third to two-thirds less than men. Ideologi-cally defined early in the nineteenth century as mothers rather than as workers, they could not demand workers' wages. Because employers were able to base wages on gender, they increased their profits. In times of economic depression, women were hired to replace better-paid men or to deter the male workforce from striking; in general, this pattern created a kind of insecurity based on suspicion between the sexes. Employers also hired more women when the skill level needed to work in an industry decreased. For example, as fine metalwork became more highly mechanized and less craft-based in France at the turn of the century, the number of women employed in this type of manufacturing increased and wages dropped. In the Khar'kov province of Russia, the fraction of women workers in pottery and ceramics went from none in 1885 to two-fifths in 1911 as these handicrafts became industrialized. On the Continent women's participation in mechanized industry began to increase slowly but

Active Female Population of Three Spanish Provinces, 1900–1930

| Province | Economic sector | Active Female Population | | | |
| | | 1900 | | 1930 | |
		Total female workers	% of total workers	Total female workers	% of total workers
Barcelona	*Primary*				
	Agriculture	19,558	18.91	442	0.17
	Secondary				
	Industry	48,922	47.29	164,050	65.23
	Tertiary	34,958	33.6	56,943	34.57
	Commerce	4,909	4.7	4,642	1.8
	Clergy	5,183	5	6,327	2.5
	Liberal professions	1,826	1.7	6,969	2.8
	Domestic service	21,842	21	37,609	15
	Post and telegraph			567	0.2
	Public administration			727	0.3
Granada	*Primary*				
	Agriculture	1,082	10.1	228	2.47
	Secondary				
	Industry	2,989	27.9	1,463	15.87
	Tertiary	6,643	62	7,526	81.65
	Commerce	419	4	369	4
	Clergy	1,119	10.4	1,329	14
	Liberal professions	351	3.3	641	7
	Domestic service	4,602	43	5,138	56
	Post and telegraph			28	0.3
	Public administration			14	0.2
Madrid	*Primary*				
	Agriculture	4,936	8.18	268	0.28
	Secondary				
	Industry	11,428	18.93	11,208	11.57
	Tertiary	44,000	72.89	85,362	88.14
	Commerce	1,605	2.7	4,760	5
	Clergy	3,810	6.3	6,818	7
	Liberal professions	1,372	2.3	4,607	4.8
	Domestic service	36,927	61.2	67,329	69.5
	Post and telegraph			647	0.7
	Public administration	39		860	0.9

Source: Rosa Capel Martinez, *El trabajo y la educcación de la mujer en España* (Madrid: Ministerio de Cultura, 1982), 74.

perceptibly in the early twentieth century. Men concluded that they did not like women as co-workers because they drove men out, drove down wages, and diluted working-class skill by encouraging employers to simplify work. Then tasks could be separated from a complex process and given to lower paid workers. The use employers made of gender proved decisive in shaping male working-class opinion about women workers. By the end of the nineteenth century, a dual labor market existed—male and female workers were paid differently and lacked solidarity.

The seasonal nature of women's work continued to exacerbate the problem of low wages. Many women worked in producing consumer goods, such as clothing, rather than capital goods, such as iron and steel. Consumer purchasing occurred according to seasons. There were two seasons for clothing purchases, another season for the purchase of household linens, and so on. In what was known as the dead season, January to March and July through September, consumer purchasing stopped, and so therefore did women's work and wages. One milliner reported that she and her mother turned to making dolls' clothing to earn a little something during these times. Because their boutique was on the way to the cathedral, they might count on one or two sales a week. Manufacturers who put out work to women at home also did so sporadically; where there was no money invested in machinery or a plant, they had little incentive to keep productivity constant. Therefore, women might be given enough work to fill fifteen hours a day at one period and then nothing for months. Even factory workers in textiles might be employed for less than two-thirds of the year. The periods of unemployment necessitated a turn to something else—taking in boarders, doing laundry, caring for others' children, or cleaning. Some factory workers returned to rural areas to work during harvests; others constantly sought new jobs. In the long run, the variety of jobs that women took and their movement from one to another had much less to do with their own desires than with the nature of the work available to them. In addition, women who did piecework in isolated settings had little recourse to organizational support. Rather, they had to depend on their own resourcefulness.

Sexual harassment also shaped worklife. In the late nineteenth-century, gender-based power in the workplace translated into sexual coercion. Austrian Adelheid Popp's (1869–1939) autobiography tells of such harassment on the job by superiors. She watched a succession of her co-workers in the factory become favorites of the foreman and then leave as he grew tired of them. She herself quit a job because one of the managers forced her to kiss him in exchange for higher wages. A German barmaid cried "bitterly" because so many customers tried "to kiss me or otherwise fondle me, which I always vigorously forbade. I usually heard in reply, 'This is no cloister, my child!' or 'That's only your first reaction, you'll like it better.' "[3] Getting jobs, keeping them, advancing—sexual favors often played an important role in women's working lives and in their ability to support or try to support themselves and their families. Moreover, despite job segregation, the workplace was often a sexually charged arena. Taunts and roughhousing around factories could create a constantly unpleasant, even dangerous atmosphere for women.

Women's work also differed from men's in its connection to household and family. Some historians believe women chose to work in ways that allowed them to connect family and income-generating activity. Others have seen this characteristic of women's work as the result of a consistent policy—by businessmen or politicians—to force women to maintain working-class family life. In either case, the fact remains that women's productive and reproductive lives were entwined in ways that made them difficult to disentangle. The household had to advance both kinds of activities at the same time, and this made special demands on women's working lives and shaped them in particular ways. For one thing, from early childhood, girls saw the house as the locus of constant activity. Talking of her girlhood in the early twentieth century, an English girl noted how from the youngest age she resented her brothers' freedom to play and romp while she had to do household tasks, especially mending and sewing. Sometimes the entire family engaged in household production, and children of both sexes learned such skills as weaving or knitting at a young age and began to work at home. But as fewer and fewer men engaged in such household production, fewer and fewer boys had anything to do at home. Even after they entered the workforce—between the ages of ten and fourteen years—girls and boys had different relationships with their families. In Germany at the turn of the century, girls usually gave all of their wages to the family and lived at home. Boys kept more of their wages and were allowed more independence to prepare them for becoming heads of their own families. In other words, the process of socialization and arrangements within the family economy kept young working women in the household, working for the family and surrendering that modern mark of personhood—the wage—to it.

The life of Jeanne Bouvier (1865–1964) illustrates how families relied on their daughters' efforts and how varied women's working life could be. Bouvier's father was a barrelmaker for the wine industry. Jeanne Bouvier grew up south of the city of Lyons doing odd jobs such as tending the family cows and knitting while she did so. When her father lost his job because phylloxera destroyed the vineyards, Jeanne, at the age of eleven, began her life of work for wages in a silk factory. At that time, she was the only person in her family with a regular wage because her unemployed father had begun drinking. She moved among factories several times in search of a higher wage or because her mother moved. She had one job caring for children when she herself was only thirteen. After her mother found jobs as domestics for both of them in Paris in 1879, Bouvier spent the next few years in one domestic post after another. She lied about both her age and her abilities, which, for the bourgeois clients she served, were usually insufficient. Some cousins in Paris helped her find a job in the hat-making industry, but she lost it because of the replacement of felt hats by woollen ones. In her moves from one job to another and from one living place to another, Bouvier was cheated out of money, became indebted to relatives, and never accumulated clothing or cash reserves of any sort. Finally, she ended up working for a fairly good couturière. By that time she had a drive for security that led her to work extra hours and to save in order never to be hungry. To accomplish her end, Bouvier not only worked the regular twelve-hour day of a seamstress, she also worked for private clients from 8:30 p.m. until midnight and from 4:00 a.m. to 8 a.m. Such additional work prevented her from experiencing the worst effects of the dead season, but she paid for her financial security with ill health. She spent several months in hospitals at different times. Despite what was obviously a debilitating schedule, she persevered. She felt proud of herself for being an exception; she did not commit suicide, did not fall into prostitution, and did not squander her money on passing fashions. Until she turned to trade unionism, her major goal in life was to have "a small house in the country with chickens and rabbits." Teased by her friends that she would be bored, Bouvier responded: "No, my dears, I could never be bored knowing that I had enough to eat."[4]

Rural Work

Jeanne Bouvier's dream of returning to rural life is evidence of the powerful effect the countryside had on the urban imagination and how much Europeans remained connected to their agricultural roots. At the turn of the century, the number of rural people continued to decline, though national censuses in most countries showed they still dominated. In Central Europe, the majority of women worked on the land. For example, in Hungary in 1914, 56 percent of the population farmed, and even in the West—in France, for instance—rural people still made up two-fifths of all workers. However, technology and new ways of agricultural production had produced changes in agricultural work. For one thing, metal plows and scythes replaced wooden plows and sickles, and combination machines speeded up harvesting. Scythes and reapers could eliminate women from harvest work and were so efficient as to leave nothing behind for gleaning. In England, the country where the smallest proportion of people worked in agriculture, women wielding sickles continued to appear in work crews, but less frequently. Some gleaners still tried to get a bit of grain for their families. Older women sometimes worked a short day weeding, hoeing, or digging stones. Often, however, the farmer's or day laborer's wife no longer did much work outside the home, except perhaps for tending a flower garden. In Denmark, the dairymaid's job disappeared because of a combination of the mechanization of dairying and the rise of dairy cooperatives. These examples suggest that modernization in the form of new machinery or extensions of scale sometimes undermined women's traditional ways of contributing to the family economy.

Despite modernization, their work in rural areas generally remained as complex as before. In parts of Germany and France, women continued weaving at home and doing agricultural or even factory work as part of a productive package allowing them to make their economic contribution. An observer in County Mayo, Ireland, noted that "women besides all the ordinary domestic duties, carding, spinning, etc., take part in field labour with the men and gather sea-weed for manure."[5] However, statistics show the decline of piecework as a means by which rural women could cut the losses caused by agricultural modernization. Whereas in Ireland in the 1840s approximately half a million women did domestic textile work, in the 1880s that figure had dropped to less than 100,000. In Eastern Europe, they continued to do various kinds of piecework, fieldwork, and housework. Rural women who lived close to industry might work in a factory until the season for agricultural work came around. Indeed, a husband finding factory work for himself could sometimes depend

Early twentieth century women hauling a barge in Russia. Notice the male overseer of the team.

on his ability in off season to put together a team of cultivators and harvesters including women. Although the husband kept the account book and received the pay, the family acted together in harvesting, just as in the winter months it would reallocate all forms of household chores. In Russia, however, men could move back and forth between industry and agriculture more readily than women could. Once in the city, a young Russian female did not have so easy a time returning to the farm to work as a hand but instead had to endure the dead season by finding some kind of other urban work.

Sexual harassment also posed problems for rural women. Domestic servants who hoed and harvested alongside men knew—through hearsay or experience—of sexual brutality or sexual advances. Some Russian landowners even kept harems of peasant women. In the extended family, the patriarch could exact sexual favors. Still living in proximity to their masters, rural laundresses, seamstresses, or day workers might commit themselves to fleeting or extended extramarital relationships.

Given the continued labor-intensive nature of agriculture and the uneven effects of industrialization, rural women still had plenty to do. In many places they maintained a vital role in farm activities and continued their complex way of life. First, the interior of the home was the woman's sphere, and she was responsible for all activities connected to food, fire, water, and clothing. Though cooking was simple for the most part, women served food as often as five or six times a day during planting or harvest seasons. From observations of a French family on the eve of post–World War I agricultural changes, one sees what serving food meant: first a snack of bread and cheese at 5 a.m. then a breakfast of bread and perhaps bacon or sausage; at noon a lunch of soup, boiled meat, and vegetables; another snack of bread followed by a soup of leftovers, or a dish of potatoes, or an omelette. This menu omits the large quantities of bread that accompanied meals, and the varied diet is obviously that of a prosperous farm. Women were still responsible in many places for baking bread as well as for procuring (or raising) all other food, but in some areas bakers and itinerant grocers were changing these practices. Like urban women, rural women generally hauled all the water, which often took enormous amounts of time and energy. They maintained the interior of the house, which in more prosperous peasant areas involved a domestic ritual of its own, including waxing wood and whatever furniture the family had. From the Rhineland area in Germany comes another account of peasant women's activity. During the haying season, Frau K rose at 4:30 a.m., prepared the fire, cared for pigs, and did the milking by 6 a.m. Then she made and ate breakfast and did her housework, including preparing a snack and lunch. After a morning of haymaking, she and her husband had lunch, then returned to the fields until 6 p.m. She returned home to do the evening milking and care for the pigs; then she made supper and afterward sewed until 11 p.m. This arduous schedule only varied in winter when peasant couples rose an hour or two later.

Findings in women's history have profoundly affected historians' view of the effects of industrialization. Instead of bringing steady progress toward opportunity, the application of technology to production had uneven effects and caused many people to have to piece together working lives that allowed them to maintain themselves and their families. For rural women these pieced-together lives sometimes involved combinations of agricultural work, factory work, doing outwork, and gardening for home consumption as well as raising a few animals wherever space permitted. Rural and industrial distinctions were hardly neat in actual experience.

Marriage, the Family, and the Home

Rural Lives

Rural Europe was enmeshed in change but still governed in many ways by longstanding customs. For instance, many farms continued to employ young women as servants. Arranged by yearly contracts, such service lasted a decade or more and remained necessary for many women in order to earn money to set up housekeeping. Late in the nineteenth century a German woman who wanted to get married found a certain young man pleasing. She passed near where he was working, and "he put down his axe and told her that if he knew for certain that she could raise a thousand marks, perhaps they could talk."[6] The subject, once the young servant had earned the thousand marks, would be marriage. Where land passed down to children and formed the basis for prosperity, parents continued to control marriages. In southern Italy, only pregnancy or elopement could offset parental authority. In Germany, statistics show many single rural mothers of the propertyless classes totally abandoned by their lovers. In such instances, women could plead only for child support, marriage being out of the question.

The continued growth in number of landless rural workers affected the rate of remarriage. In the eighteenth century and earlier, a spouse's death was usually followed by a hasty remarriage to form a new agricultural partnership. Studies of Scandinavia find this pattern declining. In Norway, for example, early in the nineteenth century almost 10 percent of all marriages involved widows, whereas by 1880 this percentage had declined by half. Italy saw the same decline in remarriages, from 19 percent of marriages in the mid-1860s to 11 percent just before World War I. This kind of change resulted from male migration out of rural areas and from the decline of farming as a way of life demanding marital partnerships.

Although the extended rural family stayed viable, subtle innovations appeared. In the Hungarian *zadruga*, modern notions of individualism altered family habits. Around the large main building, couples built themselves one-room cabins or bedrooms. Wives in some cases cooked individual meals for their families, and reports of friction among women working together also became more common. Like the *zadruga*, whole communities experienced factionalization, especially an increasing division between landed and landless. The former were able to afford certain novelties, for example, dietary additions such as meat, coffee, sugar, and processed foods. Tourists and vacationers or workers returning from the city brought fashions, books, and urban customs to the countryside. Rural people who owned land increasingly practiced birth control so that their property would not be divided into so many pieces that it would support no one. In many areas, landless peasants married late to limit fertility. Yet among the rural poor, infants still had a high mortality—in central Italy at the turn of the century 50 percent died before the age of five.

As industrialization was overwhelming Europe as a whole, the peasant woman and peasant family seemed to some anachronistic and to others a touchstone of stability in a changing world. Country women met life's burdens, including childbirth, with such expressions as "I didn't flinch," or in praising a friend, "she didn't flinch neither."[7] Ethnographers began studying the habits, dress, and proverbs of country people; upper-class landholders began making notes of disappearing folkways. What emerged was an idealized picture of a rural mentality, representing enduring values and a community-centered life. In fact, the peasant family had, in some people's view, grown tighter in the face of increasing challenges to its way of life. Whereas some urban women were emancipating themselves from domesticity and becoming "modern,"* rural women sometimes became more tightly integrated into family strategies for survival. They also developed a "folk" clothing stressing difference from urban people. By the end of the century, peasant costume evolved into ornate, cum-

---

*See Chapter 8.

Customs of the Country

Southeastern Europe by the late nineteenth century had become the focus of Slavic nationalist aspirations, particularly the independent state of Serbia. This area—the present-day Yugoslavia—remained one where tasks had clear gender definition and where people in their everyday, rural lives expressed a powerful belief in male supremacy.

In Servia, and still more in other Servian lands, parents prefer to have a son rather than a daughter. . . . It is interesting to note how eager the women are to have a son, and how many sisters give up their lives for their brothers or how much more grandmothers rejoice over the birth of a grandson than over a granddaughter. A Montenegrin fires his gun when a son is born to him. "I have a little son, and forgive me, two daughters," he says. There are some who do not mention their daughters when asked how many children they have. A Servian woman may never cross the road when a man is passing. Whatever number of men enter a house their hands are kissed by womenfolk; even old women kiss the hands of youths young enough to be their sons. The respect and awe with which a husband is regarded is also evident from the fact that the wife never calls him by name.

In Montenegro it is a disgrace for a man to carry a burden on his back; this is done by women. In some parts of Montenegro adjoining Dalmatia the women are regarded as beasts of burden, carrying wood, dried meat, fish, etc., on their backs to and fro between the mountains and the sea-coast. When a heavy snowfall makes it impossible for horses to draw goods, the Montenegrins, mostly women, take up burdens of 30 to 50 kilogrammes, and carry them uphill a distance of seven hours walk. On account of the excellent industry of their women, the Montenegrins often say, "A house is not based on the ground, but upon a woman. . . ." Notwithstanding that woman is made such an indefatigable living machine of in Montenegro, men never act as tyrants, nor beat or scold them.

Source: Adapted from *Servia by the Servians,* Alfred Stead, ed. (London: William Heinemann, 1909) 176–178.

bersome, and highly distinctive clothing delineating community, gender, and marital status. Marriage within one's community or even between relatives was another way of defending the agricultural way of life against further intrusion.

Swedish holiday racers, arranged along gender lines and clothed in elaborate peasant dress. For country people these highly decorated costumes were actually features of modern, rather than traditional experience.

So popular did this solution become that observers noted high incidences of inherited physical abnormalities in rural areas. With agriculture so precarious and with new land therefore constantly coming on the market, the rural family aimed at one thing—acquiring land or maintaining the closest possible relationship to it.

The illiteracy of rural women began to decline at the end of the nineteenth century. The law now required them to attend school for at least two or three years, often in spite of the opposition of parents who still believed in the uselessness of education for farm women. Women who had grown up in the country and learned how to write excelled as chroniclers of rural ways and people. Daughter of a prosperous peasant, Grazia Deledda (1871–1936) was raised in Nuova, Sardinia, after the unification of Italy. With no more than four years of formal education, she published her first story and her first novel while she was in her teens. Deledda wrote intricate tales of Italian peasants, their lives in nature, and their resignation (and her own) to the force of fate in human destiny. Celebrated throughout Italy, she won the Nobel Prize for literature in 1926. Another Nobel laureate, Selma Lagerlöf (1858–1940), also cast her literary net locally. Like Deledda, she longed for a wider world and for time off from the constant round of household activities so she could write. Yet, when she did write, her focus was the Swedish village and farm, local legends, and those who spread them. Similarly, Margaret Penn (b. 1896) wrote *Manchester*

Fourteen Miles, and Flora Thompson (1876–1947) produced *Lark Rise to Candleford;* both became classics of the rural experience. Many such writers, however, were among those who left the countryside to find a different kind of life, one they hoped would be less onerous.

Urban Lives

Under industrialization, sexual roles dating from earlier centuries continued to influence the way most men and women of the working class treated each other in cities and towns. Even at the beginning of the twentieth century, things in the home were women's responsibility—including more often than not, providing financial support for the domestic sphere. Some men did not turn their wages over to women, and a few did not even contribute to the costs of food and shelter. Women took in boarders or did piecework because centuries-old tradition mandated that, at the very least, they support themselves. Children were also associated with women and seen as their responsibility in every way, including financially. A husband would give his wife a set amount of money periodically for expenses. Often this amount never changed despite the birth of children—an indication that the wife was responsible for their support.

Conversely, though women might participate in the industrial world, men had little knowledge of the domestic sphere—even less perhaps than children, who often helped their mother carry out her household strategies. Older children tended the others, foraged for fuel, and carried water. Girls added more responsibilities as they grew older. Male children often removed themselves from this sphere as they gained a mature sexual identity. If the mother died, the children were often farmed out to female relatives or other women. Society did not expect a father to care for his motherless children or to have the knowledge to do so. Working-class men had little capability when it came to household maneuvers such as the constant resort to pawnshops. In many cases men seemed strangers to the household and its inhabitants; for example, one Austrian working-class woman could not remember her father ever talking to her or she to him.

Food was the centerpiece of domestic life in working-class homes but in a way far different from middle-class homes. For working-class women, obtaining sufficient food occupied their lives and thoughts. Across Europe the most important dietary staples were bread and potatoes, which whenever possible served as vehicles for some type of fat or protein, such as lard, butter, margarine, or cheese. Or the bread or potatoes appeared with some kind of broth that contained scraps of meat in the best times and was simply watery in the worst. Women engaged in daily activity to obtain these bits of food; relationships with butchers were crucial to getting meat scraps for special meals or the broth in which sausages had been cooked. Even in more affluent working-class homes, women saw food only as a necessity during these decades, never as a consumer item meant for pleasure. This is not to say that there were not occasional feast days, but for the most part cooking was minimal and based on physical necessity. Working women often purchased precooked food, and so did those who had no fires, stoves, or utensils. As well as food procurement and preparation, women took care of the apportionment of food. Generally, as observers noted, they apportioned the most food to wage earners, less to children not earning, and the least to themselves. Men often demanded "extras" and larger portions, but most had never had to develop the skill of making ends meet. Consequently, a woman's illness could mean extreme privation for her children unless female relatives or women from her social network intervened. In these circumstances, where food was never taken for granted, tradespeople with domestics in their homes or those with the good fortune to have a cupboard always kept food under lock and key.

Domestic violence—sexual and nonsexual—plagued many working-class homes. Perhaps prompted by sentimental feelings or romantic love, marriage operated according to negotiated obligations and the performance of services. If women failed to serve meals on time, overworked their pawnshop connections so that something did not reappear, or seemed remiss in other ways, they might be beaten. Women often gave as good as they received in this regard, many of them being muscular from hard domestic or factory work. Perpetrated by boarders, stepfathers, or even blood relatives, sexual assaults on women also took place in working-class homes. Such events form a constant theme in autobiographies from every country and in accounts to social investigators. Both sexual and nonsexual violence often sprang from the use of alcohol. At the heart of a good deal of working-class sociability, alcohol served a variety of purposes among both men and women. It provided at least a temporary feeling of warmth for those whose homes often lacked the most elemental forms of heating. It also temporarily induced feelings of well-being among the overworked. In addition, the *bierstube*, café, or pub was the one meeting place available to the working class, and drinking alcohol was a ritual of friendship. But often drinking led to drunken rages, with beatings not far behind. Alcoholic men who could not support their families even in a minimal way turn up in the autobiographical writings of countless working women, including Italian Teresa Noce, Austrian Adelheid Popp, and English Margaret Penn.

Although working-class women's sexuality was apparently less constrained than that of middle-class women, the oppressive aspects of sexual relations also remained a theme in these autobiographies. Moreover, sexual and nonsexual violence perpetrated against women was intended to keep them within certain behavioral bounds. In Germany, female victims of homicides were more often single working women living alone than women living in families. Jack the Ripper's murders of single women in London's East End started an enduring myth about the consequences of certain kinds of free behavior. The possibility of sexual harassment or violence constituted a menacing shadow under which working women lived.

Working women of this period developed a sense of self based on their experiences and skills. First came a belief in their own strength and competence arising from a relatively independent accomplishment of tasks. Although some women gave in to sexual advances in order to keep a job, others stood up to employers who made unreasonable demands. In the 1880s, in Hamburg, servant Doris Viersbeck took revenge on demanding employers by keeping to her room until the mistress "pleaded" with her to come out. Even then, she refused to return to cooking right away: "It was their problem to get their meals prepared; they deserved some sort of punishment. This I told her straight out."[8] When bosses denied minimal standards of living, workers resisted in whatever ways they could. Hired by a family that deprived its servants of ordinary coffee or table wine, cook Yvonne Chabot "discreetly lifted a few grains of coffee and put aside this ration for the servants who savored—as soon as the coast was clear—this forbidden fruit."[9]

Finally, like their rural counterparts, urban working-class women created a domestic environment resembling on a superficial level that of the middle class. Women prided themselves on domestic skills such as making a special wine or tending a small flower garden. Photos of the interiors of working-class homes of this time show pictures on the wall, trinkets or souvenirs on surfaces, and flowered curtains at the windows. Many women made a special ritual of cleaning hearths, doorsteps, and front walks. Although the poor faced such basic problems as ridding their bodies of lice and their furniture of bugs, cleaning also involved some procedures with strictly decorative intent such as working designs on front steps or walks or chalking hearths or walks. Wooden furniture, panels, and windowsills often gleamed from constant polishing. As products like cleaning soda fell in price because of improved productive techniques, working-class families substituted it for sand, ashes, and other natural products that had served their cleaning needs. Relying on an array of homemade implements such as brooms made of twigs and brushes or mops made of scraps and rags, housewives made domestic cleaning a way of life. In England, for example, an "Auntie Mabel . . . used to black-lead the coal stove, scrub the coal cellar floor and, upon the return of her husband from work, turn out his pockets and trouser turn-ups to brush them down."[10] Women took the charge to care for their families beyond the realm of necessity by developing clear cultural imprints.

Interventions in Working Women's Lives and State Building

Despite the vital culture of working people, their way of life and living conditions in urban areas caused immense concern and even disapproval among the upper and middle classes. To a large extent, this concern arose from the very force of the urbanizing experience. Some in Eastern Europe viewed the process of industrialization in their societies as they would have regarded an outbreak of the plague. "I have frequently seen women workers coming to the dinner table and falling on the bench without the strength to eat," wrote one observer in Moscow just before World War I. As for the factories and workshops there, "the premises are filthy, the walls covered with torn wallpaper. Bedbugs, lice and cockroaches emerge from the filth. The odor of the toilets permeates the room."[11]

By the end of the nineteenth century, European cities were teeming with young working-class women and men who had migrated from rural areas. Housing shortages existed everywhere, and slums abounded. Moreover, from 1873 on, a prolonged depression lasting several decades exacerbated urban misery. Unemployed or underemployed for long stretches of time, workers unionized, struck, and protested in a variety of ways. As cities grew, new patterns of urban living also developed. Tight community social structures weakened. The mixed neighborhood in which artisan and aristocrat lived side by side became less common. Instead, the middle and upper classes created distinct neighborhoods for themselves as city limits expanded. These new neighborhoods were often built around parks and other open spaces. There a privileged domestic life flourished that sharply contrasted with that of working-class sections.

The contrast between the classes was clear among women. Women's fertility began dropping sharply among the upper classes, as did infant mortality. Among the poor and working urban population, such changes occurred more slowly, so class differences became highly visible. Underpaid and overworked women, with several children at a minimum, were constantly burying their young. In contrast to the image of the upper- or middle-class woman as the "angelic" mother, the image of a turn-of-the-century working-class woman reflected poverty, misery, social protest, crowding, and a burdened family life. Artists painted her as drugged or drunk, with little grace or even dignity. The sharp contrast of middle-class and working-class women caused alarm.

Both state administrators and reform-minded individuals focused on the condition of working women and their families as the key, they claimed, to social health in general and to solving international problems. Nations were embattled during the *belle époque*. Not only did urban decay exist amidst prosperity and progress, but international economic and political competition intensified the ups and downs of booms and busts. Countries resorted to imperialist assaults on other continents to bring them new markets and raw materials. These expansions often provoked new rivalries and military contests. Moreover, most nation-states experienced working-class protests that left politicians feeling shaky. The expansionist efforts of imperialism would solve the problem of working-class unrest, politicians believed. Increasing the size of the army would bring more members of the working class into a body that taught loyalty to the state. Moreover, imperialism would test the mettle of countries and upgrade its physical well-being by engaging armies and work force alike in contests of readiness. Also, politicians saw in imperial expansion a way to renew industrial prosperity and thus end those grievances around which trade unionism and strikes arose. In other words, a policy of imperialism seemed to hold a remedy for visible troubles in the cities. To prepare the working class for this national venture, improvements in its health became the order of the day. For one thing, an imperial army needed fitter men than the working class could provide at the time. Second, it needed more men than the high infant mortality rates and falling birth rates would allow. In fact, French and English politicians, for example, attributed both strikes and business depressions to scarcity of labor, stemming in part from high infant mortality. Urban blight did not merely offend middle-class sensibilities; it also seemed to hold the seeds of social unrest.

To ensure progress and restore well-being, policymakers ultimately put women in charge of working-class health. Whereas once workers' morality had preoccupied the upper classes, now their health caught the attention of politicians, businessmen, and reformers. It was a sign of the modern, scientific world view that the body, not the soul, was the focus of such massive concern. The first government efforts involved working-class housing and infant mortality. In France, infant mortality had alarmed officials since the defeat of France by Germany in 1871. The unexpected German victory and the simultaneous working-class uprising of the Commune had left officialdom in a state of panic. They observed not only high rates of infant mortality but also low birth rates. Even among peasants, "only one child is wanted. At the second, one groans and laments."[12] In fact, the decline in fertility had begun in France a century earlier, but only after 1871 did politicians start perceiving the country a declining nation. From the 1870s on, the French government launched a concerted effort to decrease infant mortality. Following the example of English legislation of 1872, called the Infant Life Protection Act, the French government enacted a law that required public health doctors to examine children put out to nurse or even those cared for on a daily basis in other women's homes. This was followed by municipal and industrial efforts to set up clinics for infants, which provided physical examinations and financial support for mothers who nursed their children. Nurses made visits to homes to examine subsidized mothers to ensure compliance with provisions for breast-feeding. Other countries, such as Germany, began following these French and English initiatives, though the Germans had preceded most nations in providing health insurance for workers in 1878. Continental leaders seemed alert by the early twentieth century to the need for assistance to mothers and newborn children.

Reformers next began to look at housing. Many governments tore down slum housing at an unprecedented rate. In Paris, this process had begun under the Second Empire, where interest in security, or, to put it another way, the fear of revolution, had motivated the government to tear down and rebuild neighborhoods dating from the Middle Ages. Streets that were winding and narrow would be easier for inhabitants to barricade than for authorities to control. Elimination of older neighborhoods was also justified on the basis of several devastating cholera and typhus epidemics, which established the necessity for improvements in urban water supplies. Housewives living in older neighborhoods thus operated within a precarious universe, watching the modernizers at work nearby and waiting to know whether their housing would be upgraded or torn down. The poor moved when hard times hit their families; they also moved to new neighborhoods or suburbs as new—usually more costly—housing replaced the old. When modernization threatened, they responded with rent strikes, protest meetings, and by attending socialist party meetings.

Finally, governments initiated a round of protective legislation controlling women's work. From the 1870s on, industrial countries enacted laws that limited the time women could put in at work and controlled their conditions of work and to some extent the work patterns of pregnant women or those who had recently given birth. Under the Factory and Workshops Acts of 1874 and 1878, English women could work no more than fifty-four hours per week. Between 1890 and 1910 additional laws were passed to protect women in the match industry from phosphorus poisoning, to end the system of compulsory meals shop assistants bought from their employers, to set minimum wages in certain trades where the sweatshop conditions prevailed, and to give some insurance benefits to women, who were not normally covered because of their low wages or irregular patterns of work. Women were also prohibited from working at night in England and in most other countries. In Germany in 1891, legislation prohibited women from working at night or underground, mandated a paid maternity leave of four weeks after childbirth, limited women's workday to eleven hours, and forbade work on Sunday. Earlier German insurance benefits covering accidents and retirement had excluded the needle trades, laundering, and ironing. By the beginning of the twentieth century, France put similar restrictions on working women in terms of hours, nighttime work, and work in mines. Only after World War I did most paid maternity leave programs go into effect.

Much of the protective legislation was regarded with distinct acrimony by some working women who did not view all the efforts said to be made on their behalf as being helpful. "How can a person whom I deprive of her daily bread have any use of my advice on how to keep her health?"[13] was how the first Swedish woman doctor, Karolina Widerstrom, interrogated an audience considering protective legislation and other health measures for women. Widerstrom referred to the law enacted in 1900 by the Swedish parliament that mandated that no woman be allowed to work for four weeks following childbirth. Because the legislation provided for no economic support to women during this unemployed period, it actually detracted from their well-being while purporting to improve it. The contradiction in Swedish legislation—passed to protect women but ultimately affecting them adversely—existed in almost every other law passed in the pre–World War I period. On the one hand, such things as limitations on hours and health regulations in the workplace benefitted them. On the other hand, such things made women less competitive in the employment market. Forbidden to work at night, they could not, for example, serve as printers for morning newspapers. The reduction of women's hours meant that they could not hold the same jobs as male workers. Moreover, many restrictions made women less desirable as employees. In addition, legislation covering pay and hours sometimes exempted sweatshops and work farmed out to women to do at home. The sweated trades, where most of the exploitation occurred, were thus able to continue in their particularly harsh and low-paying treatment of women. Making factory women noncompetitive and more neatly ghettoizing female work, the legislation did improve the lot of some factory workers by giving them more time for sleep or perhaps for recreation. But, simultaneously, it channeled women into the lowest-paying jobs in domestic service and in sweatshops by making these alternatives more obviously than ever work meant for women.

Some women protested this growing power of the state over women's work. In 1911, "pit brow" women in England, who worked on the surface of coal mines, criticized proposals to eliminate them from mine areas with banners: "We Claim the Right to Sell Our Labour Even as Our Brothers."[14] The claim to equal treatment was a pertinent comment on protective legislation, for the laws' clearest effect was the singling out of women workers. This singling out occurred not just ideologically as it had earlier in the nineteenth century. Governments took measures to create a legal representation of the woman worker as someone different from the male worker, someone who needed the protection of the state. While giving such protection, the state built itself up institutionally with systems of regulations, factory inspectors, penalties, fines, and the like. Thus, while weakening the economic position of the woman worker, the state set itself up as her stronger partner. In many cases, legislation also reinforced male economic superiority by offering, as in Germany, pensions for male workers but not female ones. The intention of protective legislation was also state building, as German Chancellor Hans von Bulow clearly stated in the 1890s: "The national aspect of these policies must be moved into the limelight time and time again so that the national ideal will never cease to move, integrate and divide."[15] Legislation endeavoring to work some kind of transformation on the working class had three similar results. First, such legislation created activity and institutions that enhanced unending state growth. Second, it integrated women into the functioning of the nation-state as they interacted with inspectors, public health officials, and other functionaries dispensing assistance. Finally, protective legislation divided male from female in an official way with sharp economic results and an impact on family life and working-class politics.

Intersections with Middle-Class Women

Government efforts prospered with the help of middle-class women, both as volunteers and, later, as paid factory inspectors and social workers. Their motivations for doing such work ranged from a general concern for the conditions facing poor mothers to an interest in making working-class life more modern and scientific. In the 1860s in London, for instance, Octavia Hill (1838–1912) began buying houses, renovating them, and then renting them to the poor. She distinguished herself as an improving landlord, but she was also a woman of charity. Hill intervened in the lives of the poor. According to her, they needed to build their character by learning frugality and paying bills promptly. So, as her housing expanded, she trained teams of rent collectors to teach middle-class household-management skills and see that they were applied. Hill's successes gave rise to imitators and brought other landlords, such as the Church of England, to ask her to manage their properties. Hill herself was an unusual version of the traditional charity woman, in that she adapted moral concerns to the ongoing process of systematization and rationalization of relief. Her peers in almost all countries were doing likewise, that is, multiplying their efforts in the homes of the poor, organizing them better to fit the new mood of social welfare as social discipline.

For many poor women, the result of all this attention was an invasion of interlopers, often with different priorities depending on the type of charity practiced or the degree to which the visitor was motivated by social science or religious affiliation. Housing as a priority meant that working-class homes were hardly private. Housewives responded in a variety of ways to these invasions. In England, for example, many of them geared their strategies in dealing with charitable visitors to obtaining public housing, which began appearing in many places by the turn of the century. An Austrian worker remembered her mother's various relationships with charitable women, including her refusal of their demands for religious conformity. They also refused to adopt middle-class suggestions for nutritious meals, partly out of taste and partly out of poverty.

Common middle-class wisdom held that poor women were slovenly, poor homemakers hardly capable of caring for their children properly. This view attributed these faults less to poverty than to ignorance; that is, working-class women existed outside the reach of advances in science that had benefited other classes. The first way of changing this involved raising the age at which children could leave school and enforcing it for girls as well as boys. Because pulp journalism was growing in popularity and often dealt with topics of domestic improvement, fashion, and health, women's literacy seemed to hold the key to the democratization of hygienic concern. An entire body of household knowledge was placed at every woman's disposal, providing she could read. Working-class women could usually not afford middle-class women's journals, but clinics, welfare workers, and industrialists did provide free books and pamphlets on every aspect of housekeeping. For example, the big metallurgical firms in Germany gave away 200,000 copies of *Household Happiness. Complete Information on the Rules of Housekeeping for Workers' Wives*, which included "Directions for Cooking." From the 1880s on, the Suchard chocolate factory in Switzerland handed out a version of this book to its workers' families. It contained household instructions, recipes to suit the worker's budget, and hints on interior decoration with flowers and pictures as well as moral precepts and the principles of child care. Industrialists' wives sometimes set up schools and courses on domestic skills for female workers or workers' wives. Individuals also started schools to teach domestic skills to future generations of mothers, the modern ways their own mothers lacked. In Germany, Lina Morgenstern (1830–1909) instituted an array of such schools to foster more up-to-date housewifery and more accomplished motherhood.

The raising of domestic standards took place at the same time as the end of child labor. Having lost their children's wages, mothers now had to clothe them to meet a national standard. Children in Germany, for example, were sent home from school if their clothing was not up to regulation. A mother also lost childrens' labor around the house when they went to school; she had then to haul more water, provide better clothing, and improve general clean-liness through her own efforts alone. At the same time, she herself was always out-of-date in relation to the next generation, her own children. Reformers, of course, never meant this to occur; they aimed at improving working-class health and living conditions. However, working women were expected to meet official standards on a small income, and the results were measured by school-teachers, public health nurses, and bureaucrats.

An interlocking system of assistance and scrutiny focused on working-class women. The interest in disseminating household knowledge generated a need for an inside view of working-class women's lives. Pinpointing what working women did not know demanded constant observation of them and compilation of the knowledge thus gathered. By the early twentieth century, most countries had teams of investigators operating from governmental of-fices, social science associations, reform groups, and the academic world. Such investigators studied factory women in Munich, needleworkers in France, and homemakers and their budgetary strategies in England. Hundreds of books and pamphlets about working-class women were published. These publica-tions were not intended to be read by the workers but to inform the upper classes about what the workers were like. They created a portrait of the work-ing woman, often using her own words but just as often presenting her words and behavior as interpreted by reformers and social scientists. It also became fashionable for middle-class reformers to pose as or imitate working people. In Berlin in the 1890s, for example, Minna Wettstein-Adelt (b. 1869) com-posed her *3½ Months as a Factory Worker*; in London, Mary Higgs (1854–1937) pretended to be a vagrant.

The gatherers of social data encouraged working women's participation in the creation of the data and even encouraged the production of worker auto-biographies. Along with many lesser-known working women, union leaders Adelheid Popp of Austria and Jeanne Marie Bouvier of France wrote their memoirs long before their careers were over. In England, the Women's Coop-erative Guild Collective produced a volume entitled *Maternity: Letters from Working Women* (1915), which described their experiences in childbirth, sex-ual relations, and housekeeping. The encouragement to publish and the vig-orous response that followed were new developments. Working-class women had spoken out before, but had never been published in such volume. Also noteworthy were the semi-official nature of some publications, their interac-tion with the needs of social science, and the self-creative aspect inherent in the autobiographical mode.

Middle-class women constituted a good portion of the reformers, and they had their own motives in this enterprise. As charity grew less and less fashion-able, they turned from philanthrophy to social welfare. In the place of the moral vision of charity, there developed an interventionist view that govern-mental agencies could use the findings of social science to reshape society. Lib-eral theory could accommodate this role for government; thinkers such as Jer-emy Bentham had postulated that public servants could calculate the good or bad effects of laws and thus legislate so as to achieve the good ones. The grow-

Poor Mothers' Writing

Politicians and government officials fixed their attention on working women and poor mothers at the end of the nineteenth century. At the same time, social investigators encouraged them to speak about their condition as a way of bringing about reform. Such an undertaking—speaking out and writing—coincided with working women's own organizing efforts. In order to bring about legislation that would benefit women during pregnancy and after, the members of the Women's Cooperative Guild in England were asked to write about their life experiences. Published in 1915, the letters told of relentless hardship in the years before World War I, but, as in the following example, entitled "Almost a Wreck," they also showed a determination to survive.

I was married at the age of twenty-two (barely twenty-two years), and by the time I had reached my thirty-second birthday was the mother of seven children, and I am sure you will pardon me if I take the credit for bringing up such a family without the loss of even one, seeing that it entailed such a great amount of suffering to myself on account of having to nurse them through all illness, and in addition (after sitting up many nights in succession) being compelled to do all household duties.

During pregnancy I suffered much. When at the end of ten years I was almost a mental and physical wreck, I determined that this state of things should not go on any longer, and if there was no natural means of prevention, then, of course, artificial means must be employed, which were successful, and am happy to say that from that time I have been able to take pretty good care of myself, but often shudder to think what might have been the result if things had been allowed to go on as they were. Two days after childbirth I invariably sat up in bed knitting stockings and doing general repairs for my family. My husband at that time was earning 30s. per week, and out of that amount claimed 6s. 6d.* as pocket-money, and when I tell you that through all my difficulties there were no debts contracted on my part, you will be able to form some idea of what women are, in some cases, called upon to endure.

*s. is an abbreviation for shilling and d. for penny.
Source: Maternity: Letters from Working-Women Collected by the Women's Co-operative Guild (London: G. Bell and Sons, 1915), 60–61.

ing popularity of positivism, whose aim was to study society in order to discover "positive" social laws, fostered the organization of social science societies. These societies offered their findings to appropriate branches of the government or to reformers to be used to develop further legislation or activity. Middle-class women formed the backbone of many such organizations or fact-finding agencies; indeed, they were often founding members. Pioneers such as Marie Bernays (b. 1883) in Germany, Beatrice Webb (1858–1943) and Maud Pember Reeves (b. 1865) in England, and Caroline Milhaud in France called themselves feminists, socialists, or scientists; in so doing, they made new claims for the importance of what women did. Such middle-class women believed that the understanding that would arise from applying modern social science would eliminate class conflict by serving as a social glue and a social corrective at the same time. In other words, the process of getting working women to explain their lives as precisely as possible yielded information, but it also caused those women to recognize their dilemma and to seek scientific solutions. Such beliefs motivated these new social activists, who also thought their beliefs had universal applicability. Endorsed with varying degrees of self-consciousness, these beliefs motivated middle-class women in a variety of endeavors to make new connections with the working class and to repair the separation that had developed among women of different classes.

Certain older inspirations, such as a feeling that gender brought unity of experience, grew in importance. A pro-woman attitude characterized increasing numbers of groups aimed at reform. Some of these groups appeared anti-scientific and antistatist. The most notorious centered on the campaign in England to repeal the Contagious Diseases Acts.* Led by Josephine Butler, the Ladies National Association was formed by women who had been excluded from men's groups that favored repeal. The view of Butler and her associates was that the acts discriminated against women and that they converted men's immorality into public policy. Men's groups took shape from older, moralizing rescue efforts, whereas Butler's group drew on nationwide support from feminist organizations. Maintained for almost two decades, the campaign soon made it clear to those women involved that not only were men implicated in the spread of syphilis, but that economics, not immorality, was the basis of prostitution. Though encounters with prostitutes were sexual for men, for women they were means to make money. It was this insight into prostitutes' lives that separated these particular middle-class reformers from those who only moralized about women's sexuality. Challenging glib definitions of whorish behavior, Butler saw sexual mores of the working class as complex and "so gradually and imperceptibly shaded off, that . . . it would be impossible to affix a distinct name."[16] Moreover, this insight transformed the views of these middle-class women and gave substance to their social vision. They saw that social

---

*See Chapter 6.

These pictures of the forbidden life—that of prostitutes—constitute a kind of secret viewing. Their interior surroundings almost imitate those of the home, as do certain articles of clothing, such as the huge hat, which seem almost those of "respectable" women.

evils such as prostitution should be blamed on male-dominated society, and this recognition fortified them in the face of intense social stigma. Butler and her associates came to be called "shrieking sisters," because they spoke out boldly, breaking stereotypes that women should not speak about sex. They shocked polite society by calling ruling-class men immoral, whereas prostitutes were moral in their efforts to support their children. Promoted in speeches, tracts, and newspaper articles throughout the country, the repeal campaign eventually (by 1886) succeeded and meanwhile forged temporary cross-class alliances.

By the 1890s, Butler's position on prostitution had inspired women in almost every European country. As it had in England, the issue divided reformers and feminists and challenged the working of public welfare systems. By this time, women interpreted prostitution in two different ways. First, Butler and her followers saw its economic origins and were willing to leave the issue of women's sexuality to themselves. They favored individual self-regulation combined with an awareness of class differences in such matters. Conversely, welfare programs of the day were designed to reshape working-class sexuality. Claiming to be creating healthier families through new educational programs and the like, social workers and officials were also aiming at changing lower-class patterns of sociability by engaging young women and men in activities that would keep them constantly occupied. Interventionism was in the air, not only to improve economic or physical well-being, but to change sexual behavior.

Challenges to Butler's leadership and programs materialized quickly. Some middle-class women and men opposed the Contagious Diseases Acts because they were not strict enough: they did not affect everyone and failed to create tough, uniform sexual monitoring. Other middle-class people worked toward reforming prostitutes' morals, not their economic situation. Across the Continent, the issue of the regulation of prostitution created divisions along these same lines. For example, in Germany, where the sexual avant-garde was prominent,* women were nonetheless conservative in their reform efforts. Some of the first initiatives sponsored by Hanna Bieber-Böhm, who founded the Association for the Protection of Young Persons in 1889, called for deporting foreign prostitutes, incarcerating all others, and abolishing brothels. Josephine Butler's viewpoint, however, ultimately caught on with other prominent German feminists, including Anita Augspurg (1857–1943), Minna Cauer (1841–1922), Käthe Schirmacher (1865–1930), and Marie Stritt (1856–1928). Some of them decided to force the issue in Hamburg, a city that both allowed women's political activity and had a heavily regulated system of prostitution. Led by Lida Gustava Heymann (1867–1943), the campaign involved suits against brothel owners, public discussions of sexuality, and a formulation of the prostitution issue in terms of women's rights. As in every other campaign about prostitution, gender-related battle lines were drawn, as male control over female sexuality was questioned. Although meetings of the Hamburg group were banned, its members fined, and their efforts ultimately unsuccessful, their campaign represented the first time middle-class German women's political activity moved into a radical terrain investigating sexual order.

Thus, although the intersection of middle-class and working-class women was intended to foster conformity, it sometimes had the opposite effect. Women who worked against the regulation of prostitution connected gender and class in ways that were highly disruptive. Middle-class women strengthened such a connection by starting new types of institutions, neither correctional nor reformist in intention. In France, for example, late in the nineteenth century, middle-class women with charitable intentions overcame their preoccupations with the legitimacy of children or whether women had been legally and religiously wed and began to help prostitutes and unwed mothers economically instead of just lecturing them on morality. Although a Parisian charity organization had been established in the 1830s to help prostitutes, such soci-

---

*See Chapter 8.

eties were very uncommon in the early nineteenth century. Organizations offering assistance without moral strings developed rapidly at the turn of the century across the Continent. In Italy, the Mariuccia Asylum founded by Milanese women brought under its protection young prostitutes, children resulting from incest or rape, and those who had been sexually abused. Like other similarly minded reformers, the Mariuccia founders and administrators raised questions of sensuality and pleasure, economics and socialism, and the relation of religion to all of these. Despite such questioning by some reformers, many in the working classes, especially skilled workers and artisans, had adopted middle-class attitudes spread by other reformers and government institutions. One German woman remembered that, despite her socialist father's contempt for the middle class and its morality, he chased her from the house when she announced her pregnancy out of wedlock. However, the alliances between classes, wherever they arose and however temporary, over the right to sexual expression proved mutually illuminating in a society that for the time being sought to restrict women through restricting such expression.

Moving into the Service Sector

For the most part, such cross-class connections increasingly occurred through state-sponsored agencies. As education, health, and supervision of the family became bureaucratized, women took advantage of the opportunities offered by professionalization of these fields to move into the workforce. Service work, however, encompassed a wide range of jobs, not merely those directed by the government. Businesses also started depending on non-industrial, "white-collar" workers. So did banks, telephone companies, and private or public libraries. The first place women appeared, however, was the classroom: public schools had become more widespread because of society's need for a more literate and more disciplined workforce in the technological age. After 1870, almost every European country passed legislation mandating universal primary education. As long as education had been available only to upper-class children, teaching had been considered a masculine profession. Early in the century the governess made the first inroads into this profession, as well as widening the education of a new and growing bourgeoisie. Later, society became convinced of women's suitability for educating the young of the working class. In some countries, women came to outnumber men in primary education: in England, they constituted 75 percent of elementary school teachers by 1914, whereas in France female teachers outnumbered male teachers in 1909. In 1900, 60 percent of Swedish public school teachers were women. In Germany, where women constituted almost 20 percent of elementary teachers at the turn of the century, their mere presence was a sign of change. Male teachers resisted these inroads, for women teachers represented a significant challenge to their position. Not only did women drive down salaries, their presence threatened to undermine the men's efforts to get teaching recognized as a profession and get it more social power. However, men would continue to control secondary school teaching, even though they had been outnumbered on the elementary front.

Teaching had complex overtones and consequences for women. First, teachers were expected to be inculcators of a new discipline in the working class. At the same time, they served as mother surrogates, perhaps simultaneously calling attention to the inadequacies of working-class mothers. The woman teacher was more often than not unmarried, thereby implicitly demonstrating the desirability of sexual restraint to her pupils. Many countries enforced this by not allowing married women in classrooms and by forcing those who did marry to resign. Teaching also connected women with knowledge, although the lesser amount of knowledge needed to teach in elementary schools made the connection almost symbolic.

Suddenly many women acquired a sense of profession and a new role as the demand for teachers mushroomed. Teaching brought many of them into the workforce for the first time. This new profession had its own ambiguities, however. Although it demanded some knowledge and offered clean, safe working conditions, teaching paid women less than men, as did most jobs. In England, in particular, the majority of the first wave of women teachers were drawn from the working class. They experienced upward mobility through their new profession. The social origins of teachers would gradually become more lower-middle-class throughout Europe. Many middle-class women also saw opportunities in the field. When secondary teaching opened up to women, it offered even greater opportunity for prestige and expert work. Thus, while serving in elementary schools for the most part, many women teachers throughout Europe had their sights set on secondary schools and universities. With men monopolizing most of the academic subjects in advanced education and with women relegated to teaching such subjects as needlework in secondary schools, much room for improvement existed.

Women teachers began to demand a variety of improvements. They sought the opportunity to improve their skills as well as better training for the next generation of teachers. They also sought to eliminate salary differences between men and women teachers, limitations on the subject matter studied and taught, and inequality in numbers of women in secondary teaching and in administrative positions. In the process of making these demands, women teachers developed powerful and often feminist professional organizations. Helene Lange (1848–1930) founded the General German Women's Teachers' Association in 1890, one of the most forceful groups making such claims. All women teachers represented a new brand of women, who intervened in workers' lives, who devoted only a portion of their own lives to domesticity by entering the working world, and who became political in order to improve their working lives.

By the early twentieth century, teaching had attracted thousands of European women—both those from the upper working class who sought upward mobility and those from the lower-middle class who needed to support themselves. Yet this semiprofessional job was only one of a cluster of new jobs that opened up for women at this time. One official in northeast Scotland complained: "Our girls about the country are all getting an education and finding their ways into shops as cashiers, and bookkeepers, and into business."[17] Between 1870 and 1914, government bureaucracies throughout Europe grew by as much as half. Many of the new clerks, inspectors, postal workers, typists, and other office workers were women. In addition, the managerial functions of modern industrial production required teams of managers and large supporting staffs who replaced the traditional single owner-manager. Secretaries, typists, stenographers, bookkeepers, and file clerks—increasingly women— were hired to staff offices in manufacturing firms. Banks, insurance companies, and other commercial enterprises had to develop, disseminate, and store more information than ever, and thus needed more service personnel. Stores and shops also became larger and more numerous to accommodate an increase in the production of consumer goods. Young, unmarried, and attractive women were hired as salesclerks or shop assistants. Often they worked longer hours, up to twelve or fourteen hours a day, than their factory counterparts without any place to sit—sitting, in fact, was initially forbidden. Salesclerks often had to live in company-owned accommodations and follow a strict set of rules that governed their behavior even when not on the job. Yet for many women such work was more attractive than more highly paid industrial jobs or onerous farm work. The working environment was clean, and social interaction was possible. Salesclerks dealt with consumer, not industrial, goods. Finally, nursing had also become a major career for women. Like teaching, it had its ambiguities, seeming desirable in terms of status and attractiveness and drawing from several socioeconomic groups, but having such decisive disadvantages as low pay.

Although the opening of these jobs to women constituted a real revolution in women's work, the nature of the jobs changed in ways invisible to those who first entered them. Most of these positions appeared at first to have high status, and many had in fact been filled by men. Secretaries, for example, had formerly been young well-educated males, serving a kind of apprenticeship in leadership. The first women secretaries and typists were also well-educated, or at least fairly literate, but they were given no opportunity to move into higher positions. Once women took the job, it ceased being an apprenticeship. The same was true for sales positions, which men had entered in order to learn about commerce before embarking on their own ventures. The position of salesclerk became a dead-end job for women, although sometimes they did become fairly powerful heads of departments or buyers for large stores. In general, however, sales jobs had a certain impermanency because of employers' emphasis on youth and beauty. As department stores developed, women hired to do sales had to be youthful and as enticing as the goods they sold. After the first generation of literate, educated women, employers stopped seeking experienced women for some of these jobs and instead demanded more pliable girls.

In sum, as soon as women entered a field, it seemed that both the status and the salary declined. In fact, women factory workers at this time often earned more than shop assistants, and many women who might have wanted the more attractive sales jobs realized they could not earn enough at them to support themselves and their families. In addition, a division of labor was usu-

New office workers. Even by the early twentieth century, typists are arranged in regular lines that allow for regular observation and direction.

ally established as soon as women appeared in jobs. Men became floor managers while women remained clerks; in government agencies such as the post office, women earned less than men doing the same work and were often assigned to the most isolated rural postal stations where no possibility of advancement existed. There were exceptions: Mathilda Fibiger (1830–1872) became head of the Danish national telegraph service, for instance. For the most part, however, women's white-collar work had definite disadvantages in conditions and pay. To improve matters, schoolteachers often unionized; so did postal workers and office workers in some countries. Health practitioners were slower to take this step, although Swedish nurses had unions by 1910. But for many women in white-collar jobs, the sense of being a non–factory worker, of being close to management and even sharing the interest of owners, prevented them from seeing that, despite their centrality to the entire managerial process, they were often being exploited more than machinists in terms of hours and pay. For the time being, they took satisfaction in having employment that utilized their skills, paid some salary, and provided a sense of social worth.

Varieties of Political Action

Working women's lives were multifaceted and full, incorporating a broad cast of characters and a wide array of complex activity. It is not surprising then that working women's politics were correspondingly varied. Urban male politics developed in male-dominated spaces—the factory, workshop, and tavern. For women, political consciousness could develop in the industrial or commercial workplace, but other spaces were also important. The common sidewalks, stoops, and streets of the neighborhood, the cafés and pubs, the tenements—all of these were meeting places in which solidarity of interests developed. In addition, opinions or discontent would be passed along kin networks or gossip channels. Traditional evening work sessions, laundering in public areas, hauling water, and attending markets provided other occasions for fostering solidarity.

Unions also developed. Though the majority of working-class women were not involved in unions, hundreds of thousands of activists were unionizing by the beginning of the twentieth century. In Germany, in 1910, there were over a quarter of a million women union members; in France, a year later, more than a hundred thousand women were members. In 1913, over 430,000 women belonged to unions in England; whereas in Italy, where unionization was less prevalent and where industrialization was uneven, 45,000 or less than 1 percent of women workers were unionized. Forms of unionization varied, with socialist unions most popular on the Continent and, in some cases, more popular among women than among men. In Germany, for example, a greater percentage of women than men chose socialist and religious unions, whereas a greater percentage of men chose independent unions, ones without an explicit political goal other than workers' solidarity. In the Habsburg empire, close to 30,000 women belonged to socialist organizations in 1914. Finally, among the many types of unions available were exclusively women's unions, mixed-gender ones, or leagues, such as the Women's Trade Union League in Great Britain, that involved collaboration between middle-class and working-class to protect women's economic position.

Trade unionism flourished at the end of the nineteenth century. By that time, industrialists had generally amassed such economic and political power that they were able to determine a good deal of public policy. Oddly enough, workers' organizations helped structure the workforce, and the most forward-looking industrialists could see their beneficial nature. As governments slowly removed restrictions on worker organizations, the old "friendly societies" and mutual benefit and insurance groups turned into unions. These new organizations were created by workers seeking to maintain some influence on the work process, its conditions, hours, and wages. Instead of trying to squeeze a penny or two out of wages to put into a community emergency fund, workers began to demand such benefits from employers. Workers' attitudes toward employers altered; they began to see them as people who were taking far more than they returned in the form of wages.

Women workers shared the grievances of men and added others of their own. Attending her first meeting of the Association of Working Women in Berlin, Emma Ihrer noted that the most important debates centered on the yarn tax and prices. The Women's Protective and Provident League (WPPL), formed in the 1870s in England, fought for equal pay and equal access to jobs. Simultaneously, middle-class English women sponsored Women's Industrial Councils intended to teach working women their rights under protective labor legislation. Whatever women demanded or aspired to through unions, however, proved to be controversial, even among women themselves. Unions never attracted a majority of women workers prior to World War I, with union membership staying somewhere under 10 percent of each national workforce. In some industries, particularly those like textiles, that were dominated by women, they constituted anywhere from 40 to 60 percent of union membership. These union members did better economically than nonmembers in the same industries. Yet, despite this fact, most shunned union membership.

Several factors contributed to this lack of participation in organizations that might have improved their lives. First, the precariousness of their economic situation prevented them from being able to pay union dues. Usually earning half or less of what men earned, women could barely support themselves, let alone pay fees that were based on male wage scales. Second, all women had domestic responsibilities, and some had to work several jobs just to make ends meet. They had no time for union activity. Moreover, women's working lives had an irregular pattern compared to men's, many worked outside of factories, and many women workers were young. All of these factors contributed to making them uninterested in organizations geared to those who had sustained engagement in regular factory work. Third, many working men had little use for women in unions or even in the workforce. These men may have pressured their wives and daughters to stay out of unions.

Even when admitting women to membership, men's unions drew up such regulations as this one from a French textile union in Roubaix: "Women may address observations on propositions to the union only in writing and by the intermediation of two male members."[18] It was understandable that male workers would be antagonistic to women and see them as those who pulled down wages, who took men's jobs in hard times, who could be supported by someone else. Their antagonism led union men to invoke domestic ideology. They fought for a substantial or "family" wage for the breadwinner so that women would stay out of the labor market. Like bourgeois men, workers relished the comforts and status a wife at home could bring them. They built their sense of self on precisely this sense of difference.

Some labor organizers recognized that the discriminatory position of working women was always a threat to men; they made common cause for all workers across gender bounds. But the typical union position around the turn of the century was that women should not be working; a pro-woman stance in union policy would, it was felt, only encourage their competitive entry into the workforce. The constitution (1872) of the cigar makers union in Copenhagen made this opposition official: "Any cigar maker who teaches a woman, apart from his wife, how to roll a cigar cannot be a member."[19] Organized male labor also called women's work in factories a disaster. Union after union proposed legislation to prevent women from entering particular trades: two examples from Britain are the chain and nail trades in 1872, and the Amalgamated Brassworkers in 1908. Men wanted women out of the workforce for the obvious reasons that employers used women to cut wages and thereby to increase their profits. In addition, a wife working in public to a male worker was a sign of his degradation. A working man should be able to support his wife and family—as the middle-class man did. Some men supported legislation for equal pay on the grounds that women would then no longer be hired.

In sum, unions' activity and approaches were based on models of the male worker and on his desires and fears as well. Few took into account the complex lives of women. Even unions that were not hostile to women failed to consider that the intermeshing of women's work and domestic lives created a different pattern than that of men's work, with different problems. As a result, unions were not able to attract the majority of working women.

Thus, women's experience with unions mirrored the general situation between men and women in the entire social order. In unions, however, there were some notable examples of cross-gender solidarity. Unions were perhaps the only public organizations other than the church that had women from the lower classes as members. Unlike the church, unions even allowed women to hold leadership positions, though never as many as their numbers entitled them to. Women's leadership first developed in a strong way within female unions. In England, for example, clerk's assistant and former bookbinder's apprentice Emma Smith Paterson (1848–1886) founded the WPPL, which encouraged the development of women's unions. This group evolved during the next fifty years into the Women's Trade Union League, which had branches and rivals that sprang from within its own ranks. Later its most prominent leader was the aristocratic Lady Emilia Dilke (1840–1904), a believer in both positivism and good works. At the turn of the century, women's unionism in England began to be more working-class with the appearance of leaders such as Margaret Bondfield (1873–1953), a shop clerk, although Mary MacArthur (1880–1921), her father's shop assistant and an effective strike leader, was actually recruited from the middle class. In the industrial north of England, Selina Cooper (1864–1946) and Ada Nield Chew (1870–1945) became vigorous orators among textile workers, and had a great deal of support from the active union women there. In Germany, where unions were especially vigorous, Luise Zietz (1865–1922), Helene Grunberg (1874–1928), and Gertrud Hanna (1876–1944) rose to leadership out of the ranks of labor. Before finding union activity, these women saw their lives as debilitating. "Life's bitter needs, overwork, and bourgeois family morality [though she worked as a seamstress] had destroyed all joy in me," wrote Ottilie Baader (1847–1925), a leading German labor activist.[20] A daughter of miners who became a leading Spanish Communist, Dolores Ibarruri (b. 1895) lived miserably in rural poverty until, as a young mother, she read Marx. An organizer from then on, she found that politics "was a window opening on life."[21] For all the frustrations and problems of union work, many women found satisfaction in lives devoted to worker organizations.

The *belle époque* was an age of union building and also of labor action, particularly in the form of strikes. Unionization and strikes aimed at pulling industries out of that primitive stage where a good many laborers were prematurely destroyed by the inhuman hours and poor remuneration. The London matchgirls' strike in 1888 constitutes one of the best examples of how such activity aimed at humanizing the industrial process. Among the mass of unskilled women laborers, matchworkers in the Bryant and May factory were highly exploited. Like many other workers in industry, they endured a fining system that took a good part of their wages. Workers in general complained that they could lose a whole day's wages in fines assessed for being even a minute or two late, for making a mistake (after twelve or more hours of work), for having any debris around the work area, for talking or laughing, and so on. The amounts of fines depended on the whim of management or owners, as did the definitions of infractions and the enforcement. The particular situation at Bryant and May Company came to the attention of reformers, in particular, Annie Besant. Besant had led crusades against child prostitution and other social inequities. She went to the factory and easily roused the girls to strike for an end to fines and higher wages. One thing that provoked the matchgirls to strike, they themselves said, was their fury at having to contribute from their meager wages to the building of a statue of Liberal Prime Minister William Gladstone. Some seven hundred joined the strike, and the public and the press took their side. Fines and low wages, it was announced widely, made possible a more than 22 percent return on investment for stockholders. Moreover, the bad working conditions—women quickly ate their lunches amidst the phosphorus—led to a deterioration of the workers' facial bone structure, a condition called "phossy jaw." Rather quickly the matchgirls won higher wages, an end to the abuses of the fining system, and a union of their own. Many people saw in this one strike the beginning of a new kind of unionism involving unskilled workers who had previously had no chance of winning much.

There were many strikes by women across Europe, and there were other protests more difficult to describe because of their complexity. Only protests and strikes centering on working conditions in factories have been defined as constituting labor action. Yet men's union activities concerned more than just work; their demands also involved ideas about gender and about women's role in the workplace. Women's protests often incorporated all ingredients of their universe. For example, in Catholic countries religiously based unions often vied with other types for women's allegiance. In Italy, at the turn of the century the majority of working women belonged to Catholic unions, and for several decades secular ones seemed to spend less effort on reforms than on trying to win women away from the Catholic unions by name-calling. When women protested in Catholic countries, their rhetoric was influenced by religious debates and the pervasiveness of religion in the society. In the 1890s, Sicilian peasants protesting their general misery carried signs saying "Jesus was a true socialist . . . but the priests do not represent him well."[22] However, in the 1901–1906 strikes of rice weeders in the Po Valley of Italy, women made no allusion to religion when they demanded an eight-hour day in their very arduous job:[23]

If eight hours seem few to you
Try working
And you'll see the difference
Between work and giving orders.

These workers wanted a shorter day to escape from the malarial conditions in the fields and to have more time for their children and household responsibilities. In Russia in 1893, women weavers virtually destroyed a plant in the Riazan province because of sexual harassment of women workers, and earlier in the 1880s weavers in Narva had struck for the right to nurse their babies for longer amounts of time at breaks during the workday.

Not all protests were by unions or workers. In some cases, housewives exploded into violence using a combination of domestic language and union gestures. For example, across France in 1910 and 1911, waves of housewives protested the high price of commodities, especially butter, milk, and eggs. Destroying goods at markets or confiscating them to sell at lower prices, they developed a solidarity of purpose that led them to compose songs and slogans. One of their songs concerned the price of butter:[24]

Tomorrow in the market of every big city
All the women will gather
To protest strongly
The price of butter now.
We've had enough suffering
Without this increase in the price of butter and milk.
Tomorrow all the women of France,
Will sell it at a discount.

A year earlier, union leaders had tried to organize similar protests without much success. Then, however, conditions had not affected women's lives enough to lead to action. This time, at the end of summer when harvests began coming in, women expected price reductions or stabilization, not increases. Their family budgets depended on such expectations being realized; there was no extra money to cover price increases. This had a very real effect on women's ability to get food for their families and provoked them to act. Though the unions were caught by surprise, they quickly recouped and organized many of the women into consumers' leagues or took them into the unions.

Thus, protest activity as a public expression of dissatisfaction with conditions arose not only when union leaders directed it. Women formed crowds when their communities were threatened by eviction officers forcing people from their homes or by school officials trying to find truant children. Knowing how much children were needed in home production, neighbors banded together to protect the many aspects of household life necessary to survival. They lied to factory inspectors and almost anyone else who threatened their neighbors' livelihood. But the high cost of living was often the core of protest and could unite factory women and housewives into huge bands that were unpredictable because they were outside the usual labor controls. In Barcelona in 1913, housewives supported Catalan women textile workers. During the summer months, crowds of them marched daily on their own route—not necessarily the traditional union one—to make public officials aware of the condition of working women and their families. Whereas people whose consciousness was centered on trade unionism might petition owners of factories or organize strikes against them, women directed general protests toward those responsible—as they themselves were—for social welfare that ranged beyond economic issues alone. "Everyday life," in the words of one historian "became a political process."[25] Thus, the politicization of women was as varied as everyday life itself.

Socialism and the Woman Question

Trade union activity and protest movements occurred in the midst of new and old ideas about the nature of work and society and about improvements in both these areas. Anarchists sought a society free from the rule of law and governmental structures, while the Catholic church struggled to strengthen working class faith and religious practice. Social Darwinists adhered to ideas of "survival of the fittest" when they preached rational mating and started programs for bodily improvement. These were but a few of the many ideological systems in competition for preeminence among workers during the *belle époque*. From the many ideologies of the period, Marxism grew in popularity and came to offer a powerful challenge to liberalism and the tenets of capitalism. From the 1880s on, the works of German Karl Marx (1818–1883), affected worker politics and union debate. Marxism, socialism, or communism—the names were used interchangeably at that time—attracted workers, reformers, and women. Whereas liberalism posited economic harmony, Marxism envisioned conflict. Instead of liberalism's autonomous individual, Marxism identified classes with class interests. Instead of steady progress, Marxism postulated "dialectical" movement involving assertions of class interests that would be negated by other interests, leading to resolutions and then another beginning of the process. Marxism did agree with liberal ideology as to the nature of human life. For Marx, as for Locke and others, human beings developed their identity from the need to support themselves. Natural needs and wants shaped individual and social life. Rather than enabling goods and services to be exchanged harmoniously, however, social systems arose with a single group dominating the way in which economic production was carried on. The other groups or classes submitted, though influencing and engaging in this process. The way in which economic production was carried on was called the "mode of production" by Marx; the tools, land, and other equipment for production were called the "means of production." Those controlling the means of production constituted the ruling class—in the past they had been slaveowners or feudal lords, whereas in industrial times they were the bourgeoisie, that is, the industrialists, merchants, and financiers. Contesting the ruling class were first slaves or serfs, and then modern factory workers, or the proletariat.

The clash of forces during slave uprisings, peasant revolts, or revolutions was how history moved toward a final moment. Marx thought this final moment would arrive when the proletariat unseated the bourgeoisie. Then, the system of private property and bourgeois control of the means of production would end. The working class as a whole would assume command of the forces of production. Individual would no longer exploit individual; class would no longer exploit class. Ending the system of private property would end the system of exploited labor that had previously existed. For Marx and for Marxists, socialism would bring the triumph of social justice.

Socialists addressed the condition of women in two major books, *Woman and Socialism* (1879) by German socialist August Bebel and *Origins of the Family, Private Property and the State* (1884) by Marx's collaborator, Friedrich Engels. These works came as a revelation to working-class women, for both addressed their working lives and personal lives. Bebel and Engels saw women's oppression as rooted in the system of private property. Before private property had existed, mothers had had power in communal society as the bearers of life. Once private property came into being, men subjugated women because women's fidelity was necessary to ensure that property could be legitimately transmitted from father to son. In a blow, the argument went, all the power in women's reproductivity was made to serve the sanctity of property. Bebel's work presented figures on the condition of women in the nineteenth century. Moving from theoretical to practical problems, he demonstrated women's inferior position in almost every aspect of life. He saw women as doubly oppressed—first as workers and second as women. The working woman was to her husband, he said, as the proletarian man was to the capitalist.

Mainstream socialists, however, ignored Bebel's attention to gender questions *per se*. They believed the solution to the poor condition of women was nothing more nor less than socialist revolution. They saw oppression as being rooted only in the system of private property; women had but to collaborate in its overthrow. Though important, questions of gender were merely by-products of the mode of production. Socialist theory offered hope to women as well as men. From the 1880s on, women organized, theorized, and proselytized on socialism's behalf, because it alone spoke, however minimally, to both work and gender experience and promised better things to come.

Socialists took notice of women and set out to organize them. As in unions, women tended to take charge of this task once an initial group had taken shape. That is, they took over the recruitment and educational activities aimed at other women because they believed that gender difference played an important role even in class analysis. This belief always provoked conflict, but women also undertook this job because men were often less than enthusiastic about doing it. Women's commitment to such recruiting was an affirmation of their labor. Only the woman worker, most believed, could fully understand the class struggle and be capable of revolutionary action. Work put women truly into the proletarian situation, made them real members of the working class. To increase female membership in socialist groups, these women scoured their countries on organizing tours, gave lectures, proselytized at factories, did extensive journalistic work, investigated the conditions of women's work and home life, and created innumerable women's enclaves within socialist parties. One such organizer was Eleanor Marx, daughter of Karl Marx, who supported herself by taking in typing, doing research and writing for others, and translating. She organized workers, particularly women, and during strikes would travel to the area of the strike, often several times a day, to give speeches. As a result of similar, though paid, organizing efforts, by the outbreak of World War I about 175,000 German women were affiliated with the Social Democratic Party (SPD)—by far the most successful of the national efforts. In no other country did women's response to socialism match German women's enthusiasm, but everywhere there were thousands who gave it vigorous support.

The German party's vigor was largely due to the resourcefulness of a committed leadership. The inspiration provided by Bebel's book drew in women like Ottilie Baader, a seamstress who led one of the party sections in Berlin and who served on the national SPD executive board for years. Her vigorous comrade in arms in many struggles was Clara Zetkin (1857–1933). A brilliant theorist and writer, Zetkin directed the SPD women through the newspaper *Die Gleichheit* (*Equality*) for several decades. After Bebel, Zetkin became the major formulator of the party position on women and maintained at all times a radical commitment to preparing women for revolution. Constantly engaged in one struggle or another, Zetkin was particularly concerned with keeping working-class men and women in the same movement by preventing any alliances of working-class women with middle-class feminists. Although *Die Gleichheit* ran stories and passed information that appeared feminist and that at times seemed removed from classic socialist issues, the paper's reports on "feminist" meetings were filled with vitriol and ridicule. Zetkin and Baader were violently opposed to the aristocratic Lily Braun (1865–1916). An SPD member since the 1890s, Braun had wide-ranging rather than disciplined interests and broached questions that were jarring to more conventional socialist women leaders. Her consideration of scientific investigation, political alliances, and family reform all took Braun outside the confines of class theory into a theoretical realm potentially disruptive of the tenuous connections of women to the socialist party and of men to women in it. By the early twentieth century, Zetkin and Baader had triumphed over Braun only to find themselves superseded by moderates like Luise Zietz and Marie Juchacz (1879–1956).

A Socialist's Analysis

Clara Zetkin's paper *Die Gleichheit* had more than 100,000 subscribers in the early twentieth century. Zetkin was a powerful theoretician of women's place in socialism and a forceful advocate on their behalf. At meetings of the Second International—the assembly of socialists from around the world that met between 1889 and 1914—Zetkin harangued, educated, and led often reluctant men to support suffrage, equal wages for women, and the incorporation of women into socialism. In the following vivid passage she explains the need for men to understand the threat from wage inequities based on sex and the need for women to organize.

It is not just the women workers who suffer because of the miserable payment of their labor. The male workers, too, suffer because of it. As a consequence of their low wages, the women are transformed from mere competitors into unfair competitors who push down the wages of men. Cheap women's labor eliminates the work of men and if the men want to continue to earn their daily bread, they must put up with low wages. Thus women's work is not only a cheap form of labor, it also cheapens the work of men and for that reason it is doubly appreciated by the capitalist, who craves profits. The economic advantages of the industrial activity of proletarian women only aid the tiny minority of the sacrosanct guild of coupon clippers and extortionists of profit.

Given the fact that many thousands of female workers are active in industry, it is vital for the trade unions to incorporate them into their movement. In individual industries where female labor plays an important role, any movement advocating better wages, shorter working hours, etc., would be doomed from the start because of the attitude of those women workers who are not organized. Battles which began propitiously enough, ended up in failure because the employers were able to play off non-union female workers against those that are organized in unions. These non-union workers continued to work (or took up work) under any conditions, which transformed them from competitors in dirty work to scabs.

Certainly one of the reasons for these poor wages for women is the circumstance that female workers are practically unorganized. They lack the strength which comes with unity. They lack the courage, the feeling of power, the spirit of resistance, and the ability to resist which is produced by the strength of an organization in which the individual fights for everybody and everybody fights for the individual. Furthermore, they lack the enlightenment and the training which an organization provides.

Source: Excerpted from "Women's Work and the Trade Unions," in *Clara Zetkin. Selected Writings*, Philip S. Foner, ed. (New York: International Publishers, 1984), 54–56.

Struggles involving socialist women and their parties occurred throughout Europe. The specific issues were multiple, but they boiled down to a handful of major questions. In France, for example, men and women split over the relationship of women to the party. Should women have their own sections in which to discuss the unique problems of women workers as well as more general socialist theory? French leaders Louise Saumoneau (1875–1950), Elisabeth Renaud (1846–1932), Aline Valette, Madeleine Pelletier (1874–1939), and Hélène Brion struggled with the pros and cons of special sections within the party, sometimes reaching the point of not speaking to one another. In 1896, Austrian Adelheid Popp maintained that "women comrades have the right, where they find it necessary, to create free organizations next to the trade union organizations."[26] In Germany, this problem had not arisen at first because of laws prohibiting women from attending political meetings at all. So women's organizations were initially separate and were built around lectures and other purportedly nonpolitical activities. After repeal of that law in 1908, German women were absorbed into the Socialist party, much to the dismay of the radical leadership, who predicted subsequent weakening. In other countries, where governmental fiat did not provide an answer, the issue of women's role in the socialist party often dominated other matters.

Another problem was that socialist women, though allied closely with union women, often split with them over tactics. Should organizations collaborate with governments to get benefits such as higher wages, maternity benefits, insurance, and so on? Unions supported all measures that would provide amelioration of workers' lives, but socialists claimed that the price to be paid for such measures was a watering down of support for the eventual class struggle. Moreover, many of the goals of union women involved gender as well as class issues; they often looked like feminism rather than socialism.

Relationships with "bourgeois feminism" constituted a third problem for socialist women. For example, Zetkin despised the middle-class but radical *Frauenwohl* (Women's Welfare) group, which aimed at organizing working women and training them to agitate for improved working conditions. She believed that such middle-class activity drained off support for socialism and weakened solidarity with proletarian men. The "feminist" issue of suffrage also posed problems. Although various workers' parties in France and Germany had announced their support for women's suffrage, in Italy the socialist party refused to. Cofounder of the party, Anna Kuliscioff (1854–1925) supported the vote for women, though she believed that feminist parties only duplicated what middle-class men had been striving for since the democratic revolutions of the late eighteenth century. She also criticized "generic" legal reforms covering everyone "from the humble worker to the countess" for their failure to see women's distinct interests according to class.[27] Nonetheless, whereas her party opposed suffragism as bourgeois, she had to take a stand in its behalf and thus appear to substitute gender solidarity for party unity. In fact, there were hardly any socialist women—Rosa Luxemburg may be the exception— who did not discuss gender in ways that sounded feminist.

The final difficult problem for socialists involved the nature of the working-class family. Bebel had outlined women's relationship to men and noted that women faced double oppression. In her 1890 paper "The Monopoly of the Male," Anna Kuliscioff came right out and said that the working-class woman was oppressed by her husband. But when Lily Braun wrote in the early twentieth century about oppression in the individual household, Zetkin and others denounced her for dwelling on reformist matters and for calling into question the place where workers received their comfort. Braun's plans for socialized housework (and for many other kinds of cooperatives) sounded much like the ideas of radical feminists. All questions concerning the working-class family implicated the men with whom the women had to collaborate on class issues if the class struggle was to succeed. Questioning the working-class home ultimately amounted to questioning the backbone of socialism—the working-class male. Yet had not Engels gone so far as to say that the proletarian male was to his wife as the industrialist was to the worker? Such views divided the proletariat along gender lines and thus weakened the conceptual framework of socialism by saying that, within the working-class, solidarity did not exist because of men's treatment of women. One solution was to concentrate on economic issues by seeing the woman only as worker. The party would work for economic settlements and political skills to give women parity with men. Both Marxism itself and socialist leaders such as Zetkin repressed reproductive analysis. Concerning such issues as socialized household work, birth control, and sexuality, socialist leaders often upheld the Victorian synthesis. That is, Zetkin emphasized the socialist woman as "forward-stepping companion of her husband who will fulfill her task as a wife and mother," especially by "educating her children to Socialist principles."[28] Looking squarely at cultural roles seemed counterrevolutionary at the time. Despite this stance of the majority of socialists, some of them joined other radicals to agitate around gender-based issues. Although socialist parties shunned such agitation for strategic and tactical reasons, it was a sign that something new was happening to women.

A Complex Legacy

Socialism and trade unionism made their contribution toward generating new ideas about women. Socialists and trade unionists sought to increase the numbers of working women and to improve their condition. In this way, these activists affirmed work and challenged dominant ideas about women. Though professing support for contemporary standards of sexuality, reproduction, and domestic life, socialist women actually undermined them by restoring the positive value of work for women and by agitating to make the workplace more receptive to them. Some historians argue that socialists' affirmation of the workplace and the home at the same time only intensified women's oppression and compounded dilemmas that would resurface in the twentieth century. Others, however, argue that working-class ideas gave women choices for the first time and put them in a new situation. Something else was new: socialism posited equality and comradeship between the sexes in the workplace. Gone, at least in theory, was the sexual division of labor. Complementarity in the reproductive sphere was to be balanced by identity in the productive sphere. This theory—though theory it remained—validated the rich work experience of everyday life, and offered hope that in the future reality would become less cruel.

NOTES

1. Emma Ihrer, "Die proletarische Frau and die Berufstätigkeit," in Gisela Brinker-Gabler, ed., *Frauenarbeit und Beruf* (Frankfurt am Main: Fischer, 1979), 300.

2. Cited in Mary Nolan, *Social Democracy and Society: Working-Class Radicalism in Düsseldorf* (Cambridge, England: Cambridge University Press, 1981), 121–122.

3. Quoted in Alfred Kelly, ed., *The German Worker* (Berkeley: University of California Press, 1987), 259.

4. Jeanne Bouvier, *Mes mémoires* (Paris: Maspero, 1983), 97.

5. Mary E. Daly, "Women, Work, and Trade Unionism," in Margaret MacCurtain and Donncha O. Corràin, eds., *Women in Irish Society. The Historical Dimension* (Westport, Conn.: Greenwood, 1979), 71.

6. Quoted in Regina Schulte, "Peasants and Farmers' Maids. Female Farm Servants in Bavaria at the End of the Nineteenth Century," in Richard J. Evans and W. R. Lee, eds., *The German Peasantry* (New York: St. Martins, 1985), 158.

7. Flora Thompson, *Lark Rise to Candleford* (London: Oxford University Press, 1945 [1939]), 38.

8. Doris Viersbeck, *Erlebnisse eines Hamburger Dienstmädchens* (Munich: 1904), 56, quoted in Katharina Schlegel, "Mistress and Servant in Nineteenth Century Hamburg: Employer/Employee Relationships in Domestic Service, 1880–1914," *History Workshop Journal*, 15 (Spring 1983):67–68.

9. Paul and Michel Chabot, *Jean et Yvonne. Domestiques en 1900* (Paris: Pierre Belfond, 1980), 164.

10. Caroline Davidson, *A Woman's Work is Never Done. A History of Housework in the British Isles 1650–1950* (London: Chatto and Windus, 1982), 134.

11. E. A. Oliunina, quoted in Rose Glickman, *Russian Factory Women. Workplace and Society, 1880–1914* (Berkeley: University of California Press, 1984), 64–65.

12. M. B. Lavigne, quoted in Angus McLaren, *Sexuality and Social Order. The Debate over the Fertility of Women and Workers in France, 1770–1920* (New York: Holmes & Meier, 1983), 21.

13. Quoted in Ann-Sophia Ohlander, "Maternity Benefits and Population in Sweden, 1900–1945," unpublished paper (1986), 5.

14. Quoted in Angela V. John, *By the Sweat of Their Brow. Women Workers at Victorian Coal Mines* (London: Routledge and Kegan Paul, 1984), 226.

15. Quoted in Volker R. Berghahn, "On the Societal Functions of Wilhelmine Arma-

ments," in George Iggers, ed., *The Social History of Politics* (Leamington Spa, England: Berg, 1985), 178.

16. Quoted in Judith R. Walkowitz, *Prostitution and Victorian Society* (Cambridge: Cambridge University Press, 1980), 185.

17. Parliamentary Papers, 1896, cited in Ian Carter, *Farmlife in Northeast Scotland 1840–1914* (Edinburgh: John Donald, 1984), 95.

18. Cited in Patricia Hilden, *Working Women and Socialist Politics in France* (Oxford: Clarendon Press, 1986), 132.

19. Quoted in Inger Dübeck, "Female Trade Unions in Denmark," *Scandinavian Journal of History,* Vol. 5, No. 1 (1980):28.

20. Quoted in Jean H. Quataert, "Unequal Partners in an Uneasy Alliance: Women and the Working Class in Imperial Germany," in Marilyn J. Boxer and Jean H. Quataert, eds., *Socialist Women* (New York: Elsevier, 1978), 120.

21. Dolores Ibarruri, *They Shall Not Pass. The Autobiography of La Pasionaria,* (New York: International Publishers, 1966), 61.

22. Quoted in Lucia Chavola Birnbaum, *Liberazione della donna. Feminism in Italy* (Middletown: Wesleyan University Press, 1986), 13.

23. Elda Zappi, " 'If Eight Hours Seem Few to You . . .': Women Workers in Italian Rice Fields, 1901–1906," in Barbara J. Harris and JoAnn K. McNamara, eds., *Women and the Structure of Society* (Durham: Duke University Press, 1984), 211.

24. J. M. Flonneau, "La crise de vie chère, 1910–1914," *Le mouvement social,* 72 (1970):60–61.

25. Temma Kaplan, "Female Consciousness and Collective Action: The Case of Barcelona, 1910–1918, *Signs,* 7 (Spring, 1982):564.

26. Quoted in Thomas Hamer, "Beyond Feminism: The Women's Movement in Austrian Social Democracy," Ph.D. dissertation, The Ohio State University, 1973, 7–8.

27. Quoted in Franca Pieroni Bortolotti, *Socialisme e questione femminile in Italia 1892–1922* (Milan: Mazzotta, 1974), 74.

28. Clara Zetkin, "Only with Proletarian Women," in *Selected Writings,* Philip Foner, ed. (New York: International Publishers, 1984), 83.

SOURCES AND SUGGESTED READING

Bachrach, Susan. *Dames Employées. The Feminization of Postal Work in Nineteenth-Century France* (1984). A study of one branch of the service sector.

Bell, Rudolph M. *Fate and Honor, Family and Village. Demographic and Cultural Change in Rural Italy Since 1800* (1979).

Black, Clementina, ed. *Married Women's Work* (1915). A classic portrayal of the varieties of labor.

Bortolotti, Franca Pieroni. *Socialismo e questione femminile in Italia 1892–1922* (1974). Italian socialism and the woman question.

Bouvier, Jeanne. *Mes mémoires* (1983). An important memoir of a French childhood, of work life, and of union politics.

Boxer, Marilyn, and Jean Quataert. *Socialist Women: Socialist Feminism in the Nineteenth and Twentieth Century* (1978). Studies of major European socialists.

Clark, Linda. *Schooling the Daughters of Marianne* (1984). On the education of girls in France.

Franzoi, Barbara. *At the Very Least She Pays the Rent: Women and German Industrialization* (1985). A revisionist study of the effects of industrialization.

Grafteaux, Serge. *Mémé Santerre. A French Woman of the People.* Tr. Louise A. Tilly and Kathryn Tilly (1985). A moving memoir of work and family.

Gunda, Bela. "The Ethno-Sociological Structure of the Hungarian Extended Family," *Journal of Family History* (1982). The changing nature of the *zadruga*.

Hausen, Karin. *Frauen suchen ihre Geschichte* (1983). A collection of major articles about German social and political history.

Hilden, Patricia. *Working Women and Socialist Politics in France 1880–1914* (1986). Women at work in northern France.

Holcombe, Lee. *Victorian Ladies at Work: Middle Class Working Women in England and Wales, 1850–1914* (1973). On the nature of the new careers for women.

Honeycut, Karen. "Clara Zetkin: A Socialist Approach to the Problem of Women's Oppression," in Jane Slaughter and Robert Kern, eds., *European Women on the Left* (1981).

Kertzer, David I. *Family Life in Central Italy, 1880–1910: Sharecropping, Wage Labor, and Coresidence* (1984).

Quataert, Jean H. *Reluctant Feminists in German Social Democracy 1885–1917* (1979). An important study of the complexities of socialist women's politics.

Roberts, James S. *Drink, Temperance and the Working-Class in Nineteenth-Century Germany* (1984).

Ross, Ellen. " 'Fierce Questions and Taunts': Married Life in Working-Class London 1870–1914," *Feminist Studies* (1982). Pathbreaking studies of working women's experience.

———. "Labour and Love: Rediscovering London's Working-Class Mothers, 1870–1918," in Jane Lewis, ed., *Labour and Love* (1986).

———. "Survival Networks: Women's Neighbourhood Sharing in London before World War I," *History Workshop Journal* (1983).

Schmiechen, James Andrew. *Sweated Industries and Sweated Labor. The London Clothing Trades 1867–1914* (1984).

Sowerwine, Charles. *Sisters or Citizens? Women and Socialism in France Since 1876* (1982). The conflicting politics of French women socialists.

Springer, Beverly Tanner. "Anna Kuliscioff. Russian Revolutionist, Italian Feminist," in Jane Slaughter and Robert Kern, eds., *European Women on the Left* (1981).

Tilly, Louise. "Paths of Proletarianization: Organization of Production, Sexual Division of Labor, and Women's Collective Action," *Signs* (1981). An important delineation of the forms of women's protest.

Walton, Ronald G. *Women in Social Work* (1985). The rise of social work in England.

8

The New Woman

Breaking
Away

Dora Russell (1894–?), English activist and writer, remembered that "like young men," she and her friends "demonstrated our physical endurance on long bicycle rides; fifty miles on a machine without a free wheel was no joke. We took, like men, to walking tours," mountain climbing, round-the-world travel, and weeks of hiking.[1] In the *belle époque*, the craze for cycling and hiking was not confined to women of privileged classes. Among the "new women" who bicycled and went on adventures were working women, who bicycled to spread socialist information or to share a worker holiday with friends. Other new women such as Cambridge don Jane Ellen Harrison (1850–1928) and reformer Beatrice Potter Webb (1858–1943), as well as liberated heroines in novels, smoked in defiance of old rules concerning feminine behavior. Swedish feminist Ellen Key (1849–1926) saw the new woman deriving happiness from an unmarried state, living with a woman friend and yet being a mother. In most respects the new type of woman seemed to reject Victorian concepts of home and domesticity or at least wanted these concepts modified. New women did not accept standard roles for what was ladylike or many other accepted gender definitions.

The activities of new women stood out, even amidst the tumult in Western European societies at the turn of the century. The depressions that began in the 1870s, the challenge that socialism and anarchism posed to liberal politics, the contests for colonies that were waged by the major powers, the arms buildup that went along with imperialism—none of these overshadowed the new woman. Instead much cultural comment centered on her and her bicycle. Anxiety about the other current events doubtless influenced the outpouring of comment about the new woman. By controlling their fertility, new women caused those in power to fear national population declines—industrialists feared a shortage of workers, and imperialist politicians feared there would be insufficient troops to extend or defend the power of the nation-state. What seemed even worse to society was that a good many new women had political opinions

Although this young woman poses appropriately enough by a house, in fact the bicycle could take her miles away from it. Observers correctly saw this invention in the hands of women as a matter of grave concern.

that were socialist or feminist or in other ways radically different from the ruling middle-class consensus of the Western European democracies or the monarchism that prevailed elsewhere.

Some leading male writers portrayed the phenomenon of the new woman in fictional works. The main characters of George Gissing's *Odd Women* (1893) refused marriage and focused their emotional and productive lives on women's issues. Gissing developed these characters fairly fully as he also worked out his own ambivalent feelings toward them. For some readers, H. G. Wells's *Ann Veronica* (1909) was so sympathetic a treatment of the new woman that they modeled their lives on that of the book's heroine. Arthur Schnitzler's *The Road to the Open* (1908) has a socialist heroine who falls in love but returns to her political activity with the recognition that love is only part of life. Dozens more men wrote about new women—as doctors, teachers, struggling workers, and writers. Similarly, female authors portrayed this type. Sarah Grand's *The Beth Book* (1897) describes the unhappy marriage of her protagonist to the doctor of a "lock hospital." Leaving her husband brings the heroine hardship, but it is also the only possible road to happiness, individual fulfillment, and a commitment to women's values. Norwegian Nobel-prizewinner Sigrid Undset wrote about a new woman in *Jenny* (1911); the heroine, though pregnant, leaves the father of the child because she finds his love oppressive. Hedwig Dohm (1833–1919), Marcelle Tinayre (1877–1948), Gabrielle Reuter (1859–1941), Colette (1873–1954), Grete Meisel-Hess (1879–1922), Marie Antin (1881–1949), Ricarda Huch (1864–1947), Colette

Yver (pseudonym for Antoinette Huzard) (1874–?)—all of these artists and activists and their many less well-known contemporaries depicted the passionate adventures, the changed relationships, and the iconoclastic behavior of Europe's new women.

Literature depicting the new woman took Europe by storm, shocked some members of society, and encouraged others to emulate the heroines. The new woman was more than a literary type, however. Although fiction made the new woman a prominent phenomenon, it merely mirrored real women's lives as innovators and activists. New women registered and even intensified social concern. Innovative women marked out new roles for women. First, new women worked outside the household. This in itself broke the domestic stereotype, especially because many of these new workers were middle-class. Second, some new women pursued higher education with the opening of universities during the end of the nineteenth century as the result of feminists' efforts. Still others participated in a developing debate over marriage, reproduction, and sexuality. This debate signaled important changes with respect to the terms of gender identity. Finally, as part of that debate, isolated feminist groups became a mass movement, which increasingly focused on suffrage. Winning this one right, suffrage proponents believed, would end women's dependence on male chivalry and legal protection—neither of which could be relied on under male political leadership.

Marriage: Reform and Debate

In the last three decades of the nineteenth century, parliaments enacted substantial reforms that made the new woman possible. These resulted from intense lobbying activity and from the first organized feminist efforts. In the 1870s and 1880s, English women won the right to control their own property and wages. Although inequities remained, many were straightened out after World War I. The right of English husbands to incarcerate their wives at home or have them imprisoned for such things as refusing sexual intercourse ended during this period. Estranged wives were also given the right to petition for financial support, for custody of their children in case of separation, and for other benefits hitherto denied them. The French government enacted a divorce law in 1884 and by 1910 allowed married women to have control of their property and wages. In addition, French reform ended restrictions mandating that the wife live wherever her husband decreed. Russian upper-class women had greater control of their property than did Western European women and often managed large estates. Nonetheless, in Russian society husbands and fathers had extreme personal authority, and this hardly changed. Yet Russian fathers and the patriarchal, autocratic government alternated between allowing women favors such as higher education and then forbidding them. When Russia established a Duma, or congress, in the early twentieth century, some propertied women could vote if a man cast their ballot.

Germany, in contrast, had had fairly liberal laws on divorce and remar-

The New Woman

Sigrid Undset's *Jenny* (1911) portrayed a young schoolteacher who struggled to be an artist. Jenny also longed for love. In trying to love as a woman and yet remain an artist, she ultimately uncoupled marriage from both sexuality and reproduction. In so doing, Jenny represented the new woman. Finding out that she is pregnant, Jenny refuses to marry the father of her child, whom she does not love, and speculates on the life of a single parent.

What if it were true? The dread of having a child is really a senseless superstition; it happens every day. Why should it be worse for her than for any poor working girl, who was able to provide for herself and her child. The anxiety was a remnant from the times when an unmarried woman in similar circumstances had to go to the father or her relations and confess that she had had a good time, and that they had to pay the expenses—with the sad prospect of never afterwards having her provided for by somebody else—a quite sufficient reason for their anger.

Nobody had any right to be angry with her. Her mother would, of course, be sorry, but when a grown-up person tried to live according to his conscience the parents had nothing to say. She had tried to help her mother as much as possible, she had never worried her with her own troubles, her reputation had never been spoilt by any tales of levity, flirtation, or revelling, but where her own opinions about right and wrong differed from that of other people, she meant to follow them, even if it would be painful to her mother to hear disagreeable things said about her. . . .

She could provide for a child just as well as many a girl who had not a tenth a part of her knowledge. . . .

If it was true how dreadful that it should happen now. If it had happened when she loved him, or thought she did, and she could have gone away in good faith, but now, when everything that had been between them had crumbled to pieces, torn asunder by her own thinking and pondering. . . .

During these weeks at Tegneby she had made up her mind not to go on any longer. She was longing to go away to new conditions, new work. Yes, the longing for work had come back; she had had enough of this sickly desire of clinging to somebody, to be cuddled and petted and called little girl.

Source: Excerpted from Sigrid Undset, *Jenny,* W. Emme, trans. (New York: Knopf, 1929), 214–215.

riage, because of the state's great interest in promoting fertility. German women's situation, however, was complicated by the continuation of local customs even after the various states united in 1871 under Prussian leadership. German women had partial voting rights in many states and localities; property law differed from one region to another, though generally husbands had control. When a new code took effect in 1900 in Germany, many trappings of patriarchy disappeared. Women gained a legal personality and no longer were subject to dominant principles such as "obedience" and "paternal power." Though property generally remained under the husband's control, wages could belong to the wife who earned them. However, women were shocked by the tightening of divorce law in the new German code. Moreover, not until almost a decade after the new code did the government rescind the prohibition on women's attendance at political meetings. Affecting all of Central Europe between Germany and Russia, the General Civil Code (1811) of the Habsburg empire maintained male authority in the household right through the mid–twentieth century. Even with changes in property law, many European law codes similarly retained expressions of male privilege in familial and cultural affairs. The General Civil Code did allow many propertied women local suffrage provided they cast their vote through a man.

Despite only partial success, reforms in response to women's activism did prove encouraging. First, it fostered further activism where inequity remained striking, and women took heart from their victories. Yet they also remembered that men had made them walk a tortuous road to equitable treatment under the law. Their gains in rights did not make them trust men more. Second, the gains were real. Being able to keep their wages helped working women, even though this was the only contribution politicians made toward solving the problems of these women. Changes in property law also brought middle- and upper-class women into the modern system of property, while it weakened male control over them. This too constituted a kind of empowerment. The new woman rode the crest of these victories; she was, in fact, born of them.

Clearly, the condition of women in marriage refuted the claim of nineteenth-century society to progress and enlightenment. George Sand had seemed an anomaly to those in the best circles in the 1830s, but fifty years later protests such as hers about marital laws and gender relations influenced many playwrights, novelists, and other literary types. These writers, along with reforming politicians, examined the existing conditions in marriage and found a great deal lacking. The debate on marriage accompanied persistent efforts at reform and aroused both disgust and support of the status quo. While sociologists and anthropologists such as Herbert Spencer labeled monogamous marriage the sign of high civilization, others saw the darker side of the institution. They pointed to the lack of symmetry in marriage, especially in the coercive privileged status of men and the attendant powerlessness of women.

Norwegian playwright Henrik Ibsen's *A Doll's House* (1879) was among the first literary portrayals of marriage as a problematic institution. Sponsor of a married women's property bill and champion of women's rights, Ibsen created an unforgettable protagonist, Nora, in this play. Finding her relationship to her children and husband degrading in certain ways, Nora opted to leave them all, an act that put Europeans on the edge of their theater seats. Audiences either applauded Nora or hated her; no one remained neutral. Later, in England, South African–born Olive Schreiner (1855–1920) produced *The Story of an African Farm* (1889), in which the heroine held a less than rosy picture of life: "In truth, nothing matters. This dirty little world, full of confusion, and the blue rag, stretched overhead for a sky, is so low we could touch it with our hand." Schreiner's female protagonists struggled for independence because they perceived marriage's asymmetry: "I'm not in so great a hurry to put my neck beneath any man's foot," says one, explaining her reluctance to marry.[2] Schreiner's later analysis of gender relations, *Women and Labor* (1911), revealed the parasitical nature of women's position with respect to men when they were forced to remain apart from the productive world. A theme also explored by American Charlotte Perkins Gilman, women's commitment to sexual rather than productive concerns stood behind male power in both writers' theories.

Imbalances in gender relations grew from law and culture, critics charged. Affecting the entire social sphere, but particularly marriage, inequity poisoned all relations between men and women. The sensational novel, *Una Donna* (1906), by Italian Sibella Aleramo (pseudonym for Rina Facci 1876–1960) explored how unpleasant marital relations actually were for women. Facci's real-life marriage was the basis for her novel. The heroine is raped by a man who then marries her. The husband's insensitivity highlights the mental and physical misfortune of a woman in marriage. Norwegian author Björnstierne Björnson described the difficulties of being an emancipated women in *Leonarda* (1879). In *Glove* (1883), he portrayed a woman's suffering before marriage because of her fiancé's sexual activity with another woman. In Sweden, Victoria Benedictsson (1850–1888) became famous for two novels depicting unhappy marriages, *Money* (1884) and *Fru Marianne* (1887). Benedictsson's own marriage was terribly unhappy, and she committed suicide after being seduced by an eminent Danish author, who was a notorious womanizer. To prevent unhappy marriages, French intellectual and later prime minister Léon Blum advocated long periods of living together beforehand as a way of ascertaining compatibility. Although the French middle class saw new women in their midst and read any number of novels about them, it was scandalized by Blum's suggestions as well as frightened by the thought that all was not well in this sancrosanct institution.

The Promise of Higher Education

Before World War I, the system of higher education gradually opened up to women in the face of a concerted onslaught by activists. First in Switzerland and then in France, medical schools and universities began admitting women in the 1860s. Women students flocked to them, especially women from Eastern Europe, such as socialist Rosa Luxemburg, Polish-born scientist Marie Curie,

Women in universities democraticized the pursuit of knowledge, while they simultaneously threatened male privelege and their monopoly in higher education. Like these students at Cambridge, men across Europe rioted, especially as more and more women took first place in exams.

and Russian doctor and feminist Anna Shabanova. In the early 1870s, thanks to the efforts of women like Emily Davies, the first women's colleges were established: Girton and Newnham at Cambridge, followed by Somerville College and Lady Margaret Hall at Oxford. Although women at Oxford and Cambridge did not receive degrees for more than half a century after this, the more fortunate women who did receive diplomas from other schools acquired the kind of institutional sanction that was becoming ever more important in an increasingly bureaucratic world. Italian universities had never closed their courses to women, and women there received degrees in the eighteenth and nineteenth centuries. While activists in other countries struggled to get young women admitted, a very few Italian women actually held university teaching posts. In contrast, the talented Greek scientist Angeliki Panajiotatou's (1875–1954) first lecture at Athens University made male students hysterical: "Back to the kitchen," they screamed, "back to the kitchen."[3] Panajiotatou left for Alexandria to become the director of its leading hospital and a pioneer in battling cholera and typhus. Students in Spain stoned the first women medical students in 1881. The situation in Germany was less violent but more repressive. Individual professors could instruct young women, but most refused. In addition, many German universities actually barred women from attending lectures, and activists devoted energy to this situation until the very end of the century. The quest for liberal political rights that had been defeated in 1848 metamorphosed into a drive for *Bildung,* or culture and education. Thus feminism in Germany centered on education. Wherever women entered university life, the world of abstract thinking, modern scientific skills, and social analysis opened up to them. Moreover, the fact of obtaining a higher education legitimized a variety of aspirations.

Even as women gained access to the legitimizing process of higher education, the academic and medical world developed theories designed to keep women out or at least to discourage them. In 1872, for example, Dr. Theodor von Bischoff published *The Study and Practice of Medicine by Women.* Bischoff believed that women had smaller brains than men, had evolved less satisfactorily, and therefore were wholly unsuited to academic work, especially medical study. In addition, he stated that women who studied would cause irreparable damage to their reproductive organs. Bischoff was but one of a number of influential intellectuals, medical men, and scientists who developed this line of argument. In 1889 in England, Patrick Geddes and J. Arthur Thomson elaborated on this analysis with their theory of male katabolic, or active, cells and female anabolic, or passive, ones. The energy women did have, they maintained, was centered in the uterus; therefore, any energy used to study drained energy from reproductivity. Doctors, particularly those in obstetrics and gynecology, sounded the alarm across Europe.

Like doctors, social commentators used the new language of social analysis to brand what women were doing in the realm of higher education as pernicious to the well-being of the public, the family, and the individual woman. Not much separated these writers' views from traditional common wisdom about women, except that these new arbiters of opinion used the language of science and social science. In his *Principles of Sociology* (1876), the prominent social scientist Herbert Spencer spoke of the nuclear family, as well as the existing sexual division of labor, as the most advanced form of civilization. Spencer proceeded to describe the harm done by educating women to new kinds of thinking; he maintained this was not progress, but rather mischief.

Despite the protest from doctors and social scientists, intelligent women gathered in universities and ended their domestic isolation. In fact, at the turn of the century, European women generally took advantage of changing laws and customs to cluster together more frequently in all-female surroundings such as settlement houses, women's clubs, women's colleges, nursing orders, and boarding houses for factory and department store workers. Living away from direct male and familial authority, they developed a community life that focused on women. These new groups experienced the uncertainties that accompany the founding of communities, especially those without precedent. Thus, conflicts arose—for example, about the role of the principal at the new British women's colleges. Was she a maternal or paternal head of family? Or was she a kind of corporate head or a scholarly one? What was her relationship to the scholars, who outranked her in knowledge but not in authority? Such roles were still evolving well into the twentieth century.

Across Europe, higher education attracted women precisely because it offered an escape from familial patterns into a community of scholars, allowed for community building, and promised the further freedom of a career. Many women's colleges deliberately excluded men from their purview. A Russian woman enrolled in Zurich wanted none of them in her study group for "even the most stupid man would try to gain the upper hand over women."[4] Lack of confidence and authoritarianism haunted women's community-building efforts in the late nineteenth century. Naturally, some leaders of women's groups generated passionate attachment, whereas others only caused rebellion. The excitement of such release from male domination and such adventurous experimentation triumphed, however, over all odds. As a result, the first generations of European women who went to the colleges or to universities proceeded to organize further social institutions after they left school. They established clubs, philanthropic societies, and settlement houses. In this way, the new women multiplied by creating communities and constantly inventing different ways for women to live on their own. Grouped together, these women attracted attention.

Buying and the New Body

Women also began to dress differently. The new woman depended on a certain bodily freedom allowed by changing fashion from the 1860s onward. About then, the most advanced women began wearing suits, composed of blouse, jacket, and long but streamlined skirt. This new-style women's costume was an imitation of what men were wearing and ushered in less ornate styles. In England, proponents of the arts and crafts movement introduced dresses without defined waistlines that freed the body from corsets and other restrictive garments, including voluminous petticoats. By the 1870s, the German reformer and professor Dr. Gustav Jaeger began publicizing the connections between clothing and health. Jaeger's ideal fabric was unbleached and undyed wool, which, he maintained, improved bodily vigor. His emphasis on activity and vigor instead of the Victorian languor pertained to women as well as men. Although others were making similar points, Dr. Jaeger's rejection of massive crinolines and the tight lacing of corsets influenced advanced segments of society. Jaeger recommended a wool corset, whose fiber, he said, would lend the body natural support and thus obviate the need for tight lacing. In addition, he substituted the springed steel used in watch mechanics for the bones used in most corsets. Some considered these only small advances, but watch springs did allow for easier bodily movement. Moreover, Jaeger became such a respected authority, that although many women still wore corsets, they often ended their tight-lacing practices. Soon after, a more straight-lined corset was introduced by a French couturière. Although potentially an advance, this corset was worn laced tightly, so as to constrict the body into the famous S-shaped or Gibson girl figure. Nonetheless, this would be the last of the tightly laced genre. New women were generally influenced by Jaeger or by arts and crafts styles in their clothing.

By the early twentieth century, women's clothing had been drastically re-formed. By then, Henry van der Velde had designed high-waisted, loose gowns, and French designer Poiret made the slim skirt smart. Petticoats diminished in size and number, and for many new designs a corset was unnecessary. The evolution of women's costume from the suit of the 1860s to the slim dress of the early twentieth century intersected with a changing way of life for women and particularly with the appearance of the new woman. As much as anything, the bicycle influenced the trend. Whereas women had played sports such as lawn tennis for several decades dressed in fairly traditional attire, the intro-duction of the bicycle into women's sphere could not have occurred without modification of clothing. In order to ride bicycles, women adopted the once highly ridiculed bloomers, the divided skirt, or knickerbockers. Simultane-ously, advice literature often suggested that the corset be abandoned during strenuous sports in favor of bodice support—a precursor of the brassière. So the freedom the bicycle brought was not only social, it was a kind of physical release from constraint that must have affected the new women in dramatic ways. Moreover, this release affected all classes, for the bicycle expedition was a venture taken just as often by working-class women as by upper-class women. Thus, at the beginning of the twentieth century, the waists, hips, and legs of women were being freed from excess clothing that had constricted movement and had been generally encumbering. As a result, women increased their activity, especially in calisthenics, swimming, hiking, and bicycle riding. New women looked different, and they moved around more and more vigor-ously.

Such developments in the consumer economy had two faces for women—one expressive and liberating, the other oppressive in its emphasis on constant change. The start of the Industrial Revolution had been characterized by in-creased production of consumer items in textiles and small iron goods, but for a good part of the nineteenth century industry concentrated on producing large machinery and railroads. The consumer market developed slowly after the ini-tial push in textiles. After mid-century a spurt of inventions such as the sewing machine and new kinds of stoves set the stage for increasing abundance in consumer goods. The sewing machine hardly changed the nature of garments, nor did woodburning cast-iron stoves change the nature of food. Rather each allowed more sophistication, more intricacies with less effort, and objectively made basic tasks less onerous.

The idea of "good taste" in household items also expanded the home's potential as a consumer outlet. William Morris and his collaborators in En-gland and the Viennese Workshops developed the idea that the home could be the place for artistic goods. Furniture, carpets, drapery, dishes, and utensils could be artistically designed objects that even workers could have. Although these innovators in domestic design never began to realize their intentions con-

Nettie Honeyball, captain of the British Ladies Soccer Club in the 1890s, dressed in a completely new type of clothing for women. In fact, her clothing and participation in sports threw gender stereotypes into disarray.

cerning the working-class home, they did cause a revolution among segments of the middle class, who began to regard the home as a place that had to be artistic, tasteful, and up-to-date. In the first wave of this never-ending enthusiasm, women such as William Morris's daughter, May Morris (1862–1938), and later Margaret Macdonald Mackintosh (1865–1933) did a great deal of needlework and other kinds of design. In the Viennese Workshops, Jutta Silka (1877–?) and Therese Trethan (1859–?) set new trends in dishware and furniture. In Russia, artist Natalia Goncharova (1881–1962) applied her talent to designing costumes for the innovative Ballets Russes. She revived peasant motifs that then became fashionable on an array of textiles. Moving away from centuries of tradition that limited home decoration to fabrics such as brocades and silks and certain classic styles in dishware and furniture, these designers continued the process of making the home modern. They saw themselves as more akin to craftspeople than to the leisured classes from which they came. At the same time, by promoting good taste as a household necessity, they hastened the appearance of another new woman—the twentieth-century consumer.

In the past, market women and small proprietors had sold household necessities, but a type of modern entrepreneur stepped forth to contribute to the consumer revolution. The modern department store was a group achievement of entrepreneurs such as Aristide Boucicaut in Paris, A. T. Stewart in New York, Whitely in London, simultaneously appearing in different countries across industrial society. Although each "founder" contributed individual embellishments and differences, these soon became standard in all such stores. Department stores not only amassed a greater variety and quantity of goods on one site than ever before, but they also developed a new aura around the process of purchasing consumer goods. The first stage of this process involved impressing consumers with the masses of goods and commodities, which became overwhelming by their sheer number and diversity. The idea of having an abundance of goods took shape gradually among the middle and working classes, which had previously thought in terms of restraint and even scarcity. Sold in a new way at a fixed instead of negotiable cost, consumer goods cut into household production by being so readily accessible as to discourage domestic toil yet simultaneously encouraged home production to add to the abundance. The goods themselves provoked these changes, but the site where they were sold worked its own kind of revolution.

The department store created a space connecting the productive world of industry and the reproductive world of the home. Although this new social space was an urban phenomenon, part of its success rested on the ability to draw more and more people into the world of consumption, initially through the use of mail order facilities. To be effective, the department store had to exist as a special world—a dream world as some have called it or a site that worked the "reenchantment of the universe."[5] To this end, stores offered a new kind of total environment different from the home or business. As entrepreneurs became more innovative, stores became more elaborate, more appealing to the senses, more fulfilling of almost every human need, and more imposing on the human psyche. First came the idea of the monster store that would act as a "Universal Provider"—a fulfiller of every need. Then came the store as source of pleasurable experiences. Entrepreneurs discovered the technique of displaying goods so attractively and skillfully that even basic necessities could be converted into enticing commodities. They added constantly to the variety of commodities until the most unessential and frivolous articles entered their stores and spoke to customers' fancy and imagination. Alongside commodities appeared services that had formerly been provided only in private space: lounges, concert rooms, restrooms, and restaurants were but a few of the special facilities that contributed to making the department store a world unto itself. The final accomplishment of the department store was a revolution in

This Berlin department store features certain aspects of cathedral architecture, skylights to create airiness, and a sumptuous chandelier to incite desire for luxury.

architecture, not just in scale, but in form. The department store building incorporated ornamentation borrowed from other spheres—the religious, the palatial, the domestic. Galleries, rotundas, balconies, and walkways were constructed of iron, marble, brass and gilt, and glass. Well-planned lighting, both artificial and natural streaming in from skylights served to highlight both the goods and the store itself. In this way department stores gave birth to the consumer world and made consuming a modern way of life.

In the past, purchases of commodities had often been made by men, but the department store introduced shopping as a woman's activity, though men certainly also engaged in it. As consumption became more demanding, given the array of goods and the time entailed in moving from one part of the store to another, women increased their consumer activity. This constituted a natural extension of domestic activity, but one that moved women outside the home. In fact, a large part of the appeal of the department store was that it constituted a new social space that women could justifiably occupy. Necessity and pleasure worked hand in hand. The pleasure afforded women by the sensuality, visual stimulation, and appeals to the imagination of the store coincided with women's role as provisioner.

The department store also changed rural women's lives—not because they went to the store, but because the store came to them. Many stores sent patterns to women workers in the countryside and thus updated their ideas about fashion. Also, many peasant women somehow got their hands on stores' mail-order catalogues. Though these women usually lacked the financial means necessary to be fashionable, nonetheless, the catalogues contributed to the demise of peasant costumes. An image of women as "new" emanated from those catalogues and ultimately reached even into the countryside.

New Directions

In 1899, Dr. Maria Montessori (1870–1952) made a triumphant tour of Italy giving a lecture entitled "The New Woman." Having struggled to acquire the first medical degree awarded to a modern Italian woman, Montessori characterized the new woman as someone who, above all, based her thinking on science. Indeed, Montessori saw science as the key to solving social problems, which for her meant problems of abnormal children and social deviancy. At the time, in Italy and elsewhere, the so-called "idiot child" was generally locked in institutions and left imprisoned in idleness. While doing her clinical practice in hospitals for the insane and retarded, Montessori through careful observation had detected these children's need for neural stimulation; she was able to train her charges to perform the seemingly miraculous feat of reading and writing. After this early success, Montessori proceeded to devise a celebrated system of childhood education that emphasized freedom and useful activity. Though she worked long hours as a doctor, Montessori also made lecture tours in order to speak out concerning women's condition. Her insights were numerous and apt: the graceful tilt of a woman's head was the posture of a slave, working women of Italy deserved equal pay for equal work, and equality in pay should start in the many state-owned Italian industries. Montessori's modernism manifested itself in striking ways, notably in that she was a professional woman who became an unwed mother. Her chief ambition, however, concerned education and was based on the combination of science and social reform. It resulted in the founding by the early twentieth century of many Montessori schools throughout the world.

Maria Montessori's scientific outlook made her a quintessential new woman. Observation rather than prejudice, rational thinking rather than the force of tradition informed her world view. During the *belle époque*, scientific professions were one gateway to power and prestige. Many new women—like Montessori—chose medicine, but a few made their names in mathematics and theoretical science. In England Sarah Mertha Ayrton (1854–1923), after studies in mathematics at Girton, worked on theories of wave and electric arc behavior. Lise Meitner (1878–1968) studied radioactivity in Vienna and became an expert in nuclear fission. Struggling against official hostility to her studies, Amalie Noether (1882–1935) pioneered in modern algebra. Marie Sklodowska Curie (1867–1934) worked at the leading edge of modern scientific knowledge. Born in Poland, Marie Sklodowska first put her sister through medical school in Paris and then went there herself to study science and math-

Maria Montessori, new woman par excellence, was a doctor, a pioneer in childhood education, and an unwed mother. Others cared for her son until they were reunited later in life.

ematics. Working with her French husband, Pierre Curie, she discovered polonium and radium and developed insight into the recently discovered phenomenon of radioactivity. The Curies jointly and later Marie on her own received Nobel prizes for their contributions to the revolution then occurring in physics and chemistry. Her scientific thought, like that of Albert Einstein and Werner Heisenberg, reopened basic questions about energy and matter and contributed to the overturning of the Newtonian universe of the seventeenth century.

A more common path for new women was social science rather than natural science. Approaches and attitudes toward the working class and the poor fundamentally changed during the crises of the late nineteenth century. Social science, social analysis, social programs, and social policies began replacing moralizing activities of charity and philanthropy. Women studied social science at universities, but they also discovered it on their own in study groups or

A Young Polish Woman's Intellectual Ambitions

In the fall of 1891 Marya Sklodowska set out from Warsaw to attend science classes at the Sorbonne in Paris. At twenty-four she had already served as governess and taught peasant children in order to support an older sister's medical studies. When her turn came, she became a committed student, forgetting to eat and living simply in order to give full attention to science. In 1893, she received the highest grade in the master's examination for physics and in 1894, the second highest in mathematics. A new woman, she devoted herself to her work and even repeatedly turned down the proposals of Pierre Curie that they marry. Even after Sklodowska decided to marry Curie, even after becoming the first person to win two Nobel Prizes, she remained committed to work. She was, as Albert Einstein put it, "of all celebrated beings, the only one whom fame has not corrupted." This letter to her brother in September 1893 reveals a new woman's commitment and her simplicity.

I have already rented my room on the sixth floor in a clean and decent street which suits me very well. Tell Father that in that place where I was going to take a room there was nothing free, and that I am very satisfied with this room. It should not be cold here, especially as the floor is of wood and not tiles. Compared to my last year's room it is a veritable palace.

I hardly need say that I am delighted to be back in Paris. It was very hard for me to separate again from Father, but I could see that he was well, very lively, and that he could do without me—especially as you are living in Warsaw. As for me, it is my whole life that is at stake. It seemed to me, therefore, that I could stay on here without having remorse on my conscience.

Just now I am studying mathematics unceasingly, so as to be up to date when the courses begin. I have three mornings a week taken by lessons with one of my French comrades who is preparing for the examination I have just passed. Tell Father that I am getting used to this work, that it does not tire me as much as before, and that I do not intend to abandon it.

It seems that life is not easy for any of us. But what of that? We must have perseverance and above all confidence in ourselves. We must believe that we are gifted for something, and that this thing, at whatever cost, must be obtained.

It is difficult for me to tell you about my life in detail; it is so monotonous and, in fact, so uninteresting. Nevertheless I have no feeling of uniformity and I regret only one thing, which is that the days are so short and that they pass so quickly. One never notices what has been done; one can only see what remains to be done, and if one didn't like the work it would be very discouraging.

Source: Excerpted from Eve Curie, *Madame Curie*, Vincent Sheean, trans. (New York: Doubleday, Doran and Co., 1938), 115–116.

action groups such as the Fabian Society or the Men and Women's Club in London, the Musée Social in Paris, and the Union for Social Politics in Germany. These small but vigorous groups engaged in free discussion and investigation of social issues. Through their participation in these groups, women's world view changed. For one thing, they studied and worked for the most part with men. This practice ended the segregated nature of many charitable societies. Although many charitable and philanthropic groups had had men as titular leaders, women had organized themselves or acted as all-female subsections. The new organizations integrated the sexes in studying social and public matters.

Many of the groups raised issues concerning gender itself. A unique example is the Men and Women's Club, launched in the 1870s but particularly active through the next decade. After tentative beginnings, the club took as its goal "the unreserved discussion of all matters in any way connected with the mutual position and relation of men and women."[6] Membership was exclusive because the club centered on informed discussion and researched papers. Presentations and subsequent discussion were carefully recorded in order to perpetuate insights that could lead to socially significant action. Annie Besant (1847–1933) presented a paper on "The State and Sexual Matters," and Maria Sharpe (d. 1927), who married eugenicist and co-member Karl Pearson, spoke on "The Regulation of Prostitution." Topics such as "State Interference in Marriage" and "Hebrew Women" reveal the range of the group's investigative mission. Thus, social research came to mean, among other things, gender research, especially as it touched on public policy.

The influence of social science lessened the domestic content of public activity. The beliefs behind social welfare differed fundamentally from the traditionally personal, moral, hierarchical, and charitable nature of philanthropy. One of the most famous women to break away from that tradition was Beatrice Potter Webb (1858–1943). Born into an upper-middle-class family of many daughters, she started her work as a social investigator by helping her brother-in-law, Charles Booth, with his studies of life in East London. Miss Potter disguised herself and worked in a sweatshop; this experience, as well as earlier observations of the working class, enabled her to write some of the most interesting sections of Booth's book. During this time Joseph Chamberlain, a widower and prominent English politician, began an intense courtship of Potter that left her constantly at odds with her own feelings of independence.

Chamberlain had an overpowering personality, and his insistence on masculine domination convinced her that, for women to accomplish anything, they would have to create a class of celibate reformers. She wrote, ". . . from the flight of emotion away from the service of God to the service of man and from the current faith in the scientific method, I drew the inference that the most hopeful form of social service was the craft of social investigator."[7] In 1890, she met Sidney Webb, a leader of the Fabian Society, a group devoted to socialist principles and to the evolution of a classless society through study and planning. Wary of him at first, she finally committed herself to him in what became a famous "partnership," a new kind of relationship based on sharing both the public and the private worlds. Her marriage to a man from the lower middle class shocked many and alienated friends and even some members of Beatrice's family. For the couple, it initiated a life committed to leadership of a powerful reform group, participation in politics and government, and writing.

Reform groups such as the Fabians concerned themselves with studying industrial production and working-class conditions. Using the analytical methods of social science, they also began looking at the precise connections between public and private worlds. One product of this analysis was the organization of consumers, now mostly women. Consumer leagues soon developed all over the industrial world, and the first international meeting was held in Geneva in 1904. These groups aimed at improving working-class life both by buying products whose manufacturers were humane in their treatment of workers and by practicing educated purchasing. One did not buy from manufacturers who demanded Sunday work or were known for sweating labor. These groups also believed that consumer restraint and consumer education were necessary. Members made a point of placing orders well in advance of the season. In this way they aimed to prevent long hours for seamstresses, but also got lower prices. They tried to combat inflation by searching out good buys and rejecting products whose prices were too high. Such groups flourished in the first decades of the twentieth century and in so doing began creating a consumer language, a self-conscious consumer role, and a consumer science. Women reformers of this breed were beginning to shape a domestic role that incorporated the advances in social science. The consumer movement coincided with the development of a marketing apparatus that relied on this kind of attention to consumption. Consumer concerns began to take over the domestic sphere and crowd out moral and reproductive interests. In a larger sense, scientific thinking and scientific issues modified the republican ideal that had dominated public discourse about women for a century.

Women and Modernism

High art and philosophy also aroused passionate interest in new styles called "modern." Born out of late Victorian dissent and maturing in the cataclysm of World War I, "modernism" developed in the thinking of certain intellectuals and the works of some artists. The writings of Friedrich Nietzsche (1844–

Paula Modersohn-Becker refused to sentimentalize women, as this painting of a peasant woman (c. 1905) shows. Hailed immediately as a masterwork, this portrait, like many others, was nonetheless seen as transgressive because of its subject's ugliness and coarseness.

1900) revolted against middle-class society and its values, conventional concepts of reality, the domination of scientific thought, and academic tradition. The art of Paul Cézanne (1839–1906), with its eccentric coloration and deformed shaping of familiar objects, was part of an ongoing challenge of realism in the visual arts. Such revolts and many others made up the ill-defined movement called modernism. Literature, art, music, philosophy, and even scientific thought were affected by its force. Meanwhile, the general public often felt its sensibilities battered by this cultural revolution.

The new woman was closely connected with modernism. Her singular newness jolted middle-class sensibilities the way modern art did and she participated in modernism's formation. French painter Berthe Morisot (1841–1895) joined the impressionists, who were characterized by their use of everyday subjects, less realistic brushwork, and a fascination with light. American Mary Cassatt (1844–1926), who spent most of her life in Paris, also belonged to the impressionist school. Never a sentimentalist in technique, Cassatt developed a consistent subject matter in her paintings of mothers and children. This subject matter, despite Cassatt's progressively less realistic style, fit in with the public attention given to both motherhood and small children. The German artist Paula Modersohn-Becker (1876–1907) also painted women, mothers, and children, but by the early twentieth century she adopted the antirealistic style known as expressionism. Censured by critics for their lack of conventional beauty, her paintings of peasant and poor women expressed the powerful emotions called forth by her subjects. Modersohn-Becker only reached this style close to the end of her short life and after much searching for her own way of painting. Rebellious at an earlier age, her compatriot Gabriele Münter (1877–1962) was co-organizer of an exhibit in Munich, mounted by the Blue Rider group, which had seceded from an already avantgarde movement. Münter's paintings, many of which were landscapes and sometimes human figures, shocked the viewing public because of their intense, disturbing colors and the simplification of objects. Part of an ongoing challenge—some called it a crisis—of Western civilization, these women's paintings and many other less famous ones formed the background for even more disturbing work to come.

In literature, works such as Schreiner's *The Story of an African Farm* (1883) undermined the beliefs on which middle-class propriety and optimism about life were based. Less immediately popular were the first volumes of *Pilgrimage* (1915–1917), by Dorothy Richardson (1873–1957), which captured the modernist form, also used by James Joyce and Marcel Proust. This multivolumed novel depended on the heroine's interior monologue. This use of a female narrator was a significant aspect of the modernism of Richardson's work. Hungarian Margit Kaffka (1880–1918) similarly experimented with psychological techniques and unresolved feminist themes. Finally, German expressionist poet Else Lasker-Schüler (1869–1945) wrote verse that was Nietzschean in that it rejected an exclusively rational basis for the self or one's relations with others. She used the mysticism of the Near and Far East to express her commitment to love and transcendence:[8]

> Both my soul and yours, which loveth mine,
> In the Tibetan rug are intertwined.
>
> Ray in ray, infatuated colors,
> Stars that heaven-long wooed one another.
>
> On this jewel our feet rest side by side
> Thousand-upon-thousand-meshed wide.
>
> Sweet Lama son upon a musk-plant throne,
> How long will your mouth likely kiss my own
> And cheek on cheek the brightly knotted times go on.

Lasker-Schüler not only wrote a new kind of verse but lived a new kind of life, sleeping in railroad stations and bearing a child out of wedlock.

By the end of the nineteenth century, science had simultaneously influenced some novelists to adopt a naturalist or realist form. Realist and naturalist writers scorned romantic versions of people's lives. Instead, like Emile Zola (1840–1902), who pioneered naturalism in France, they described the power of nature to destroy whole families and distort human relationships. Spanish writer Emilia Pardo Bazan (1851–1921) imported naturalism into Spain. Her great masterpieces, such as *The Manor of Ulloa* (1886), portrayed village life and the decay of aristocratic families. Illegitimate children, neglected property

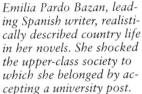

Emilia Pardo Bazan, leading Spanish writer, realistically described country life in her novels. She shocked the upper-class society to which she belonged by accepting a university post.

and health, and most of all ignorance and sloth ruined the family and many of its dependents. The sequel, *Mother Nature* (1887), opened with the legitimate daughter of the Ulloan seigneurs and her illegitimate half-brother succumbing to the force of sexual passion—that is, nature. In this case, the force of nature was stronger than that of social or familial order; as a result, further deterioration of the lineage ensued. Pardo Bazan complemented her naturalism with doses of feminism. Refusing to be limited by the minimal intellectual standards set for upper-class Spanish women, Pardo Bazan edited journals, engaged in notorious literary arguments, and vigorously championed improved education for girls. Because of her social status as a female aristocrat, her appointment to a university post stunned society. By the end of the century, she became interested in psychology, which led her to develop an even more complex view of the problematic chances for a happy resolution of human affairs. Constantly engaged in a literary quest, Pardo Bazan joined the modernist revolt and is now acknowledged to be the greatest Spanish writer of short stories.

Other modernist writers rejected what is often called the sociological approach. Meticulous, realistic narratives of social life, customs, and character had less interest than experimentation with artistic forms and the quest for spiritual values. So, Lasker-Schüler, for example, employed an Oriental motif in her poem about the carpet, which suggested the vibrant colors of the East but also its higher spiritual values in comparison to Western commitments to profit and production. This side of modernism flourished among Russian women writers. Mirra Lokhvitskaya (1869–1905) depicted the decadence then flourishing in the West with a poem about the Queen of Sheba, surrounded by slaves and trembling in remembrance of passion. But ten years later (c. 1903) she abandoned this praise of excess: when "Desires are gone . . . Blessed, blessed is Nirvana's rest."[9] Lokhvitskaya's contemporary, Zinaida Hippius (1869–1945), concentrated on the modernist concerns of groups that composed St. Petersburg's philosophical and literary elite. At the center of these groups, she was the inspiration for the journal *Novy Put* (*The New Way*) and wrote short stories and poems of an intensely spiritual nature. Her story "The Mad Woman" describes the clash of a scientific, secular, and rational public official with his wife, who aspires to communion and spirituality. Overwhelmed by the power of her husband's world view, both within their marriage and as expressed in society at large, the wife opts to live in an insane asylum. For Hippius, middle-class optimism was a delusion; she viewed contemporary life not as happy but as "Terror. And groans. And darkness . . . but above these/The unflinching light."[10] In sum, modernist artists and writers rejected or reworked the rational and optimistic vision of reformers and liberals from the eighteenth century on.

Uncovering the Psyche

Thinkers of the *belle époque* were acutely aware of the darker side of human existence. Crowds of striking workers or the terrorism of anarchists frightened society in general, and the violence of imperialism hardly went unnoticed. Charles Darwin's *Origin of the Species* (1859) and *Descent of Man* (1871) postulated that human beings were mired in a struggle for survival with nature and with each other. By the end of the century, a Viennese physician, Sigmund Freud (1856–1939) saw an equally intense struggle occurring within each person. Freud's psychoanalytic ideas, based in good part on observations of women, posited a realm of psychic activity apart from, and even unknown to, rational mental processes. His understanding of psychoanalysis as a "talking cure" and as a therapy involving emotions transferred from patient to physician developed from the case of the young Bertha von Pappenheim (1859–1936)—later the leader of the feminist League of Jewish Women. Freud wrote about the unconscious and the subconscious and about the importance of dreams, slips of the tongue, forgetfulness, and all kinds of behavior that previously had seemed accidental or trivial. For Freud, however, all these things were powerful indications of being. Also, Freud saw the psyche not as a unity, but as divided into parts competing for a finite pool of psychic energy. The id was a vast reserve of sexual needs and wants; the ego was a kind of reality center that faced the social world and was active in it; and the superego provided injunctions, laws, and moral principles, a whole realm of dos and don'ts that the individual had to adhere to. With a war for control occurring within the self, individuals, according to Freudian theory, should no longer see themselves in liberal terms as rational, laboring, and autonomous. Rather they were conflicted and irrational and engaged in a constant struggle against mental breakdown.

Freud had much to say about sexuality and gender, and most of it was shocking to society. Freud believed that individuals were sexual beings from the time of birth, with anal, oral, and genital drives. To a culture that seemed to deny publicly the sexual nature of existence, Freud's explicit recognition of sexual components in the makeup of the tiniest infant ran against the grain. Moreover, Freud challenged ideas about inherent gender identity. For him, people developed a gendered way of thinking and behaving through painful experiences over time, and never achieved an untroubled masculine or feminine state. Both masculinity and femininity were relative and existed on a continuum of possible gender definitions. Little boys and little girls started to become men and women during catastrophic moments in childhood when they had to reject their sexual feelings for their parents as well as their many perverse kinds of sexual longing. Children only entered into full adult sexual identity, however, during the terrifying experience that Freud described in terms of the Greek myth of Oedipus. Freud believed that in the Oedipal moment, the child recognized the father's power of castration and adopted a conventional psychosexual code that demanded rejection of incest and perverse sexuality and adherence to proper gender identity. Failure to pass through this stage successfully would result in a range of adult states from homosexuality to mental illness. Thus, becoming a man or woman could not be taken for granted nor would it result automatically from one's anatomical makeup; instead gender was psychic, cultural, and always difficult.

The implications of Freud's psychoanalytic theories for women would only emerge clearly after World War I when he himself wrote more about them. Nonetheless, his *Studies in Hysteria* (1899), which began his notoriety, refuted the common belief that hysteria was a disease confined to subnormal, less intelligent, and morally degenerate women. Freud's observations showed hysterics to be more than normally intelligent and also hypermoral. The many physical symptoms of hysteria—tics, fits, fainting, paralysis, and others—developed in the course of their psychosexual development and indicated profound psychic distress. Some of this distress, Freud maintained, would never have arisen had not society demanded so much repression of women's sexual drives. In other words, he pronounced that the sickness of a good many women was due to the moral codes of the time. Freud announced and publicized women's sexual nature. This, in itself, threatened middle-class morality and middle-class versions of what constituted proper gender roles. Even more shocking was Freud's later work, *Dora* (1905), a calm and accepting portrayal of a woman dealing, so he theorized, with incestuous and lesbian feelings.

Despite Freud's new ideas, psychoanalysis hewed to a normative line. Thus, psychoanalysts took it for granted that it was important for civilization that individuals develop masculinity and femininity. Freud saw a range of possible gender behavior, but he assumed that women should develop the traditional traits of female passivity within the domestic interior, to complement the fortified masculine ego that created civilization in the first place. Yet Freud's ideas posed a challenge and offered certain hopes to feminist theorists. Though arriving at the same conclusions as antifeminists, Freud opened a realm of psychic sexuality, explosive both in society and in the individual. The family, too, was now seen in a different light—rather than being the training ground for virtue and sweet sentiments, it was an arena where murderous and incestuous desire played itself out. Offering this revolutionary analysis, Freud raised frightening questions and yet still gave many conventional answers.

The Discussion of Sex Becomes Explicit

Freud's frankness in sexual matters and his view of the human personality and human society as based in sexuality was not strange for the times. Since the 1870s, along with the debate on marriage, sexual discussion in Europe had become more frequent, more clinical, and more wide-ranging. Preceding Freud were two Germans, Richard von Krafft-Ebbing (1840–1902) and Magnus Hirschfeld (1868–1935), who pioneered these discussions. In the beginning, medical interests seemed to dominate books that created new classifications of human sexuality. Hungarian Karoly Benkert (1824–1882) first coined the term "homosexual" in 1869, and in his *Psychopathia Sexualis* (1886), Krafft-Ebbing saw homosexuality as derived from both congenital and learned tendencies. Later, Hirschfeld popularized the idea of the homosexual as a person born into a third, or intermediate, sex. Partly due to Hirschfeld's leadership, homosexual culture thrived in Berlin, though not free from persecution. Societies such as the Scientific Humanitarian Committee and the Community of the Special consolidated, studied, and promoted homosexual culture. In England, Havelock Ellis's (1859–1939) *Sexual Inversion* (1894) described thousands of kinds of homosexual behavior. Ellis investigated historical and medical manifestations and built out of them a description of the homosexual or sexual invert.

For Ellis, sex was part of nature; thus, sexual life was not susceptible to moral categorization, only to scientific description. Interest like that of Ellis in fact created a new type of person—the homosexual. Previously considered isolated acts, same-sex relationships took on new import as the behavior of a human type. As a result, the definition of normality itself became more confined. With homosexuality and perversion carefully described and classified, heterosexuality was simultaneously limited. Heterosexuality meant never crossing the boundary separating the "normal" person from the "homosexual." Yet, ironically, doctors and theorists had charted homosexual behavior as rich and complex. Thus, enrichment for one subtracted from the sum of possible behavior acceptable to the "normally" sexed person. From such a self-contradicting view, twentieth-century sexual mores arose.

Many writings also affirmed women's sexuality. For example, Magnus Hirschfeld included in his annual *Yearbook for Intermediate Sexual Types* that began in 1899 pro-lesbian accounts of sexual life. There women announced that heterosexual marriage was not the only alternative, as many women had believed. Lesbians could develop their productive and creative talents and their vitality and be open to the new possibilities awaiting them now that remaining unmarried was no longer such an undesirable state. There were also stories of torment, but Hirschfeld believed such witnessing was "indispensable" to the lifting of sexual proscriptions. Interest in sexual reform stemmed from such concerns but still aimed at women's sexual welfare. For all his ambiguities and uncertainties, Havelock Ellis was concerned with women's sexual feelings and sought to liberate them in matters of physical sensation. Freud advocated ending the excessive repression of women that caused hysteria and its attendant miseries. Thus, a certain consideration for women's happiness motivated the debate over marriage, morals, and sexuality. It combated the conventional wisdom that virginity was necessary for brides but husbands must be "experienced," that love was irrelevant to marriage, and that same-sex relationships were "unnatural." This debate also introduced a new way of talking about women that neither spiritualized them into angels nor made them into beasts of burden or vessels for reproduction. Economic, sexual, and moral debate edged women closer to a parity with men in cultural discussion; however, the discourse occurred within a body of literature they still did not participate equally in creating.

Literature also discovered lesbianism, in ways at once fascinating and disturbing to society. In his *Remembrance of Things Past* (1913–1927), Marcel Proust (1871–1922) fixated on women dancing together, doing new dances in which bodies touched. His interest marked, however, but the culmination of several decades during which male artists such as Charles Baudelaire (1821–1867), Stéphane Mallarmé (1842–1898), and Theophile Gautier (1811–1872) in France had used lesbian eroticism as a literary device for challenging middle-class morality. Writings by women at the turn of the century expressed the self-discovery inherent in lesbianism. In 1903 in Berlin, Aimée Duc (pen name of Minna Adelt-Duc, 1869–?) published *Are These Women?*, a novel about highly talented women who build a social circle based on love for each other. The heroine, Minotchka Fernandoff, and her friends believed marriage worse than death for women. Like goods on display, women who pleased men were masculine rather than feminine. Minotchka's circle defended its femininity and its right to love in feminine ways. In the same year, Maria Janitschek's (1860–1927) story "The New Culture and the Old Morality" and Maria Eichhorn's (1879–?) *Fraulein Don Juan* appeared, both describing the comforts of lesbian love, especially during adolescence. A year later, the English writer Renée Vivien (pen name of Pauline Tarn, 1877–1909) wrote another modern lesbian classic, *A Woman Appeared to Me*. In it Vivien expressed her love for Nathalie Barney (1876–1972), whose Paris *salon* would soon become celebrated as a center for intellectual rebels, and especially for lesbians. Vivien's love for Barney fed her art and allowed her to discover a female literary tradition beginning with Sappho. This discovery involved sisterhood and oneness, a new aspect of women's unity. The appearance of lesbianism in major capital cities in the 1890s announced a major change. Author Oscar Wilde's notorious trial and imprisonment for sodomy in that decade showed how threatened many people were by these new developments. Disturbing the European psyche and undermining social customs on the one hand, lesbianism's emergence into the public eye marked a new synthesis, solved mysteries, resolved personal dilemmas, and stimulated art among many women on the other.

Some who called for new sexual standards also adopted "bohemian" ways of life. Setting up freer living arrangements, new women and men scorned Victorian, middle-class, or heterosexual morality. They did so in the name of love, companionship, artistic and economic independence, and individual fulfillment. Artist Gabriele Münter, actress Sarah Bernhardt (1844–1923), writer Rebecca West (1892–1983), political activist Rosa Luxemburg (1870–1919), reformer Helene Stöcker, suffragist Lida Gustava Heymann—a variety of women had different motives for living with men or women outside of wedlock. As the number of single people increased in western Europe by comparison with eastern countries (see tables on page 343), theorists justified the change. Political radicals, for example, saw marriage as a symbol of bourgeois hypocrisy and thought the marital state existed to uphold the system of private property. Anarchists felt that the state had no business regulating individual behavior and that state licensing had nothing to do with love. These rebels believed in love as the polar opposite of governmental institutions. The couple should create a private realm where interests of all kinds intermingled and where the human personality could develop. Many men liked the idea of intimacy with a new, liberated kind of woman who was educated and conversant in politics or the arts. A companion and sexual partner attracted them more than a traditional mother/wife who guarded a separate sphere. Also, the formation of companionable relationships defied arranged marriages based on family interest. In so doing, it fostered the twentieth-century trend of forming couples on the basis of desire rather than prudence or productivity. Moreover, this desire rested on individual choice.

Individual choice depended first of all on women's being able to speak freely. The work of Josephine Butler marked a crucial first step in women's becoming more outspoken, as did that of Nelly Roussel (1878–1922), who advocated birthstrikes in France, Lida Gustava Heymann, who attacked regulation in Germany, and the founders of the Mariuccine, who helped sexual victims in Italy.* First, all of these women broke the taboo that said respectable women kept silent on sexual issues. They brought every issue having to do with sexuality and reproduction to the fore in an assertion of women's sexual needs. In this assertive atmosphere, the prostitute served as the symbol of sexual nonfreedom because her sexuality was linked to economic need. This insight directed women's sexual discourse along economic lines. Swedish feminist Ellen Key led the way in advocating an economic security for mothers. For her, sexual harmony and reproductive well-being only existed in the context of material independence. Economic dependence meant sexual slavery for

---

*See Chapter 6.

women. This assertion was in direct opposition to the idea that the economic world was unrelated to the domestic; ultimately, it was an attack on separate spheres based on compulsory sexuality in the home. The propertyless state of the housewife or prostitute, along with her silence on sexual matters, served only to hinder worthwhile relationships between men and women.

The parallels between prostitution and middle-class women's sexual lives inspired reformers to act and write. Waging war against regulation, women launched their own dialogue about sexuality. First, they saw the "normal" sex-

Comparison of Single Population in Europe and Eastern Europe around 1900 (Single population as percent of total population in age group)

Europe (except Eastern Europe)

Country	Men			Women		
	20–24	*25–29*	*45–49*	*20–24*	*25–29*	*45–49*
Austria	93	51	11	66	38	13
Belgium	85	50	16	71	41	17
Denmark	88	50	9	75	42	13
Finland	84	51	14	68	40	15
France	90	48	11	58	30	12
Germany	91	48	9	71	34	10
Great Britain	83	47	12	73	42	15
Holland	89	53	13	79	44	14
Iceland	92	66·	19	81	56	29
Ireland	96	78	20	86	59	17
Italy	86	46	11	60	30	11
Norway	86	54	11	77	48	18
Portugal	84	48	13	69	41	20
Sweden	92	61	13	80	52	19
Switzerland	91	58	16	78	45	17

Eastern Europe

Country	Men			Women		
	20–24	*25–29*	*45–49*	*20–24*	*25–29*	*45–49*
Greece	82	47	9	44	13	4
Hungary	81	31	5	36	15	4
Romania	67	21	5	20	8	3
Bulgaria	58	23	3	24	3	1
U.S.S.R.	51	18	3	28	9	4
Serbia	50	18	3	16	2	1

Source: J. Hajnal, "European Marriage Patterns in Perspective," in D. V. Glass and D. E. C. Eversley, *Population in History. Essays in Historical Demography* (London: Edward Arnold, 1965), 102–103 [101–143].

ual life as diseased. In 1910, a German physician, Grete Meisel-Hess, wrote *The Sexual Crisis*, in which she used Darwinian motifs to talk about contemporary marriage. Male breadwinners were accorded an inflated value and a disproportionate power, she wrote, in a civilization that prohibited women from similar activity. Moreover, because marriages were based on this unnatural power, they were unhealthy and so were the offspring. Meisel-Hess prescribed, first, economic independence for women, and second, trial sexual relations until the final love match took place. Translated into English, her work complemented much else that pointed to a diseased state of male sexuality and the general sexual compulsion men exercised. Throughout Europe, women discussed male immorality and the absence of the much vaunted "chivalry" on which the sociosexual order was supposed to rest. Meisel-Hess was only one who said that, toward a woman who was unprotected or who responded to sexual advances, a man would be the "basest of roughs," his behavior "the very reverse of chivalrous."[11] The final and most extreme form of this argument appeared in Christabel Pankhurst's (1880–1958) *The Great Scourge* (1913), which called marriage a dangerous institution because of men. Not only did men mistreat their wives in many obvious ways, they infected women with venereal disease as a result of their own unchecked sexuality. Therein lay the secret, according to Pankhurst, of most households: no one was immune—not women, not children—from male disease. Rather than being protectors of society, men were its scourge.

From these assertions arose others about women's sexuality and women's rights. A French writer affirmed that "woman is not just a desired being; she desires; the sexual instinct speaks in her also."[12] German sex reformer Helene Stöcker (1869–1943) proclaimed the need to refute middle-class ideas of woman's sexuality. A Nietzschean and head of the German Society for the Protection of Mothers, Stöcker believed that new ideas about sex could alter its nature. Changing people's vocabulary and attitudes toward physical relations would make those relations more vibrant and more elevated. Spanish anarchist and schoolteacher Teresa Mañé (who used the pen name Soledad Gustavo), in *La Revista Blanca* in 1898, denounced "a society that makes children a burden for their parents . . . and that makes love a matter of commerce."[13] Groups such as Stöcker's were scattered across Europe, and their concern with marriage and motherhood led them to focus on changing the cultural context in which these social institutions operated. Thus, Nelly Roussel lectured to enthusiastic French audiences about the mother as "the eternally sacrificed one" and called for a birth strike, or abstinence from sex, until women's conditions improved. Many spoke of motherhood and child care in terms of "improving the race." However, women were interested in improving conditions in the home for different reasons from those motivating governments. When women argued for improved health and hygiene for themselves and their children, they were not thinking in terms of better armies, more colonial conquests, or winning wars. (In fact, many of these sex reformers were pacifists who remained so even during World War I.) For these reformers, the benefits would accrue to individuals and to the general social well-being. Ellen Key spoke of preserving motherhood as a way of maintaining the "critically symmetrical woman" who could bring about social balance.[14] Thus, the theory of republican motherhood branched out in new directions at the turn of the century.

Birth Control and Sexual Rights

The debate on sexuality involved a range of topics, but nothing provoked more controversy than birth control, or the right to limit fertility. Falling fertility was perhaps the main ingredient in changing the roles and perceptions of women. By the early twentieth century, Europeans had started dramatically reducing family size in one of the most striking changes in history. In the forty-year period before World War I, most countries began a population decline that leveled off at figures that represented half the earlier population. France, the canton of Geneva, and a small section of Hungary began this steady decline by the mid–nineteenth century, whereas Ireland and Albania only started in the late 1920s and 1950s, respectively (see graph on page 346). In the "high" Victorian period, the average family in England had 6.6 live births; by the 1920s and 1930s family size had declined to slightly more than 2 children per couple. Besides geographical variations, there were also class differences in fertility rates. In the city of Rotterdam, professional couples who married between 1879 and 1893 had only three-fifths as many children as did shopkeepers and half as many as artisans or manual workers. In London in 1901, the fertility rate per 1,000 married women was 282 in working-class Bethnal Green and 183 in upper-class Hampstead. Where birth control propagandists were active, fertility dropped among some working-class constituencies. In Roubaix and Tourcoing in northern France, the birth rate fell by a third and more between 1894 and 1908 alone.[15]

Whatever their class, women took a variety of measures to reduce their fertility. In the 1880s, Dutch doctors recommended the individually fitted cervical cap, known as the Dutch cap, which had been invented by a German physician, Wilhelm Mensinga. Condoms were available from birth control organizations and some pharmacists. Some women used a kind of vaginal sponge and also various solutions, including quinine and plain water, for postcoital cleansing. *Coitus interruptus,* or withdrawal, was widely practiced as well. A handloom weaver in northern France recalled how birth-control information spread in the early twentieth century: "We didn't want any children yet. My brother-in-law Paul had explained to [my husband] how one could have kids only when one wanted them. Auguste followed his advice scrupulously."[16] Finally, many types of practitioners administered abortions. This form of fertility reduction was so popular in Paris in the 1880s that an estimated 100,000 abortions took place.

The birth-control cause spawned efforts by individuals and organizations. In the Netherlands, Aletta Jacobs (1854–1929) popularized the Dutch cap. The first woman to win a medical degree in a Dutch university, Jacobs practiced among the poor in Amsterdam and quickly understood how central birth

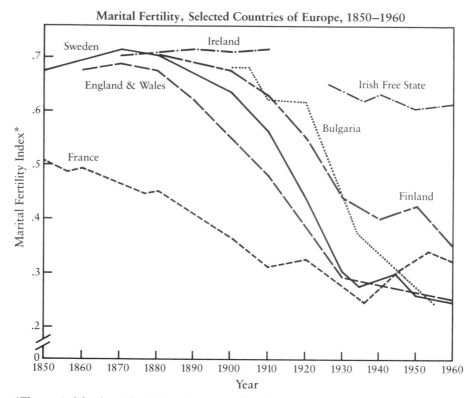

Marital Fertility, Selected Countries of Europe, 1850–1960

*The marital fertility index is based on the fertility of a group called the Hutterites. These people marry young, practice no contraception, and thus have what demographers call "absolute fertility." The scale in this graph represents a complex formula which was developed to measure fertility of women in various countries at various times against Hutterite fertility.

Source: Ansley J. Coale, "The Decline of Fertility in Europe from the French Revolution to World War II," in S.J. Behrman, Leslie Corsa, and Ronald Freedman, eds., *Fertility and Family Planning: A World View* (Ann Arbor: University of Michigan Press, 1969) 23 [3-24].

control was to improving their health. A neo-Malthusian league took shape in the Netherlands as did similar groups in many countries in the late 1870s and early 1880s. These organizations took their name from Thomas Malthus, the economist who had written early in the nineteenth century about the close connection between fertility control and economic well-being. The chief proponent of the English neo-Malthusian movement, Dr. George Drysdale, hoped to alleviate social problems through birth control: "The error of Socialism is, that it attributes to the constitution of society and to *competition . . .* the evils, which really spring from the principal of population."[17] From the mid-1850s to 1905, Drysdale's *Elements of Social Science; or Physical, Sexual, and Natural Religion* went through 35 editions and was translated into most European languages including Swedish and Hungarian. In general, the neo-Malthusian leagues sought to improve marital harmony through birth control and improved sexual knowledge, but also to bring social peace by improving the condition of the working class. Although neo-Malthusianism attracted working-class adherents, it was basically a middle-class movement. Well-being depended on knowledge and rational control of the body, these reformers argued, as they extended Enlightenment principles to new areas of behavior.

French physician Madeleine Pelletier (1876–1939) was among those who argued for birth control and abortion as being women's particular rights. Having obtained her medical education in spite of objections and harassment, Pelletier herself performed abortions and provided information on birth control. As more and more public officials in France advocated increasing family size to boost the French population, she became outspoken in her denunciations of such "barbarism." For her, intensive reproductivity indicated a civilization on an "inferior rung of the biological ladder."[18] Higher forms of development were manifested in a concern for individual well-being. For Pelletier, women as individuals had greater rights than the species as a whole, and people who asserted the rights of the race or species above those of the individual only betrayed their inferior state of evolution. Her theories applied the classical ideal of rights to reproductive issues rather than to market or productive ones alone.

Thus, birth control moved toward being a fact of reproductive life at the end of the nineteenth century as most European populations started a dramatic decline. Perhaps more than anything else occurring at the time, this change in fertility affected the lives of women and made them "new." Birth control and changing patterns of fertility were also part of a debate that tried to accommodate people's cultural beliefs to their actual practices. Birth control led society to face unprecedented questions about the terms of replenishing the human species. The old subsistence organization of population had disappeared for good and brought new suggestions for gender definition. The changes threatened male sexuality insofar as it was constructed around generating life. Politicians worried about impotence—not just in terms of reproduction but as affecting society as a whole. In particular, they focused on the "new" woman and even the middle-class woman in general as somehow selfish in her demands for rights, which seemed to imperil the social structure. Yet these demands were expressions of a rapidly changing reproductive and productive situation. For one thing, what Ellen Key called "the rapturous chivalry"[19] on which nineteenth-century society had built itself had not protected women from poverty and inegalitarianism. The debates over wages, sexuality, and motherhood made this much clear. Instead women had to fight for education, jobs, and good health without any chivalric aid from males, who instead provided resistance all along the way. Second, the conditions attending motherhood—the much praised role of women—were so miserable they could scarcely bear any scrutiny. Social investigation had uncovered only disjuncture and inequity. By the 1890s many women had fastened on the vote as the mechanism by which these social inequities would be righted.

Women's Politicization Continues

Across Europe as the nineteenth century ended, representative politics was becoming the order of the day. With the reform bill of 1884, more men could vote in England than ever before, and the French Third Republic (1870–1940) reestablished universal male suffrage. Male citizens of newly united Italy or Germany could vote, and even Russian peasants participated in making decisions about the use of land within villages and in the local *zemstvos*, or councils. Excluded from this system, women nonetheless participated in national politics in a variety of ways. For example, many female activists worked for Home Rule in Ireland. As teachers, missionaries, and health professionals, they furthered the European imperial mission in the colonies. They also continued the tradition of conducting political *salons*: Juliette Lamber's *salon* in Paris, for example, built the short-lived power of Gambetta in France. German and English women formed auxiliaries to political parties and sometimes served in local government. Finally, their presence adorned the increasingly elaborate ceremonials of European court life, which were part of the world of political ritual and served as a glamorous façade for politics.

However, many women wanted the same kind of citizenship that men had. By the turn of the century, a women's movement of significant size had taken shape. In 1915, the National American Women's Suffrage Association boasted two million members. Until recently, this huge suffrage society had dwarfed the significance of other movements. In France, much smaller societies drew approximately 100,000 adherents, but this number was greater than the membership of French trade unions for both sexes. Somewhere between these two in size, the English movement created the greatest stir as a result of its audacious tactics. In Germany, suffragism met with hostility from other activists on women's behalf. Whatever its size, the suffrage movement in each country marked a divide, in that it represented the first mass organization of women on a political terrain far more extensive than that of the 1850s and 1860s. German feminist Käthe Schirmacher called it "the most radical demand made by organized women."[20] Because of their organization in great numbers to try to make policies beyond the home, these were indeed new women.

The suffrage movement developed from a base of varied public activities and a wide-ranging array of issues. Settlement house workers, proponents of social purity, temperance reformers, vegetarians, and other types of activists considered themselves part of the "woman movement"—the term "feminist" was only just beginning to be used. Some of these activists were "new women," but many were middle-class housewives or working-class mothers. When German women reported on the state of the movement in their country in the 1880s, they included not just Louise Otto-Peters's National Association of German Women, but also the Lette Society, which was founded by middle-class reformers to train working-class women. Broadly conceived around a range of property, marital, and cultural issues, the woman movement experienced a deliberate refocusing by the end of the nineteenth century, which produced a variety of suffrage groups. The vitality of these groups sprang from women's prior experience with reform. In fact, for many activists the emphasis on suffrage would unify the dispersed efforts that earlier reform seemed to engender and would resolve the intense debate over gender relations. The drive for the vote grew out of the liberal principles that by 1900 influenced most governments. Many women also saw the vote as a new broom for doing some social housekeeping in order to improve the conditions of motherhood. All the social service that had already been accomplished by women and the century of their raising citizens served as their credentials, their claim to the franchise. If that did not suffice, they were prepared to use the expertise at organizing, publicizing, raising funds, influencing politicians, and political analyzing that had been gained over the decades.

The organization of a suffrage movement involved the coordination and consolidation of the other women's groups. In the 1890s in England, more than fifty suffrage associations joined to form the National Union of Women's Suffrage Societies. In France, all women's groups united into a moderate feminist council, which grew from 21,000 members in 1901 to close to 100,000 members in 1914. This group was rivaled by the French Union for Women's Suffrage, founded in 1909, which took a more forthright pro-suffrage stand. In Germany, two groups also arose, and, as in France, attempts at unity revealed strong differences among feminists. In Russia, the first strong feminist "union" was made up of philanthropic and other women's groups, in which commitment to suffrage was initially weak. In all cases, however, the unification of groups into a movement generated a bureaucracy with paid employees and organizers—that is, professional staffs that worked for wages, communicated via newspapers and mailings, and maintained permanent headquarters. Moreover, women in these organizations not only developed networks among themselves, but also maintained contacts with male allies and male feminists. Thus an initiation into the workings of politics became an ongoing aspect of suffrage work. Finally, national societies began regularly holding congresses for suffragists. At such meetings, hundreds of delegates gathered to study women's issues in general. Usually the programs had sections on labor, suffrage, marriage and family, education, and similar subjects. Knowledgeable women spoke, differences received an airing, and women from all parts of a given country could receive inspiration for what was in some cases difficult, though increasingly collective, activity.

Women forged the final organizational link in the suffrage chain when they created an international women's suffrage association. Proposed in the 1880s by the American suffrage leader Susan B. Anthony (1820–1906), the idea was dropped when European support seemed insufficient. At the turn of the century, the drive for an international association revived, and a congress convened in 1904 in Berlin. The International Women's Suffrage Alliance that subsequently developed served as a policy-making group, often pushing national organizations and councils toward greater determination and parallel efforts. For example, the more committed suffragists from France received encouragement from alliance leaders of more "advanced" countries. Sometimes such encouragement was necessary to reassure women that suffrage was a worthy and even proper aspiration. Although many women had no problem supporting changes that would improve the conditions of motherhood, they had a more difficult time agitating for suffrage. In 1896, for example, Ellen Key attacked women's desire to vote in a speech entitled "The Abuse of Women's Strength." Others, however, saw the vote as a proper thing for mothers. Once international feminism had moved beyond its early goals of the 1850s and 1860s, it had two ideological threads: one that perpetuated the emphasis on motherhood as the source of rights, and a second that refuted this emphasis on motherhood in the name of liberalism. Austrian Rosa Mayreder (1858–1938) put the second viewpoint in a 1913 essay: "The woman who omits to develop any talent of her own, because of her belief that it is possible to develop it in her son will, in ninety-nine out of a hundred cases, be grievously cheated."[21] Nonetheless, because motherhood touched powerful political interests and debate on it might open up new questions of sexuality, it remained a vigorous motivating force.

Toward the Vote

In England, women had failed to obtain the national franchise in the electoral reforms of the late 1860s, but they had gained the right to vote locally (1869) and to serve in local offices as poor law guardians and on school boards. Despite these gains the quest for suffrage seemed to falter in the 1870s and 1880s. The death of John Stuart Mill was a setback; so was the persistent refusal of Liberal leaders in Parliament to help, even though women saw themselves allied to liberalism. While they were ignored, British suffragists watched the franchise extended to more men in the 1880s. Were that not enough to deflate their resolve, they began quarreling among themselves over sexual morality. In particular, Josephine Butler's crusade against regulated prostitution provoked dissension because it pitted women against those in the government from which they hoped to get support for female suffrage. In addition, the topic so contradicted some women's concept of virtuous motherhood that they could not bear being associated with the champions of prostitutes' rights. Thus, although feminism was thriving during these decades as women gained property rights, educational opportunity, and marital reform, the middle-class suffragists of London split into groups based on their attitudes toward sexual debate. Until her death in 1890, Lydia Becker continued the struggle for suffrage in her *Women's Suffrage Journal*, but for many women these decades were discouraging.

Late in the 1890s, women set aside their differences to form the National Union of Women's Suffrage Societies (NUWSS) with Millicent Garrett Fawcett (1847–1929) at its head. Several stories circulated about how Fawcett became a feminist. One story says she got her first inspiration when just a child from Emily Davies while sitting around the fire one evening. Davies assigned herself the mission of opening education to women and the conquest of medicine to

Millicent's older sister, Elizabeth, who did become a doctor; "Milly" received the task of getting women the right to vote. Another story fixes the origins of Fawcett's activism at the trial of a thief who had stolen her purse. Although she was the victim, the law said the purse—being a piece of property—belonged to her husband, and so the charge read. The wording of the charge, so Fawcett later claimed, made her seem culpable as well. From that moment, she began working for property reform; by the 1890s, she was undisputed leader of the women's suffrage movement in England.

Accounts of the suffrage movement in England have generally characterized it as middle-class. Despite the dominance of women like Millicent Garrett Fawcett, England did have a powerful working-class suffrage movement among textile workers in the north, women miners, and sweated workers. Just as suffrage groups in the United States had memberships that included black and working-class and bourgeois women, so by the turn of the century did every occupational group in England want its own representatives in the NUWSS. The most vigorous of these groups was the Lancashire and Cheshire Women Textile and Other Workers' Representation Committee, which took the campaign for suffrage into the countryside by giving speeches to crowds of working men and women. In the working class, winning the vote seemed to have a different air, an urgency that came from economic facts of life. One organizer, Selina Cooper, bluntly lectured against an abstract equality with men, which she claimed, motivated middle-class suffragists. She said that suffrage was crucial to meet "the needs of the people" and to achieve such practical ends as "the feeding of children." The vote was not, she maintained, "a plaything."[22] Understanding the connection between political impotence and low wages, Ada Nield Chew had started her reform activities by pointing to the terrible conditions in the sweatshop where she worked. For this young activist, women earned not a "living wage," but a lingering, "dying wage."[23] From her individual protest, she proceeded to trade unionism and finally became a charismatic and tireless suffrage speaker. The English suffrage movement thrived where women constituted a relatively better paid segment of the female labor force. Having greater contact with the public and better working conditions then sweated laborers, industrial workers promoted a measure of cross-class alliance.

A third force in English feminism, the Women's Social and Political Union (WSPU), formed no alliances with other groups. Founded by Emmeline Pankhurst (1858–1928) and her daughters Christabel (1880–1958) and Sylvia (1882–1960), the WSPU took a militant stand. Emmeline Pankhurst had gotten her first taste of feminist politics at the side of her husband, Richard, an activist in the cause of women's rights. She also became interested in the Independent Labor Party in her native city of Manchester. Forced to support herself and her family after her husband's death in the 1890s, Emmeline Pankhurst opened a small store and also began running for local offices for which women had become eligible. Her first victory was election to the Manchester School Board in 1900. From then on, Pankhurst accelerated her political activity and founded the WSPU in 1903. Her rationale for forming a new suffrage group was simple and striking: other groups were too timid. Men understood only violence; they respected only property. So the WSPU engaged in attacks on property and spectacular kinds of civil disobedience. The first attention the group attracted was in 1905 when Christabel and her working-class friend Annie Kenney (1879–1953) broke up a political rally by heckling the speakers concerning women's suffrage. The two were physically mistreated and thrown from the lecture hall and arrested. Released from prison with great fanfare, they, as well as the other WSPU leaders, realized the importance of drama, publicity, and a certain kind of martyrdom. From then on the members of the WSPU, led always by the Pankhursts, made spectacular mass parades, chained themselves to the gates of Parliament whenever a suffrage issue was to be voted on, and staged hunger strikes whenever they were arrested. Their activities became increasingly violent and later included acts of terrorism such as planting bombs, slashing works of art, and smashing plate-glass windows of urban businesses. The WSPU was often racked by internal dissension and defections from the Pankhursts' increasingly dictatorial control, but it certainly marked a new stage in the suffrage movement.

Suffragists had initially acted within the liberal credo of a harmonious social order, consensual politics, and the rights of property. The WSPU overturned all these principles by bringing violence, militant dissent, and deliberate destruction into English public life. Many historians have claimed these inversions were part and parcel of the decay of a previous European way of life. "Liberal" England declined in part because of the WSPU. The WSPU was a manifestation of the challenge to the entire gender order of liberal society. It was not that other groups failed to pose such a challenge, but they did it less visibly. Other suffragists certainly announced their intention of improving male morality via the female vote; many wanted a new power for motherhood via the vote as well. In making these claims, suffragists of other groups usually maintained their decorum and a certain respect for established social norms. All suffragists were announcing change, but the WSPU made that announcement violently and thus aroused overt fear of and hostility toward women. Meeting up with WSPU demonstrators, men grabbed them by their breasts, punched them, dragged them by the hair, and generally expressed the hostility that might otherwise have been covered over by social convention. Sexual warfare became stark rather than controlled. Forces of irrationality, which people saw everywhere in Europe on the eve of World War I, built to a fevered pitch until Derby Day, May 31, 1913. Then WSPU activist Emily Wilding Davison (1872–1913) ran in front of the King's horses and was trampled to death. This ghastly moment dramatically punctuated a decade during which the WSPU had held the attention of the world. During that decade, women and men had regarded its activities in England with hope, with fear, with disdain. WSPU members, along with writers, artists, and thinkers, proclaimed a new world that the twentieth century had in store for everyone.

Other national movements were far less violent. French feminists had to promote their programs during threatening times for the nation they wanted to participate in. The Third Republic (1870–1940) was born of defeat at the hands of the Germans and had barely triumphed over both monarchists and socialists. Feminists had to try to make progress in an atmosphere charged with uncertainty, and, in addition, they sympathized with the goals of moderate political leaders. When Leon Richer and Maria Deraismes (1828–1894) organized two groups, The French League for Women's Rights and The Society to Improve the Condition of Women and Claim Their Rights, respectively, in the 1870s, French feminism began its modern era. Wealthy and single, Deraismes supported the second group with her money and with her captivating speaking ability. She passionately attacked well-known men who criticized women writers or poor women. She also pointed out the inconsistencies of the Third Republic, which had taken the place of Napoleon's Second Empire. To her way of thinking, the republic was no advance at all and was in fact in power on false grounds because it obviously did not even believe in that minimal word of its creed—equality. Deraismes's quest for women's rights met strong resistance from the national government. At various times in the 1870s and 1880s, the republic was threatened by growing socialism on the left or monarchism on the right. As a sign of its stability, the government began to use language that invoked family stability. Republican politics shored itself up by invoking the family as the "backbone" of French order and patriotism. To further ensure stability, the government sent prominent troublesome women (such as Louise Michel) into exile, prevented Richer's and Deraismes's first women's group from meeting, and kept other feminists from lecturing. Constantly harassed by the republic whose principles it believed in, the French feminist movement tried to demonstrate its loyalty by good behavior. Republican propriety—which meant middle-class good manners—characterized the majority of French feminists up until World War I.

Hubertine Auclert (1848–1914) was also a well-to-do woman, but unlike other French feminists, she did not display ladylike behavior. Nor did she believe in a moderate kind of feminism. Starting late in the 1870s, she began championing suffrage despite republican arguments against it. In those days, with the republic proclaiming that security came first, women's suffrage was labeled just one more radical threat. Most women, so the argument ran, were ignorant, superstitious, and hyperreligious. If granted the vote, their first use of it would be to return the monarchy, with Catholicism as its official religion. Auclert saw herself as a republican and was undeterred by such an argument. For her, republicanism was fraudulent if it failed to allow universal suffrage for both sexes. Moreover, she boldly pointed out, the word "français" meant French people of both sexes when it came to paying taxes. Why did it mean French men only when it came to voting? Auclert made her radical demands in radical ways—by refusing to pay taxes, by toppling voting urns in 1907, and by staging protests and demonstrations. She also ran a newspaper. Auclert called attention to herself and her cause and found allies wherever she could. One of her first pro-suffrage acts, for example, involved getting the socialist party's commitment to women's suffrage—hardly likely to make her cause respectable. Though an embarrassment to moderates, Auclert pushed feminism in France unwillingly toward suffrage for more than forty years.

Following these pioneers, a whole range of women's groups agitating for rights appeared in France by the 1890s. Nonetheless, their activities still focused on basic issues long since settled in England and the United States. For example, Jeanne Schmahl (1847–1915) and her group, The Forerunner, lobbied singlemindedly for women's right to keep the wages they earned. Other groups sought guardianship of children, the right to serve as a civil witness, or the right to bring paternity suits against the fathers of illegitimate children. For French women, these and other issues rested on rational, Enlightenment principles. In fact, the entire movement was directed toward uprooting the gender system established by the Napoleonic Code. From women's point of view, there was little that was rational in this much touted code of laws. Instead, it gave French women a legal identity as propertyless, subordinate wives and mothers, and this identity shaped their feminist struggles.

Class and religion divided French feminists. The legacy of Catholicism continued to have a strong effect. By the early twentieth century, Catholic women developed a language that affirmed womanhood in the strongest terms. Because the Catholic Church in France saw itself as engaged in a battle with the Third Republic and its politicians, Catholic women avoided the language of republicanism and rationalism. Though adopting the cause of women, they never abandoned the rhetoric of duty and subordination. Instead they emphasized the power of female saints, religious women, and Catholic benefactresses in a compelling way. On the other side of the political fence, republican feminists, whose leaders such as Sarah Monod (1836–1912) and Julie Siegfried (1848–1922) were overwhelmingly Protestant and upper-middle-class, continued their allegiance to the politics of their husbands—many of them prominent politicians. Suspicious of Catholicism, only a few tried to form alliances with the multitudes of potential feminists who supported the church. This middle-class and republican form of feminism had a vitality in France in the pre-war decades. Marguerite Durand (1865–1936) ran and funded her famous *La Fronde,* a daily newspaper written and printed by women. Its title referred to the seventeenth-century rebellion against the monarchy. The National Council of French Women grew in numbers and spread to the provinces. By the early twentieth century, women had even held a few mass demonstrations: these would not, however, become an established form of activity for French feminists.

Most French women first thought in terms of advancing the tradition of French rights and French rationality when they suggested an amelioration of women's condition. No matter what their politics, they saw themselves as preserving embattled French values—the legendary "rights of man." Thus, French feminists were always torn on issues such as birth control that threatened French glory. Though some, Madeleine Pelletier, for example, recognized that the most important issue for feminists was gender, all too many feminists put other issues first, such as French nationalism, republicanism, or Catholicism. As a result of such priorities, France remained, in Auclert's words, a nation of "well-trained sheep," with women "excommunicated from public life."[24]

The French feminist movement kept to a middle course because of the alignment of political forces, and so did many in the German movement. In Germany, however, conservatism was the middle way. After unification of the German states under the Prussian monarchy, the national ethos became increasingly royalist and imperialist. Although there was a heritage of liberal principles from which feminists could draw, the accomplishment of German unification after a series of victorious wars made ideas of natural rights, equality, and rationalism seem rather dull. Simultaneously, Germany was rapidly industrializing, and capitalist values of progress and mobility competed with those of caste and duty, which had long dominated German life. In this atmosphere of political conservatism and economic growth, German women developed many organizations reflecting the whole spectrum of political and social views. Philanthropic organizations patronized by the empress coexisted and competed with those advocating free love. As a result, the alignment of German women was perhaps the most interesting in all of Europe. Like French feminists in the 1830s, some Germans at the beginning of the twentieth century seemed to have a theoretical lead.

The clash of ideological forces made the German movement exciting. On the one side, Social Democrats—advocates for women, though opponents of a "women's movement"—complained constantly about the policies and programs of middle-class organizations. At another extreme, radicals within the movement contested entrenched conservatism by adopting a range of causes, including prostitution, a new morality, and the legalization of abortion. Neither social democracy nor radicalism pleased the mainstream feminist movement, which had begun during the blossoming of German conservatism after 1848. In 1865, Louise Otto-Peters, once a fairly fiery revolutionary, had founded (along with Augusta Schmidt, Henrietta Goldschmidt, Ottilie von Steyber, and Lina Morgenstern) the General German Woman's Association (Allgemeiner Deutscher Frauenverein, or ADF), which concentrated for decades on issues such as education and women's work. Because of the laws against women attending political meetings, the ADF constantly claimed to have nonpolitical purposes and focused on *Bildung*, or cultural self-development, as did feminists in Austria. Working for improvement in middle-class women's secondary education and for their gradual admission to universities, the association also monitored legal changes, especially the revising of the legal code. Its tactics were always ladylike, which some have interpreted as ineffective. Nonetheless, the ADF did achieve the admission of women to German universities, though many believe it failed dismally because the law code of 1900 made divorce more, rather than less, difficult to obtain.

Around the ADF there developed competing and coordinate organizations for charitable and self-help purposes. By the 1890s, these had become so numerous that, following the example of organizations in other countries, they united to form the Union of German Women's Associations (Bund Deutscher Frauenvereine, or BDF). It was within the BDF that the struggles over the direction of the women's movement took place. Initially dominated by conservatives such as Helene Lange and Augusta Schmidt, the BDF was both inspired and divided for the next decade and a half by three issues: regulation of prostitution, new morality, and suffrage. In 1876, Hedwig Dohm, in *Women's Nature and Privilege*, doubted that "men have always been so just, so noble, that the fate of more than half mankind can be safely entrusted to their pure hands."[25] Reciting men's deeds against women throughout the course of history, Dohm pronounced chivalry nonexistent and declared the need for suffrage to be urgent. Yet such a pronouncement had little effect in a country still dominated by aristocratic military men. Moreover, the government blocked women's progress at the fundamental level of culture by such measures as forbidding the opening of college preparatory schools unless there were already schools for domestic training in the area. The many issues with which German women were concerned gave the movement diversity and spawned a host of splinter groups working for (or against) each particular cause. Women of these groups were constantly in motion, going from city to city, holding rallies and lectures to educate on behalf of their chosen cause.

Perhaps the most striking modern women in Russia had first appeared in the 1860s.* By the last decades of the nineteenth century, the descendants of these new women had gone beyond the individualistic self-improvement and liberated living arrangements. They developed interest in the lot of peasants and urban workers. By the 1880s, young radicals had formed bands that went into the countryside to educate, nurse, and organize whoever would listen to them. The more the police pursued them, the more daring the groups became and the more directly they began attacking the Russian government. In 1877, Vera Zasulich (1849–1919), daughter of a landowner, shot the governor-general of St. Petersburg after hearing that he had had a prisoner beaten for not removing his cap. Zasulich's act, as well as the stirring defense she made, inspired further terrorism, which increased right up until the revolution in 1917. One of the radical groups, the People's Will, focused on assassinating the czar, whose very existence, they believed, prevented any amelioration of the peasants' conditions. On March 1, 1881, they succeeded. One-third of the People's Will executive committee was female, and the key to the successful assassination was Sophia Perovskaia (1853–1881), the daughter of a major czarist official and a rebel against her father since her teens. Perovskaia exemplified the tendency of Russian women revolutionaries to be at the forefront of their group's activities. She appeared to her friends as someone committed to the peasantry and driven by a hatred for those who treated peasants as less than human. Moving from participation in a radical study group to living with the peasantry and finally to terrorism, Perovskaia became the first woman executed for political activity in Russia.

Compared to all that women had done earlier—assassinating the czar, setting up cooperatives, and participating in the most radical associations—Russia's feminist movement of the 1890s seemed tame. In 1895, Anna Nikitichna Shabanova (1848–1932), a doctor educated first in Helsinki and then in the

---

*See Chapter 6.

Russian women's educational system, and an older feminist, Anna Filosofova (1837–1912), organized the Mutual Philanthropic Society. Dominated by upper-class women, this society sponsored everything from housing for working women to day-care centers. Its emphasis on charity was a sign of the problems facing Russian feminists after the radical seventies and eighties. By the time women were ready to join the feminist movement developing internationally, the Russian government was too fearful of women's activism to allow anything but the mildest and most innocuous kind of activity. The empress would not even allow her picture to appear on diplomas for women's courses that had traditionally received the imperial blessings. But the restrictions were soon loosened by events, and when a new uprising against autocracy erupted in 1905, feminists were ready to make the most of it. A group of women journalists and their supporters founded the All-Russian Union for Women's Equality. Their demand was for rights, particularly local voting rights in the *zemstvos,* or regional councils, and in city government. Shabanova inspired her group to make similar demands. Finally, a Women's Progressive Party arose with a broad platform of civil and political rights for women.

In the first decade of the twentieth century, all these groups demanded rights from the Russian parliament, or Duma, that had just been established. In the atmosphere of insecurity that pervaded the parliament, support for women's rights seemed a luxury and also dangerous, given the average woman's alleged potential for conservative behavior such as support for the church and imperial family. In the face of opposition from all but radical and socialist parties, some women took to the streets, invaded the Duma, or went out into the countryside in imitation of their more radical contemporaries to rouse the peasantry and to educate them. Less glamorously, others kept up constant lobbying of politicians of every persuasion, and even formed women's auxiliaries for those parties that seemed promising. Harassed from both right and left, the feminists-turned-suffragists had a difficult time. Until the outbreak of World War I, they suffered official and unofficial reprobation and constantly regrouped around a range of issues from motherhood and prostitution to women's labor and the vote.

Antifeminism and Pre-War Tensions

"The normal woman has many characteristics which she shares with the savage and the child (irascibility, vengeance, jealousy, vanity) as well as other characteristics . . . which prevent her from approximating the conduct of men—that equilibrium between rights and duties, egotism and altruism"[26] wrote a French criminal anthropologist at the end of the nineteenth century. Comparing woman to the savage, who was being conquered by imperialists at this time, this writer was but one of many who attempted to downgrade feminist activities because of fear of the results. Crowds of English men greeted working-class suffragist speakers with jeers: "Go home and wash the pots" or "what about the old man's kippers?"[27] In the 1880s, Swedish author August Strind-

An Appeal Against Female Suffrage

Many educated women opposed the vote for women, among them Mrs. Humphrey Ward (1851–1920), a highly respected and popular author. Disturbed by the agitation for female suffrage, she penned the following statement and published it with the endorsement of a number of leading upper-class women.

> We, the undersigned, wish to appeal to the common sense and the educated thought of the men and women of England against the proposed extension of the Parliamentary suffrage to women.
>
> While desiring the fullest possible development of the powers, energies, and education of women, we believe that their work for the State, and their responsibilities towards it, must always differ essentially from those of men, and that therefore their share in the working of the State machinery should be different from that assigned to men. Certain large departments of the national life are of necessity worked exclusively by men. To men belong the struggle of debate and legislation in Parliament; the working of the army and navy; all the heavy, laborious, fundamental industries of the State, such as those of mines, metals, and railways; the lead and supervision of English commerce, the service of that merchant fleet on which our food supply depends.
>
> At the same time we are heartily in sympathy with all the recent efforts which have been made to give women a more important part in those affairs of the community where their interests and those of men are equally concerned; where it is possible for them not only to decide but to help in carrying out, and where, therefore, judgment is weighted by a true responsibility, and can be guided by experience and the practical information which comes from it. As voters for or members of School Boards, Boards of Guardians, and other important public bodies, women have now opportunities for public usefulness which must promote the growth of character, and at the same time strengthen among them the social sense and habit. But we believe that the emancipating process has now reached the limits fixed by the physical constitution of women, and by the fundamental difference which must always exist between their main occupations and those of men. The care of the sick and the insane; the treatment of the poor; the education of children: in all these matters, and others besides, they have made good their claim to larger and more

extended powers. We rejoice in it. But when it comes to questions of foreign or colonial policy, or of grave constitutional change, then we maintain that the necessary and normal experience of women does not and can never provide them with such materials for sound judgment as are open to men.

In conclusion: nothing can be further from our minds than to seek to depreciate the position or the importance of women. It is because we are keenly alive to the enormous value of their special contribution to the community, that we oppose what seems to us likely to endanger that contribution. We are convinced that the pursuit of a mere outward equality with men is for women not only vain but demoralizing. It leads to a total misconception of women's true dignity and special mission. It tends to personal struggle and rivalry, where the only effort of both the great divisions of the human family should be to contribute the characteristic labour and the best gifts of each to the common stock.

Source: Excerpted from "An Appeal Against Female Suffrage," *The Nineteenth Century*, CXLVIII (June, 1889): 781–785.

berg denounced the matriarchal implications of feminism while supporting equal education and even female suffrage. By the early twentieth century, antifeminism had become more vicious, with Russian politicians branding middle-class suffragists as "whores" and Irish men attacking new women on bicycles and throwing them to the ground. Corset-makers organized against feminism and so did male schoolteachers. The wealth of antifeminist organizations and newspapers, as well as the proliferation of cartoons and filthy jokes, showed how anxious Europeans were in an age of challenge and transition.

Those fearing change had increasing cause for fear. "The miracle has happened," wrote Finnish author and activist Alexandra Gripenberg (1857–1913) in 1906.[28] She referred to women's suffrage and eligibility for national office just voted by the Finnish Diet. Soon thereafter in 1913, Norwegian women also received their right to vote in national elections. Activism spread with urbanization and industrialization in the years before World War I. Women in the Austro-Hungarian empire held hundreds of public rallies seeking the vote. In Prague, Eliška Krásnohorská (1847–1926), editor of *Ženské listy* (*Women's Gazette*), led a drive to open women's higher education. Karla Machova founded a women's journal for Czech readers at the turn of the century, and Františka Plamínková led a movement demanding representation in the Bohemian Diet. Hana Gregorova (1885–1958) founded a similar review, *Denica*

(*Morning Star*), for Slovaks, in 1898. These developments encouraged feminists, but also produced such dramatic woman-hating outbursts as Viennese Otto Weiniger's *Sex and Character* (1903), who saw "a woman's demand for emancipation . . . in direct proportion to the amount of maleness in her." For Weiniger, the greatest danger to civilization was the women's movement. He believed that women's true nature was sensual, and that her current ascendency would mean the destruction of religion, philosophy, and a higher sense of social order. Along with Jews, women were always "in constant close relation with the lower life."[29] Anti-Semitism and antifeminism intertwined in Weiniger's work (which sold very well). For him, both Jews and women directed the decline of civilization in the early twentieth century.

Throughout Europe politicians and intellectuals attributed social chaos to feminism. In France, the feminist movement, according to politicians, was depopulating the country and causing its attendant weakness. English and German orators feared a rising tide of inferior breeding by the poor and declining births of superior children among the elite. The woman worker also supposedly endangered national well-being by overtaxing her reproductive body while neglecting her children—a nation's heritage. Political fears and gender fears were part of a single phenomenon shaping international life. The new women or feminists undermined gender order, so the critics believed, and thus nations and cultures were imperiled. Though feminists such as Italian Anna Mozzoni saw the women's movement as affirming "the roots of democracy," to other groups, such as the German Commercial Employees Union, suffragists were, like Jews and socialists, a "foreign body in our national life," that threatened the state's survival.[30] Such national feelings of insecurity led to arms buildups, more colonies, new welfare programs, and many secret diplomatic maneuvers.

In embracing science, in speaking of sexuality, in controlling fertility, and in forming massive groups for public political action, women were rejecting separate spheres, the patriarchal family, and their former cultural innocence. Joining clubs, political parties, pressure groups, and all-female communities, they demanded, finally, the vote, in some cases to redeem motherhood and in others to ensure an egalitarian future. All such claims pointed to a reworking of the gender order in keeping with the transformations in productive life. A new political culture was developing to express, in particular, the end to subsistence reproduction. As a result of such demands and such changes, politicians saw their worlds on the verge of collapse. In August of 1914, these and other tensions exploded in World War I.

NOTES

1. Dora Russell, *The Tamarisk Tree*, 3 vols. (London: Elek, 1975), 1:40.
2. Olive Schreiner, *The Story of an African Farm*, 2nd ed. (Boston: Little, Brown, 1905), 217.

3. Quoted in Jennifer Uglow, ed., *The International Dictionary of Women's Biography* (New York: Continuum, 1982), 356.

4. Quoted in Barbara Engel, *Mothers and Daughters: Women of the Intelligentsia in Nineteenth-Century Russia* (Cambridge: Cambridge University Press, 1983), 132.

5. William Leach, "Transformations in a Culture of Consumption: Women and Department Stores, 1890–1925," *Journal of American History,* vol. 71, no. 2 (September, 1984):319–342.

6. Record of a Men and Women's Club, 1879–1885, Pearson Collection, 10/4, University College, University of London. (The author thanks Judith Walkowitz for directing her to this collection.)

7. Beatrice Webb, *My Apprenticeship* (Harmondsworth, England: Penguin, 1938), 165.

8. Else Lasker-Schüler, "An Old Tibetan Rug," quoted in Robert P. Newton, trans. and ed., *Your Diamond Dreams Cut Open My Arteries* (Chapel Hill: University of North Carolina Press, 1982), 137.

9. "Before Sunset," in Temira Pachmuss, *Women Writers in Russian Modernism* (Urbana: University of Illinois Press, 1978), 113.

10. "The Light," in Pachmuss, *Women Writers in Russian Modernism,* 28–29.

11. Grete Meisel-Hess, *The Sexual Crisis,* Eden and Cedar Paul, trans. (New York: 1917), 6–56 passim.

12. Madeleine Pelletier, *L'émancipation sexuelle de la femme* (Paris: Giard et Brière, 1911), 39.

13. Quoted in Lucienne Domergue, "Le feminisme dans *La Revista Blanca,*" in *La femme dans la pensée espagnole* (Paris: CNRS, 1984), 87.

14. Ellen Key, *The Woman Movement,* Mamah Bouton Borthwick, trans. (Westport, Conn.: Greenwood, 1976 [1912]), 132, 160.

15. Sources for the information in this paragraph are: Aynsley J. Coale, "The Decline of Fertility in Europe from the French Revolution to World War II," in S. J. Behrman et al., *Fertility and Family Planning: A World View* (Ann Arbor: University of Michigan Press, 1969); Etienne van de Walle, *The Female Population of France in the Nineteenth Century* (Princeton: Princeton University Press, 1974); J. Sanders, *The Declining Birthrate in Rotterdam* (The Hague, Netherlands: Nijhoff, 1931); Ellen Ross, "Labour and Love: Rediscovering London's Working Class Mothers 1870–1918," in Jane Lewis, ed., *Labour and Love: Women's Experience of Home and Family* (London: Blackwell, 1986), 76–77; Francis Ronsin, "La classe ouvrière et le néo-malthusianisme: l'exemple français avant 1914," *Mouvement social,* 106 (Jan.–Mar., 1979):114.

16. Serge Grafteaux, *Mémé Santerre,* Louise Tilly and Kathryn Tilly, trans. (New York: Schocken, 1985), 62.

17. Quoted in Rosanna Ledbetter, *A History of the Malthusian League 1877–1927* (Columbus: Ohio State University Press, 1976), 62.

18. Pelletier, *L'emancipation sexuelle,* 62.

19. Key, *Woman Movement,* 115.

20. Käthe Schirmacher, *The Modern Women's Rights Movement,* Carl C. Eckhardt, trans. (New York: Macmillan, 1912), xii.

21. Rosa Mayreder, *A Survey of the Woman Problem,* Herman Scheffauer, trans. (London: William Heinemann, 1913), 67.

22. Jill Liddington and Jill Norris, *One Hand Tied Behind Us: The Rise of the Women's Suffrage Movement* (London: Virago, 1984), 185.

23. Doris Nield Chew, *Ada Nield Chew. The Life and Writings of a Working Woman* (London: Virago, 1982), 14.

24. Quoted in Steven Hause, *Hubertine Auclert. The French Suffragette* (New Haven: Yale University Press, 1987), 126.

25. Hedwig Dohm, *Women's Nature and Privilege,* Constance Campbell, trans. (Westport, Conn.: Hyperion, 1976 [1896]), 98.

26. Dr. Ryckere, "La femme criminelle et la prostitution," *Archives de l'anthropologie criminelle* 12 (1897):306, in Susanna Barrows, *Distorting Mirrors* (New Haven: Yale University Press, 1981), 57.

27. Liddington and Norris, *One Hand,* 216.

28. "The Great Victory in Finland," *The Englishwoman's Review* (July 16, 1906), quoted in Susan Groag Bell and Karen Offen, eds., *Women, the Family, and Freedom: The Debate in Documents, 1750–1950* (Stanford: Stanford University Press, 1983) 2:229.

29. Otto Weiniger, *Sex and Character* (London: Heinemann, 1906), 64, 320, 329.

30. Ludwig Langemann, quoted in P. S. Pulzer, *The Rise of Political Anti-Semitism in Germany and Austria* (New York: Wiley, 1964), 221–222.

SOURCES AND SUGGESTED READING

Albisetti, James. "Could Separate Be Equal? Helene Lange and Women's Education in Imperial Germany," *History of Education Quarterly* (1982).

Edmondson, Linda H. *Feminism in Russia, 1900–1917* (1984). On the middle-class movement.

Evans, Richard. *The Feminist Movement in Germany 1894–1933* (1976). An early survey.

Ewing, Elizabeth. *Underwear, a History* (1972). Góod on nineteenth-century changes.

Faderman, Lilian, and Birgitte Eriksson. *Lesbian-Feminism in Turn-of-the-Century Germany* (1980). An important study of activists and social change.

Foster, Jeannette H. *Sex Variant Women in Literature* (1956). A classic and detailed study.

Fromm, Gloria G. *Dorothy Richardson. A Biography* (1977). An important literary life.

Garner, Les. *Stepping Stones to Women's Liberty* (1984). The British movement and its issues.

Gravier, Maurice. *D'Ibsen à Sigrid Undset. Le feminisme et l'amour dans la litterature norvégienne 1850–1950* (1968). Recaptures the excitement of Norwegian literature.

Greven-Aschoff, Barbara. *Die bürgerliche Frauenbewegung in Deutschland 1894–1933* (1981). The classic study of German feminists.

Hause, Steven, with Anne Kenney. *Women's Suffrage and Social Politics in Third Republic France* (1981). The trials of French feminism.

Kaplan, Marion A. *The Jewish Feminist Movement in Germany. The Campaigns of the Jüdischer Frauenbund, 1904–1938* (1979). A story of one dynamic group of feminists.

Kent, Susan Kingsley. *Sex and Suffrage in Britain, 1860–1914* (1987). A major reassessment of the nature of the suffrage movement.

Knodel, John. *The Decline of Fertility in Germany, 1871–1939* (1974). A statistical study.

Lauritsen, John, and David Thorstad. *The Early Homosexual Rights Movement* (1974). Important information on the European scene.

Ledbetter, Rosanna. *A History of the Malthusian League 1877–1927* (1976). Birth controllers in Britain.

Liddington, Jill, and Jill Norris. *One Hand Tied Behind Us: The Rise of the Women's Suffrage Movement* (1984). An exciting reinterpretation of working-class women and suffrage.

Lundell, Torberg. "Ellen Key and Swedish Feminist Views on Motherhood," *Scandinavian Studies* (1984).

McLaren, Angus. *Sexuality and Social Order: The Debate over the Fertility of Women and Workers in France 1770–1920* (1982). A study of French Malthusianism.

Newton, Stella Mary. *Health, Art, and Reason: Dress Reformers of the Nineteenth Century* (1974).

Offen, Karen. "Depopulation, Nationalism, and Feminism in Fin-de-Siècle France," *American Historical Review* (1984). An excellent revision of views of depopulation.

Pachmuss, Temira. *Women Writers in Russian Modernism* (1978). Women in the Russian avant-garde.

———. *Zinaida Hippius: An Intellectual Profile* (1971).

Scanlon, Geraldine M. *La polemica feminista en la España contemporanea (1868–1974)*. A survey of Spanish debate and politics.

van de Walle, Etienne. *The Female Population of France in the Nineteenth Century* (1974). Statistics on fertility.

Vicinus, Martha. *Independent Women: Work and Community for Single Women* (1985). New women in action in England.

Weeks, Jeffrey. *Sex, Politics and Society* (1981). An overview of sexual policies and social change over two centuries of British history.

Wolchik, Sharon L., and Alfred G. Meyer, eds. *Women, State, and Party in Eastern Europe* (1985). Important information on pre-war feminist activity in Eastern Europe.

CHAPTER
9

Warriors, Pacifists, and Revolutionaries

Facing
War

World War I brought mass slaughter and mass warfare into European lives. Tens of millions of people were killed or wounded, billions of dollars of property damage occurred, and billions of dollars were spent on arms. It was a war that played itself out not only on the battlefields of many countries, but in factories and politics and in millions of human hearts. German artist Käthe Kollwitz (1867–1945) was one of those whose life seemed transformed by this new experience of total war. In her pre-war art, Kollwitz depicted starving weavers and had taken up the cause of the poor of Berlin. A gutter art, the kaiser had called it, when refusing her a gold medal. When war broke out, Kollwitz wept, but her two patriotic sons immediately enlisted. Peter was killed in the first few months; Hans remained at the front for four years. Pouring her genius into a memorial for her child and his dead companions, Kollwitz felt within herself "upheaval, turmoil." This way of dying differed from the natural death of a child unwell enough to go on living. In the case of the "great war," Kollwitz saw a general agreement among European nations to slaughter their young men: "down with all the youth!" Along with despair, she felt she could no longer sort things out as she had once been able to. One thing, however, became finally clear: "The young men who are still alive, Germany must keep. . . . Therefore *not another day of war*."[1] Her sense of a world gone mad was eventually shared by others. By the end of the war, Europeans agreed that the old way of living and thinking had been destroyed.

Few reacted like Kollwitz, however, to the outbreak of war. Instead, all over Europe people rejoiced, and men gladly enlisted. Caught up in a cheering demonstration for departing soldiers, a young German believed that "war had made everything beautiful." It had eliminated traditional distance and social restraint: "My mother kissed me, strange men lifted me on their shoulders, strange ladies gave me chocolate. . . . I was giddy with this incomprehensible human love."[2] The war was seen by many at the start as "a majestic, rapturous,

Scenes similar to this joyful one in Berlin on August 2, 1914 took place across Europe. War, most believed, would set things right and even make life "beautiful."

and even seductive something," by which, according to one writer's perspective from Vienna, "the clerk, the cobbler, had suddenly achieved a romantic possibility in life: he could become a hero, and everyone who wore a uniform was already being cheered by the women."[3]

When World War I broke out in August, 1914, it ended years of international and intranational disputes. The struggle for colonies as sources of raw materials and markets for industrial products had pitted nation against nation in the *belle époque*. To strengthen their positions, governments had built huge fleets of warships and invested heavily in military arms. Incidents erupted in Asia, Africa, and just before the war, in the Balkans—very close to home. It was there, in June of 1914, that a Serbian nationalist assassinated the heir to the Habsburg throne and his wife. Beset like other countries with internal challenges such as anti-Semitism, socialism, and feminism, the Austro-Hungarian empire suddenly decided to meet this particular outbreak with force and declared war on Serbia at the end of July. Because of the system of alliances among European countries, war spread. Germany, Austria, Turkey, and Bulgaria were soon at war with Russia, France, and Britain, and later, Italy (1915) and the United States (1917). A war unlike any previous wars, this one ultimately surpassed the recent ones in length, devastation, and effects on the lives of soldiers and citizens alike.

Within countries, the war smothered tensions, and those who had been at odds with society were swept up with everyone else by feelings of social unity. Suffragists were among those who experienced an end to conflicted loyalties. Not that their struggle to obtain the vote was the same as the struggle for power in the Balkans or the nationalistic and ethnic conflicts of Central and Eastern Europe. The suffragists' demands for the rights of citizens meant they wanted a closer relationship to the nations in which they lived. Although not an explicit testament of loyalty, the desire to vote was an aspiration to direct participation in national decision-making. At the outbreak of war, women in general surrendered all contestatory platforms to the single cause of national victory. Many who were pacifists became militarists; many new women contributed their skills to the national cause. Many socialists jettisoned the concept of international working-class solidarity to support their own country. Thus, many feminists and socialists were suddenly welcomed into the national fold. Soon they would be given specific civic responsibilities, for governments at this point needed women's loyalty.

Like most women in every belligerent nation, Gertrude Bäumer of the Union of German Women (BDF) welcomed the new situation. In times of peace, she wrote, women had worked for their countries, but without recognition. Now, in wartime, their relationship to the state was becoming reciprocal, with the state finally recognizing its dependence on women. In England, women displayed a similar enthusiasm. Millicent Garrett Fawcett appealed to readers of *Common Cause,* the English suffrage magazine. "Women, your country needs you. . . . LET US SHOW OURSELVES WORTHY OF CITIZENSHIP."[4] Changing the name of their paper from *The Suffragette* to *Britannia,* the Pankhursts of the WSPU—except for Sylvia, who opposed her mother and sister on war—undertook militant warmongering. For four years, they traveled extensively, even to the United States to speak at bond-selling or recruitment rallies, and worked to raise the level of psychological support for war. The two militant Pankhursts also encouraged their followers to beat up pacifists, many of whom had earlier been comrades in the suffrage movements. In France, suffragists and feminists had been less violent in their expressions of political sentiment, but their patriotism was nevertheless strong. In fact, it was perhaps stronger there than elsewhere, for a good measure of the battles of the war took place on French soil. The newspaper *La Française* spoke for most French feminists when it declared in November, 1914, that "while the ordeal our country is suffering continues, it will not be proper for anyone to speak of her rights."[5] So many French feminists closed down their newspapers or converted them to organs of wartime propaganda. They also used their experience as organizers to set up all kinds of groups aiding the war effort. The war changed their aspirations. For the most part, new women reverted to the ideology of republican womanhood or motherhood, as did suffragists.

Gender tensions also dissolved as men went off to the battlefield. There, they chivalrously protected the home front, which meant their mothers, sweet-hearts or wives, the young and the aged. Soldiers on both sides dwelt on the familial, supportive roles of mothers. In 1915, a German soldier from the trenches imagined his mother back home:[6]

> Sadly she turns away from dainty fare
> "Perhaps my son is hungry over there!"

The ideal of the traditional home may have faded a bit before 1914, but war made it vivid again. Men were doing their duty, being manly. "I don't loathe war," one English soldier admitted to his wife in 1916. "I love 95% of it, and hate the thought of it being ended too soon." At the same time, he "yearn[ed] most for the touch of your lips and a sight of my boys."[7] Another English soldier wrote to his fiancé in the same year: "I told you Dear that I was happy well so I am." And yet another declared that he would die "with your dear face the last vision on earth I shall see and your name on my lips."[8] War made the feelings of men and women toward one another clear again. Across the great divide that split home from battlefield—an extreme version of separate spheres—societies resurrected gender harmony.

Women and War Work

No one expected a long war; the opposing troops believed they would take either Paris or Berlin in a few weeks. In the meantime, most working women went back to the home—thrown out of work. Within a few months, women's employment in many sectors fell to 30 or 40 percent of what it had been before the war. War subordinated consumer needs and interests to those of the nation and the military. Industries or fields outside the realm of military necessity, such as dressmaking, textiles, furniture making, upholstering, candy making, jewelry, and shoemaking, declined immediately. In addition, many farms became difficult, if not impossible, to run because of the scarcity of male labor. Because each side believed it would win quickly, unemployment caused little stir. Initially, governments made no plans to shift women to production for the military. At first, older men substituted in factories for young workers going off to fight. In fact, *Gewerkschaft* (*Trade Union*), the Austrian paper, continued to denounce women working in factories, especially now that men had such good opportunity for jobs. Not until 1915 did women begin substituting for men in heavy industry, and only in 1916 did the German general staff give serious attention to the deployment of female labor. Therefore, out of work or suddenly lacking the support of a male breadwinner, women first felt the war as an economic catastrophe.

Women's charitable groups, workers' cooperatives, and even municipalities set up workshops to provide minimal employment for the displaced. French trade unionist Jeanne Bouvier ran several different workshops that made shirts, slacks, and ground cloths for the soldiers. However, such workshops provided only half-time employment, and were therefore criticized heavily for their inability to support those working there. But women soon were needed to fill industrial jobs, most of which they had not held before. In all combatant countries, munitions factories, which had generally hired few women, took them on in great numbers. In heavy metallurgical plants, the composition of the workforce also changed drastically. In Vienna and its suburbs the number of female metalworkers increased to almost half of all metalworkers. Most visible to the public, however, were the women who worked in transportation, as tram conductors or workers on railroads or subways. In Vienna, women made up only 2.5 percent of streetcar workers in June of 1914 but constituted 54 percent four years later. In Germany, as in other countries, the move to industry came late: only after 1916 did the proportion of factory workers who were women rise from 22 percent to 33 percent. In industries where women had already been a large part of the workforce, notably textiles, job segregation abated, and they moved into formerly male jobs, such as piecing. In places where weaving had been male-dominated, as men went off to war, women took over their jobs. In clothing workshops, women performed cutting tasks that had formerly been done by men. Nevertheless, the number of women working in textiles diminished throughout the war, as did the number of domestic servants and seamstresses. These declines came about because women switched to the more lucrative work offered in heavy industries and munitions factories.

Women entered or re-entered the workforce for a variety of reasons. Wives of soldiers went to work because they could not support themselves and their children on meager government allotments. Single middle-class women also entered the workforce out of necessity: one English munitions worker endured a work week of 72 hours because she was "young and always hungry."[9] Patriotism or feelings of solidarity with loved ones at the battlefront drew some women out of the home and so did propaganda. By the time English women had started shifting to men's work, the government was offering them the psychological incentive of constant praise for their efforts. In the summer of 1915, Mrs. Pankhurst led tens of thousands of women through London demanding war work from the government. By 1916, such demonstrations were no longer necessary, and such slogans as "Shells Made By a Wife May Save a Husband's Life" were posted in public spaces. Newspapers also pointed out what women could do in wartime. They often highlighted the female tram conductor or subway worker as a war worker in her own right.

Fellow workers, however, were less welcoming to women. There were obviously many individual cases of men offering female co-workers kindness or assistance in learning a new trade—which men's work was for the majority of women. Yet the atmosphere was sometimes tense in the industrial workplace. Women modified their clothing to fit their new jobs. They wore overalls or went uncorseted; such deviations in dress made them conspicuous. An English labor paper said that working women were coming to look like characters in a "comic opera." Some people criticized the way women seemed to spend their extra wages on ribbons and baubles, but Austrian Adelheid Popp declared that

The streetcar conductor and munitions worker helped in the war effort by filling in for men. They became powerful symbols of what women could do, as the poster shows. But as symbols of war and its ultimate disorder, women workers of all types were criticized severely once the soldiers returned home.

a work week of 70 or more hours and the struggle to find food justified women in seeking a little pleasure in colorful clothes. Many people agreed with one French doctor's diagnosis that the war was leading to the "masculinization" of women. Women walked about freely, earned wages, and lived independent lives. Indeed, the whole world came to appear more out of joint than ever with women outside the home, on the shop floor, in men's jobs, wearing "unfeminine" clothing, and flaunting finery while men were dying. The refusals of men to help their co-workers, the ridicule, and the criticism were all symptomatic of the sexual tensions that resurfaced after the first euphoria of going to war.

Conflict between the sexes in the workplace was nothing new; it was part of an age-old problem. But new accusations arose: French munitions workers made the common charge that hiring women in men's jobs enabled more and more men to be sent to the front to be slaughtered. Because of women—not because of war—men were becoming "cannon-fodder." Besides such accusations specific to wartime, other more familiar ones were made. Men feared women's encroachment at every level of work because they saw it as a source of both male unemployment and lower wages in the future. Men also feared the loss in their social and domestic position that high wages and employment had secured. The position of breadwinner that men had held seemed undermined for good. Women, of course, had expectations of receiving the same wages when they did the same work as men, but both employers and the government thought differently. Paying lower wages to women, who replaced men going off to war, ensured profits for manufacturers and was supposed to lower prices for war material. Although unions had temporarily given up their right to strike in return for government assurances of fair treatment, union members had difficulty extending that right to fair treatment to women. Nor were the workingmen interested in solidarity with women to ensure fair wages for all. Industrialists found that divide and conquer remained applicable in wartime as a strategy to maintain control over the workforce. Many unions did support equal pay for women who did a man's skilled job up to standard, but were not always successful in obtaining it.

Employers used the emergency as an excuse for further dilution of jobs and increased streamlining of work processes. One German factory official in 1917 announced great advances in arms production due to simplifying and further mechanizing: "The previous manufacturing process required 6 skilled men and 1 woman to produce 42 pieces a day. Under the present one only 1 man and 3 women are needed."[10] In this case, the savings in wages for the employer amounted to 50 percent. Many jobs were broken down into components so that unskilled women could be given parts of jobs that had formerly been done entirely by skilled men. In some instances, workers and employers agreed to go back to pre-war practices when peace came. Another innovation that was supposed to be eliminated at the end of the war was new machinery that was introduced to improve production or to enable women to do jobs they did not have the physical strength for. The goal of technological regression was only a dream, but male workers agreed to the changes because they believed that they would later be able to eliminate both women and technology. In England, union men who obtained written statements from employers promising to reintroduce "the practice prevailing before the war" were supported by women who believed that "men should certainly be safeguarded on their return from any undercutting by women."[11] The disadvantageous position of workers would not have taken shape had the men agreed to train women or to make them union comrades. Employers were able to continue using gender to improve their position in relation to all workers. The union elite, as well as the rank and file, opted for gender solidarity with male industrialists. In this regard, too, the war reinforced a social order that socialists and feminists had challenged.

Gaining skills or becoming craftswomen seemed as unattainable to women working during the war as it was undesirable to their employers and fellow workers. Most women entered heavy industry totally ignorant of technology; they had prior background in fields like domestic service or seamstressing or had done piecework at home. Training women in wartime would have taken the combined effort of skilled male workers and of employers. Neither thought it in their interest. Women were warned that their jobs were transient, so intensive training made little sense to them either. German journalist Emma Stropp reminded women educating themselves for clerical jobs that men might replace them at any time. Being convinced that one should seek, in Stropp's words, "narrow limits in order to avoid later disappointments," not all women performed their jobs eagerly.[12] Many women workers had additional responsibilities besides their jobs, which meant they lacked energy to learn new skills. Some who worked also had children to care for. Their rates of absenteeism were high because they had to stay home if children were ill. Also, it became increasingly clear in wartime that working women were exhausted from twelve-hour shifts in addition to housework and child care. As civilian life became increasingly difficult to manage because of food shortages and increasing costs, for example, the double burden under which women labored took its toll. Their lower wages that had to feed whole families only exacerbated their poor health.

The energetic home front where women were active in public life became symbolic of the war. Propaganda efforts launched by both sides put women in the headlines. On the one hand, newspapers censored those who undertook peace efforts and made them look like silly-headed girls; on the other, they applauded the woman war worker who could do a job as well as a man. As the relationship between press and government became more cooperative, journalists tried to fill the national need for women in industry by publishing stories of women's bravery, dexterity, and energy. Beginning with Belgian women, whose neutral homeland was overrun by the Germans, propaganda organs in England, France, and Italy proceeded to glorify women such as Edith Cavell, a British nurse executed in 1915 by the Germans for hiding soldiers, and seventeen-year-old Maria Vallini, condemned to death in the same year for sending information about the Austrian army to her cousin, an Italian soldier. A negative image was the woman spy, such as Mata Hari, but more often the worker, nurse, and housewife were portrayed as vital to the war effort. Such attention contributed to the creation of the "public" woman. Initially a suffragist wanting to participate in mass politics and decision-making, the image changed into that of a patriotic working woman, contributing to the war effort and in solidarity with men. Once isolated in the home, women stood boldly outside it, with their activities providing grist for the press and organs of public information.

The propaganda effort in which government agencies released news and guided reporting also generated volunteer activity on behalf of the national cause. In the English countryside, Women's Institutes sprang up to organize and inform rural women. Farm and village women shared their knowledge about conservation of food or better methods of doing housework. These

Mata Hari became a symbol of women's power to seduce men away from their duty to the fatherland. Women like her threatened individual men, but also the nation.

women called on the new centers of women's higher education to instruct them in large-scale organizing of volunteers. In Germany, the General German Women's Association by the middle of the war was able to put into operation its plan for a Women's Year of Service, in which women would devote an entire year's effort to the nation-state, just as men did in the military. Run by a variety of women's club activists, the program served as means of communication and contact between the countryside and the national government by setting up relief operations and reporting on civilian morale and material conditions. So effective was this undertaking that its leaders were soon given government positions from which they could coordinate women's work better. These two cases suggest the way town and country women developed a public and national identity during the war. In France, the female schoolteachers often took over the mayoral functions in small towns. In Germany women moved into municipal functions that men had filled, and in many places in Europe they became policewomen. The role of volunteers grew increasingly important to the war effort, and in 1917 French feminist Cécile Brunschwicg (1877–1946) sponsored the founding of a school for training inspectors and social workers who would assume supervisory positions in industry and government. Admission to this school required the equivalent of a baccalaureate degree, a nursing certificate, and character references. As the war continued, the female presence spread throughout industry, relief organizations, and government, and women became ever more professional. As one Italian woman put it in 1917, the one "certainty of the war" was that "women had undertaken a great integrative task."[13]

No woman's role drew so much popular attention or remained so vivid in popular memory as that of the military nurse. For many, she symbolized all that was sacrificial about women, a perpetual reminder of the nineteenth-century ideal of virtue. Throughout the war women did knitting, sorted bandages, and ran homes for wounded soldiers, as their ancestors had performed charitable activities to alleviate urban poverty. When she was only 22, Louise Weiss (b. 1893), who would become a leading French journalist and feminist, converted an abandoned building in Brittany into a hostel for refugees from northern France. Soon the military got wind of her efficiency and ordered her to change the hostel into a hospital for convalescing soldiers. At first, she provisioned the place with donations gathered from the countryside until she realized that the government, rather than her family and friends, should provide the means for her work. Weiss did not even like nursing: "My heart always in panic, my spirit always revolted, I continued this task, which brought me general approval."[14] Ultimately, she switched to journalism and more casual help for the wounded in the last year of the war. Vera Brittain (1893–1970), in England, took a different circuit. Pursuing studies at Oxford during the first year of the war, she abandoned them to share the agony of the men at the front, among whom were her brother, her fiancé, and many friends. Starting in a London hospital, Brittain moved first to Malta and then to the French front. The experience changed her life. Nursing brought toughness and the conviction that the war was not worth a single life. Other women wrote of similar transformations as they carried away amputated arms and legs, as brains spilled out into their hands, as they endured the smell of pus and rotting flesh.

Not all views of the war nurse were favorable. Some people attributed changing morals to her existence. Living apart from familial supervision and amidst male society, she loosened nineteenth-century standards by traveling alone and trading her innocence for experience of the world—of the worst the world had to offer. Vera Brittain returned to Oxford with new values and commitment to a variety of activities she had never before conceived of. More-

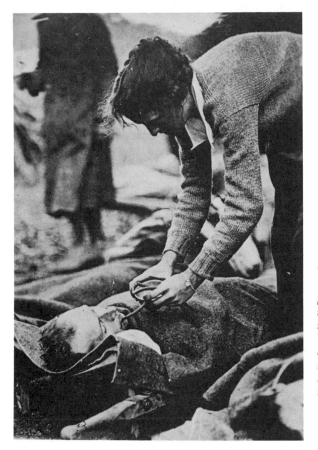

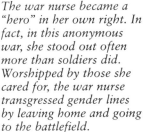

The war nurse became a "hero" in her own right. In fact, in this anonymous war, she stood out often more than soldiers did. Worshipped by those she cared for, the war nurse transgressed gender lines by leaving home and going to the battlefield.

over, she, like other nurses, had learned ways of getting things done, very different from those available in domestic experience or even in the university. Some have even said the war nurse acquired a whole new type of personality. By being "one of the boys" for so long, she helped break down gender role boundaries and gained for herself a strengthened ego. Though a focus of attention and even a kind of emblem of the war effort, the nurse also threatened the gender structure of the society she served.

War increased women's productive responsibilities, but it also made their consumer role more onerous. Those whose men were at the front lived on lower family budgets even if they worked themselves. The problem of reduced income was compounded by soaring prices. Inflation occurred in almost every European country during the war, so even though workers gained wage increases, their standard of living fell. This was especially true for households headed by women. Soon even securing basic commodities became difficult. As

Vienna in Wartime

Anna Eisenmenger, a wealthy doctor's wife, spent a good deal of the war trying to find food for her family. Before the war, feeding a family of four children, a son-in-law, grandson, and aunt posed little challenge for someone in her circumstances. By the end, after her husband and one son had died, it was Frau Eisenmenger's main undertaking. Alarmed by having the three remaining men in her family sent home from war as invalids and by her daughter's and aunt's illness from malnutrition, she illegally hoarded food, bartered away her dead husband's tobacco, and overcame any number of middle-class scruples to get that most precious commodity—food.

Ten dekagrammes [3½ ounces] of horse-flesh per head are to be given out to-day for the week. The cavalry horses held in reserve by the military authorities are being slaughtered for lack of fodder, and the people of Vienna are for a change to get a few mouthfuls of meat of which they have so long been deprived. Horse-flesh! I should like to know whether my instinctive repugnance to horse-flesh as food is personal, or whether my dislike is shared by many other housewives. My loathing of it is based, I believe, not on a physical but on a psychological prejudice.

I overcame my repugnance, rebuked myself for being sentimental, and left the house. A soft, steady rain was falling, from which I tried to protect myself with galoshes, waterproof, and umbrella. As I left the house before seven o'clock and the meat distribution did not begin until nine o'clock, I hoped to get well to the front of the queue.

No sooner had I reached the neighbourhood of the big market hall than I was instructed by the police to take a certain direction. I estimated the crowd waiting here for a meagre midday meal at two thousand at least. Hundreds of women had spent the night here in order to be among the first and make sure of getting their bit of meat. Many had brought with them improvised seats—a little box or a bucket turned upside down. No one seemed to mind the rain, although many were already wet through. They passed the time chattering, and the theme was the familiar one: What have you had to eat? What are you going to eat? One could scent an atmosphere of mistrust in these conversations: they were all careful not to say too much or to betray anything that might get them into trouble.

At length the sale began. Slowly, infinitely slowly, we moved forward. The most determined, who had spent the night outside the gates of the hall, displayed their booty to the waiting crowd: a ragged, quite freshly slaughtered piece of meat with the characteristic yellow fat. [Others] alarmed those standing at the back by telling them that there was only a very small supply of meat and that not half the people waiting would get a share of it. The crowd became very uneasy and impatient, and before the police on guard could prevent it, those standing in front organized an attack on the hall which the salesmen inside were powerless to repel. Everyone seized whatever he could lay his hands on, and in a few moments all the eatables had vanished. In the confusion stands were overturned, and the police forced back the aggressors and closed the gates. The crowds waiting outside, many of whom had been there all night and were soaked through, angrily demanded their due, whereupon the mounted police made a little charge, provoking a wild panic and much screaming and cursing. At length I reached home, depressed and disgusted, with a broken umbrella and only one galosh.

We housewives have during the last four years grown accustomed to standing in queues; we have also grown accustomed to being obliged to go home with empty hands and still emptier stomachs. Only very rarely do those who are sent away disappointed give cause for police intervention. On the other hand, it happens more and more frequently that one of the pale, tired women who have been waiting for hours collapses from exhaustion. The turbulent scenes which occurred to-day inside and outside the large market hall seemed to me perfectly natural. In my dejected mood the patient apathy with which we housewives endure seemed to me blameworthy and incomprehensible.

Source. Excerpted from Anna Eisenmenger, *Blockade. The Diary of an Austrian Middle-Class Woman 1914–1924*, tr. Winifred Ray (New York: Ray Long and Richard R. Smith, 1932), 63–68.

production for civilian use declined, new clothing became rare. Food became increasingly scarce, even impossible to obtain in some areas. German and Austrian women experienced the lack of food most desperately because of the effectiveness of the British blockade. They stood in queues for hours to obtain bread, when it was available. By 1918, the average German civilian was consuming only 1,000 calories per day—half the number necessary to maintain an average adult. Early in the war the potato crop failed, and turnips—often themselves in short supply—became the standard German fare. This diet was supplemented by all sorts of ersatz and adulterated products. What passed for coffee was a mixture of grains. Bakers added a variety of noxious and non-nutritious substances to bread. Sausages, so relished by Germans, were scarce, and those that were available were reportedly made of offal, dog meat, horse meat, and rutabagas.

Europe became a society focused on the boys at the front and on food. In Paris where food was less scarce than in the east, but unaffordable nonetheless, a hungry Parisian seamstress and woman-of-all-work made the situation into poetry: "White, plump, and round like the bouquet of a country bride, cauliflowers are a good buy today."[15] But for most, escape through literature was impossible. Famine amennorhea set in: that is, women were so malnourished, they stopped menstruating and became sterile. By the end of the war, the defeated civilians, even the well-to-do, in both the German and Austrian empires were starving. Children died in great numbers of tuberculosis and even the mildest diseases. An epidemic of influenza spread throughout Europe, killing millions. At the first congress of feminists after the war ended, the Austrian and German women were visibly deteriorating and even had trouble thinking because of their malnutrition. American pacifist and reformer, Jane Addams, recalled in her memoirs the emaciated condition of Viennese representative Frau Kulka, who died soon after. At the conference, Kulka asked fellow feminists to urge their governments to lift the ongoing blockade of food shipments.

Throughout the war, conditions on the home front were of concern to governmental leaders. Behind the leaders' concern lay an interest in women's role as producers and reproducers for the embattled nation. State interference in people's lives assumed its modern shape during this war; in fact, the bureaucratic state came of age then. An extreme example of state interference in women's lives consisted of proposals by the German generals that all women be officially conscripted into national service. The government refused to enact such a measure, not because it was so severe, but because the available women's labor actually outstripped demand for it. Although the question of whether women should work abated, their health once more became an issue. In order to provide better nutrition to workers, France in 1917 decreed that workers' cooperatives could organize canteens in munitions factories with expenses paid by the state. Local governments such as that in Lyons also recognized the difficulties working women had in providing food for themselves and their families, and many paid for food kitchens organized by women's charities. Working women could get cooked food at these kitchens to take home with them after what were usually twelve-hour shifts. In another instance of this state intervention, in 1915 the French government encouraged productive work at home by passing a minimum wage bill that specified that a woman engaged in domestic production had to earn the equivalent of a ten-hour day's pay in a factory. Many of the efforts of the French government toward the end of the war were directed by the Committee on Female Labor under the supervision of the undersecretary of state for artillery and munitions; its officers were all male. In contrast, in Germany and England, women entered government service to provide similar supervision and control of women's work. Meanwhile, Austrian industry operated under a 1912 decree that nullified all protective legislation affecting working women; this lack of protection was aimed at allowing women to participate fully in Austria's struggle for control of the Balkans. Yet even such temporary elimination of regulation, which happened elsewhere too, was part of the circle of control, and it expanded or contracted as the state saw fit. Thus, the bureaucratic state made significant growth during World War I, partly to direct the modern army and partly to control the home front. Intervention by governmental agencies in civilian life became accepted as part of the order of things.

Protesting War and Conditions on the Home Front

For decades, people had been opposing the arms buildup that seemed to signal that war was inevitable. By the twentieth century, governments had become major consumers of industrial products—weapons for the most part. The Crimean Wars (1854–1856) and those in the 1850s and 1860s preceding German and Italian unification had generated a peace movement. During the imperialist 1890s, peace advocates began meeting regularly at The Hague, Netherlands, established a permanent organization in Switzerland, and lobbied internationally against the arms race. The center of this movement and head of the Austrian Peace Society was Bertha von Suttner (1843–1914). After her family lost its fortune, she became a governess. While serving in this role, she fell in love with her employer's son, Arthur Suttner. Their marriage forced them into a life of travel and exile, where they supported themselves by writing. In 1889, Bertha von Suttner published *Lay Down Your Arms*—a book that soon became a European best-seller. The heroine's husband dies in one of the battles for Italian unification. A second husband's disappearance during the Austro-Prussian war causes the heroine to undertake an emotionally devastating search of the battlefields, where she views the dying and the dead. The story touched middle-class sensibilities so strongly that it added respectability to the pacifist movement. The friendship of Bertha von Suttner with Alfred Nobel contributed to the establishment of the Nobel Peace Price—an honor she won in 1905. At the lower end of the social scale, pacifism was more political than personal or sentimental. In 1911, women workers demonstrating in Vienna demanded suffrage and something more: "We also want to struggle against the millions that are squandered on murderous ends and in the war of brother against brother. We want an end to armaments, to the means of murder and we want these millions to be spent on the needs of the people!"[16] By 1914, pacifism had become a powerful force; but it remained vital for relatively few once war stimulated patriotic feelings.

Many feminists had seen pacifism as central to their creed. They agitated to end war as another manifestation of male violence. From the war's opening pacifism had enough force to split the suffrage movement in more than one country. In England, Millicent Garrett Fawcett's pronouncement that pacifism was close to treason led to the resignation of many women from the NUWSS.

Catherine Marshall, Helena Swanwick, Kathleen Courtney, Cary Schuster, Margaret Ashton, Maude Royden, and dozens of other leading feminists left in bitterness to organize what they saw as more internationalist feminist groups. From the German middle-class feminist movements, Anita Augspurg, Helene Stöcker, and Lida Gustava Heymann spoke out vigorously against their country's militarism. Although earlier feminists had often supported military expansion because it had created the German nation, Heymann, who had attended international peace conferences, called the declaration of war "nonsense." First, she pledged to "perform no work to further military goals, such as hospital service or casualty duty." And second, like many others who believed that "help could only come from women," she started to organize pacifists.[17] Dissenting voices developed into an international women's peace movement led by Rosa Schwimmer, a Hungarian feminist stranded in England at the outbreak of the hostilities, along with Aletta Jacobs of neutral Holland and Jane Addams of the United States. Traveling and writing letters, Schwimmer organized many peace initiatives that took place over the next four years. Her strongest support came from her initial operating base in England—home of many peace activists. Working to nourish and shelter refugees, these activists supported the call for an international women's peace congress, which actually met at The Hague at the end of April 1915.

Governments put every obstacle possible in the way of this meeting; the government of supposedly peace-loving and liberal-minded England closed the North Sea to shipping just as the English delegates were about to embark. Schwimmer had prepared other pacifists to expect bad treatment by publicly writing that those making initiatives "must not be offended if the combatant Governments refuse their offer in a rude or purposely offensive tone."[18] Despite opposition from many countries and dangerous traveling conditions, the congress met and outlined a course of constant pacifist lobbying until peace was achieved. First approaching neutral governments and the belligerent ones to get commitments to negotiate peace, two sets of delegates travelled throughout Europe immediately after the congress. Successful in all cases, they came away with written agreements to such negotiations. Moreover, the congress drew up twenty resolutions on which negotiations would focus. Woodrow Wilson's subsequent "Fourteen Points" bore a strong resemblance to these resolutions. Although thousands observed its proceedings, the congress ultimately failed to reach its goal—immediate negotiations. Moreover President Wilson's attempt to take center stage for himself alienated both neutrals and belligerents. In spite of this failure, the international women's peace movement continued its activities, and its members braved increasing abuse from government.

Some socialist women were just as courageous as the middle-class pacifists in opposing the war, particularly the socialists in Germany. There, the SPD, the largest Socialist party in the world, had abruptly ended its commitment to internationalism to cooperate in the wartime government. Though remaining in the party, some women, such as Clara Zetkin, began using their powers of persuasion to oppose this defection from socialist principles. Still editor, Zetkin continued *Die Gleichheit*'s policy of promoting international solidarity; in it, she denounced war. In 1916, the SPD dropped all support for Zetkin and founded a competing paper for women, *Die Gewerkschaftliche Frauenzeitung* (*The Trade Union Women's Paper*), edited by Gertrude Hanna. Next, Zetkin, Louise Zietz, and Ottilie Baader were relieved of their responsibilities within the SPD. By 1917, many women like Zetkin had thrown their efforts behind a new left-wing splinter party, which worked for peace but also for the cause of working women. Constantly agitating for both causes, such women, Zetkin among them, served jail sentences not only for pacifism but for agitation among working women, whose loyalty in wartime was seen by the government as especially crucial. (After the war, Zetkin became a communist and went to the Soviet Union.)

Intense conflict among socialists and between women and governments occurred repeatedly throughout Europe. In France, activists Louise Saumoneau and Hélène Brion were tried and jailed for making pacifist protests. So were Hana Benešová and Alice Masarykova in Prague. In Vienna, Adelheid Popp and Therese Schlesinger continued to work within the socialist party but constantly criticized the breakdown of international solidarity. In England, Sylvia Pankhurst focused her attention not on winning the war but on the welfare of women in the East End of London. In Lancashire, Selina Cooper denounced the war despite opposition from many of her Labor Party comrades. Although she put most of her energies into a group called No Conscription Fellowship, Cooper maintained her suffrage connections and worked to establish maternal centers for prenatal and family care, needed more than ever in wartime. Women who were tried, as Hélène Brion was, for treason, countered the charges that pro-women activism masked attempts to undermine the nation with the response that the tight connection between pacifism and feminism would make for public lives based on principle, not might. Other women socialists and pacifists had to go through the ordeal of watching those with whom they had worked, perhaps for decades, turn against workers in other countries and pacifist friends in their own towns. The international conflagration had made the nation-state everyone's first friend, the center of all loyalties and an end in itself—everyone except those who rebelled. Thus, for pacifists and internationalists the war was an intense agony. For them, the defection of comrades; constant harassment by former friends, strangers, and officials; public hostility in newspapers; and even jail sentences compounded ordinary wartime privation.

Outside the women's movement and even scornful of it, Rosa Luxemburg (1871–1919), Polish socialist and leader in the Second International,* reacted to the outbreak of war by falling mute. At first utterly depressed, as Clara Zetkin had also been, she quickly regained her journalistic power and started organizing an opposition socialist party in Germany where she lived. Of Jewish background, Luxemburg had received an education in Warsaw that did justice

---

*See Chapter 7.

to her natural intelligence. She produced increasingly definitive socialist analyses of capitalism, the question of nationalism, and finally, the war and imperialism. Contemptuous of her German socialist comrades who were participating in the *Burgfrieden* (Peace among Classes), Luxemburg began organizing leftist members of the party to oppose war, and became the central figure of this opposition. She believed the war had destroyed decades of effort in building proletariat internationalism and had won workers back to patriotism. By 1917 and 1918, however, the glory had gone from combat, and German society pursued war grimly, even grudgingly. While smuggling tracts, letters, and proposals out of prison, Luxemburg maintained the unshakable conviction that she could woo workers away from their participation in nationalist politics and support of the war. With William Liebknecht, she formed the Spartakus League, which by 1918 was trying to instigate a working-class revolution in Germany.

Luxemburg's efforts were grounded in her perception of the growing unrest in Europe. By 1917 the cost of living had reached such heights that civilian revolts broke out. Already in June, 1915, newspapers in Glasgow, Scotland, reported "intense excitement." The issue was increased rent: "Women pickets were everywhere armed with all sorts of weapons; children would not go to school and a flag flew bravely from Mrs. M'Hugh's house as a signal."[19] Soldiers' wives for the most part, these women had themselves taken up arms over civilian conditions. In Austria the cost of living had doubled by 1916. Membership in the socialist party rose as fast as prices did. At the same time Viennese women instigated work stoppages, demonstrations, and finally a series of strikes, culminating in a widespread one in January, 1918. From then on regular work disruption and looting occurred. Challenging demands for national unity, housewives everywhere in the last year of the war were protesting food prices; workers, their overwork and low wages. In noncombatant Spain women set up organizations to march on stores during the coal shortage in the winter of 1918. In Turin in 1917, they swelled crowds of food rioters. Such protests accelerated as the war progressed, as conditions grew desperate, and as the outbreak of revolution in Russia provided inspiration to work not for war but for social change. The length and effects of the war had begun to undermine solidarity and the peaceful coordination between the home front acting on behalf of soldiers and those soldiers fighting far away. Although every country experienced such turmoil, the greatest breaches of solidarity came in Ireland and czarist Russia.

Rebellion and Revolution

Ireland

"We came into being to advance the cause of Irish liberty and to organize Irishwomen in furtherance of that object," announced the *Cumann na mBan* (Irishwomen's Council) in November 1914.[20] Even though the male-dominated independence movement in Ireland had little use for activist women, the Irishwomen's Council was vigorous in its opposition to the hated British. Irish activists refused to support the cause of Allied victory while the British still held Ireland in a tight grip. The war, the Irish maintained, would help the status of national groups oppressed by more powerful countries; that is, the Serbs, Czechs, Croats, and other Slavic groups would benefit from an Allied victory. Why not Ireland too, they asked, especially since on the eve of war the British Parliament had voted through the much sought after provision for Irish home rule? When war erupted home rule was suspended and the activists began driving for independence and the formation of an Irish republic. Centuries of English rule had turned Ireland into an economic backwater. English land policies had impoverished the peasantry, while English landlords prospered. Being part of the empire had also meant an end to Irish manufacturing because its products competed with English goods and the decimation of Irish culture. Yet, although Irish men wanted liberal rights and self-determination for themselves, they opposed such rights for Irish women. As one of them put it: "The movement was one in which there was no room for the ladies."[21]

The first to appraise many of the Irish issues was Maud Gonne (1866–1953), who became an activist after noticing that all the Irish literary clubs were closed to women. She made numerous attempts to join existing organizations that fostered Irish nationalism. When rejected, she set out on her own to alleviate peasant conditions as both a political and compassionate gesture. Urging rural people to protest the terms of landholding, she believed "the agrarian and National struggle were inherently one."[22] For all Gonne's successes, few wanted women's help, even despite the Ladies' Land League's notable achievements helping impoverished tenant farmers in the 1880s. Then, in 1900, after a great protest against the practice of bribing children to salute Queen Victoria on her Irish visit, a group of women, with Gonne as their inspiration, formed the Daughters of Erin (*Inghinideh na hEireann*). They made their goals Irish independence; the rebirth of Irish culture, including art, literature, and music; opposition to all English culture; and the promotion of Irish industry and crafts. The group's emphasis on culture resembled that of Polish and Czech women, who also were working toward independence in their countries. The Daughters of Erin opened the Irish National Theatre and fostered the flowering of many cultural ventures, especially among the young. About eight years later, the first women's newspaper in Ireland, *Bean na hEireann* (Women of Ireland), started, with Helena Moloney as its editor. Its goal was "to be a women's paper, advocating militancy, Irish separatism and feminism."[23] Most Irish male nationalists had little use for the Daughters of Erin or any of the other women's organizations that succeeded it. For them, nationalism was an assertion of virility, too long suppressed by several centuries of English domination. In the view of these Irish men, even worse than female nationalists were suffragists, such as those in the Irish Women's Franchise League. This league, until open rebellion broke out, condemned "Irish and English alike" as "little legislators blindly making little laws" to which all women submitted.[24] Nationalist Irish men approved of women's organizations only if their purpose was to raise money for the men's activities or to cook, sew, and clean uniforms. The nationalist men saw women who wanted to take part in policy-making, speech-making, or combat, or who wanted rights as emasculating as the English. They blurred the gender identity men received from national political struggles.

As Irish nationalism evolved into various armed societies such as the Irish Citizens Army and the Irish Volunteers, women, despite the attitudes of Irish men, also made themselves ready for a violent confrontation with the English. Their organizations conducted intensive training in signaling, medical assistance, care of military equipment, and marksmanship. In the early years of World War I, many Irish women were able to succeed as couriers and gunrunners because it was inconceivable to police and soldiers of that time that women would be capable of such activity. Throughout the next decades, female nationalists would also excel at distributing propaganda, making tours of foreign countries, fund-raising, and spreading news to prisoners' relatives and information for general public consumption about the mistreatment of prisoners and even brutality in English prisons.

On Easter Monday in 1916, a variety of groups attacked British outposts in cities throughout Ireland. Countess Constance Markiewicz (1868–1927), head of the Irishwomen's Council, and Dr. Kathleen Lynn were among the

---

Letters from Prison

Constance Markiewicz was sentenced to execution for participating in the Easter Rebellion of 1916. Instead, the English government commuted her sentence. A woman of privilege, Markiewicz had several relatively luxurious stays in prison, during one of which she was elected to Parliament. Nonetheless, the last ten years of her life spent either in jail or in hiding were trying. Her letters to her sister, poet and activist Eva Gore-Booth, show how boring, emotional, and very political the prison atmosphere was with war and rebellion going on outside.

> We cannot accept the new scheme they have offered us for visits, as I don't see how one could possibly keep the promise one is asked to give.
>
> They want us to promise not to talk "politics." To-day life *is* "politics." Finance, economics, education, even the ever popular (in England) subject of divorce is all mixed up with politics today. I can't invest my money without politics, buy clothes without politics. Art is all political, music is battle tunes or hymns of hate or self-glorification, and so I simply do not know what they mean when they say we must not talk politics.
>
> What the Censor lets through is no criterion. He did not like some of the Christmas cards sent me, I find.

That blockading and starving the enemy's children is an old trick of the English. I have just been reading about Carew in the reign of Elizabeth, who destroyed harvests with machines and killed cattle with the avowed purpose of starving women and children.

Do you know that we, Cuman na-mBan, have already sent £500 for the starving in Europe?—mostly collected in pennies all through Ireland. Every collector risked jail! Mind you, it was entirely a rank-and-file collection. Just the girls. I call it so splendid.

Mrs. Skeffington has been awfully knocked about. She interfered with the police who continued to hammer an unconscious man with clubbed rifles and she was clubbed over the head. She lost a lot of blood and will have to keep quiet for a bit.

I have nothing to say to-day. It's too hot to think, except about you, darling. Write and tell me how your health is and how everyone is going along and would there be any chance of your getting over here in the Autumn (I don't mean to jail!) but to the Republic.

Source: Excerpted from an undated letter (1918?) and from letters of August 2 and 14, 1919, to Eva Gore-Booth in *Prison Letters of Countess Markievicz* (London: Virago, 1987 [1934]), 208, 235, 237.

dozens of women who supplied medical help, courier service, and food for the troops. Trained as a sharpshooter, Markiewicz soon was second in command at Stephen's Green in Dublin. Like other women combatants, she surrendered after the fight was lost at the end of the week. The male leaders were executed, and the rest, including the women, received stiff jail sentences; Markiewicz's death sentence was commuted to life imprisonment because of her sex. Her taste for battle, she said, had developed when she noticed the injustices to women and heard of the movement. "That was my first bite, you may say, at the apples of freedom and soon I got on to the other freedoms, freedom to the nation, freedom to the workers."[25] For many women involved in the Easter uprising and subsequent civil struggles, visions of women's rights and women's place in the new Irish republic made their commitment to the cause all the stronger. But, as at all times when gender issues are brought into national politics, discord was the order of the day.

After the uprising, the publicity that women gave to the constant brutality and injustice of the English made Irish separatism increasingly more popular. Into the 1920s their role in the nationalist movement increased as civil war erupted. Those who favored accepting a semi-dependent dominion status within the British Empire fought those who wanted to hold out for complete independence for Ireland. Until the end of the civil war in 1923, both women and men were shot, executed, or beaten, watched their houses set ablaze, and had their jobs taken away. On both sides, women spied, carried guns, and served as nurses. While fighting for the cause, nationalist women kept questioning: would male leaders pledge themselves to parity for women in political and economic rights; would a new government mean a new day for women as well as for men? Most of the men had little interest in such questions and pleaded the urgency of the "larger" struggle. The situation in which Irish nationalist women found themselves had an interesting parallel to that of pacifist women in other countries. The latter connected national struggles to questions of an equitable peace and women's rights, whereas men saw victory for the nation-state as the primary issue. Irish nationalist women connected the war of independence with women's issues, only to be told that victory against England was the primary goal and would change everything.

Russia

"Not a single state and no democratic legislation has done even half of what the Soviet government did for women in the very first months of its existence."[26] This claim by Bolshevik leader V. I. Lenin (1870–1924) came less than two years after he and his followers had taken power in the fall of 1917. In the short run, the Russian Revolution threatened Allied victory, because Lenin quickly made peace with the Germans. The peace freed them to turn all their energies to a major offensive against the British and French on the western front. More significant were the long-run implications of the revolution. Socialist programs challenged European ideas about property and gender relationships. Overnight, Russia was transformed from being a friend of Western culture into a threat.

The revolution had been brewing for over a decade. In 1905, hardships generated by the Russo-Turkish war had intensified demands for reform. In the winter of that year, workers petitioning Czar Nicholas II for help had been shot down. As a result of the ensuing outcry, the czar created the Duma, a parliamentary type body. The Russian leadership, however, had trouble sharing power, so the representatives in the Duma were repeatedly sent home. World War I produced more intense difficulties. To compensate for their lack of modern weapons, Russian leaders sent their troops into battle in massive numbers. A war based on technology and modern production methods, World War I gave bloody evidence of how backward Russia actually was. Even before the war, workers in St. Petersburg and elsewhere had struck time and again demanding better conditions. Members of the middle class also recognized Russian technological, cultural, and political backwardness. Thus, by March of 1917, when women began demonstrating for better food supplies, the revolution that erupted involved many classes, including members of the armed forces, all wanting a new Russia.

The tradition of women's radicalism that provided the impulse to revolution in Russia was older and more powerful than anywhere else in Europe.

After Sophia Perovskaya's assassination of the czar in 1881, women remained prominent in the radical movement through the early twentieth century, as terrorists—such as Mariya Spiridonova (1880–1930), who in 1906 assassinated a tyrannical general—or as organizers of the peasantry and of workers. From this history, Lenin himself had drawn the conclusion that women's role in revolutionary activity would be crucial. On the eve of World War I, Lenin's wife, Nadezhda Krupskaya (1869–1939), his sister Anna Elizarova, his devoted friend Inessa Armand (1874/5–1920) and other women published seven issues of *Robotnitsa* (*The Woman Worker*) as a way of introducing to women the Bolshevik brand of socialism. Meanwhile, the rival Social Revolutionary group organized women schoolteachers, and many other radicals recruited activists from the upper classes. Terrorist acts died down before World War I because the czarist government had by then incarcerated or exiled most of the prominent women radicals. However, their collective activity continued in waves of strikes ranging from that involving 11,000 textile workers in 1905 to sporadic ones between 1912 and 1914. When World War I broke out in 1914, such activity abated in a rush of patriotism, but only for a few years.

At the beginning the war led Russian women, as it did women in other countries, to express nationalistic fervor and to explore new opportunities. Women filled the factories and the civil service and continued their regular network of services to other women. In addition, many Russian women became soldiers; foremost among them was the eccentric and formidable Mariya Bochkareva (1889–?). Though particularly known and decorated for her bravery under fire, she was but one of thousands of Russian women who fought on the battlefield. The massive outpouring of patriotic energy perhaps blinded officialdom to problems brewing on the home front—in the households of poor women, of women workers, and of workers' and soldiers' wives. Many of them were finding it very difficult to live on the small governmental allowances to soldiers' families; before they had had their husband's and their own regular wages. Even those who had some money could often not buy food because the government's bureaucracy was extremely inefficient when it came to provisioning civilians. Finally, massive numbers of Russian soldiers were dying, and many began to desert. All of these factors produced intense and mounting civilian discontent. Women in Petrograd (St. Petersburg) began demonstrating after waiting hours in food lines. They then turned to pillaging and general destruction, and, on International Women's Day in 1917, they spontaneously coordinated a series of protests. Seizing streetcars and confiscating food from stores, they filled the streets by the hundreds of thousands in an outburst of disobedience the government could not control. They literally disarmed the troops by boldly urging soldiers protecting the streets to turn disloyal: "Put down your bayonets—join us."[27]

With those protests, the Russian Revolution began. Those who initially came into power after the czar's abdication were of the middle classes and upper-class liberals who had been pushing for parliamentary and economic reforms for decades. Continually pressed by feminists, the government in July of 1917 spread its reforms in their direction. Russian women obtained the right

Demonstrations by Russian women in 1917 concerned food prices and access to commodities. Historians often label such demands "backwards" or "traditional." In this case they provoked the Russian Revolution.

to vote in all elections and an array of civil rights, including the right to equal pay. Although feminists applauded this victory, radicals turned their fury on the government for its inattention to the starving masses and its failure to stop Russia's involvement in the war. Under the banner of "bread and peace," exiled radicals, including Lenin, Krupskaya, and Alexandra Kollontai (1872–1952), returned to Russia to push the Revolution leftward. After a series of maneuvers and outright battles, the Bolsheviks, who were led by Lenin, Trotsky, Zinoviev, and others and who stood for consolidated and strict leadership of the masses, took control of the government in the fall. Their position did not become secure for several years. Meanwhile, in the midst of military and political challenges, the Bolsheviks attempted a series of reforms, including the abolition of private property, the democratization of production and politics, and numerous social changes affecting the individual, the couple, and the family.

Women participated in every step of the radicalization of the Russian Revolution, but a small and particularly motivated group guided the Bolshevik program about women, the family, marriage, children, and social welfare in general. In the vanguard was Alexandra Kollontai, who in the first days of the revolution urged workers' councils and women workers to even greater radicalism. Kollontai's speech-making abilities had developed from years of organizing women and heckling feminists. Her early life, however, had not seemed likely to lead her among revolutionaries. Kollontai's father was a Russian general, and her wealthy mother had married for love, but only after Kollontai had been conceived. Kollontai acquired her first liberal tendencies from observing her father's commitment to modernization in Russia. Her mother, too, had a modern style—she managed farms and seemed to thrive on constant activity and ascetic, health-reforming habits. Her parents' departures from traditional Russian conservatism were mild compared to Kollontai's abandonment of her engineer husband and her young son in order to study in Switzerland. When taking this step at the age of 26, her motives were clearly political and social. A witness to the economic misery of most Russians, she would investigate—as her father had done—the source of this situation. From then on, Kollontai's revolutionary course was set; as soon as she reached Switzerland, she fell in with international socialists and other radical activists.

Like many other Russian expatriates of that time, Kollontai wavered for almost two decades between the more gradualist and democratic Mensheviks and the Bolsheviks, who called for planned and centralized leadership of revolutionary activity. Always in touch with Lenin, Krupskaya, and Inessa Armand, Kollontai became a powerful writer and speaker, able to address audiences in half a dozen languages. While traveling around Europe and in the United States on behalf of revolutionary socialism, she developed a theoretical and practical interest in the woman question. For Kollontai, the development of the "social personality" of women was a key to both revolutionary success and women's own liberation from the double oppression Engels and Bebel had mentioned. The extremely backward conditions under which Russian women lived made Kollontai fear their potentially reactionary role if socialists did not provide them a political education. Equally frightening to Kollontai, as it had been to Clara Zetkin, was feminism's undermining of the loyalties of working-class women to their male co-workers. So she attacked feminists constantly and tried to get her comrades to direct socialist party efforts toward developing a female constituency. This goal became the backbone of her program. However, other socialist leaders relegated her concern for women to a theoretical and organizational limbo. When World War I broke out, Kollontai switched her efforts away from women and toward peace by pointing to war's capitalist inspiration and profits. She wrote leaflets addressed to almost every part of the potential socialist family: "Who Wants War?" "The Defence of the Fatherland or International Solidarity?" and "Why Was the German Proletariat Silent During the June Days?" When the revolution began in 1917, Kollontai returned to Russia to bring women around to the socialist viewpoint and to give them its benefits.

The new Soviet government passed a number of reforms directly affecting women as a way of making gender relations anew. Within the first few months, the government declared marriage a civil, rather than a religious, act and made divorce obtainable when requested by either partner. In 1920, a law permitted women to obtain abortions in hospitals, though it called abortion itself an "evil." All Russians were enlisted by law to work as a duty of citizenship. Since most women had always worked as peasants, this provision was hardly new in substance. However, Bolsheviks gave legitimacy to women's working for pay and ended the questioning of it that had existed for a century. In addition, mothers began to benefit from a series of supportive measures such as those providing prenatal education and medical care, most of which were enacted during the first months of the new regime. Behind these lay a recognition that the work of motherhood was, as stated by Bolshevik leader Vera Lebedeva, "every bit as important as that of the engineer who constructs roads."[28] Buttressing this appreciation of motherhood were measures that gave women legal rights over their children and others that granted them political and economic rights, such as equality in courts of law and in the workplace, to safeguard the rest of these gains. Finally, the Bolsheviks announced a campaign to end illiteracy, which affected 85 percent or more of women. Not only would women be educated, they would learn subjects other than sewing and other domestic skills. Engineering, agronomy, and veterinary medicine were a few of the fields party leaders envisioned women in. Lenin's boast was true insofar as there was official commitment to sweeping changes in women's social and political role.

What the Soviet government did next gave substance to this commitment. In the first days of the revolution, the Bolsheviks recognized that women were vital; women's allegiance must be won away from other competing political tendencies, including the liberal party, the Social Revolutionary organizations, and Menshevism. The journal *Robotnitsa* reappeared, and activists went into factories and workshops to teach women about Bolshevism. Although many male Bolsheviks only wanted to change women's politics, Kollontai, as Minister of Social Welfare, created Palaces for the Protection of Maternity and Childhood not only to give women and children complete healthcare, but to serve as symbols of the new government's concern for them. When revolution turned into civil war, a group of leaders went into the countryside with messages about Bolshevism and women's place in it. These two activities—providing information and forming an institutional structure—led to the All-Russian Congress of Women Workers and Peasants in November of 1918. Expecting 300 or so women, the organizers greeted 1200 enthusiasts, who discussed topics ranging from how to obtain party positions to working for the civil war and socialization of housework.

The highly visible success of the All-Russian Congress paved the way for the setting up of a women's bureau, or *Zhenotdel,* headed by Inessa Armand at the central office and with branches in major cities. *Zhenotdel* functionaries continued the proselytizing in the countryside. Their status as representatives of a government bureau made their activities more vigorous and at the same time incurred more opposition. Some leading Bolshevik women, such as Klavidya Nikolaeva and Konkordiya Samoilova, distrusted anything that looked like feminism, as did many party men. Assuming the directorship of the *Zhenotdel* after Armand's death in 1920, Kollontai—always an opponent of feminism—supported the organization's goals of the "full liberation of woman" and "defending her interests. . . . This does not lead to parallelism with the

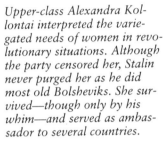

*Upper-class Alexandra Kol-
lontai interpreted the varie-
gated needs of women in revolutionary situations. Although
the party censored her, Stalin
never purged her as he did
most old Bolsheviks. She survived—though only by his
whim—and served as ambas-
sador to several countries.*

work of the party, but supplements it."[29] To further these goals, *Zhenotdel*
functionaries struck at the heart of the patriarchal Russian family by educating
women in their rights, by teaching them a variety of liberating skills such as
how to organize day-care centers, and by giving them confidence. Although
internationally the *Zhenotdel* was a showpiece for the Bolsheviks and attracted
numerous admirers, it faced significant resistance from the party and localized
harassment from threatened heads of families. In the Far East, *Zhenotdel*
workers were hacked to death, stoned, and beaten for encouraging women to
take off their veils and to challenge tribal customs. Closer to the capital, workers were attacked and sometimes killed. The *Zhenotdel* suffered waning support among party leaders despite evidence of its success. For leaders, social
stability and economic productivity took precedence over women's rights, and
only a few could imagine that the activities of *Zhenotdel* might eventually
produce a healthier economy and more progressive workforce. By 1930, the
government liquidated this and many other such programs.

The demise of *Zhenotdel* was only one event in the narrowing of social
goals that took place in the Soviet Union, reminiscent of the fate of social
reform during the French Revolution. Kollontai, like French activists more

than a century earlier, had connected changing the condition of women with the onward process of revolution. Such changes demanded transformed gender relations, the complete egalitarianism professed by the Bolsheviks. If patriarchal and marital power could survive the revolution, so could any other kind of domination. Thus, Kollontai worked to establish a participatory situation among workers in their councils, or *soviets,* and within the family. However, she was swimming against the political tide of bureaucratization, planning, and centralization produced by the civil war, massive economic disaster, and the legacy of the old regime. In the early 1920s, as part of her attempt to bring a personal message to women everywhere, she wrote novels in a simple style about women, love, and work. Two of the most famous, *Love of Worker Bees* (1923) and *A Great Love* (1927), tell about productive female party members who become love slaves to useless or unworthy men because they lack the subjectivity that comes from work. Most of Kollontai's heroines finally reject their lovers when those lovers ask for sacrifice of self. Like these women, workers were to develop all their potential and constantly participate, not slavishly, but with the full dignity their productivity gave them. As the Soviet government took more control of the workers' *soviets,* Kollontai and others were discredited. The government, faced with mounting social and political problems, invoked the restabilization of the family as central to the new state. Civil war and ensuing famine had made millions of children into wandering orphans. In addition, relaxed sexual customs had led to the exploitation of women, who often found themselves abandoned with no means of support for their children. Kollontai received much of the blame for this result. She had, said Lenin, equated sexual love with drinking a glass of water, but who wanted to drink from a soiled glass? What the Bolsheviks once scorned as "bourgeois morality" became useful again to restore order.

Reworking Love in the Soviet Union

In addition to working for economic and social revolution, Alexandra Kollontai saw a transformation of sexual relations as an integral part of socialism. In contrast to those who saw this transformation as an automatic result of socialist victory, Kollontai believed that it would come through the same kinds of struggle with old and repressive forms that made socialism victorious in the economic sphere. The following excerpt from her famous essay "Make Way for Winged Eros" (1923) attacks promiscuity, which she calls "wingless eros," and urges young people to consider how central love is to the new social order.

Bourgeois ideology has insisted that love, mutual love, gives the right to the absolute and indivisible possession of the beloved person. Such exclusiveness was the natural consequence of the established form of pair marriage and of the ideal of "all-embracing love" between husband and wife. But can such an ideal correspond to the interests of the working class? Surely it is important and desirable from the proletariat's point of view that people's emotions should develop a wider and richer range? And surely the complexity of the human psyche and the many-sidedness of emotional experience should assist in the growth of the emotional and intellectual bonds between people which make the collective stronger? The more numerous these inner threads drawing people together, the firmer the sense of solidarity and the simpler the realization of the working-class ideal of comradeship and unity. The complexity of love is not in conflict with the interests of the proletariat. On the contrary, it facilitates the triumph of the ideal of love-comradeship.

The hypocritical morality of bourgeois culture resolutely restricted the freedom of Eros, obliging him to visit only the "legally married couple." Outside marriage there was room only for the "wingless Eros" of momentary and joyless sexual relations which were bought (in the case of prostitution) or stolen (in the case of adultery). The morality of the working class definitely rejects the external forms of sexual relations. The social aims of the working class are not affected one bit by whether love takes the form of a long and official union or is expressed in a temporary relationship. But at the same time the ideology of the working class is already beginning to take a thoughtful attitude to the content of love and shades of emotional experience. In this sense the proletarian ideology will persecute "wingless Eros" in a much more strict and severe way than bourgeois morality. "Wingless Eros" contradicts the interests of the working class. In the first place it inevitably involves excesses and therefore physical exhaustion, which lower the resources of labor energy available to society. In the second place it impoverishes the soul, hindering the development of inner bonds and positive emotions. And in the third place it usually rests on an inequality of rights in relationships between the sexes, on the dependence of the woman on the man, and on male complacency and insensitivity, which undoubtedly hinder the development of comradely feelings.

Source: Excerpted from Alexandra Kollontai, *Selected Writings,* Alix Holt, ed. and trans. (Westport, Conn.: Lawrence Hill and Company, 1978), 288–289.

Millions died in the Russian Revolution and many mourned the passing of their world. For example, after losing family members, her livelihood, and all possessions, aristocrat and wartime nurse Marie Bariatinsky called the execution of the imperial family in 1918 "the greatest sorrow I have ever known . . . a shadow across whatever sunshine is left in my life."[30] Nonetheless, many viewed the new Russian experiment with hope. For some, it seemed a vote for peace when Russia defected from the Allied side in World War I. As news traveled westward about the programs in the Soviet Union, women such as Emma Goldman from the United States, Clara Zetkin from Germany, Beatrice Webb from England, and Madeleine Pelletier from France made pilgrimages to the new promised land. They scrutinized the condition of women, of the family, and of social life in general. In the first few years, as Lenin maintained, the promise for women's progress was great. No other major government supported mothers with such concrete help. None made the guarantee of equal pay. Nowhere else had a political movement garnered the allegiance of women to such a degree: conservative estimates say there were at least 80,000 female combatants in the civil war. Even when the Bolsheviks started questioning some of their own reforms, reformers in other countries still saw Russia as a model when it came to changing women's lives for the better. However, the Soviet Union's promises to transform women's lives took a back seat to many other socialist goals. After watching Lenin denounce Kollontai's democratic and pro-women position using sexual slurs, one revolutionary called her defense "courageous" and "calm."[31] The goals of Kollontai were defeated early in the 1920s as the Soviet Union consolidated its repression of democracy. "Life in Russia had become a torture to me," wrote the American anarchist Emma Goldman (1869–1940) of her decision to leave the country in 1921. Having visited old friends who were in prison or living at home in fear of what the Revolution might still have in store, she described her tormented resolve to go: "It was like the tragic end of a great love."[32]

Germany

The Russian Revolution led to revolutionary activity in other countries. The red flag hung from city hall in Glasgow. As the war drew to an end in 1918, some German towns turned communist. Socialist leaders across Europe thought that the moment had arrived for an international socialist revolution. In many places, as governments negotiated peace, workers and housewives began pushing for change. Marxists had always assumed that industrialized Germany was the logical place for the revolution to begin, not backward Russia. In fact, before the war the German socialist party (SPD) had been the largest and most apparently successful one in the world. During the war itself, the SPD apparently abandoned the cause of international revolution as it took part in the war government. The war's end brought Allied demands that the kaiser abdicate, and the reformist SPD leaders assumed control of a government that was threatened by revolutionary uprisings in many areas, beginning with the short-lived "Democratic and Social Republic of Bavaria." Some former revolutionaries such as Frederick Ebert became, by virtue of their new positions, members of the establishment. To them, the Spartakus League, organized during the war by Rosa Luxemburg, Clara Zetkin, and Karl Liebknecht, among others, appeared treasonous in its demands for such socialist goals as internationalism and workers' political activism.

Luxemburg, after years of contributing to the theory and politics of socialism, was not willing to see her ideal watered down. Emphasizing constant endeavor in applying theory, she saw socialism as process. For her, the members of the Spartakus League and striking workers elsewhere in Europe were demonstrating that workers could forget their own destiny and seize hold of history. Encouraged, she hoped that the flaws developing in the Russian Revolution would "be healed by the European revolution. And this is coming!"[33] Luxemburg spent a few months after the armistice editing a new revolutionary paper, *The Red Flag*. Then, in January of 1919, workers renewed their demonstrations in Berlin. Even though Luxemburg and Liebknecht believed these strikes were premature in terms of actually bringing about a revolution, they were blamed as the instigators and were forced into hiding. On January 15, the government captured and shot Luxemburg and Liebknecht on the spot.

Like Kollontai, Luxemburg had posed questions to socialist leaders and had challenged the dictatorial positions they assumed as leaders of the working class. Both of these dangerous women were eliminated—Kollontai from powerful positions and Luxemburg totally. No country in Europe was to take the directions these women envisioned; in most countries, even bureaucratic socialist revolutions of the Russian variety or socialist governments of the German variety did not materialize. As uprisings or protests failed elsewhere, the Soviet Union gained more prestige among socialists internationally by the very fact of its success. It sought to direct all socialist movements through a new international workers' organization, or "Comintern." A split then occurred in every country between the old-line social democrats or socialists and those supporting the Soviet Union, who took the name "communists"—both groups that had formerly been united in the Second International and in pre-war socialist parties. At the time, only in Germany did the split have such a dramatic and disastrous end.

Aftermath of the War

When the fighting finally stopped on November 11, 1918, Europeans faced a host of changes and bore the scars from a war more horrible than any before. Battlefield deaths alone are estimated at 8 to 9 million, with the numbers of wounded being double those figures or more. The total number of civilian deaths during the war is unknown. Historians have calculated it to be anywhere from 2 to 13 million, and the global influenza epidemic of 1918 claimed another 20 million lives. The impact of death resonated in every European household. Although World War I was a conflict among nations, people experienced it as individuals. Assessing what had changed, many thought of their personal losses. But changes also resulted from the way people had had to live during the war, which involved "making do" and sometimes even defying the rules that had applied in peacetime.

A young Hungarian woman's experiences during the war show this undramatic side of things—not the life of a war nurse or revolutionary, but rather of the kind of new women who seemed to surface everywhere. One of eight children, Ilona Elek was fourteen, poor, Jewish, and living in Budapest when the war began. Her father had abandoned the family; her mother died when Ilona was eleven. The older boys supported the children and, at the same time, worked their way through the university. Ilona remembered that in school they would knit one hour each morning for the soldiers and then for two hours more each afternoon. The schoolteachers frequently recited prayers for the Austro-Hungarian emperor and his armies. One of Ilona's brothers died in an early battle of the war. Meanwhile, Ilona and her sisters did odd jobs around Budapest. Ilona had had great experience; from the age of four she had gone door to door begging, had sold at the market, and had run errands for neighbors, including the mistress of a lawyer. Ilona's most successful wartime *coup* concerned food. Although many left the city for the countryside, where food was more plentiful, Ilona and her sister helped local merchants who were hard pressed by long food lines. Once they helped on a day when brown sugar had arrived. Collecting ration tickets for the merchant, they pocketed many of them for the next distribution and were also paid in that scarcest of commodities—sugar. In the midst of the war, Ilona grew up, did various office jobs such as stenography, and fell in love with a wounded soldier on leave. Three times she became pregnant. The first two times her brother insisted she have an abortion, but the third went unnoticed until it was too late. The baby arrived in the midst of the 1919 workers' revolution in Hungary. Ilona observed this revolution and was, in fact, closely affected by it because her brother served as a local official of the socialists. But for her, political events were minor incidents. Though always looking to a better future without anti-Semitism and without inequities, she seemed unconcerned with the political cataclysm going on around her: "nothing interested me except pleasing men, that they courted me as much as possible. I wanted to live, I was free, that was enough for me."[34] Elek's sense of freedom and her sense of sexual adventure were what many saw as major social changes wrought by the war. The dislocation that split up families and couples, that wrecked so many lives, caused many like Ilona Elek to seek the consolations of pleasure and release.

Suffrage Gains

Certain pleasures and freedoms once defined as male were now women's, and, in addition, women increasingly gained political privileges, including direct participation in representative government. During the war neutral countries such as Denmark (1915), Iceland (1915), and the Netherlands (1917) gave women the vote. Belligerent governments also considered extending the franchise. In England, parliamentary leaders realized during the war that a new voting law was needed—the right to vote could no longer be based on residence or millions of soldiers could not vote. As the new voting law was being drawn up, the question of giving the vote to women came to the fore again. By this time little remained of the previously vociferous objections to women's participation in public life; they were already active in noticeable and crucial ways. Finally, in 1918 Parliament awarded the franchise to women who were over 30 years old and either had established residence or were married to a man who did. At the same time, virtually all men received the vote. The compromise left millions of women still disenfranchised and aroused the fury of many. It seemed clear that, for one thing, men still feared women voters: if the law had included all women, they would have outnumbered men voters. In addition, as labor leaders pointed out, precisely those young working women who had contributed to the war and who needed representation to protect their rights could not vote. Militants of the NUWSS, such as Millicent Garrett Fawcett, agreed that some progress had occurred, but a good deal remained to be done. Some remained skeptical about whether men had acted in good faith, whereas others waited for the extension of suffrage to younger women, which they believed to be inevitable. After the passage of the 1918 law, NUWSS changed its name to the National Union of Societies for Equal Citizenship, reflecting the fact that many believed the struggle for votes was over and, perhaps, even the need for feminist activism. All that remained, the majority declared, was to make the most of this new power and begin to use it to right the wrongs of women. The first elections following the end of the war took place in December of 1918 and threw a damper on women's optimism. The fifteen English women who were candidates for election to the House of Commons all failed. The Irish rebel Constance Markiewicz, then in jail, became the first woman elected to the British Parliament, but, like all other Irish nationalists, she refused to serve as a symbol of defiance.

Women won the vote in new nations carved from the defeated Habsburg empire: Czechoslovakia (1918), Austria (1920), Poland (1921), and Hungary (1925, but limited to women over 30). Suffragist efforts continued in Germany, where, under pressure, the kaiser had promised a new political system in 1917. When revolution erupted in various cities at the war's end and the Social Democrats took charge of the national government, one goal was the vote for women. Because workers' councils promised women's participation, the Social Democrats who were setting up the new national government finally got the liberals and the Centre Party to agree to give women the vote. In the end, women of the Weimar Republic, as the new German government was called, received the vote in an ambiguously phrased constitution. Although it pronounced men and women equal, one of its articles gave them "basically" the same rights and duties. While elaborating some rights, the constitution also announced its concern for women as housewives and mothers. According to some historians, phrases like these indicated that, despite the franchise, little had changed where women were concerned.

French women had been affected by the war even more than others. They had been imprisoned, and their country occupied. Many lost their homes and members of their families: 1.3 million Frenchmen had died on battlefields and 3 million were wounded. French feminists found reason to hope, however, in the winning of the vote elsewhere in Europe and expected similar recompense for their own contributions and suffering during the war. Even critics of the suffrage movement seemed to have changed their minds somewhat: some antisuffragists thought that widows and those who had lost male relatives should take their places at the polls. Belgium voted in suffrage for war widows only in 1919. In the same year, the French Chamber of Deputies passed a sweeping suffrage bill by more than a three-to-one margin. Then the Senate delayed and finally, in 1922, defeated the bill, as it would defeat similar ones for several more decades. It is clear from an analysis of the 1922 vote that every political group, but especially republicans, opposed women's suffrage. Though each opponent gave his own particular reasons, none wanted to share political power with women. Political participation by women would blur gender lines more than war had done.

Restoring Gender Order

After the revolutionary upheaval and its bitter defeat, Germany in general grew more conservative, although there were some pockets of avant-garde activities. The Social Democrats who procured the vote fit this pattern. Marie Juchacz (1879–1956), a former factory worker and seamstress who replaced Clara Zetkin, was loyal to the party and a constant worker on women's behalf, but she did not press women's issues with the radicalism, understanding, or stubbornness of the earlier generation. Juchacz's strategy was to maintain a low profile and to comply with socialist leaders' wishes that she and her women's groups leave them in peace. In another major arena of women's activism, Gertrude Bäumer, after directing German women's efforts during the war, began to identify the cause of the BDF more in patriotic terms than in feminist ones. In 1919, she stated that her group's new program would enable women to "express their national identity"; in the post-war world, women would use their franchise and political efforts to bring "unity . . . , internal peace, and . . . the conquest of social, confessional and political antagonisms through a spirit of self-sacrifice, a sense of civic duty and a strong, unified national consciousness."[35] In Germany, the impact of war on the feminist consciousness had caused a rebirth of the ideology of republican motherhood.

Besides defeating the suffrage bill after the war, the French legislature passed a significant law that had ominous intent. On July 31, 1920, a bill was enacted that outlawed the sale and distribution of all contraceptive devices and literature; it also made any public discussions of birth control punishable with hefty fines and prison terms. In addition, abortion became a major crime for the abortionist, the woman procuring one, and any other involved in the process. France now had "the most oppressive laws in Europe" in the area of fertility and reproduction.[36] For decades, the French had cited a lack of "virility" behind both their defeat by the Germans in 1870 and their falling birth rate. Moreover, even a few feminists calling for birth strikes until the conditions of motherhood were improved were evil portents. French politicians and physicians chastised "militantly emancipated women, the unbridled sportswomen, the cosmopolitanites, and 'brains,' " to return to their womanly duty to reproduce.[37] French politicians refused women the vote and enforced male control of reproduction through legislation in a burst of patriotic rhetoric that invoked the restoration of national power. Although the war had started out in a female return to the home and in initial acts of republican motherhood, and although in contrast men had chivalrously taken up arms to protect them, gender definitions had weakened as the war progressed. Women filled men's jobs, while men had had spectacular trouble winning battles. Men returned home from war maimed, shell-shocked, and hysterical—like women. So the control of reproduction by the French legislature amounted to an attempt to show, after so much uncertainty, who was male and who female.

Troubles on the Literary Front

Other instances of blurring occurred. The war produced a vigorous but, until recently, largely unnoticed body of literature by women. Most sensational and moving were accounts from nurses on both sides of the war about their experiences. Some of these emphasized endurance and danger. Others described how wartime activity and energy meant a new sexuality quite different from that confined to houses, the etiquette of courting, and the ethos of female passivity. Those on the home front also wanted to let people know that they had a war story as much as men did. "Why should these young men have the war to themselves?" asked Vera Brittain, explaining why she had written her *Testament of Youth* (1933).[38] Didn't women live through the war as well? It was in the spirit of telling what the home front had been like for women that Brittain produced her account of losing loved ones, stopping one's normal female life, fearing the telegrams that eventually came. Other women writers showed a sense of contrast in seeing smiling faces that they imagined dead the next week, or French rivers once serenely glimmering but now flowing with blood and body parts. The war led many writers to question the nature of reality. Was the battlefield real and the household not? Was the factory or the hospital real and the university not? For many women and men, the only real place in the wartime world was a battlefield; anyplace else was somehow lesser, less worthy. Women writers often took up this theme, once thought common only to men. They also picked up male attitudes of hatred for women and things civilian. Like Brittain, many female authors deplored their mothers' domestic stupidity, their pettiness and selfishness, and their insulation from reality. Poet Siefried Sassoon (1886–1967) expressed hatred of the silly, impotent, old men politicians as well as the mothers who knitted for sons dying in rat-filled trenches. So did many women writers. Whatever the content of women's writing, however, the act of writing itself seemed to consolidate the role of the new woman. Believing that something enormous had occurred and that they had bravely acted in the world, women writers gave themselves a wartime persona far different from that previously acceptable for women. Many claimed to be heroes.

Gender Crisis

At the war's end people had become acutely aware of gender in troubling ways. On the one hand, the war had blurred gender differences by allowing women to replace men in the workforce. On the other, the war segregated society by gender more than in peacetime, with millions of men on the front and women and children at home. War itself was a "male" event in which those fighting had priority in all concerns. All other interests were subordinated to supporting "the boys" who were sacrificing themselves for the nation. And men on the front wrote of sacrificing themselves for those back home. As writers expressed it, a great divide arose between the battle front and the home front, between men and women.

When the war ended, the first question asked was whether women would hold on to those jobs they had taken over. Bad feelings generated by women's new-found strength only intensified when men returned to find society saturated with women working in jobs that had been male-dominated in pre-war life. Returning French schoolteachers were enraged that they received "a rather cold welcome" and that women's lobbies wanted to make diplomas a prerequisite for teaching. "What does it matter to them that [the veteran] could not take his exams because he was in the trenches?"[39] In England, veterans wrecked streetcars and physically abused women still working in what were supposed to be men's jobs. Women had crossed the gender boundaries the war had erected so clearly in the first few months. Not only was it economically important for men to reclaim jobs from women, but eliminating working women from public view had psychic value as well. The women munitions workers and streetcar conductors had symbolized war on the home front; regaining a peacetime mentality meant eliminating them and reasserting men's position as breadwinners. Acutely aware of what should be male and what female, men in general, not just politicians, violently attempted to set things back the way they had been.

As many observers noted, the war undermined the entire tradition of male heroism—a tradition that had developed over several millenia. Instead of individual heroes, machines had become crucial to warfare; cannons and machine-guns, submarines and airplanes, trucks, trains, cars, and tanks were the determinants of victory. Also, for the first time, uniforms were drab, not brightly colored and decorated. A single soldier stood for nothing in the face of fire and transport power, nor did he stand out in his uniform. For millenia, men's myths had defined masculinity in terms of besting other men in combat and dominating women in the sexual arena, but only dominating women remained after this unheroic war. The "Hollow Men" of T. S. Eliot's poem seemed to dominate mythical formulations of manhood after the war. These hollow men were propped up by the power of sexuality and a desperate search for renewed conquest to prove the myth of military prowess had not died. In the search for post-war identity, men would fall back on fighting and gender dominance. A nation could only live by fighting, they asserted, and "it can only fight if it maintains its masculinity."[40] Beating up female streetcar conductors was one expression of men's desperate post-war plight. Yet feminists, such as Helena Swanwick in 1915, had predicted as much from national policy based on war: "The sanction of brute force by which a strong nation 'hacks its way' through a weak one is precisely the same as that by which the stronger male dictates to the weaker female."[41]

The war caused a psychic crisis in all the men who fought it, but particularly those who were defeated. Because the terms of the Versailles Treaty that ended the war were so onerous to Germany and because the treaty pronounced Germany "guilty" in bringing on the war, German soldiers and generals posited theories of their own. To the generals' way of thinking, the civilian government had stabbed them in the back by making peace. For many soldiers, women at home had abandoned them economically, emotionally, or even sexually. What did it mean, poets asked, that women had sent them off to war with roses, laughter, and kisses? Mothers who had tucked their sons into their beds seemed just as easily to tuck them into shrouds. But if mothers and sweethearts had let their men down, women strikers, hoarders, and pacifists were even worse. Such feelings were common among many German veterans. From 1918 on, they produced an antidemocratic sentiment against the new Weimar Republic that had replaced a military monarchy and an intense masculinism, evidenced in the wandering armies of tens of thousands of men who beat, raped, and pillaged in their own country in the early 1920s.

However, the war had been a collaborative effort in certain other respects. Many feminists had relaxed their rhetoric, though not given up their belief in their cause. Most men and women had struggled together for their nation or a revolution. Efforts to better women's situation more often than not fell by the wayside, except when those efforts would also help the nation-state. Thus, the nations' mighty effort to win women to the imperialist cause and then to that of national victory had reached fruition. Of the many women who subsequently received the vote, more were patriots than feminists; once intensely pro-woman, their allegiance had become nationalistic. Feminism survived the war but its strength was weakened. Although activists in most countries had worked right through war and revolution to affirm causes such as the right to work, equality in work, support for motherhood, and the like, by 1920 women such as Sylvia Pankhurst and Alexandra Kollontai were perceived as eccentrics more than anything else. Masses of people who had previously constituted the base for such activism had turned their support to "the boys at the front." In those countries where men and women had joined forces in a socialist revolution, supporting the revolutionary goals had weakened women's commitment to change gender conditions. What remained was collaboration without the strong affirmation of equality. War and revolution served as goals outweighing all others. Male and female efforts were fused in being directed to these ends.

The few short years of World War I ushered in a world in which the premises of social organization were essentially changed. Before the war, activists had tried to assert the dignity of women as individuals in the Enlightenment sense of the word. However, war and revolution enshrined the state and mass power and left the individual in the position of being merely instrumental to that power. A generation of young men had been sacrificed to ensure that nations would live; the individual, as conceived of in the eighteenth century, hardly mattered at all. This priority of the state left the feminist struggle in trouble. Feminists had worked toward gender balance in marriage, the family, and society. War and revolution instead gave priority to conflict on behalf of the collectivity. The unleashing of the "irrational" and male physical force was something feminists from Mary Wollstonecraft on had feared. Yet organized aggression as a general political tactic became the major fact of twentieth-century culture. Feminist analysis had affirmed the human and humane society, but World War I marked the start of an era in which machines and technology undermined the primacy of that most sacrosanct of Western values—the human individual. Thus, all the assumptions on which women's social analysis rested fell by the wayside as war and revolution fundamentally weakened eighteenth-century principles. Feminists had to regroup over the next half century, adjusting their efforts and their understanding of women's experience in this modern world.

NOTES

1. Käthe Kollwitz, *Diary and Letters*, Hans Kollwitz, ed., Richard and Clara Winston, trans. (Chicago: Henry Regnery, 1955), 63, 88.

2. Ernst Gläser, *Class of 1902* (New York: Viking, 1929), 210–211, 214.

3. Stefan Zweig, *The World of Yesterday* (New York: Viking, 1943), 224.

4. Millicent Garrett Fawcett, *The Common Cause, August 14, 1914*, quoted in Anne Wiltscher, *Most Dangerous Women. Feminist Peace Campaigners of the Great War* (London: Pandora, 1985), 27.

5. Steven Hause with Anne Kenney, *Women's Suffrage and Social Politics in Third Republic France* (Princeton: Princeton University Press, 1984), 192.

6. A. F. Wedd, ed., *German Students' War Letters* (New York: E. P. Dutton, 1929), 86.

7. Letter of Captain Alfred Bland to Violet Bland, January 14, 1916, in Annette Tapert, ed., *Despatches from the Heart. An Anthology of Letters from the Front During the First and Second World Wars* (London: Hamish Hamilton, 1984), 31.

8. Letter of Daniel Sweeny to Ivy Williams, c. July, 1916, and James Milne to his wife, July 20, 1917, in Tapert, *Despatches from the Heart*, 43, 56–57.

9. Peggy Hamilton, *Three Years or the Duration: The Memoirs of a Munitions Worker, 1914–1918* (London: Peter Owen, 1978), 33.

10. Quoted in Jürgen Kocka, *Facing Total War. German Society 1914–1918*, Barbara Weinberger, trans. (Cambridge, Mass.: Harvard University Press, 1984), 33.

11. Quoted in Irene Osgood Andrews, *The Economic Effects of the War upon Women and Children in Great Britain* (New York: Oxford University Press, 1918), 47, 57.

12. Quoted in Bell and Offen, *Women, the Family and Freedom*, 2:280.

13. Donna Paola (pseud.), *La Donna nella nuova Italia* (Milan: Riccardo Quintieri, 1917), 161.

14. Louise Weiss, *Mémoires d'une européene*, 6 vols. (Paris: Payot, 1968), 1:192.

15. Louise Delétang, *Journal d'une ouvrière parisienne pendant la guerre* (Paris: E. Figuière, 1935), 151.

16. Quoted in Beatrix Kempf, *Bertha von Suttner. Das Lebens einer Grossen Frau* (Vienna: Österreichischer Bundesverlag, 1964), 192.

17. Lida Gustava Heymann (with Anita Augspurg), *Erlebtes-Erschautes. Deutsche Frauen Kämpfen für Freiheit, Recht und Frieden 1850–1940* (Meisenheim am Glan: Anton Hein, 1972), 121.

18. Quoted in Wiltscher, *Most Dangerous Women*, 24.

19. *Forward*, June 19, 1915, quoted in David Englander, *Landlord and Tenant in Urban Britain 1838–1918* (Oxford: Clarendon Press, 1983), 219.

20. Quoted in Margaret Ward, *Unmanageable Revolutionaries. Women and Irish Nationalism* (London: Pluto, 1983), 101.

21. Quoted in Ward, *Unmanageable Revolutionaries*, 92.

22. Quoted in Nancy Cardozo, *Lucky Eyes and a High Heart. The Life of Maud Gonne* (Indianapolis: Bobbs-Merrill, 1978), 150.

23. Ward, *Unmanageable Revolutionaries*, 67.

24. Hanna Sheehy-Skeffington, "An Impression from the Platform," *Irish Citizen*, June 8, 1912, quoted in Leah Levenson and Jerry Natterstad, *Hanna Sheehy-Skeffington. Irish Feminist* (Syracuse: Syracuse University Press, 1986), 36.

25. Jacqueline VanVoris, *Constance de Markievicz* (Old Westbury, N.Y.: Feminist Press, 1972), 122.

26. Stefan T. Possony, ed., *The Lenin Reader* (Chicago: Henry Regnery, 1966), 73.

27. Quoted in Richard Stites, *Women's Liberation Movement in Russia* (Princeton: Princeton University Press, 1978), 291.

28. Quoted in Fannina Halle, *Women in Soviet Russia* (London: Routledge, 1934), 149.

29. Quoted in Carol Eubanks Hayden, "Feminism and Bolshevism: The Zhenotdel and the Politics of Women's Emancipation in Russia, 1917–1930" (unpublished Ph.D. dissertation, University of California, Berkeley, 1979), 162.

30. Princess Anatole Marie Bariatinsky, *My Russian Life* (London: Hutchinson, 1923), 312.

31. Angelica Balabanoff, *My Life as a Rebel* (New York: Harper, 1938), 251–52.

32. Emma Goldman, *My Further Disillusionment in Russia* (Garden City, N.Y.: Doubleday, 1924), 139.

33. Letter to Adolf Warski, November–December, 1918, in Stephen Bonner, ed., *The Letters of Rosa Luxemburg* (Boulder, Colo.: Westview Press, 1978), 258.

34. Hélène Ilona Elek, *La mémoire d'Hélène* (Paris: Maspero, 1977), 57.

35. Quoted in Richard Evans, *The Feminist Movement in Germany 1894–1933* (London: Sage, 1976), 235.

36. Angus McLaren, *Sexuality and Social Order* (New York: Holmes & Meier, 1983), 1.

37. Françoise Thébaud, *La femme au temps de la guerre de 1914* (Paris: Stock, 1986), 276.

38. Vera Brittain, *Testament of Experience* (London: Fontana, 1980 [1957]), 77.

39. Jean-Louis Robert, "La CGT et la famille ouvrière, 1914–1918. Première approche," *Mouvement Social*, 116 (July–September, 1981): 54–55.

40. Quoted in James Steakley, *The Homosexual Emancipation Movement in Germany* (New York: Arno, 1975), 84.

41. Helena M. Swanwick, *Women and War*, Blanche Wiesen Cook, ed. (New York: Garland, 1971), 4.

SOURCES AND SUGGESTED READING

Braybon, Gail. *Women Workers in the First World War. The British Experience* (1981). An informative study.

Brittain, Vera. *Testament of Youth* (1970[1933]). A woman's story of the war.

Cardozo, Nancy. *Lucky Eyes and a High Heart. The Life of Maud Gonne* (1978).

Clements, Barbara Evans. "Working-Class and Peasant Women in the Russian Revolution," *Signs* (1982).

———. *Bolshevik Feminist: The Life of Aleksandra Kollontai* (1979). An impressive biography.

Farnsworth, Beatrice. *Alexandra Kollontai* (1980). An excellent study of this major figure.

Gersdorff, Ulricke von. *Frauen in Kriegsdienst, 1914–1918.* (1969). Documents from German women's experience.

Harrison, Brian. *Separate Spheres: The Opposition to Women's Suffrage in Britain* (1978).

Higgonet, Margaret Randolph, Jean Jenson, Sonya Michel, and Margaret Collins Weitz, eds. *Behind the Lines. Gender and the Two World Wars* (1987). An impressive collection of essays.

Holtman, Sandra. *Feminism and Democracy. Women's Suffrage and Reform Politics in Britain* (1986). The end of the suffrage campaign.

Kaplan, Temma. "Women and Communal Strikes in the Crisis of 1917–1922," in Renate Bridenthal, Claudia Koonz, and Susan Stuard, eds. *Becoming Visible. Women in European History* (1987). A comparative study of women's protest and its relationship to the political crisis of the late and post-war period.

Kent, Susan Kingsley. "The Politics of Sexual Difference. World War I and the Demise of British Feminism," *Journal of British Studies* (1988). An exciting interpretation.

The Letters of Rosa Luxemburg. Stephen E. Bronner, ed. (1978). Especially moving letters from prison.

Norman, Diana. *Terrible Beauty. A Life of Constance Markievicz* (1987).

Porter, Cathy. *Alexandra Kollontai* (1980). Dense with information.

Rigler, Edith. *Frauenleitbild und Frauenarbeit in Österreich* (1976). Particularly good on women's work during and after the war.

Stites, Richard. "Alexandra Kollontai and the Russian Revolution," in Jane Slaughter and Robert Kern, eds. *European Women on the Left* (1981).

Thébaud, Françoise. *La femme au temps de la guerre de 1914* (1914). An engaging survey of women's lives in war.

Theweleit, Klaus. *Male Fantasies* (1986 [1977–1978]). German soldiers' depictions of women.

Ward, Margaret. *Unmanageable Revolutionaries. Women and Irish Nationalism* (1983). A comprehensive survey of women's involvement in the nationalist cause.

Wiltscher, Anne. *Most Dangerous Women* (1985). The struggles of pacifists to be heard in wartime.

PART
IV

The Fruits of Twentieth-Century Technology

By 1925 millions of women had acquired the right to vote. Suffrage and changing conditions of work and domestic life indicated that modernity now affected women as much as it did men. Between 1925 and 1985 most homes acquired a range of domestic machinery and also were run with the help of electricity and gas. Childbirth and childcare moved to centralized institutions like hospitals, clinics, daycare centers, and schools. The development of reliable birth control technology also transformed reproduction. Worklife in the service sector became automated with the application of electricity to office machines. Women learned to operate dictaphones, photocopiers, and most importantly, computers. These advances brought benefits such as improved health, increased longevity, declining infant mortality rates, and higher levels of education.

Technological changes occurred in an increasingly insecure world. Twentieth-century people still felt the psychological and material effects of World War I and the socialist revolution in Russia. Imperialism left a legacy of dominated peoples eager to become as free as their masters. As a result, conflict continued and intensified. Technology then gave these wars and struggles for freedom their particular character. Mass propaganda via radio and television, mass control of fertility and breeding through medical techniques, and efficient mass murder were hallmarks of the new politics in an age of technology. The Spanish Civil War, World War II, the Holocaust, and colonial wars for independence all continued to make the twentieth century the bloodiest in history. By 1985 people lived with unprecedented material goods but also with an unprecedented fear that technology in the form of nuclear weapons could annihilate the human species.

During such perilous times, people directed their energies not only toward survival but toward making the uses of technology beneficial and liberating. All questions that had once been answered by liberal and republican theory were reopened in an age of dictators, genocide, and atomic weaponry. Theoreticians in pre–World War II Germany, for instance, asked what family structure had to do with the development of authoritarian personalities. What, others asked, did repressed sexuality have to do with the rise of dictators? What, indeed, was mass society and what was its relationship to technology? After the Holocaust, people questioned all European values and cast some of their hopes toward those in the Third World.

In the midst of this ferment, a new women's movement arose. Political disasters had so thoroughly masked the role of gender questions that many new activists had no idea that there had ever been earlier movements of women. Many of their goals merely repeated those of a century earlier. Parity in wages and political power were hardly new aims, but they were still unattained ones. Other feminist activists, artists, and theorists took their lead from developments in psychoanalysis, philosophy, and technology. They revised, and still revise, visions of what a just gender order will look like.

Time Line

- **1921** Women receive the suffrage in Poland
- **1922** Mussolini's March on Rome
- **1925** Art Deco exhibition in Paris
- **1926** Grazia Deledda wins the Nobel Prize in Literature
- **1928** Sigrid Undset wins Nobel Prize in Literature
- **1929** Stock market crash in New York, depression follows
- **1931** Spanish Republic founded
- **1932** Reform of divorce and marriage law in Spain
- **1933** Hitler becomes chancellor of Germany
- **1936–1939** Spanish Civil War
- **1938** Virginia Woolf publishes *Three Guineas*
- **1939** Germans open Ravensbrück, the largest concentration camp for women
  World War II begins
- **1944** Allies invade Normandy beaches
- **1945** Atom bomb dropped
  World War II ends
  Women receive the suffrage in Italy
- **1948** Czechoslovakian constitution declares equality of men and women
- **1949** NATO formed
  Germany divided into Federal Republic (West) and Democratic Republic (East)
  West German constitution declares equal rights
  Simone de Beauvoir's *Second Sex* published
- **1950–1953** Korean War
- **1953** Death of Stalin
  First issue of *Playboy* magazine
  Conflict in Algeria
- **1954** Equal pay legislation for women civil servants and teachers enacted in Britain
- **1955** Sex education made obligatory in Sweden
- **1960s** Uprising of university students
- **1963** Vietnam War
  Valentina Tereshkova of the Soviet Union becomes first woman in space
- **1967** Sale of contraceptives legalized in France
- **1968** Pope Paul VI condemns birth control
- **1969–1970** Feminist movements take shape in Western Europe
- **1970s** Laws permitting and easing divorce enacted in Europe
- **1979** Margaret Thatcher becomes Prime Minister of Great Britain
- **1980** Vigdis Finnbogadothhir elected President of Iceland
- **1981** Increased family benefits for women in the Soviet Union
  Marguerite Yourcenar becomes first woman elected to Académie Française
- **1986** Referendum in Republic of Ireland rejects legalization of divorce

10

Consumer Culture and the Routinization of Work

Emergence of the Modern Woman In 1921, Victor Margueritte's novel *La Garçonne* caused a public uproar in France. It told the story of a young woman's last-minute refusal to marry a man who both coveted her family's money and intended to keep his mistress after marriage. Freeing herself from the traditional fate of many French women, the heroine became a career woman and searched for fulfillment in her work and in truly companionate and sexual relationships. Translated into thirteen European languages, *La Garçonne* became a fashion, but also a code word like "flapper." Its author, however, became an outcast, mostly—it was said—because he told the truth about women's changing behavior. The French government even rescinded Margueritte's membership in the Legion of Honor. Reactions to the book showed the clash of the old and new worlds and stirred anxiety about the fate of society after the war. In fact, many young women could not follow the normal cycle of work followed by marriage and children because so many millions of men had been killed. The number of "surplus" women skyrocketed. In addition, revolutionary ideas about women's conduct that had developed before the war had become commonplace during it. The new woman seemed to be everywhere, and, of the many who noticed the change, more than a few were frightened.

During the *belle époque*, a small minority had dared to dress and act in new ways, but the 1920s saw the new woman's way of life gain more acceptance. Women's roles and terrain were visibly transformed. Specifically, both the modern middle-class housewife and the career woman emerged. Women had more rights than ever, and some were in parliaments and ministries. Meanwhile, women intellectuals and artists helped form the cultural avant-garde. Intertwined with these developments was the rise of modern communications and marketing, which combined to project even more powerful images of women than religion had centuries earlier. From the 1920s on, media power would vividly portray women in association with the new household goods and office technology. In the meantime, feelings of release and a quest for vitality absorbed Europeans, along with concern about new warnings of war.

Yearning to forget the past, society focused, for instance, on the exploits of women pilots, tennis champs, mountain climbers, and daredevils, who all seemed fantastic creatures. People also focused on new consumer products, instead of saving for a rainy day. And many of these were meant for women. During these years, the restraint, prudence, and productivity demanded of nineteenth-century people were replaced by a world view based more on material wishes and consumption. From all these ingredients, there emerged a modern notion of womanhood that included efficiency at home and work, energy in sports and sexual life, companionship with her mate, and consumerism.

Yet most women determined their destiny less freely than did the fictional *garçonne*. Even as Europe experienced war weariness, new dictatorships prepared an even greater cataclysm. Europe—and most of the rest of the world—moved from crisis to crisis. First, Europeans became even more urgent about boosting the birth rate than they had been before the war. The 50 percent decline in fertility and the war losses had taken their toll everywhere. Europe hardly faced demographic catastrophe. Rather, the post-subsistence population situation still had people in a quandary. Second, the health and political loyalty of the workforce were of concern to industrialists and politicians. A falling birth rate seemed to make labor shortages a threat, and the repetitive nature of many modern jobs used up worker vitality, as industrialists increasingly recognized. Because women constituted an important part of the workforce and a key to both increased reproduction and working-class vitality, public policymakers focused on women's role in the family and their sexuality. Although the granting of modern rights to women prevented politicians or even husbands from coercing women to perform any number of duties, other methods of persuasion existed. Direction came through incentives from the welfare state and through overwhelming publicity about how to use one's body, from the point of view of both health and sexuality. In fact, the image of the erotic woman developed its contemporary intensity during these years. Publicized and officially encouraged because it could lead to reproduction, sexual activity provided an outlet for energy left over after work was done. Rather than directing this energy into political activity, many women expended it on consumerism and fashion. Restraints on sexual behavior seemed to fall away, replaced by the guidance or, some would say, the manipulation of social scientists, social workers, doctors, and other officials concerned with the public welfare. More sexual activity would help reach that goal and also, it was hoped, reestablish gender complementarity. Having passed through the "Great War" and come out scarred, the nations reminded their citizens of the patriotic duty to replace life.

The Modern Household

Putting the household back in order was one way to restore European society after World War I. It meant readjusting the interaction between the sexes, returning all members of the family from the battlefront to the hearth, and even using improved sexual life between marriage partners as a way of alleviating gender tensions. Margueritte's *La Garçonne* contested the familial aspects of this goal and even suggested that restoration amounted to an impossible task, given all that had transpired between 1914 and 1918. Pre-war society had already chosen the road modern society was to take, and nowhere more obviously than with respect to women's sphere. But some people tried to maintain the illusion that bygone domestic life would continue. For instance, women's magazines for several years after the war still published sample meals more like the heavy food of the mid–nineteenth century than the quicker and lighter fare that wartime work and shortages had introduced into most homes. Such illusions that all was normal on the home front were perpetrated by many, even though everything from household technology to sexual technology was transforming actual experience. Thus, two opposing trends affected women's lives. The first sought a return in every aspect of life to an idealized version of the *belle époque,* or the good old days of pre-war Europe, the patriarchal family and harmoniously hierarchical gender relations. The second trend was that toward technology and modern ways of doing things. The second trend created the modern housewife while the first kept her a housewife nonetheless.

By the 1920s, household efficiency and modernization had long been in the air. Late nineteenth-century health movements and the discovery of the germ theory of disease only added to interest in eliminating dirt and decay within the domestic sphere. Architectural experiments in Austria, the Soviet Union, Germany, Switzerland, and Sweden worked to modernize the house itself—to make it airy, sunny, and free from intricacies that could attract and hold germs. Detailed moldings, ornate fixtures, alcoves, and small cluttered spaces disappeared from post-war domestic architecture. Such changes in housing were the result of several factors. One was that the nineteenth-century home was viewed as outmoded; efficiency became the byword for domestic space as well as work space. Some architects aimed at eliminating the artifical from the domestic space and opening the home up to nature, especially to light, air, and greenery. Also, particularly in the Soviet Union and in Vienna, some urban planners tried to make housing more socialized. During the years between the two world wars, their experiments in large-scale architecture emphasized the collective services that people such as Alexandra Kollontai and Lily Braun had envisioned. Tenants enjoyed facilities for laundry, childcare, and bathing. In the West, however, politicians initiated the building of hundreds of thousands of inexpensive, scaled-down housing units to allay unrest. One member of the British Parliament volunteered to show his fellow legislators slum housing "which had I to live in them I should be not only a Bolshevik but a leader of Bolsheviks."[1] Fearful that unemployed veterans of World War I would become socialist agitators, the House of Commons in England, like other parliaments, voted to undertake vast projects of "homes for heroes." Displayed in pulp magazines or on the urban landscape, the new models of domestic space were visible in one way or another to all women.

Particularly within the middle-class home, new industrial products made significant changes in housekeeping. First, stoves employing gas or electricity began replacing those fueled by coal or wood. By the end of the 1930s, the electric company of Paris reported annual rentals alone of 50,000 stoves in the city. Electric refrigerators also appeared in the 1920s. These new appliances eliminated perhaps the most strenuous aspects of kitchen work, hauling fuel and ice, while also improving the regulation of temperature for cooking. Electricity started to transform washing and ironing, cooking procedures such as mixing, and household heating. By the end of the 1930s, millions of households were adding electricity each year. The vacuum cleaner had appeared before World War I but now came into widespread use. Originally intended for use by servants in middle-class and upper-class homes, many labor-saving appliances became widely popular among middle-class women who no longer had servants. Machines also appealed to upper-class women, whose increasing level of education inclined them toward a more scientific orientation to domestic work. The kitchen as a whole began to look more like a factory or laboratory. From the school of modern design called the Bauhaus, Marcel Breuer constructed kitchens that were white and had, for almost the first time, hung cupboards to give both easy access to equipment and the appearance of efficiency. The kitchens of some 60,000 units of working-class housing in Vienna had a similarly efficient and modern look. The labor-saving effect of appliances allowed the servantless household to gain a more respectable aura. Planners thought women would more readily do housework if the strenuous and dirty aspects were performed by machines. The first appliances, large and small, had an industrial-type design to suggest the transfer of work from housewife to machine. This was superseded by a decorative, less functional one in order to eliminate reminders of the "work" aspect of using them in the household. Streamlined casings soon covered the exposed mechanisms of appliances, which at first had appealed to scientifically minded housewives.

Whether or not appliances raised the standards for home cleanliness and comfort and therefore increased the demands on housewives' time is a question that still provokes debate. That was certainly what happened in the nineteenth century with the sewing machine and the upscaling of women's clothing. On the other hand, in 1926 an impoverished manicurist and her seamstress mother got a small gas stove for their one-room apartment, which had no running water; that one appliance seemed to them a blessing that saved immense time in cleaning, hauling fuel, and the like. Yet the next round of consumer products introduced more activities into the middle-class household and fed expectations that the home would be increasingly sanitary and comfortable for everyone. Implementing such improvements in domestic life was left to the housewife, running her machines. However, public images of the housewife perpetuated a significant illusion: that she was not working. It was on the assembly line where "real" work occurred; in contrast, the housewife's activities were said to be craftlike and essentially pleasurable. In "real" industrial work, the worker had no actual ownership of the tools, whereas at home, women owned more and more of them. Although the home gained certain aspects of modernity, including machines, the image of the twentieth-century housewife, like that of her nineteenth-century counterpart, counterbalanced the industrial side of society.

The pre-war arts and crafts movement had initiated the distancing of the home's image from industrial ones. By the 1920s, prominent female designers and artists were contributing heavily to enhancing the crafts. German Gunta Stözl (1897–?) was probably the most gifted weaver in all of Europe. Part of the Bauhaus school, she executed wall hangings and also designed textiles for manufacturers. In England, Vanessa Bell (1879–1961) was as celebrated for her book, textile, floor, and screen designs as for her paintings. Major modern artists like Swiss-born Sophie Taeuber-Arp (1889–1943) and Russian expatriate Sonia Delaunay (1885–1979) did high fashion textiles, embroidery, stained glass windows, and furniture. Charlotte Perriaud so excelled at modern furniture design that architect Le Corbusier teamed up with her in the late 1920s. Exhibited at numerous expositions around Europe, their products created a new household look. Women went in great numbers to these expositions, especially the Exposition des Arts Decoratifs in Paris in 1925. There, it was reported, wealthy women ordered furnishings and decorations for complete households to replace their Victoriana. Historians identify this exhibition as the initiation of the idea that the home is part of the ongoing process of modernization and, therefore, a receptacle for large consumer purchases. The products themselves looked simultaneously modern and craftlike. Such a style echoed the nonindustrial symbolism of domestic life, now made modern and up-to-date in its artisanal (even antimodern) motif.

Despite the nostalgia for pre-war innocence, many women accepted the idea of technological modernity in the home, though obviously the more affluent led the way. Sales of small items such as alarm clocks, electronic irons, modernized washtubs with wringers, cutlery, and gadgets soared. Chain department stores such as Marks and Spencers or Woolworths that sold to people of very modest income were growing fast. Consumer goods for the lower classes were displayed alongside more expensive goods at exhibitions, which made these annual events attractive to everyone. In Western Europe and Scandinavia, annual income (corrected for inflation) rose, for instance, by 40 percent in Sweden and 30 percent in Great Britain during the period between the world wars. Thus, people could afford the new consumer goods. As in the nineteenth century, the identification of women with their households remained. A modern woman consisted of someone whose tools were "without smoke, clean, and fast." Magazines summoned them to be "tempted by the whiteness, the scientific precision, the elegance of the electric oven."[2] Machines were precise and trouble-free, unlike servants who could be troublesome or defiant. Moreover, the machine in the household was also modern in that it was economical. In the early appeals to upper-class women, magazines suggested that readers compare the cost of a stove, refrigerator, and vacuum cleaner with the wages of domestics, who were unreliable in addition to being more costly. Modernity also consisted of paying for major purchases in a new way, via installment buying. At expositions of new household products, in magazine reports, and in advertising, prices were broken down into monthly payments. Like production itself, buying was made easier through the modern process of fragmentation. Basic household commodities were also modernized, especially food, which became available in tin containers. In some countries, such as England, tens of millions of cans sold to all social strata, but in others, magazines were less successful in touting the modernity of such prepared food to women.

By the end of the 1930s, the modern woman was portrayed as someone who had eliminated old-fashioned stoves and old-fashioned domestic help, who used canned foods or healthier ones like raw vegetables, and who was an expert in do-it-yourself ways of running the household. By this time, the cutting edge of household modernity had led to the total isolation of middle-class women in their houses and a translation into scientific terms of much of the nineteenth-century drive to look fresh and fertile. In addition, the trend of acquiring household machinery masked a declining post-war standard of living for middle-class women. The general crisis affecting domesticity that had been the result of the wartime priority on military goods had carried over into peacetime. Few modern households would have servants.

In 1928, Paulette Bernège published *On the Household System* (*De la méthode ménagère*), a guide to scientific home management that would be reissued for the next four decades. Taking the work of efficiency expert Frederick Taylor as her model and appropriating many of the ideas of Americans Christine Frederick and Mary Pattison, Bernège advocated systemization, order, and efficient use of time. Bernège was the most enduring of Christine Frederick's many followers. In 1921, Mlle. Cavaignac had first presented Frederick's principles to French women, and Irene Witte (1894–?) did a German translation, *Rational Household Management*. Later, both Witte and Erna Meyer (1899–?) adapted American domestic science to German households. Whatever the country, the principles of domestic science remained the same: women should plan household work by the clock and divide work into series of comparable tasks. To avoid fatigue, they should perform as many tasks as possible sitting down and should reduce, streamline, or eliminate movements whenever possible. Smaller kitchens—an innovation that was usually accessible only to middle-class and upper-class women—would also conserve energy. Propagated by magazines, social workers, homemaker's courses, and developments in architecture and interior design, domestic science joined older rationales—such as "duty" or "love"—that encouraged good household performance. The modern housewife did things in a scientific way to ensure her own health and that of her family. Scientific principles underlay domestic advice from the twenties on. The drive of domestic science toward modern efficiency was obvious; less so was the idea that household efficiency, as one efficiency expert said, would give women free time for "dreaming."

Efficiency and "dreaming" formed a team not only in literature about the household but in advertising that sold household equipment. In fact, the household became, during this period, an arena incorporating technology that led to both of these ends. For, in addition to the modern stoves, refrigerators, bathrooms, and small appliances, "dream" machines such as radios and phonographs became necessities to middle- and even working-class homes. These two machines transformed the interior atmosphere of the home to one of disembodied voices, music, dramas, and imposed moods. Early in the 1930s working women in Vienna said their favorite domestic recreation came from listening to the radio, and they also enjoyed housework more when they listened to it while performing their chores. Great Britain had approximately one radio per household at this time. Similarly, magazines brought advice and news of technology, but they also carried an escape from reality in the form of romantic stories, glamorous photos of celebrities, and sensual pictures of fashions. One breakthrough in printing technology during this period was the mass production of color photography; magazines such as the Parisian *Marie-Claire* (1937), with half its photos in color, became instantly popular. Color magazine pictures made fantasies about products or movie stars more vivid, more lifelike, and more inescapable. In the barrage of dreams, two themes became clear: one sexual, in the form of romance and cinema stars; the other material, in the form of more and better commodities. The household in the twentieth century was supposed to serve as the focus of both desire and efficiency.

"Know how to buy" was the message of one magazine in the 1930s, and this message was repeated thousands of times. The message no longer circulated outside the home in department stores; pulp journalism carried it right to the interior of the household, where it could shape habits and thoughts on a more regular basis. The invasion of monthly magazines and daily papers went hand in hand with the new consumer ideal of a household based on up-to-date equipment. The magazines simultaneously encouraged the desire for goods in their advertisements and the quest for romance in their short stories. Indeed, magazine stories often featured romantic, even erotic couples. Desire, not calculation, inspired marriage, and married couples would then fulfill materialistic wishes in the marketplace. Writers, advertisers, and publishers placed the pleasures of love and consumption at the heart of the home.

Women's Bodies

New ways of life, new fashions, new concern for the body, new things to buy, and new anxieties all combined to produce a transformation in women's physical appearance. Technological and erotic motifs were blended in the household, and women's bodies also displayed both themes. Fashion made women at once more desirable, more efficient, and in need of new goods. First, in the decade after the war, skirt lengths climbed approximately a foot to show half the leg. In addition, sleeves disappeared from clothing intended for warm weather or for evening. Clothing now revealed the most muscular and active parts of the body—the arms and legs—which were used in sports, work, and dancing. For a time, the boyish figure was stylish, emphasizing vigor and energy. Corsets structuring women's curves gave way to undergarments similar to brassieres that flattened the breasts. Women adopted men's slacks, trench-

By the mid-1920s, the body was boldly displayed in comparison with the preceding century. Women's bodies stood for health, reproduction, and sexual compatability.

coats, and even berets and wore shorts and abbreviated bathing suits for sports. A less boyish figure returned to style in the 1930s, but it was still more exposed than before. Between 1875 and 1925, women's general appearance changed strikingly.

Women's faces changed, too. Short, streamlined hair was the most striking change. Because it was such a deviation from the tradition, it had a modern aspect, especially when framing a face made up with lipstick, rouge, powder, mascara, and beauty marks. Cosmetics began to be widely used to accentuate individual features of ordinary women's faces. The cosmetics industry itself grossed billions of dollars almost overnight. Some women, such as Polish-born Helena Rubenstein, made fortunes selling "beauty secrets" they incorporated

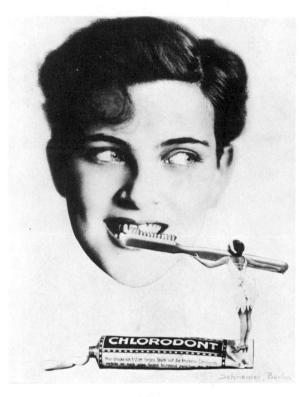

Inciting sexual desire, women also incited the desire to buy. Their photos, often disembodied, sold new consumer items.

into products. Before the war Rubenstein's products were sold in exclusive salons, but later they became, like other cosmetic lines, over-the-counter items. Even in the depression of the 1930s cosmetic sales remained high, since working women were using lipstick and powder. Once used only by prostitutes, cosmetics became a necessity for most women. Their faces portrayed a carnivalesque aspect of modern society—colorful faces supplemented colorful clothing to make a contrast to the drabness of machinery, factories, and offices.

The care women gave to their faces was indicative of a major change in the treatment of the body—especially the female one. Scantier clothing revealed more, and more of the body was observed by others. This led to a new focus on the body's tone, color, size, texture, and cleanliness. A Swiss doctor, before the war, had advocated sunshine as a cure for tuberculosis. By the 1920s, the fashion of suntans and more colorful complexions had replaced a centuries-old cultural preference for pale or white skin. A tan now stood for health, and people of all classes crowded to beaches. Soap became an important consumer product around which intensive marketing campaigns developed. To get people to buy soap, advertisers promised that using it would bring financial success, love, and happiness. Commenting on new baths installed at mines in the late 1920s, an English miner's wife endorsed the soap, brushes, and polish that allowed for "a sweeter atmosphere in the home."[3] Deodorants and depilatory products first appeared during World War I but made their way only slowly into the market. Because more of the body was revealed, people became more conscious of nuances of its appearance. Shiny noses, facial pores, cuticles, freckles, acne, wrinkles, bags, callouses, and sagging were of concern for increasing numbers of women. In the post-war period doctors began to perform cosmetic surgery on faces, breasts, and hips as fashion demanded less covering, corseting, and coiffeuring. Finally, menstrual products became a major consumer item around which advertising slogans developed. The advertisements' messages emphasized hygiene and "feminine daintiness," but also the active life of modern woman.

Work in the Post-War World

At the end of World War I, most countries made some effort to remove women from jobs they had held in wartime. The German government issued the following statement: "As a result of the radical change that has occurred in women's industrial work in Germany during the war, the question of the transition from a war to a peace economy is of great significance for the economy and the strength of the nation. It is necessary to re-integrate the labor of women into the traditional areas."[4] Almost without exception, people applied gender terms to the achievement of a healthy peacetime economy. That is, a healthy economy meant a workforce without women in the better-paying, skilled jobs. Women in these jobs should go back to the "traditional" realms of unskilled, often domestic labor. German Social Democrats, though wanting the new votes of women, generally agreed with trade unionists that massive numbers of women must leave the industrial workforce. Women were fired en masse— even those who had worked at their jobs before the war. Filling the ranks of the unemployed, many women did turn, at least temporarily, to "feminine" work in agriculture, domestic service, textiles, and so on.

The real problem, as many people saw it, was not that women worked— though many objected to that—but that the better-paying jobs in industry that women had filled during the war were now sought after by the returning veterans who had previously held them. At the same time, the least attractive work, such as domestic service and agricultural labor, suffered shortages. So the dramatic firings in Germany aimed at working a redistribution of the labor force. Other programs also served this end. In Great Britain, the government administered the unemployment insurance program in such a way that women were forced into domestic service, so as to solve the "servant problem" brought on by the war. To begin with, the "dole," as it was called, paid women much less than men and certainly not enough to live on. In addition, an unemployed person only received the dole after providing proof of a thorough search for work. Women had a difficult time proving there were no servant jobs available.

In Germany, the mass firings coincided with lobbying by the German Housewives Association, a group that formed in order to find a solution to the shortage of domestic labor. Confronting the fairly recent servants' unions, this organization of several hundred thousand housewives developed its own wage scales and household hierarchies—the latter an attractive option offering upward mobility in jobs that were normally more static than others. Ultimately, the group, under the leadership of Berta Hindenberg-Delbrück, proposed a mandatory year of domestic service for all young women either in households or on farms. An explicit expression of the aim of the mass firings, this proposal was unpopular with many and would remain so even after the Nazis converted it into law in the 1930s. But women still avoided domestic labor, which not only paid poorly but demanded work from 5 a.m. to midnight with virtually no time off. Moreover, the servant crisis, according to some, had made employers not less demanding but more so of any servant they finally hired. A taste of factory work—even with long wartime hours—had made domestic service unpalatable. Yet, to some extent, the policy succeeded: during the interwar years, between 10 and 20 percent of the female workforce in Germany was employed in some kind of service, although this was a drop from the higher levels of the late nineteenth century. Only the continuation of severe economic sanctions, political decrees mandating firing from other jobs, and virtually enforced domestic service in some cases could have achieved this result.

The work of farm women also provoked attention from politicians, researchers, social workers, and women's groups. The collapse of the wartime boom in prices of agricultural produce led to post-war problems. Falling prices and urban demands for even lower ones coincided with the appearance of motorized farm machinery, which made men's fieldwork easier. This mechanization only made household farm labor seem more and more onerous, more and more backward. Women in rural areas often lacked stoves, cupboards, running water, sinks, and sewing machines to say nothing of electricity. Working thirteen to eighteen hours every day, these women experienced a falling standard of living in comparison to all other segments of the workforce. In Spain and Eastern Europe, rural women's living and working conditions deteriorated even further than elsewhere as agriculturalists in these places competed in a rapidly modernizing international market. As their incomes were threatened in this competitive market, big landowners raised rents. In more modern countries, men created cooperatives and syndicates to improve their bargaining position both as producers and as consumers of seed, fertilizers, and equipment. Many attributed the rush for nonagricultural jobs—a female exodus to manufacturing centers—to the failure to modernize rural women's work as men's was growing more co-operative. To avoid poverty and harsh conditions in Central Europe, bands of hundreds of women would make seasonal migrations, from Poland, for instance, to more advanced agricultural areas such as Denmark. There, protective legislation regulated working conditions and mandated minimum standards for room and board. Elsewhere, population experts and philanthropists pushed for agricultural laws comparable to those applying to industry. However, even fairly prosperous countries that had such agricultural codes rarely enforced them. Meanwhile, a rupture was occurring on farms. The symbiotic interaction of housework and fieldwork was destroyed as large capital investments became necessary for machines and the farm became fully market-oriented, with cash crops gaining priority over everything else.

Movements for the improvement of women's work in agricultural areas took hold in the 1920s, though their impetus came from earlier expressions of dissatisfaction. In the 1890s, German groups had tried to enhance women's agricultural work by emphasizing commercial fruit growing and horticulture. In 1907, Ida Kortzfleisch von Reifenstein had lectured on the value of women's agricultural labor. Farm housekeeping and farm prosperity were intertwined. The connection, she thought, should be officially recognized, especially since "scarcely any other profession better suited female nature than the maternal creativity and governance of a house and courtyard manager."[5] After the war, similar sentiments resulted in the formation of national groups to aid farm women, international congresses on their welfare, statistical studies, and rural assistance programs to provide social services similar to those for urban women. Behind such efforts lay complex motivations. First, the agricultural sector was losing political power to industrial interests; many leaders of the national agricultural aid groups were large landholders eager to strengthen rural values, including religious ones, in order to maintain their own position. They issued religious and moral encouragement, but also scientific information. Rural women, they believed, needed labor-saving machines and technological advice. "All human effort," wrote the Countess Keranflech-Kerezne, a leading force in the French farm women's movement, "gains from being rationally organized."[6] Though their numbers were few, rural social workers brought some farm women the latest news on health, machines, and domestic science and suggested possible forms of female association. Correspondence courses, home economics lessons, and rural clubs all aimed at making the farm home modern. Those promoting rural modernization hoped it would strengthen religious values and conservative politics.

During the years following World War I work diversified within the range of women's occupations. The percentage of women working reached a peak between 1905 and 1920 and then declined in the 1920s. For example, in Vienna before the war, 95.7 percent of all able-bodied men and 50.8 percent of all able-bodied women were employed, but in 1923, the percentage of employed women had already declined to 48 percent. Male employment had risen by then to 97.7 percent. Domestic service continued to decline steadily, but the service sector in general had begun to represent a larger percentage of women's occupations. More and more women found jobs as office workers of all sorts, government clerks, department store salesclerks, and telephone and telegraph operators. In Germany, for example, the number of women in commerce and transport—a number made up largely of store clerks—rose 82.3 percent between 1907 and 1925. In France, out of every 1,000 nonagricultural female workers in 1921, 236 were in the service sector, 195 in the clothing trades, and 169 in domestic service. In 1921 in Czechoslovakia, recently carved from the Austrian empire and already the seventh leading industrial country, almost 2 million women worked in agriculture, half a million in industry, another half a million in domestic service and household work, and 200,000 in the service sector. Within the service sector itself, new areas opened up, especially in the booming beauty, cosmetics, and entertainment industries. At the lower end of the pay scale in these fields were hairdressers, stylists, and manicurists; at the other, more lucrative but precarious end were chorus girls, actresses, writers, singers, and radio announcers. Society's focus on physical beauty, spectacle, and glamour made these fields attractive to many women, even though they generally paid poorly.

Conditions within women's work also varied. In a large French dyeworks, women stood on their feet for 10 hours a day, worked with no protection from noxious chemicals, had no time off for pregnancy, and received no benefits such as canteens, recreational programs, and the like. But they could gossip, get lighter assignments from the foremen if they were pregnant, and help each other out of difficulties. Women in larger, modernized factories often had more comforts and were better paid, but their jobs were more monotonous. In many of these factories, psychic stress increased as managers and efficiency experts eliminated human judgment from the work routines. Increasingly, workers' roles were to serve machines' productive capacities; to perform precise and repetitive tasks; and often to care for, repair, and clean the machines that, in effect, directed their actions. In fact, many benefit programs offered by the most up-to-date industrialists were motivated by a wish to provide expensive factory machinery with healthier, more attentive tenders. A machine tender whose health and vitality were promoted in the service of productivity was one view of the modern working woman.

Taylorization, named after the influential American engineer Frederick Taylor, involved the reorganization of work according to results of time-and-motion studies of the work process. Efficiency experts measured how long human movements took in hundredths of a second, watched for unnecessary motions, and divided workers' tasks into subtasks of a specified number of motions. Applying their results, they set rates, for example, of the number of holes a worker should drill in an hour. Workers received premiums for producing more than the specified rate. If too many workers exceeded the quotas, they were generally increased. Many of these studies, especially of women's work, took place during the war when worker fatigue and illness due to long hours and poor nutrition threatened productivity. After the war, such studies were part of the increasingly competitive industrial scene as more and more countries became industrialized. Taylorization demanded greater output of physical power by workers while it reduced worker's intellectual contribution. Organizational charts and time rates guided the productive process. Efficiency studies also determined what characteristics to look for in potential employees. For example, across Europe, experts observing the process of typewriting calculated its mechanical attributes to develop standards for number of words per minute and studied the personal qualities necessary for good typing. Writing for the International Labor Organization in Geneva, researcher Dora Bieneman concluded from studies in the 1920s that although typing seemed merely mechanical, the best typists were not necessarily those with the greatest physical dexterity but those with intellectual talents such as knowledge of lan-guages, spatial ability, memory, and so on. Nonetheless, by stressing mechan-ical measurements in job descriptions, efficiency experts claimed publicly that such jobs required little more than physical motion—no matter what other talents they might actually demand. With the rapid development of physiolog-ical and psychological testing, workers were scrutinized to determine the point where maximum productivity without extreme fatigue could be reached.

Philosopher Simone Weil, who worked in automobile and metallurgical plants in the 1930s, wrote that from these experiences she knew what it was like to be a slave without control of one's own movements or one's thoughts. "The tragedy is that the work is too mechanical to offer material to think about and it nonetheless forbids all other thought. To think is to go more slowly; but there are standards of speed set by merciless bureaucrats and that one must reach both to keep one's job and to earn enough."[7] This was what work was like when guided by Taylorization. Others, including Weil, noticed how con-sistently women were given the most menial and least skilled work on assembly lines. The clustering of women in these menial jobs reduced men's hostility toward them for being in the workplace. A common gender ratio in industry at this time was 90:10. For example, where men predominated numerically, such as in printing, the 10 percent of the workers who were women were clustered in such unskilled jobs as counting sheets, labeling, and so on, while men did the skilled tasks of typography. In contrast, in textiles, where men were in the 10 percent minority, they served as the more highly paid mechanics and foremen. Whether men were in the majority or minority, they always con-stituted the elite group of workers. In either case, the menial status of women ensured that men would keep the more desirable jobs. But the hiring of women in order to make work less skilled kept male workers suspicious of them.

Those areas where women's work had, to some extent, been highly skilled experienced a decline in employment. For example, across Europe careers in the clothing industry—a stronghold for women—declined by as much as 25 percent between the world wars. The streamlining of women's fashion was responsible for much of this decline: in France between 1921 and 1936, a quarter of a million jobs in millinery, embroidery, corset-making, and working in feathers came to an end. Although women could still get apprenticeships in needlework, sewing machine operation, and knitting machine operation, they, nonetheless, often gave these skills up. War refugees and rural people who moved to cities found that a highly skilled job was more difficult to obtain than a menial one. Strangers, according to one newcomer to Paris in the twen-ties, "don't know the right door to knock at. If one doesn't have a little pull or know someone, you wander around like that for weeks and weeks and months, and then that's it—boom!"[8] Many skilled migrants—and in some cit-ies, they constituted as much as half the female workforce—became chamber-maids or domestics or joined women on the assembly line.

The process of Taylorization expanded managerial functions. Concern for the health and efficiency of the workforce led to a continuing reorganization of the workplace that increasingly generated jobs in both government and in-

Workday and Weekend in Germany

In 1930 women of a textile union in Berlin made a project of writing about their work and their leisure. They then produced a fascinating book describing a variety of working lives. This account of a workday comes from a married, thirty-year-old woman without children, whose life combines housework, factory work, and activities with her husband.

At six o'clock my alarm clock wakes me up and thus begins my workday. Washing and dressing are my first jobs; as for grooming, there's not much to do in that regard because I have short hair. Then I put on water for coffee and get some bread and butter ready for my husband and me. With that I'm ready and it's also time to wake my husband because he has a half hour bike ride to his workplace. *While he's getting dressed, I get his bicycle ready.* I pump air in the tires and fasten on his lunchbox. He drinks his coffee and soon he's on his way. I go to the front window and wave him good-bye. Now it's 7:45 and I must quickly bring a little order to the place. I have only a small apartment, but it nonetheless takes some doing in order to make it look right. At 8:15 I also have to leave. I work in the colored-pattern weaving section from 8:30 to 12:30 without stop. I eat my breakfast about 9. *But I don't let my looms stop; they continue working, for when one works by contract, one has to keep going in order to earn something.* At 12:30 it's time for lunch and I return home quickly. After eating, I clean the hall and stairs, and meanwhile it's 1:45 and time to go. Work then goes from 2 to 5 without stop. But when it's five, I go back to my little place with a happy heart. Then my husband soon returns, and I have always taken great pains to have his dinner ready on time. Then I wash the dishes and my husband reads me the newspaper. When I'm ready, we go for a walk. If I had children, I'd probably have to stay home. In addition I go to women's meetings of the union or SPD.* I never miss a general meeting of the SPD and so it goes one day after another until the weekend.

Saturday I get home from work at about 1 and quickly warm up the soup that I made Friday evening. Today I have to clean thoroughly, because for the rest of the week it only gets done superficially. After we have bathed and had some

*SPD is the abbreviation for the German Social Democratic party.

coffee, my husband goes to perform his union duties, and I help him. He is the first president of the metal workers' union. When he's finished, we go home well satisfied. After dinner we quietly read the union paper. Happy because we don't have to work the next day, we go to bed. I usually wake up at 8:30 Sunday morning and we have a pleasant breakfast. Then I start preparing lunch. Today I have time to make a really elaborate meal. After that we fix ourselves up nicely and go for a walk. We attend union events or public associations of which my husband is a member. We always return home with the consciousness of having served a good cause. We go to sleep with the intention to struggle further for the trade unions, for trade unions are the stronghold of the workers' movement.

Source: Adapted from Deutscher Textilarbeitverband. *Mein Arbeitstag—mein Wochenende* (Berlin: Textilpraxis, 1930), 80–81.

dustry in social and personnel work. When factory legislation first took effect in late-nineteenth-century England, philanthropic middle-class women had been the first inspectors. Especially during the war, when overwork was particularly pronounced, the role of such inspectors grew progressively important for both sides in the conflict. In England and in other countries, charity became professionalized into social work, with little difficulty in the transition. As workers, as mothers of potential workers, or as both, lower-class women constituted the clientele of social workers. For modern factory owners, social workers provided "a service that pays off." Trained to observe workers' health, fatigue, sanitary conditions, and morality, social workers were part of a new class of employees that connected the realms of manual laborers and of owners, of citizens and the government. Their skill—as they themselves saw it—was in bridging the gaps that separated these worlds, creating social health and harmony in a scientific way.

Although World War I had ended on a revolutionary note, with workers claiming political control, the working class suffered in the 1920s from underemployment, wage cuts, and swings in the employment market. For women, these conditions were exacerbated by obligatory unemployment, downgrading of occupational skills, and their return to doing piecework at home. Not surprisingly, women's participation in unions dropped sharply, after having risen during the war. In England, membership dropped from a high of 1,342,000 women trade unionists in 1920 to 731,000 by 1933. In Germany, women socialists in the 1920s tried to reach pre-war membership figures. Male membership in unions also dropped during these difficult times. Even the women who remained lost some of their special relationship to unions. In England, waves of mergers occurred, with small unions joining larger ones and female unions merging with male. In new mixed-gender unions, women's activism declined because they lost their leadership positions to men. Women were considered second-class members because they paid lower dues, in accordance with their lower salaries. Having lost their women representatives and stewards, they saw unions as less vital to them than ever before. In 1926, the first of several annual women's conferences took place to bring together English trade unionists. Protests began immediately, with one woman claiming the condescending atmosphere reeked "of a happy evening for the poor."[9] Then, women pointed out the lack of women speakers and of women delegates in leadership roles, the conditions in sweated industries, and so on. Future conferences were marked by similar protests because women's work continued to have such a low status. Observing the disinterest in trade unions by women in Germany, activist Mathilde Wurm noted that the two-tier system, with men in an upper strata of work and women in an inferior one, gave male unionists a set of privileges to defend against women's possible advances. Many unions in Germany had, in fact, dismantled their special groups for women and gotten rid of the special organizers. Such actions, as well as the merging of female unions into male ones, may have been an expression of union members' belief, perhaps subconscious, that sexuality and similar issues were attracting too much attention, away from labor issues.

Sexual Debates

Attacking the erotic journalism of the day, a left-wing journalist wrote: "Lake Como a place for romance, you say. *No!* center of the region's textile industry."[10] This journalist was taking note of a twentieth-century phenomenon: an exhibition of and accent on the sexual aspects of most ingredients of everyday life. Images of women's sexuality saturated post-war society. The notoriety of *La Garçonne* was due to the sexual looseness portrayed in the book. In Germany, cabaret singers, transvestites, and highly made-up prostitutes appeared at night in search of pleasure. Sensuous actresses such as Marlene Dietrich (b. 1901) and Greta Garbo (b. 1905) dominated the public imagination and even determined ideas of what women's sexuality should be. Representing the heights of female eroticism, black dancer Josephine Baker (1873–1945) toured Europe with an all-black troupe. She settled in Paris, where, in exotic and scanty costumes, she captivated audiences for years with her fluid movements. Even the achievements of female aviators, mountain climbers, and Olympic athletes drew attention to women's bodies by emphasizing physical prowess. Beauty contests heightened the emphasis on the physical and erotic aspects of women's lives. Dressed in swimsuits, young women displayed their bodies to be judged and discussed. Finally, the publication in 1928 of *Well of Loneliness*, Radclyffe Hall's (1883–1943) novel about lesbian identity, and the sensational prosecution of its author for obscenity added new intensity to a multifaceted debate. Although there was wide variety in concerns about sexuality, one as-

A depiction of the so-called new morality in a Berlin nightclub. Another part of this painting shows maimed soldiers looking on at the revelry and sexual display.

pect remained constant. Even though sexual activity involved both genders, the debates concerning sexual relations and portrayals of the sexual side of life more often centered on women than on men. These debates became a major preoccupation from the post-war period on.

Some suggest that World War I opened the floodgates of eroticism, with women on the home front reputedly enjoying unprecedented amounts of sexual activity, mostly outside of marriage. After the war, the rate of marriage and the rate of both illegitimate and legitimate births rose. Then came a perceptible decline in births. These fluctuations in reproduction demonstrated that couples were consciously manipulating fertility. The increased interest in contraception and sexual activity in general was reflected in the offerings of the mass media. In England, Marie Stopes's (1880–1938) *Married Love* was first published in 1918 and sold hundreds of thousands of copies over the next decades. Because of her rhapsodic descriptions of physical love, Stopes received countless re-

Marie Stopes and her new-born son in 1924. Stopes wrote rhapsodically about sexual pleasure in marriage. She combined a celebration of sex with scientific information about birth control and thus ushered in the modern reproductive age.

quests for information on birth control. She answered these by writing *Wise Parenthood* (1918), *Radiant Motherhood* (1920), and *Enduring Passion* (1928). Translated into more than a dozen languages and issued in countless editions, her work coincided with the post-war rise in the marriage rate and was part of the swelling tide of writing about sex. More technically accurate, wide ranging, and popular was Dutch physician Theodor van de Velde's *Het Volkomen Huwelijk* (1926), which soon overshadowed all other similar publications. Translated immediately into German, it went through forty-two printings in four years and soon had editions in every European language. The English edition (*Ideal Marriage: Its Physiology and Technique,* 1928) was translated by socialist sex reformer Stella Browne (1883–1955). Others of van de Velde's numerous and popular publications covered child care, eugenics, and exercise (*Sex Efficiency through Exercises: Special Physical Culture for Women*). Both he and Stopes provided the physiological information women had been demanding for decades. They did so in a way that still equated women's being with her sexuality; it is especially notable that the works of these writers emphasized female performance and fitness, less than male. Such books and many others in a similar vein formed part of the dense culture of sexuality in post-war Europe.

Although some published works about sexual life were very technical, many discussions of this topic still occurred on the old and familiar moral terrain. With images of women's sexuality all around them, people debated its characteristics, desirability, and regulation. Although nineteenth-century reformers had criticized the conventional double standard, some sexual modern-ists still wanted women to be purer sexually than men—virginal before mar-riage and faithful afterward. As before, the dominant middle-class morality suggested that somehow the working-class woman could not live up to this ideal. Working-class organizations—especially socialist and communist parties and trade unions—found themselves torn between the old and new ways of thinking about sex. The disarray of the sexual debate manifested itself in a series of contradictory and confusing utterances. The relative unanimity with which parties approached the theory of production gave way when it came to sexual and reproductive matters. Many in the French Communist Party scorned working women who dressed in ways that were sexually enticing. In 1934 Elsa Triolet, for instance, found seamstresses too "flirtatious and well-dressed." Although they were women of the people, "the air of [high society] slowly poisons them."[11] Hating bourgeois hypocrisy and repression in sexual matters, workers nonetheless sometimes labeled sexual display on the part of working women as an absorption of bourgeois immorality or decadence. An Austrian leader, expressing a common fear of working women becoming pros-titutes, warned that "sexual relations meet a physiological and psychological need" but also had "social consequences."[12] Finally, many labor leaders be-lieved the emphasis on sexuality only provided a new way of distracting people from politics and from class struggle. The "real" working-class woman led a conventionally moral sexual life, so that she might use her energy for political action.

Germany had been the center of sex reform movements, and many work-ers' parties and liberal thinkers there definitely advocated sexual freedom. Pro-moting sexuality and pacifism even before the war, Helene Stöcker's magazine, *Die Neue Generation (The New Generation)*, aimed "to make human sexual-ity a powerful instrument not only of reproduction, but of progressive evolu-tion, and concurrently of a heightened and cultivated joy of life."[13] A sympa-thizer with socialist aims, Stöcker was able to lead her sex reform organizations to alliances with working-class parties based on common inter-ests in sexual issues. In Germany, the Nietzschean rebellion against bourgeois sexual morality had more thoroughly permeated society than had similar chal-lenges elsewhere. The German Communist Party ran sex counseling and birth control clinics and made money selling contraceptives. Many German workers had learned the language of sexual fulfillment and connected sexual happiness with the attainment of economic goals. Although most political parties of the time did not display consistency in their attitudes on sexual and reproductive matters—and few at any time did—nonetheless, leaders had learned over the decades that affirming that the party was concerned about such issues was essential to winning women's support.

In England, it was also on the political left that explicit affirmations of women's sexuality most often occurred. Pre-war feminists everywhere had been leery of affirming women's rights to sexual pleasure, for they saw the sexual arena as the locus of women's inferior status. When viewed as only sexual—indeed, as "the sex"—women had no standing in the political or economic world. In places where women had received the vote, some feminist leaders refused to make sexuality and birth control public issues, because they saw them as matters that would only lead to further exploitation and renewed disrepute. Other women—some influenced by the discussion of sexual issues in the Soviet Union—agreed with the feminists' analysis, but not with their tactics. "I believe that the conventional estimate of women's sexual apathy . . . is not true. . . . The sexual emotion in women is not, taking it broadly, weaker than in men. But it has an enormously wide range of variation; and much greater diffusion."[14] That was Stella Browne's opinion, and she made women's sexuality into a cause within the context of working women's politics. She, and other women throughout Europe, believed that ideas about women's sexual feelings—that nice women did not have them, that prostitutes had them in abundance—had been constructed by men to maintain control over women. For Browne, the determination of reproductive activity and the description of women's sexuality belonged to women themselves as a primary right. Fitting her constructions of sexuality into the framework of liberal rights, she spoke to crowds of English working women. In her speeches, she joined reproductive rights to economic rights and knowledge of contraceptive methods to dignity and the struggle for well-being. As the *Letters from Working Women* (1915) had shown and as numerous studies of working wives in the first three decades of the century had clearly demonstrated, reproductive and economic issues

---

Ideal Marriage

Theodor van de Velde's *Ideal Marriage* was an international best-seller well into the 1950s. Providing information about female and male anatomy, Dr. van de Velde also described birth control techniques and encouraged male responsibility in sexual matters. In certain respects the book perpetuated stereotypes, for instance, in regarding men as the teachers and initiators of their wives. Van de Velde, director of an obstetrical hospital in the Netherlands, articulated a contemporary view of marriage based on sexual knowledge and sexual activity as the mainstay of both the individual personality and of gender harmony.

> Sex is the foundation of marriage. Yet most people do not know the A B C of sex. The average husband does not even know that his wife's sexual sensations develop and culminate to a slower rhythm than his own. He does not know *at all* that he must *awaken* her with delicate consideration and adaptation.
>
> If erotic genius does not characterize him, the man needs *explicit knowledge* if he is to be capable of inspiring such desire and imparting such joy.
>
> He must *know how to make love*.

The ensuing chapters may be of help to him here. They can, in certain portions, be read by educated laymen without any difficulty. Other portions, however, need close and careful study. For I aim at giving my instructions and deductions an entirely scientific tone and basis, though keeping free from superfluous pedantry. This manner of treatment, as well as the nature of the theme, make it impossible to avoid the use of many foreign words and technical terms. Readers who do not exactly comprehend any of these words can ask a doctor to explain their precise meaning.

Among civilized races, the urge to reproduce has ceased to "play the lead" among the components of the sexual impulse, which appears as a further stage of evolution; an advance in psychic power and complexity.

We must reflect that sexual activity is not necessarily identical with complete intercourse; that the urge to such activity generally, if not always, exists in children, long before they have any idea of the possibility of intercourse.

The sexual impulse *is an urge or impulse to sexual activity which has its original origin and irradiation not only in the genitals, but in the whole body and the whole psychic personality.* Hence its power is almost supreme.

Source: Adapted from Theodor van de Velde, *Ideal Marriage: Its Physiology and Technique*, Stella Browne, trans. (New York: Random House, 1957 [1926]), 8–9, 11–12.

were united for women. By the 1920s, this particular connection came from the grass roots, unlike the early assertions of women's right to pleasure, which had been advocated by upper-class feminists.

During the 1920s and 1930s, Sigmund Freud also focused efforts on explaining women's psychosexual development. In the last two decades of his life, he wrote on the origins of sexual differences and on femininity. Freud turned his attention to the pre-Oedipal attachment little girls had to their mothers. Though admitting always his lack of complete understanding, he postulated that female psychosexual development was based on rejecting this attachment by recognizing women's lack or inadequacy compared to men. That is, the little girl, as she reached the Oedipal—or, in her case, Electral—stage, rejected her mother for not having a penis. Unlike a boy, however, the little girl had no worries about castration; therefore, instead of having to repress her desire for the parent of the opposite sex, she could throw herself into his arms. Thus, according to Freud, women developed no principled superego as men did, nor did they develop an unproblematic ego. Instead, their constant valuation of the penis would make them long to reproduce, like their mothers, of course, but also as a way of gaining a substitute penis in the form of a child.

Many women came to Freud's home in Vienna for analysis and training, and Freud welcomed some into the ranks of psychoanalysts. Freud's youngest daughter Anna (1897–1986) would be the most prominent of the latter. As in other new fields such as social work and anthropology, there were no structures barring women's entrance into psychoanalysis. Some women psychoanalysts made breakthroughs in theory; specifically, they added a theoretical concern about women. In the 1920s, Ruth Mack Brunswick (1897–1946), Helene Deutsch (1884–1982), Melanie Klein (1882-1960), and Marie Bonaparte (1882–1962) were in one way or another among those associated with the fortunes of Freudianism. Ruth Mack Brunswick directed Freud's attention and that of her co-workers to the pre-Oedipal phase. She focused on the child's relations with the mother, and her findings allowed Freud to refine his work on the Electra complex. Melanie Klein drew attention to the child's relationship to the mother's breast, and she and Anna Freud (in opposition to one another) opened the field of child analysis. Princess Marie Bonaparte was part of France's aristocracy, but gave up much of her social life for serious study with Freud, who unfortunately viewed her mainly as the cause's philanthropist.

Karen Horney (1885–1952) would eventually maintain that a male vision dominated psychoanalysis. A physician trained in Berlin, Horney first described what she called "womb envy," or men's general awe in the face of women's reproductive power. Critics believed that Horney failed both to integrate her theories successfully into the whole body of psychoanalytic thought and to appreciate the way in which psychoanalysis had uncovered the dominance in the psyche of such male symbolic constructs as the ever present fear of the father's power to castrate. In spite of such criticism, strong pro-woman theories such as Horney's served an important purpose in times when feminism seemed on the decline as an organized movement. This was especially true because some of Horney's peers, notably Helene Deutsch, insisted on emphasizing some of the least attractive features of Freudian thought concerning women. In her major work, *The Psychology of Women* (1945), Deutsch elaborated on such concepts as penis envy, female narcissism, and women's general inferiority in the creative and public world. Work such as Deutsch's would have a restraining effect on efforts to maintain women's position in economic and political life.

Freud's theories had their greatest impact from the 1920s onward. Although suspect in the medical profession, they were a major force among other intellectuals in Central Europe. As the pulp media developed, ideas of complexes, neuroses, the libido, the unconscious, and so on became common. Except in France, where psychoanalysis would not be accepted until after World War II, throughout the rest of Europe and in the United States ideas of gender started to be based on certain aspects of Freudian theory. European thought on gender issues became more psychological and therapeutic, and this, in turn, posed a challenge to all former ways of thinking about women. Freudianism called certain aspects of gender definition into question and thus made it more complicated. At the same time he pushed gender identity into the most hidden recesses of the human psyche. On the one hand, one's gender identity was no longer just based on unambiguous biology; rather, it was built up over a lifetime, was never certain or untroubled, and was established through a difficult manipulation and interpretation of cultural symbols. On the other hand, because gender identity worked in unseen and relentless ways in the unconscious, gender relationships were no longer open to the rational modification pre-war feminists had espoused. How could nineteenth-century feminist rationalism affect the irrational psyche? Moreover, gender identity was deemed to be a historical process within each psyche. How could reformist feminist thought, which wanted to erase the bad parts of gender history by creating new institutions, deal with psyches in which gender had been established over time? That is, could feminist thought cling to ideas of harmony and to rational social panaceas that seemed to have little connection with the realms of the unconscious? From the 1920s on, it now seems clear, feminism went through a quiet period during which it made an almost imperceptible readjustment to deal with the psychological thinking about gender and society. Feminism had to face the psychological twentieth century.

Historians still argue the merits of the debate over sexuality that had such prominence in the first half of the twentieth century. Some believe sexual liberalization gave women a new arena of control—their own bodies—by giving them access to increased knowledge of how female physiology and sexuality functioned. Birth control techniques and sexual permissiveness seemed to free women from the sexual norms of their parents and from the consequences of sexual activity. Moreover, these historians point out, the new literature stressed consideration of women's sexuality: brutal sexual initiation by the male and passivity in the female were no longer acceptable. Other historians, however, believe the sexual debate narrowed women's options. First, it emphasized sexual intercourse in such a way as to make spinsterhood and celibacy less acceptable than ever before in history. Second, as the debate became popularized by the media, it imposed on the public yet another standard of behavior, that of attaining expertise in sexual intercourse. Sexologists and Freudians, for instance, set a standard of "vaginal" orgasms and the overcoming of the problem of female "frigidity." In addition, the sheer weight of words devoted to the debate made it seem that heterosexuality and marriage were the only acceptable outlets for sexuality. Finally, hardly a book or organization failed to describe sexual life and women's role in it in old-fashioned terms. Women should concern themselves, for example, with marital "adjustment." Critics claimed that the portrayal of women's sexual feelings and behavior in many sex manuals was simply an updated version of passivity, receptivity, and sensitivity. Given the drive to increase women's fertility after World War I, the emphasis on sex seemed just a new means to the old end of reproduction. Stressing the goal of sexual compatibility also opened a new arena in which men and women should find harmony and restore stable relations. Attention to sexual happiness would obliterate gender tension and finally restore peace. The widespread discussion of sex had another long-range consequence. Once sex was a subject for public debate, its practices could easily be manipulated—withholding or allowing contraceptives, for instance—merely through media attention. Improved knowledge of one's body provided many social and personal benefits, but the dispersal of such knowledge also made attitudes toward bodily experiences more easily influenced by the media, government, and other institutions controlling knowledge.

The Battle for the Family and Population

After World War I, an onslaught of public debate over ways to increase population coincided with the debate on sexuality. Except for a brief surge in births right after the war, fertility, in general, continued to decline. In Belgium the high of 176,000 births in 1910 was halved to 85,000 in 1918. In 1921, the number of births reached 163,000, but had dropped to 151,000 by 1930 and fell even lower subsequently. Although some rural or poor areas such as Ireland kept a constant birth rate throughout the 1920s, others such as Bulgaria dropped from 39 births per thousand inhabitants between 1921 and 1925 to 32 per thousand in 1928. This declining Bulgarian birth rate was still one of the highest in Europe, with Norway, Britain, France, Switzerland, and Austria having rates of 17 or 18 births per thousand inhabitants at the end of the 1920s. Declining birth rates occurred despite a legal framework banning abortion, contraception in some cases, and even, in France, discussion of contraceptive issues. In spite of article 218 of the German legal code, an estimated 800,000 to 1 million German women had abortions every year. Birth control literature and lectures there drew vast audiences.

Long a concern of government, women's fertility became elevated to a major policy question in the 1920s as decreasing birth rates were interpreted as a national security problem. Jules Courmont, a French physician and professor of hygiene, had announced in 1916 that the Germans would continue to be a threat after the war ended because of their higher birth rate. In fact, Courmont believed the pre-war decline in French fertility had made the country so weak as to invite the war. "Our families are too small," Courmont said, echoing earlier advocates of increasing the birth rate. For Courmont "the restriction of fertility is voluntary"; the problem for government involved undermining couples' resolve and replacing it with a desire for more children.[15] He cited numerous ways to achieve this: aid to pregnant and nursing women, a program to fight slums, the severe repression of abortion, and so on. By the mid-1920s, most countries were concerned about this problem. Declining fertility remained a sign to some of national impotence: "The complexities of modern life are assumed to have weakened the drive toward the potency of coitus, particularly on the part of men," explained Swedish sociologist and politician Alva Myrdahl (b. 1902).[16] To strengthen the nation, more than three children per family would be necessary. Although World War I had taught two lessons—one, that massive armies meant nothing in the face of modern firepower, and two, that modern warfare gobbled population—only the second preoccupied politicians.

Even neutral countries and those who suffered few wartime casualties were worried about how to get women to reproduce and how to get them devoted to the cause of national population growth. Church leaders, especially the pope, spoke in menacing tones about contraception being a sin and childbearing a duty, but a more voluntaristic approach was also shaping up. Late nineteenth-century debates on marriage, as well as the reform of divorce and property law, had led post-war theoreticians and cultural leaders to generate a more romantic and less mercenary model of how couples would form. "Companionate" was what Americans called this type of twentieth-century marriage. Governments and welfare institutions started trying to shape marriage to conform to the state's needs for population control and consumption. For the time being, the specific goal was population increase, and the means used to win the battle for increased family size were medical, financial, and educational benefits. Those governments that lacked social programs for the support of childhood now implemented some. An Austrian law enacted in December of 1921 made family allowances for workers obligatory throughout industry. Workers were to receive extra money for each child. European businesses had gradually, but erratically, introduced a similarly tiered kind of wage system by which unmarried men without families received lower wages. Though announced as a bonus to encourage people to have children, to labor leaders such a system looked like a wage cut for some. In England, where a proposal for government-controlled family subsidies out of tax monies drew fierce debate, *The Labour Woman* maintained in 1923 that such subsidies "should be from national funds and not from employers," who touted their payments as generosity.[17] Having initiated payments to poor mothers in 1913, the French government in 1932 converted the voluntary system to a state-run program of family allocations. This was a fairly comprehensive alternative to the piecemeal state and employer efforts that had developed in response to depopulation and employees' wage demands. As the social programs of Bismarck in the late 1870s and 1880s had made clear, subsidies to workers and political questions were closely intertwined, but so were those of subsidized reproduction.

Sweden had by far the most comprehensive program for encouraging parenthood through welfare programs. By 1940, the government had put various benefits into effect: prenatal care (1937), payment of delivery costs (1937), a maternity bonus (not dependent on income) and special subsidies to poor mothers (1937), dental care for children (1939), and protective medical care including innoculations and vitamins (1940). At the same time, legislation in 1934 made it compulsory for imbeciles to be sterilized, and a law in 1939 legalized hospital abortions under a range of conditions. These programs clearly intended to shape reproductive habits. Government-funded housing projects, like those in other European countries, also encouraged marriage and fertility by providing people with the space to raise a family.

Welfare programs sought to improve the conditions under which families cared for children and mothers gave birth. In Sweden, and elsewhere, medical attention centered on increasing the longevity of the existing population. Publicity campaigns begun earlier against tuberculosis, venereal disease, and alcoholism were supplemented by networks of clinics and teams of visiting public health nurses. Mothers took their babies to dispensaries—more extensive than ever before—for free medical check-ups. If they failed to do so, a public health nurse went to them. The most striking development, however, was the increasing popularity and availability of hospital maternity care for European women. Between 1920 and the 1970s, the percentage of hospital deliveries rose from a small proportion to virtually 100 percent. Visiting nurses, agents working for family allowance and insurance plans, social workers, and other public officials all advised against relying on midwives. Meanwhile, the number of health personnel increased dramatically and gave the hospital a more substantial presence. While paying lip service to the intimacy of home deliveries presided over by relatives, journalists touted the convenience and affordability of spacious clinics, scientific procedures, and abundant, knowledgeable personnel. This kind of persuasive effort was necessary to combat the earlier vision of hospitals as death houses or places for the indigent and unwed. Meanwhile, as giving birth in a hospital grew in popularity among the middle classes, workers, and professional people, the process of birthing was as transformed as work was.

Because of their importance to the state, pregnancy and birth demanded, first of all, close observation and intervention. When social security and insurance plans started paying for prenatal and postpartum medical care, hospitals set up gynecological clinics. Within hospitals, childbirth became a fragmented procedure, but one more easily monitored. Instead of giving birth in one room at home, women entered an institution that was divided by medically or managerially determined stages into a succession of rooms: a reception room; a room for making tests on blood and urine; one for shaving, bathing, and even pedicures; one for early labor; one for intense labor; a delivery room; a recovery room; and finally a postdelivery ward. Specialized personnel guided each procedure, as the mother moved along a kind of assembly line in a way that minimized her control over the delivery. In addition, mother and newborn child were usually separated—there were discrete spaces for specialized treatment of both. Women themselves reported their reactions to the new custodianship of childbirth: the lack of privacy and the loneliness in the midst of strangers appalled them; the cries of others in pain disturbed them; they appreciated others doing the laundry, but hospital staff filled their days with the increased duties of modern motherhood. However, between 1900 and 1938, infant mortality fell dramatically in countries where hospitals were abundant: in Germany, from 206 to 62 per thousand live births; in England and Wales, from 152 to 52; in France, from 142 to 66; in the Netherlands, from 149 to 36; in Sweden from 101 to 42; in Italy, from 166 to 106. This definite drop in infant mortality marked a singular change in the conditions of reproduction.

More and more women participated in the medical hygienic endeavor as thinking and behaving hygienically became a way of life. Once only the concern of reformers who talked in terms of social progress, children and women became the objects of intense medical interest, and women themselves became involved in medical care. Women learned to report physical changes during the course of pregnancy; they could time labor pains. Diet, exercise, and postpartum care, as determined by doctors, were things they learned about and could talk about as well. Dr. Anna Fischer-Dückelmann's *The Housewife as Doctor* (1910) had been translated into ten languages by 1922 and continued to be published in Germany through the 1950s. Also an author of books on sexual techniques and marriage, Fischer-Dückelmann provided her readers with doz-

A public-health worker in the Soviet Union explains scientific nursing of infants. In the twentieth century, governments across Europe focused on the bodily development of their citizenry and made maternal instruction a priority.

ens of clinical drawings illustrating the individual organs of the body, childbirth, and the development of the child. Under her guidance, women could even learn the chemical composition of dust—to which she devoted eight pages. Although the book's massive amount of scientific detail seemed to be intended to undermine the need to consult a doctor, in fact, Fischer-Dückelmann asserted that knowing so much would enable the housewife to have a better relationship with her doctor instead of relying on nonmedical advice. In fact, the thrust was to eliminate rivals such as the neighbor woman, the grandmother, the midwife. With books such as hers, Fischer-Dückelmann maintained, "the public" would be "on guard not to trust its own abilities too much." Scientific knowledge and reproduction went hand in hand now. "Every woman should have a medical visit to learn about her own body before making a decision about marriage or motherhood,"[18] recommended Fischer-Dückelmann. Many rivals to her work appeared by the 1930s, but all had the same end of involving women in the hygienic and medical enterprise.

"We must restore to contemporary society the idea that the child exists,"[19] announced Suzanne Lacore, on taking office as Under Secretary of State for the Protection of Children, in France in 1936. The way to do this, according to Lacore, involved fighting maternal ignorance: therefore, her *Guide for*

Mothers would reach not just urban women—as did hospitals—but rural ones as well. Lacore's activities reflected the international flowering of scientific childrearing, which involved developing women's objective knowledge about children and thus forging a new kind of tie between mother and child. Whereas once mothers were urged to be concerned about the moral development and generalized well-being of their children, twentieth-century mothers now weighed and measured their children or had them weighed and measured in clinics or by visiting nurses. Statistical models developed charting normal growth, appetite, and sleep patterns, and mothers were given charts and record books in which to keep track of illness, vaccination, teeth, weaning, and toilet training. The mother's time optimally involved making sure that the child received the correct amount of food, scheduling the sleeping and waking periods, and spending designated amounts of time in the open air and sunlight. The transformation of child care involved the entire social service system, the medical profession, journalists, and women themselves. Starting in the 1920s, courses on childrearing became obligatory for French girls in public schools. A typical course of ten sessions included lectures on the following: the importance of scientific childrearing and the struggle against infant mortality; cleanliness and bathing; clothing; room cleaning, play, and outings; normal growth, innoculations, and diseases; four lectures on food, feeding, weaning, and nutrition; and a final lecture on social services and laws. From the 1920s on, new ways of relating to children and new skills and knowledge about child care were becoming part of women's mentality and came to constitute part of daily life. Accepting the tenets of scientific childrearing, women made the decline in infant mortality possible. They interacted with agencies of state power and thus legitimated that power while also serving the national need for a strong, alert workforce. However, though European women answered the call for healthier children, they resisted governments' summons to increase their fertility. In this respect, the settlement of population issues and the rearrangement of reproductive life remained unstable.

Politics and the Women's Movement

What would suffragists do once women got the vote? Many people wondered how parliaments would function with women in them and how women's groups would behave politically. Others thought that little more could happen once women had been released from the home to do war work. Some thought the combative spirit of the pre-war days was bound to be a thing of the past, but others thought it might resurface.

When Marie Juchacz entered the German parliament in 1919, she made a conciliatory move in taking a stand with her fellow party members. In a spirit of national solidarity, she announced that women and men no longer had differences of opinion and goals. Moreover, women would not contest their rights anymore, for the defeat of the nation made such claims appear trivial. Juchacz not only allowed national interest to supersede all other claims, including those for rights and justice, she also revived the ideology of separate spheres. At caucuses and congresses of her party, she pleaded that women be authorized to turn their political efforts toward welfare activities. "Women are the born protectors of humanity," she announced in 1921, "and, therefore social work corresponds so well with their nature."[20] German feminists, seeing the franchise as the climax of a long series of victories, redirected their efforts toward the welfare of working women and mothers and even toward promoting reproduction for the sake of the nation. The violence of World War I made the domestic interests seem safer to pursue, while the sacrifice of life enshrined the nation as everyone's first priority.

Everywhere that women voted, they also entered parliamentary life. In some places, the first results were encouraging. In the 1919 election in Germany, 9.6 percent of the deputies elected to the Reichstag, or 41 of its members, were women; in 1926, there were only 26 female deputies. In the British elections of 1918, only one woman was elected among 17 who were candidates for the House of Commons; in 1929, after the vote was extended to all women over twenty-one, 14 out of 69 women candidates became members of Parliament. In the Netherlands between the world wars, the number of women deputies in the legislature never rose above eight. In Finland, which had led the way in national suffrage for women, the 1908 high of 25 out of 200 parliament members declined to 8, or only 10 percent, during the period between the wars. In the Soviet Union, where the handful of nationally prominent women had disappeared by the 1930s, women's representation on local councils rose continuously. Already making up 20 percent of local representatives in the mid-1920s, they increased their official participation from then on. In almost every country, the depression of the 1930s marked a sharp decrease in the number of women in parliaments. By 1933, the percentage of German parliamentarians who were women had fallen to 3.3 percent; in Britain, the 1935 elections returned only nine women members. However, in the 1930s they gained the equivalent of ministerial rank and cabinet posts in those countries that did not turn toward totalitarianism. In England, Margaret Bondfield (1873–1953) served as Secretary of Labor from 1929 to 1931; the beginning of the depression was a challenging time to become the first woman cabinet member. In republican Spain, Clara Campoamor served as Director of Public Welfare in 1933. In France, women's advocate Léon Blum gave Suzanne Lacore, Cécile Brunschvicg, and Irène Joliot-Curie (1897–1956) positions in his 1936 Popular Front government, even though French women could not vote. Voters and politicians of all parties watched these trends carefully, charting the health of feminism, the threat of a female voting block, and the general status of women as wielders of governmental power.

In the countries where women failed to get the vote—France, Italy, and Spain—suffrage groups continued their efforts, though many historians believe the war weakened them and fundamentally changed both their will and their sense of purpose. Where the suffrage movement had triumphed, however, they fragmented into numerous smaller groups, often competing and hostile to one another. In England, the National Union of Women's Suffrage Societies (NUWSS) became the National Union of Societies for Equal Citizenship (NUSEC). Headed by Eleanor Rathbone (1872–1946), the new group stressed

New Voices

During the 1920s the cause of freedom and rights gained new activists and moved to other parts of the world. Countries under the control of European imperialist policies developed independence movements, often influenced by liberal, socialist, and nationalist ideas from the West. In India poet, feminist, and activist Sarojini Naidu (1879–1949) became a follower of nonviolent leader Mahatma Ghandi. In the 1930s she led groups to protest British control of salt and was jailed several times. She also rallied mass audiences with her oratory and particularly urged wealthy women to feminist activism and to useful work. Poor women in imperially controlled countries had had their livelihoods destroyed by the economic power of Europeans and their standing in local communities undermined by European ideas of women's role. These women Sarojini Naidu also led to Ghandi's movement, which emphasized the restoration of Indian economic health. Finally Naidu directly confronted the British, as in this notorious speech given in London in 1920. The ideas of "Third World" women activists and their immense physical courage inspired and troubled Westerners particularly from the 1920s on.

> I speak to you today as standing arraigned because of the blood-guiltiness of those who have committed murder in my country. I need not go into the details. But I am going to speak to you as a woman about the wrongs committed against my sisters. Englishmen, you who pride yourselves upon your chivalry, you who hold more precious than your imperial treasures the honour and chastity of your women, will you sit still and leave unavenged the dishonour, and the insult and agony inflicted upon the veiled women of the Punjab?
>
> The minions of Lord Chelmsford, the Viceroy, and his martial authorities rent the veil from the faces of the women of the Punjab. Not only were men mown down as if they were grass that is born to wither; but they tore asunder the cherished Purdah,* that innermost privacy of the chaste womanhood of India. My sisters were stripped naked, they were flogged, they were outraged. These policies left your British democracy betrayed, dishonored, for no dishonor clings to the martyrs who suffered, but to the tyrants who inflicted the tyranny and pain. Should they hold their Empire by dishon-

---

*Purdah is a practice in which Indian women screen themselves from view through special clothing such as veils and special enclosures in buildings.

oring the women of another nation or lose it out of chivalry for their honor and chastity? The Bible asked, "What shall it profit a man to gain the whole world and lose his own soul?" You deserve no Empire. You have lost your soul; you have the stain of blood-guiltiness upon you; no nation that rules by tyranny is free; it is the slave of its own despotism.

Source: Adapted from "The Agony and Shame of the Punjab," quoted in Padmini Sengupta, *Sarojini Naidu: A Biography* (London: Asia Publishing House, 1966), 161–162.

housing and family allowances. Some older leaders such as Millicent Garrett Fawcett resigned because of the lack of focus on feminist issues, and a smaller Six-Point Group was formed to continue the push for women's rights. With feminist groups apparently fragmenting, in 1919 politicians could pass the Sex Disqualification (Removal) Act, which gave British women access to "any public function" but which still permitted discretionary regulations (for example, no women in the civil service could be married). Nevertheless women formed many new all-female groups. This was an expression of the vitality war work and the suffrage movement had generated. Under the aegis of NUSEC, Towns-women's Guilds were started to give women in towns and cities a base for social activities and civic concerns; most of their members seemed primarily interested in housekeeping and crafts. In Italy, the most active women's groups were church-based. In Germany, there were church-based groups or groups of housewives who became politically active because of the servant problem and the deterioration in conditions affecting the home. At the other extreme, some women converted feminism into the fight for sexual freedom or pacifism. In defeated Central Europe, such pacifism seemed disreputable or remote from practical issues. Whatever stand was taken, the array of political positions and the number of women's groups organized made some people think that feminism was dying out, a cause from the pre-war world.

Gender struggles were simply not fashionable for almost half a century after the beginning of World War I. It was an age of national solidarity in times of international turmoil and of solidarity of women with men because of men's sacrifice in military service and their threatened economic position. In this climate feminists were not viewed sympathetically. Also, most feminists were of the pre-war generation, and whereas post-war women who were active in politics were young and sleek, these older feminists were dowdy and dumpy in their persons and out-of-date in their combative ideology. The younger activists could distance themselves from feminism simply by refusing the mass politics of the older generation. Or, as Winifred Holtby did in her 1931 novel, *Poor Caroline*, they could gently mock the older feminists. Younger women also distanced themselves from feminism by focusing on the one area that would give them solidarity with men: the family. Whereas interest in mother-hood, health, and housing had once been seen as a gauntlet thrown in the face of industrial society, now such interests were socially acceptable. Adopting them made one smart, modern, and eligible for a governmental post such as statistician, factory inspector, or public assistance worker. One of the most prominent women in this shift away from earlier feminist concerns was Eleanor Rathbone, who built her "new feminism" on support for motherhood consisting of a family allowance. Making this the major focus of NUSEC, she worked to improve the position of women but at the same time was fixing their image in a maternal role. Although truly wanting to help mothers, many took this position out of fear generated by the war. As feminists had seen in the war and its aftermath, "the forms of chivalry and deference . . . inevitably turn into brutality . . . and express their political opinions.[21] By focusing on welfare issues, women could escape the dangers of chivalry that were still at the heart of the public, gendered world.

By the 1930s the status of the home, the mother, and the woman worker had become matters serving the freedom of women less than the state's interest and the strength of national culture. The tensions between rights and national strength proved particularly intense in the newly-organized countries of Eastern Europe such as Czechoslovakia, Yugoslavia, Hungary, and so on (see map on page 443). While a range of women's groups pursued basic legislation to broaden rights, rural political parties urging dutiful mothering to aid the strengthening of nationality groups attracted hundreds of thousands of women. Croation women in Yugoslavia and Ukranian mothers in Poland became eager upholders of ethnicity.

On the fringes, however, some women turned the issue of "welfare" back to "rights." Until the 1970s, most organized women's groups did not focus on the connection that had arisen between women's economic well-being and the control of reproductive technology. Until her 1939 arrest for performing abortions, Dr. Madeleine Pelletier continued to link the two. So did the women who lobbied against the anti-abortion article of the German law code throughout the 1920s. In 1931, it became dramatically clear that the issue of women's right to reproductive control was joined to economic well-being. Upset by difficulties finding work, which were intensified by a widespread campaign against the "double-earner"—that is, a wife whose husband also worked—women felt an additional grievance when two prominent doctors, Else Kienle and Friedrich Wolf, were arrested for performing abortions. The prosecution of these two came at precisely the moment when family size was more critical than ever for working women. As a result, women began a series of demonstrations against unemployment and high prices and for reproductive control. Briefly, these grass-root protests attracted sexual reformers, women pacifists, and members of workers' parties in a kind of pro-woman political action reminiscent of Kollontai's broad vision. In England, too, some observed the postwar position of women, as Ray Strachey put it in 1928, "like a specter across the lives of working girls." Without economic rights, a women would be forced to accept "the conditions which her grandmother endured," only this time with some amenities provided by the welfare state, when and if it chose to distribute them.[22]

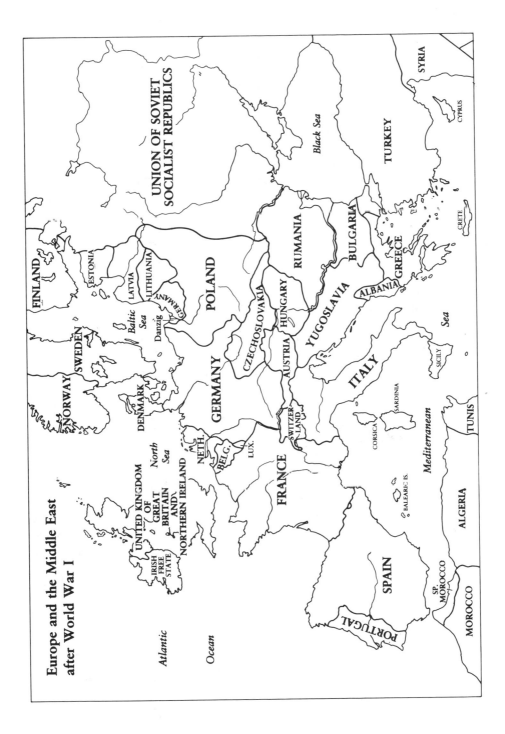

Europe and the Middle East after World War I

Dream Palaces and the Development of Mass Culture

Although many women apparently did not dream of entering Parliament or of pursuing grass-roots politics, they did dream about following another new path—becoming a movie star. Films, like radio and phonograph, provided cultural experience to millions of people on a more uniform basis than the local varieties of "popular culture," hence the name "mass culture." By the 1920s movie theaters were everywhere in urban Europe, though many of the most successful ones were American-owned. Women constituted the majority of filmgoers, and surveys from London to Vienna showed going to the movies to be working women's preferred leisure activity outside the home. Large numbers of British people under forty attended films once a week; of these, as many as two-thirds were women. These audiences overwhelmingly preferred American films: "Action, horror, low-brow comedy, and musicals, if not too elaborate, are what we go for here," as one British viewer put it.[23] The active British film-making industry lagged behind American in output and innovation (in part because of the war). The French first excelled in making silent films, and German film-making flourished with expressionistic classics such as *The Cabinet of Doctor Caligari* (1919) and influential masterpieces such as *The Blue Angel* (1930). After the revolution, Soviet films celebrated Russian culture, the revolution, and the new political and economic progress. From East to West, films became popular and influential, displaying hours of larger-than-life images to mass audiences of predominently working-class people. From the movies, these audiences learned how to behave and how to look. Audience members could think, feel, and empathize with the vividly portrayed characters. Gender roles, sentiment, sexuality, and women's daily lives (if only fantasy lives) dominated the stories. Besides offering the possibility of a glamorous career, the movie industry projected powerful visions of womanhood.

Films depicted both male and female behavior, sticking for the most part to stereotypes of stronger, more adventurous men and weaker, less venturesome women. Silent pictures spread these images internationally; without spoken words, no language barriers existed for most of these movies. When "talkies" took over in the 1930s, studios often made several versions of the soundtrack of a film in different languages. Movies weakened national boundaries; thus, cultural impressions of womanhood became internationalized. For example, farces of the 1920s embodied a view of a new domesticity based on sexuality, comradeship, and joking. The Italian film *Separate Rooms* (1918) and the German one *Comedy of the Heart* (1924) showed couples getting themselves in and out of difficulties arising from manners, sexual expectations, and gender roles. Some movies featured the woman who, as a drudge or frump, lost her husband but then won him back by becoming glamorous. To be companionate, the message was, one had to be chic in dress and smart in manners. In some films, the flapper—an emancipated working woman like the *garçonne*—dominated the screen with her physical energy and derring-do. Working, flirting, dancing, and eventually marrying, she personified the new sexuality and energy that brought couples together. On the screen, showgirls, office workers, and career women dramatized a new range of work experience. In general, such heroines projected youth and freshness; then success, it was implied, came from those qualities rather than from experience. The tension in these films, however, developed from the entangling of love and work lives. Movie images of working women exemplified the values of entire nations during the Depression of the 1930s. In England Gracie Fields took a series of working-class roles in such films as *Sally in Our Alley* (1931), *Looking on the Bright Side* (1932), *Sing as We Go* (1934), and *Shipyard Sally* (1939). Portraying a range of good-natured and upright working women, Fields seemed the model Briton, who rose above all economic trials and class envy in a display of good sportsmanship and joviality. All these films offered role models, instruction in how to look and behave, and even words to fit situations that might occur in real life.

Movies offered the public an assortment of angelic, demonic, whorish, sensual, and dangerous women. In 1933 Greta Garbo starred in *Queen Christina*, one of her more breathtaking films. This story of a powerful Swedish monarch captured some of the vigor of the new woman. Christina wore men's clothing, drank with men, and ruled like one. Unlike the real Christina, the film heroine gave up her throne for a man and then suffered agonies when he died. The movie industry often combined real and fantasy women in this way. Many powerful films involved female destroyers and evil ladies. Among these was Austrian G. W. Pabst's *Pandora's Box* (1929), which had lesbian scenes and a heartless, never satiated antiheroine, played by Louise Brooks, who drags down everyone around her. She is finally murdered by a Jack the Ripper–like figure. Joseph von Sternberg made the classic film of female destructiveness—*The Blue Angel* (1930). Before making it, he looked around Germany for a star and found the plump unknown he would transform into Marlene Dietrich. Throughout the 1930s, Dietrich became the vehicle for von Sternberg's obsession with the disasters ensuing from role reversal. Women were supposed to be passive recipients of male attentions. *The Blue Angel* depicts an emasculating, sexually demanding, evil woman, Lola Lola, always ready to destroy men. After moving to Hollywood, von Sternberg and Dietrich continued to portray this type of destructive woman in a series of films; the plots revolved around efforts to destroy such a constant, ever-threatening menace. Such portrayals of the evil woman provided social and psychic tension for millions of Europeans, who then found release in counterbalancing images of angels. The angelic parts fell to blond, innocent-looking types, especially those who looked like children. By the 1930s these soothing apparitions had taken the fanciful form of showgirls. Because the depression dashed the male ego, a common fantasy showed woman cheerfully and amusingly giving her all for the rehabilitation and restoration of "her man." Especially in the popular, large-scale Hollywood musicals, showgirls were on the one hand machine-like in chorus lines and on the other angelic because of the miracles they could work. Although the nineteenth-century visions of womanhood had changed little in substance, they now were displayed in the psychically powerful form in film.

Marlene Dietrich in her celebrated role as the destructive Lola Lola. The woman worker but also the so-called "emasculating woman" threatened male identity in the postwar years.

Movies took their place alongside magazines, newspapers, books, and radio as part of the mass culture with which people filled their leisure time. Though for the most part men directed movies and generally determined the substance of mass culture, some women rose to prominence alongside them. Working at first for the Ullstein publishing firm in Berlin, Austrian-born Vicki Baum (1896–1960) wrote one best-selling novel after another while she also wrote filler copy and did a variety of jobs for the editorial department of *Berliner Illustrierte* (*The Berlin Illustrated*). After the success of her novel *Grand Hotel* (which became a play and then a movie starring Greta Garbo, John Barrymore, and Joan Crawford [1904–1977]), Baum worked permanently in the Hollywood film industry. Similarly, Margarete Böhme's (b. 1869–?) *Tagebuch einer Verlorenen* (*Diary of a Lost One*, 1929) was first a best-seller and then a popular movie. In England, Agatha Christie (1890–1976) and Dorothy Sayers (1893–1957) built careers writing successful detective stories, which helped make that genre an ingredient of mass culture.

A few European women made films. German director Lotte Reiniger (b. 1899) became famous for her silhouette films. At first an actress, Leni Riefenstahl (b. 1902) took up directing. In *Das Blaue Licht* (*The Blue Light*) (1932), she explored the ravages that reason and science wrought on the intuitive and magical. Riefenstahl herself starred as a mysterious "nature-woman" destroyed when the blue light she worships is confiscated as a valuable collection of crystals. She reached the height of her career making lavish Nazi propaganda films, such as *Triumph of the Will*. Austrian Leontine Sagan's

(1899–1974) *Girls in Uniform* (*Jeunes Filles en Uniforme* or *Mädchen in Uniform*, 1931) expressed a horror of the increasing militarization of society and captured the attention of female movie-goers all over Europe.

The most envied women involved in producing mass culture were movie stars. Actresses such as Birgette Helm (b. 1906), Françoise Rosay (1891–1974), Gracie Fields (1898–1979), and Lyda Borelli (1884–1959) became celebrities whose images served as role models for women and whose daily lives offered them an equal fascination. Fairly quickly, however, many European actresses—Pola Negri (1894–?), Greta Garbo, Marlene Dietrich, Claudette Colbert (b. 1905), and Ingrid Bergman (b. 1915)—opted for even greater stardom by moving to the United States, which was dominating the film industry by the 1930s.

A Culture of Difference

In post-war culture, the concern that defined the twentieth century for decades was the search for personal identity. Among men, this search led, in some cases, to forceful assertion of masculinity, as seen in the works of D. H. Lawrence (1885–1930), Gabriele d'Annunzio (1863–1938), and Ernest Hemingway (1899–1961). Conquest of territory, of enemies, and of women was the key in this literature. Other male writers, such as Thomas Mann (1875–1955), tried to discern what had happened to nineteenth-century civilization, its values and myths. Exploring the crisis of culture, Mann wrote *Joseph and His Brothers* (1933–1943), *Death in Venice* (1913), and the *Magic Mountain* (1924). To James Joyce (1882–1941) and Marcel Proust, art was personal and sacred, an exploration of the interior universe of the artist. Their works were ironic, but also epic, presenting the sweep of Western culture and customs in the form of remembrances or personal monologues. Meanwhile, in philosophy, Ludwig Wittgenstein (1889–1951) and the growing school of logical positivists asserted that traditional metaphysics were nonsense and turned to language instead. Truth lay, not in speculations about nature and the universe, but in clear statements that could be dissected according to the principles of logic. In Germany, under the influences of Nietzsche, there was also a move away from metaphysics toward theories called phenomenology, existentialism, and hermeneutics, all of which emphasized human experience in history.

Women writers moved in parallel, yet unique directions. One of the leaders was French writer Colette (1873–1954), who produced the first of the famous Claudine series at the turn of the century. Colette was forced to write each day by her husband Willy, who published her work as well as that of other writers as his own. Colette tired of surrendering her work to him, of catering to his many mistresses, and of being dressed up and displayed by him to decadent Parisian society. Breaking away, she became a music hall and café dancer but continued to write. All her stories were considered shocking and depraved. *La Vagabonde* (1911), *Mitsou* (1918), and several other works described those who frequented the cafés and night spots of Paris and especially the interior lives of the women who entertained them. In 1919, Colette wrote *Cheri*, a story about an older woman who initiates a twenty-five-year-old into true love. Among the distinguishing characteristics of her work is her vivid description of sexual desire—such as that generated by a kiss that spreads anticipation of pleasure throughout the heroine's body or that felt by a young man seeking the breast of his fifty-year-old mistress. Colette's work also explored the role of memory, first in the Claudine series and then relentlessly throughout *Cheri* and *The End of Cheri* (1926). In the latter work, the hero is past thirty and cannot adjust to post-war life or to his mistress's sixty-year-old face and enormous figure; instead he fixates on her old pictures from the pre-war days, but he finally blows his brains out. Colette's own memories were mingled in the stories she told, most notably memories of her mother and of nature and of animals. Though always considered unsuitable, her novels endured, despite critics' suggestions that she write about more elegant people and more elevated topics, such as politics. She continued to write about love, incest, adultery, and lesbianism—this last in *The Pure and the Impure* (1932), which she thought was her best book. Relentlessly pursuing the theme of love, even during the Nazi occupation of Paris, when she had to hide her Jewish husband each day and night, she produced *Gigi* in 1944. Differing from the elevated philosophical works about the French resistance then being composed by many authors, *Gigi* described an old courtesan and an older man who was in love with the courtesan's granddaughter, the title character. Destined to be a courtesan herself, Gigi is another of Colette's not-quite-respectable characters who manifest both sexuality and virtue. Unlike most male novelists of the period, who searched for male identity, Colette expressed female identity rather than engaging in a quest for it.

Colette participated in many society circles, including the celebrated one of Natalie Barney, American expatriate and lesbian intellectual. Barney introduced Colette to Radclyffe (born Marguerite) Hall (1880–1943), whose *Well of Loneliness* (1928) was the subject of most discussions of women's literature at the time. Marguerite Hall was born into a wealthy but troubled English family. Her father left the house when she was born, and she and her mother had a tempestuous relationship. By the time Marguerite reached young adulthood, she knew she was a homosexual. This side of her nature soon flourished in two successive relationships—the last being with her lifelong companion Una Troubridge. John—as Hall came to call herself—began publishing poems and novels under the name Radclyffe Hall. Although many of her novels indirectly raised the problem of lesbian identity, *The Well of Loneliness* forthrightly narrated the life of Stephen Gordon, a young woman who should have been born a man. In describing the torments of "sexual inversion," Radclyffe Hall followed Havelock Ellis's formulation; in fact, Ellis wrote a preface in which he called *The Well of Loneliness* a "book on a high level of distinction."[24] Stephen Gordon manifested not degeneracy but exemplary moral concerns—for her family, her lovers, and for the social order in general. Yet the book outraged many in English society for its explicit mention of women's intimacy. As a result, the Conservative government prosecuted Hall and her publisher. Though banned, the book was published in many languages and in many editions, and Hall herself received the thanks of women around the world. Most of Radclyffe Hall's correspondents felt the book to be a liberation and a declaration of high principles, though some disapproved of her delineating her heroine in masculine terms because it seemed to cast lesbianism too formulaically.

Women had introduced lesbian characters in other major works, for example, in one chapter of Rosamond Lehmann's *Dusty Answer* (1927). Clemence Dane's *Regiment of Women* (1917) was an entire book devoted to lesbianism, but her tale was one of seduction and sadism. In Germany, Sophie Höchstetter's (1873–1943) *Selbstanzeige: Die Letzte Flamme (Self-Proclamation: The Last Flame)* (1917) was privately printed; and Anna Weirauch's (1887–?) *Scorpion* (1919–1921) had wider circulation and was translated in other languages after Hall's work had made lesbianism a topic of public interest. Mary Renault's (1905–1983) sensational writing career included *The Friendly Young Ladies* (1944), which differed from Hall's static and deterministic interpretation of sexual identity by describing it as more fluid.

Among the giants of twentieth-century literature, Virginia Woolf (1882–1941) was not only one of the great stylists and innovators but an unforgettable character herself. Woolf and her husband Leonard established the Hogarth Press, which published not only her works but those of other avant-garde writers including a complete translation of Freud. She was also the focus of the Bloomsbury circle of intellectuals and artists, and a major literary critic. She struggled with recurring mental breakdowns that punctuated intense productivity and complete lucidity. Woolf perfected the technique of inserting the interior monologue into the normal progression of the novel's narrative. In *Jacob's Room* (1922), the reader only learns about events from hundreds of individual impressions. Like a painter, Woolf created a literary canvas of splotches joined together by their proximity in the text rather than by a narrator interpreting the events and people for the reader. Woolf's writing set new formal standards, but it also captured the rhythm of women's lives. Her characters Mrs. Dalloway and Mrs. Ramsey are unforgettable in the way they radiate domestic competence and sensibility. Fascinated by the flow of time and the illusiveness of character, Woolf wrote *Orlando* (1928) in which the protagonist has several centuries of adventures and problematical love affairs while metamorphosing from a man into a woman. In all these works, she explored the relationships of characters, as literary forms, to one another and the ties of women to other women and to men.

Woolf's critical writing was especially clear concerning the condition of women and the mess she felt men had made of the world. *A Room of One's Own* (1929) posed questions about Shakespeare's sister: Did he have one? Did she write? How could one find out about her? This literary device allowed Woolf to explore the question of women's writing and, indeed, women's intellectual activity. For Woolf, the answer was clear: to achieve what men had, a woman needed money and "a room of one's own"—that is, economic support and protection from the demands of domesticity or reproduction. *Three Guineas* (1938) was a later, powerful work that continued these themes, only here Woolf made stronger connections between inequities in the world at large and inequities against women. Specifically, Hitler's persecution of the Jews, the per-

Russian poet Anna Akhmatova and her family.

secution of colonial peoples, and the threat of compulsory killing, she wrote, made people angry. Suddenly, men could see what it had been like for women to live in a world where principles of liberty, individual rights, and justice did not apply at all. The rule by exclusion and scapegoatism, the rule, that is, of fascism, as it was then arising across Europe, just took the old way of doing things and applied it to new groups.

Many consider Anna Akhmatova (1889–1966) to be the greatest Russian poet of her time. Even before World War I she had achieved fame for her stark love poetry written in the Acmeist style. Revolting against symbolism and decadence in poetry, Acmeists—who included Ossip Mandelshtam (1891?–1940) and Akhmatova's husband Nikolay Gumilyov (1886–1921)—affirmed the goodness of life, of nature, of earth. Akhmatova's own search for meaning led her to write of being unloved and to combine this with religious themes. Was there, she asked, in women's different love stories as well as her own, "an angel pointing out a light we cannot see?" Akhmatova's quest was for this light and for those who could see it. Akhmatova, though searching for an extraordinary vision, attracted a wide Russian following with her use of ordinary speech and her intense portrayal of human feelings. When war, revolution, and civil war came, she first thought to turn away but instead interpreted what people felt. Described by the new regime as a useless writer, unless one wanted to observe the foolish preoccupations of idle women, she nonetheless caught the attention of Kollontai because her poetry captured the ways women had suffered unjustly in old-fashioned types of love affairs. Like Kollontai, Akhmatova became silent as her husband was executed, her work censored, her son imprisoned. In those years of continuing horror, Akhmatova discovered the heart of modern times. Standing in line before prisons where her friends and loved ones might receive packages and where she might receive an indication of their existence, she felt part of Russian womanhood in a new age:[25]

> And the happy word "home"
> Is known to no one now.

This destruction of the common trappings of life was what revealed life to her more starkly than ever before.

A Fragile Peacetime

Like Colette's novels, Akhmatova's poetry served as popular rallying points when hard times continued to strike European people. Material goods and a rising tide of prosperity healed some wounds of World War I. People bought more and earned more, especially in Western Europe. Household life became technologically more complex, and couples took on marriage as a venture that would bring them personal pleasure and emotional satisfaction. Governments tried to ensure reproductive health and productive stamina through a variety of new programs.

Active to rebuild a prosperous citizenry, nations nonetheless remained hostile and belligerent toward one another. The crisis of personal identity and the competitive quest that fueled pre-war European politics continued to produce feelings of insecurity. Popular protest and governmental actions became increasingly violent. Confronted by economic and social problems, yet driven by private demons and the culture of dreams, Europeans were soon to unleash on one another all the technology they had built up in two decades of peacetime. Using modern methods, governments tried to reshape entire races through both welfare and genocidal policies. Resorting to conquest, they pursued yet another devastating war.

NOTES

1. Laurence F. Orbach, *Homes for Heroes: A Study of the Evolution of British Public Housing, 1915–1921* (London: Seeley, Service, 1977), 79.
2. *Journal de la femme*, no. 223 (February 13, 1937).
3. "A Durham Guildswoman" in Margaret L. Davies, ed., *Life as We Have Known It* (London: Hogarth Press, 1931), 139.
4. Quoted in Renate Pore, *A Conflict of Interest: Women in German Social Democracy* (Westport, Conn.: Greenwood, 1981), 21.
5. Ida Kortzfleisch von Riefenstein, *Weibliche Dienstpflicht: Zwei Vorträge* (Berlin: A. Duncker, 1907), 29.
6. Simone de Keranflech-Kerenze, *La vie et les oeuvres de la campagne* (Autun: Pernot, 1920), 181.

7. Simone Weil, *La condition ouvrière* (Paris: Gallimard, 1923), 23–24.

8. Catherine Rhein, "Jeunes femmes au travail dans le Paris de l'entre-deux guerres," doctoral dissertation, University of Paris VII, Paris, 1977, 120.

9. Quoted in Norbert Solden, *Women in British Trade Unions 1874–1976* (Dublin: Gill and McMillan, 1978), 124.

10. "Popolo d'Italia," *Regards,* September 1, 1933, quoted in François Delpla, "Les communistes français et la sexualité, 1932–1938," *Mouvement social,* vol. 81 (April-June 1975):122.

11. Elsa Triolet, "L'industrie souriante," *Regards,* February 9, 1934, in Delpla, *Mouvement social,* vol. 81 (April-June 1975):132.

12. Quoted in Helmut Gruber, "Sexuality in 'Red Vienna': Socialist Conceptions and Programs and Working-Class Life, 1920–34," *International Labor and Working-Class History,* vol. 31 (Spring 1987):37.

13. Amy Hackett, "Hélène Stöcker: Left-Wing Intellectual and Sex Reformer," in Rénate Bridenthal et al., *When Biology Became Destiny: Women in Weimar and Nazi Germany* (New York: Monthly Review Press, 1986), 115.

14. F. W. Stella Browne, "The Sexual Variety and Variabilty among Women and Their Bearing upon Social Reconstruction," quoted by Sheila Rowbotham, *A New World for Women: Stella Browne, Socialist Feminist* (London: Pluto 1977), 92–93.

15. Jules Courmont, "La guerre et la repopulation," *Musée social* (1918):1–30.

16. Alva Myrdahl, *Nation and Family. The Swedish Experiment in Democratic Family and Population Policy* (New York: Harper, 1941), 49.

17. *The Labour Woman* (June 1, 1923), 93.

18. Anna Fischer-Dückelmann, *Die Frau als Hausartin* (Munich: Süddeutsches Verlagsinstitut J. Müller, 1929), passim.

19. Suzanne Lacore, in newspaper clipping, Bibliothèque Marguerite Durand, Paris, File LAC.

20. Quoted in Jean Quataert, *Reluctant Feminists in German Social Democracy, 1885–1917* (Princeton, N. J.: Princeton University Press, 1979), 233.

21. Marie Juchacz, quoted in Werner Thönnessen, *The Emancipation of Women. The Rise and Decline of the Women's Movement in German Social Democracy 1863–1933,* Joris de Bres, trans. (London: Pluto, 1973), 130.

22. Ray Strachey, *The Cause: A Short History of the Women's Movement in Great Britain* (London: Bell, 1928), 392.

23. Interviews from *World Film News,* vol. 1 (December, 1936): 3–4, quoted in Jeffrey Richards, *The Age of Dream Palaces* (London: Routledge and Kegan Paul, 1984), 29.

24. Michael Baker, *Our Three Selves. The Life of Radclyffe Hall* (New York: Morrow, 1985), 205.

25. Amanda Haight, *Anna Akhmatova,* (London: Oxford, 1976), 33, 86.

SOURCES AND SUGGESTED READING

Anscombe, Isabelle. *A Woman's Touch: Women in Design from 1860 to the Present* (1984). A fascinating portrayal of women's major role in modern design.

Appelt, Erna. *Von Ladenmädchen, Schreibfraulein und Gouvernanten: Die weiblichen*

Angestellten Wiens zwischen 1900 und 1934 (1985). On the development of women's work in Vienna.

Baker, Michael. *Our Three Selves. The Life of Radclyffe Hall* (1985). A vivid portrayal of Hall's life and ideas.

Benstock, Shari. *Women of the Left Bank: Paris, 1900–1940* (1986). Recaptures the excitement of avant-garde life.

Davies, Margaret L., ed. *Life as We Have Known It* (1931). English working-class women write about their lives.

Dobkowski, Michael N., and Isidor Wallimann, eds. *Towards the Holocaust: The Social and Economic Collapse of the Weimar Republic* (1983). Particularly excellent articles by Atina Grossman on working-class sexual reform and by Renate Bridenthal on women's conservative organizations.

Forty, Adrian. *Objects of Desire* (1986). An engaging study of household appliances and other objects and their use in the twentieth century.

Foucault, Annie. *Femmes à l'usine, ouvrières et surintendants dans les entreprises françaises de l'entre-deux guerres* (1982). Women workers and their supervisers in France.

Gittins, Diana. *Fair Sex: Family Size and Structure in Britain, 1930–1939* (1982). An important study.

Gruber, Helmut. "Sexuality in 'Red Vienna': Socialist Conceptions and Programs and Working-Class Life, 1920–1934," *International Labor and Working-Class History* (1987). A look inside socialist activities and ideology.

Haight, Amanda. *Anna Akhmatova* (1976). A moving biography.

Heller, Geneviève. *"Propre en ordre": habitation et vie domestique 1850–1930* (1979). On household tools, design, and schedules among the Swiss.

Henrey, Madeleine. *Madeleine Grown Up. The Autobiography of a French Girl* (1953). The story of a manicurist in London.

Holzman, Ellen M. "The Pursuit of Married Love: Women's Attitudes Toward Sexuality and Marriage in Great Britain, 1918–1939," *Journal of Social History* (1982).

Martin, Martine. "Femmes et société: le travail ménager en France entre les deux guerres," unpublished thesis, University of Paris VII (1984). On household work and household utensils between the wars.

Mitchell, Juliet. *Psychoanalysis and Feminism* (1974). A clear presentation of Freud's ideas about women.

Petrement, Simone. *Simone Weil: A Life* (1976). A major French philosopher and activist.

Pore, Renate. *A Conflict of Interest: Women in German Social Democracy* (1981). An important study of women in German politics.

Rosen, Marjorie. *Popcorn Venus: Women, Movies and the American Dreams* (1973).

Sarde, Michele. *Colette* (1980). An engaging life story.

Solden, Norbert. *Women in British Trade Unions 1874–1976* (1978). Explores the fate of trade unionists between the wars.

Thébaud, Françoise. "Donner la vie: Histoire de la maternité en France entre les deux guerres," unpublished thesis, University of Paris VII (1982). A major work on the development of hospitalized childbirth.

New Battles: The Rise of Dictators and War

Global Upheaval   In 1931, the Spanish people overthrew their monarch and declared Spain a republic. At the time, Constancia de la Mora (1906–1950) and two friends "talked for hours" in Madrid about what a republic would mean for their people. "We saw a backward country suddenly blossoming out into a modern state. We saw peasants living like decent human beings. We saw men allowed freedom of conscience. We saw life, instead of death in Spain."[1] Others, however, preferred what de la Mora called the "backward" state of things. An Englishman who had settled with his Spanish wife in Barcelona just before the fall of the monarchy described it as a country to "love and admire." In particular, he liked that there were "few childless couples and large families are the rule." In fact, Spanish women gave birth to 648,000 children in 1921 and to 664,000 in 1928—thus, the decline in fertility so disturbing to politicians in other countries was not occurring there. For conservatives and monarchists, Spain differed from the decadent, modernizing nations where "young married couples . . . secure a motor car before they will have any children at all."[2] In 1936, the army rebelled against the young republic. Big landowners and the church supported this rebellion, and workers and landless peasants fought against it. The fight between old and new involved many women. Having fought at the front for the republic, like thousands of other women, Lina Odena became the first martyr to the cause by killing herself just as the rebel forces started to overrun her position. In her position, suicide was preferable to capture, because the forces had free reign to rape and mutilate republican women. On the rebels' side, Pilar Primo de Rivera (b. 1912) organized the public activities of hundreds of thousands of women defending the church, monarchy, and their domestic life. The rest of the world watched this drama with great concern, while hundreds of thousands of Spaniards died.

The Spanish Civil War (1936–1939) was not an isolated occurrence of war. On the contrary, beginning with the Italian invasion of Ethiopia in 1931, war erupted both in European colonies and on the Continent until the globe seemed a theater for perpetual warfare. World War II (1939–1945) and the unprecedented slaughter of the Holocaust distributed the terror fairly evenly across Europe. Modern weapons wiped out both men at the front and civilians at home, and new technologies such as gas chambers combined with the old killer, malnutrition, to destroy concentration camp populations by the millions. Even when World War II ended, the Cold War began and so did many wars for independence in Europe's colonies. By 1948, George Orwell in his celebrated novel *1984* described life as an ongoing news footage from various war fronts. In the midst of this devastation, gender seemed to play little role: the primal struggle for everyone was not to die.

Not surprisingly, however, the wars of the thirties, forties, and fifties arose in an atmosphere of anxiety over and preoccupation with gender definition and arrangement. One reason was that the economic dislocation in the twenties and the worldwide depression that began with the stock market crash in the United States in 1929 showed the fragility of male identity based on breadwinning. Even those with jobs felt their identities threatened as they watched the emasculated unemployed stand on street corners or in breadlines. Military demonstrations and war itself provided some relief by restoring men's gender identity through combat. Those rebelling against the Spanish Republic firmly said that fighting was man's work and refused to allow women soldiers, but the Republicans pointedly did the opposite. Yet even for Republicans, such as an American volunteer who wrote to his brother, a sense of manly difference from women accompanied soldiering: "I wouldn't miss the show here for all the weeping of all the mothers in the world."[3] The drive to assert manhood through performance in combat was particularly powerful in countries that had been defeated in World War I. In Germany, Italy, and Austria, strong militaristic movements ultimately took control of the countries and began World War II. Powerful dictators, cheered by mass audiences, set about reestablishing order, morale, and a clear articulation of gender difference. All countries sought such order, but Fascists and Nazis used violence to achieve it.

Psychic, economic, and social problems resulting from World War I were evident throughout Europe. In Spain, where the country's neutrality had made suppliers into millionaires, the great discrepancies in wealth were made highly visible in magazine and tabloid photos showing the wealthy and their limosines on display. Newspaper headlines around the world reported how soldiers, refusing to disband at the end of the war, marched by the tens of thousands through German and Austrian streets. Pacifist women in several countries organized themselves into the Women's International League of Peace and Freedom. Lobbying among politicians, they distributed leaflets by the tens of thousands: "Women of Germany," said one pamphlet, "we call on you. The possibility of world war, of civil war demands that you take action."[4] The league also held mass demonstrations, such as one involving more than 10,000 women in London's Hyde Park in the summer of 1920. Diplomats who had drawn up the Treaty of Versailles, which ended World War I, publicly declared

Germany's guilt as part of the document. As a result of many post-war problems, a menacing, combative style came to color mass society. Even after the war was over, militarization or brutalization of society remained.

The Trauma of Mass Society

World War I had created a society in which many people worked and sometimes even thought along lines planned out by governmental agencies. Though civilian life was restored in 1918, governments continued to direct daily life through welfare programs and other projects such as building public housing and public transportation systems. At the same time, nation-states increasingly influenced economic life through continued military spending and staffing of large service bureaucracies. Radio, film, and pulp journalism also helped to unite populations in their thinking and behavior and thereby to shape societies into mass entities. Popular sports events such as soccer games and the Olympics and mass transport in subways, trains, and tramways made individual experience more uniform. So did large institutions such as corporations and unions and the modern assembly line pattern of work. Governmental policies affected millions, and a newspaper headline or news program could enrage millions or delight them.

The Great Depression began in 1929 and deepened in the first half of the 1930s. As the depression spread through almost all sectors of the modern international economy, financiers and manufacturers called in debts and refused to circulate their capital, all of which restricted production. Governments initiated tariffs on imported goods, which served as barriers that cut the circulation of goods even more. Heavy industry suffered the most, but so did consumer production. Manufacturers stopped ordering new machinery, although they did not stop producing goods that people needed. With some manufacturing severely curtailed, many men lost their jobs. Protected to some extent by their exclusion from the most affected areas of heavy industry, women were able to continue working throughout the worst depression years. For one thing, women formed a high proportion of the workers in menial, indispensable jobs such as agricultural work. They were also predominant in white-collar jobs in the service sector that were less affected by the economic hard times. For instance, the number of Austrian women in service jobs went from 89,000 in 1920 to 280,000 in 1934 and 299,000 in 1939. The number of Swiss women in all service fields increased from 162,000 in 1920 to 256,000 in 1930 and then took a small drop to 251,000 by 1941. Moreover, during the depression women were often able to find work more easily than men were. Women's usual last resorts in hard times, such as taking in boarders, laundry, and sewing, continued to be used, though they were scarcely a secure living. An English woman in the 1930s, for instance, compensated for her husband's unemployment by helping the public-health visiting nurse with childbirths and other health-related tasks. After a bout of sickness brought on by strenuous efforts for the nurse and patients, this woman resumed helping the nurse and, in addition, did laundry for four families as well as taking on several hours of cleaning each week.

Some developments throughout the years between the wars gave the impression that women were becoming a larger part of the labor force at the expense of men. For instance, in doing piecework at home such as in sewing, making cutlery, making artificial flowers, stone finishing, and some aspects of shoemaking, women maintained a steady presence, despite the depression. In France in 1936, about 1 million were so engaged, whereas many men in artisanal jobs were replaced by machines. For example, most aspects of shoemaking were done in the factory, except inserting shanks for laces, which continued to be done in homes. Although any cutback in shoe production affected domestic workers as well as industrial ones, other forms of household production—such as routine sewing—continued to thrive as ready-made goods became too expensive. Outside the home, the female part of the workforce continued to grow, especially in white-collar occupations. In Germany, the number of women working in jobs that earned them benefits from government insurance programs increased from 5 million to 6 million between 1925 and 1929. In France, 23 percent of the female workforce was in white-collar work by 1936; this meant 1,034,000 women, compared with 344,000 thirty years earlier. The same trend affected Germany where three times as many women (1.5 million) had white-collar jobs in 1925 than had had them in 1907. Meanwhile, women continued making inroads in manufacturing wherever employers were demanding less skills or fundamental new development was occurring, for example, in chemical production.

The increasing numbers of women in parts of the workforce seemed a menace to those who wanted to blame them for the depression, rather than those who structured industry. At issue was men's work identity. For men in white-collar and professional ranks, accepting women as civil servants, professors, and lawyers proved more threatening than seeing them as maids or seamstresses. Hans Fallada's *Little Man What Now* (1932), about a German engineer, examined the fractured male psyche that resulted from war and economic and professional dislocation. People fixed their attention, as they had after the war, to women's labor. In France, Eve Baudoin's important *The Mother at Work and the Return to the Home* firmly blamed women workers for falling birth rates and the state of the economy. She urged the government to use every means available to restore men's work and health by keeping women home. In Belgium, those in favor of increasing the birth rate similarly blamed working women and those with small families for the depression: "Would not twenty thousand more children each year increase the consumption of milk, leather, cotton, wool and even—cradles? What we must rekindle in people is a taste for the family."[5] The depression only increased this type of propaganda. It proposed that the solution to economic problems was, as it had been to political tensions, large families, with women staying at home to care for family members.

In the meantime, social investigators uncovered more about working women and about how working-class mothers actually fared at home. From

Margery Spring Rice (1887–1970) in London to Käthe Leichter in Vienna, observers assessed work behavior, household habits, and social patterns. Continuing a trend begun in earlier studies, new works often discussed budgets and food allocation, but their middle-class writers were also interested in feelings, health, leisure activities, and sometimes sexual practices or reproductive knowledge. The picture that emerged showed that women continued to be responsible for managing household funds so as to ensure the health of the breadwinner and the children. During the depression this responsibility remained the mother's even when she became the main breadwinner. Mothers in the lower economic levels lived a life of neverending toil; many of them got up at anywhere from 4:30 to 6 in the morning and were not done working before 10:30 or 11 at night. Mending or sewing the family clothing was considered leisure activity, compared to laundry, food preparation, cleaning, child care, and doing odd jobs for pay. Some lower-class women had never even seen a film, though some occasionally had "a read," went to club meetings, or had a day-long or even a week-long outing. The social investigators exposed the facts of life in poverty-stricken areas, particularly those about impoverished motherhood, and thus continued to keep motherhood a public matter. Yet the reality printed in such little read works as sociological studies could hardly compete with the vehement voices on the radio, in mass meetings, and in popular journalism that berated women who worked and those who had few children. Although incorporated into the nation-state, either by the vote or through welfare benefits, women still served as scapegoats for its problems.

An Italian Solution to Social Problems

Benito Mussolini (1883–1945) was the first peacetime ruler to organize a government around warfare and wartime planning in order to solve the dilemmas of twentieth-century life. He appealed to many Italians because of their experiences following World War I. Although Italy had switched to the winning side before the end of the war, Italy did not receive at the Versailles peace conference the preferential treatment of other winners. Also, Italian civilians mocked the soldiers, who had suffered some stunning defeats. Mussolini and his *Fascisti* (the Italian *fascio* means group or band) countered quickly with violent affirmations of patriotism. Out to purge Italy of its old, incompetent leaders and its cynics and nonpatriots, Fascists beat up socialists or pacifists who denounced war. They abhorred feminists, who were often pacifists and who questioned the virile kind of spirit the Fascists saw as necessary to win wars or to be one of the great nations. In 1922, long before similar bands of violent men came to power in Germany and Spain, the king of Italy asked Mussolini to form a government. Having stirred up the disorder and violence, Mussolini promised to restore Italian greatness as well as social order.

From the mid-1920s on, Mussolini made it clear that order meant virility for men and fertility for women. Even though he announced that women would stay out of the public sphere in his new society, he nonetheless drew

Mussolini touted this type of Italian family as the key to national greatness. Men could again be manly, virile, and heroic in battle.

them into his mass following. Mussolini attracted women both as individuals in sexual liaisons and as mass audiences. Crowds of 60,000 to 100,000 women filled plazas wherever the Duce, as Mussolini was called, appeared. When he stepped out on a balcony, they held up their babies and chanted "Thank you, Duce." After Mussolini acknowledged their tribute, they would continue holding up their babies and chanting. Mussolini also played on the feelings of mothers who had lost sons or husbands in World War I. For years, the war widow was a constant image in his calls for support. In December of 1935, women poured into the streets of major cities by the hundreds of thousands to contribute their gold wedding rings to the Duce. In calling for this sacrifice, Mussolini intended to overcome the economic sanctions imposed on Italy by the League of Nations. Responding to the women's devotion like a lover might, he gave them iron rings to replace the gold ones. This mass adulation constantly reaffirmed allegiance to the state, but it was an allegiance charged with gendered ritual and meaning. Although men had often participated in rituals of mass allegiance as parts of a national guard, army, or militia, highly coordinated public gestures on behalf of the state marked a new step in most women's lives as citizens.

In Italy, and elsewhere, World War I had fostered a political style of intense patriotism, aggression, and violence that continued into peacetime. Politics took on the violent attributes of war. The war, however, commented Social Democrat Theresa Labriola approvingly, had matured Italian women. They learned to support a great cause beyond petty female interests and thereby had come to be "inscribed in the history of the world."[6] Modern women had been trained in the school of wartime work and wartime nationalism. They participated actively in the politics that followed. Luisa Brolis, secretary of the Fascist women's movement, explained her early and temporary devotion to Mussolini as a result of her father's participation in the war. When middle-aged and older citizens began mocking soldiers and Italian patriotism, she and other young people took issue and became Fascists. "At the beginning it was a youth movement. . . . And all these young people started fighting—at least this is what one said—for the fatherland, for the mutilated, the invalids and the heroes of the war—who were insulted every day."[7] On the other side, Anna Bechis remembered her father and uncle being brutalized by the Fascists because they were socialists, and also the consumers' cooperative being destroyed. Only twelve at the time, she was warned not to display the red flag on the veranda any more, but did so nonetheless because "I wanted to demonstrate that I was a socialist."[8] Drawn into the brutal contests of political life at an early age, during World War II Bechis became a partisan in the Italian Resistance.

In the midst of violent political struggles, Mussolini reconstructed a traditional vision of the Italian woman, using modern technology and mass publicity. In the 1920s, Italy had a large peasant population and many of those women were illiterate, but movie newsreels brought political and cultural images to them. A former journalist, the Duce carefully monitored film footage of mass demonstrations and ceremonies. Such ceremonies as one occurring in December of 1940, which honored 58 couples who had produced 1544 living children, conveyed the message that women were made primarily for reproduction. Mussolini's speeches about women and Fascist laws governing their work further emphasized this message. Mussolini attributed both the falling birth rate and the series of post-war depressions to the working woman. First, by competing in the workforce, she filled men's jobs and thereby caused unemployment. Her employment might feed a child or two, but it caused misery for more people than it helped. Work made men virile; unemployment caused their impotence. According to Mussolini, women had no talent for public life, for "synthesis," or the world of creativity. So their withdrawal from the workforce would have little effect on prosperity. Once they were gone, however, "legions of men could lift their heads again" and begin both supporting families and siring even larger ones.[9] Earning money gave man back his virility, and distance from the machine gave woman back her femininity.

Mussolini revived old ideas about sexuality, where gender identity came from, and what distorted it. In a country with many rural districts, peasant ideas of gender differences could be exploited successfully to bring social order in troubled times. However, Mussolini's ideas about gender moved him to extreme positions, ludicrous even to the faithful. For instance, disapproving of the excitement about women in the Olympic games in the 1930s, he demanded that Italian women give up even the mildest athletic pursuits as being too virile. By that time, the rhetoric of the Duce's propagandists had become more extreme than ever. For example, both Ferdinando Loffredo's *Politica della famiglia* (Politics of the Family, 1938) and Giovanni Gentile's *La Donna et il fanciulo* (Women and Child, 1934) declared that, under Fascism, women should become "silent."

Telling blows against Italian women came in the form of legislation that undermined their position in the urban workforce. In January of 1927, all women's salaries were cut 50 percent. In November of 1933, government offices received authorization to exclude women from working there, but in 1938 this order was modified to allow women to fill 10 percent of all positions. As official instructions that welcomed women to certain jobs, such as stenography, typing, and filing, made clear, the Fascist government did not really oppose women's working. It only opposed their having good jobs and being well-paid. Fascists believed not only that the machine denatured women, but so did any connection with books. Young women studying in secondary schools and universities found their fees doubled; by decrees of 1927 and 1928, they could not teach the humanities in universities or high schools, nor could they run any liberal arts establishments. A corollary effort of the Fascist government aimed at keeping women in agricultural work and preventing them from migrating to urban areas to find higher-paying jobs. Counseling, social work, and clubs were instituted in rural areas. These social services and leisure activities provided by the Fascists, though unsuccessful in reversing the longstanding trend of rural depopulation, did attract many female agricultural workers, in fact, a higher percentage of them than of any other occupational group.

"Everything in the state, nothing outside the state, nothing against the state"[10] was Mussolini's platform. To implement it, he closed down the political opposition and independent workers' associations. Initially recognizing women as potential allies, he promised them the vote. After elections were canceled in the mid-1920s, however, that promise was worthless. Mussolini also stopped the feminist movement from operating, first by promising suffrage and then by censoring it virtually out of existence. Fascist clubs and charitable groups were the only women's organizations available, and middle-class women flocked to join the latter. In the National Organization for Maternity and Childhood, such women recreated the nineteenth-century persona of the lady of charity while promoting the modern state's reproductive policies. A similarly ironic organization was the Fascist Professional Women's Association, which fostered the professional woman's cause in a society where she theoretically did not exist. Many conversions of intermediate organizations— those that mediated between the individual and the state—to official ones were accomplished violently. Yet the efforts of Mussolini and the Fascists to restore patriarchal society, the workplace that favored men, and the family devoted to male virility received little challenge. Of course, in his attempt to break down mediating institutions, Mussolini never thought of attacking the male-headed family, for its principle of virility mirrored the goal of state power.

When it came to day-to-day life, Mussolini's system worked imperfectly. First, despite his pronouncement that women had no analytic ability, the number of women enrolled in Italian universities continued to grow. In 1911, women comprised 3.9 percent of students; in 1935, 17.4 percent; and in 1942, 29.9 percent. Female students were most common in the areas of letters, science, and pharmacy and least common in engineering, law, political science, and economics. Although the percentage of women in the Italian labor force declined steadily after the 1921 censuses, the percentage of women workers increased in certain fields. For instance, between 1921 and 1931, the percentage of women in public administration rose, which became a sore spot for white-collar men. Moreover, according to some analysts, the decline of women in industry was due to Italy's failure to mechanize, a process that drew women into factories, and to an excessive supply of labor in general.

Fascist ideology received support for its aims in 1930 in a papal encyclical entitled "Casti Connubii." In this pronouncement, Pope Pius XI lambasted the working woman who was also a mother for injuring her husband, children, and herself. By working outside the home, "she descends from her truly regal throne."[11] Part of a general reconciliation between the Catholic Church and Mussolini, this encyclical also included a condemnation of any birth control other than abstinence, which remained church doctrine and thus had an effect in Italy long after the fall of the Duce. The pope proclaimed that women's primary and natural duty was to procreate. Even after the encyclical, the birth rate failed to fulfill either Mussolini's or Pius XI's hopes: women (or couples) refused to double or triple the size of their families. Although the mean age at marriage for Italian women dropped between 1922 and 1941 from 25.11 to 23.84 and the percentage of women who were or had been married rose from 86 percent to 93 percent, family size declined slightly. The mean number of children per family was 2.56 in 1916 to 1920 and 2.42 between 1936 and 1940. The refusal of women to increase their fertility and the Fascist regime's increasing dependence on women to provide future soldiers and laborers posed a clear danger as war approached. Depending on violence as the expression of both governmental potency and masculine personality, Mussolini needed war. Although many Italian women accepted Mussolini as a symbolic lover, they clearly refused to provide him with the number of soldier-sons he demanded. Nonetheless, his policies and his psychic manipulation of the population, male as well as female, was early evidence of how directly the modern state would intervene in people's lives.

The Rise of Nazism

The Third Reich—the German government under Adolph Hitler (1889–1945)—was far more interventionist and more cruelly violent than any previous government in human history. When Hitler came to power in 1933, however, neither observers nor his supporters expected such an outcome. Those who supported him believed he held the cure for the psychic wounds of World War I. German men came home from the war shaken by defeat and convinced that their prowess in combat had not really received a true test because of civilian, including female, shirking. In addition, they found the German state disarmed, new women everywhere, and, for a while, high unemployment and massive inflation. In 1924, inflation wiped out middle-class savings, as prices rose by thousands of marks every hour. It literally required wheelbarrows full of money to buy necessities. For what had been the most powerful country on the Continent to have the lowest prestige, enforced military impotence, and a sick economy shocked all of its citizens. Moreover, when soldiers had failed at the front, socialists and communists had for a time succeeded in controlling municipal and state governments. They, too, threatened German sensibilities by looking eastward to the new Soviet state for inspiration. The National Socialist, or Nazi, Party aimed at righting all these wrongs. Claiming to be the voice of the German people, or *Volk,* the party was controlled by a small group of men led by Hitler. Roughing up citizens and marching in massive numbers through the streets, Nazis gave an impression of force and power in a nation that felt a need for this.

Nazism united a set of ideas about German society and the German race with a violent political style. Marching stormtroopers entered towns to brutalize individuals and destroy property. Nazism also involved modern techniques of psychological manipulation and intimidation. For example, in his book *Mein Kampf* (1925–1927), Adolf Hitler recommended that mass rallies be held at night when people's psyches were, to his way of thinking, most open to suggestion and to demonstrations of power. The power of the German race needed to be exercised triumphantly worldwide to restore Germany's international prestige. The German race had been sold out, Hitler propagandized, by Jewish intellectuals, feminists, and Bolsheviks—all of whom expressed ideas and ways of life that were un-German. The influence of these "inferior" racial types—social and racial inferiority are fused here—had brought defeat in the war, inflation, confusion between the sexes, and ultimately the depression. Like the Fascists, the Nazis created chaos in localities, then showed how they could clean it up, and thus gained a following among the unaffected. Nazism combined anti-Semitism, concern over sexuality, and fear of socialists and new women. They added to this mixture a belief in eugenics—the organization of procreation around scientific knowledge of breeding rather than around political, economic, or emotional needs. Hitler and his propagandists excelled at negative political integration—that is, at bringing people to political unity by involving them in a common attack on minority groups within the society. Nazis never came close to winning a majority of seats in parliamentary elections, yet Hitler became chancellor because he seemed the best alternative, the one person with a solid following and the potential for leadership.

In the 1920s and early 1930s, women enthusiastically joined Hitler's following, and several particularly strong women became prominent speakers on behalf of Nazism. Nazis proclaimed their movement to be "a male phenomenon. . . . We believe that every *genuine* woman will, in her deepest feelings, pay homage to the masculine principle of National Socialism. Only then will she become a total woman."[12] Women were encouraged to support Nazism as a cause that would bring them a unique identity. As one member analyzed it: "[Women] had discovered they could once again serve the Fatherland. Women have something to offer their *Volk*—the purity of their hearts and the power of their spirit."[13] Serving the party by raising money, sewing, and cooking, Nazi women envisioned a special terrain, a kind of renewed separate sphere, controlled by women. Energetic leaders such as Guida Diehl of the New Land Movement and Elsbeth Zander of the Order of the Red Swastika vied with others for control of the swelling numbers of female Nazis.

Nazi policies were built on theories of race and gender that had existed for centuries. For the Nazis, the perfect expression of German superiority was a healthy, fertile mother at home tending five or six children while the father worked or went off to war. Other social types—including prostitutes, alcoholics, agitators, the poor and unemployed, women working in men's jobs—were the result of poor reproductive habits. According to the Nazis' theory of eugenics, the breeding of Jews, Slavs, gypsies, the physically or mentally deformed, or those with deformations in their ancestry and the breeding of fit people with any of these types produced social disorder and, ultimately, political impotence. Orderly reproduction, based on a clear racial and gender order, solved the problems of class conflicts, poverty, and erratic business cycles. Thus, by scientific breeding at home, German women would end the depression. Similarly, the forced sterilization of hundreds of thousands of the poor and non-Germans would eliminate the country's political problems. "The number of degenerate individuals born," Nazis argued, "depends mainly on the number of degenerate women." Thus, they advocated "the sterilization of degenerate women" as far "more important than the sterilization of men."[14]

Hitler promised a restoration of German power and prosperity. According to the general principles of gender order, the first way to achieve this involved getting women out of men's jobs and into breeding more children. On June 1, 1933, the government enacted the Law to Reduce Unemployment. The law provided marriage loans of 1,000 marks to the husband of a newlywed couple on the condition that the wife had been a worker and gave up her job right after their marriage. Repayable after three months at 1 percent interest per month, the loan was reduced by a fourth at the birth of the first child. Accumulation of interest and repayment then stopped for a year. If a second child was born, another fourth was forgiven and another year's hiatus followed. When the immediate cessation of work by the wife proved too onerous a burden on working-class couples, that stipulation was relaxed. Later laws gave fathers direct subsidies for children. Finally, late in the thirties, Gestapo chief Heinrich Himmler instituted the Mother Cross, an award honoring mothers of large families. By regulation Nazi youth had to give the Hitler salute to women wearing the Mother Cross, and Himmler hoped that some day all Germans would have to do so. In addition, Himmler set up a chain of *Lebensborn*, homes where unwed mothers-to-be received care. If a mother could not support the child, he or she became the property of the SS, an elite security force of some 50,000 men. In fact, the *Lebensborn* developed into quasi-bordellos where members of the SS could have sexual relations and, it was hoped, procreate. Although Nazi women strongly objected to the *Lebensborn*, they were not heeded. The general Nazi program to increase breeding also focused on eliminating birth control and abortion. Though formerly outlawed, abortionists were actually arrested and prosecuted. The government scrutinized doctors' and hospitals' lists of miscarriages and closed down birth control societies. Traditional morality and the privacy of personal life were of less concern than governmental control of breeding.

Undermining the economic situation of women was a corollary of the Nazis' reproductive policy. The Law to Reduce Unemployment also called for eliminating women from men's jobs and channeling them into onerous, low-paying domestic service and farm work jobs, that according to one official, "correspond to the nature and talents of women."[15] Putting women in these jobs restored male economic dominance and also made women economically dependent and, therefore, more eager to marry. In fields where men felt particularly threatened—in the civil service, for example—the push to eliminate women was so overwhelming that the Nazis had to urge caution; they still relied on women social workers. Professional men also eagerly purged women from their ranks. University teachers and the men they trained who had felt women students posed a threat to their control of knowledge regained total sway with official government sanction. The elimination of women from such positions was not just a German phenomenon—in the Western democracies and fascist countries alike, the numbers of women in higher education and the professions dropped sharply in the 1930s as society in general tried to eliminate the economically independent new women. Conversely, women's employment in domestic and agricultural jobs, which they had left in the greatest numbers during and after World War I, rose. Although ideological inducements to be a good German mother were powerful, officials acknowledged that "change will be possible only through use of force."[16] Women were legally forbidden to hold jobs in rolling mills, mines, salt works, and so on. Thus the Nazi government established the principle of state control of women's activity in the productive as well as the reproductive sphere.

The Nazi gender scheme was fortified by constant discussion of sexuality, as intense as the debate of the 1920s and earlier. However, this debate rejected many of the modern ideas that had taken shape, especially where homosexuals were concerned. In 1933, Nazi troops attacked Magnus Hirschfeld's Institute for Sexual Science, which had for years advocated freer sexual behavior and less rigid sexual identities, and destroyed its library. Lesbians were among the first female political prisoners under the Nazis. The radical feminist couple Lida Gustava Heymann and Dr. Anita Augsberg fled, and all their possessions were confiscated. Yet, by most accounts, lesbians received less attention than male homosexuals. Nazis maintained that lesbians could still be impregnated, whereas male homosexuals were not likely to father children. The attack on homosexuality occurred despite the fact that there was a substantial but covert homosexual component among the Nazi leadership. Many Nazis, however, were misogynists and male supremacists who despised Hirschfeld's egalitarianism. Though the Nazis did oppose homosexuality, they did not oppose sexual behavior considered immoral by middle-class society, such as adultery or pregnancy outside of marriage, as the *Lebensborn* show. They did not necessarily prize modesty. Although looking pure and virginal, girls in the Nazi youth movement in fact received lessons in eroticism. Hitler himself emphasized time and again that Nazi virility was not subject to the restrictions of middle-class morality. Imitating a middle-class slogan about the home being a haven, propaganda minister Joseph Goebbels stated that creative men in particular needed not one but numerous sources of sexual recreation and renewal. Thus, the Nazis could practice whatever sexual behavior struck their fancy. Persecuting homosexuals in an apparent display of middle-class morality or setting up *Lebensborn* that went against it showed that the Nazis' intense interest in sexuality had less to do with moral behavior than it did with controlling reproduction.

Hitler's government exercised the most direct and repressive control over those it wanted to prevent from breeding—Jews, Slavs, and people deemed biologically unfit. Unlike Aryans, or people of Germanic stock, "inferior" groups had access to abortions and birth control; conversely, they were not eligible for marriage bonuses, subsidies for children, or even the *Lebensborn*. More threatening, 250 sterilization courts were instituted to permanently prevent such people from reproducing. Many countries practiced forced sterilization during this period, but nowhere to such an extent and with such theoretical commitment as in Hitler's Third Reich. Nazi officials estimated that between 5 and 30 percent of the population should be sterilized, and some 320,000 people were sterilized before 1939. The idea of controlling reproduction also led to many inhumane medical experiments. Nazi doctors were allowed to try the effects of X-rays in such procedures as sterilization and to perform breeding experiments. Finally, to achieve racial control, the Third Reich set up the system of death camps in which millions of the so-called unfit—particularly Jews—were systematically executed. The horror of the Holocaust lies not only in the number of innocent people killed—civilian deaths in the Soviet Union during World War II are estimated at 20 to 25 million. What is equally horrifying is that concentration camps killed in the name of reproduction, that is, in order to further the breeding of a supposedly superior Aryan race. Marriage bonuses, economic deprivation of women, and the Holocaust formed a continuum of increasingly brutal coercion to carry out a policy of reproductive domination by the state.

The Nazi program for women was neither as original nor as popular as they themselves claimed. For one thing, the initial impulse to eliminate women from the workforce had emanated from the democratic Weimar Republic that had governed after World War I. Going against the expressed equality of opportunity in the Weimar constitution, a law in 1932 allowed the firing of any woman who was the second earner in her family. Also, women who joined the Nazi movement constantly protested attacks on professional women. Al-

Young women and girls in German youth movements learned athletics, house-keeping, civics, and also, in some cases, "erotic expression." The perfect Nazi wife and mother, some have suggested, was the ultimate form of republican motherhood.

though believing that the new woman was a product of "Jewish intellectual" ideas or of "democratic-Marxist" ones, Nazi enthusiasts, such as Irmgard Reichenau, Paula Siber, and Sophie Rogge-Börner, all believed that Hitler's vision of separate spheres left a place for excellent and talented women in positions of power running the female sphere. Ignoring misogynist rhetoric from both the rank and file and leaders of the Nazi Party, they called warnings from liberal feminists "nothing other than the last big lie of an age that is past."[17] In the universities, those women students who survived the marked drop in female enrollment tried to demonstrate that they could be what might be called "new" Nazi woman, that is, an intellectual and at the same time wholesome, athletic, heartily domestic, and Nazi. In other words, some Nazi women believed it would be possible to create an important niche for themselves even in areas closed off by party theory. The rush to support Hitler included long-time feminist leaders such as Gertrude Bäumer of the BDF, even though one of the Nazis' first acts after coming to power was to fire her from her government post with a minimal pension. After a number of power struggles among women who had supported the Nazis from their start, the party found a leader for women in Gertrud Scholtz-Klink (b. 1902), who became the National Women's Leader (*Reichsfrauenführerin*) in 1934. A true believer in Hitler's program, she succeeded in centralizing a great many activities by gradually attaching the leadership of existing women's groups to her office. After disbanding independent groups, she then persuaded women left without an organizational home that the Nazis wanted them. It is difficult to say whether she succeeded, for although by World War II some 4 million women had joined the Nazi Women's Group, this was only a small percentage of those eligible in the Third Reich, which at the time included Austria and the Sudetenland, a region in northern Czechoslovakia. In fact, those who failed to join were precisely the housewives the Nazi Party courted. Isolated and motivated by an ideology of a private sphere for women, many of these housewives had no intention of participating in outside organizations, not even Nazi ones.

Committed under Hitler to displaying masculine prowess and national might, Germany began rearming massively and building an army after the mid-1930s. As a result, labor became scarce, making a change in policy toward women advisable. At that point Nazi indoctrination about women's domesticity was not as much of an obstacle as might be thought. In one sense, the ideology that valued women as reproducers and called them worthless as producers paved the way for lowering industrial costs even when labor was short. Thinking themselves of little worth in the workplace, women were prepared to receive a small wage, and this made them desirable to employers. The downgrading of women's education under the Third Reich and the replacement of technical skills with domestic ones gave women additional reasons for regarding work as a temporary expedient and not as something that would improve. In addition, the induced preoccupation with household and family, labor managers in the Third Reich believed, would make women excellent workers on the assembly line at monotonous, nontaxing jobs. While they performed these routine, subdivided tasks, they would be able to think of their children. These theories, in which labor rationalization and Nazi gender ideology complemented each other, would prevent a repetition of the World War I situation in which women took on complex jobs formerly held by men and then expected equal pay. By 1939, bureaucrats had advised employers to routinize their operations before women came on board. Finally, Nazi managers proposed a system of wages that disregarded skill, apprenticeship status, or difficulty of tasks. Instead, gender categories alone determined the assignment of wages. During the Third Reich the methods for ascertaining worth by gender were perfected in a complex classification system that endured for decades after Hitler's downfall. Although working-class women had little recourse, many middle-class women refused to work at all. Committed to the system of subsidies for not working and to the theory of separate spheres, they had little reason to accept ill-paying, miserable jobs from the late 1930s on. Just when Hitler needed full female employment, a good proportion of women refused to leave the domestic sphere for the male world.

Sexual division of labor, eugenics, better conditions for mothers, and sterilization and birth control for "inferior" groups made up the Nazi position on sexuality and reproduction. And that theory developed into state policy, not to benefit the individual, but to enhance the power of the nation. Like Mussolini, Hitler took the feminist and progressive aim of improving the condition of motherhood for women and turned it into a chauvinist and reactionary program. Throughout Eastern Europe, states enacted this new policy by political violence. Although many democratic nations enacted similar policies, they did so in piecemeal fashion, sometimes with fewer racial overtones, less violence and coercion, and some concern for liberal principles, including the well-being of the individual.

Regression in the Soviet Union

Progressive women had viewed the changes wrought during the Russian Revolution as among the most promising developments in the modern world. In 1932, English intellectual and reformer Margaret Cole (1893–1980) "went to the U.S.S.R. believing it to be the hope of the world." Like Cole, scores of European women visited the Soviet Union in the 1920s and 1930s to find models for their own reform efforts. According to Cole's account, they saw certain dreams come true: "paid rest for mothers during and after pregnancy, equal pay and equal opportunity for both sexes, equal marriage laws and easy divorce, abortion officially performed in State hospitals—factory and district crèches [day-care centers]."[18] In Soviet factories, both conditions and personnel had been transformed. Within twenty years of the revolution, many women had left peasant ways and the sense of inferiority behind them. A 1930s Russian novel described the metamorphosis of a typical peasant woman into a factory worker. Originally, the heroine shrank from the industrial world: "Even more than people did she fear machines. She did not understand what they were for, nor how one should deal with them."[19] By the end, she had become an official and highly skilled technician. In the late 1930s, in fact, the general "industrialization" of Soviet women took place, with the number of women in factory jobs tripling in a decade. By 1945, women constituted 50 percent of the workforce.

Yet, even as Cole witnessed what seemed like a miracle in 1932, forces were at work that were quite different from what had originally inspired these changes. For one thing, a new leader, Joseph Stalin (1879–1953), came to power following Lenin's death in 1924. In certain areas, he altered Soviet development by ushering in an age of purges and prison camps, of forced industrial growth, and of governmental bureaucratization. Stalin lacked any appreciation of women's existence as individuals struggling in a revolutionary way against oppressive conditions. For him, they served the cause of revolutionary progress, but progress in no way needed to serve them. Whereas the opening phase of the Soviet experiment saw an outpouring of initiative toward changing traditional gender roles, the Stalin years revived many prerevolutionary attitudes.

Lenin had secured the Russian Revolution's success by getting the country through a period of civil war. To do so, he held up some of the economic reforms socialism was supposed to bring and allowed a mixed system of individual and collectivized production. Beginning in the late 1920s, Stalin initiated a system of five-year plans to begin immediate collectivization and industrialization of all production. To achieve these difficult goals, he strengthened the already powerful government bureaucracy by adding planners, statisticians, demographers, and engineers. Meanwhile, social conditions in the Soviet Union seemed to stand in the way of the proposed centralization and collectivization. Children roamed the streets, sometimes formed bands of delinquents, and stirred up trouble. Though many of these had been orphaned in the civil war, officials said their presence and activities were due to the breakdown of the family and the emancipation of women. Men complained that the revolutionary policy of granting divorced women alimony and child support in the form of land was destroying productivity by diverting agricultural resources to women. At a time when famine, disease, and the malfunctioning of public services plagued Soviet society, the revolutionary government seemed in danger. Publicly, these problems were rarely attributed to economic or political difficulties; instead, the condition of the family and the emancipation of women were said to be the causes.

A significant shift occurred in the 1930s and 1940s in Soviet policy and Soviet ideas. In the nineteenth century, socialists had scorned the family as a form of middle-class hypocrisy and of male property. By the 1930s, Stalin called it the birthplace of communist values. Soviet theoreticians also reassessed revolutionary ideas about relationships based on companionate values. By the 1930s, they judged the previous reforms that encouraged marriage for the mutual satisfaction of spouses to be individualistic, egotistic, and therefore counterrevolutionary. After years of population decline, the Soviet Union launched a drive urging couples to have more children on the grounds that the large family was more like the large collective unit on which communism was based. Moreover, women must demonstrate their own lack of egotism by producing these large families. When the birth rate was cut almost in half between 1930 and 1935, Stalin revised the revolutionary program that had liberalized government control of reproduction and sexuality. Between 1935 and 1945, he made abortion illegal, divorces difficult to obtain, and homosexuality a criminal offense. Some of the services envisioned by revolutionary women remained. Maternity leaves (though shortened), day-care centers (though insufficient in number), and some modernized obstetrical facilities served primarily to encourage women to reproduce. Government policy did zigzags, giving benefits and then taking them away. For example, a maternal subsidy system went into effect under Stalin, but in 1947 allotments were reduced by half, even though the rhetoric of maternal heroism continued. As in Nazi Germany and Fascist Italy, programs and facilities in the Soviet Union resembled those in the democracies. What made them different was the level of compulsion, the intensity of women's domestic difficulties, and the silencing of those voices that protested on behalf of women.

Domestic life proved particularly difficult in the Soviet Union. Industrialization occurred with a brutality affecting men and women alike, and purges touched millions of lives. But the forced modernization in military production and heavy industry and the pursuit of a devastating war put a special burden on women because of the attendant demand on them to breed. Women's employment increased dramatically between 1930 and 1945, but this was due to the poverty that resulted from social dislocation and widowhood caused by purges and war. Yet women's entry into the paid workforce occurred without any increase in the availability of consumer goods to relieve the burden of household work. In countries such as England, France, and Germany, consumer and industrial goods were provided to make the reproductive duty easier. In the Soviet Union, in contrast, heavy industry developed at the expense of consumer goods and services. Even in 1953 two-thirds of all urban Soviet households lacked running water and only 3 percent had their own hot water supply. Thus, Soviet women, like nineteenth-century working women, had to spend hours each day carrying water, and they did this while working a full shift outside the household. Shortages abounded. In the early 1930s, an English woman married to a Russian scientist reported that it was difficult to obtain not only aspirin, razor blades, and cleaning supplies, but such basics as bread and coal as well. A strong supporter of the regime, she nonetheless wrote in a letter home in 1931, "I stood and froze in a queue for kerosene an hour or more today." Leaving without getting any of the fuel, she explained "I'm not so Russianized I can wait for ever."[20] In response to some of the other problems, including lack of housing and adequate child care, women teamed up—generally, mothers and their grown daughters—to share living space and divide the child care and housework into manageable units. In the Soviet Union, the multigenerational, predominantly female household was more common than in most modernizing societies.

The most surprising development of the Stalin era was the return of the ideal of female domesticity in the form of glorified motherhood. Such romanticism contradicted early socialist principles just as the new emphasis on the family did. Images of the woman on the tractor and as technician and active party worker seemed to be pointing to a new way of life opened up by the revolution. But, as socialism developed in the Soviet Union, it seemed unable to reconcile the conflict between the goal of work and that of motherhood. In the early 1930s, Alexandra Kollontai's successor in the *Zhenotdel,* Sofia Smidovich (1872–?), maintained publicly that for women love had little to do with sexual passion for men. Instead, women's love revolved around maternity and an attendant concern for children's health and education. In the 1930s Soviet fiction still appeared confused as far as issues about women's personal lives were concerned. Maternity and sexuality confounded writers who portrayed women mainly as factory workers, until a consensus took shape around Stalin's own policies emphasizing maternity in women. Prominent Communist writer Fedor Panferov's novel *Bruski* (4 vols., 1928–1937) showed a shift in attitude during the decade of its publication. Although the first volume concurred with the Leninist condemnation of domesticity, the fourth volume, published right after the new family code of 1936, focused on Motherhood: "I love the mother in woman," a party leader says to his pregnant wife. "When I see a pregnant woman, I feel like going up to her . . . and saying, 'You're an adornment to the earth.' "[21] In 1943, Stalin abolished coeducation in order to tailor instruction to gender stereotype. Boys could thus receive education emphasizing military skills and attitudes, whereas girls' concentrated on maternal and domestic ones.

Two images characterized Stalin and his regime. First, Stalin embodied the Soviet drive for communist modernization in the face of implacable enemies. Second, though standing for progress, he was the Great Father of the Soviet people. The Stalin years highlighted patriarchal motifs and revitalized the cruelty and brutality of the old-style head of household. Through the collectivization of farms and the purges of party members in the 1930s, Stalin brought his country into the modern world and terrorized it. Many have called him demented; others have said that Stalin had to weed out disloyal elements that might have challenged his authority when it was most needed in the fight against Hitler. Whatever its motivation or cause, Stalin's reincarnation of the brutal father affected many Soviets but especially those tortured, imprisoned, and exiled by his orders. In his purges, Stalin worked on familial principles by imprisoning and even executing relatives of the main offender, including children and aged grandparents. Also, he seemed to subscribe to the traditional idea that only other men could be major threats, since women were often spared execution. Women were sent to forced labor camps in Siberia, however. Oddly enough, according to one account at least, imprisonment created a new kind of women's community and a totally different relationship to the patriarch. "For the first time in my life I was faced by the problem of having to think things out for myself" wrote Eugenia Semyonovna Ginzburg, a young party member who kept a journal of her eighteen years of trials and labor camp experiences from 1937 on.[22] Women prisoners made up their own rules about some behavior; for example, they never talked about children, a subject that brought on emotional weakness. Solitary confinement often made them feel liberated and able to think about life on new and more profound terms. Notwithstanding any small personal compensations such as that, the camp system and the purges had millions of victims and depended on a kind of rule that was violent, militaristic, explicitly patriarchal, and brutal.

Women and the Spanish Civil War

As other countries moved toward fascism and one-man rule, Spain opted temporarily for another kind of political system. For decades, the country had shifted from one political ideology to another, including liberalism, monarchy, and dictatorship. Governed unofficially by the Catholic Church and large landowners, Spain's people were desperately poor, undernourished, ill-housed, and in poor health in comparison to most Europeans. Unlike the most progressive countries, Spain had not reformed its agricultural system to make property ownership more widespread and equitable. Instead, in 1930 the different holdings of fourteen individual landlords covered approximately 1 million acres, and the majority of the population had barely enough to live on. An industrial, mining, and manufacturing sector had emerged, especially in northern Spain, and along with it an array of republican movements and labor politics that ranged from socialism and communism to a popular anarchism supported by a mixture of factory workers, housewives, and peasants. A middle-class feminism also developed that focused on women's education and public role. The greatest surge of ideas and energy developed in 1931, when, after the fall of dictator Miguel Primo de Rivera who had controlled the royal family, the monarchy itself fell. Passing quickly through Republican, Socialist, Conservative, and Popular Front governments, Spain became the focus of international attention. The Popular Front of 1936 particularly inspired hope because it rested on a coalition of liberals and republicans, communists and socialists. Like Russia earlier, Spain seemed to be a testing ground for a variety of experiments and to hold somehow a key to the future.

When the Second Republic was first formed in 1931, women could not vote but could be and were elected representatives to the parliament, the Cortes. Among the most prominent of Republicans, Clara Campoamor served on the commission that wrote a new constitution giving women the vote. A leading proponent of women's suffrage, Campoamor had a difficult time persuading her colleagues that a republic was not a republic unless all adults voted. In 1933, she took a government position as Director General of Public Welfare, but resigned after less than a year to protest the severe repression by the government of both church and workers. In January, 1932, divorce legislation and provisions for civil marriage were enacted despite conservative papal pronouncements. This attack on the power of the Catholic Church also loosened the control Spanish families held over daughters, who were still being forced into marriage. Spain and its women entered the twentieth century, but under a cloud. Although many women, such as Constancia de la Mora and Clara Campoamor, appreciated the new freedom, many more continued to find their main comfort in the church and traditional household arrangements.

In the midst of these early and ongoing attempts at reform, the right and left were involved in increasingly violent struggles. Though a liberal republic, the government outlawed the Communist Party and imprisoned its leaders. The most prominent of these was Dolores Ibarruri—known as La Pasionaria—who, as editor of the party paper, expert organizer, and charismatic orator, had begun attracting support. Although republicanism should have meant free expression and the play of political parties, the Spanish tradition of repression of dissent—and brutal repression at that—survived. This repression made the new leaders bitterly resented and their rule contested. Since reforms concerning women were associated with the new government, they too found disfavor.

By the mid-1930s, the Republican government faced a particularly strong rival in the combined forces of right-wing military leaders, large landowners, and the church, which aspired to bring back the old order, in some cases by using Fascist techniques. Workers and peasants also were discontent with the new order because it seemed to favor the middle classes. Some Spanish women were particularly alarmed by the threat from Fascism, especially as embodied in Mussolini and Hitler. In 1933, the Worldwide Committee of Women Against War and Fascism was formed to oppose the political current in Europe. Approached by the French representatives who initially dominated the committee, Spanish women created a broad coalition including both conservative Republicans and Communists. Under honorary president Doria Catalina Salmeron, daughter of the president of the First Spanish Republic of 1883, the organization developed a large and diverse following. Maria Martinez Sierra, a playwright, member of the Cortes, and intellectual; Campoamor; and Victoria Kent, Republican leader and head of the prison system, were members, as was Ibarruri. Within a few months, the Spanish government outlawed this group, as it did almost all others. Immediately the Spanish Women's Committee changed its name to the Organization for Working-Class Children, which still maintained contacts with the original international group but also tried to relocate children orphaned or displaced by the ongoing violence. In addition, on the initiative of Salmeron, it demonstrated against calling up reserves for military actions.

Other Spanish women flocked to the right-wing Falange, or the Nationalists, as those opposed to the so-called radicalism of the Republican government were called. Advocating a limited domestic role for women, the Falangists, who later merged forces with military leader Francisco Franco, became even more adamant about separate spheres for men and women as their support from Mussolini and Hitler increased. The Catholic Church's sponsorship of the Falange made it attractive to many women because of its centrality to their social and emotional lives. The more the Republic tried to draw people away from the church and the harder it pressed for secularism, the more anti-Republican many Spanish women became. After her manuscripts were destroyed by Republican forces, the celebrated writer Concha Espina (1869–1955) became an ardent supporter of the Falange because she thought it would preserve Spanish traditions. Whereas in 1929 she had favorably described the Spanish new woman in her feminist novel *The Prudent Virgin,* by 1938 she was praising Franco for waging "the most admirable war in the universe" on behalf of values and a threatened way of life.[23] Formerly a pacifist, Espina came to espouse war. Just as ironically, other women worked publicly for the Falange because it favored separate spheres and a private life for women.

As civil war erupted in 1936, Pilar Primo de Rivera, the daughter of the dictator who was ousted in 1931, started a women's branch of the Falange. This group had its own military-style uniform and members gave the Fascist salute. Like many others, Primo de Rivera hated divorce legislation and the "flood of weird things" that representative government had seemed to bring forth. Instead, the Falange offered guidance "by the Church, by Catholic morality," to make life "much more constructive and orderly."[24] Thus, the Falange cause drew out hundreds of thousands of women to work in a host of programs, which were coordinated by Mercedes Sanz Bachiller through an umbrella agency, the Auxilio Social (Social Auxiliary). These programs helped war orphans, widows, and the infirm and set up hospitals and soup kitchens. Their mission, they maintained, was divinely ordained: "It was when God said 'let the Auxilio Social be born' that the Auxilio Social . . . arose spontaneously and effectively, by its own impulse in the midst of pain and weeping."[25] By 1937, young women in Falange-controlled parts of Spain were being conscripted into service to support the rebels' efforts. Even as these women were participating in a very public war, they pledged themselves to rigid adherence to the Falangists' regulations for women of the future: no reading of novels or newspapers, ankle-length dresses, and strict religious piety. As they fought for military control of Spain, the Nationalists did not make their control of women appear "modern" as did the Nazis; rather they rearticulated nineteenth-century standards—often explicitly Catholic ones.

From 1936 to 1939, the Spanish people participated in and endured a bloody civil war fought by both professional and citizens' armies. During this struggle, a system of popular militias formed to fight the Falangists; these represented a challenge to the idea of an army led by aristocrats. The people would defend the Republic, for it directly represented them as citizens. Thus, the heroic defense of Madrid, inspired by the fervent speeches of La Pasionaria, was accomplished by militiamen and many militiawomen. Foreign reporters

The militia woman was a common sight in the Spanish Civil War. While many foreigners sought to reestablish male definition as warrior heroes, Spanish republicans needed women as well as men to be heroic in battle.

photographed women throughout the Republican ranks. In fact, the militia system seemed to embody a revolution in gender relations. In addition, by 1936, social reform more extensive than that initiated by the Republican government had become the order of the day in certain parts of the country, particularly in Catalonia in the industrial north. In its major city, Barcelona, the anarchist-dominated municipal government closed down brothels and tried to find prostitutes new jobs in collectivized industries. At first sponsoring free unions, the anarchist leaders soon saw the advantages of offering civil marriage ceremonies to those who wanted them. A divorce could be obtained just by burning the marriage certificate. This system engendered both complaints and enthusiasm.

Within the atmosphere of liberation, or at least of its promise, yet another set of women's groups took shape. The most active, and many believe the most successful, was the Mujeres Libres, or Free Women, a wide-ranging organization that started among an anarchist segment of the working class in the Barcelona area. Within a year or so, the Mujeres Libres had 30,000 official members, and many more women were influenced by their writings and activities. The group's newspaper covered feminist issues and others indigenous to anarchism. Its writers criticized the prejudices of the typical anarchist man, who happily reported at meetings that his wife was home caring for his needs and those of the children. The Mujeres Libres broke ranks with other anarchists by pointing out that such attitudes would retard social progress because women would still be slaves once men were liberated. Under these conditions, society would hardly be transformed.

The insight that made the status of women central to anarchism had developed gradually in anarchist writing in Spain. In the 1920s, Soledad Gustavo, co-editor with her husband of a major anarchist paper, encouraged her daughter Frederica Montseny (b. 1905) to write. During the late 1920s, Montseny produced a series of articles on women and sexual questions, in which she pushed the gender debate beyond the terms laid down by mainstream Spanish feminists. By the autumn of 1936, Montseny had become the first woman minister in the Popular Front government that was fighting the Falangists. In founding the journal *Mujeres Libres,* Mercedes Comaposada and Lucia Sanchez Saornil took up where she left off. A third founder, Dr. Amparo Poch y Gascon, represented another aspect of the aims of Mujeres Libres, that of bringing hygienic information and medical aid to working women. The new journal took up gender questions with great vigor in an effort to combat what it called Spanish women's triple oppression: stemming from her ignorance, from her existence as a woman, and from her life as a worker. Each local branch of the organization sponsored multiple activities based on counteracting the triple oppression. Foremost among their goals was teaching all women to read; that was followed by providing a range of social services that would lighten the burden of motherhood. The ultimate goal was human liberation, of which the liberation of women was requisite. How could the male worker ask a woman to help in the cause of workers' freedom, wrote Sanchez Saornil, "when she isn't even master of her own hands and feet?"[26]

A Leader in the Spanish Civil War

Dolores Ibarruri inspired the Spanish citizenry to resist the efforts of those trying to overthrow the republic. Her slogan "They shall not pass," echoed throughout the Spanish Civil War. As a result, Ibarruri (La Pasionaria) was beloved by many, but also loathed. After the republican forces were defeated, she fashioned her account of what had happened in the war. This extract from her autobiography—a story that is disputed—shows how historical figures shape their own character as it will be seen by later generations. Ibarruri's reviewing of her career and her controversial status remind us how complicated heroine's lives and analyses of them actually are.

[January 1939] The situation in Madrid was anything but encouraging. The day after my arrival I went to see Colonel Casado, since he was Commander-in-Chief of the Army. After the loss of Barcelona the busy little rats of capitulation now left their holes, biting wherever they could.

Instead of finding an office reflecting the feverish life of a country at war, I found the silence of a cemetery. Casado was inside his office, thin, pale, preoccupied, nervous.

"I'm going to talk with you as I've never talked to anyone, except perhaps with the President of the Republic," he said.

"Thank you for your confidence. Go ahead, I'm listening."

He began telling me what he thought of the war. In his opinion "the war, from beginning to end, was a mistake. The Republic, when it found itself without an army, should have renounced the idea of resistance and accepted the situation, until the political pendulum once again swept back to a situation favorable to the Republic. Now there was only one solution, to abandon Madrid."

I thought for a moment that I was listening to the ramblings of a mentally unbalanced person, like the people who had so often come to see me to propose fantastic schemes to end the war quickly with ingenious weapons of their own invention.

I let him finish and then I said:

"I don't think you've given sufficient thought to what you've just told me, because almost three years of war prove that your opinion about resistance is wrong. If we analyze the situation from a narrow, academic viewpoint, a military viewpoint, then you could arrive at the conclusions you have just drawn. But there is a factor you haven't taken into account, a fundamental factor—the people. The people did not accept quick surrender to fascism; they organized militias. The people resisted in the savage enemy attempts to besiege Madrid; they defended Madrid. And they have resisted until now. And if there were errors in waging the war they were not the fault of the people but of those who, underestimating them, failed to do their utmost to help them militarily. It's the fault of those who didn't know what to do with the Republic's victories.

"No, Senor Casado, you're wrong. I don't know anything about military matters, but I still have enough common sense to know that your proposal amounts to collective suicide."

Source: Adapted from Dolores Ibarruri. *They Shall Not Pass: The Autobiography of La Pasionaria* (New York: International Publishers, 1966), 325–329.

Like other revolutions and wars, the Spanish Civil War aroused women to intense activity, as Spain itself became a testing ground for new and old ideas. For the Fascists, trying out new military techniques, such as terrorizing civilians with bombs, was a test of their ability to conquer other countries. The deliberate bombing by the Germans of the city of Guernica in 1937 served as the model for a successful and innovative military policy. For others, Spain became a testing ground for democracy and a place where it seemed that the individual heroism destroyed by the heavy gunfire, chemical warfare, and mass slaughter of World War I might be reborn. American and European intellectuals by the score shouldered rifles because this looked like a heroic venture; Ernest Hemingway, George Orwell, and many others saw a chance to determine the course of events.

Working as a major propagandist in the drive to gain support for the Republic outside of Spain, La Pasionaria made speeches in Paris and other places that roused the people she addressed. Her watchword was *"non* pasaran," or "they shall not pass," and it became the slogan of those protecting the Republic. From Madrid in the darkest days of the civil war, she made radio broadcasts calling for resistance and invoking the women of the French Commune. "To the extent that we know how to get the value from this resource, from this inexhaustible treasure which is our women, we will create the conditions for resistance."[27] And it was not just men from around the world who flocked to Spain; women went as well. British Labor Party leader Ellen Wilkinson co-authored *What We Saw in Spain* (1937), and American journalist Anna Louise Strong wrote *Spain in Arms* (1937). There were dozens of other women's memoirs, and many women attended the International Writers' Conference in 1937 in Valencia. Designed as an anti-Fascist demonstration, the conference attracted—among others—novelist Anna Seghers (b. 1900), in exile from German persecution, and writer Ludmilla Litvanova of Bulgaria, as well as Spanish feminist writers such as Margarita Nelken (1898–1968). French philosopher Simone Weil worked for the Republic at the front. Though opposed to what she called the male cult of force that war represented, she had joined up, nonetheless, to help those she believed in when they were under fire. Weil reported, however, that in wartime conditions the use of force soon dominated all other considerations; even her supposedly more upright comrades slaughtered innocent women and children to avenge their own losses.

Both sides bathed the countryside and towns in the blood of Spanish citizens—even children. Horror followed horror; deliberately strafing innocent civilians such as occurred at Guernica would become a common tactic. Even before this, however, American Emma Goldman had reported on the increasingly desperate condition of women and children in wartime Spain. Women needed material assistance, but they also needed education, which might lead to more enlightened politics. "But our comrades are too engrossed in winning the anti-Fascist war," Goldman wrote in 1936, "to devote much time to this kind of necessary labor."[28] Superstitious and under the wing of local priests who gave them comfort and provided for female camaraderie in church activities, most Spanish women gave their allegiance to the Franco forces, which they hoped would restore the monarchy. Even pro-women activists shifted their efforts to helping Republican men. "School teachers are peeling potatoes, nurses are washing floors, clerks form an avalanche heading to get preparatory instructions, all feminists are caring for children and hospitals, seamstresses are taking up their guns."[29] Although feminists saw such activity against the hated enemy as a liberation of women from the tyranny of a former way of life, nonetheless their explicit concern for the welfare of women was weakened.

In Spain's civil war, Falangists and anarchists—from opposite ends of the political spectrum—had worked for national political goals, both with a clear sense of what women's lives would be like when peace returned. In 1939, the forces of the right won, after hundreds of thousands of deaths in battle, executions, and atrocities on both sides. Pilar Primo de Rivera attended Franco's victory celebration to promise that women would return to their homes and to religion: "We appear in public now, only to celebrate your triumph and to honor your soldiers."[30] From then on, Franco instituted a one-man regime based on a traditional social structure that included rigid gender divisions.

World War II

The Spanish Civil War laid the psychic groundwork for World War II, which began in 1939. Since the early 1930s aggressive Fascist leaders had undertaken expansionist activity, with Mussolini conquering Ethiopia and Hitler grabbing Austria and Czechoslovakia and intervening in Spain. Although Britain and France initially seemed to acquiesce, the invasion of Poland in 1939 brought them into open combat with Germany and then Italy. Using techniques practiced earlier in Spain, the German forces looked invincible as they blitzkrieged their way to victory in almost every European country except Britain and the Soviet Union. Holland, Belgium, and France quickly fell in 1940, which led Hitler to take on the Soviet Union in defiance of a mutual nonaggression pact. By 1941, Britain, the United States, and the Soviet Union were allied against Germany, Italy, and Japan in a struggle that would eventually claim at least 50 million lives. In the beginning, the odds against the Allies seemed high, for Germany had conquered most of Europe and had access to its labor force, industrial and natural resources, and monetary wealth. To most, Hitler seemed unbeatable; just the sight of his troops, tanks, and bombers evoked terror. Within months, Germany had started integrating the many conquered countries into what was planned to be a thousand-year empire, or Reich, based on the supremacy of the "master" Aryan race and the elimination of all inferior peoples. To this end, conquered nations had to support the German army and civilian population through forced labor and confiscation of property. Fascism offered a final, bloody challenge to liberal values and free economic development; it also explicitly aimed to destroy socialism in the Soviet Union. Thus, another total war began, with both sides organized for the purpose of completely destroying the other through mass slaughter (especially with bombing), starvation, and the obliteration of military forces. The destructive capacity of this war was greater than that of previous wars; new technology increased the power of bombs and chemicals to kill people and devastate industrial and civilian resources. With all energies directed to the end of winning, most of the world suffered.

With the outbreak of this war, tens of millions of women again became heads of households and war workers overnight. In countries occupied by Hitler's armies, the men were often prisoners of war or had been deported to work in German factories or on farms. Obtaining food, clothing, coal, medicine, or almost any other necessity of life was a daily struggle. With their men gone, women pooled their resources, especially by sharing housing. In occupied countries conditions deteriorated rapidly as resources were drained into Germany and the Nazi war effort, with no concern for civilian life. After the fall of Warsaw in the autumn of 1939, a volunteer hospital worker used her scalpel as she joined a street crowd dividing up a horse that had died recently. Others who shared her apartment took turns heading for the countryside when the curfew lifted at 5 a.m. There they stole a cabbage or any other food they could get quickly or unobtrusively. Stealing, hiding, and lying became a way of life for many, particularly when women were caring for children. Everyone lost a lot of weight during the war, a Frenchwoman maintained, except the butchers. Only in Germany could women obtain necessities, at least until the last year of the war. A minority government, Hitler's Third Reich had to avoid discontent at home if possible. Thus, starving the rest of Europe was both a military and domestic imperative for Germany. Even there, long lines for food indicated the priority of military life over the civilian. "As soon as food rationing was introduced," wrote one Berlin woman, "everything not on the ration cards disappeared like magic from every shop counter. . . . Cows no longer had livers, hearts, kidneys, or tails and hens had vanished off the face of the earth."[31] All such uncontrolled items were sold on the black market, an unofficial and illegal source of food and other items for those with money.

In all countries, war generated a great increase in governmental control and organization of civilian life. All the means of nourishing and caring for the workforce came under official direction, albeit with the black market available on the side. By the 1940s, scientific information gathered on the individual body guided public policy toward food. Ration books or cards allowed each person to purchase so many ounces of meat, so many eggs, so much sugar, and so on. In Germany, rationing became an intricate and immense bureaucratic operation. Caloric intake—and therefore the number of ration coupons allocated—was gauged according to one's function in the wartime machine. Even different job categories had caloric differentials. In some countries school lunch programs came into fashion to make sure that children from the poorest homes and those with "ignorant" or "lazy" mothers would receive proper nourishment. Cod liver oil and supplements of all sorts, along with the standardization of food processing, aimed at improving bodily endurance. As more women went to work outside the home, official anxiety about nutrition and housekeeping intensified. Radio broadcasts included recipes touted as crucial to winning the war and reminded women to visit cod liver oil dispensaries. Beyond nutrition, radio, motion pictures, and other media propagandized in support of wartime aims and told people how to think and feel. The capacity for affecting the collective psyche had intensified dramatically since World War I. Civilians, especially women civilians, received constant prompting about the way they looked, dressed, and behaved. In the midst of wartime shortages and the scramble for basic necessities, women were expected to look better than ever in order to ensure military morale. As a result, hairstyles became more elaborate—that did not take a ration coupon—and more attention was paid to the face and hands. The housewife's century-old absorption with the bodies of herself and her family now received direct management from the central government, acting through a multitude of agencies from the coupon dispensers to public broadcasters.

As the war spread, the nonworking, domestically oriented woman became suspect and was no longer praised by the government or its propaganda organs. In England, the government conscripted women into the workforce. Filling men's jobs as they had done twenty-five years earlier, women questioned the entire scheme of inequitable conditions in the workplace right from the start. The issues of equal pay and equal benefits arose immediately, along with more qualitative concerns about working conditions affecting women in the workforce. The Women's Power Committee established itself to deal with those qualitative issues and in general with the conscription of women into industry. Not wanting to tread on union territory, the leaders initially avoided demands for equal pay but organized a campaign for equal insurance and benefits. Winston Churchill's government opposed even these attempts at equalizing women's status. His excuse was that such equalization might upset male workers and cause labor unrest. However, the equal compensation proposal

Women flooded armaments factories again in World War II. Conditions remained unequal when it came to pay.

gained parliamentary support and was passed in 1943. Concerning the issue of equal pay, some agreements, notably one with the Amalgamated Society of Engineers, had been negotiated during the war, but few were fully observed because they contained numerous loopholes. The committee for equal pay began by asking the government to legislate equity in the civil service, which women had come to dominate during the war. (By war's end, women held 57 percent of local governmental posts and 49 percent of national ones.) The proposal offered in Parliament narrowed this to equal pay for schoolteachers, and the bill passed by one vote. Incensed by the issue, Churchill had the measure brought up for another vote, calling for votes against it as a sign of confidence in his government's conduct of the war. Under that circumstance, the measure failed. Thus, although women in Britain performed war work with vigor—if the soaring employment figures mean anything—the British government did not reward their efforts with equal pay. The government played on feelings of patriotism to defeat this campaign for equality.

The Holocaust

In most countries, women's issues were swept aside in the face of forced labor, the struggle to survive, and the constant terror of destructive technological warfare. Bombing destroyed cities and killed or wounded millions of civilians. What made World War II more horrifying than any others, however, was the

Nazi program of genocide, an attempt to wipe out certain racial and cultural groups. The Holocaust—as this mass murder is called—began when Hitler came to power, spouting ideas of racial purification. The first concentration camps were built in the 1930s, though initially they were intended for political prisoners rather than racial segregation. In 1939, the Germans established Ravensbruck, the largest concentration camp for women; at first, it held more political prisoners than Jews. Although Nazis killed, tortured, imprisoned, and stole from Jews and other people they considered racially unfit from the very beginning of their rise to power, because of civilian resistance Hitler's "final solution" did not take its ultimate, well-organized shape until 1942. Before that, Nazis performed mass executions by shooting after the "unfit" had been worked almost to death in factories and other labor projects close to the camps. The largest and most destructive camp was Auschwitz, built in the spring of 1940 near Kraków, Poland. The complex contained factories of major German industries such as I. G. Farben, along with a gas chamber that killed 2,000 people at one time and in which, during the heaviest period of its use, approximately 34,000 people died in one day. At this and other camps, prisoners not only worked in factories but sorted clothes and possessions of incoming victims; removed hair and gold inlays in teeth from the living and the dead; and moved corpses from infirmaries, places of work, barracks, and the gas chambers to the crematoria. Prisoners performed their work on a diet of no more than 500 calories a day, which lacked most vitamins and led to many diseases as well as exhaustion and starvation. In this cycle of work, starvation, and death, men and women were separated both for greater efficiency and in keeping with gender stereotypes. The Nazis added chemicals to the women's food to keep them from menstruating, although malnutrition by itself was often enough to cause famine amenorrhea. Any signs of pregnancy meant automatic execution, for the major goal of the concentration camps,

---

Auschwitz, 1944: A Transylvanian Woman's First Days

Olga Lengyel's husband was an important doctor in the city of Cluj. Less than cautious in his criticisms of Nazis, he was rounded up—or so his wife thought—to be sent to work in Germany. She insisted on "resettling" with him and brought along their children and parents. The trip ended not in Germany but in the concentration camp in Auschwitz, Poland. There family members were all separated from one another. Entering the women's section, Olga Lengyel showered, had all her body hair removed, was examined vaginally and rectally, and given an old, transparent evening dress as her only clothing. But this humiliation, a starvation diet, and inhuman conditions did not immediately end her hopes, as the following passage from this rare survivor's memoirs shows.

When I learned that our barrack chief, a Polish woman named Irka, had been in the camp for four years, I felt reassured.

However, when I hinted at these thoughts to Irka, she made short work of my illusions.

"You think they are going to let you live?" she jeered. "You are burying your head in the sand. All of you will be killed, except a few rare cases, who will have, perhaps, a few months. Have you a family?"

I told her the circumstances under which I had taken my parents and my children with me, and how we had been separated from one another when we arrived at camp.

She shrugged her shoulders with an air of indifference, and told me coldly:

"Well, I can assure you that neither your mother, your father, nor your children are in this world any more. They were liquidated and burned the same day you arrived."

I listened, petrified.

"No, no, that's impossible," I mumbled. This timid protest made the block chief beside herself with impatience.

"Since you don't believe me, look for yourself!" she cried, and dragged me to the door with hysterical gestures. "You see those flames? That's the crematory oven. It would go bad with you if you let on that you knew. Call it by the name we use: the bakery. Perhaps it is your family that is being burned this moment."

[Olga Lengyel hears that someone has seen her husband and finds him on the other side of the barbed wire fence.]

Though I had lost my sensitivity after the first experiences in the camp, I still was painfully shocked when I saw my husband again. He, too, stared at me with unbelieving eyes. In my tattered dress, in which I was half exposed, in my stripped drawers, and with my clipped head, I must have shocked him even worse than he did me.

We stood there silently, clocking our emotions.

As briefly as I could, I told him about the deaths of our two sons and of my parents. I spoke without expression in a tone that rang strangely in my own ears.

I said: "I cannot believe that human beings, even Germans, would be capable of killing little children. Can you believe it? If it is true, then there is no longer any reason for living."

Source: Excerpted from Olga Lengyel, *Five Chimneys: The Story of Auschwitz* (Chicago: Ziff-Davis, 1947), 31–34.

Women guards were rounded up at the Bergen-Belsen concentration camp in 1945. Their cruelty was legendary and reinforced an idea of women as savages or saints.

which became explicit after 1942, was not work but racial control. Of the 11 or 12 million who died in the camps, almost 6 million were Jews; the rest were other "inferior" peoples, including Slavs, Poles, gypsies, homosexuals (some say in the hundreds of thousands), and many political prisoners and resistance workers.

Because the Third Reich was essentially based on gender principles, women endured punishments and tortures designed specifically for their sex. In the first place, though both male and female socialist and communist politicians were rounded up, female relatives of male prisoners were persecuted also. Their men being arrested could mean confiscation of property, no employment, no ration tickets, and no access to government services. As one Transylvanian woman described it, by 1944 Nazis so persuasively described the concentration camps as zones of resettlement, that she, like her neighbors, clamored to join her husband. Thus, she, her children, and her parents inadvertently placed their fates in the hands of the Nazis. Any civilian suffering paled next to that in the camps. Survivors said that women prisoners were seldom used as prostitutes, first, because, shaved and emaciated, they were so unappealing, and second, because of the racial stigma attached to them in Nazi eyes. This did not preclude sexual harassment and abuse, the most minor being the stares and comments as women entering the camp were stripped, bathed, and shaved of all hair. There was also deliberate sexual torture including breasts being cut off for punishment or to entertain sadistic officials or provide them with souvenirs. As the "final solution" became better organized and the biological and racial plans of the Nazis outweighed other goals, women were killed immediately with their children without the interlude of labor.

For those in the camps, death sometimes came at the hands of doctors. Doctors with Nazi credentials could go to the camps to perform any type of reproductive or other medical experiments. Women (and men) became guinea pigs for experiments that Nazis thought might help the war effort. Injured and injected with any of a number of infections, including gangrene, typhus, and tetanus, they were observed until they died. Doctors sawed off prisoners' limbs to attempt grafting on wounded Nazi soldiers; donors were left to die from the amputations or were gassed or even cremated alive. Finally, in an effort to control reproduction by increasing that of Aryans and eliminating that of non-Aryans, Nazi doctors—of whom Joseph Mengele was but the most notorious—performed all sorts of violent, painful, and usually lethal experiments to cause sterility or to develop ways to induce multiple births. These included inventing procedures for rapid hysterectomies or ovariectomies and often practicing them on nonanaesthetized patients, who were, again, then gassed or left to die. The reproductive project also involved experiments with radiation or painful injections and artificial insemination. By the closing days of the war, however, such experiments ended as the speedup of the "final solution" meant that 99 percent of incoming prisoners were immediately executed.

Death spared few in the camps, but women who stayed alive managed to recreate domestic networks to which they attributed their survival. "One thing makes me lose my temper here: when I see that men are much weaker and less able to resist than the women. Physically and often morally"[32] wrote Hanna Lévy, a Yugoslav partisan imprisoned at Bergen-Belsen, in her prison diary. Her ungenerous attitude, though not necessarily typical, revealed the kind of feelings toward one another that Nazism could provoke among camp inmates. Quarrelsomeness and bad feeling toward fellow prisoners often erupted, as Lévy herself noted, because the lethal conditions made each fight the other for survival. Nonetheless, her observation had some truth, for other inmates noticed women's seemingly superior ability to endure. One reason was that women had specific survival skills, many of them developed from the business of keeping house. Thus, they found nourishment where none seemed to exist and made clothing from scraps of all sorts. One story describes a prisoner who somehow cleaned her clothing before her trial out of an unweakened sense of dignity and despite the fact that her cell lacked a sink and water. To nourish a bunkmate who had typhus, a group of women somehow found a cucumber. Women created networks among entirely new sets of companions. They maintained religious observances even though these were prohibited, preserved ethnicity, and kept up patriotic customs. Responsible in outside life for anniversary, death, and birth rituals, they continued them in the midst of the Holocaust. Czech prisoner Vera Laska wrote about a death march from Auschwitz near the end of the war. It was her birthday. Defying death, a woman companion reached down and pulled a few bits of grass for a birthday gift. Laska ate them, drew strength, and soon after escaped. Such stories of courage gained from bonding with others and upholding rituals are common among survivors. In peacetime, bonds between neighbors had been created as they did pawnbroking, laundering, and shopping. In the women's camp at Ravensbruck or in other camps, bonds developed through shared endurance of forced labor, harsh conditions, and violence. New skills evolved as they were needed. Women taught each other languages—such as Hebrew—and ways to make do by crafting needles from bits of wood, thread from the smallest bits of hair, and so on. Witnesses claim that these bonds and skills increased women's rate of survival.

Resistance

Both the Fascist occupation of Europe and the Holocaust inspired widespread opposition, known now as the Resistance. Resistance to Fascism on an organized international scale began in the 1930s with the formation of the Worldwide Committee of Women Against War and Fascism, presided over by French feminist and pacifist Gabrielle Duchêne. Delegates travelled throughout Europe to set up branches. Many members of this organization were Communists, since that party, directed by Soviet policy, sponsored a good deal of the initial opposition to Hitler until 1939, when Germany and the Soviet Union became allies. Picked up by the German police, women involved in this early opposition were the first in the Nazi concentration camps. Resistance sometimes had a domestic form. During the 1930s and even during the Nazi occupation of Europe, women made protests about food, prices, and shortages and demanded unobtainable items. Many of these protests were orchestrated by political groups with definite goals. Women were also attracted to anti-Fascist organizations working for the protection of children or the welfare of orphans, thus making civilian demands on Fascist governments that wanted to direct full attention to war. Any protest, inquiry, or petition served to draw some of the enemy's attention from the battlefront, from taking political prisoners, or from tracking down resisters.

With the outbreak of World War II, civilian resistance took on larger proportions. Hundreds of thousands were involved in resisting Fascism, usually working toward discrete goals. For example, the work of widow Ellen Nielson, who lived near Copenhagen, depended on the access her job as a fish-seller gave her to the port and boats. Nielson hid escapees in her home until they could get transportation from Denmark to Sweden. She was caught by the Gestapo in 1944 and sent to Ravensbruck. Other women were part of highly organized border teams that led Jews, escaping soldiers, and other hunted peo-

Soviet women dominate this particular wartime effort to dig antitank trenches around Moscow. By the time the war ended, Soviet women were half the Russian workforce.

ple on complicated escape routes across the Pyrenees or the borders of Slovakia, Hungary, Yugoslavia, or Switzerland. Vera Laska has described her experience as part of teams skiing and hiking across these borders, often leading city dwellers with little background in such pursuits. Laska was also caught and sent to Auschwitz.

The Resistance also involved sabotaging Fascist efforts by assassinating leaders; destroying railroad track, roads, and bridges; and performing other acts of violence, destruction, and propaganda. Complicated networks developed for Resistance workers involving "safe" houses and constant moving in and out of them, passwords, and code names so that networks would be protected even if individual members were captured and tortured. Women often excelled at assignments such as carrying arms to an assassination point or passing on letters and instructions because their presence in certain public spaces, like markets, caused less suspicion than did that of men. "Naturally the Germans didn't think that a woman could have carried a bomb," explained one Italian resister, "so this became the woman's task."[33] In Fascist ideology, women were pictured as so docile and of such limited intelligence that they could hardly dream of, much less execute, a plot. Such stereotypes gave the women in the Resistance a better chance of success and encouraged them to resist.

Being part of the Resistance meant constant danger. If caught, one faced imprisonment, torture, and execution. One's family would certainly suffer, too. Top leaders were hunted; some were denounced by neighbors or acquaintances in exchange for favors or even turned in for revenge. In France, almost all those in the forefront of the Resistance fell. Danielle Casanova, who converted the Communist Party's Union of French Young Women (Union des Jeunes Filles Françaises) into the Union of French Women, a Resistance organization, was executed during the war. Former social worker and activist Bertie Albrecht cofounded with Henri Frenay a major network of sabotage and opposition politics called Combat and was killed in 1943. Olga Bancic from Eastern Europe became the major arms carrier and retriever for the Manouchian section of the Immigrant Workers Group, which carried out major assassinations and violent sabotage in the Paris area. She was decapitated in Germany in 1944. France Bloch-Sérazin, a university chemist who provided the Resistance with grenades, explosives, and guns she had refurbished, was also decapitated in 1943.

Another important Resistance goal was gathering information for the Allies. Many espionage networks existed in Europe, but the principal one was in France and was organized and led by Marie-Madeleine Fourcade. At the start of the war, she was a thirty-year-old executive secretary, working for a publisher who was obsessed with espionage and intelligence gathering in the event of a new war with Germany. The Germans arrested her boss soon after the fall of France, but Fourcade rebuilt their intelligence network, called Noah's Ark, after each round of Gestapo arrests. Before the invasion of North Africa, Fourcade provided the Allies with information from various Mediterranean ports. Before the Normandy invasion, she built up a network of sources of particularly valuable information. One of these sources was a seamstress who repaired life vests for German submarine crews just before they were heading out. The seamstress sewed well and also listened closely to the sailors' talk. Fourcade was proudest of providing the Allied command with a fifty-foot map of the Normandy coastline where the successful invasion of Europe ultimately took place. Her sex initially protected her; it even stunned the British to find out that the main French intelligence chief was a woman.

Like most Resistance women, Fourcade used time-honored ways of caring for her children—relatives, boarding schools, and the like—as she pursued a new kind of "career." Other civilian women's traditions became central to the Resistance. To maintain local sources of information and spread news throughout communities, women published underground newspapers. In France, they had such titles as *The Housewife of Aisne* (*La Ménagère de l'Aisne*) and *The Echo of Women* (*L'Echo des Femmes*). Housewives were encouraged to hide food, forge ration coupons, and to lie about the size of harvests. When civilians became prisoners, flyers went out announcing arrests and urging protests to authorities: "Don't throw this paper away. Circulate it."[34] Suddenly, women's

The beautiful woman could seduce men to betray the nation. In wartime, the government vividly portrayed women's bodies to convey emotional messages just as commercial advertisers depicted them in peacetime.

informal communication networks had a status as part of international warfare. Civilian morale was all important during the effort to keep the dignity of oppressed peoples. Resistance brought exaltation from injuring the enemy and such organizations served as "a grand fraternity." In the meantime, household skills and the ideas of neighborliness saved lives on a daily basis. In 1944, the French writer Colette published *From My Window*. Although it appeared to be seemingly mindless chatter about Colette's neighbors and their households, the book actually passed on recipes for rations and other survival techniques. More obviously Resistance-oriented were the cookbooks, circulated by women, that had recipes for grenades and bombs. Some women learned how to pack boxes for prisoners, which were permitted in the early days of the war. Every quarter inch was used, and every possible hiding place was taken advantage of. Women wrote letters on cigarette papers and then unhemmed and rehemmed gloves or shirts with the messages sewn inside.

Art Helps Out in War

The incomparable French writer Colette, who had seen most of what there was to see in life, experienced the Nazi occupation of Paris. During World War II she published *De ma fenêtre* (*From My Window*), a simple tale of what happened in her neighborhood every day. The patriotism of the work was apparent from the opening sentence: "But how do we know that we are in France?" The answer arose from the description of people and life. Like the following narrative, these descriptions were deceptively simple in that they told of French ways while conveying practical information—such as how one kept a fireplace going with little fuel or how to do without meat—to those who suffered the privations of Nazi policies.

A childhood, an adolescence in the country saved me from one of the absolute necessities of urbanites—that of revered, ineluctable meat, the monotonous object of Parisian feasting. A dishful of white cheese (well-peppered) makes a lunch for me and so does a pumpkin quiche or a *gratin* of leeks. A hollowed out tomato, a large onion, squash stuffed with meat or vegetables rival a minute steak. But in the South, I often watched, astonished, as vacationing Parisians turned away from peppers, love apples, polished eggplants, and sweet onions. So, it would probably be, that Hindus would turn up their noses at wheat when deprived of their rice. My "fawhriners" signed after their traditional steak and fried potatoes.

The French family summons up great principles each time it is put in the presence of something that is new and therefore suspect: "My mother dislikes any fowl. . . . My son is like his father; he would rather die beside a fried rabbit rather than eat it!" Picky eaters, gourmands without curiosity who are finicky as much as you choose, will you now eat "whatever there is," including green vegetables, so despised by the stronger sex? I wish you luck.

Meanwhile I will continue to steal from my little saucepan of chestnuts. What admirably white skin on the brown chestnut, what a heaven-sent complement to the limited meal. You are the delicate bread brought by this cold season, which is stingy with lentils or dried beans; you are abundant when all else is rare, when the earth closes down. I will allow myself to point out that the boiled chestnut—one must salt the water it's boiled in—shelled, cleaned of its inside skin, crushed into a fine dough mixed with a bit of confectioners sugar, and finally pressed into small cakes with a fine cloth, makes a healthy and simple feast, a complete dessert if you serve it with a bit of red jelly.

Source: Excerpted from Colette, *Oeuvres complètes: De ma fenêtre,* 15 vols. (Paris: Flammarion, 1950), 12:290–291.

Peace Again

When the liberation of Europe occurred, some of the comradeship that had developed through common resistance remained. Tens of thousands of men appeared at town halls across the Continent to receive certificates and medals honoring their participation in the Resistance. Generally, women were less likely to apply for such honors; their participation was slowly forgotten. But in 1945, their participation received some of its due. General de Gaulle returned to France in 1944 with a promise that women should vote. Having gained suffrage in 1945, Italian women first participated in elections in 1946. Moreover, in both of these countries, unions and governments announced their support of the principle of equal pay. In contrast to the lack of representation by women at trade union congresses in the 1930s, sixty-eight French women were delegates for the Federation of Metal Workers in 1946. Manifesting a similar spirit of participation for women, the Italian constitution of 1947 not only gave women the right to vote but announced the equality of the sexes and affirmed the right of women to work and to an equal partnership in marriage. Such affirmations, which unraveled the threads of Fascist rule, resulted from the claims women had established and, indeed, the work they had done during the Resistance. Thus, their wartime activities had had a twofold benefit. Not only had they fought the general horror of Fascism, they had also worked against a system that was explicitly anti-women.

At the war's end, Europe lay devastated; 50 million people had been killed and billions of dollars of damage done. The Holocaust alone had wiped out generations of families among its 11 or 12 million victims; the Soviet Union had lost 20 million people, or more than 10 percent of its population; Poland had lost nearly 17 percent of its people. Bombing had destroyed roads, bridges, and factories everywhere. The modern military tactic of terrorizing civilians had been carried out in the razing of entire cities—Dresden was destroyed by the Allies and up to 200,000 of its citizens were killed. Cathedrals and works of art had been destroyed; civilization and even the concern for civilization seemed to have perished. For Europeans, the most immediate problem was survival, followed by rebuilding. At the time, the United States, with its vast industrial and agricultural capacity, held the key. Even as people tried to get enough to eat, however, new troubles arose. First, the Cold War between the United States and the Soviet Union soon threatened European peace. These two powers began to act so menacingly toward one another that war appeared to continue. Second, the war itself had destabilized the entire world, so that revolution, civil war, and nationalist struggles erupted everywhere, but especially in the old European colonies.

"There is too much fathering going on just now and there is no doubt about it fathers are depressing" wrote American ex-patriate Gertrude Stein from France late in the 1930s. Pointing to "father Mussolini and father Hitler and father Roosevelt and father Stalin," Stein noted the intense masculinity the twentieth-century nation-state embodied on the eve of World War II.[35] Both Hitler and Mussolini set out to conquer in the name of male supremacy and masculine prowess. By 1945, their empires lay in shambles but so did most of the rest of Europe. Defeated by highly organized armies employing lethal technology, the ideals of Mussolini and Hitler fell as the liberalism and socialism espoused by the Americans, British, and Russians triumphed. The war had drawn people in all countries more closely together in the great cause of national victory, before which all other causes disappeared. Most agreed that feminism was a dead issue, killed by the overwhelming need to support the military and by the leveling effects of terror, starvation, and death. On the one hand, it seemed that post-war society could be more egalitarian, especially since women in the army and those working double shifts in factories had once again proved their solidarity. The age of high military technology ushered in by World War II distributed violence equally in wartime. When peace returned, French women got the vote and so did the Italians. On the other hand, old views were once again espoused. "We men like our women to be a little effeminate," said an Englishman in 1945 criticizing wartime auxiliary organizations.[36] Charles de Gaulle returned victoriously to France and told women there that the country immediately needed "twelve million healthy babies," and a French Communist leader called for a society of "virile" young men and of "mothers with strong haunches."[37] Amidst conflicting aspirations, Europeans confronted the technological age.

NOTES

1. Constancia de la Mora, *In Place of Splendor. The Autobiography of a Spanish Woman* (New York: Harcourt, Brace, 1939), 140–141.

2. Charles Wicksteed Armstrong, *Life in Spain Today* (London: Blackwood, 1930), xvi, 30, 173–174.

3. Quoted in Peter Wyden, *The Passionate War. The Narrative History of the Spanish Civil War, 1936–1939* (New York: Simon and Schuster, 1983), 244.

4. Internationale Frauenliga für Frieden und Freiheit (Women's International League of Peace and Freedom), Deutscher Zweig, *Flugblatt Nr. 3* (Munich: n.d. [1920s]), 1.

5. Jean Denis (writing in 1936), quoted in Hedwige Peemans-Poullet, "Crise et Antiféminisme," in Maria Macciocchi, ed., *Les femmes et leurs maîtres* (Paris: Christian Bourgeois, 1978), 116.

6. Quoted in Franca Pieroni Bortolotti, *Feminismo e partiti politici in Italia 1919–1926* (Rome: Riuniti, 1978), 41.

7. Rosana Rossanda, *Le altre* (Rome: Bompiani, 1979), 228–229.

8. Bianca Guidetti Serra, *Compagne: Testimonianzo di parteci pazione politica feminile*, 2 vols. (Turin: Einaudi, 1977), 2:489.

9. These particular quotations come from Mussolini's "Donna e Machina," *Popolo d'Italia*, 206 (August 21, 1943) but express his earlier ideas. Cited in Macciocchi, *Elements pour une analyse du fascisme* (Paris: Union Générale d'édition, 1976), 184–186.

10. George Seldes, *Sawdust Caesar* (New York: Harper and Row, 1935), 432.

11. *Casti Connubii*, quoted in Susan G. Bell and Karen Offen, *Women, the Family, and Freedom. The Debate in Documents* (Stanford: Stanford University Press, 1983), 2:314.

12. Quoted in Claudia Koonz, *Mothers in the Fatherland: Women, the Family, and Nazi Politics* (New York: St. Martin's Press, 1987), 54.

13. Speech by Irene Seydel, quoted in Claudia Koonz, "The Competition for a Woman's *Lebensraum*, 1928–1934," in Renate Bridenthal et al., eds., *When Biology Became Destiny: Women in Weimar and Nazi Germany* (New York: Monthly Review Press, 1984), 217.

14. Quoted in Gisela Bock, "Racism and Sexism in Nazi Germany: Motherhood, Compulsory Sterilization and the State," *Signs*, vol. 8 (Spring, 1983): 406.

15. Fritz Junghaus, *Der Weibliche Arbeitsmarkt des Arbeitsamtbezirkes* (Jena, 1934), 78, quoted in Annemarie Tröger, "The Creation of a Female Assembly-Line Proletariat," in *When Biology Became Destiny*, 243.

16. Tröger, "The Creation of a Female Assembly-Line Proletariat," in *When Biology Became Destiny*, 243.

17. Sophie Rogge-Börner quoted by Jill McIntyre, "Women and the Professions in Germany, 1930–1940," in Anthony Nicholls and Erich Matthais, *German Democracy and the Triumph of Hitler* (New York: Allen and Unwin, 1971), 190.

18. Margaret Cole, *Growing Up into Revolution* (London: Longmans, Green, 1949), 139, 160–161.

19. Ilya Ehrenburg, *Out of Chaos*, Alexander Balshy, trans. (New York: 1934), 72, quoted in Louise E. Luke, "Marxian Women: Soviet Variants," in Ernest J. Simmons, ed., *Through the Glass of Soviet Literature* (New York: Columbia University Press, 1953), 52.

20. Letter of "Eddie Kira," November 16, 1931, in Lucie Street, ed., *I Married a Russian. Letters from Kharkov* (New York: Emerson, 1947), 205.

21. Quoted in Luke, "Marxian Women," in Simmons, *Through the Glass of Soviet Literature*, 90.

22. Eugenia Semyonovna Ginzburg, *Journey into the Whirlwind*, Paul Stevenson and May Hayward, trans. (San Diego: Harcourt, 1967), 74.

23. Quoted in Mary Lee Bretz, *Concha Espina* (Boston: Twayne, 1980), 115.

24. Quoted in David Mitchell, *The Spanish Civil War* (New York: Franklin Watts, 1983), 113–114.

25. *Auxilio Social*, December 1937, quoted in Geraldine Scanlon, *La polemica feminista en la España contemporanea (1868–1974)* (Madrid: Siglo Veintiuno, 1978), 315.

26. Lucia Sanchez Saornil, *Solidaridad Obera*, November 8, 1935, quoted in Mary Nash, *Mujeres libres* (Barcelona: Tusquets, 1975), 65.

27. Newspaper clippings in Dossier IBA, Bibliothèque Marguerite Durand, Paris.

28. Letter of Emma Goldman to Stella Ballantine, November 18, 1936, in David Porter, ed., *Emma Goldman and the Spanish Revolution* (New Paltz, N. Y.: Commonground Press, 1983), 254.

29. *Mujeres Libres*, vol. 10 (July 1937) in Nash, *Mujeres libres*, 91.

30. Pilar Primo de Rivera, *Discursos circulares* (Madrid: n.d.), 152–153, quoted in Scanlon, *Polemica feminista en la España*, 319.

31. Christabel Bielenberg, *The Past Is Myself* (London: Chatto and Windus, 1970), 61.

32. Hanna Lévy, "Notes from the Camp of the Dead," in Vera Laska, *Women in the Resistance and in the Holocaust* (Westport, Conn.: Greenwood Press, 1983), 251.

33. Carla Capponi, interviewed in Shelley Saywell, *Women in War. From World War II to El Salvador* (New York: Penguin, 1986), 82.

34. *La Ménagère de l'Aisne*, vol. 2 (August 1942), quoted in Anita Francos, *Il était des femmes dans la Résistance* (Paris: Stock, 1978), 55.

35. Gertrude Stein, *Everybody's Autobiography* (New York: Vintage, 1973 [1937]), 133.

36. *Among You Taking Notes . . . The Wartime Diary of Naomi Mitchison, 1939–1945*, Dorothy Sheridan, ed. (London: Victor Gollancz, 1985), 316.

37. Renée Rousseau, *Les femmes rouges* (Paris: Albin Michel, 1983), 88.

SOURCES AND SUGGESTED READING

Alcalde, Carmen. *La mujer en la guerra civil española* (1976). An exploration of women's various activities.

Bandettini, Pierfrancesco. "The Employment of Women in Italy, 1881–1951, *Comparative Studies in Society and History* (1959–1960).

Bock, Gisela. "Racism and Sexism in Nazi Germany: Motherhood, Compulsory Sterilization, and the State," *Signs* (1983). A provocative thesis.

Bortolotti, Franca Pieroni. *Femminismo et partiti politici in Italia* (1978). On women's politics and the rise of fascism.

Bridenthal, Renate, Atina Grossman, and Marion Kaplan, eds., *When Biology Became Destiny. Women in Weimar and Nazi Germany* (1984). A collection of excellent articles.

Calder, Angus. *The People's War, Britain 1939–1945* (1969).

de Grand, Alexander. "Women under Italian Fascism," *Historical Journal* (1976).

Fredricks, Shirley. "Feminism: The Essential Ingredient in Federica Montseny's Anarchist Theory," in Jane Slaughter and Robert Kern, eds., *European Women on the Left* (1981). A central figure in anarchist politics.

Gasiorowska, Xenia. *Women in Soviet Fiction, 1917–1964* (1968). Changing views of women in this formative period.

Higonnet, Margaret R., Jane Jenson, Sonya Michel, and Margaret Collins Weitz. *Behind the Lines. Gender and the Two World Wars* (1987). Very good articles on France, Germany, and England.

Kern, Robert. "Margarita Nelken: Women and the Crisis of Spanish Politics," in Jane Slaughter and Robert Kern, eds., *European Women on the Left* (1981). Good study of this socialist deputy.

Koonz, Claudia. *Mother in the Fatherland: Women, the Family and Nazi Politics* (1987). A rich study of women participants, victims, and resisters in the Nazi system.

Lapidus, Gail. *Women in Soviet Society* (1978). A detailed examination of policy toward women before and after the Revolution and in post–World War II society.

Laska, Vera. *Women in the Resistance and in the Holocaust* (1983). Stunning eyewitness accounts.

Mason, Tim. "Women in Germany, 1925–1940, *History Workshop* (1976). An interesting analysis.

Mora, Constancia de la. *In Place of Splendor. The Autobiography of a Spanish Woman* (1939). A republican look at the changes in Spain.

Passerini, Luisa. *Fascism in Popular Memory. The Cultural Experience of the Turin Working Class* (1987). An exciting collection of women's and men's first-hand accounts.

Rousseau, Renée. *Les femmes rouges* (1983). On left-wing women in the French Resistance.

Rupp, Leila. *Mobilizing Women for War: German and American Propaganda, 1939–1945* (1978). Crucial differences in policies toward women and how they shaped war efforts.

Saywell, Shelley. *Women in War. From World War II to El Salvador* (1986). Memories of Resistance fighters and women soldiers.

Scanlon, Geraldine. *La polemica feminista en la España contemporanea (1868–1974)* (1978). An excellent survey.

Smith, Bonnie G. *Confessions of a Concierge. Madame Lucie's History of Twentieth Century France* (1985). A French woman's experience of the depression and war.

Smith, Harold. "The Problem of 'Equal Pay for Equal Work' in Great Britian During World War II," *Journal of Modern History* (1981).

Stephenson, Jill. *The Nazi Organization of Women* (1981). On women's professional, work, and political activity.

———. *Women in Nazi Society* (1975).

Thibert, Marguerite. "Economic Depression and the Employment of Women," *International Labour Review* (1933).

CHAPTER
12

Technology and Power in the Late Twentieth Century

Remaking Europe

In 1947, the Dutch public first read the sensational diary of Anne Frank (1929–1945). Soon published around the world, the diary described a young Jewish girl's experience of the war and her family's clandestine life hiding from the Nazis. Others also wrote of their wartime experiences. Luise Rinser's (b. 1911) diary described her life in prison, where the Nazis had incarcerated her on charges of treason and antimilitary activity. Natalia Ginzberg (b. 1916) described life under Mussolini, and Madeleine Henrey wrote about the Blitz in wartime London. Nelly Sachs (1891–1970) shared the Nobel Prize in 1966 for her poems commemorating the victims of the Holocaust. Yet it was Anne Frank who captured the public's imagination as people sought to understand what civilization had lost during the frightening wartime years. Recounting the daily emotional life of an adolescent, including problems with parents and encounters with a young man who was also hiding in the same house, she often saw the war as a mere background to personal life. At the same time, she revealed a human idealism amidst barbarism and a natural longing to develop into an adult. After the war, readers marvelled at the message of this young woman, who died at Bergen-Belsen concentration camp in the closing weeks of the war. Her ideals remained mostly intact, she wrote, "because in spite of everything I still believe that people are really good at heart."[1]

Anne Frank's diary portrayed the plight of an individual at the mercy of the modern state. The post–World War II tensions arising from the individual's confrontation with the technological and interventionist state also produced such novels as George Orwell's *1984*. In this work, published in 1949, governmental technology, communications, and systems of knowledge ultimately outwit the hero and his colorful friend Julia, who represents life and humanity. While Europeans struggled to rebuild and to repopulate, such themes understandably preoccupied them. Picking up the pieces of a devastated social and political order, Europeans quickly confronted the demands of lives both traumatized and transformed by war. As well as having to deal with memories of unprecedented and massive cruelty, Europeans faced a technological society, unified by communication systems, public planning, and governmental order- ing of many aspects of everyday life. Even agricultural workers in barely mod- ernized rural areas of Eastern Europe toiled under their relatively primitive conditions because of centralized bureaucratic decision-making. Two hundred years earlier, local communities had controlled work and marriage with cha- rivaris and other folk rituals, but different and more massive structures now guided individuals in the late twentieth century.

By the 1980s, technology influenced production and reproduction in pow- erful ways, the latter through the birth control pill and test tube babies. Com- munications technology enabled vivid messages about behavior to be dissem- inated widely via the medium of television. Who would control such technologies, women asked, and to whose benefit? Driven by such questions, as well as by older ones concerning economics and education, a new feminist movement arose. It was prominent, included diverse points of view and, iron- ically, interacted with all the new technologies.

The Economic Miracle and Technological Transformations

At the end of World War II, much of Europe existed only as heaps of rubble. Two decades later, however, many countries, especially in Western Europe, had become highly competitive participants in the sophisticated international mar- ketplace led by multinational corporations. That recovery was labeled the "economic miracle," particularly with regard to Germany. The United States gave aid to both its former allies and its former enemies. The Marshall Plan, for example, gave financial assistance in a variety of forms to rebuild Europe. Right after the war, women worked in greater numbers than ever before in such menial jobs as removing rubble as well as in a wide array of industrial posts.

Ongoing inequity in pay in the rebuilding countries helped make the "eco- nomic miracle" possible and continued to keep women at a disadvantage long after the war was over. The system that allowed for this kind of exploitation continued the work classifications advanced by Nazi administrators who had lowered the skill ranking of any jobs women did and raised that of ones men performed. Instead of rising with wartime and post-war demand, women's pay did not increase in proportion to the need for their labor. In West Germany, now separated from the eastern half, specific wage scales for women, as Nazi bureaucrats had organized them, only became illegal in 1956; even then they continued to be applied surreptitiously because of their benefit to employers. In Great Britain in the 1960s, women earned no more than 60 percent of men's earnings and usually less. Even though women in French printing firms could make 15,000 strokes per hour at keyboards compared to 10,000 by men, they earned one-half what the men did because of different job titles. In 1958, Bel- gian women working in manufacturing earned 56.5 percent of men's wage

Civilians cleared rubble in Berlin and other bombed cities and thus allowed the "economic miracle" of European revival.

level, and in West Germany in that same year, women in all occupations except agriculture earned 62.9 percent of what men did. These patterns changed during the next decade, but not in the same way everywhere. British women in manufacturing in the 1960s went from earning 62 percent of what men earned to 57 percent a decade later. Danish women in all occupations other than agriculture, however, improved their earnings level from 67 percent of men's level to 73 percent. Thus, Europe's post-war economic recovery was partially based on women's pay remaining inequitable, thus allowing industries to make their profits.

Women's participation in the labor force reached new highs in the 1970s and 1980s, and they became more visible as workers because more worked outside the home. Although cultural norms stressed their role as mothers, in fact, the percentage of married women in the workforce exceeded wartime levels. In 1979 in Sweden, 64 percent of married mothers worked, and in Britain 60 percent did. In France and West Germany, 41 percent of married mothers had jobs. In countries showing lower percentages, such as Italy with only 30 percent of all women working in 1970, those percentages did not include the large number of women working at home, for instance, doing hand-finishing of luxury goods such as leather purses. Although these percentages for

Western Europe are high, they are even higher for socialist countries. In the Soviet Union, well over 90 percent of adult women were working in the 1970s, up from something over 25 percent of women in the early years after the revolution. Early in the 1980s in the German Democratic Republic (East Germany or GDR), almost 90 percent of adult women held jobs or were in training programs for entry-level positions. In fact, socialist countries encouraged women to do productive work as well as family work.

In some places, such as Italy, Czechoslovakia, Greece, and elsewhere, doing piecework at home continued to be a source of income for many women. Also, improvising some contribution to the family income remained crucial for many married women. A Norwegian mother reported in the late 1970s that her worklife included caring for others' children, office cleaning, and later several waitressing jobs. A woman in Paris worked as a theater usher and also as a seamstress for an upholstery firm. In the 1970s, her daughter-in-law did part-time leather work for a small firm that avoided contributing to social security for its employees by not listing them. In Greek villages, housewives sewed tablecloths, napkins, handkerchiefs, and dress scarves for Athenian wholesalers and luxury shops. These working women were uncounted in many instances; if they had been counted, women's employment figures would be even higher.

Although industrialization in general remained partial, from the late 1940s on, increasing numbers of women worked in technological jobs or had their work lives organized by technology. Those jobs that had few technological aspects declined noticeably in the period between 1950 and 1970. In particular, domestic service dropped from being a major form of employment to one of the smallest ones. In Germany, where the largest percentage of women workers in the nineteenth century had been domestics, in 1950 only 12.4 percent were, and this figure dropped further to 1.7 percent in 1970. Farm work fell to below 1 percent of women's jobs in Germany in 1970. The percentage of German women workers employed in factories hovered between 27 and 30 throughout the twentieth century; the service sector, including sales, employed more than 50 percent of all female workers by 1970. Whereas in Italy women's unemployment rose in the recessions of the 1970s and the early 1980s, in England employers used these cycles as an excuse to eliminate more highly paid male workers and streamline businesses by introducing woman-operated technological systems.

Technology dominated much of work life after the 1970s with computers and other systems of knowledge used to control machines in industry as well as sales and marketing and financial operations. In short, technology became the major influence in productive life, and this marked a shift to so-called post-industrial society. For example, in the British clothing industry, mass production of garments under the industrial system involved a designer, a pattern-maker who converted the design into pattern pieces, a grader who sized those pieces, a layout person who arranged the pieces for optimal use of cloth, and a cutter who used machinery on layers of fabric that were rolled out by the operator of a bale and roller machine. Post-war developments, especially since 1970, have transferred most of these processes to computers, which are fed

Distribution of Employed Women in Germany, 1882–1970

Sector	1882	1895	1907	1925	Year 1933	1939	1950	1961	1970
Agriculture	34.8%	31.9%	28.2%	17.0%	13.7%	11.0%	8.0%	1.7%	0.9%
Household service	40.0	34.4	26.2	21.7	19.0	18.4	12.4	4.9	1.7
Trade	1.6	2.4	4.9	9.0	12.5	11.2	11.9	16.7	17.5
Old service*	3.4	5.6	6.2	6.1 } 18.6		11.5	12.1	15.8	15.8
New service†	3.0	3.7	5.4	8.8 }		10.3	14.6	20.1	23.4
Clerk	0.1	0.2	1.2	5.2	5.1	6.3	6.7	10.4	13.4
No permanent post or not indicated	2.5	1.3	0.9	1.3	0.7	0.1	5.2	0.3	—
Industry	14.5	20.5	27.0	30.8	30.4	31.2	29.1	30.1	27.4
Number in millions	3.494	4.351	5.08	6.264	6.398	7.321	4.8	6.999	7.638

*Old service occupations: public administration and military, church, culture, personal service (innkeeping, beautician), cleaning.

†New service occupations: education, health, hygiene, welfare, legal, transport and commerce, banks and insurance, architecture and laboratory.

Source: Walter Müller, Angelika Willms, Johann Handl, *Strukturwandel der Frauenarbeit, 1880–1980* (Frankfurt/New York: Campus Verlag, 1983), 176.

information about design modifications by operators who are predominantly women. The expertise of cutters and pattern-makers is now stored in a computer, which can be operated by a worker of far lower skill. "It puts management in the driver's seat," said the manager of one English firm. The control of programmed industries lies with those possessing knowledge of how to design and maintain computer systems, not those with mechanical or craft skills. In technological enterprises, those having the high-level knowledge are predominantly male. Women operating the computers need intellectual resources, but the people with technical knowledge of the machine itself are in control. Managers tell computer operators "it's dead easy." In contrast, women see this work as demanding "someone who's bright" or taking "more skill to it because the computer gives you feedback," thus calling for further response.[2] Despite workers' interpretation of their new role, the gender segmentation of the workforce has continued to mean inferior status for women in the technological age. At the same time, some male industrial workers have surrendered their blue-collar work with machines to computer-driven systems and taken on unskilled, feminized jobs. After the onerous years of reconstruction, technology has changed the nature of power in the workplace without making that power gender-neutral.

In socialist countries, there is almost total participation by women in the workforce. In the Soviet Union at the end of World War II, women continued to replace men in the manual jobs in industry, and the number of women in

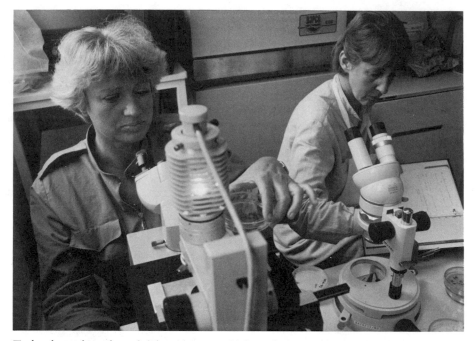

Technology shaped work life and personal life in the post-war world. It both provided and organized work. At the same time, scientific breakthroughs improved health and changed reproduction.

agriculture declined from 60 percent in 1939 to just over 20 percent in 1970. Large numbers of Soviet women obtained highly skilled jobs. Most notably, they dominated medicine and constituted more than three-quarters of Soviet doctors in the mid-1970s. They also took jobs in science, engineering, and other technical fields, in addition to making inroads into the judicial and legal professions. Stressing the importance of work, socialist countries have encouraged women's participation in the workforce. Yet, in general, women's work in socialist countries shows more similarities to than differences from that in the West. First, women have dominated in the worst-paying jobs in the least-valued fields: in Eastern Europe, these include agriculture, service, education, food, and health. In the Soviet Union, often the most arduous work was women's: in 1970 69 percent of women loggers but only 37 percent of men loggers did arduous work, and 80 percent of women in construction did heavy work but only 6 percent used machinery. Moreover, many jobs remained female "ghettos"; for instance, typists and stenographers in the Soviet Union in 1970 were 99 percent female. And women's high level of representation in medicine did not bring them economic or political power. On the contrary, as a female-dominated profession, medicine in the Soviet Union has far less prestige than it does in the West. Women in socialist countries entered apprenticeships more often than did women in the West, but their wages remained low and so did their skill level. Those who made the grade of foreperson or manager received lower wages than did men in the same jobs—the explanation often being that men had to support families. In socialist countries, women held few leadership positions, and those that they held were in lower ranks. In Czechoslovakia in the early 1960s, for example, women filled approximately 25 percent of administrative positions in communications, financial auditing, and housing administration, but 5 percent or less of such positions in more important areas such as production, transport, technical fields, and government. In the Soviet Union, the percentage of women directors of enterprise rose from 6 to 9 percent between 1963 and 1973. In comparison West Germany had virtually no female directors of businesses in 1987. The question of leadership and equity in the workplace is still a problem across Europe.

Rural Life and Continuing Migration

For the small proportion of rural women in Western Europe, the farm remained the center of life after the war, yet it was profoundly transformed by the mechanization and consolidation of small farms into large ones. These occurred widely following World War II as American techniques spawned the rise of European agribusiness. Polyculture—that is, raising a mixture of several crops and different animals—gave way to either large livestock farming or grain production. In addition, cooperatives were formed to monitor the marketing of produce, set agricultural policy, and lobby the government. Although the market-oriented aspects of farm life intensified, those traditionally maintained by women declined. For one thing, though food consumed on the farm became more diversified, women's connection with it diminished. A variety of sources could provide food, including itinerant grocers in their trucks or supermarkets from which months of canned provisions could be purchased. On very large farms, labor intensive kitchen gardens seemed anachronistic and even wasteful of space that could produce cash crops. After the war, children went regularly to school, and therefore instruction in chores at home diminished. Household clothing production also became a thing of the past. Even the extended household, with its multiple generations, declined as young couples set out on their own, in tune with the national economy and national culture. The modernization of the farm household certainly simplified the rural woman's life; it also diminished her traditional usefulness to the family and her contribution to farm life in general. The farm became the province of the farmer; his occupation alone created family prosperity.

From the time of the Russian Revolution, socialists had made much of the rural woman. She was wooed politically, and she was valued for her labor, which remained crucial to prosperity. During World War II, Soviet women maintained the agricultural sector, and just after the war they constituted about half of all agricultural workers. Newly trained to run the heaviest and most modern machinery, they played an important role in the modernization of rural life. At the same time, they faced prejudice against their doing this kind of work; men continued to think of machinery as part of their sphere. In any case, after the war, machine operation did not usually fall to women's sphere in the rural division of labor. Instead, much of their work remained traditional, onerous, and very poorly paid. The Soviet government put less effort into improving agriculture than into building heavy industry and improving military capability during the Cold War. Thus, calls for women to reproduce received little cooperation from women in rural areas, already working to capacity in what remained a major occupational sector in socialist countries.

In the Mediterranean region, where peasant holding remained intact, the forces of mechanization coexisted with the strictest patriarchal control of family life. A study of the Greek town of Pouri, whose economy was based on charcoal, chestnuts, apples, and olive trees, showed increased paternal power in the 1960s and 1970s. The civil war in Greece in the 1940s reflected international tensions between communism and capitalism but it affected individual lives by destroying women's networks for sociability in the town. Families were too suspicious of one another, for example, to continue participating in traditional shared evening work sessions. Also, indoor plumbing was installed in some individual houses, which brought an end to the sociability of communal laundering. Since electricity and plumbing were the only innovations in household technology allowed by the village men, women's work actually increased during the decades of the study. Controlling all family budgetary decisions, men refused to buy washing machines, vacuum cleaners, or electric mixers. "Why did I marry her except to do the washing?" one man explained in the early 1980s.[3] They did increase the size of homes and added bathrooms, but most money went to purchase land, fertilizer, and machinery. In order to produce more crops for the market, the men cleared more and more hill country. As a result, women's labor intensified because, for work outside of the home, no sexual division of labor existed. While trading with middlemen and fixing machinery, men sent the women to the fields and pastures. The women's workday—as opposed to their husbands—was observed to be nineteen to twenty hours a day and men's, several hours shorter. The only ones in touch with the market and with money, men had all the prestige in the new commercial society. Simultaneously, they ruled in such matters as meals, marriages, and sexuality through the traditionally accepted exercise of violence. By the 1980s, many young women of Pouri, who had had some schooling and who caught glimpses of urban life—since some of their fathers bought televisions—rejected such miserable lives for themselves by moving to larger towns. Thus, they forced young men who stayed in Pouri to find hard-working wives in more impoverished, neighboring villages.

Whether on small holdings or in large modernized agricultural enterprises, the eighteenth-century balance of tasks of rural life had given way to total direction by men. Unlike their nineteenth-century predecessors who had fled to cities just for employment, twentieth-century rural women sought not only urban jobs but social benefits and the easy lives they thought urban women had. Migrations resulted from displacement in the war, from decolonization,

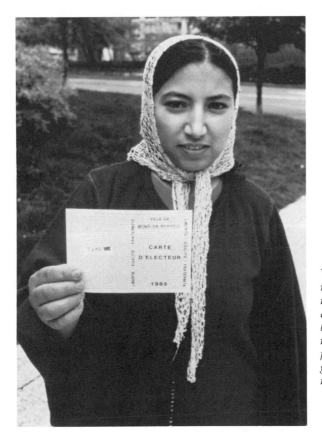

The new workforce in Europe included millions of immigrants from former colonies. Western nations became multinational, which allowed for different forms of job segregation by gender and also by ethnicity.

and from general economic insecurity as Europe continued to modernize, as well as from rural women's discontent. In the mid-1940s, families and individuals fled from advancing armies and political strife or were driven out by a dearth of economic opportunity due to the general devastation of industrial plants, farmland, and commercial institutions. Europe was full of refugees. Meanwhile, as decolonization occurred, people in newly liberated Asian and African countries come to the Continent, which they believed to be more secure politically and economically than their own nations. Finally, surplus labor from impoverished areas such as Sicily moved to more prosperous northern regions as news of opportunity spread in the 1960s and 1970s. Belgium in the mid-1970s, for example, harbored close to 700,000 new immigrants, of which 45.8 percent were women. Among these immigrants, 113,000 were Italian, 33,400 Spanish, and 15,000 Moroccan, with roughly 10,000 each from Greece, Turkey, and Poland. This population constituted the less fortunate sector of workers, whereas Germans, French, and Dutch made up a more privileged group within the immigrant pool. Of the immigrant women 35 percent worked, whereas 37 percent of all Belgian women did.

In general—and Belgium provides a microcosmic instance of a northern European phenomenon—women immigrants from Mediterranean and non-European countries held the lowest-paying, least-skilled jobs. An Italian woman whose former employment had been painting on crystal moved into an unskilled position oiling machinery in the Herstal armaments factory. Arriving in 1946, she needed the work to support her five children and eventually started working swing shifts to earn more. Although this worker supported every union job action out of a belief in "equal pay for equal work," she did so fearfully because her work permit was at stake. By the 1970s, however, Turkish women had replaced her in the cleaning jobs that were the lowest-paid in the Herstal plant. She and her co-workers, understanding the necessity of solidarity, always "tried to give them a hand."[4] She recognized that the woman immigrant, in addition to having few opportunities, suffered extreme alienation in a new culture. Children educated in the adopted country had little use for the woman's native tongue or for values of the homeland. As in the nineteenth century, although the city offered opportunities for survival, life there was tarnished with cultural trauma. Also, patriarchal customs often came along with immigrants. One worker in a British hosiery plant noted about some co-workers that "Indian women are so malnourished," mostly because husbands or heads of extended families claimed their pay.[5] As technology improved production and drew women into its orbit, familial and social inequities remained powerful influences in shaping women's relationships to such improvements.

The Revolution in Reproduction

Although natural increase and immigration replenished the population, the birth rate fell everywhere and the plea for women to reproduce echoed from east to west. The first few years after the war saw some increase in reproduction that replaced the decline of the war years. From then on limited fertility was the order of the day. In Poland, the birth rate fell from 32.8 per thousand inhabitants in 1921 to 29.4 in 1949 and 16.3 in 1969; in Yugoslavia it went from 36.7 to 30 to 18.2, and in Denmark from 24 to 18 to 14.6. The birth rate in France had a slight increase to 20.7 per thousand inhabitants after the war, but by 1969 it had fallen to 16.7 per thousand. On the average, women's childbearing ended before they reached the age of thirty, although menopause did not occur until around fifty. In other words, couples practiced birth control for longer periods and thus curtailed reproductivity for decades of each woman's life.

This changing pattern was in large part due to technological intervention, particularly the birth-control pill, which was perfected in the 1950s and tested on Third World women before going on the market in the early 1960s. Many women adopted the intrauterine device (IUD) and condoms, diaphragms, sponges, and contraceptive creams remained important in preventing pregnancy. Both men and women could easily have themselves permanently steri-

Childbirth: The Soviet Union in the 1970s

The average number of children a woman bears has declined a good deal since the eighteenth century, and nowhere more than in the Soviet Union. Although in the Moslem area of Central Russia family size averages almost seven people, in the European areas women have two children at most and often just one. The experience of childbirth also differs widely. Sveta, a young worker, went to a state hospital in her neighborhood, and Masha, a higher ranking health care functionary, gave birth in the hospital where she worked. The passage shows how the experiences of twentieth-century life are viewed in diverse ways.

Q. Did you have any preparation for childbirth?

Sveta: No, there was no talk of anything like that.

Q. Were you given medication during the birth? If so, who made the decision, and was the reason for it explained?

Sveta: Yes, during labour they do a number of injections, they call it setting the scene for labour. But if the labour is normal they don't need to. Of course I protested, argued with them. I think it's better to suffer for ten hours, and do it all myself. The doctors insisted on the injections. There isn't a chief doctor, they're midwives. They rush around, they have a plan—they have to see that everything goes quickly. They also give castor oil, and they force you to drink it, I protested, but the labour pains began and she brought me the castor oil—she did it very rudely, I felt she was ready to beat me to get me to drink the stuff. They don't explain anything, they just do what they think necessary.

Masha: No, you see if they give you some kind of drug you don't have the same strength to push the baby, the contractions are reduced. So even though I was in hospital through connections with good doctors, and even though I had a very hard time they couldn't do anything to help me, so they didn't give me any anesthesia. . . . Later on, though, the baby turned over and I had to lie on my side for a whole day, hoping it would right itself—they gave me morphine injections then. But no, they don't ask if you want them.

Q. Were you left alone during labour? And what was the attitude of the doctors and midwives?

Sveta: There were two beds in the room, but I was alone. The doctors went out and didn't come in very often. If the mother calls them they come and start kicking up a fuss— why do you keep crying like a mad thing, you're giving birth. Well that's true, but still they ought to watch, to calm you. The thing is that there aren't enough doctors, the staff is very small. . . . Yes, the mother has to call out; of course, there are all sorts of ropes on the wall that you're supposed to pull to call the doctor, but nothing works. Childbirth is considered a normal happening, so the bells don't work.

Masha: I was with two other women in the ward when labour began. A midwife was with me all the time. I wasn't left alone.

Q. How did you get on after the birth, on the postnatal ward?

Sveta: Straight after the birth I felt a great relief. The rest of the time I felt tired, weak. I wanted to rest, to sleep, but it's hard to sleep much because it's painful. I was allowed out of hospital on the fifth day but I think that's too soon. I found it was an effort to keep on my feet. In the hospital the babies are kept separate in the children's ward. I was shown her after the birth and then I didn't see her for 24 hours. . . . No one is allowed in the ward to visit, no one at all. I looked out of the window and saw B [the father]. The father has to ask about the birth at the information desk, he can't see the baby. They don't even allow us mothers into the children's ward. They don't say why. They don't know why themselves. . . . To be honest, I have to say they treat people badly, like a dog that gives birth and that's it. That's how they see childbirth. And afterwards, things are always happening that wear down the nerves—they all have their own rules, one comes and says like this, another comes and says like that. They're all so bossy and like giving orders. It's very unpleasant, as if we were small children.

Masha: After the birth I felt a wonderful bliss, all the pain left me immediately. But later in the hospital my mood was terrible. The cuts didn't heal and because the birth was diffi-cult, I was there a long time and all the other women left. The nurses tried to cheer me up, they would come in and sym-pathise, talked with me as if I were a baby, but I wanted to go home very much. Yes, it was difficult, but you forget the pain very quickly, it's hard to describe it all now.

Source: Barbara Holland and Teresa McKevitt, "Maternity Care in the Soviet Union," in Barbara Holland, ed., *Soviet Sisterhood* (Bloom-ington: Indiana University Press, 1985), pp. 170–172.

lized by the late 1970s. On the one hand, the decline of nontechnological meth-ods such as abstinence and the rhythm method allowed for more reliable choice in reproductive matters. On the other hand, women only consumed the technology and did not control it; their access was susceptible to limitations.

For instance, some countries, such as France and Italy, banned the sale of birth-control products. Moreover, quick profitability had motivated manufacturers of both the pill and the IUD. Neither product was tested thoroughly enough before being marketed, and thus there were side effects, some of which were eliminated in the next decades. Many women implanted with the Dalkon shield became sterile from its use.

Technology for both inducing pregnancy and monitoring it developed rapidly. Hospitals' physical rearrangement in the 1920s and 1930s into separate rooms for each phase of pregnancy and birth had set the stage for applying technology to pregnant bodies and those in childbirth. Scientists worked out methods to help women to conceive through artificial insemination and fertility drugs. Finally, in 1978 Louise Brown, the first "test tube" baby, was born in England. Her birth resulted from an artificial conception achieved by mixing egg and sperm from her parents in a "dish" and then implanting the fertilized egg in her mother's uterus. Called "in-vitro" fertilization, this process also allowed women to bear children for couples in which the wife was infertile by using the husband's sperm and implanting the egg in the surrogate's uterus to gestate there. Amniocentesis and ultrasound were among an array of technological monitorings of pregnancy. The infant and maternal mortality rates continued to fall, but at the expense of greater technological intervention in the birth process. The number of Caesarian births increased as did the instances of artificial inducement of labor. Most obstetricians used drugs to make labor last an optimal 8 to 12 hours. To facilitate all these interventions in the birth process, doctors encouraged their patients to surrender themselves to technology and medical know-how. As one pamphlet printed in the 1970s for pregnant women put it: "You are going to have to answer a lot of questions and be the subject of a lot of examinations. Never worry your head about any of these."[6]

The Sexual Revolution

In the late 1970s, a Spanish country woman, born during World War I, lamented modern sexual freedom: "If a boy wants to be alone with a girl there's no problem; they go off alone and whatever fires they have can burn." She was upset that engaged couples and even married ones kissed—something not done even in private, she maintained, in the 1930s and 1940s.[7] In the 1960s and 1970s, public space did indeed seem to see more demonstrations of sexual affection, including bodily closeness when dancing, embracing in restaurants and cafés, and even intimate contact on beaches.

Late in the 1940s, fashion designer Christian Dior revealed his "new look" for women. This look involved a pinched-in waist, longer skirts, and a closer fit about the chest. This fashion development was part of a revolution in which the sexual aspect of a woman's body received sharper emphasis. The breasts especially became a symbol in advertising for womanhood and for the unleashing of desires. In the 1950s, crinolines and even waist-reducing corsets reestablished emphases that dated from a century earlier. In the 1960s, the bikini bathing suit became the most common beachwear. It too attracted attention to women's sexuality by giving an emphasis to the breasts and genitals it skimpily covered. During the 1970s even the bikini top was dropped, and most European young women bathed or sunned topless.

The sexual revolution not only brought women's bodies more into public view, it also restructured male psychosexual norms. In the mid-1950s, *Playboy Magazine* made its first appearance, leading to an international array of similar magazines catering to male sexual fantasies. Containing many well-written and interesting features, such magazines also highlighted photos of nude women and of bachelor parties in penthouse apartments or on luxury yachts. In so doing, they portrayed male sexual fulfillment as occurring outside of the family; wives and children were nowhere to be seen in these magazines. Instead of generating offspring and supporting a family, the playboy left responsibility behind and pursued personal gratification, especially sexual pleasure. Although society had long recognized male sexual desire, such desire had always been accompanied by familial duty, at the very least in financial terms. The playboy mentality emphasized the stressfulness of such responsibility and its ability to retard personal fulfillment and growth. With sufficient population, Western Europe could afford a diminished emphasis on the paternal male, and in Eastern Europe the emphasis on masculinity was aimed at improving the birth rate. Simultaneously, occupational dislocation because of technological change made gender identification for men hinge more on sexual prowess and less on occupational definition.

The importance attached to men's fulfillment resulted in women being encouraged to take better care of their men. Magazines such as the French *Elle,* while running recipes regularly, featured articles about cholesterol—women needed to protect masculine vitality. Some women workers saw their placement in nonskilled jobs as protective of masculinity and creativity. Boredom was better borne by women than by men: "Men'd go mad. It'd kill them with boredom," said a young English tobacco worker in the 1970s.[8] Other constructions of femininity aimed at inciting male desire as well as preventing male boredom. The brassiere, now worn by nearly all women, focused the male eye on the breasts, as did the bikini. Women's bodies became prime consumer items for the roaming male, the playboy, the hunter. Sex shops opened, the divorce rate soared, and public space became saturated with seminude, voluptuous women on commercial posters in subways, on magazine covers, and in clubs for middle-class men.

Images of the post-war man lacked an essential decency, uprightness, and fidelity that had once so characterized man's "official" persona. Feminists and traditionalists alike entered the debate over man's character. At first, women in the 1960s fell for the sexy, macho politicians of the middle-class left; later, as feminists, they rejected them. Traditionalists who realized what was happening to the male persona lobbied for increased protection for women. A poster for a campaign against legalizing divorce in Italy showed a sad middle-

New fashions of the 1970s had contradictory aspects. Supposedly less confining, they were designed to accentuate sexual difference. This photo depicts a modern male-female relationship.

aged mother and her two children: "You betrayed me, you wanted a divorce, you abandoned me with two children and gave me pennies for food."[9] That part of the sexual revolution stressing male sexual liberation did not change sex roles, nor did it mean that parents had a more equitable interest in children. If anything, the sexual revolution meant that women had more responsibility for children, as the new norms encouraged men who wanted to be "all man" to be more sexually promiscuous and less family-oriented.

Reports from countries where the sexual revolution had progressed the farthest gave an interesting picture of what such liberation actually involved. Sweden, for example, decriminalized homosexuality in 1944 and made sex education obligatory in 1955. As early as the 1930s, the Swedish government rescinded laws prohibiting contraceptive information. By the 1960s, sexually explicit scenes appeared in Swedish films, including such works as Ingmar Bergman's *The Silence,* and Vilgot Sjoman's *491,* which depicted a girl being forced to have sexual relations with an animal. By the 1970s, there was no longer any official censorship, except where violence was mixed with sexual scenes. Finally, Swedes began having sexual relations early; studies early in the 1980s show the average age for a girl was 15 years, 2 months and for a boy, 15 years, 5 months. However, 43 percent of all young women indicated that they did not take any pleasure in early sex. Ten percent of young women between the ages of sixteen and twenty-five complained that their first experiences had been physically forced on them. Insecurities also played their role. For instance, finding herself paired off at a party with a man known for sexual exploits, one young woman worried whether she should have intercourse as he suggested: "I dared not say no, I dared not say anything for fear of losing him."[10] Sexual liberation in Sweden did not mean that gender relationships became egalitarian, but simply that old stereotypes were reworked. Sixty-one percent of all women between the ages of twenty and twenty-four lived in free unions, but many still fulfilled the domestic ideal of a century ago, remained at home, and were unemployed. Led on by communications technology, young adults displayed masculine or feminine characteristics and roles at earlier and earlier ages.

Women and the Welfare State

The late–twentieth-century nation-state applied its power differently from the way governments had two centuries earlier. Once power had been focused on directing international diplomacy and expansionism and on the workings of internal political groups seeking control. In contrast, using the social scientific knowledge of its officials and of intellectual elites, the state in the twentieth century reached out to influence the everyday lives of its citizens. Concern for the health of children as potential laborers had first led the modern state to give help to impoverished women and children. After 1945, with the help of statistical, scientific, and technological expertise, those early welfare programs for the poor had multiplied and been extended to every citizen—rich and poor alike—of just about every European country. The state particularly shaped the relationship between reproductive and productive lives.

Some say the state maintained welfare provisions—as the imperial state had—to replenish the population after each catastrophe in the ongoing series of wars. In this way, the military and welfare aims of the state were coordinated. Others contend that the welfare state was needed to help the family so that the workforce could be maintained in good condition as technology demanded people with greater powers of concentration and more stamina. Still others see the welfare state as being necessary to supplement the income of those who had been discriminated against by law and governmental rules. Finally, in an age of gender redefinition that was diluting the importance of financial responsibility to male identity while maintaining the lower wages of women, the state stepped in as women's financial partner. In this view, the state now supported women and their children, as husbands used to. In any case, the welfare state is a phenomenon of post-war life with profound if varied implications for women.

The welfare state tried to integrate social expectations about women's behavior with knowledge about that behavior. Thus, welfare provisions functioned differently according to national expectations and needs. In England, the welfare state adopted its post-war form from the 1942 report of economist William Beveridge (1879–1960). Heeding warnings about inflation and underemployment after the war, Beveridge and those who enacted his program worked to eliminate the worst features of that unemployment. First a comprehensive national health program was put into effect to keep people healthy and fit for work whether employed or not. Beveridge directed his attention to women and the family as keys to the employment situation: "During marriage most women will not be gainfully employed. The small minority of women who undertake paid employment or other gainful employment or other gainful occupations after marriage require special treatment differing from that of single women." Just after the war, Beveridge stressed that women had "vital work to do in ensuring the adequate continuance of the British race."[11] As a result, women received small subsidies for children, but as workers they received fewer benefits if they were married. Beveridge envisioned that married women in the workforce would have no welfare benefits. Thus, the post-war state in Great Britain initially reemphasized women's maternal role as well as stressing gender difference.

In France, in contrast, welfare legislation was based on liberal concepts of individual rights. Some attribute this egalitarianism to memories of recent events held by those making social policy: women had contributed equally in the Resistance and in all efforts to liberate the country. At the same time, a higher percentage of French women worked toward rebuilding, making them more in need of assistance in their activities as mothers. They received benefits before and after pregnancy in addition to free health care; they had more children's services, such as early education, after-school programs, and day care, at their disposal. Moreover, the government made women's benefits equal to men's in pensions, health insurance, and other job-related plans. The welfare state, then, varied in its attitudes toward women and in the roles toward which it directed them.

Some governments committed themselves to helping the unwed mother or the single female parent as a way of shaping and reacting to the new sexual morality. In that case, children qualified for aid depending on the means of their parents. In Sweden, welfare programs provided a single mother and her two children 93.8 percent of the money earned by an average worker, and other programs gave housing allowances and an "advance maintenance allow-

Women at work on the assembly line in socialist Sweden. The gender division of labor remains intact, as the "line" itself is female, while managers are male.

ance" for children whose father provided no support. In addition to these three forms of aid, single parents could apply for personal welfare, but few did because of these child-centered programs. Because these packages of allowances focused on children, they did little to help women upgrade their skills and did not address the problem of women's low wages. In other words, after children left the home and allowances declined, the mother still had no job training. While staying at home to watch her children, she developed no marketable skills and would enter the workforce in her late thirties or forties in a vulnerable position. Defining the problem as one centered on children, the Swedish state perpetuated the situation in which women would remain impoverished.

Socialist countries generated policies concerning women in their childbearing and childrearing capacity in connection with the state's productive needs. Committed to having women work outside the home as part of socialist doctrine, the socialist states faced enormous difficulties in balancing work with reproduction. Although post-war devastation mandated women's labor, labor shortages simultaneously demanded an increase in birth rates. Unlike Western European countries, which were flooded with migrant labor from virtually the entire world, Eastern Europe received almost no outside workers. Women who worked full-time, and most did in socialist countries, naturally cut back on the number of children they bore, especially since wages and public support systems hardly permitted them to do otherwise. Concerned about population decline, socialist states recapitulated the nineteenth-century ideology of gender difference by officially emphasizing woman's gentleness and emotional connection with children. Girls should be raised so as to prepare them for maternity, whereas boys needed more discipline and less demonstrative affection in preparation for their role as head of the family. By the post-war era, governments were able to fine-tune the beliefs of their citizens through psychological, educational, and even pulp literature. In order to benefit production, the state gave increasing support for motherhood. In East Germany and elsewhere, governments imitated the Third Reich's program of loans to newly married couples, which would be gradually forgiven with the birth of the first through the fourth child. Sociologists charted the housework done by socialist women and found that consumer shortages, for one thing, made for additional daily housework of five to six hours. Yet planners faced difficulty in reducing concern for household care because of the official emphasis on gender difference in domestic affairs that was supposed to incite female desire for children. By 1981, the Soviet Union undertook even more drastic measures to ensure demographic stability by reducing the hours women worked outside the home and increasing child care subsidies. Also, improving the consumer side of things marked a major shift in Soviet policy as part of the incentives to increase reproduction undertaken by the welfare state. In order to remain both productive and reproductive, socialist society has seen fit to define all childrearing—and not just childbearing—as the duty of the female. In this way, the state maintains the situation in which reproducers remain at the low end of the production cycle with the most demeaning and lowest-paying jobs through such measures as mandatory part-time work for women. At the other extreme, women who have career aspirations will disregard the state's inducement to enhance fertility. In any case, official socialist welfare shows a firm allegiance to the family that is headed by the men and serviced by the woman.

Increasingly in post–World War II Europe, the state and its citizenry interacted on these crucial issues via an array of social institutions. From England to the Soviet Union, for instance, almost all prenatal care and births took place in national hospitals and were paid for by the state. Although most European countries in the early 1970s provided a range of medical services to children, Sweden had public doctors caring for 99.7 percent of all newborns and carrying out a mandatory check-up of all four-year-olds. Sweden also offered state-supported day care for the newborn, nursery schools, and all other education, including compulsory state sex education. European women in general received increasing amounts of information through clinics and adult courses about their own reproductive functioning and about children's development. The prominence of Dr. Benjamin Spock (b. 1903) as an international expert of

Welfare State Developments in Maternal and Infant Health Care in Czechoslovakia, 1948–1978 (population 13 million)

	1948	1957	1967	1976	1978
Resources					
Prenatal clinics	434	1,625	1,812	1,840	1,840
Obstetrical/gynecological beds	6,531	12,624	14,856	15,932	15,935
Specialized obstetricians	326	1,030	1,865	2,341	2,407
Midwives	2,643	4,648	5,570	6,387	6,510
Activities					
Deliveries in maternity homes (%)	41	86	99.2	99.8	99.8
Average number of visits to prenatal clinics per woman	0.6	3.9	7.1	9.2	9.4
Outcome					
Maternal mortality rate per 100,000 deliveries	137	63	28	15	13
Cases of eclampsia per 100,000 deliveries		122	68	35	34
Perinatal mortality rate per 1,000 live births	51	26.3	20.9	20.3	18.5
Stillbirth rate per 1,000 live births	19	11.6	7.1	6.8	6.0
Early neonatal mortality rate per 1,000 live births	32	14.7	13.8	13.5	12.5

Source: Alena Heitlinger, *Reproduction, Medicine and the Socialist State* (London: Macmillan, 1987), 79.

children's well-being and of his counterpart Jean Piaget (1896–1980) in child development served these same interests by awakening women's interest in the scientific aspects of childrearing. The mass information system operating in private enterprise and the welfare state's services to the individual and family formed a context for each woman's reproductive life. The local community control of the eighteenth century had gradually given way to more intensive, centralized, and depersonalized monitoring.

The welfare state, like technological industry, depended on an educated citizenry. European men and women increased their average years of school attendance at state-run educational institutions after World War II. In the Soviet Union, urban women and girls aged ten and over had an average of 7.6 years of schooling in 1959 and 9 years in 1970. In 1970 and again in 1976, more employed urban women than men had had some secondary education. In the West, figures on women's participation in higher education fluctuated. In France in 1967, women constituted 44 percent of university students, but in West Germany they were little more than 25 percent. Moreover, twice as many German women as men gave up their studies before completion. In France, almost half of all women studied under faculties of letters—the French route into schoolteaching. Men, in contrast, went into science, engineering, and schools for national administration.[12] Indeed, the prestigious engineering schools only started admitting women in the 1980s. The complete post-war democratization of general education showed that people needed a minimum standard of knowledge to participate in modern society. The dominance of men in technological fields, however, showed that they were the ones getting the skills to run both state and economy. Initially educated together, young women and men took divergent paths when it came time for higher education, routes that consolidated gender difference in economic power.

The Quest for a Meaningful Culture in the Technological Age

After World War II, most women still built their lives as a complex series of encounters with the state, their jobs, and families. Public culture empowered them to individualized activism both inside the home and as citizens. For example, in the 1950s, French politicians tried to break the grip of male post-war alcoholism. "If women would take note of their power," one magazine stated, "they could aid in the development of a movement for sobriety."[13] In fact, many women felt a general responsibility for familial well-being and order. In family relations, wrote one West German department store worker in the 1980s, "I am always the one who has to nag others."[14] To this concern for familial well-being others added an interest in consumer goods, working in order to buy new wallpaper, appliances, or carpeting. The standard of consumption rose, and standards of domestic comfort did, too. In the 1970s in Bergen, Norway, a part-time worker and mother prided herself on her living room furniture, a year old and "still like it was new." Her work outside the home helped to buy the new furniture, and her household activities generated familial culture: "In this house it happens only twice a year that dinner is not ready when my husband comes home."[15] Late in the 1970s a bride in Budapest boasted of marrying for love, unlike her friends who married to be entitled to an apartment. Even though the state marriage official suggested she wear white as "more romantic," this young rebellious Hungarian refused and even kept her maiden name. She did, however, receive premarital counseling in birth control as part of government benefits.[16] As all these cases show, domestic culture had become more open to outside influences than ever before.

Some women developed post-war culture on a public level. In the first two decades after the war, certain questions nagged them, in particular, the general status of civilization and enlightenment values after the Nazi experience. Some searched for a new spirituality, others for a new philosophy, and still others considered the question of women's role and the treatment of women. Among the most prominent in this public quest was Simone de Beauvoir (1908–1986), an influential existentialist and a rebel against her Parisian family's middle-class values. Raised by a devout mother, de Beauvoir attended fashionable religious schools as a child. Her father practiced law in a desultory fashion and led the restless life usual for some men of his background. After the family's prosperity was ruined by World War I, Simone de Beauvoir and her younger

Simone de Beauvoir and Jean-Paul Sartre were premier intellectuals in postwar Europe. Her insight about the interrelationship between gender definitions of women and men and their interlocked nature influences theorists to the present day.

sister suddenly faced a new reality: unlike their mother, they would need some way to support themselves. Against her family's wishes, de Beauvoir chose the arduous road of higher education. While attending the Sorbonne, she fell in love with Jean-Paul Sartre (1906–1980), who was to become the most celebrated intellectual in France. Refusing to marry, they maintained an intense free union, though often separated by their early teaching careers and by other love affairs. Their intellectual lives developed in tandem, though Sartre was far more famous even after de Beauvoir's *The Second Sex* (1949) appeared.

The Second Sex discussed women in terms of existential theory, biology, Marxism, Freudianism, and the literary tradition. It was a work researched and written in two years, just after World War II. Earlier, de Beauvoir had produced several philosophical novels dealing with human relationships, the construction of a self through those relationships, and the fundamental question of twentieth-century European philosophy—the nature of being. De Beauvoir began with the existential premise of an absurd world, a world of nothingness. This premise rejected attempts to find the "essence" of human life; it also was motivated by a post-war appraisal of Fascism, the Holocaust, the dropping of the atomic bomb on Hiroshima and Nagasaki, and the Cold War. Instead of searching for "essence" or the "spirit" of being, one created existence through constant action. In addition, interaction with the objective world, including people, established a self. The process of creating the self, however, remained ongoing, constantly demanding reflection and analysis. Each action, reaction, and subsequent reflection on these actions counted toward existence. Simone de Beauvoir's four volumes of memoirs are the best evidence of existential philosophy in action; there, she reports her own self-creation through her relationships with Sartre and others.

The Second Sex, oddly enough, started out as a book about de Beauvoir. Setting out in the summer of 1946 on a new project, she "wanted to write about myself."[17] It became clear that to do so she would have to consider womanhood, something that had had little influence on her philosophy before. Therefore, de Beauvoir jettisoned the project about herself for a consideration of women, especially in the myths she felt had been constructed about them and that determined their situation. The book that was published in 1949 consisted of two volumes, some 1200 pages, and sold 20,000 copies almost immediately. Part of readers' fascination was de Beauvoir's connection with Sartre. In fact, it was rumored that Sartre had written the book, as it had been rumored that he had written de Beauvoir's earlier books. In spite of high sales, de Beauvoir was vilified by many for examining philosophically matters that these people believed were best left undiscussed: women's physiology, lesbianism, misogynous myths, and the creation of a female self. Men who freely give their opinions about women castigated de Beauvoir for daring to do so. Not having borne a child, she could know little, they claimed, of what womanhood was really like.

Simone de Beauvoir had produced a masterpiece, perhaps the best and most thorough book about women ever written. It began by pointing out that a man would never think of writing about the peculiarities of men or of defining what men were: "there is an absolute human type, the masculine. . . . He is the Subject, he is the Absolute—she is the Other."[18] Starting from this proposition, de Beauvoir wove her analysis. Each individual saw those with whom he or she came in contact as Other; but there also existed generalized Others—particularly, for white Christian males, de Beauvoir maintained, women, blacks, and Jews. For those seen as generalized others, the problem of life centered on creating a self and freedom to act in the face of an oppressive definition of being that was determined by dominant groups. For women, those imposed definitions—the situation of Otherness—involved aspects of female life found in "femininity" or the "Eternal Female." Women could easily lead lives based on externally produced definitions of femininity, but in so doing they surrendered their freedom. By living in cultural and economic dependence and thereby failing to create their own lives, they failed to reach beyond the givens of nature. Choosing to accept Otherness meant choosing "immanence" (or nature) instead of "transcendence" (or existence). De Beauvoir maintained that many women found it easier to surrender, for the feminine life had its attractions. The "independent woman," however, always chose the more difficult road of work, self-definition, and ongoing and vigorous interaction with the male Other.

In 1954 the sexually explicit *Story of O*, written by Pauline Réage (pen name of Dominique Audry), further examined the cultural choice of unfreedom and sexual slavery. The story shows how men and women assume master and slave roles and how they become dependent on one another as partners in a very unequal relationship. Once a photographer, the heroine has become dehumanized by the end of the story—an animal led willingly on a chain by her lover. Although both Réage and de Beauvoir saw that some women might find satisfaction in this kind of Otherness, they advocated an ongoing attempt at life, the very process of which constituted a "liberation." In fact, de Beauvoir would be criticized by feminists for minimizing the need for liberationist movements for women and for adopting what were called "male values," such as transcendence. De Beauvoir, however, eventually changed her mind about organized activism. Long after she had become a symbol and almost a cult figure, she gave her support and leadership to the new women's movement of the late 1960s.

In addition to de Beauvoir's questioning of traditional values, many people who had looked to the Soviet Union and to socialism to reform public culture and private life suffered an enormous shock. Accounts of deportation camps and Stalinist purges began at the end of the 1940s and increased in number right on into the 1960s and 1970s. The promised perfection of socialism now appeared unobtainable. News of Stalinist purges and camps was often met with disbelief. Some people attributed the reports to the passions of the Cold War and to the anti-Bolshevism that had existed in Europe since the Russian Revolution. Nonetheless, some evidence was incontrovertible. Margarete Buber-Neumann (b. 1901) was a Communist for more than two decades before World War II and the companion of a Communist representative in the German Reichstag, Heinz Neumann. Shortly after the war, she published an account of her experiences in both Soviet and Nazi camps. Escaping from Hitler's terrorism in the 1930s, the couple fled to Moscow, only to be arrested. Then Neumann disappeared; presumably he was executed. A year later, after trying to track him from prison to prison, Margarete Buber-Neumann found herself imprisoned. Her account dwells first on her anger and humiliation, as the trumped-up charges were followed by the horror of a judicial system based on lies and made-up confessions signed through trickery. Only secondarily did the terrifying conditions of the prisons and concentration camps come into play. In these camps, the common criminal held power over the other inmates, both officially and unofficially. Ruling with the sanction of the guards and robbing all the other inhabitants, the criminal had higher status because he or she had no unpatriotic or—in the case of Buber-Neumann—counterrevolutionary thoughts. The most despicable crimes in Soviet society grew from not having correct ideas. Similar stories of Soviet repression came from other sources, for example, Aleksandr Solzhenitsyn's *Gulag Archipelago* (1974–1976) and Eugenia Semyonov'na Ginzburg's *Journey into the Whirlwind*

(1967) and *With the Whirlwind* (1979). As the once important alternative of Russian socialism grew tarnished, cultural values were ripe for further exploration.

Artists' Portrayals of Modern Life

For most artists, the Nazi experience and post-war technology had finally buried the art of previous centuries. The entertaining novels and easy rhymes that had been loved by earlier generations were as outmoded, artists believed, as myths and epic poetry. Twentieth-century artists continued the kind of experimenting that had begun in the works of Proust and Woolf and further explored the relationship of art to modern life and to the individual. Just before World War II broke out, Nathalie Sarraute's *Tropismes* (1939) was published in France. It marked a new genre—neither poem nor novel nor short story. Sarraute presented short sketches based on human "movements," a term that indicated both emotions and gestures. As she explained in later writings about fiction, the novel as it had evolved during the eighteenth and nineteenth centuries belonged to a pre-psychological world. The individual's plight and the resolution of that plight had been the source of the novel's drama. In her own time, Sarraute had seen the belief in a collective unconscious dispel any notions of the autonomous individual. To illustrate this point, she used "sub-conversations," interior monologues, ambiguous narrators, and indefinite characters as a way of presenting twentieth-century conditions. Armed with unique wit and influenced by James Joyce and Marcel Proust, she, along with Alain Robbe-Grillet, Marguerite Duras, and others, wrote "new novels" in the post-war decades.

Austrian Ingeborg Bachmann (1926–1973), in contrast, focused on intense, individualistic experience. Her protagonists in such works as "The Thirtieth Year" and *Malvina* (1971) engaged in such intense thinking that the premises underlying the modern social world fell into question and all the ambiguities of the self came to the fore. In her unfinished novel *The Franza Case* (1978), Bachmann used the metaphor of disease to challenge the idea of the perfectible nature of being that was propounded by the rational tradition and espoused by technocrats. In England, Doris Lessing (b. 1919) undertook a psycholiterary quest in her novel *The Golden Notebook* (1978). Its heroine narrates the different aspects of her life—the psychic, the personal, the political, the womanly—in different notebooks. Reared in the British colony of Rhodesia, Lessing understood the fragile mental positioning of those outside the dominant power structures and culture. In her most celebrated work, she presented a woman's fractured psyche as she moves toward madness while struggling to recognize her different and minority status. Having been a Communist, Lessing became increasingly disillusioned not only with left-wing politics but with the drift of mass society in general. Her *Memoirs of a Survivor* (1974) provide a running commentary on a world gone mad outside the apartment of an old woman. To Lessing, the higher the technological level of a

Making Art from War in Austria

Ingeborg Bachmann (1926–1973) was an internationally known poet and playwright. Growing up during World War II, she contributed to the post-war literary rebirth, some of which involved turning war experiences into literature. The bleakness and inversion of wartime childhood appear in this passage from her short story, "Youth in an Austrian Town."

> The children get one more surprise: the next lot of Christmas trees really do fall from heaven. On fire. And the unexpected present which the children receive is more free time. During air raid alarms they are allowed to leave their exercise books lying on their desks and go down into the shelter. Later they are allowed to save up sweets for the wounded, to knit socks and weave raffia baskets for the men who are fighting on land, on sea, and in the air. And to write a composition commemorating those under the earth and on the ground. And later still they are allowed to dig trenches between the cemetery and the airfield, which is already paying tribute to the cemetery. They are allowed to forget their Latin and learn to distinguish between the sounds of the engines in the sky. They don't have to wash so often any more; no one bothers about their fingernails now. The children mend their skipping ropes, because there are no longer any new ones, and they talk about time fuses and landmines. The children play "Let the robbers march through" among the ruins, but often they merely sit there staring into space, and they no longer hear when people call out "Children" to them. There are enough bits of rubble for hopscotch, but the children shiver because they are soaking wet and cold.
>
> Children die, and the children learn the dates of the Seven Years War and the Thirty Years War, and they wouldn't care if they mixed up all the hostilities, the pretext and the cause, for the exact differentiation of which they could get good marks in history.
>
> They bury the dog Ali and then his owners. The time of veiled hints is past. People speak in their presence of shooting in the back of the neck, of hanging, liquidating, blowing up, and what they don't hear and see they smell, as they smell the dead of St. Ruprecht, who cannot be dug out because they have been buried under the movie theatre into which they slipped surreptitiously to see "Romance in a Minor Key." Juveniles were not admitted, but then they were admitted to the

great dying and murdering which took place a few days later and every day after that.

There is no more light in the house. No glass in the windows. No door on hinges. Nobody stirs and nobody rises.

Source: Ingeborg Bachmann, "Youth in an Austrian Town," in *The Thirtieth Year,* Michael Bullock, trans. (New York: Knopf, 1964), pp. 14–15.

---

society, the more primitive its emotions seemed to become. After that novel, much of Lessing's fiction featured a kind of science fiction utopianism that many critics called ultra-conservative.

Right after the war, film directors found themselves with few resources but full of ideas about portraying modern experience. A new kind of realism began to characterize film-making in such works as Roberto Rossellini's *Rome Open City* (1945) and Vittorio de Sica's *Bicycle Thief* (1948). Shot out of doors and without complicated or expensive sets, these films portrayed the realities of poverty and suffering that most Europeans were experiencing. Liliana Cavani (b. 1936) later continued the most political aspects of this post-war tendency in such works as *Galileo* (1968), *The Cannibals* (1969), and the *Night Porter* (1974). Fearful of the rebirth of Fascism, she also made documentaries about the Third Reich and about Marshall Petain, head of the French government under the Germans. The themes of state power, modernism, technology, and brutalization of innocents dominated her films; the perennial interplay of sadism and masochism in the human personality and society was the theme of the brilliant *The Night Porter.* Another Italian, Lina Wertmuller (b. 1928), had a good deal of commercial success with her caricatures of modern people. In such works as *Seven Beauties* (1976) and *Swept Away* (1974), she showed how grotesque and cruel modern life could be. In so doing, she often incorporated stereotypes of women into her films. Czech filmmaker Vera Chytilova (b. 1929) also based her work on excess, surrealism, and role inversions. *Something Else* (1963) depicted a woman making her way to the top of the sports world, whereas *Daisies* (1966) showed two women involved in lives of lechery and perversion. *Fruit of Paradise* (1969) portrayed a lush, mythic world distant from all that was modern; this film was so radical in form that Chytilova had difficulty getting financing for her subsequent films. Some of these successful directors objected to being called "women filmmakers." Cavani, for example, announced that such a title resembled that of "paraplegic painter."[19]

Some other directors and screenwriters during the post-war era explicitly aimed at challenging what they began to describe as the "male gaze," which had heretofore determined the movements of the camera, the portrayal of women, and even the way spectators viewed films. Some poked fun at male behavior, as Chytilova did in *Daisies;* others tried to reshape the whole internal movement of the film. For instance, Belgian Chantal Akerman commented on her *Jeanne Dielman* (1975): "I give space to things which were never, almost never, shown in that way, like the daily gestures of a woman. They are the lowest in the hierarchy of film images. A kiss or a car crash come higher."[20] *Jeanne Dielman* minutely depicted the daily life of a supposedly ordinary mother at home. However, the woman routinely alternated her domestic routine with prostitution, and the film is dramatically punctuated by her murder of a client. This film says that beyond the social welfare bureaucracy and its norms, life is different. Helke Sander and Laura Mulvey—theorists and film-makers—worked toward the same kind of avant-garde feminist end. However, Marguerite Duras gained the most fame for such endeavors, both in writing and in cinema, and she did so with an explicit acknowledgment of feminist possibilities in what she was doing. The screenplay for *Hiroshima, Mon Amour* (1959) displays her characteristic use of voices and intimate conversation to develop a heightened awareness. Duras often limited herself to two or three characters; she uses a couple in her novel *The Square* (1955) and another in *The Truck* (1977), a film featuring her and Gerard Depardieu. Not highly plotted and hyperemotional, her films and novels sometimes aim at finding a character's own "original voice, the feminine one that she possessed before society conditioned her."[21] Duras, like other writers and artists, partook in a conscious reawakening of pro-women inclinations and a rethinking of modern life that ultimately contributed to a rebirth of feminist organization.

The New Age of Reform

In 1956, a London journalist wrote in *The Evening Standard* about feminism: "Today, the spirit of the old pioneers is so dead it seems a miracle it ever existed."[22] This was the conventional wisdom at the time. However, many goals of the supposedly dead women's movement were achieved during these years. For example, in Great Britain, legislation during the first fifteen years after the war mandated equal pay for equal work in government posts. In Italy, in the 1950s, the government, spurred by the Union of Italian Women that developed out of the Resistance, passed a series of programs to move toward equality in the workplace, including a prohibition against firing women just because they got married. The ongoing women's lobbying that produced such legislation was accompanied by more dramatic movements aiming at a variety of reforms, even in the face of the Cold War. The new movements for reform drew their real inspiration from civil rights movements and nationalist movements in overseas colonies, which awakened millions to modern brutality. Democratic society, while proclaiming its virtue for defeating Hitler and for defending the cause of democracy in the face of communism, still contained violence and racism. Europeans followed civil rights activism in the United States and the often bloody process of decolonization in Africa and Asia. Frantz Fanon's *The Wretched of the Earth* (1961) called for violently throwing off oppressors and shaped the mind-set of many who worked for reforms in the 1960s. But European women had been active in reform movements beginning in the early 1950s with the "Ban the Bomb" movement and international peace activities. They made major protest demonstrations in London against the possible outbreak of nuclear war but also against the dangers posed by the radioactive fall-out from nuclear testing. The series of colonial wars in Algeria and elsewhere, the invasion of Hungary by the Soviet Union in 1956, and finally the eruption of the Vietnamese War out of the ongoing battle for independence in Southeast Asia all kept the cause of reform and peace activism alive.

A movement composed of young people, especially those in universities, spread throughout Europe and the United States during the 1960s. French writer Françoise Sagan (b. 1935) had given premonition of this result in her novel *Bonjour Tristesse (Hello, Sorrow)*, (1954), which was about adolescent rebellion against the older generation. Frustrated and angered by the technological society growing around them, young activists struck out at conditions of education, at middle-class values, at war and colonialism, and at the general political climate. Women threw themselves into these movements and took part in mass protests, public discussions, and university demonstrations. Even while flexing their political muscle, women became aware of gender discrepancies within the political groups of the left. That is, men made most of the political pronouncements; women made few. In fact, women were often expected not to be political comrades but to serve as women—doing cleanup, providing refreshments, and performing clerical and secretarial work for the many groups that developed. In Europe, as in the United States, the inequities of women's situation in groups championing equitable and participatory societies became apparent. By the end of the 1960s, many women had split off from their male comrades, founding feminist groups to take issue with the treatment of women everywhere. These groups multiplied nationally and internationally, with some of the first international contacts being made at the first meeting of the new women's movement in Oxford, Great Britain, in the summer of 1970. By the late 1970s, over 5,000 Trotskyite women from twenty countries—to name only one group—had met in Paris; others from around the world met annually in summer camps to discuss feminist strategy and theory. Causes within the women's movement multiplied and so did women's points of view. Furthermore, within each country, different women had their own

---

Speaking Bitterness in Portugal

Part of the women's movement involved testifying, or consciousness-raising. Some portion of this phenomenon sprang from the revolutionary idea of "speaking bitterness" as a way of building commitment to change. Also, speaking about bad conditions transgressed the age-old belief that things happening between men and women were "private" and therefore inviolable. Instead of acquiescing to the fixture of middle-class social order—embodied in the Napoleonic Code and its many copies—European women spoke out. In Portugal, Maria Isabel Barreno, Maria Teresa Horta, and Maria Velho Da Costa produced an outspoken work, full of accounts of brutality and hardship as well as of love and erotic experience. The government tried them on charges of obscenity, though after two years their trial suddenly ended. This excerpt from *The Three Marias: New Portuguese Letters* is part of a fictitious monologue addressed by a maid to her mistress.

My mother was right when she kept saying "Maria, be careful, you never know how a marriage is going to turn out, sometimes it's better for a woman to be an old maid. . . ." But how was I to know that my Antonio was going to come home from Africa a changed man, he used to be such a fine person, if you'll pardon my immodesty, Senhora, so good-hearted, but ever since he came back from the wars everything is all mixed up in his head and I'm frightened of him, he shouts night and day, he beats me till his arms get tired and I'm lying there stretched out on the floor. That was when I began having these attacks, one day he came home drunk and I called him a pig. "You pig," I said, begging your pardon, Senhora, "where's the money for us to eat?" And he said: "Shut your mouth you bitch or I'll kill you," and then I started screaming and he lost his head and started to beat me with all his might, and the blows rained down on me from head to foot till I started gasping and spittle came dribbling out of my mouth as I lay there writhing on the floor and he kept beating me and beating me, and the only reason he didn't kill me was because my little boy, the poor thing, flung himself on top of me as I lay there and clung to my body and when he saw the poor child clinging to me like that, so frail and so terrified, he was ashamed of himself and went away, leaving me lying there unconscious, all alone with my little boy and then he came back a month later to beg my pardon, and apologized so politely that I forgave him, what else could I do, Senhora, everybody has his weak points and then after that everything went along the same as before at first but then he started drinking again and keeping other women and not working and I had to go on doing housework by day, and thank the Good Lord I always have places to work, the hardest part though is my little boy, they won't take him at the day nursery because he's always ailing.

Source: Maria Isabel Barreno, Maria Teresa Horta, and Maria Velho Da Costa, *The Three Marias: New Portuguese Letters*, Helen R. Lane, trans. (New York: Bantam, 1974), pp. 179–180.

favorite programs and, in some cases, suspicions about the thrust of other groups.

French Feminism

The rebirth of feminism in France had as its background the towering theoretical work of Simone de Beauvoir as well as the student movement. In the years since World War II, contraception, in particular the 1920 law abrogating women's reproductive rights, had come to the fore as a major issue through the work of Dr. Marie-Andrée Weill-Hallé, who founded the Mouvement Française pour le Planning Familial (French Movement for Family Planning) in 1956. Also part of the presidential campaign of François Mitterand in 1965, the issue persisted thereafter until the sale of contraceptives was legalized in 1967. Sociologists Andrée Michel, P.-H. Chombart de Lauwes, and Géneviève Texler wrote massive studies of women in contemporary society. When students at the Sorbonne erupted into revolutionary activity in 1968, the French women participating soon saw that their status in the student movement depended on the position of men with whom they associated. They also saw that their value depended on doing secretarial and household-type chores. In 1968 and 1969, they began forming women's groups of diverse tendencies—Marxists, Maoists, housewives, those interested in psychoanalysis, workers—in a variety of locales throughout the country, although Paris had the most groups.

Certain dramatic incidents marked the first years of the new feminist activism. In the summer of 1970, men yelled at a "women-only" conference: "Power lies at the tip of the phallus." Soon after, authors Christiane Rochefort, Monique Wittig, and others shocked many in French society by placing a wreath at that sacred spot the Tomb of the Unknown Soldier—in honor, they maintained, of someone even more unknown: the Unknown Soldier's Wife. Soon, women's groups were stunning the respectable middle classes even more than students had done by publishing newspapers such as *Le Torchon Brulé* (*The Burning Rag*). Feminists used shock tactics to break up a complacent conference on women sponsored by the fashion magazine *Elle*. To mock *Elle*'s questionnaire, which had predictable questions about women's role and happiness, feminists wrote their own. A sample question was "When a man talks to a woman, should he address (a) her tits and her legs? (b) her arse and her tits? (c) just her arse?"[23] Incident followed incident in a concerted attack on French culture. Like women in other countries, French feminists had decided that political questions had a basis in cultural portrayals. The situation that women found themselves in would only be rectified if the cultural fabric were changed.

Although there was some underlying consensus on that point, profound differences existed among women's groups. Arising at a time of crisis and change in manufacturing, women's sections in labor unions and in socialist and communist parties were intricately involved in the struggle for worker participation in management and in the protection of workers in threatened industries. Such women were committed to their alliance with men, but at the same time they questioned the gender-based divisions of labor and sexual attitudes in the workplace. In the post-war period, the CGT (Confédération Générale du Travail), the major union of French workers, began publishing a women's periodical *Antoinette*, diligently recruiting women members for labor unions, and agitating on behalf of maternity leaves and child care for workers. With the rise of feminism, women in labor unions intensified their efforts in the belief that they were the best representatives of women's interests—other women being "petty bourgeois." The focus of union women—and ultimately of many unions—was on the double oppression of working women by patriarchal and capitalist interests, which they saw as a single entity. In fact, French union women were so persuasive that eventually the unions they belonged to agitated not only against bosses but against women's oppression within the working-class household. It was a great achievement for these women to have forced unions to acknowledge a women's cause at the center of union identity and to turn toward personal issues. By the late 1970s, some union leaders in France moved beyond traditional economic interests to announce that the working class should "strike over the issue of abortion."[24]

Other women's groups arose within intellectual and professional milieus. Most prominent among them was Politique et Psychanalyse (known as Psych et Po), which relied on the leadership of psychoanalyst Antoinette Fouque. Unionism had been transformed by new efforts of women, and feminism would also be transformed by the insights of such radical groups. Since World War I, crucial changes in European thought, including Freudianism and the end of liberal consensus and optimism, posed a challenge to everything feminism had originally taken as its base. Psych et Po, along with other groups such as Feministes Revolutionnaires (Revolutionary Feminists), incorporated, almost in a single stroke, twentieth-century philosophic advances. Psych et Po rejected both feminism and women's past accomplishments and said that they were but manifestations of masculinity. The theories of Jacques Lacan (1901–1981) became the starting point for Psych et Po's ventures into analyses based on language and writing. Lacan maintained that each human psyche was simultaneously controlled by the power of the father and the structures of language. Language was a system dominated by male, or, in Lacan's terms, phallic, power. That is, as a child one learned the "non" (the prohibitions) of male laws simultaneously with the "nom" (or name) of the father (the pronunciation of these two words in French is virtually the same). Such analyses based on word play, puns, homonyms, and so on became standard fare for Psych et Po and its sympathizers.

For writers influenced by Psych et Po or by contemporary French philosophy, the written word became the battleground for women. Because these writers believed the individual to abide in language, they saw revolutionary action taking a written form. However, the sense that they could escape from the father's language separated many of these women from Lacan's theories. Influenced as well by Jacques Derrida's (b. 1930) theory of "deconstruction," they believed in exposing the myth that written language corresponded easily with objective reality. Instead of being centered or focused, deconstructive analysis moved to the "margins" of a text to uncover, pull apart, and demonstrate what lay around the perimeters of any discourse. Rather than looking for sameness and uniformity, deconstructionists searched for gaps and differences. What this meant to women writers was nothing less than a revelation. Intellectuals such as Lucy Irigaray (b. 1939) and Hélène Cixous (b. 1937)—the most celebrated among outstanding pioneering writers—in the 1970s began "writing the body"—that is, writing from a sense of female difference located in woman's body and its unique sexuality. Male writing and male existence were centered on the phallus; female writing would be as diffuse as female sexuality itself. The very posing of an opposition in language would in and of itself unseat male dominance. "Let the priests tremble," wrote Hélène Cixous in a summarizing wordplay on "sex" and "text," "we're going to show them our sexts."[25]

West German Movements

In 1968, film-maker Helke Sander (b. 1937) made a rousing speech on behalf of women before a convention of the German students' movement. A woman in the audience then proceeded to hurl tomatoes at the male steering committee. That moment gave the women's movement in West Germany its symbol of defiance—tomatoes. Like the movement in other countries, the West German one created a network of countercultural institutions such as bookstores, cafés, refuges, publishing houses, small newspapers, and mass circulation magazines, for example, *Courage* and *Emma*. Best-sellers appeared, such as Verena Stefan's *Shedding* (1975), which sold over 100,000 copies in four years. This and subsequent commercial successes convinced a few publishers to print women's writings, among them many translations of works written by those in the women's movement in the United States. For the most part, however, feminist activism in Germany remained even less mainstream than elsewhere. In the first place, there was no strong middle-class feminist organization comparable to the National Organization of Women (NOW) in the United States. In a country aiming for respectability after the Nazi experience, women in the professions and at home hesitated to take any step indicating political difference. Also, the shadow of the Cold War made West German feminists eager to distinguish themselves from their socialist and Marxist feminist tradition despite its many alternatives and historic strength. In fact, being a feminist-socialist was likened to having a man inhabiting one's self.

So the isolated movement set out in 1971 by convening a national conference and drawing up an abortion petition. These concrete acts led to the organization of women on a local level, but drew little positive response from the government. The abortion drive in fact ended in yet another infamous law, article A18, by which a woman's right to an abortion was denied unless psychological or medical reasons made it imperative. In addition, the 1970s witnessed persecution of women and feminists as officialdom reacted to the terrorist violence then taking place throughout Europe. Police raided offices of abortion groups that offered lists of doctors willing to overlook the provisions of article A18, and officials denied jobs to those appearing politically suspicious—a broad and vague category—under the provisions of a series of repressive laws. Without being directly named, feminists, socialists, and lesbians were singled out as being among the politically suspicious.

Feminist practice consequently developed in a direction determined by the harshness of the West German political situation. Along with doing local organizing, feminists devoted themselves to theoretical investigations of women's experiences, the inequities they faced, and their work lives. Because of the historical interest of Germans in motherhood and service to the state, theorists focused in their analyses on the work of women as mothers and housewives. In 1976, Ulrike Prokop's *Weiblicher Lebenszusammenhang* (*The Context of Women's Daily Life*) appeared. In it, Prokop declared that housework is a form of productive labor on which all social relations rested. Although it is unpaid, as feminists had pointed out for more than a century, housework and mother's work give the laboring human a psychic context so that he or she may produce in the social world. Thus, Prokop asserted, it is important not "to reduce production to 'functions,' that is, not merely cite isolated aspects of women's work, but understand the power to create everyday life in the housewifely role."[26] At the same time, she saw women's isolated household activities as an "underdevelopment" of their productive forces similar to the oppression of the worker in the factory through his relationship to the "private" industrialist. Focusing on women's psychic labor added a new ingredient to feminist analysis. However, this type of analysis received a good deal of criticism from those who maintained that women's actual productive activity in the home was masked precisely by its ideology that stressed the love behind women's work instead of the muscle power. Such activists supported a campaign in favor of wages for housework.

Still other West German feminists focused on motherhood and called for its release from the coercive context in which it operated. These feminists maintained that women had never really known what motherhood is because it had been defined by patriarchal society. Like the Psych et Po group in France, another group of West German feminists focused on the question of language. Influenced by both German philosophy and the work of French feminists, writers such as Verena Stefan investigated the male power structure embedded in language. They emphasized women's writing as a revolutionary and feminist practice. Others disagreed, maintaining, as did the editors of the feminist journal *Die schwarze Botin* (*The Black Messenger*), that this kind of linguistic analysis lacked a practical purpose. Instead of righting wrongs, so critics said, the analyses represented a sterile kind of exercise that dragged the entire movement down.

Some women in West Germany branched out into politics at large. Ulrike Meinhof (1934–1976), leader of the Baader-Meinhof terrorist group, had first become politically oriented while attending a university in the 1950s. The fact that her parents had opposed Nazism from the beginning gave Meinhof a different background from that of many German activists. In 1961, Meinhof married Klaus Rainer Röhl and edited the pro-communist journal *Konkret* with him. Financed by the East Germans, the paper nonetheless took a critical view of Communist Party politics and ultimately broke with its sponsors. Röhl then began using sexy cover stories to sell the paper, and ultimately he and Meinhof parted company. In the meantime, Meinhof had started putting feminist articles in *Konkret* and covered feminist meetings. It was she whose writings made tomatoes the symbol of West Germany's feminist movement. Pointing to the enormous number of women in the workforce, she asked where the day-care centers and the part-time job opportunities were. In 1970, Meinhof joined forces with Andreas Baader to create the Red Army Faction, a group that spread terror in the form of murder, arson, and robbery throughout West Germany. This group had a lot of internal conflict over the question of women's role. Some women activists turned to terrorism during the 1970s, but the terrorist movement itself was hypermasculine, even sexist, in its orientation. For women, terrorism was a way of behaving like men; for men, it was a way of using more force and power in a world that had robbed them of male definition. Caught in 1972, Meinhof was found hanged in her prison cell, officially a suicide but not definitely so. Some called the step from feminism to terrorism obvious, whereas others felt Meinhof had parted company from the goals of most feminist movements, which were pacifist. In any event, the government made her activities an excuse for rounding up and harming the careers of "suspicious" people, including many women.

From a different place on the political spectrum, women entered the Green Party, a grass-roots political movement concerned with the environment and aimed at creating an ecological society. From the late 1970s, the Greens flourished because of the usual office work done by women and, some said, because of the sexual excitement their mere presence in the party caused. In contrast, many felt the party represented a "women's perspective" and their "closeness to nature." One activist wrote: "In pregnancy and childbirth the continuity between human beings and nature is fully realized. Because women are raised for these social functions they are kept away from all technical matters from an early age."[27] Because the party emphasized nature and employed the same political tactics as the feminist movement, it seemed that it should also have supported women's issues and endorsed their efforts to participate at the highest levels if only for consistency. Yet that did not happen. Instead, women complained about remaining in menial posts in the party, and when women's health issues, such as abortion, came to public debate, the male leadership declared them too controversial. Moreover, women faulted the party for failing to connect the destruction of nature with male supremacy and patriarchal power. In addition, they charged the party leadership with relegating women's issues to a position of minor importance by saying—in something like an echo of male socialists—that women's wrongs, like many other problems, would resolve themselves immediately with the triumph of ecology. Women in the Green Party discovered that movements interesting to them needed remaking to eliminate gender stereotypes within party organization and programs. Many in West Germany continued to interest themselves in reshaping the ecology party and, like women in Great Britain, agitated against atomic warfare and nuclear power in particular.

Italian Feminism

When the new feminist movment began in Italy in 1968, the Union of Italian Women had been active for more than two decades. Originally connected with the Italian Communist Party, the group had shown a good deal of independence in organizing women. From the beginning, prominent members of the Communist Party who had been luminaries in the Resistance, for example, Camilla Ravera (1889–1988), praised Soviet egalitarianism where women were concerned. Yet slowly both the party and the Union had become disillusioned with Soviet-style politics. Meanwhile, the Italian situation for women was one of the most repressive in Europe. Not only did women work extensively in sweated trades, but virtually no modern legislation existed on their behalf. The proclamation of equal rights in 1945 meant little. Thus, many feminist groups sprang up alongside radical student ones. Announcing their determination, hundreds marched on International Women's Day in 1968, carrying a revised leftist slogan: "There is no revolution without liberation of women. There is no liberation of women without revolution."

The major gains made by these Italian women involved political reforms, beginning with the campaign to allow divorce, which succeeded in 1970, and including a drive for economic and reproductive rights. Around these issues developed the Women's Liberation Movement in Rome, the Feminine Revolt in Milan, and other groups employing a variety of tactics, such as women chaining themselves to the gates of the Vatican. In response to mass demonstrations and heavy lobbying, the government made birth control information legal in 1972. After that, women began an intense drive to obtain abortions in Italian hospitals. They achieved this goal in 1978, as the sequel to a program of legislation on equal rights in the family and in careers. Several times right-wing forces allied with the conservative Christian Democrats tried to repeal these decrees, but the educational campaigns of the mainstream feminists proved too effective. Tens of thousands of women demonstrated on behalf of these rights, and voters gave both divorce and abortion huge margins at the polls. These legislative victories involved a great deal of lobbying of male politicians, even those who professed to support women's causes. Although Italian feminists seemed united in these efforts, there was enormous theoretical and political variety among the activists.

The Catholic Church had long had enormous spiritual and ideological power over the terms for women's existence in Italy. Long after other countries had moved toward secular policies, Italy relied on church doctrines to set its own laws. Divorce and birth control were banned for religious reasons, and the power of the father in the family rested on ecclesiastical interpretations of the Bible. However under the leadership of Pope John XXIII from 1958 to 1963, a new spirit entered the Catholic Church. This pope specifically advo-

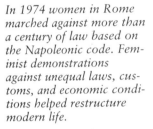

*In 1974 women in Rome
marched against more than
a century of law based on
the Napoleonic code. Fem-
inist demonstrations
against unequal laws, customs, and economic condi-
tions helped restructure
modern life.*

cated an awareness of the spirituality of the people and favored giving women
both public and private rights. The message influenced lay Catholic groups as
well as the clergy. When feminism became prominent in Italy in the late 1960s,
the many Catholic feminists based their activism precisely on this kind of invitation to popular Catholicism and to change. In particular, they pointed out
that the early Church had not been based on patriarchy as the modern Church
was. The early Church had concerned itself with the well-being of all its members. Such concern, in practice, the new Catholics argued, involved standing
by women who had to have abortions, saying "no" to backroom practitioners,
and working for a better society in which people would want to have children.
The most influential book in connecting women with a revitalized faith was
Franca Long and Rita Pierro's *The Other Half of the Church: To Be Feminist
and Christian* (1981). Another work, Roberta Fossati's *And God Created
Women* (1977), pointed out that all the ideas about women's uncleanliness and
sensuousness and other misogynist ideas had developed after the early days of
the Church. Fossati and the feminist nun Adriana Zarri, along with other
Catholic activists, had devoted their studies to this kind of unraveling of
Church history after a 1975 conference in Assisi. The springboard for con-

cerned Catholic feminist efforts in Italy, this conference invoked the life of Francis of Assisi, his spirit of revolt and concern for the poor. From this point on, Catholic feminists, meeting in many different groups around the country, worked toward revolutionizing the position of women and fundamentally restructuring the shape of organized Catholicism.

While some feminists pursued an ongoing and sometimes satisfying dialogue with Church officials, other Italian feminists displayed an extreme diversity. Because of the Resistance heritage and communist orientation of many members, debate within the Union of Italian Women was charged with a sense of history but also with a vision of women's future. Before long, this large and influential group split from the Italian Communist Party to pursue more focused policies and to create a more democratic organization. The issue of lesbianism came to the fore in feminist circles in Italy later than in other countries, that is, not until the early 1980s. Although startling at first to many Italian women, lesbian sexuality drew wide attention and support from almost every branch of the movement. All over the world, the lesbian cause reshaped the movement by showing how central the control of sexuality was to male power. In addition, lesbians made feminists aware of the sexual arena in general as site of differentiation, pleasures, and dangers that needed addressing.

On another front, some very powerful and pointed activism occurred in Sicily and Naples in the 1970s and 1980s, where thousands of women generated a concerted attack on the Mafia. Women in southern Italy faced problems specific to that region. Economic underdevelopment accentuated poverty, and southern culture and control by the Mafia particularly affected women. Addressing peasant women, Senator Simona Mafai (b. 1928) had taken up the economic issue early in her career: "First one must have running water in the house, then one can think of higher things."[28] Because many men had left the region to work in industry in the north or in other countries with labor shortages, women were left by themselves to deal with underdevelopment and poverty. At the same time codes enforced by the Mafia kept them in their place. For activist women, Mafia violence was an extreme, but not unusual, form of male activity. Using the threat of violence, men not only restrained women, but controlled their sexuality and their economic activity. Women in Naples held rallies protesting Mafia control of the system by which they earned money doing piecework at home and the extreme exploitation that control engendered. Throughout the south, women rallied at every instance of Mafia atrocity. They opposed, they said, all such expressions of *machismo*—the term used to characterize Latin men's demonstrative sense of superiority. The Mafia took revenge by subjecting many women to beatings, threats, and other retributions. This struggle in Naples seemed to bear out the famous and early analysis of Mariarosa Dalla Costa, *Potere femminile e souversione sociale* (*Feminine Power and the Subversion of the Community*, 1972), which maintained that housework formed the core of women's exploitation. For this reason, Dalla Costa said, the uprising of women around domestic exploitation was what would bring down the male-dominated system. Though this kind of analysis resembled others demanding pay for housework, in fact, it grew out of a situation indigenous to Italy, where women did much work for pay in the home.

Socialist Feminism in Eastern Europe

Women living in communist countries have the full legal protection of their governments and the explicit commitment of leaders to sexual equality. Employment figures allow officials to point with pride at the strides women have made. Also, in such countries, which are theoretically worker-states, no place exists for movements other than those endorsed or specifically sponsored by the government. When many Eastern European countries became socialistic in the late 1940s, their women's movements ended. Therefore, Eastern Europe has no groups, centers, or other organizations designed to advocate or reform women's situation. Westerners point to the obvious "double burden" of socialist women, who work full-time and also do the full complement of household chores. In fact, socialist women spend even more time at housework because of the time in lines to obtain commodities. These states have not developed the consumer side of their economies, and women must deal with shortages and distributional inefficiency in trying to purchase even everyday necessities. Defenders of the system maintain that the concept of the double burden is a Western one: socialist women don't think in terms of measuring every minute they contribute to the family or to their work; they draw their entire self-definition from work experiences and from the sociability of work. As one researcher notes, for women in East Germany "it is the social-centered aspect of the personality that is clearly given primary significance."[29] At the same time, women across Eastern Europe have in fact manifested discontent—a discontent to which policy-makers have given some heed. State-run journals for workers or peasants invite letters outlining specific problems at work, in housing management, and in social services. Even though the concept of individual rights is foreign, given the socialized nature of work, general grievances have arisen about the functioning of socialist systems and in particular about the behavior of male comrades toward female ones. Eastern European governments have reacted to such critics in varied ways, from censure and imprisonment of critics to acceptance and demonstrations of concern.

The fall of 1979 saw the appearance of the daring *Almanach: Women and Russia*, a journal designed to deal with the problems of women in the Soviet Union. Among the editors were Yuliaya Voznesenskaya, a poet; Tat'yana Goricheva, a philosopher; and Tat'yana Mamonova, a writer and former translator. The first issue circulated as only ten copies, but articles began coming in from many quarters. These ranged from descriptive essays about grandmothers to more accusatory ones about conditions in the Soviet Union. Women compared their experiences to those one had in prison camps; they revealed the abominable conditions of childbirth in a country that purported to revere the mother. Certain features distinguished this small, grass-roots publication from Western women's journals: "If needs be, the women from our journal will come and see you and give whatever help they can."[30] Although promising such personal attention seemed to put a limit on what might be accomplished, the *Almanach* writers did have wider ambitions. Not only was the relation of male to female an issue for these writers, so was the entire operation of the Soviet state a matter that concerned them. The state treated women badly and in so doing manifested a pervasive sexism. In addition, sexism and bad treatment pointed to a failure to meet the Soviet Union's aspirations to be a state fully representative of its citizens. In making such charges, *Almanach* seemed to be reviving the dissident movement that had started in the 1960s, during the so-called thaw that developed after the death of Stalin. Even though the *Almanach* writers accused those dissidents of caring nothing for women's issues, they shared a common breadth of purpose with them: "We believe that it is possible to democratize the country,"[31] wrote Mamonova later from exile. As the KGB interrogated one after another of the editors, a split developed among the group. Some of them split off to form a Christian feminist group, among them Goricheva, Voznesenskaya, and Natalya Malakhovskaya. They focused their efforts on reviving devotion to the Virgin Mary as a symbol of women's power. Although the Russian Orthodox Church offered no support of feminist leadership (rather the contrary), it had long offered a place from which dissidents could launch opposition programs. The split may have weakened the group somewhat, but the secret police finished it off. Eventually four of the original members went into exile in the West to continue publishing about Soviet women; others went to prison, to camps, and to mental hospitals.

Another center of socialist feminism appeared among writers in East Germany. Not overtly critical of socialism, many of these authors in fact praised it and made slighting remarks about the individualism and bourgeois mentality of Westerners. These writers did, however, mark out inconsistencies between theory and practice, between East German laws and the day-to-day treatment of women by their male comrades The most famous of these explorations was a collection of interviews with East German women done by Maxie Wander (1953–1977). In compiling *Guten Morgen, du Schöne* (*Good Morning, Beautiful*, 1978), Wander interviewed dozens of women from young waitresses to artists and bureaucrats. She wove these testimonies together to create a powerful work revealing the daily lives and daily observations of typical socialist women. A young waitress described her unsatisfactory, but continuous relationships with men. Whenever they planned together, she explained, the plans always reflected the man's aspirations, not her own: "Where do *I* fit in in all these stories? What's *mine*, anyway?"[32] Others expressed the satisfaction they achieved from work, whereas still more dreamed of different work in the future. The emphasis was on dreams, on hopes for better relationships, and often on the desire to see socialism become more fully realized, especially where women were concerned.

Irmtraud Morgner (b. 1933) produced fantasy after fantasy, often written in a light or ironic style. In "The Turnip Festival," she portrayed a collective farm manager who was turned into a woman and gained an appreciation of his lowly workers' wit and wisdom. In the fantastic "The Duel," a streetcar conductor manages to buy herself a motor scooter—precisely the deluxe model she wanted—after much threatening, outsmarting, and fooling of the manager of the store. The antics of the heroine recall the disruption that women can make in public with carnivalesque behavior. Although the heroine got away with such behavior for a while, ultimately she ran up against the authorities who reproved her for her wild ways. In the end, however, she returned to the scooter store, stood before the manager, and "laughed him to death."[33] Critique and frivolity intertwined in Morgner's stories and in other women's writings in the German Democratic Republic.

The innovative genius of Christa Wolf (b. 1929), editor and author, presided over this renaissance in literature in East Germany. Wolf's first works made her famous, but incurred official displeasure. Ostensibly her novels dealt with the plight of Germans, specifically East Germans. *A Model Childhood* (1976) chronicled childhood under Nazism, whereas *Divided Heaven* (1963) described a woman's sacrifice of a lover in West Germany for the possibilities the socialist state offered for individual fulfillment. *The Quest for Christa T.* (1966) continued the theme of self-realization. Annoyed by this bourgeois theme, the East German government forbade its publication temporarily and then heartily criticized it thereafter. This novel, Wolf's masterpiece, centered on a young woman, unusual for her time and setting because she rejected the official commitment to facts and to reason. Instead she had imagination, pondered situations, and took emotional pleasure in relationships. She was odd, a woman doctor analyzed, because she believed "everything depends on how you look at it," and would "disregard the objective facts."[34] Christa T. accommodated herself to the reasoning about her, but nonetheless continued her quest into subjectivity.

Wolf produced collections of stories in the 1970s, many of them focused on the theme of finding perfection or utopia—also a theme in *Christa T.* Wolf became a leader not only in writing feminist fiction, but also in raising women's issues through her own statements and her endorsements of the work of other women writers. In fact, Wolf directed the attention of socialists to the women's movement in capitalist countries. Although not sympathetic to capitalism, she did admire the cohesiveness at the grass-roots of feminism and programs that attacked problems at their base without the help of the state. "I cannot believe," she wrote, "that we in the GDR have nothing to learn from this."[35] Finally, Wolf also produced fantastic stories, for example, about sex transformations. Like other East German women, she stressed complementing the materialist analyses of socialist life with the fanciful. Constantly a controversial figure, Wolf raised difficult questions, but always within socialist context.

Toward the Future

By 1980, the women's movement in Europe had transformed itself. The attack on male privilege was as central to the cause as it had been a century earlier. Union women struck, took over factories, and demonstrated in the streets in an effort to right economic imbalance and develop meaningful work lives. Women ran for public offices and some succeeded. Motivating the quest for office in many cases was the long-standing belief that only by political participation would women end abuses to their cause. Old liberal notions of justice, reason, equality, and rights fortified such efforts. Yet twentieth-century events had changed the premises of the original movement. For many, the two world wars and the Holocaust had virtually destroyed faith in humanistic or liberal values. Also, since psychoanalysis had revealed the dark side of human nature, many turned toward the unconscious. Few had a clearer appreciation of the pessimistic consequences of the psychoanalytic discipline than Juliet Mitchell in her *Psychoanalysis and Feminism* (1974). Mitchell focused on the psychic consequences for women of male power. She was joined by others who talked in terms of sexual pleasure, desire, and violence. The "unconscious" became the locus of feminist analysis and tactics in a way hitherto unknown, because they saw its power in male-directed areas such as war, violence, consumerism, and sexual pleasure. Thus, women's quest to control supposedly rational areas, such as economics and politics, generated subgroups interested in the irrational or pleasurable sides of power—poetry, the body, and work. The nuts and bolts struggle to achieve ends such as divorce, abortion, and equal rights legislation coexisted with lyrical celebrations of female physicality. Works such as the irreverent *The Female Eunuch* (1970) by Germaine Greer (b. 1939), though frank, were far less explicit than the explorations of the feelings, couplings, and beauties of the female body in such works as Monique Wittig's *The Woman Warriors* (1969) and *The Lesbian Body* (1973). Even in the austere moral climate of Eastern bloc countries, writings aimed at dreaming, utopias, and fantasy.

The campaign for decent treatment along liberal lines ran up against harsh realities. The defeat of the United States in Vietnam, the widespread recession and oil crisis of the 1970s, and the intrusion of the Third World countries' claims changed the temper of the times. In 1979, Margaret Thatcher, a politician committed to cutting the benefits of the welfare state, became the first woman prime minister in England. Although Thatcher initially endorsed a public work life for women, nonetheless her internal programs cut public expenditures that allowed many women to support themselves. During the late 1970s, Eastern bloc countries enhanced their grants to women so that they might have more children. Such programs—different in means but similar in intent—demonstrated that the state still controlled women's reproductivity and potential to support themselves as it had two hundred years earlier. At the same time, two popes of the 1970s and 1980s—Paul VI and John Paul II—committed the Catholic Church to maintaining women's lack of physiological freedom and economic inferiority. John Paul II seconded Paul VI's condemnation of birth control. In addition, he reaffirmed the Catholic Church's doctrine on the sinful nature of homosexuality, on the celibacy of the priesthood, and on the unfitness of women to be priests. In March of 1987, Prime Minister Jacques Chirac of France launched an attack on magazines dealing in sexual matters, especially those mentioning homosexuality. The pope and Chirac were but two of the influential leaders obviously confounded by the outbreak of AIDS. A fatal illness at first believed to affect only homosexual men, the disease made many people demand the enforcement of monogamous heterosexual behavior and curtailment of rights according to sexual preference.

These conservative campaigns, aimed at controlling the reproductive and sexual side of human endeavors, conformed to an age-old pattern. Threatened by the Third World, facing economic troubles, and menaced by the threat of nuclear war, European leaders created an aura of solving their problems by invoking the family, "decent" standards of morality, and the cause of children. In such rhetorical campaigns, women were invoked as the metaphor for prosperity and the return to stability. Getting women back "where they belonged" and righting gender order would ensure an end to crisis and a smoothing out of the social and political fabric; anything else would spell disaster. Facing immense problems, rulers constructed images of women—not for the first time—as either potent threat or potential panacea. In the face of the "Star Wars" defense system and energy crises, such constructions indicated just how pertinent was the road feminist analysis was taking. As well as organizing for political and economic equality, feminists searched out the roots of the irrational, embedded so deeply in psychoanalytic and historic renderings of what was male and what was female. Like the Italian activist Evelina Zaghi, they continued to agitate: "Just last April we had a big demonstration for better day-care facilities, and I mean it was big."[36] Feminists also tried to take control of modern culture, especially to change media constructions of womanhood so detrimental to women's well-being. Finally, the movement looked at the reproductive and productive facts of women's lives and reopened the drive to give women their full measure of human dignity and worth in both areas.

NOTES

1. Anne Frank, *The Diary of a Young Girl*, M. B. M. Mooyaart, trans. (New York: Simon and Schuster, 1953), 237.

2. The example of computerization and managerial and workers' attitudes in the clothing industry comes from Cynthia Cockburn, *Machinery of Dominance. Women, Men, and Technical Know-How* (London: Pluto Press, 1985), 44–77, 61, 64–65.

3. Marie-Elisabeth Handman, *La violence et la ruse. Hommes et femmes dans un village grec* (Aix-en-Provence, France: Edisud, 1983), 114.

4. Jean Guyot et al., eds., *Des femmes immigrées parlent* (Geneva: Comité des églises auprès des travailleurs migrants, 1978), 47.

5. Sallie Westwood, *All Day, Every Day. Factory and Family in the Making of Women's Lives* (London: Pluto, 1984), 176.

6. *Family Doctor Publications* (1977):8, quoted in Ann Oakley, *Women Confined: Toward a Sociology of Childbirth* (New York: Shocken, 1980), 10.

7. Hans C. Buechler and Judith-Maria Buechler, *Carmen. The Autobiography of a Spanish Galician Woman* (Cambridge, Mass: Schenkman, 1981), 35–36.

8. Anna Pollert, *Girls, Wives, Factory Lives* (London: Macmillan: 1981), 99.

9. Poster in Lucia Chiavola Birnbaum, *Liberazione della donna* (Middletown, Conn.: Wesleyan University Press, 1986).

10. Ann-Maria Gaillard, *Couples suèdois: vers un autre idéal sexuel* (Paris: Editions Universitaires, 1983), 64.

11. Quoted in John Stevenson, *British Society 1914–1945* (London: Penguin, 1984), 177.

12. Statistics are taken from Alastair McAuley, *Women's Work and Wages in the Soviet Union* (London: Allen and Unwin, 1981), 134–162; Michele Tournier, "L'accès des femmes aux études universitaires en France et en Allemagne," doctoral dissertation, University of Paris, 1972.

13. From *Elle*, no. 796, quoted in Evelyne Sullerot, *La presse feminine* (Paris: Armand Colin, 1966), 227.

14. Margaret Riedel, "Living with a Family and Living with a Job," in T. Scarlett Epstein et al., eds., *Women, Work, and Family in Britain and Germany* (London: Croom Helm, 1986), 173.

15. Marianne Gullestad *Kitchen-Table Society: A Case Study of Family Life and Friendships of Young Working-Class Mothers in Urban Norway* (Oslo: Universitetsforlaget, 1984), 50–59.

16. Quoted in Anita Rind, *Etre femme à l'est* (Paris: Stock, 1980), 39–60.

17. Simone de Beauvoir, *The Force of Circumstance*, Richard Howard, trans. (New York: Knopf, 1965), 267.

18. Simone de Beauvoir, *The Second Sex*, H. M. Parshley, trans. and ed. (New York: Bantam, 1961), xvi.

19. Quoted in *Elle*, no. 1494 (August 5, 1974):17.

20. "Chantal Akerman of 'Jeanne Dielman'," *Camera Obscura*, vol. 2 (Fall, 1977): 118.

21. Quoted in *Elle*, no. 1494 (August 5, 1974):13.

22. Jill Craigie, *The Evening Standard* (1956), quoted in Elizabeth Wilson, *Only Halfway to Paradise: Women in Postwar Britain: 1945–1968* (London: Tavistock, 1980), 184–185.

23. Cited in Claire Duchen, *Feminism in France from May '68 to Mitterand* (London: Routledge and Kegan Paul, 1986), 10.

24. Quoted in Margaret Maruani, *Les syndicats à l'épreuve du féminisme* (Paris: Syros, 1979), 64, n. 18.

25. Hélène Cixous, "The Laugh of the Medusa: Viewpoint," *Signs*, vol. 1, no. 4 (Summer, 1976):875–893.

26. Ulrike Prokop, "Production and the Context of Women's Daily Life," *New German Critique*, vol. 13 (Winter, 1978):32.

27. Ulla Terlinden, "Women in the Ecology Movement—Ecology in the Women's Movement," in Edith Hoshino Altbach et al., eds., *German Feminism. Readings in Politics and Literature* (Albany, N. Y.: SUNY Press, 1984), 318.

28. Quoted in Lucia Chiavola Birnbaum, *Liberazione della donna*, 160.

29. Maria-Barbara Watson-Franke, "'I Am Somebody?'—Women's Changing Sense of Self in the German Democratic Republic," in Marilyn Boxer and Jean Quataert, eds., *Connecting Spheres* (New York: Oxford, 1987), 257.

30. Quoted in Alix Holt, "The First Soviet Feminists," in Barbara Holland, ed., *Soviet Sisterhood* (Bloomington: Indiana University Press, 1985), 237.

31. Tat'yana Mamonova, *Women and Russia: Feminist Writings from the Soviet Union* (Boston: Beacon, 1984), xx.

32. Maxie Wander, "Waiting for a Miracle," in Altbach et al., *German Feminism*, 176.

33. Irmtraud Morgner, "The Duel," in Altbach et al., *German Feminism*, 212.

34. Christa Wolf, *The Quest for Christa T.*, Christopher Middleton, trans. (New York: Dell, 1970), 49.

35. Quoted in Edith Hoshino Altbach, "The New German Women's Movement," in Altbach et al., *German Feminism*, 14.

36. Quoted in David I. Kertzer, "The Liberation of Evelina Zaghi: The Life of an Italian Communist," *Signs*, vol. 8, no. 1 (Autumn, 1982)1:56.

SOURCES AND SUGGESTED READING

Altbach, Edith Hoshino, Jeanette Clausen, Dagmar Schultz, and Naomi Stephan, eds., *German Feminism: Readings in Politics and Literature* (1984). Important presentation of essential writings of contemporary German feminists.

Birnbaum, Lucia Chiavola, *Liberazione della donna* (1986). A broad survey of twentieth-century Italian feminism.

Chamberlain, Mary, *Fenwomen. A Portrait of Women in an English Village* (1983).

Cockburn, Cynthia, *Machinery of Dominance. Women, Men and Technical Know-How* (1985). Studies of computerization of industries and how technology affects gender relations in work.

Cornelison, Ann, *Women of the Shadows* (1977). A vivid portrayal of Sicilian women's lives.

de Beauvoir, Simone, *The Second Sex* (1953). The classic theoretical study of women.

Duchen, Claire, *Feminism in France. From May '68 to Mitterand* (1986). An account that particularly outlines ideological differences.

Ehrenreich, Barbara, *The Hearts of Men* (1983). An outline of the "new" man.

Freier, Anna-Elisabeth, and Annette Kuhn, eds., *Frauen in der Geschichte V* (1984). An important collection on women in post-war Germany.

Handman, Marie-Elisabeth, *La violence et la ruse. Hommes et femmes dans un village grec* (1983). The play of familial power in a Greek town.

Heitlinger, Alena, *Women and State Socialism: Sex Inequality in the Soviet Union and Czechoslovakia* (1979). A detailed comparison of demographic, family, and working conditions of women in socialist countries.

Holland, Barbara, ed., *Soviet Sisterhood* (1985). An anthology of important articles covering politics, popular culture, and work.

Jenson, Jane, "Both Friend and Foe: Women and State Welfare," in Renate Bridenthal, Claudia Koonz, and Susan Stuard, eds., *Becoming Visible: Women in European History* (1987). A good comparison of British and French programs after World War II.

Kemerman, Sheila B., "Women, Children, and Poverty: Public Policies and Families in Industrialized Countries," *Signs*, 10 (Winter, 1984). A comparative statistical study of aid in Europe and the United States.

Kramer, David, "Ulrike Meinhof: An Emancipated Terrorist?" in Jane Slaughter and Robert Kerns, eds., *European Women on the Left* (1981). An intriguing and balanced account.

Lamartine, Thérèse. *Elles cinéastes ad lib 1895–1981* (1985). An encylopedia of women directors.

McAuley, Alastair, *Women's Work and Wages in the Soviet Union* (1981). Statistical and in-depth view of occupations and opportunities.

Mamonova, Tat'yana, ed., *Women and Russia: Feminist Writings from the Soviet Union* (1984). Original writings from *Almanach*.

Marks, Elaine, and Isabelle de Courtivron, eds., *New French Feminisms* (1980). A pioneering anthology.

Meyer, Donald, *Sex and Power. The Rise of Women in America, Russia, Sweden, and Italy* (1987). A massive and unique comparative work.

Weigel, "Contemporary German Women's Literature," *New German Critique*, 31 (Winter, 1984), 32 (Spring-Summer, 1984). A survey of the latest writings and literary activity, noting its debt to the work of Bachmann and Wolf.

Westwood, Sallie, *All Day, Every Day. Factory and Family in the Making of Women's Lives* (1985). Resistance, work, and ritual among British hosiery workers.

Willis, Sharon, *Marguerite Duras: Writing on the Body* (1987). A fresh and stimulating interpretation of Duras's work.

Wilson, Elizabeth, *Women and the Welfare State* (1977). An analysis of the interconnections between government and women.

Wolf, Christa, *The Quest for Christa T.* (1970). A classic from East Germany.

Yedlin, Tova, ed., *Women in Eastern Europe and the Soviet Union* (1983). An anthology with excellent statistical data on work, fertility, and political participation.

Young, Michael, and Peter Willmott, *Family and Kinship in East London* (1957). A detailed study of the separate worlds of men and women in a working-class community.

In addition to the works cited in notes at the end of chapters, the following general sources informed the writing of this book and will be of interest to those wishing to increase their knowledge of women in history. For statistical material, including population, fertility, income, and consumption, I relied on Brian Mitchell, *European Historical Statistics* (1981), the League of Nations *Yearbook*, and statistical annuals for individual European countries.

General works on women in Europe include the pioneering collection of articles edited by Renate Bridenthal and Claudia Koonz, *Becoming Visible: Women in European History* (1st ed. 1977) and Renate Bridenthal, Claudia Koonz, and Susan Stuard, eds., *Becoming Visible: Women in European History* (2nd ed. 1987); Marilyn Boxer and Jean Quataert, eds., *Connecting Spheres: Women in the Western World, 1500 to the Present* (1987); Priscilla Robertson, *An Experience of Women: Pattern and Change in Nineteenth Century Europe* (1982); *Frauen in der Geschichte* (1979), an ongoing series of anthologized articles on women in Europe, especially Germany, whose general editor is Annette Kuhn. General collections of documents are Susan Groag Bell and Karen Offen, eds., *Women, the Family and Freedom: The Debate in Documents*, 2 vols. (1983); John Fout and Eleanor Riemer, eds., *European Women: A Documentary History, 1789–1945* (1980); Erna O. Hellerstein, Leslie P. Hume, and Karen Offen, eds., *Victorian Women: A Documentary Account of Women's Lives in Nineteenth-Century England, France, and the United States* (1981); and Julia O'Faolain and Lauro Martines, eds., *Not in God's Image: Women in History from the Greeks to the Victorians* (1973).

There are numerous sources for material on women and culture. For art and design, see Isabelle Anscombe, *A Woman's Touch: Women in Design from 1860 to the Present Day* (1984); Anthea Callen, *Women of the Arts and Crafts Movement, 1870–1914* (1984); Ann Sutherland Harris and Linda Nocklin, *Women Artists: 1550–1950* (1979); Nancy Heller, *Women Artists: An Illustrated History* (1987); Claire Richter Sherman, ed. (with Adele M. Holcomb), *Women as Interpreters of the Visual Arts, 1820–1979* (1981). For literature, see Beverly Allen, ed., *The Defiant Muse: Italian Feminist Poems from the Middle Ages to the Present* (1986); Susan L. Cocalis, ed., *The Defiant Muse: German Feminist Poems from the Middle Ages to the Present* (1986); Angel Flores, ed., *The Defiant Muse: Hispanic Feminist Poems from the Middle Ages to the Present* (1986); Carolyn L. Galerstein, ed., *Women Writers of Spain* (1986); Sandra M. Gilbert and Susan Gubar, *The Norton Anthology of Literature by Women: The Tradition in English* (1985); Hiltrud Gnüg and Renate Mohrmann, *Frauen Literatur Geschichte: Schreibende Frauen vom Mittelalter bis zur Gegenwart* (1985); Ellen Moers, *Literary Women: The Great Writers*

(1977); Domna Stanton, ed., *The Defiant Muse: French Feminist Poems from the Middle Ages to the Present* (1986).

Comparative studies in politics and society include Bonnie Bullough and Vern Bullough, *Women and Prostitution: A Social History* (1987); Lillian Faderman, *Surpassing the Love of Men: Romantic Friendship and Love between Women from the Renaissance to the Present* (1981); Gisbert H. Flanz, *Comparative Women's Rights and Political Participation in Europe* (1983); Catherine Gallagher and Thomas Laqueur, eds., *The Making of the Modern Body: Sexuality and Society in the Nineteenth Century* (1987); Peter Gay, *Education of the Senses* (1984) and *The Tender Passion* (1986); Helga Maria Hernes, *Welfare State and Woman Power: Essays in State Feminism* (1987); Margaret Randolph Higonnet, Jane Jenson, Sonya Michel, and Margaret Collins Weitz, *Behind the Lines: Gender and the Two World Wars* (1987); Sheila Lewenhak, *Women and Work* (1980); Michael Mitterauer and Reinhard Sieder, *The European Family* (1982); George L. Mosse, *Nationalism and Sexuality: Respectability and Abnormal Sexuality in Modern Europe* (1985); Shelley Saywell, *Women in War: From World War II to El Salvador* (1986); Phyllis Stock, *Better than Rubies: A History of Women's Education* (1978); Louise A. Tilly and Joan W. Scott, *Women, Work and Family* (1978).

On women in England see Sandra Burman, ed., *Fit Work for Women* (1979); Olive Banks, *British Feminists* (1985); Anne Crawford et al., *The Europa Biographical Dictionary of British Women* (1983); John Gillis, *For Better or Worse: British Marriage, 1600 to the Present* (1985); Brian Heeney, *The Women's Movement in the Church of England, 1850–1930*; David Levine, *Reproducting Families: The Political Economy of English Population History* (1987); Jane Lewis, ed., *Labour and Love: Women's Experience of Home and Family, 1850–1940* (1986); Jane Lewis, *Women in England, 1870–1950* (1984); Alan Macfarlane, *Marriage and Love in England: Modes of Reproduction, 1300–1840* (1986); Linda A. Pollock, *Forgotten Children: Parent-child Relations from 1500 to 1900* (1983); Norbert C. Soldon, *Women in British Trade Unions, 1974–1976* (1978); Jeffrey Weeks, *Coming Out: Homosexual Politics in Britain, from the Nineteenth Century to the Present* (1977) and *Sex, Politics, and Society: The Regulation of Sexuality since 1800* (1981); Sybil Wolfram, *In-Laws and Outlaws: Kinship and Marriage in England* (1987). On women in Ireland, see Margaret MacCurtain and Donncha Ó'Corráin, eds., *Women in Irish Society: The Historical Dimension* (1978).

For Austria and Eastern Europe see Edith Rigler, *Frauenleitbild und Frauenarbeit in Österreich von ausgehenden 19 Jahrhundert bis zum Zweiten Weltkrieg* (1976); L. Muziková-Nosilová, *Les femmes tchéchoslovaques* (1947); Sharen L. Wolchik and Alfred G. Meyer, eds., *Women, State, and Party in Eastern Europe* (1985); Tova Yedlin, ed., *Women in Eastern Europe and the Soviet Union* (1980).

General works on women in French history include Jean-Paul Aron, ed., *Misérable et glorieuse, la femme du XIXᵉ siècle* (1980); Maïté Albistur and Daniel Armogathe, *Histoire du féminisme français* (1977); James F. McMillan, *Housewife or Harlot: The Place of Women in French Society, 1870–1940*

(1981); Michelle Perrot, ed., *Une histoire des femmes est-elle possible* (1984); Samia Spencer, ed., *French Women and the Age of Enlightenment* (1984); *L'Histoire sans qualités* (1979).

For Germany, general sources are Barbara Beuys, *Familienleben in Deutschland* (1980); Richard J. Evans and W. R. Lee, eds., *The German Family* (1981); John Fout, ed., *German Women in the Nineteenth Century* (1984); Karin Hausen, ed., *Frauen suchen ihre Geschichte* (1982); Ruth-Ellen B. Joeres and Mary Jo Maynes, eds., *German Women in the Eighteenth and Nineteenth Centuries: A Social and Literary History* (1986); Walter Müller, Angelika Willms, and Johann Handl, *Strukturwandel der Frauenarbeit, 1880–1980* (1983); Hans-Jurgen Schultz, ed., *Frauen: Portrats aus zwei Jahrhunderten* (1985).

General works on women in Italy include Mirella Alloisio and Marta Ajo, *La donna nel socialismo italiano tra cronaca et storia, 1892–1978* (1978); Betty Boyd Caroli, Robert F. Harney, and Lydia F. Tomasi, eds., *The Italian Immigrant Woman in North America* (1978); Ginevra Conti Odorisio, *Storia dell'idea femminista in Italia* (1980); Camilla Ravera, *Breve storia del movimento femminile in Italia* (1978); Fiorenza Taricone and Beatrice Pisa, *Operaie, borghesi, contadine nel XIX secolo* (1985).

For Russia, see Dorothy Atkinson, Alexander Dallin, and Gail Lapidus, eds., *Women in Russia* (1977); Gail Lapidus, *Women in Soviet Society* (1978); David Ransel, ed., *The Family in Imperial Russia* (1978); Richard Stites, *The Women's Liberation Movement in Russia: Nihilism, Feminism, and Bolshevism, 1860–1930* (1978).

On Spanish women see Anabel Gonzalez, Amalia Lopez, Ana Mendoza, Isabel Uruena, eds., *Los origenes del feminismo en España* (1980); Temma Kaplan, *The Anarchists of Andalusia, 1868–1903* (1977); Mary Nash, *Mujer, familia y trabajo en España (1875–1936)* (1983); Geraldine M. Scanlon, *La polemica feminista en la España contemporanea (1868–1974)* (1976).

For Scandinavian countries see Inga Dahlsgård, *Women in Denmark Yesterday and Today* (1980); and the many articles in *The Journal of Scandinavian History, The Scandinavian Economic History Review,* and *Scandinavian Studies.*

INDEX

PHOTO CREDITS

PART I opener (p. 2): An upper-class woman reading in the eighteenth century (Historical Pictures Service).

p. 8 North Wind Picture Archives; p. 10 North Wind Picture Archives; p. 25 North Wind Picture Archives; p. 30 Alinari/Art Resource; p. 34 North Wind Picture Archives; p. 42 Bildarchiv foto Marburg; p. 56 Bettmann Archive; p. 63 Archiv für Kunst and Geschichte, Berlin; p. 66 Sammlung der Bayerischen, Alte Pinakothek, Munich; p. 67 Bettmann Archive; p. 73 Michele Medici, Eligio di Giovanni e di Anna Morandi Mahzolini. Bologna: San Tommaso D'Aquino; p. 77 Giraudon/Art Resource; p. 89 Archiv fur Kunst and Geschichte, Berlin; p. 94 Historical Pictures Service; p. 98 Historical Pictures Service; p. 105 Bettmann Archive; p. 115 Mary Evans Picture Library; p. 124 Archiv für Kunst and Geschichte, Berlin; p. 127 bildarchiv preussischer kulturbesitz.

PART II opener (p. 134): Honoré Daumier's caricature of women demanding the right to divorce (Historical Pictures Service).

p. 140 Topham/The Image Works; p. 156 Bettman Archive; p. 157 North Wind Picture Archives; p. 160 (both) North Wind Picture Archives; p. 166 Archiv für Kunst and Geschichte, Berlin; p. 171 Mary Evans Picture Library; p. 182 Mary Evans Picture Library; p. 185 Archiv für Kunst und Geschichte, Berlin; p. 191 Archiv für Kunst und Geschichte, Berlin; p. 196 Bettmann Archive; p. 201 Mary Evans Picture Library; p. 217 Bettmann Archive; p. 223 Historical Pictures Service; p. 232 Bettmann Archive; p. 239 Réunion des musées nationaux, Paris; p. 243 bildarchiv preussischer kulturbesitz; p. 250 Historical Pictures Service; p. 253 Städelsches Kunstinstitut und Stadtische Galerie, Frankfurt; p. 259 Mary Evans Picture Library.

PART III opener (p. 268): Emmeline Pankhurst being carried off by the police (Mary Evans Picture Library).

p. 273 Mary Evans Picture Library; p. 275 Archiv für Kunst und Geschichte, Berlin; p. 281 Tass from Sovfoto; p. 285 North Wind Picture Archives; p. 297 (both) Historical Pictures Service; p. 302 Bettmann Archive; p. 318 Bettmann Archive; p. 323 Topham/The Image Works; p. 327 Mary Evans Picture Library; p. 329 bildarchiv preussischer kulturbesitz; p. 331 UPI/Bettmann Newsphotos; p. 335 Paula Modersohn-Becker, German 1876–1907. "Old Peasant Woman" c. 1905, oil on canvas. © the Detroit Institute of Arts, Gift of Robert H. Tannahill; p. 337 Historical Pictures Service; p. 366 bildarchiv preussischer kulturbesitz; p. 370 (left) Archiv für Kunst und Geschichte, Berlin; p. 370 (right) Imperial War Museum, London; p. 373 Bettmann Archive; p. 375 Bettmann Archive; p. 388 Sovfoto; p. 391 Novosti from Sovfoto.

PART IV opener (p. 406): Lina Wertmüller, post-World War II film director (UPI/Bettmann Newsphotos).

p. 417 UPI/Bettmann Newsphotos; p. 418 bildarchiv preussischer kulturbesitz; p. 427 Archiv für Kunst und Geschichte, Berlin; p. 428 Topham/The Image Works; p. 437 Sovfoto; p. 446 Archiv für Kunst und Geschichte, Berlin; p. 450 Tass from Sovfoto; p. 459 bildarchiv preussischer kulturbesitz; p. 467 bildarchiv preussischer kulturbesitz; p.

475 UPI/Bettmann Newsphotos; p. 482 Bettmann Archive/BBC Hulton; p. 485 bildarchiv preussischer kulturbesitz; p. 488 Tass from Sovfoto; p. 490 Imperial War Palace, London; p. 499 UPI/Bettmann Newsphotos; p. 502 Martine Franck/Magnum; p. 505 A. Duclos/Gamma-Liaison; p. 511 Bettmann Archive/BBC Hulton; p. 514 UPI/Bettmann Newsphotos; p. 518 Gilles Caron/Gamma-Liaison; p. 533 UPI/Bettmann Newsphotos.

Sonia Terk Delaunay, "Study for Portugal," 1936–37
Gouache on paper, 14¼ x 37"
The National Museum of Women in the Arts, Gift of Wallace and Wilhelmina Holladay

TEXT CREDITS

p. 225 (excerpt) *Granny: Scenes from Country Life* by Božena Němcová, translated by Edith Pargeter. Greenwood Press, 1976, pp. 195–196.

p. 307 (poetry) From *Le Mouvement Social*, 72, July–September 1970, pp. 60–61. © Editions Ouvrières, Paris. *Le Mouvement Social* is the French journal of social history.

p. 336 (poetry) from *Your Diamond Dreams Cut Open My Arteries*, translated and edited by Robert P. Newton. © 1982 The University of North Carolina Press. Reprinted by permission.

pp. 392–393 (excerpt) Copyright © Alix Holt, 1977. Reprinted from *Selected Writings of Alexandra Kollontai*, translated by and with introduction and commentaries by Alix Holt, by permission of the publisher, Lawrence Hill & Co. (Westport, Conn.).

pp. 430–431 (excerpt) Adapted from Theodor van de Velde, *Ideal Marriage: Its Physiology and Technique*. Stella Browne, trans. Random House, Inc. 1926, 1957, pp. 8–9, 11–12.

p. 501 (table) Published and copyright 1983 Campus Verlag Frankfurt/New York.

pp. 507–508 (excerpt) From *Soviet Sisterhood*, edited by Barbara Holland, pp. 170–172. Copyright © 1985 by Indiana University Press. Reprinted by permission.

p. 516 (table) St. Martin's Press, 1987.